The Works of John Dryden

General Editor

ALAN ROPER

Textual Editor

VINTON A. DEARING

Volume Twenty

EDITOR

A. E. Wallace Maurer

TEXTUAL EDITOR

George R. Guffey

I Closterman Pinxit.   W Faithorne fecit.   Cum Privilegio Regis.   Sold by E. Cooper at ye 3 Pidgeons in Bedford street.

JOHN DRYDEN, FROM AN ENGRAVING BY W. FAITHORNE
AFTER A PAINTING BY JOHN CLOSTERMAN
Mounted in the Clark Library's large-paper copy
of Dryden's Virgil

VOLUME XX

The Works
of John Dryden

Prose 1691-1698

DE ARTE GRAPHICA
AND SHORTER WORKS

University of California Press

Berkeley   Los Angeles   London

1989

UNIVERSITY OF CALIFORNIA PRESS
Berkeley and Los Angeles, California

UNIVERSITY OF CALIFORNIA PRESS, LTD.
London, England

The copy texts of this edition have been drawn in
the main from the Dryden Collection of the
William Andrews Clark Memorial Library

*In Gratitude
for Years of Advice and Assistance
since the Inception of this Edition
This Volume of the California Dryden
Is Dedicated to the Past and Present Staffs
of the William Andrews Clark Memorial Library*

The preparation of this volume of the California edition of The Works of John Dryden *has been made possible in part by a grant from the Editing Program of the National Endowment for the Humanities and by a matching grant from The UCLA Foundation.*

Preface

The editors of this volume divided their labors as follows: George R. Guffey prepared the text; A. E. Wallace Maurer researched and drafted most of the commentary, which was put into final form by Alan Roper, who also collaborated with Maurer on the research for and then wrote the commentary to Dryden's translation from Tacitus.

The editors are particularly indebted to the following: To the staffs of these libraries for their advice and assistance: the William Andrews Clark Memorial Library, the UCLA Research Library, the Belt Library of Vinciana at UCLA, the Henry E. Huntington Library, the Newberry Library, the Bancroft Library at UC Berkeley, the British Library, the University of Michigan Rare Books Room, and the Ohio State University Library, especially the Rare Books Room for furnishing the Editor with a table and special privileges during some eight years.

To the late Professor Samuel Holt Monk for notes and suggestions used in the commentary to Dryden's Parallel betwixt Painting and Poetry.

To Professor Clarence A. Forbes for the translation of Latin passages from Casaubon's edition of Polybius and Pichon's edition of Tacitus used in the commentary to The Character of Polybius.

To Professor Kim D. Gainer for assistance in the collation of editions of Dryden's French original for De Arte Graphica.

To Professor Steven N. Zwicker for exchange of findings on a variety of topics.

To Professors Charles L. Babcock, Alan K. Brown, A. R. Braunmuller, David E. Hahm, Phillip Harth, Philip Levine, Franklin M. Ludden, Albert N. Mancini, Earl Miner, Mark P. O. Morford, Ronald C. Rosbottom, Carl C. Schlam, John M. Wallace, and Charles G. Williams for researching and answering many questions.

To the present or former graduate students of the departments of English and History at UCLA: Jane Abelson, Dianne Dugaw, Walter Ellis, Robert Hunt, Jill Kuhn, Ronald Lear, Janette Lewis, Kathryne Lindberg, Geraldine Moyle, and Eric

Schroeder for their assistance in gathering and verifying materials used in the commentary, and for their help in preparing and proofing the text.

To Mrs. Geneva Phillips, Managing Editor of the edition, and to Mrs. Grace Stimson for preparing the manuscript with care for the printer, and to the former for coordinating the work of editors and research assistants, and for overseeing the production of the volume.

To the William Andrews Clark Memorial Library for Short-Term Resident Fellowships awarded to the Editor.

To Professor Jack M. Hollander, Vice President for Research and Graduate Studies, Ohio State University, for a grant supporting the Editor's work on this volume at UCLA.

To Professors Diether H. Haenicke, former Dean, G. Micheal Riley, present Dean of the Humanities College, and James L. Battersby of the research committee of the Department of English—all of Ohio State University—for encouragement and support in the form of grants-in-aid and research leave.

To the Academic Senate Research Committee of the University of California, Los Angeles, for annual grants-in-aid and, in addition to support separately acknowledged on a previous page, to Chancellor Charles E. Young of UCLA for sabbatical leaves and for continued support of the edition in the form of supplemental funding.

The Editor of this volume values the memory of H. T. Swedenberg, Jr., his earlier General Editor, and the happy collaboration with Alan Roper, his present General Editor, whose acumen, learning, and hand drive up the worth of all our work.

A. E. W. M.
G. R. G.

Contents

Illustrations

PROSE 1691–1698

DE ARTE GRAPHICA AND SHORTER WORKS

A
DIALOGUE
Concerning
WOMEN,
Being a
DEFENCE
Of the
SEX.

Written to *EUGENIA.*

LONDON, Printed for *R. Bentley* in *Ruffel-
ftreet* in *Covent-Garden*, and *J. Tonfon* at the
Judge's-Head in *Chancery-Lane*. **1691**.

Preface to A Dialogue Concerning Women

T HE *Perusal of this Dialogue, in defence of the Fair Sex,*
Written by a Gentleman of my acquaintance, much sur-
pris'd me: For it was not easie for me to imagine, that one
so young, cou'd have treated so nice a Subject with so much judg-
ment. 'Tis true, I was not ignorant that he was naturally In-
genious, and that he had improv'd himself by Travelling; and
from thence I might reasonably have expected that air of Gallan-
try, which is so visibly diffus'd through the body of the Work,
and is indeed the Soul that animates all things of this nature:
10 *But so much variety of reading, both in Ancient and Modern*
Authors, such digestion of that reading, so much justness of
thought, that it leaves no room for affectation, or Pedantry, I
may venture to say, are not overcommon amongst practis'd Writ-
ers, and very rarely to be found amongst Beginners. It puts me
in mind of what was said of Mr. Waller, *the Father of our* English
Numbers, upon the sight of his first Verses by the Wits of the
last Age, that he came out into the World Forty Thousand strong,
before they had heard of him. (Here in imitation of my Friends
Apostrophe's, I hope the Reader need not be told, that Mr.
20 Waller *is only mention'd for Honour's sake, that I am desirous*
of laying hold on his Memory, on all occasions, and thereby
acknowledging to the World, that unless he had Written, none
of us cou'd Write.)
I know my Friend will forgive me this digression; for it is not
only a Copy of his Stile but of his Candour. The Reader will
observe, that he is ready for all hints of commending merit, and
the Writers of this Age and Country are particularly oblig'd to
him, for his pointing out those Passages which the French *call*
Beaux Endroits, *wherein they have most excell'd. And though*
30 *I may seem in this, to have my own interest in my eyes, because*
he has more than once mention'd me so much to my advantage,

---

9 *animates*] annimates O.   15 English] *English* O.
24 *I*] *no paragraph break in* O.   31 *me*] ~, O.

yet I hope the Reader will take it only for a Parenthesis, because the Piece wou'd have been very perfect without it. I may be suffer'd to please my self with the kindness of my Friend, without valuing my self upon his partiality: He had not confidence enough to send it out into the World, without my Opinion of it, that it might pass securely, at least amongst the fair Readers, for whose service it was principally design'd. I am not so presuming, to think my Opinion can either be his Touchstone, or his Passport: But I thought I might send him back to Ariosto;* 10 who has made it the business of almost Thirty Stanza's in the beginning of the* 37th *Book of his* Orlando Furioso, *not only to praise that Beautiful part of the Creation, but also to make a sharp Satyr on their Enemies; to give Mankind their own, and to tell them plainly, that from their envy it proceeds that the Vertue and great Actions of Women are purposely conceal'd, and the failings of some few amongst them expos'd with all the aggravating Circumstances of Malice. For my own part, who have always been their Servant, and have never drawn my Pen against them, I had rather see some of them prais'd extraordi-* 20 narily, than any of them suffer by detraction: And that in this Age, and at this time particularly, wherein I find more Heroines than Heroes. Let me therefore give them joy of their new Champion. If any will think me more partial to him than really I am, they can only say I have return'd his Bribe: And the worst I wish him, is, that he may receive Justice from the Men; and Favour only from the Ladies.*

John Dryden.

---

23 *Champion.*] ~: O.

MISCELLANEOUS
ESSAYS:

BY
Monsieur St. EUREMONT.

Translated out of French.

WITH
A CHARACTER,
BY
A Person of Honour here in *England*.

CONTINUED
By Mr. *DRYDEN*.

LONDON,
Printed for John Everingham, at the
Star in *Ludgate-street*, near the West-End
of St. *Paul*'s Church-Yard, 1692.

TITLE PAGE OF THE FIRST EDITION (MACDONALD 137)

A Character of Saint-Evremond

THE Discourses which compose this Book, being printed already, in another Language, there may be several amongst us, who have only heard in general of *Monsieur St. Evremont,* and the Reputation he has with the Men of Sence, and therefore may be well enough pleas'd to know what it is, wherein he Excels, and which distinguishes him from other Writers: For it is not with the Wits of our Times, how Eminent so ever, as with those who lived under *Augustus* when the Empire and Language were in some Sence Universal; they properly wrote
10 to the World: the Moderns, even the *French* Authors themselves, write at most but to a Province of the *Roman* Empire; and if they are known beyond their own Country, and become a Common Benefit to Mankind, it is, in a great measure, owing to their Translators. *Monsieur St. Evremont* hath establish'd his Fame where-ever the *French* Language is understood, and yet surely he cannot be displeas'd with an attempt to carry it farther, by making him speak that of a Country, where he has resided so many Years.

    Whoever reads these Essays will acknowledge, that he finds
20 there a Fineness of Expression, and a Delicateness of Thought, the Easiness of a Gentleman, the Exactness of a Scholar, and the Good Sence of a Man of Business; that the Author is throughly acquainted with the World, and has conversed with the best sort of Men to be found in it. His Subjects are often Great and Noble, and then he never fails to write up to them; when he speaks of the Ancient *Romans,* you would believe you were reading one of the same Age and Nation: the same Spirit, the same Noble Freedom, the same unaffected Greatness appear in both; if the Subject he chuseth be of a lower Nature, he is sure to write that

3–4 *Evremont*] O2; *Euremont* O1. [These sigla are identified in the Textual Notes, where also fluctuations in the texts cited are explained.]
6 Writers:] ∼. O1–2.   9 Universal; they] ∼. They O1–2.
10 *French*] French O1–2.   11 Empire] *Empire* O1–2.
14 *Evremont*] O2; *Euremont* O1.   22 Business; that] ∼: That O1–2.

which is not common upon it: there is still somewhat New and
Agreeable, and beyond what you could expect. However you
were affected when you began to read him, he gains upon you
insensibly, and before you have done, you take a pleasure to
be of the same Opinion with him.

    The Variety and Choice of his Subjects pleases you no less,
than what he writes upon them. He perpetually entertains you
with new Objects, and dwells not too long upon any of them. As
for Method, it is Inconsistent with his Design, neither pretends
10 he to write all that can be said. He sets not up for a Teacher,
but he Instructs you unawares, and without pretending to it.
Every thing appears so Natural, that the Art is hidden, and yet
the Observer finds all the stroaks of a Master's Hand. He knows
exactly when to give over: All is so well, you'll wish he had said
more; and yet when he concludes, you believe he could not have
ended better. He has truly studied Nature in that point, that it
is with the Mind, as with the Body, they are to be treated alike:
the desires of both should be satisfied, yet so that you are to rise
with an Appetite.

20   *Mr. D.* Cha.

    I know, how Nice an Undertaking it is to write of a Living
Author: Yet the Example of Father *Bouhours,* has somewhat
encourag'd me in this Attempt. Had not *Monsieur St. Evremont*
been very considerable in his own Country, that Famous Jesuit
wou'd not have ventur'd to praise a Person in Disgrace with the
Government of *France,* and living here in Banishment. Yet in
his *Pensees Ingenieuses,* he has often cited our Author's Thoughts
and his Expressions, as the Standard of Judicious Thinking, and
Graceful Speaking; an undoubted sign that his Merit was suf-
30 ficiently establish'd, when the Disfavour of the Court cou'd not
prevail against it. There is not only a justness in his Conceptions,
which is the Foundation of good writing, but also a Purity of

7   them.] O2; ~: O1.   10   said.] ~: O1; ~; O2.
11   it.] O2; ~: O1.   13   Hand.] O2; ~: O1.
19–21   Appetite. / ————— / *Mr. D.* Cha. / I] ~. *Mr. D.* Cha. / ————— / I
O1 (*corrected form*); Appetite. / I O1 (*uncorrected form*); Appetite. / **Character of
Monsieur de St. Evremont, by Mr.** *Dryden.* / I O2.
23   *Evremont*] O2; *Euremont* O1.   29   Speaking; an] ~. An O1–2.

Language, and a beautiful turn of Words, so little understood
by Modern Writers; and which indeed was found at *Rome,* but
at the latter end of the Commonwealth, and ended with *Petro-
nius,* under the Monarchy.

If I durst extend my Judgment to particulars, I wou'd say that
our Author has determined very nicely in his Opinion of *Epi-
curus;* and that what he has said of his Morals, is according to
Nature, and Reason. 'Tis true, that as I am a Religious Admirer
of *Virgil,* I cou'd wish that he had not discover'd our Father's
10 Nakedness. But after all, we must confess that *Æneas* was none of
the greatest Hero's, and that *Virgil* was sensible of it himself.
But what cou'd he do? The *Trojan* on whom he was to build the
Roman Empire, had been already vanquish'd; he had lost his
Country, and was a Fugitive. Nay more, he had fought unsuccess-
fully with *Diomedes,* and was only preserv'd from Death by his
Mother-Goddess, who receiv'd a Wound in his Defence. So that
Virgil, bound as he was to follow the Footsteps of *Homer,* who
had thus described him, cou'd not reasonably have altered his
Character, and raised him in *Italy* to a much greater height of
20 Prowess than he found him formerly in *Troy.* Since therefore
he cou'd make no more of him in Valour, he resolved not to
give him that Vertue, as his Principal, but chose another, which
was Piety. 'Tis true this latter, in the Composition of a Hero,
was not altogether so shining as the former; but it intitled him
more to the favour of the Gods, and their Protection, in all his
undertakings: And, which was the Poets chiefest aim, made a
nearer Resemblance betwixt *Æneas* and his Patron *Augustus
Cæsar,* who, above all things, lov'd to be flatter'd for being Pious,
both to the Gods and his Relations. And that very Piety, or
30 Gratitude, (call it which you please,) to the Memory of his Uncle
Julius, gave him the Preference, amongst the Soldiers, to *Mark
Antony;* and consequently raised him to the Empire. As for
Personal Courage, that of *Augustus* was not pushing; and the

---

5   If] *no paragraph break in* O1-2.   13   Empire] *Empire* O1-2.
16   Mother-Goddess] S-S; Mother Goddess O1-2.
17   *Virgil,*] ~ₐ O1-2.   18   cou'd not] O2; cou'd O1.
26   undertakings:] ~. O1-2.
31   Preference, . . . Soldiers,] ~ₐ . . . ~ₐ O1-2.
32   *Antony*] *Anthony* O1-2.

Poet, who was not ignorant of that Defect, for that reason, durst
not ascribe it, in the supream degree, to him who was to repre-
sent his Emperour, under another name: which was manag'd by
him, with the most imaginable fineness: for had Valour been
set uppermost, *Augustus* must have yielded to *Agrippa.* After
all, this is rather to defend the Courtier, than the Poet; and to
make his Hero escape again, under the covert of a Cloud. Only
we may add, what I think *Bossu* says, That the *Roman* Common-
wealth, being now chang'd into a Monarchy, *Virgil* was helping
to that Design; by insinuating into the People the Piety of their
New Conquerour, to make them the better brook this Innova-
tion; which was brought on them by a Man, who was favour'd
by the Gods. Yet we may observe, that *Virgil* forgot not, upon
occasion, to speak Honourably of *Æneas,* in point of Courage,
and that particularly in the Person of him by whom he was
overcome. For *Diomedes* compares him with *Hector,* and even
with advantage.

> *Quicquid apud duræ cessatum est mœnia Trojæ;*
> *Hectoris, Æneæque manu Victoria Grajum*
> *Hæsit, & in decumum vestigia rettulit annum:*
> *Ambo animis, ambo insignes præstantibus armis;*
> *Hic Pietate prior———*

As for that particular Passage, cited by *Monsieur St. Evremont,*
where *Æneas* shows the utmost fear, in the beginning of a Tem-
pest (*Extemplo Æneæ solvuntur frigore membra,* &c.), why may
it not be supposed, that having been long at Sea, he might be
well acquainted with the Nature of a Storm; and by the rough
beginning, foresee the increase and danger of it? At least, as a
Father of his People, his concernment might be greater for them,
than for himself. And if so, what the Poet takes from the merit of
his Courage, is added to the prime vertue of his Character, which
was his Piety. Be this said, with all manner of Respect and Def-
erence, to the Opinion of *Monsieur St. Evremont;* amongst

---

13 Gods.] ~: O1–2.
23 *Evremont*] O2; *Euremont* O1.
24–25 Tempest (*Extemplo* . . . &c.), why] ~: ~ . . . *&c.*ᴧᴧ Why O1–2 (&c. O2).
33 *Evremont*] O2; *Euremont* O1.

whose admirable Talents, that of Penetration is not the least: He generally dives into the very bottom of his Authors; searches into the inmost recesses of their Souls, and brings up with him, those hidden Treasures which had escap'd the Diligence of others. His Examination of the *Grand Alexandre,* in my Opinion, is an admirable piece of Criticism; and I doubt not, but that his Observations on the *English* Theatre had been as absolute in their kind, had he seen with his own Eyes, and not with those of other Men. But conversing in a manner wholly with the
10 Court, which is not always the truest Judge, he has been unavoidably led into Mistakes, and given to some of our Coursest Poets a Reputation abroad, which they never had at home. Had his Conversation in the Town been more general, he had certainly received other Idea's on that Subject; and not transmitted those Names into his own Country, which will be forgotten by Posterity in ours.

Thus I have contracted my Thoughts on a Large Subject: for whatever has been said falls short of the true Character of *Monsieur St. Evremont* and his Writings: and if the Translation you
20 are about to read does not every where come up to the Original, the Translator desires you to believe, that it is only because that he has failed in his Undertaking.

J. Dryden.

---

5   *Grand*] Grand O1–2.
7   Theatre] *Theatre* O1–2.
19   *Evremont*] Euremont O1–2.

THE
HISTORY
OF
POLYBIUS
THE
MEGALOPOLITAN:

CONTAINING

A General Account

Of the Tranſactions of the

WORLD,

AND

Principally of the R oman People,

During the Firſt and Second *Punick* Wars, *&c.*

Tranſlated by Sir H. S.

To which is added, a Character of Polybius
and His Writings : By Mr. Dryden.

The firſt Volume.

LONDON,

Printed for Samuel Briſcoe over againſt *Wills*
Coffee-Houſe, in *Covent Garden.* MDCXCIII.

TITLE PAGE OF THE FIRST EDITION (MACDONALD 138A)

A Character of Polybius and His Writings

THE worthy Author of this Translation, who is very much my Friend, was pleas'd to intrust it in my hands, for many Months together, before he publish'd it; desiring me to review the *English,* and to Correct what I found amiss: which he needed not have done, if his Modesty wou'd have given him leave, to have relyed on his own Abilities; who is so great a Master of our Stile and Language, as the world will acknowledge him to be, after the reading of this Excellent Version.

'Tis true, that *Polybius* has formerly appear'd in an *English*
10 Dress; but under such a cloud of Errours, in his first Transla-
tion, that his native Beauty, was not only hidden, but his Sence
perverted, in many places: so that he appear'd unlike himself,
and unworthy of that esteem, which has always been paid him
by Antiquity, as the most sincere, the clearest, and most Instruc-
tive of all Historians. He is now not only redeem'd from those
mistakes, but also restor'd to the first purity of his Conceptions:
And the Stile in which he now speaks is as plain and unaffected,
as that he Wrote. I had only the pleasure of reading him, in a fair
Manuscript, without the toyl of alteration: At least it was so
20 very inconsiderable, that it only cost me the dash of a Pen in
some few places, and those of very small importance: so much
had the care, the diligence, and exactness of my Friend prevented
my trouble, that he left me not the occasion of serving him in a
work which was already finish'd to my hands: I doubt not but the
Reader will approve my Judgment. So happy it is for a good
Author, to fall into the hands of a Translator, who is of a Genius
like his own; who has added experience to his natural Abilities;
who has been educated in business, of several kinds; has Travell'd
like his Author into many parts of the World, and some of them

---

4 *English*] English O1–2. [These sigla are identified in the Textual Notes, where also fluctuations in the texts cited are explained.]
9 'Tis] *no paragraph break in* O1–2.
9 *English*] English O1–2.
14 clearest,] O2; ~∧ O1.
19 Manuscript,] O2; ~∧ O1.
27 own;] O2; ~: O1.
28 kinds;] O2; ~, O1.

the same with the present Scene of History; has been employed
in business of the like Nature, with *Polybius;* and like him is
perfectly acquainted, not only with the terms of the Mathe-
maticks, but has search'd into the bottom of that admirable
Science, and reduc'd into practice the most useful Rules of it,
to his own Honour, and the benefit of his native Country; who,
besides these advantages, possesses the knowledge of Shipping
and Navigation; and, in few words, is not ignorant of any thing
that concerns the Tacticks: So that here, from the beginning,
10 we are sure of finding nothing that is not throughly understood.
The expression is clear, and the words adequate to the Subject.
Nothing in the matter will be mistaken; nothing of the terms will
be misapplyed: All is natural, and proper; and he who under-
stands good Sence and *English,* will be profited by the first, and
delighted with the latter. This is what may be justly said in com-
mendation of the Translator, and without the note of flattery to
a Freind.

As for his Author, I shall not be asham'd to Copy from the
Learned *Casaubon,* (who has translated him into *Latin,)* many
20 things which I had not from my own small reading, and which
I cou'd not without great difficulty have drawn but from his
Fountain, not omitting some, which came casually in my way,
by reading the Preface of the Abbot *Pichon,* to the Dauphin's
Tacitus, an admirable and most useful work; which helps I in-
genuously profess to have receiv'd from them, both to clear my
self from being a Plagiary of their Writings, and to give authority
by their names, to the weakness of my own Performance.

The taking of *Constantinople* by *Mahomet* the Great, fell into
the latter times of Pope *Nicholas* the Fifth: a Pope not only
30 studious of good Letters, and particularly of History, but also a
great Encourager of it in others. From the dreadful overthrow
of that City, and final subversion of the *Greek* Empire, many

---

1   History;] O2; ~, O1.   5   it,] O2; ~; O1.
6   Country; who,] O2; ~. Who∧ O1.   8   Navigation;] O2; ~, O1.
8   and, . . . words,] O2; ~∧ . . . ~∧ O1. 9   Tacticks:] O2; ~. O1.
14 *English*] English O1-2.   19 *Latin*] Latine O1-2.
23 Dauphin's] *Dauphin's* O1-2.   24 work; which] O2; ~. Which O1.
25 them,] O2; ~; O1.   29 Fifth] O2; fifth O1.

learned Men escap'd, and brought over with them into *Italy,* that
treasure of antient Authors, which by their unhappiness we now
possess; and amongst the rest, some of these remaining fragments
of *Polybius.* The body of this History, as he left it finish'd, was
consisting of forty Books, of which the eighth part is only re-
maining to us entire. As for his Negotiations, when he was sent
Ambassador, either from his own Countrymen, the Common-
wealth of the *Achaians,* or afterwards was employed by the
Romans, on their business with other Nations, we are oblig'd to
10 *Constantine* the Great, for their preservation; for that Emperour
was so much in love with the dexterous management, and wis-
dom of our Author, that he caus'd them all, to be faithfully tran-
scrib'd, and made frequent use of them in his own Dispatches
and Affairs with Foreign Princes, as his best guides in his con-
cernments with them.

   Polybius, as you will find in reading of him, though he prin-
cipally intended the History of the *Romans,* and the Establish-
ment of their Empire over the greatest part of the World which
was then known, yet had in his Eye the general History of the
20 times in which he liv'd, not forgetting either the Wars of his own
Country, with their Neighbours of *Etolia,* or the concurrent Af-
fairs of *Macedonia,* and the Provinces of *Greece,* (which is prop-
erly so call'd;) nor the Monarchys of *Asia,* and *Egypt;* nor the
Republick of the *Carthaginians,* with the several traverses of
their Fortunes, either in Relation to the *Romans,* or indepen-
dant to the Wars, which they wag'd with them; besides what
happen'd in *Spain,* and *Sicily,* and other *European* Countrys.
The time which is taken up in this History consists of three and
fifty Years; and the greatest part of it is employ'd in the descrip-
30 tion of those events, of which the Author was an Eye-witness, or
bore a considerable part in the Conduct of them. But in what

3   possess; and] ~. And O1–2.   4   *Polybius.* The] O2; ~: the O1.
6   us] ~, O1–2.   8   *Achaians*] O2; *Achians* O1.
16 *Polybius*] *no paragraph break in O1–2.*
18 Empire] ~, O1–2.   18 World] ~, O1–2.
19 known,] ~; O1–2.
23 *Egypt;*] *Ægypt,* O1; *Egypt,* O2.
26 them;] ~, O1–2.

particular Time or Age it was, when mankind receiv'd that irre-
coverable loss of this noble History, is not certainly deliver'd to
us. It appears to have been perfect, in the Reign of *Constantine,*
by what I have already noted; and neither *Casaubon,* nor any
other, can give us any further account concerning it.

The first attempt towards a Translation of him, was by com-
mand of the same Pope *Nicholas* the Fifth, already mention'd,
who esteem'd him the Prince of *Greek* Historians; wou'd have
him continually in his hands; and us'd to make this Judgment
10 of him—that, if he yielded to one or two, in the praise of Elo-
quence, yet in Wisdom, and all other Accomplishments belong-
ing to a perfect Historian, he was at least equal to any other
Writer, *Greek* or *Roman,* and perhaps excell'd them all. This
is the Author, who is now offer'd to us in our Mother Tongue,
recommended by the Nobility of his Birth, by his Institution in
Arts and Sciences, by his knowledge in Natural and Moral Phi-
losophy, and particularly the Politicks; by his being conversant
both in the Arts of Peace, and War; by his Education under his
Father *Lycortas,* who voluntarily depos'd himself from his Sov-
20 eraignty of *Megalopolis,* to become a Principal Member of the
Achaian Commonwealth, which then flourish'd under the man-
agement of *Aratus;* by his friendship with *Scipio Africanus,* who
subdued *Carthage,* to whom he was both a Companion, and a
Counsellour; and by the good will, esteem and intimacy which
he had with several Princes of *Asia, Greece* and *Egypt* during his
Life; and after his Decease, by deserving the applause, and ap-
probation of all succeeding Ages.

This Author so long neglected in the barbarous times of Chris-
tianity, and so little known in *Europe,* (according to the fate
30 which commonly follows the best of Writers) was pull'd from
under the Rubbish which cover'd him, by the learned Bishop,

---

6   The] *no paragraph break in O1–2.*
7   Fifth,] O2; ~ₐ O1.
7   mention'd] O2; mention,d O1.
8   *Greek* Historians;] Greek ~: O1–2.
10 him—] ~; O1–2.
22 *Aratus;*] ~, O1–2.
24 Counsellour;] O2; ~: O1.
28 This] *no paragraph break in O1–2.*

17 Politicks;] O2; ~: O1.
22 *Africanus*] *Affricanus* O1–2.
25 *Egypt*] O2; *Egyyt* O1.

Nicholas the Fifth. And some parts of his History, (for with all his diligence he was not able to recover the whole) were by him recommended to a person (knowing both in the *Greek* and *Roman* tongues, and learn'd for the times in which he liv'd) to be translated into *Latin:* and to the Honour of our *Polybius,* he was amongst the first of the *Greek* Writers, who deserv'd to have this care bestow'd on him; which notwithstanding, so many hindrances occurr'd in this attempt, that the work was not perfected in his Popedome, neither was any more than a third part of what
10 is now recover'd in his hands; neither did that learn'd *Italian,* who had undertaken him, succeed very happily in that endeavour: For the perfect knowledge of the *Greek* Language was not yet restor'd; and that Translator was but as a one-ey'd man, amongst the Nation of the Blind, only suffer'd, till a better could be found, to do right to an Author, whose excellence requir'd a more just Interpreter, than the ignorance of that Age afforded. And this gives me occasion to admire, (says *Casaubon,*) that in following times, when Eloquence was redeem'd and the knowledge of the *Greek* Language flourish'd, yet no man thought of
20 pursuing that design, which was so worthily begun, in those first Rudiments of Learning. Some indeed, of almost every Nation in *Europe,* have been instrumental in the recovery of several lost parts of our *Polybius,* and commented on them with good success; but no man before *Casaubon,* had review'd the first Translation, corrected its Errours, and put the last hand to its accomplishment. The World is therefore beholding to him for this great Work: for he has collected into one their scattered Fragments, has piec'd them together, according to the natural order in which they were written, made them intelligible to Scholars,
30 and render'd the *French* Translator's task more easie to his hands.

Our Author is particularly mention'd, with great Honour, by

---

3   (knowing] O2; ₄~ O1.   5   *Latin*] Latin O1–2.
7   him; which] ~. Which O1–2.
12   *Greek*] Greek O1–2.
13   one-ey'd man] O2; one-ey'd-man O1.
19   *Greek*] Greek O1–2.   29   written,] ~; O1–2.
30   Translator's] O2; Translators O1.
31   Our] *no paragraph break in O1–2.*

Cicero, Strabo, Josephus, and *Plutarch;* and in what rank of
Writers they are plac'd, none of the Learned need to be inform'd:
he is copyed in whole Books together by *Livy,* commonly es-
teem'd the Prince of the *Roman* History, and translated word
for word; Tho the *Latin* Historian is not to be excus'd, for not
mentioning the man to whom he had been so much oblig'd, nor
for taking as his own the worthy labours of another. *Marcus
Brutus,* who preferr'd the freedom of his Country to the obliga-
tions which he had to *Julius Cæsar,* so priz'd *Polybius,* that he
10 made a Compendium of his Works, and read him not only for
his Instruction, but for the diversion of his Grief, when his Noble
enterprise for the restoration of the Commonwealth had not
found the success which it deserv'd. And this is not the least
Commendation of our Author, that He, who was not wholly
satisfied with the eloquence of *Tully,* shou'd Epitomize *Polybius,*
with his own hand. It was on the consideration of *Brutus,* and
the veneration which he paid him, that *Constantine* the Great
took so great a pleasure in reading our Author, and collecting
the several Treaties of his Embassies: of which, tho many are
20 now lost, yet those which remain are a sufficient testimony of his
abilities; and I congratulate my Country, that a Prince of our
Extraction, (as was *Constantine,*) has the honour of obliging the
Christian World, by these remainders of our great Historian.

'Tis now time to enter into the particular Praises of *Polybius,*
which I have given you before in gross: and the first of them,
(following the method of *Casaubon,*) is his wonderfull skill in
political Affairs. I had read him in *English* with the pleasure of
a Boy, before I was ten years of Age: and yet even then, had some
dark Notions of the prudence with which he conducted his de-
30 sign; particularly in making me know, and almost see the places
where such and such Actions were perform'd. This was the first
distinction which I was then capable of making, betwixt him
and other Historians, which I read early. But when being of a
riper Age, I took him again into my hands; I must needs say,

4   *Roman*] Roman O1–2.   5   *Latin*] Latin O1–2.
5   be excus'd] O2; beexcus'd O1.
19   which,] O2; ~ᴧ O1.
24   'Tis] *no paragraph break in O1–2.*
25   before] ~, O1–2.   27   *English*] English O1–2.

that I have profited more by reading him, than by *Thucydides,*
Appian, Dion Cassius, and all the rest of the *Greek* Historians
together: And amongst all the *Romans,* none have reach'd him
in this particular, but only *Tacitus,* who is equal to him.

'Tis wonderful to consider, with how much care and applica-
tion he instructs, counsels, warns, admonishes and advises, when-
soever he can find a fit occasion: He performs all these sometimes
in the nature of a Common Parent of mankind; and sometimes
also limits his instructions to particular Nations, by a friendly
10 reproach of those failings, and errours, to which they were most
obnoxious. In this last manner, he gives instructions to the *Man-*
tinæans, the *Elæans,* and several other Provinces of *Greece* by
informing them of such things as were conducing to their wel-
fare. Thus he likewise warns the *Romans* of their obstinacy, and
willfulness, vices which have often brought them to the brink
of ruine. And thus he frequently exhorts the *Greeks* in general,
not to depart from their dependance on the *Romans;* nor to
take false measures by embroiling themselves in wars with that
Victorious People, in whose fate it was to be Masters of the
20 Universe. But as his peculiar concernment was for the safety of
his own Countrymen, the *Achaians,* he more than once insinu-
ates to them, the care of their preservation, which consisted in
submitting to the Yoke of the *Roman* people, which they cou'd
not possibly avoid: and to make it easie to them, by a chearful
compliance with their commands, rather than unprofitably to
oppose them, with the hazard of those remaining Priviledges,
which the Clemency of the Conquerours had left them. For this
reason, in the whole course of his History, he makes it his chief-
est business to perswade the *Grecians* in general, that the grow-
30 ing Greatness and Fortune of the *Roman* Empire was not owing
to meer chance, but to the Conduct and invincible Courage of
that People, to whom their own Virtue gave the Dominion of
the World. And yet this Councellor of Patience and submission,
as long as there was any probability of hope remaining to with-

---

12 *Greece*] ∼; O1–2.
15 vices] ∼, O1–2.
16 *Greeks*] O2; Greeks O1.
21 Countrymen,] O2; ∼ₐ O1.
32 People,] ∼; O1–2.

15 willfulness,] ∼: O1; ∼; O2.
15 to the] O2; the to O1.
17 *Romans*] O2; Romans O1.
23 *Roman*] O2; Roman O1.
34 remaining] ∼, O1–2.

stand the progress of the *Roman* Fortune, was not wanting to the utmost of his power to resist them, at least to deferr the bondage of his Country, which he had long foreseen. But the Fates inevitably drawing all things into subjection to *Rome,* this well-deserving Citizen was commanded to appear in that City, where he suffer'd the imprisonment of many years: Yet even then his Virtue was beneficial to him; the knowledge of his Learning and his Wisdom, procuring him the friendship of the most Potent in the Senate; so that it may be said, with *Casaubon,*
10 that the same Virtue which had brought him into distress, was the very means of his relief, and of his exaltation to greater Dignities than those which he lost: For by the intercession of *Cato* the Censor, *Scipio Emilianus,* who afterwards destroy'd *Carthage,* and some other principal Noblemen, our *Polybius* was restor'd to Liberty. After which, having set it down as a Maxim, that the welfare of the *Achaians* consisted, as I have said, in breaking their own stubborn inclinations, and yielding up that freedom which they no longer could maintain, he made it the utmost aim of his endeavours, to bring over his Countrymen to
20 that perswasion: in which, though to their misfortune, his Councils were not prevalent, yet thereby he not only prov'd himself a good Patriot, but also made his Fortunes with the *Romans.* For his Countrymen, by their own unpardonable fault, not long afterwards, drew on themselves their own destruction: For when *Mummius,* in the *Achaian* War, made a final Conquest of that Country; he dissolv'd the great Council of their Commonwealth. But in the mean time, *Polybius* enjoy'd that tranquillity of fortune, which he had purchas'd by his wisdom; in that private State, being particularly dear to *Scipio* and *Lelius,* & some of the rest
30 who were then in the Administration of the *Roman* Government. And that favour which he had gain'd amongst them, he employed not in heaping riches to himself; but as a means of performing many considerable Actions; as particularly, when *Scipio* was sent to demolish *Carthage,* he went along with him, in the nature of a Counsellor, and Companion of his enterprise. At

which time, receiving the command of a Fleet from him, he
made discoverys in many parts of the *Atlantick* Ocean; and es-
pecially on the Shores of *Africa:* and doing many good Offices to
all sorts of people, whom he had power to oblige, especially to
the *Grecians,* who in honour of their Benefactor, caus'd many
Statues of him to be erected; as *Pausanias* has written. The par-
ticular gratitude of the *Locrians* in *Italy,* is also an undeniable
witness of this truth; who, by his Mediation, being discharg'd
from the burden of Taxes which oppress'd them, through the
10 hardship of those conditions which the *Romans* had impos'd on
them in the Treaty of Peace, profess'd themselves to be owing
for their Lives and Fortunes, to the only interest and good nature
of *Polybius,* which they took care to express, by all manner of
acknowledgment.

Yet as beneficent as he was, the greatest obligement which he
cou'd lay on humane kind, was the writing of this present His-
tory: Wherein he has left a perpetual Monument of his publick
Love to all the World, in every succeeding Age of it, by giving
us such precepts, as are most conducing to our common safety,
20 and our benefit. This Philanthropy (which we have not a proper
word in *English* to express) is every where manifest in our
Author. And from hence proceeded that Divine rule which he
gave to *Scipio,* that whensoever he went abroad, he shou'd take
care not to return to his own house, before he had acquir'd a
Friend, by some new obligement. To this Excellency of Nature
we owe the treasure which is contain'd in this most useful work:
This is the Standard by which all good and prudent Princes
ought to regulate their Actions: None have more need of Friends
than Monarchs. And though ingratitude is too frequent, in the
30 most of those who are oblig'd, yet incouragement will work on
generous minds; and if the experiment be lost on thousands, yet

---

1 time] O2; tmie O1.
5 *Grecians*] Grecians O1–2.
8 who, . . . Mediation,] $\sim_\wedge$ . . . $\sim_\wedge$ O1–2 (who, O2).
9 Taxes] $\sim$, O1–2.
15 Yet] *no paragraph break in O1–2.*
20 Philanthropy] *Philanthropy* O1–2.
21 *English*] English O1–2.
27 Standard] O2; Sandard O1.
30 oblig'd,] $\sim$; O1–2.

2 *Atlantick*] Atlantick O1–2.
6 Statues] O2; Statutes O1.
11 Peace,] $\sim$; O1–2.

it never fails on all. And one vertuous Man in a whole Nation is
worth the buying; as one Diamond is worth the search, in a heap
of Rubbish. But a narrow-hearted Prince, who thinks that Man-
kind is made for him alone, puts his Subjects in a way of desert-
ing him on the first occasion; and teaches them to be as sparing
of their Duty, as he is of his Bounty. He is sure of making Ene-
mies, who will not be at the cost of rewarding his Friends and
Servants; and by letting his people see he loves them not, in-
structs them to live upon the square with him, and to make him
10 sensible in his turn, that Prerogatives are given, but Priviledges
are inherent. As for tricking, cunning, and that which in Sov-
eraigns they call King-craft, and reason of State in Common-
wealths, to them and their Proceedings *Polybius* is an open
Enemy. He severely reproves all faithless practices, and that
Κακοπραγμόσυνη, or vicious Policy, which is too frequent in the
management of the Publick. He commends nothing but plain-
ness, sincerity and the common good, undisguis'd, and set in a
true Light before the People: Not but that there may be a neces-
sity of saving a Nation, by going beyond the letter of the Law, or
20 even sometimes by superseding it; but then that necessity must
not be artificial, it must be visible, it must be strong enough to
make the remedy not only pardon'd, but desir'd, to the major
part of the people; not for the interest only of some few men,
but for the Publick safety: for otherwise one infringement of a
Law, draws after it the practice of subverting all the Liberties
of a Nation; which are only intrusted with any Government,
but can never be given up to it. The best way to distinguish
betwixt a pretended necessity and a true, is to observe if the
remedy be rarely apply'd, or frequently; in times of Peace or
30 times of War and publick Distractions, which are the most usual
causes of suddain Necessities. From hence *Casaubon* infers, That
this our Author who preaches Vertue and Probity and Plain-
dealing, ought to be studied principally by Kings and Ministers
of State: and that Youth which are bred up to succeed in the

8   Servants; and] ∼. And O1–2.   11   and] O2; ∼, O1.
12–13   Commonwealths,] ∼: O1–2.   18   Light] ∼, O1–2.
23   people;] ∼: O1–2.   24   safety:] ∼, O1–2.
26   Government,] ∼; O1–2.   29   frequently; in] ∼. In O1–2.

management of business, should read him carefully, and imbibe him throughly, detesting the Maxims that are given by *Machiavel* and others, which are only the Instruments of Tyranny. Farther-more, (continues he) the study of Truth is perpetually joyn'd with the love of Vertue: for there is no Vertue which derives not its original from Truth: as on the contrary, there is no Vice which has not its beginning from a Lye. Truth is the foundation of all Knowledge, and the cement of all Societies: And this is one of the most shining qualities in our
10 Author.

I was so strongly persuaded of this my self, in the perusal of the present History, that I confess, amongst all the Antients I never found any who had the air of it so much; & amongst the Moderns, none but *Philip de Commines*. They had this common to them, that they both chang'd their Masters: But *Polybius* chang'd not his side, as *Philip* did: he was not bought off to another Party; but pursu'd the true interest of his Country, even when he serv'd the *Romans*. Yet since Truth, (as one of the Philosophers has told us) lyes in the bottom of a Well; so 'tis hard to
20 draw it up: much pains, much diligence, much judgment is necessary to hand it to us: even cost is oftentimes requir'd: and *Polybius* was wanting in none of these.

We find but few Historians of all Ages, who have been diligent enough in their search for Truth: 'tis their common method to take on trust what they distribute to the Publick; by which means a falshood once receiv'd from a fam'd Writer, becomes traditional to Posterity. But *Polybius* weigh'd the Authors from whom he was forc'd to borrow the History of the Times immediately preceding his, and oftentimes corrected them, either by
30 comparing them each with other, or by the lights which he had receiv'd from antient men of known integrity amongst the *Romans*, who had been conversant in those Affairs which were then

---

8 Knowledge,] O2; ∼: O1.
11 I] *no paragraph break in O1–2.*
12 History,] O2; ∼; O1.
12 Antients] O2; ∼, O1.
25 Publick;] O2; ∼: O1.
29 his,] ∼: O1; ∼; O2.
31 men] O2; ∼, O1.

8–9 Societies:] ∼. O1–2.
11 perusal] perusual O1–2.
12 confess,] O2; ∼ₐ O1.
23 We] *no paragraph break in O1–2.*
26 Writer] O2; Writers O1.
30 other,] O2; ∼; O1.
32 Affairs] ∼, O1–2.

manag'd, and were yet living to instruct him. He also learn'd the
Roman Tongue, and attain'd to that knowledge of their Laws,
their Rights, their Customs and Antiquities, that few of their
own Citizens understood them better; having gain'd permission
from the Senate, to search the Capitol, he made himself familiar
with their Records, and afterwards translated them into his
Mother-tongue: So that he taught the Noble men of *Rome* their
own Municipal Laws, and was accounted more skillful in them,
than *Fabius Pictor,* a man of the Senatorian Order, who wrote
10 the Transactions of the *Punick* Wars. He who neglected none
of the Laws of History, was so careful of truth, (which is the
principal,) that he made it his whole business to deliver nothing
to Posterity, which might deceive them; and by that diligence
and exactness may easily be known to be studious of Truth, and
a lover of it. What therefore *Brutus* thought worthy to transcribe
with his own hand out of him, I need not be asham'd to Copy
after him. *I believe,* says *Polybius, That Nature her self has
constituted truth as the supream Deity, which is to be ador'd
by mankind; and that she has given it greater force than any of*
20 *the rest: For being oppos'd, as she is on all sides, and appearances
of truth so often passing for the thing it self, in behalf of plausible
falshoods, yet by her wonderful operation she insinuates her self
into the minds of Men; sometimes exerting her strength imme-
diately, and sometimes lying hid in darkness for length of time;
but at last she struggles through it, and appears Triumphant
over falshood.* This sincerity *Polybius* preferr'd to all his Friends,
and even to his Father. In all other offices of life, sayes he, I
praise a lover of his friends, and of his native Country; but in
writing History, I am oblig'd to divest my self of all other obli-
30 gations, and sacrifice them all to Truth.

Aratus the *Sicyonian,* in the childhood of our Author, was
chief of the *Achaian* Commonwealth; a Man in principal esteem,

2 Tongue,] O2; ~; O1.   7 Mother-tongue:] ~. ~. O1–2.
14 known] O2; ~, O1.   17 *I believe*] O2; I believe O1.
19 *mankind;*] O2; ~: O1.   22 *falshoods,*] ~; O1–2.
23–24 *immediately,*] O2; ~; O1.   24 *time;*] O2; ~, O1.
27 In ... [*to*] ... life] *in italics in* O1–2.
27–30 I ... [*to*] ... Truth] *in italics in* O1–2.
31 *Aratus*] *no paragraph break in* O1–2.

both in his own Country and in all the Provinces of *Greece:* ad-
mir'd universally for his probity, his wisdom, his just Administra-
tion and his Conduct. In remembrance of all which, his grateful
Country-men, after his Decease, ordain'd him those Honours
which are only due to Heroes. Him, our *Polybius* had in ven-
eration, and form'd himself by imitation of his Vertues: and is
never wanting in his Commendations through the course of his
History. Yet even this man, when the cause of truth requir'd it,
is many times reprov'd by him, for his slowness in Counsel, his
10 tardiness in the beginning of his Enterprises, his tedious and
more than *Spanish* deliberations: and his heavy and cowardly
proceedings are as freely blam'd by our *Polybius,* as they were
afterwards by *Plutarch,* who questionless drew his character from
this History. In plain terms, that wise General scarce ever per-
form'd any great Action but by night. The glittering of a Sword
before his face was offensive to his eyes: Our Author therefore
boldly accuses him of his faint-heartedness; attributes the defeat
at *Caphiæ* wholly to him; and is not sparing to affirm, that all
Peloponnesus was fill'd with Trophies, which were set up, as
20 the monuments of his losses. He sometimes praises, & at other
times condemns the proceedings of *Philip,* King of *Macedon,*
the Son of *Demetrius,* according to the occasions which he gave
him, by the variety and inequality of his Conduct: And this most
exquisitely on either side. He more than once arraigns him for
the inconstancy of his Judgment, and chapters even his own
Aratus, on the same head; shewing by many examples, produc'd
from their actions, how many miseries they had both occasion'd
to the *Grecians;* and attributing it to the weakness of humane
nature, which can make nothing perfect. But some men are brave
30 in Battle, who are weak in Counsel, which dayly experience sets
before our eyes; others deliberate wisely, but are weak in the
performing part; and even no man is the same to day which he
was yesterday, or may be to morrow. *On this account,* says our

---

10 Enterprises,] O2; ~; O1.
11 *Spanish*] Spanish O1–2.   13 *Plutarch,*] O2; ~: O1.
17 accuses] O2; cuses O1 (*but catchword on preceding page is* "accuses").
21 *Philip,*] ~ₐ O1–2.   24 He] *paragraph break in O1–2.*
25 Judgment,] ~: O1–2.   28 Grecians; and] ~. And O1–2.
33 *On this account*] *in romans in O1–2.*

Author, *a good man is some times liable to blame, and a bad
man, though not often, may possibly deserve to be commended.*
And for this very reason he severely taxes *Timæus,* a malicious
Historian, who will allow no kind of Vertue to *Agathocles,* the
Tyrant of *Sicily;* but detracts from all his Actions, even the most
Glorious, because in general he was a vicious Man. *Is it to be
thought,* says *Casaubon, that* Polybius *lov'd the Memory of*
Agathocles *the Tyrant, or hated that of the Vertuous* Aratus?
But 'tis one thing to commend a Tyrant, and another thing to
10 overpass in silence, those laudable Actions which are perform'd
by him: because it argues an Author of the same falshood, to
pretermit what has actually been done, as to feign those actions
which have never been.

It will not be unprofitable in this place, to give another famous
instance of the Candour and Integrity of our Historian. There
had been an ancient League betwixt the Republick of *Achaia*
and the Kings of *Egypt:* which was entertain'd by both parties,
sometimes on the same Conditions, and sometimes also the Con-
federacy was renew'd on other Terms. It happen'd in the 148th
20 *Olympiad,* that *Ptolemy Epiphanes,* on this occasion, sent one
Demetrius his Ambassadour to the Commonwealth of *Achaia.*
That Republick was then ruinously divided into two Factions:
whereof the heads on one side, were *Philopœmen,* and *Lycortas,*
the Father of our Author; of the adverse party, the Chief was
Aristænus, with some other principal *Achaians.* The Faction of
Philopœmen was prevalent in the Council, for renewing the
Confederacy with the King of *Egypt:* in order to which, *Lycortas*
receiv'd a Commission to go to that Court, and treat the Articles
of Alliance. Accordingly he goes, and afterward returns, and
30 gives an account to his Superiours, that the Treaty was con-
cluded. *Aristænus,* hearing nothing but a bare relation of a
League that was made, without any thing belonging to the con-
ditions of it, and well knowing that several forms of those Al-

4   *Agathocles,*] ∼ₐ O1–2.   6   general] O2; genral O1.
6–7   *Is . . .* [*to*] *. . . thought*] O2; *in romans in O1.*
12   pretermit] ∼, O1–2.   14   It] *no paragraph break in O1–2.*
19   Terms.] O1 *(uncorrected form),* O2; ∼ₐ O1 *(corrected form* [*first and second*
states]).   19   148th] O2; 148*th.* O1.
20   *Olympiad*] Olympiad O1–2.   23   *Lycortas,*] ∼ₐ O1–2.

liances had been us'd in the former Negotiations, ask'd *Lycortas* in the Council, according to which of them this present Confederacy was made? To this question of his Enemy, *Lycortas* had not a word to answer. For it had so happen'd by the wonderful neglect of *Philopœmen* and his own, and also that of *Ptolemy's* Counsellours, (or as I rather believe, by their craft contriv'd,) that the whole transaction had been loosely and confus'dly manag'd, which in a matter of so great importance redounded to the Scandal and Ignominy of *Philopœmen* and *Lycortas,* in the face
10 of that grave Assembly. Now these Proceedings our Author so relates as if he had been speaking of persons to whom he had no manner of relation, tho one of them was his own Father, and the other always esteem'd by him in the place of a better Father. But being mindful of the Law which himself had instituted, concerning the indispensible duty of an Historian, (which is Truth) he chose rather to be thought a lover of it, than of either of his Parents. Tis true, *Lycortas* in all probability was dead, when *Polybius* wrote this History; but had he been then living, we may safely think that his Son wou'd have assum'd the same
20 liberty, and not fear'd to have offended him in behalf of truth.

Another part of his veracity is also deserving the notice of the Reader (tho at the same time we must conclude, that it was also an effect of a sound judgment): that he perpetually explodes the Legends of Prodigies and Miracles, and instead of them most accurately searches into the natural causes of those actions which he describes; for from the first of these the latter follows of direct consequence. And for this reason he professes an immortal enmity to those tricks and jugglings, which the Common people believe as real Miracles, because they are ignorant of the causes
30 which produc'd them. But he had made a diligent search into them, and found out that they proceeded either from the fond credulity of the people, or were impos'd on them by the craft

6   (or] $_\wedge\sim$ O1–2.   6   believe,] O2; $\sim_\wedge$ O1.
6   contriv'd,)] $\sim_{,\wedge}$ O1–2.   14   Law] O2; *Law* O1.
21   Another] *no paragraph break in O1–2.*
22   Reader (tho] $\sim$: $\sim$ O1; $\sim$, $\sim$ O2.
23   judgment):] $\sim$: O1; $\sim$; O2.
26   describes; for] O1 *(uncorrected form and corrected form [first state]; catchword on preceding page is* "scribes;"*),* O2; $\sim$. For O1 *(corrected form [second state]).*

of those whose interest it was that they should be believ'd. You hear not in *Polybius,* that it rain'd Blood, or Stones; that a Bull had spoken; or a thousand such impossibilities, with which *Livy* perpetually crowds the Calends of almost every Consulship. His new years could no more begin without them, during his description of the *Punick* Wars, than our Prognosticating Almanacks without the effects of the present oppositions betwixt *Saturn* and *Jupiter,* the foretelling of Comets and Coruscations in the Air, which seldom happen at the times assign'd by our
10 Astrologers, and almost always fail in their Events. If you will give credit to other Authors, some God was always present with *Hannibal,* or *Scipio,* to direct their Actions: that a visible Deity wrought journey-work under *Hannibal,* to conduct him through the difficult passages of the *Alpes;* and another did the same office of drudgery for *Scipio,* when he besieg'd *New Carthage,* by draining the Waters, which otherwise wou'd have drown'd his Army, in their rash approaches: Which *Polybius* observing, says wittily and truly, that the Authors of such fabulous kind of stuff, write Tragedies, not Histories. For as the Poets, when they are at
20 a loss for the solution of a Plot, bungle up their Catastrophe, with a God descending in a Machine: So these inconsiderate Historians, when they have brought their Hero's into a plunge, by some rash and headlong undertaking, having no humane way remaining to disingage them with their honour, are forc'd to have recourse to Miracle; and introduce a God for their deliverance. 'Tis a common frenzy of the ignorant multitude, says *Casaubon,* to be always ingaging Heaven on their side: and indeed it is a successful Stratagem of any General, to gain authority among his Souldiers, if he can perswade them, that he is the man
30 by Fate appointed for such, or such an Action, though most impracticable. To be favour'd of God, and command, (if it may be permitted so to say,) the extraordinary concourse of Providence, sets off a Heroe, and makes more specious the Cause for which he fights, without any consideration of Morality, which ought to be

---

3 spoken;] ~, O1–2.
14 *Alpes*] Alpes O1–2.
17 approaches:] ~. O1–2.
34 fights,] O2; ~: O1.

13 *Hannibal*] O2; *Hanibal* O1.
15 *New*] new O1; New O2.
33 Heroe,] O2; ~: O1.

the beginning and end of all our Actions: For where that is vio-
lated, God is only present in permission; and suffers a wrong to
be done, but not commands it. Light Historians and such as are
superstitious in their Natures, by the artifice of feign'd Miracles,
captivate the gross understandings of their Readers, and please
their fancies by relations of things which are rather wonderful
than true: But such as are of a more profound and solid Judg-
ment, (which is the Character of our *Polybius,*) have recourse
only to their own natural lights, and by them pursue the methods
10 at least of probability, if they cannot arrive to a settl'd certainty.
He was satisfi'd that *Hannibal* was not the first, who had made a
passage through the *Alpes,* but that the *Gauls* had been before
him in their Descent on *Italy;* and also knew, that this most pru-
dent General, when he laid his design of Invading that Country,
had made an Alliance with the *Gauls,* and prepossess'd them in
his Favour; and before he stirr'd a foot from *Spain,* had provided
against all those difficulties which he foresaw in his attempt, and
compass'd his undertaking, which indeed was void of Miracles,
but full of conduct, and Military experience. In the same man-
20 ner *Scipio,* before he departed from *Rome* to take his Voyage
into *Spain,* had carefully consider'd every particular Circum-
stance which might cross his purpose, and made his enterprise as
easie to him as humane prudence could provide; so that he was
victorious over that Nation, not by vertue of any Miracle, but
by his admirable forecast, and wise Conduct in the execution of
his Design. Of which, tho *Polybius* was not an eye-witness, yet
he had it from the best testimony, which was that of *Lelius,* the
Friend of *Scipio,* who accompanied him in that Expedition; of
whom our Author with great diligence enquir'd concerning
30 every thing of Moment, which happen'd in that War, and whom
he commends for his sincerity in that relation.

Whensoever he gives us the account of any considerable Ac-
tion, he never fails to tell us why it succeeded, or for what reason
it miscarried; together with all the antecedent causes of its un-

1   Actions:] ~. O1–2.
12   *Alpes*] Alpes O1–2.
16   Favour;] ~, O1–2.
26   which,] O2; ~_∧ O1.
32   Whensoever] *no paragraph break in O1–2.*

8   *Polybius*] O2; Polybins O1.
14   General,] O2; ~_∧ O1.
20   *Scipio,*] O2; ~_∧ O1.
28   Expedition;] ~, O1–2.

dertaking, and the manner of its performance; all which he accurately explains: Of which, I will select but some few instances, because I want leisure to expatiate on many. In the fragments of the 17th Book he makes a learned dissertation concerning the *Macedonian* Phalanx, or gross body of Foot, which was formerly believ'd to be invincible, till experience taught the contrary, by the success of the Battle, which *Philip* lost to the Commonwealth of *Rome;* and the manifest and most certain causes are therein related, which prove it to be inferiour to the *Roman* Legions.
10 When also he had told us in his former Books of the three great Battels wherein *Hannibal* had overthrown the *Romans,* and the last at *Cannæ,* wherein he had in a manner conquer'd that Republick, he gives the reasons of every Defeat, either from the choice of Ground, or the strength of foreign Horse in *Hannibal's* Army, or the ill timing of the Fight on the vanquish'd side. After this, when he describes the turn of Fortune on the part of the *Romans,* you are visibly conducted upwards to the causes of that change: and the reasonableness of the method which was afterward pursu'd by that Commonwealth, which rais'd it to the Empire of the World. In these and many other Examples, which for
20 brevity are omitted, there is nothing more plain, than that *Polybius* denies all power to Fortune, and places the sum of Success in Providence. Συμβαινόντων τύχην αἰτιᾶσθι, φαῦλον, indeed, are his words. 'Tis a madness to make Fortune the Mistress of Events, because in her self she is nothing, can rule nothing, but is rul'd by Prudence. So that whenever our Author seems to attribute any thing to Chance, he speaks only with the Vulgar, and desires so to be understood.

But here I must make bold to part Company with *Casaubon*
30 for a moment. He is a vehement Friend to any Author with whom he has taken any pains: and his partiality to *Persius,* in opposition to *Juvenal,* is too fresh in my memory to be forgotten. Because *Polybius* will allow nothing to the power of Chance, he

29:34–1 undertaking,] O2; ~; O1.   1 performance;] O2; ~: O1.
2 explains:] ~. O1–2.   2 which,] ~ₐ O1–2.
4 17th] O2; *17th* O1.   11 overthrown] O2; over thrown O1.
23 Συμβαινόντων] O1 *(some copies)* , O2; Συμβαιν ντων O1 *(some copies).*
23–24 indeed,] ~ₐ O1–2.   26 whenever] O2; when ever O1.
29 But] *no paragraph break in O1–2.*

takes an occasion to infer that he believ'd a Providence, sharply inveighing against those who have accus'd him of Atheism. He makes *Suidas* his Second in this quarrel, and produces his single Evidence, and that but a bare assertion, neither without proof, that *Polybius* believ'd, with us Christians, God administer'd all humane Actions and Affairs. But our Author will not be defended in this case, his whole History reclaims to that opinion. When he speaks of Providence, or of any Divine Admonition, he is as much in jest, as when he speaks of Fortune: 'tis all to the
10 capacity of the Vulgar. Prudence was the only Divinity which he worshipp'd; and the possession of Vertue the only End which he propos'd. If I would have disguis'd this to the Reader, it was not in my Power. The Passages which manifestly prove his Irreligion, are so obvious, that I need not quote them. Neither do I know any reason, why *Casaubon* shou'd inlarge so much in his Justification, since to believe false Gods, and to believe none, are Errors of the same importance. He who knew not our God, saw through the ridiculous Opinions of the Heathens concerning theirs: and not being able without Revelation, to go farther,
20 stopp'd at home in his own Breast, and made Prudence his Goddess, Truth his search, and Vertue his reward. If *Casaubon,* like him, had follow'd Truth, he would have sav'd me the Ungrateful Pains of contradicting him: But even the Reputation of *Polybius,* if there were occasion, is to be sacrific'd to Truth, according to his own Maxim.

As for the wisdom of our Author, whereby he wonderfully foresaw the decay of the *Roman* Empire, and those Civil Wars which turn'd it down from a Common-wealth, to an absolute Monarchy: He who will take the pains to review this History,
30 will easily perceive, that *Polybius* was of the best sort of Prophets, who predict from Natural Causes those Events, which must naturally proceed from them. And these things were not to succeed even in the compass of the next Century to that wherein he liv'd: But the Person was then living, who was the first mover towards them; and that was that great *Scipio Africanus,* who by cajolling

4   assertion,] ~‸ O1–2.   19   farther,] O2; ~; O1.
20   stopp'd] O2; stop'd O1.   26   As] *no paragraph break in O1–2.*
27   Empire] *Empire* O1–2.   33   liv'd:] ~. O1–2.

the People to break the Fundamental Constitutions of the Government in his Favour, by bringing him too early to the Consulship, and afterwards by making their Discipline of War precarious, First taught them to devolve the Power and Authority of the Senate into the hands of one, and then to make that one to be at the Disposition of the Souldiery; which though he practis'd at a time, when it was necessary for the safety of the Common-wealth, yet it drew after it those fatal Consequences, which not only ruin'd the Republick, but also, in process of
10 time, the Monarchy it self. But the Author was too much in the interests of that Family, to Name *Scipio;* and therefore he gives other Reasons, to which I refer the Reader, that I may avoid prolixity.

By what degrees *Polybius* arriv'd to this height of knowledge, and consummate judgment in Affairs, it will not be hard to make the Reader comprehend: for presupposing in him, all that Birth or Nature could give a Man, who was form'd for the management of great Affairs, and capable of recording them, he was likewise enter'd from his Youth into those Employments which add ex-
20 perience to natural Endowments; being join'd in Commission with his Father *Lycortas,* and the Younger *Aratus,* before the Age of Twenty, in an Embassy to *Egypt:* After which he was perpetually in the Business of his own Common-wealth, or that of *Rome.* So that it seems to be one part of the *Roman* Felicity that he was born in an Age, when their Common-wealth was growing to the heighth that he might be the Historian of those great Actions which were perform'd not only in his life time, but the chief of them even in his sight.

I must confess that the Preparations to his History, (or the
30 *Prolegomena* as they are call'd) are very large, and the Digressions in it, are exceeding frequent. But as to his Preparatives, they were but necessary, to make the Reader comprehend the drift and design of his Undertaking: And the Digressions are

---

1 People] ~, O1–2.
5 Senate] ~, O1–2.
16 comprehend:] ~; O1–2.
20 Endowments; being] ~. Being O1–2.
22 *Egypt:*] ~. O1–2.
33 Undertaking:] ~. O1–2.

1–2 Government] ~, O1–2.
14 By] *no paragraph break in O1–2.*
18 them,] ~; O1–2.

29 I] *no paragraph break in O1–2.*

also so instructive that we may truly say, they transcend the profit which we receive from the matter of Fact. Upon the whole we may conclude him to be a great Talker; but we must grant him to be a Prudent Man. We can spare nothing of all he says, 'tis so much to our Improvement; and if the rest of his History had remain'd to us, in all probability it wou'd have been more close: for we can scarce conceive what was left in nature for him to add, he has so emptied almost all the Common-places of Digressions already: or if he could have added any thing, those observa-
10 tions must have been as useful and as necessary, as the rest which he has given us, and that are descended to our Hands.

I will say nothing farther of the *Excerpta,* which (as *Casaubon* thinks) are part of that Epitome, which was begun to be made by *Marcus Brutus,* but never finish'd; nor of those Embassies which were collected and compil'd by the command of *Constantine* the Great: Because neither of them are translated in this Work. And whether or no they will be added in another Impression, I am not certain; the Translator of these five Books having carried his Work no farther, than it was perfect. He, I suppose, will acquaint
20 you with his own purpose in the Preface, which I hear he intends to prefix before *Polybius.*

Let us now hear *Polybius* himself describing an accomplished Historian, wherein we shall see his own Picture, as in a Glass, reflected to him, and given us afterwards to behold in the writing of this History.

Plato said of old, That it would be happy for Mankind, if either Philosophers administred the Government, or that Governours applied themselves to the study of Philosophy. I may also say, that it would be happy for History, if those who undertake,
30 to write it, were Men conversant in Political Affairs; who applied themselves seriously to their Undertaking; not negligently, but as such who were fully perswaded, that they undertook a Work of the greatest moment, of the greatest excellency, and the most

5 Improvement;] ~: O1–2.
8 add,] O2; ~: O1.
12 I] *no paragraph break in O1–2.*
14 finish'd;] O2; ~;) O1.
30 Affairs;] ~, O1–2.
6 close:] ~; O1–2.
9 already:] ~; O1–2.
12 *Excerpta,* which] O2; ~ (~ O1.
18 certain; the] ~. The O1–2.
32 such] ~, O1–2.

necessary for Mankind: Establishing this as the Foundation whereon they are to Build, that they can never be capable of performing their Duty, as they ought, unless they have form'd themselves before-hand to their undertaking, by prudence, and long experience of Affairs; without which Endowments and Advantages, if they attempt to write a History, they will fall into a various and endless Labyrinth of Errors.

When we hear this Author speaking, we are ready to think our selves engag'd in a Conversation with *Cato,* the Censor, with *Lelius,* with *Massinissa,* and with the two *Scipio's;* that is, with the greatest Heroes, and most prudent Men of the greatest Age, in the *Roman* Common-wealth. This sets me so on fire, when I am reading either here or in any ancient Author, their Lives and Actions, that I cannot hold from breaking out with *Montaign,* into this expression: *'Tis just,* says he, *for every honest man to be content with the Government, and Laws of his native Country, without endeavouring to alter or subvert them: but if I were to choose where I would have been born, it shou'd have been in a Commonwealth.* He indeed names *Venice;* which for many reasons shou'd not be my wish: but, rather *Rome* in such an Age, if it were possible, as that wherein *Polybius* liv'd: or that of *Sparta,* whose constitution for a Republick, is by our Author compar'd with *Rome;* to which he justly gives the Preference.

I will not undertake to compare *Polybius* and *Tacitus:* tho' if I shou'd attempt it, upon the whole merits of the Cause, I must allow to *Polybius* the greater comprehension, and the larger Soul; to *Tacitus* the greater eloquence, and the more close connection of his thoughts. The manner of *Tacitus* in writing, is more like the Force and Gravity of *Demosthenes;* that of *Polybius* more like the Copiousness, and diffusive Character of *Cicero.* Amongst Historians, *Tacitus* imitated *Thucydides,* and *Polybius, Herodotus. Polybius* foresaw the ruine of the *Roman* Commonwealth, by Luxury, Lust, and Cruelty; *Tacitus* foresaw in the Causes, those events which shou'd destroy the Monarchy. They

1   this] ∼, O1–2.   10   *Scipio's;*] *Scipio's,* O1–2.
15   *'Tis just*] "Tis just O1–2.   15   says he,] '∼ ∼ₐ O1–2 (he, O2).
15–19   *for . . . [to] . . . Commonwealth*] *in romans but set off by inverted commas in O1–2.*
23   *Rome;*] O2; ∼: O1.   31   *Thucydides*] *Thucidydes* O1–2.

are both of them, without dispute, the best Historians in their several kinds. In this they are alike, that both of them suffer'd under the iniquity of the times in which they liv'd: both their Histories are dismember'd, the greatest part of them lost, and they are interpolated in many places. Had their Works been perfect, we might have had longer Histories, but not better. *Casaubon,* according to his usual partiality, condemns *Tacitus,* that he may raise *Polybius,* who needs not any sinister Artifice, to make him appear equal to the best. *Tacitus* describ'd the
10 Times of Tyranny; but he always writes with some kind of indignation against them. 'Tis not his fault, that *Tiberius, Caligula, Nero* and *Domitian* were bad Princes. He is accus'd of malevolence, and of taking Actions in the worst sence: but we are still to remember that those were the Actions of Tyrants. Had the rest of his History remain'd to us, we had certainly found a better account of *Vespasian, Titus, Nerva,* and *Trajan,* who were vertuous Emperours: and he wou'd have given the principles of their Actions a contrary turn. But it is not my business to defend *Tacitus;* neither dare I decide the preference
20 betwixt him and our *Polybius.* They are equally profitable, and instructive to the Reader; but *Tacitus* more useful to those who are born under a Monarchy, *Polybius* to those who live in a Republick.

What may farther be added concerning the History of this Author, I leave to be perform'd, by the Elegant Translator of his Work.

JOHN DRYDEN.

---

11 'Tis] O2; ,Tis O1.   12 accus'd] O2; accusd O1.
21 Reader;] O2; ~, O1.   22 Monarchy, *Polybius*] ~; ~, O1-2.
24 What] *no paragraph break in O1-2.*

ENGRAVED TITLE OF THE FIRST EDITION

De Arte Graphica.

THE

Art of Painting,

BY

C. A. DU FRESNOY.

WITH

REMARKS.

Tranſlated into *Engliſh*,
Together with an *Original Preface* containing
A PARALLEL betwixt PAINTING and POETRY.

By·Mr. *DRYDEN.*

As alſo a Short Account of the moſt Eminent *PAINTERS*,
both *Ancient* and *Modern*, continu'd down to the
Preſent Times, according to the Order of their Succeſſion.

By *another Hand.*

Ut Pictura Poeſis erit ---- Hor. de Arte Poetica.

LONDON,

Printed by *J. Heptinſtall* for **W. Rogers**, at the Sun
againſt St. *Dunſtan*'s Church in *Fleetſtreet*. MDCXCV.

De Arte Graphica

Preface of the Translator,
With a Parallel, of Poetry and Painting

IT may be reasonably expected, that I shou'd say something
on my own behalf, in respect to my present Undertaking.
First, then, the Reader may be pleas'd to know, that it was
not of my own choice that I undertook this Work. Many of our
most Skillfull Painters, and other Artists, were pleas'd to recom-
mend this Authour to me, as one who perfectly understood the
Rules of Painting; who gave the best and most concise Instruc-
tions for Performance, and the surest to inform the Judgment
of all who lov'd this noble Art: That they who before were
10 rather fond of it, than knowingly admir'd it, might defend their
Inclination by their Reason; that they might understand those
Excellencies which they blindly valu'd, so as not to be farther
impos'd on by bad Pieces, and to know when Nature was well
imitated by the most able Masters. 'Tis true indeed, and they
acknowledge it, that beside the Rules which are given in this
Treatise, or which can be given in any other, that to make a
perfect Judgment of good Pictures, and to value them more or
less when compar'd with one another, there is farther requir'd
a long conversation with the best Pieces, which are not very fre-
20 quent either in *France* or *England;* yet some we have, not onely
from the hands of *Holbein, Rubens,* and *Van Dyck,* (one of them
admirable for History-painting, and the other two for Portraits,)
but of many *Flemish* Masters, and those not inconsiderable,
though for Design, not equal to the *Italians.* And of these latter
also, we are not unfurnish'd with some Pieces of *Raphael, Titian,
Correggio, Michael Angelo* and others.
      But to return to my own undertaking of this Translation, I

6   this Authour] *this Authour* Q.   9   Art:] ~. Q.
11 Reason;] ~: Q.   21 *Van Dyck*] *Vandyck* Q.
23 *Flemish* Masters] *Flemish-Masters* Q.
27 But] *no paragraph break in* Q.

freely own, that I thought my self uncapable of performing it, either to their Satisfaction, or my own Credit. Not but that I understood the Original *Latine,* and the *French* Authour perhaps as well as most *Englishmen;* But I was not sufficiently vers'd in the Terms of Art; And therefore thought that many of those persons who put this honourable task on me, were more able to perform it themselves, as undoubtedly they were. But they assuring me of their assistance, in correcting my faults where I spoke improperly, I was encourag'd to attempt it, that I might not be
10 wanting in what I cou'd, to satisfie the desires of so many Gentlemen who were willing to give the world this usefull Work. They have effectually perform'd their promise to me; and I have been as carefull on my side, to take their advice in all things; so that the Reader may assure himself of a tolerable Translation: Not Elegant, for I propos'd not that to my self; but familiar, clear and instructive. In any of which parts, if I have fail'd, the fault lies wholly at my door. In this one particular onely I must beg the Readers pardon. The Prose Translation of the Poem is not free from Poetical Expressions, and I dare not promise that some
20 of them are not fustian, or at least highly metaphorical; but this being a fault in the first digestion (that is, the Original *Latine*) was not to be remedy'd in the second, (*viz.*) the Translation. And I may confidently say, that whoever had attempted it, must have fallen into the same inconvenience; or a much greater, that of a false Version.

When I undertook this Work, I was already ingag'd in the Translation of *Virgil,* from whom I have borrow'd onely two months, and am now returning to that which I ought to understand better. In the mean time I beg the Readers pardon, for
30 entertaining him so long with my self: 'Tis an usual part of ill manners in all Authours, and almost in all Mankind, to trouble others with their business; and I was so sensible of it before-

---

3-5 Original...Authour...Terms] *Original...Authour...Terms* Q.
5 Art;] *Art:* Q.   14 Translation:] ~. Q.
15 self;] ~: Q.
18-21 Prose Translation...Poem...Original] *Prose Translation...Poem...Original* Q.
22 second,] ~ₐ Q.   22 Translation] *Translation* Q.
26 When] *no paragraph break in* Q.
31-40:2 Authours...Readers] *Authours...Readers* Q.

hand, that I had not now committed it, unless some concernments of the Readers had been interwoven with my own. But I know not, while I am attoning for one Error, if I am not falling into another: for I have been importun'd to say something farther of this Art; and to make some Observations on it in relation to the likeness and agreement which it has with Poetry, its Sister. But before I proceed, it will not be amiss, if I copy from *Bellori* (a most ingenious Authour, yet living) some part of his *Idea of a Painter*, which cannot be unpleasing, at least to
10 such who are conversant in the Philosophy of *Plato*. And to avoid tediousness, I will not translate the whole Discourse, but take and leave as I find occasion.

God *Almighty, in the Fabrique of the Universe, first contemplated himself, and reflected on his own Excellencies; from which he drew, and constituted those first Forms, which are call'd Idea's: So that every Species which was afterwards express'd was produc'd from that first Idea, forming that wonderfull contexture of all created Beings. But the Cœlestial Bodies above the Moon being incorruptible, and not subject to change, remain'd*
20 *for ever fair, and in perpetual order: On the contrary, all things which are sublunary are subject to change, to deformity, and to decay. And though* Nature *always intends a consummate beauty in her productions, yet through the inequality of the Matter, the Forms are alter'd; and in particular, Humane Beauty suffers alteration for the worse, as we see to our mortification, in the deformities, and disproportions which are in us. For which reason the Artfull Painter and the Sculptour, imitating the Divine Maker, form to themselves as well as they are able, a Model of the Superiour Beauties; and reflecting on them endeavour to*
30 *correct and amend the common Nature; and to represent it as it was first created without fault, either in Colour or in Lineament.*

This Idea, *which we may call the Goddess of Painting and of Sculpture, descends upon the Marble and the Cloth, and becomes the Original of those Arts; and being measur'd by the Compass*

5–6   this Art . . . Observations . . . likeness . . . agreement] *this Art . . . Observations . . . likeness . . . agreement* Q.
6   Poetry,] *Poetry*ₐ Q.   9   *of a*] of a Q.
16   *Idea's:*] *Idea's.* Q.   22   Nature] *Nature* Q.

*of the Intellect, is it self the Measure of the performing Hand;
and being animated by the Imagination, infuses Life into the
Image. The Idea of the Painter and the Sculptour, is undoubt-
edly that perfect and excellent Example of the Mind; by imita-
tion of which imagin'd form, all things are represented which
fall under humane sight: Such is the Definition which is made by
Cicero in his Book of the Oratour to Brutus. "As therefore in
Forms and Figures there is somewhat which is Excellent and
Perfect, to which imagin'd Species all things are referr'd by Imi-*
10 *tation, which are the Objects of Sight, in like manner we behold
the Species of Eloquence in our Minds, the Effigies, or actual
Image of which we seek in the Organs of our Hearing. This is
likewise confirm'd by Proclus in the Dialogue of Plato call'd
Timæus: If, says he, you take a Man, as he is made by Nature,
and compare him with another who is the effect of Art; the work
of Nature will always appear the less beautifull, because Art is
more accurate than Nature." But Zeuxis, who from the choice
which he made of Five Virgins, drew that wonderfull Picture of
Helena, which Cicero in his Oratour beforemention'd, sets be-*
20 *fore us as the most perfect Example of Beauty, at the same time
admonishes a Painter, to contemplate the Idea's of the most
Natural Forms; and to make a judicious choice of several Bodies,
all of them the most Elegant which he can find: by which we may
plainly understand that he thought it impossible to find in any
one Body all those Perfections which he sought for the accom-
plishment of a Helena, because Nature in any individual person
makes nothing that is perfect in all its parts. For this reason
Maximus Tyrius also says, that the Image which is taken by a
Painter from several Bodies produces a Beauty, which it is im-*
30 *possible to find in any single Natural Body, approaching to the
perfection of the fairest Statues. Thus Nature on this account is
so much inferiour to Art, that those Artists who propose to them-
selves onely the imitation and likeness of such or such a particular
person, without election of those Idea's before-mention'd, have*

3 *Idea . . . Painter . . . Sculptour*] Idea . . . Painter . . . Sculptour Q.
9 *Species*] Species Q.   9–10 *Imitation,*] ∼ₐ Q.
11 *Species*] Species Q.   18 *Virgins,*] ∼ₐ Q.
21 *Idea's*] Idea's Q.   23 *find: by*] ∼. By Q.
31–34 *Nature . . . Art . . . Idea's*] Nature . . . Art . . . Idea's Q.

often been reproach'd for that omission: Demetrius *was tax'd for being too Natural;* Dionysius *was also blam'd for drawing Men like us, and was commonly call'd* Ἀνθρωπόγραφος, *that is, a* Painter of Men. *In our times* Michael Angelo da Caravaggio, *was esteem'd too Natural. He drew persons as they were; and* Bamboccio, *and most of the* Dutch *Painters, have drawn the worst likeness.* Lysippus *of old, upbraided the common sort of Sculptours, for making Men such as they were found in Nature; and boasted of himself that he made them as they ought to be: which*
10 *is a Precept of* Aristotle, *given as well to Poets as to Painters.* Phidias *rais'd an admiration even to astonishment, in those who beheld his Statues, with the Forms, which he gave to his Gods and Heroes; by imitating the Idea rather than Nature. And* Cicero *speaking of him affirms, that figuring* Jupiter *and* Pallas, *he did not contemplate any Object from whence he took the likeness, but consider'd in his own mind a great and admirable form of Beauty, and according to that Image in his Soul, he directed the operation of his Hand.* Seneca *also seems to wonder, that* Phidias *having never beheld either* Jove *or* Pallas, *yet cou'd con-*
20 *ceive their divine Images in his Mind.* Apollonius Tyanæus *says the same in other words, that the fancy more instructs the Painter than the imitation; for the last makes onely the things which it sees, but the first makes also the things which it never sees.*

Leon Battista Alberti *tells us, that we ought not so much to love the likeness as the beauty, and to choose from the fairest Bodies severally the fairest Parts.* Leonardo da Vinci *instructs the Painter to form this Idea to himself: And* Raphael, *the greatest of all modern Masters, writes thus to* Castiglione, *concerning his* Galatea: *"To paint a Fair one, 'tis necessary for me to see*
30 *many Fair ones; but because there is so great a scarcity of lovely Women, I am constrain'd to make use of one certain Idea, which I have form'd to my self in my own fancy."* Guido Reni *sending to* Rome *his St.* Michael *which he had painted for the Church*

---

of the Capuchins, *at the same time wrote to* Monsignor Massano, *who was* Maestro di Casa *(or Steward of the House) to Pope* Urban *the* Eighth, *in this manner: "I wish I had the wings of an Angel, to have ascended into* Paradise, *and there to have beheld the Forms of those beatify'd Spirits, from which I might have copy'd my Archangel: But not being able to mount so high, it was in vain for me to search his resemblance here below: so that I was forc'd to make an Introspection, into my own mind, and into that Idea of Beauty, which I have form'd in my own imagination. I*
10 *have likewise created there the contrary Idea of deformity and ugliness; but I leave the consideration of it, till I paint the* Devil: *and in the mean time shun the very thought of it as much as possibly I can, and am even endeavouring to blot it wholly out of my remembrance."*

There was not any Lady in all Antiquity, who was Mistress of so much Beauty as was to be found in the Venus *of* Gnidus, *made by* Praxiteles, *or the* Minerva *of* Athens *by* Phidias; *which was therefore call'd the* Beautifull Form. *Neither is there any Man of the present Age, equal in the strength, proportion, and knitting*
20 *of his Limbs, to the* Hercules *of* Farnese, *made by* Glycon: *Or any Woman who can justly be compar'd with the* Medicean Venus *of* Cleomenes. *And upon this account, the noblest Poets and the best Oratours, when they desir'd to celebrate any extraordinary Beauty, are forc'd to have recourse to Statues and Pictures, and to draw their Persons and Faces into Comparison.* Ovid *endeavouring to express the Beauty of* Cyllarus, *the fairest of the* Centaures, *celebrates him as next in perfection, to the most admirable Statues.*

Gratus in ore vigor, cervix, humeriq; manusq;
30 Pectoraq; Artificum laudatis Proxima Signis.

3 manner: "I] manner. I Q.   4 Angel] Angel Q.
6 Archangel] Archangel Q.   9 Idea] Idea Q.
10 Idea] Idea Q.   14 remembrance."] ~.ᴧ Q.
15 There] no paragraph break in Q.   17 Phidias] Phydias Q.
20 Glycon] Glicon Q.
22–24 Poets . . . Oratours . . . Statues . . . Pictures] Poets . . . Oratours . . . Statues . . . Pictures Q.
26 Cyllarus] Cillarus Q.   28 Statues] Statues Q.
29–30 lines not indented in Q.   30 Proxima] Proxima Q.

A pleasing Vigour his fair Face express'd;
His Neck, his Hands, his Shoulders, and his Breast,
Did next in Gracefulness and Beauty stand,
To breathing Figures of the Sculptour's Hand.

In another place he sets Apelles *above* Venus.

Si Venerem Cois nunquam pinxisset *Apelles,*
Mersa sub æquoreis illa lateret Aquis.

Thus vary'd.

One Birth to Seas the Cyprian Goddess *ow'd,*
10   *A Second Birth the Painter's Art bestow'd:*
Less by the Seas than by his pow'r was giv'n;
They made her live, but he advanc'd to Heav'n.

The Idea of this Beauty, is indeed various, according to the
several forms which the Painter or Sculptour wou'd describe; as
one in Strength, another in Magnanimity: and sometimes it con-
sists in Chearfulness, and sometimes in Delicacy; and is always
diversify'd by the Sex and Age.

The Beauty of Jove *is one, and that of* Juno *another:* Hercules,
and Cupid *are perfect Beauties, though of different kinds; for*
20 *Beauty is onely that which makes all things as they are in their*
proper and perfect Nature, which the best Painters always choose
by contemplating the Forms of each. We ought farther to con-
sider, that a Picture being the representation of a humane action,
the Painter ought to retain in his mind, the Examples of all
Affections, and Passions, as a Poet preserves the Idea of an Angry
man, of one who is fearfull, sad or merry, and so of all the rest:
For 'tis impossible to express that with the Hand, which never
enter'd into the Imagination. In this manner as I have rudely and

5   *line indented in* Q.   6–7   *lines not indented in* Q.
8   *Thus vary'd.] centered in* Q.   9   *Goddess*] Goddess Q.
10 *Painter's*] Painter's Q.
13–14   *Idea . . . Painter . . . Sculptour*] Idea . . . Painter . . . Sculptour Q.
14–15   *describe; as . . . Magnanimity:*] ~: As . . . ~; Q.
21 *Nature,*] ~; Q.
21–25   *Painters . . . Painter . . . Poet . . . Idea*] Painters . . . Painter . . . Poet
. . . Idea Q.
26 *rest:*] ~. Q.

briefly shewn you, Painters and Sculptours, choosing the most
elegant natural Beauties, perfectionate the Idea, and advance
their Art, even above Nature *it self, in her individual produc-*
tions; which is the utmost mastery of humane performance.

From hence arises that astonishment, and almost adoration
which is paid by the Knowing to those divine remainders of
Antiquity. From hence Phidias, Lysippus, *and other noble Sculp-*
tours, are still held in veneration; and Appelles, Zeuxis, Proto-
genes, *and other admirable Painters, though their Works are*
10 *perish'd, are and will be eternally admir'd; who all of them drew*
after the Idea's of Perfection, which are the Miracles of Nature,
the Providence of the Understanding, the Exemplars of the
Mind, the Light of the Fancy; the Sun which from its rising, in-
spir'd the Statue of Memnon, *and the fire which warm'd into life*
the Image of Prometheus: *'Tis this which causes the* Graces, *and*
the Loves *to take up their habitations in the hardest Marble,*
and to subsist in the emptiness of Light, and Shadows. But since
the Idea of Eloquence is as far inferiour to that of Painting, as the
force of Words is to the Sight, I must here break off abruptly,
20 *and having conducted the Reader as it were to a secret Walk,*
there leave him in the midst of Silence to contemplate those
Idea's; which I have onely sketch'd, and which every man must
finish for himself.

In these pompous Expressions, or such as these, the *Italian*
has given you his Idea of a Painter; and though I cannot much
commend the Style, I must needs say there is somewhat in the
Matter: *Plato* himself is accustom'd to write loftily, imitating,
as the Critiques tell us, the manner of *Homer;* but surely that
inimitable Poet, had not so much of Smoke in his writing, though

1-3   *Painters ... Sculptours ... Idea ... Art*] Painters ... Sculptours ... Idea ...
Art Q.
3-4   *productions;*] ~, Q.
7   *Antiquity*] Antiquity Q.   7   Phidias] Phydias Q.
7-11   *Sculptours ... Painters ... Idea's*] Sculptours ... Painters ... Idea's Q.
11   *Perfection,*] ~; Q.
16-17   *Marble ... Light ... Shadows*] Marble ... Light ... Shadows Q.
18   *Idea ... Eloquence ... Painting*] Idea ... Eloquence ... Painting Q.
19   *Sight,*] ~; Q.
20-22   *Reader ... Idea's*] Reader ... Idea's Q.
24   these,] ~∧ Q.
25-28   Idea ... Painter ... Critiques] *Idea ... Painter ... Critiques* Q.

not less of Fire. But in short, this is the present Genius of *Italy.*
What *Philostratus* tells us in the Proem of his *Figures* is some-
what plainer; and therefore I will translate it almost word for
word. *He who will rightly govern the Art of Painting, ought of*
necessity first to understand Humane Nature. He ought likewise
to be endued with a Genius to express the signs of their Passions
whom he represents; and to make the dumb as it were to speak:
He must yet further understand what is contain'd in the constitu-
tion of the Cheeks, in the temperament of the Eyes, in the natural-
10 *ness (if I may so call it) of the Eye-brows; and in short whatsoever*
belongs to the Mind and Thought. He who throughly possesses
all these things will obtain the whole: And the Hand will ex-
quisitely represent the action of every particular person. If it
happen that he be either mad, or angry, melancholique, or chear-
full, a sprightly Youth, or a languishing Lover; in one word, he
will be able to paint whatsoever is proportionable to any one.
And even in all this there is a sweet errour without causing any
shame: For the Eyes and Minds of the beholders being fasten'd
on Objects which have no real Being, as if they were truly Ex-
20 *istent, and being induc'd by them to believe them so, what*
pleasure is it not capable of giving? The Ancients, and other
Wise Men, have written many things concerning the Symmetry
which is in the Art of Painting; constituting as it were some
certain Laws for the proportion of every Member, not thinking
it possible for a Painter to undertake the expression of those
motions which are in the Mind, without a concurrent Harmony
in the natural measure: For that which is out of its own kind and
measure, is not receiv'd from Nature, whose motion is always
right. On a serious consideration of this matter it will be found,
30 *That the Art of Painting has a wonderfull affinity with that of*
Poetry; and that there is betwixt them a certain common Imagi-

1   Genius] *Genius* Q.   2   Proem] *Proem* Q.
4   He] "He Q.
4–47:5   *each printed italic line preceded by inverted double commas in* Q.
4   *Art ... Painting*] Art ... Painting Q.
6   *Genius*] Genius Q.   10   *Eye-brows;*] ~: Q.
12   *whole:*] ~. Q.   18   *shame:*] ~. Q.
22–25   *Symmetry ... Art ... Painting ... Laws ... Painter*] Symmetry ... Art
... Painting ... Laws ... Painter Q.
27   *measure:*] ~. Q.
30–31   *Art ... Painting ... Poetry*] Art ... Painting ... Poetry Q.

*nation. For as the Poets introduce the Gods and Heroes, and all
those things which are either Majestical, Honest or Delightfull,
in like manner the Painters, by the virtue of their Out-lines,
Colours, Lights and Shadows, represent the same Things and
Persons in their Pictures.*

Thus, as Convoy Ships either accompany, or shou'd accompany
their Merchants till they may prosecute the rest of their Voyage
without danger, so *Philostratus* has brought me thus far on my
way, and I can now sail on without him. He has begun to speak
10 of the great relation betwixt Painting and Poetry, and thither
the greatest part of this Discourse by my promise was directed.
I have not ingag'd my self to any perfect Method, neither am I
loaded with a full Cargo. 'Tis sufficient if I bring a Sample of
some Goods in this Voyage. It will be easie for others to add
more when the Commerce is settled: For a Treatise twice as
large as this of Painting cou'd not contain all that might be said
on the Parallel of these two Sister Arts. I will take my rise from
Bellori before I proceed to the Authour of this Book.

The business of his Preface is to prove, that a learned Painter
20 shou'd form to himself an Idea of perfect Nature. This Image he
is to set before his Mind in all his Undertakings, and to draw
from thence as from a Store-house, the Beauties which are to
enter into his Work; thereby correcting Nature from what ac-
tually she is in individuals, to what she ought to be, and what
she was created. Now as this Idea of Perfection is of little use in
Portraits (or the resemblances of particular persons) so neither
is it in the Characters of Comedy, and Tragedy; which are never
to be made perfect, but always to be drawn with some specks of
frailty and deficience; such as they have been described to us in
30 History, if they were real Characters; or such as the Poet began

1–3 *Poets . . . Gods . . . Heroes . . . Painters*] Poets . . . Gods . . . Heroes . . . Painters Q.
6–7 Convoy Ships . . . Merchants] *Convoy Ships . . . Merchants* Q.
10 Painting . . . Poetry] *Painting . . . Poetry* Q.
15 settled:] ~. Q.
15–17 Treatise . . . Painting . . . Parallel . . . Sister Arts] *Treatise . . . Painting . . . Parallel . . . Sister Arts* Q.
18 Authour of this Book] *Authour of this Book* Q.
19–20 Preface . . . Painter . . . Idea] *Preface . . . Painter . . . Idea* Q.
25–30 Idea . . . Perfection . . . Portraits . . . Comedy . . . Tragedy . . . History . . . Characters . . . Poet] *Idea . . . Perfection . . . Portraits . . . Comedy . . . Tragedy . . . History . . . Characters . . . Poet* Q.

to shew them at their first appearance, if they were onely fictitious, (or imaginary.) The perfection of such Stage-characters consists chiefly in their likeness to the deficient faulty Nature, which is their Original: Onely, as it is observ'd more at large hereafter, in such cases there will always be found a better likeness, and a worse; and the better is constantly to be chosen: I mean in Tragedy, which represents the Figures of the highest form amongst Mankind. Thus in Portraits, the Painter will not take that side of the Face which has some notorious blemish in it;
10 but either draw it in profile (as *Apelles* did *Antigonus,* who had lost one of his Eyes) or else shadow the more imperfect side. For an ingenious flattery is to be allow'd to the Professours of both Arts; so long as the likeness is not destroy'd. 'Tis true that all manner of Imperfections must not be taken away from the Characters, and the reason is, that there may be left some grounds of pity for their misfortunes. We can never be griev'd for their miseries who are thoroughly wicked, and have thereby justly call'd their calamities on themselves. Such Men are the natural Objects of our hatred, not of our commiseration. If on the other
20 side their Characters were wholly perfect, (such as for Example, the Character of a Saint or Martyr in a Play,) his, or her misfortunes, wou'd produce impious thoughts in the Beholders: they wou'd accuse the Heavens of injustice, and think of leaving a Religion, where Piety was so ill requited. I say the greater part wou'd be tempted so to do, I say not that they ought: and the consequence is too dangerous for the practice. In this I have accus'd my self for my own St. *Catharine,* but let truth prevail. *Sophocles* has taken the just medium in his *Oedipus.* He is somewhat arrogant at his first entrance; and is too inquisitive through
30 the whole Tragedy: Yet these Imperfections being balanc'd by great Vertues, they hinder not our compassion for his miseries;

---

2 Stage-characters] *Stage-characters* Q.
4 Original:] ∼. Q.   7 Tragedy] *Tragedy* Q.
8 Portraits . . . Painter] *Portraits . . . Painter* Q.
12–13 both Arts] *both Arts* Q.   14–15 Characters] *Characters* Q.
21 Character . . . Saint . . . Martyr . . . Play] *Character . . . Saint . . . Martyr . . . Play* Q.
23–24 Heavens . . . Religion] *Heavens . . . Religion* Q.
30 Tragedy] *Tragedy* Q.

neither yet can they destroy that horrour which the nature of his Crimes have excited in us. Such in Painting are the Warts and Moles, which adding a likeness to the Face, are not therefore to be omitted: But these produce no loathing in us. But how far to proceed, and where to stop, is left to the judgment of the Poet and the Painter. In Comedy there is somewhat more of the worse likeness to be taken, because that is often to produce laughter; which is occasion'd by the sight of some deformity: but for this I referr the Reader to *Aristotle.* 'Tis a sharp manner of Instruc-
10 tion for the Vulgar who are never well amended, till they are more than sufficiently expos'd.

That I may return to the beginning of this Remark, concerning perfect Idea's, I have onely this to say, that the Parallel is often true in Epique-Poetry. The Heroes of the Poets are to be drawn according to this Rule. There is scarce a frailty to be left in the best of them; any more than is to be found in a Divine Nature: And if *Æneas* sometimes weeps, it is not in bemoaning his own miseries, but those which his people undergo. If this be an Imperfection, the *Son* of *God* when he was incarnate shed
20 tears of Compassion over *Jerusalem:* And *Lentulus* describes him often weeping, but never laughing; so that *Virgil* is justify'd even from the *Holy Scriptures.* I have but one word more, which for once I will anticipate from the Authour of this Book. Though it must be an Idea of Perfection, from which both the Epique Poet, and the History Painter draws; yet all Perfections are not suitable to all Subjects: But every one must be design'd according to that perfect Beauty which is proper to him. An *Apollo* must be distinguish'd from a *Jupiter,* a *Pallas* from a *Venus:* and

2–3   Painting . . . Warts . . . Moles] *Painting . . . Warts . . . Moles* Q.
4   omitted:] ~. Q.
5–6   Poet . . . Painter . . . Comedy] *Poet . . . Painter . . . Comedy* Q.
7   taken, because] ~. Because Q.   9   Reader] *Reader* Q.
12   That] *no paragraph break in* Q.
13–14   Idea's . . . Parallel . . . Epique-Poetry] *Idea's . . . Parallel . . . Epique-Poetry* Q.
14   The] *paragraph break in* Q.
14   Heroes . . . Poets] *Heroes . . . Poets* Q.
16–17   Divine Nature:] *Divine Nature.* Q.   20   Jerusalem:] ~. Q.
23–25   Authour . . . Book . . . Idea . . . Perfection . . . Epique Poet . . . History Painter] *Authour . . . Book . . . Idea . . . Perfection . . . Epique Poet . . . History Painter* Q.

so in Poetry an *Æneas* from any other Heroe: for Piety is his chief
Perfection. *Homer's Achilles* is a kind of Exception to this Rule:
but then he is not a perfect Heroe, nor so intended by the Poet.
All his Gods had somewhat of humane imperfection; for which
he has been tax'd by *Plato,* as an Imitatour of what was bad:
But *Virgil* observ'd his fault, and mended it. Yet *Achilles* was
perfect in the strength of his Body, and the vigour of his Mind.
Had he been less passionate, or less revengefull, the Poet well
foresaw that *Hector* had been kill'd, and *Troy* taken at the first
10 assault; which had destroy'd the beautifull contrivance of his
Iliads, and the moral of preventing Discord amongst Confeder-
ate Princes, which was his principal intention. For the Moral (as
Bossu observes) is the first business of the Poet, as being the
ground-work of his Instruction. This being form'd, he contrives
such a Design, or Fable, as may be most suitable to the Moral.
After this he begins to think of the Persons, whom he is to employ
in carrying on his Design: and gives them the Manners, which are
most proper to their several Characters. The thoughts and words
are the last parts, which give Beauty and Colouring to the Piece.
20   When I say, that the Manners of the Heroe ought to be good in
perfection, I contradict not the *Marquess of Normanby's* opin-
ion, in that admirable Verse, where speaking of a perfect Char-
acter, he calls it *A Faultless Monster, which the World ne'er
knew:* For that Excellent Critique, intended onely to speak of
Dramatique Characters, and not of Epique.
    Thus at least I have shewn, that in the most perfect Poem,
which is that of *Virgil,* a perfect Idea was requir'd, and follow'd,

---

1–2   Poetry . . . Heroe . . . Piety . . . Perfection] *Poetry . . . Heroe . . . Piety . . .
Perfection* Q.
3–4   Heroe . . . Poet . . . Gods] *Heroe . . . Poet . . . Gods* Q.
5   bad:] ~. Q.   8   Poet] *Poet* Q.
12–13   Moral . . . Poet] *Moral . . . Poet* Q.
15   Design . . . Fable . . . Moral] *Design . . . Fable . . . Moral* Q.
17–18   Design . . . Manners . . . Characters] *Design . . . Manners . . . Characters* Q.
20   When] *no paragraph break in* Q.
20   Manners . . . Heroe] *Manners . . . Heroe* Q.
24   *knew:*] ~. Q.
24–25   that Excellent Critique . . . Dramatique Characters . . . Epique] *that Ex-
cellent Critique . . . Dramatique Characters . . . Epique* Q.
26   Thus] *no paragraph break in* Q.
26–27   Poem . . . perfect Idea] *Poem . . . perfect Idea* Q.
27–51:1   follow'd, and] follow'd. And Q.

and consequently that all succeeding Poets ought rather to imitate *him,* than even *Homer.*

I will now proceed as I promis'd, to the Authour of this Book. He tells you almost in the first lines of it, that the *chief end of Painting is to please the Eyes: and 'tis one great End of Poetry to please the Mind.* Thus far the Parallel of the Arts holds true: with this difference, That the principal end of Painting is to please; and the chief design of Poetry is to instruct. In this the latter seems to have the advantage of the former; but if we
10 consider the Artists themselves on both sides, certainly their aims are the very same: they wou'd both make sure of pleasing, and that in preference to instruction. Next, the means of this pleasure is by Deceipt. One imposes on the Sight, and the other on the Understanding. Fiction is of the Essense of Poetry as well as of Painting; there is a resemblance in one, of Humane Bodies, Things and Actions which are not real, and in the other, of a true Story by a Fiction. And as all Stories are not proper Subjects for an Epique Poem, or a Tragedy, so neither are they for a noble Picture. The Subjects both of the one, and of the other, ought
20 to have nothing of immoral, low, or filthy in them; but this being treated at large in the Book it self, I wave it to avoid repetition. Onely I must add, that though *Catullus, Ovid* and others were of another opinion, that the Subject of Poets, and even their thoughts and expressions might be loose, provided their lives were chast and holy, yet there are no such licences permitted in that Art any more than in Painting, to design and colour obscene Nudities. *Vita proba est,* is no excuse, for it will scarcely be admitted, that either a Poet or a Painter can be chast, who give us the contrary examples in their Writings and their Pictures. We

1 Poets] *Poets* Q.   3 I] *no paragraph break in* Q.
3 Authour ... Book] *Authour ... Book* Q.
6–8 Parallel ... Arts ... Painting ... please ... Poetry ... instruct] *Parallel ... Arts ... Painting ... please ... Poetry ... instruct* Q.
9–10 latter ... former; but ... Artists] *latter ... former. But ... Artists* Q.
14–15 Fiction ... Poetry ... Painting] *Fiction ... Poetry ... Painting* Q.
18–19 Epique Poem ... Tragedy ... Picture] *Epique Poem ... Tragedy ... Picture* Q.
21 Book it self] *Book it self* Q.
23–26 Poets ... that Art ... Painting] *Poets ... that Art ... Painting* Q.
28–29 Poet ... Painter ... Writings ... Pictures] *Poet ... Painter ... Writings ... Pictures* Q.

see nothing of this kind in *Virgil:* that which comes the nearest
to it, is the *Adventure of the Cave,* where *Dido* and *Æneas* were
driven by the Storm: Yet even there the Poet pretends a Marriage
before the Consummation; and *Juno* her self was present at it.
Neither is there any expression in that Story, which a *Roman*
Matron might not reade without a blush. Besides, the Poet passes
it over as hastily as he can, as if he were afraid of staying in the
Cave with the two Lovers, and of being a witness to their Actions.
Now I suppose that a Painter wou'd not be much commended,
10 who shou'd pick out this Cavern from the whole *Æneids,* when
there is not another in the Work. He had better leave them in
their obscurity, than let in a flash of Lightning to clear the nat-
ural darkness of the place, by which he must discover himself
as much as them. The Altar-Pieces, and holy Decorations of
Painting, show *that* Art may be apply'd to better uses, as well as
Poetry. And amongst many other instances, the *Farnesian* Gal-
lery, painted by *Hannibal Carracci,* is a sufficient witness yet
remaining: the whole Work being morally instructive, and par-
ticularly the *Herculis Bivium,* which is a perfect Triumph of
20 Vertue over Vice, as it is wonderfully well describ'd by the
ingenious *Bellori.*

Hitherto I have only told the Reader what ought not to be
the subject of a Picture or of a Poem: what it ought to be on
either side; our Author tells us: it must in general be great and
noble: and in this, the Parallel is exactly true. The subject of a
Poet either in Tragedy or in an Epique Poem is a great action of

---

2   *Adventure*] adventure Q.
3–6   Poet ... Matron] *Poet ... Matron* Q.
6   Besides,] ∼_∧ Q.
6–9   Poet ... Painter] *Poet ... Painter* Q.
10   *Æneids*] *Eneids* Q.
14–16   Altar-Pieces ... Painting ... Art ... Poetry] *Altar-Pieces ... Painting
... Art ... Poetry* Q.
16   And] *paragraph break in Q.*
16–17   Gallery] *Gallery* Q.
19–20   Triumph ... [to] ... Vice] *set in italics in Q.*
22–25   Reader ... Picture ... Poem ... Author ... Parallel] *Reader ... Picture
... Poem ... Author ... Parallel* Q.
26   Poet ... Tragedy ... Epique Poem] *Poet ... Tragedy ... Epique Poem* Q.

some illustrious Hero. 'Tis the same in Painting; not every ac-
tion, nor every person is considerable enough to enter into the
Cloth. It must be the Anger of an *Achilles,* the Piety of an
Æneas, the Sacrifice of an *Iphigenia* (for Heroins as well as
Heroes are comprehended in the Rule;) but the Parallel is more
compleat in Tragedy, than in an Epique Poem. For as a Tragedy
may be made out of many particular Episodes of *Homer* or of
Virgil, so may a noble Picture be design'd out of this or that
particular Story in either Author. History is also fruitfull of
10 designs both for the Painter and the Tragique Poet: *Curtius*
throwing himself into a Gulph, and the two *Decii* sacrificing
themselves for the safety of their Country, are subjects for
Tragedy and Picture. Such is *Scipio* restoring the *Spanish* Bride,
whom he either lov'd or may be suppos'd to love, by which he
gain'd the Hearts of a great Nation, to interess themselves for
Rome against *Carthage:* These are all but particular Pieces in
Livy's History; and yet are full compleat Subjects for the Pen
and Pencil. Now the reason of this is evident. Tragedy and Pic-
ture are more narrowly circumscrib'd by the Mechanick Rules
20 of Time and Place than the Epique Poem. The time of this last
is left indefinite. 'Tis true, *Homer* took up onely the space of
eight and forty days for his *Iliads;* but whether *Virgil*'s action
was comprehended in a year or somewhat more, is not deter-
min'd by *Bossu. Homer* made the place of his action *Troy,* and
the *Grecian* Camp besieging it. *Virgil* introduces his *Æneas,*
sometimes in *Sicily,* sometimes in *Carthage,* and other times at
Cumæ, before he brings him to *Laurentum;* and even after that,

---

1 Painting] *Painting* Q.
4–6 Heroins . . . Heroes . . . Parallel . . . Tragedy . . . Epique Poem] *Heroins . . .*
Heroes . . . Parallel . . . Tragedy . . . Epique Poem Q.
6–9 Tragedy . . . Episodes . . . Picture . . . Author] *Tragedy . . . Episodes . . .*
Picture . . . Author Q.
9–13 History . . . Painter . . . Tragique Poet . . . Gulph . . . Tragedy . . . Picture]
History . . . Painter . . . Tragique Poet . . . Gulph . . . Tragedy . . . Picture Q.
13–18 Bride . . . Pen . . . Pencil] *Bride . . . Pen . . . Pencil* Q.
18–20 Tragedy . . . Picture . . . Mechanick Rules . . . Time . . . Place . . . Epique
Poem] *Tragedy . . . Picture . . . Mechanick Rules . . . Time . . . Place . . . Epique*
Poem Q.
25 Camp] *Camp* Q.

he wanders again to the Kingdom of *Evander* and some parts of
Tuscany, before he returns to finish the War by the death of
Turnus. But Tragedy according to the Practice of the Ancients,
was always confin'd within the compass of 24 hours, and seldom
takes up so much time. As for the place of it, it was always one,
and that not in a larger Sence (as for example, A whole City or
two or three several Houses in it) but the Market or some other
publick place, common to the Chorus and all the Actours; which
establish'd Law of theirs, I have not an opportunity to examine
10 in this place, because I cannot do it without digression from my
subject, though it seems too strict at the first appearance because
it excludes all secret Intrigues, which are the Beauties of the
modern Stage: for nothing can be carry'd on with Privacy, when
the Chorus is suppos'd to be always present. But to proceed, I
must say this to the advantage of Painting, even above Tragedy,
that what this last represents in the space of many Hours, the
former shows us in one Moment. The Action, the Passion, and
the manners of so many Persons as are contain'd in a Picture, are
to be discern'd at once, in the twinkling of an Eye; at least they
20 would be so, if the Sight could travel over so many different
Objects all at once, or the Mind could digest them all at the
same instant or point of time. Thus in the famous Picture of
Poussin, which represents the Institution of the Blessed Sacra-
ment, you see our *Saviour* and his twelve Disciples, all concur-
ring in the same action, after different manners, and in different
postures; onely the manners of *Judas* are distinguish'd from the
rest. Here is but one indivisible point of time observ'd: but one
action perform'd by so many Persons, in one Room and at the
same Table: yet the Eye cannot comprehend at once the whole
30 Object, nor the Mind follow it so fast; 'tis consider'd at leisure,

---

3   Tragedy ... Ancients] *Tragedy ... Ancients* Q.
6–7   Sence (as ... it)] ~; ~ ... ~; Q.
8   Chorus] *Chorus* Q.
8   Actours; which] ~. Which Q.
13–14   modern Stage ... Chorus] *modern Stage ... Chorus* Q.
15   Painting ... Tragedy] *Painting ... Tragedy* Q.
18   Picture] *Picture* Q.
23–24   Institution ... [*to*] ... Sacrament] set in italics in Q.
24   his twelve Disciples] *his twelve Disciples* Q.
26   postures;] ~, Q.

and seen by intervals. Such are the Subjects of Noble Pictures: and such are onely to be undertaken by Noble Hands.

There are other parts of Nature, which are meaner, and yet are the Subjects both of Painters, and of Poets. For to proceed in the Parallel, as Comedy is a representation of Humane Life, in inferiour persons, and low Subjects, and by that means creeps into the nature of Poetry, and is a kind of Juniper, a Shrub belonging to the species of Cedar, so is the painting of Clowns, the representation of a *Dutch* Kermis, the brutal sport of Snick or
10 Snee, and a thousand other things of this mean invention, a kind of Picture, which belongs to Nature, but of the lowest form. Such is a Lazar in comparison to a *Venus;* both are drawn in Humane Figures: they have Faces alike, though not like Faces.

There is yet a lower sort of Poetry and Painting, which is out of Nature: For a Farce is that in Poetry, which Grotesque is in a Picture. The Persons, and Action of a Farce are all unnatural, and the Manners false, that is, inconsisting with the characters of Mankind. Grotesque-painting is the just resemblance of this; and *Horace* begins his *Art of Poetry* by describing such a Figure,
20 with a Man's Head, a Horse's Neck, the Wings of a Bird, and a Fishes Tail; parts of different species jumbled together, according to the mad imagination of the Dawber; and the end of all this, as he tells you afterward, to cause Laughter: A very Monster in a *Bartholomew-Fair* for the Mob to gape at for their two-pence. Laughter is indeed the propriety of a Man, but just enough to

---

1–2 Pictures ... Noble Hands] *Pictures ... Noble Hands* Q.
3 There] *no paragraph break in Q.*
4 Painters ... Poets] *Painters ... Poets* Q.
4 For] *paragraph break in Q.*
5–11 Parallel ... Comedy ... Poetry ... Juniper ... Cedar ... Clowns ... Kermis ... Snick or Snee ... Picture] *Parallel ... Comedy ... Poetry ... Juniper ... Cedar ... Clowns ... Kermis ... Snick or Snee ... Picture* Q.
12 Lazar] *Lazar* Q.   14 There] *no paragraph break in Q.*
14 Poetry ... Painting] *Poetry ... Painting* Q.
15 Nature:] ~. Q.
15–16 Farce ... Poetry ... Grotesque ... Picture] *Farce ... Poetry ... Grotesque ... Picture* Q.
16 Farce] *Farce* Q.
18 Grotesque-painting ... this] *Grotesque-painting ... this* Q.
19 *of*] of Q.   19 Figure,] ~; Q.
22 Dawber] *Dawber* Q.   23 Laughter:] ~. Q.
23–24 Monster ... Mob] *Monster ... Mob* Q.

distinguish him from his elder Brother, with four Legs. 'Tis a
kind of Bastard-pleasure too, taken in at the Eyes of the vulgar
gazers, and at the Ears of the beastly Audience. Church-Painters
use it to divert the honest Countryman at Publick Prayers, and
keep his Eyes open at a heavy Sermon, and Farce-Scriblers make
use of the same noble invention to entertain Citizens, Country-
Gentlemen, and *Covent-Garden* Fops. If they are merry, all goes
well on the Poet's side. The better sort goe thither too, but
in despair of Sense, and the just Images of Nature, which are
10 the adequate pleasures of the Mind. But the Authour can give
the Stage no better than what was given him by Nature: and the
Actors must represent such things, as they are capable to per-
form, and by which both they and the Scribbler may get their
living. After all, 'tis a good thing to laugh at any rate, and if a
straw can tickle a man, 'tis an instrument of happiness. Beasts
can weep when they suffer, but they cannot laugh. And as Sir
William Davenant observes in his Preface to *Gondibert, 'Tis the
wisdom of a Government to permit Plays* (he might have added
Farces) *as 'tis the prudence of a Carter to put Bells upon his
20 Horses, to make them carry their Burthens chearfully.*

I have already shewn, that one main end of Poetry and Paint-
ing is to please, and have said something of the kinds of both,
and of their Subjects, in which they bear a great resemblance to
each other. I must now consider them, as they are great and noble
Arts; and as they are Arts, they must have Rules, which may
direct them to their common end.

To all Arts and Sciences, but more particularly to these, may
be apply'd what *Hippocrates* says of Physick, as I find him cited
by an eminent *French* Critique. *Medicine has long subsisted in*

3–4 Church-Painters . . . Countryman] *Church Painters . . . Countryman* Q.
5 Sermon, and] *Sermon. And* Q.
5–7 Farce-Scriblers . . . Citizens, Country-Gentlemen . . . Fops] *Farce-Scriblers
. . . Citizens, Country-Gentlemen . . . Fops* Q.
8 Poet's] *Poet's* Q.
10–13 Authour . . . Actors . . . Scribbler] *Authour . . . Actors . . . Scribbler* Q.
17 Preface] *Preface* Q.
21–22 Poetry . . . Painting] *Poetry . . . Painting* Q.
25 Arts . . . Arts . . . Rules] *Arts . . . Arts . . . Rules* Q.
27 Arts . . . Sciences] *Arts . . . Sciences* Q.
27 these,] ~∧ Q.   29 *French*] French Q.
29 *Medicine*] "*Medicine* Q.

*the World. The Principles of it are certain, and it has a certain
way; by both which there has been found in the course of many
Ages, an infinite number of things, the experience of which has
confirm'd its usefulness and goodness. All that is wanting to the
perfection of this Art, will undoubtedly be found, if able Men,
and such as are instructed in the Ancient Rules will make a
farther enquiry into it, and endeavour to arrive at that, which
is hitherto unknown, by that which is already known. But all,
who having rejected the Ancient Rules, and taken the opposite*
10 *ways, yet boast themselves to be Masters of this Art, do but de-
ceive others, and are themselves deceiv'd; for that is absolutely
impossible.*

This is notoriously true in these two Arts: for the way to
please being to imitate Nature; both the Poets and the Painters,
in Ancient times, and in the best Ages, have study'd her: and
from the practice of both these Arts, the Rules have been drawn,
by which we are instructed how to please, and to compass that
end which they obtain'd, by following their Example. For Na-
ture is still the same in all Ages, and can never be contrary to
20 her self. Thus from the practice of *Æschylus, Sophocles,* and
Euripides, Aristotle drew his Rules for Tragedy; and *Philostratus*
for Painting. Thus amongst the Moderns, the *Italian* and *French*
Critiques by studying the Precepts of *Aristotle,* and *Horace,* and
having the Example of the *Grecian* Poets before their Eyes, have
given us the Rules of Modern Tragedy: and thus the Critiques of
the same Countries, in the Art of Painting have given the Pre-
cepts of perfecting that Art.

'Tis true that Poetry has one advantage over Painting in these
last Ages, that we have still the remaining Examples both of the
30 *Greek* and *Latine* Poets: whereas the Painters have nothing left

56:29–57:12   *each printed italic line preceded by inverted double commas in Q.*
13–16   these two Arts . . . Poets . . . Painters . . . both these Arts] *these two
Arts . . . Poets . . . Painters . . . both these Arts* Q.
21–22   Tragedy . . . Painting] *Tragedy . . . Painting* Q.
22–27   Moderns . . . Critiques . . . Poets . . . Modern Tragedy . . . Critiques . . .
Art . . . Painting . . . that Art] *Moderns . . . Critiques . . . Poets . . . Modern
Tragedy . . . Critiques . . . Art . . . Painting . . . that Art* Q.
28   'Tis] *no paragraph break in Q.*
28–30   Poetry . . . Painting . . . and . . . Poets . . . Painters] *Poetry . . . Painting
. . . and . . . Poets . . . Painters* Q.

them from *Apelles, Protogenes, Parrhasius, Xeuxis* and the rest,
but onely the testimonies which are given of their incomparable
Works. But instead of this, they have some of their best Statues,
Bass-Relievo's, Columns, Obelisques, &c. which were sav'd out
of the common ruine, and are still preserv'd in *Italy:* and by well
distinguishing what is proper to Sculpture, and what to Paint-
ing, and what is common to them both, they have judiciously
repair'd that loss. And the great Genius of *Raphael,* and others,
having succeeded to the times of Barbarism and Ignorance, the
10 knowledge of Painting is now arriv'd to a supreme perfection,
though the performance of it is much declin'd in the present
Age. The greatest Age for Poetry amongst the *Romans* was cer-
tainly that of *Augustus Cæsar;* and yet we are told that Painting
was then at its lowest Ebb, and perhaps Sculpture was also de-
clining at the same time. In the Reign of *Domitian,* and some
who succeeded him, Poetry was but meanly cultivated, but Paint-
ing eminently flourish'd. I am not here to give the History of the
two Arts; how they were both in a manner extinguish'd, by the
Irruption of the barbarous Nations, and both restor'd about
20 the times of *Leo* the Tenth, *Charles* the Fifth, and *Francis*
the First; though I might observe, that neither *Ariosto,* nor any
of his Contemporary Poets ever arriv'd at the Excellency of
Raphael, Titian, and the rest in Painting. But in revenge at this
time, or lately in many Countries, Poetry is better practis'd than
her Sister-Art. To what height the Magnificence and Encourage-
ment of the present King of *France* may carry Painting and
Sculpture is uncertain, but by what he has done, before the War
in which he is ingag'd, we may expect what he will do after the
happy Conclusion of a Peace, which is the Prayer and Wish of

3–7   Statues, Bass-Relievo's, Columns, Obelisques, &c. . . . Sculpture . . . Painting
. . . both] *Statues, Bass-Relievo's, Columns, Obilisques,* &c. . . . *Sculpture . . .
Painting . . . both* Q.
8–10   Genius . . . Painting] *Genius . . . Painting* Q.
12–14   Poetry . . . Painting . . . Sculpture] *Poetry . . . Painting . . . Sculpture* Q.
16–17   Poetry . . . Painting] *Poetry . . . Painting* Q.
17–23   History . . . two Arts . . . Contemporary Poets . . . Painting] *History . . .
two Arts . . . Contemporary Poets . . . Painting* Q.
24–25   Poetry . . . Sister-Art] *Poetry . . . Sister-Art* Q.
26–27   King . . . Painting . . . Sculpture] *King . . . Painting . . . Sculpture* Q.

all those who have not an interest to prolong the miseries of *Europe*. For 'tis most certain, as our Author amongst others has observ'd, That Reward is the Spur of Vertue, as well in all good Arts, as in all laudable Attempts: and Emulation which is the other Spur, will never be wanting either amongst Poets or Painters, when particular Rewards and Prizes are propos'd to the best deservers.

But to return from this digression, though it was almost necessary; all the Rules of Painting are methodically, concisely, and
10 yet clearly deliver'd in this present Treatise which I have translated. *Bossu* has not given more exact Rules for the Epique Poem, nor *Dacier* for Tragedy in his late excellent Translation of *Aristotle* and his notes upon him, than our *Fresnoy* has made for Painting; with the Parallel of which I must resume my Discourse, following my Author's Text, though with more brevity than I intended, because *Virgil* calls me.

The principal and most important parts of Painting, is to know what *is most beautifull in Nature, and most proper for that Art:* that which is the most beautifull is the most noble
20 Subject: so in Poetry, Tragedy is more beautifull than Comedy; because, as I said, the Persons are greater whom the Poet instructs, and consequently the instructions of more benefit to Mankind: the action is likewise greater and more noble, and thence is deriv'd the greater and more noble Pleasure.

To imitate Nature well in whatsoever Subject, is the perfection of both Arts; and that Picture and that Poem which comes nearest to the resemblance of Nature is the best. But it follows not, that what pleases most in either kind is therefore good; but what ought to please. Our deprav'd Appetites, and ignorance of

---

2–6 Author ... Poets ... Painters] *Author ... Poets ... Painters* Q.
8 But] *no paragraph break in* Q.
9–10 Rules ... Painting ... this present Treatise] *Rules ... Painting ... this present Treatise* Q.
11–15 Rules ... Epique Poem ... Tragedy ... Translation ... Painting ... Parallel ... Author's Text] *Rules ... Epique Poem ... Tragedy ... Translation ... Painting ... Parallel ... Author's Text* Q.
17 *The*] *no paragraph break in* Q.
20–21 Poetry, Tragedy ... Comedy ... Poet] *Poetry, Tragedy ... Comedy ... Poet* Q.
26 both Arts ... Picture ... Poem] *both Arts ... Picture ... Poem* Q.

the Arts, mislead our Judgments, and cause us often to take that
for true imitation of Nature, which has no resemblance of Nature
in it. To inform our Judgments, and to reform our Tasts, Rules
were invented, that by them we might discern when Nature was
imitated, and how nearly. I have been forc'd to recapitulate these
things, because Mankind is not more liable to deceit, than it is
willing to continue in a pleasing error strengthen'd by a long
habitude. The imitation of nature is therefore justly constituted
as the general, and indeed the onely Rule of pleasing both in
10   Poetry and Painting. *Aristotle* tells us, that imitation pleases,
because it affords matter for a Reasoner to enquire into the truth
or falshood of Imitation, by comparing its likeness or unlikeness
with the Original: But by this Rule, every Speculation in Na-
ture, whose truth falls under the enquiry of a Philosopher, must
produce the same delight, which is not true. I should rather
assign another reason. Truth is the Object of our Understanding,
as Good is of our Will: And the Understanding can no more be
delighted with a Lye, than the Will can choose an apparent Evil.
As Truth is the end of all our Speculations, so the discovery of
20   it is the pleasure of them. And since a true knowledge of Nature
gives us pleasure, a lively imitation of it, either in Poetry or
Painting, must of necessity produce a much greater: For both
these Arts as I said before, are not onely true imitations of Na-
ture, but of the best Nature, of that which is wrought up to a
nobler pitch. They present us with Images more perfect than
the Life in any individual: and we have the pleasure to see all
the scatter'd Beauties of Nature united by a happy Chymistry,
without its deformities or faults. They are imitations of the pas-
sions which always move, and therefore consequently please: for
30   without motion there can be no delight; which cannot be con-
sider'd, but as an active passion. When we view these Elevated

---

3   Rules] *Rules* Q.
9–10   Rule ... Poetry ... Painting] *Rule ...Poetry ...Painting* Q.
13   Original:] ~. Q.   14   Philosopher] *Philosopher* Q.
15   delight, ... true.] ~ₐ ... ~; Q.   16   Understanding,] ~ₐ Q.
21–22   Poetry ... Painting] *Poetry ... Painting* Q.
22   greater:] ~. Q.   22–23   both ... Arts] *both ...Arts* Q.
27   Chymistry] *Chymistry* Q.

Idea's of Nature, the result of that view is Admiration, which is always the cause of Pleasure.

This foregoing Remark, which gives the reason why imitation pleases, was sent me by Mr. *Walter Moyle,* a most ingenious young Gentleman, conversant in all the Studies of Humanity, much above his years. He had also furnish'd me (according to my request) with all the particular passages in *Aristotle* and *Horace,* which are us'd by them to explain the Art of Poetry by that of Painting: which, if ever I have time to retouch this Essay,
10 shall be inserted in their places.

Having thus shewn that Imitation pleases, and why it pleases in both these Arts, it follows that some Rules of Imitation are necessary to obtain the end: for without Rules there can be no Art; any more than there can be a House without a Door to conduct you into it.

The principal parts of Painting and Poetry next follow. Invention is the first part, and absolutely necessary to them both: yet no Rule ever was or ever can be given how to compass it. A happy Genius is the gift of Nature: it depends on the influence of the
20 Stars, say the Astrologers, on the Organs of the Body, say the Naturalists; 'tis the particular gift of Heaven, say the Divines, both *Christians* and Heathens. How to improve it, many Books can teach us; how to obtain it, none; that nothing can be done without it, all agree.

Tu nihil invitâ dices faciesve Minervâ.

---

1   Idea's ... Nature] *Idea's ... Nature* Q.
4   pleases,] ~; Q.
8–9   Art ... Poetry ... Painting] *Art ... Poetry ... Painting* Q.
9   which,] ~‸ Q.   9   Essay] *Essay* Q.
11   Having] *no paragraph break in* Q.
12–14   both these Arts ... Rules ... Rules ... Art ... House ... Door] *both these Arts ... Rules ... Rules ... Art ... House ... Door* Q.
16   The] *no paragraph break in* Q.
16   Painting ... Poetry] *Painting ... Poetry* Q.
16–17   Invention] *Invention* Q (*paragraph break*).
18   Rule] *Rule* Q.   19   Genius] *Genius* Q.
20   Stars,] ~‸ Q.   20   Astrologers] *Astrologers* Q.
20   Body,] ~‸ Q.   21   Naturalists] *Naturalists* Q.
21   Heaven,] ~‸ Q.
21–22   Divines ... Heathens] *Divines ... Heathens* Q.
22–24   it, ... it, ... it,] ~‸ ... ~‸ ... ~‸ Q.

Without Invention a Painter is but a Copier, and a Poet but a
Plagiary of others. Both are allow'd sometimes to copy and trans-
late; but as our Authour tells you, that is not the best part of
their Reputation. *Imitatours are but a Servile kind of Cattle,*
says the Poet; or at best, the Keepers of Cattle for other men:
they have nothing which is properly their own; that is a sufficient
mortification for me while I am translating *Virgil.* But to copy
the best Authour is a kind of praise, if I perform it as I ought;
as a Copy after *Raphael* is more to be commended, than an Origi-
10 nal of any indifferent Painter.

Under this head of *Invention* is plac'd the Disposition of the
Work, (to put all things in a beautifull order and harmony, that
the whole may be of a piece). The Compositions of the Painter
shou'd be conformable to the Text of Ancient Authours, to the
Customs, and the Times. And this is exactly the same in Poetry;
Homer, and *Virgil,* are to be our guides in the Epique; *Sophocles,*
and *Euripides,* in Tragedy: in all things we are to imitate the
Customs, and the Times of those Persons and Things which we
represent: Not to make new Rules of the Drama, as *Lopez de*
20 *Vega* has attempted unsuccessfully to do; but to be content to
follow our Masters, who understood Nature better than we. But
if the Story which we treat be modern, we are to vary the Cus-
toms, according to the Time and the Country where the Scene
of Action lies: for this is still to imitate Nature, which is always
the same, though in a different dress.

As in the Composition of a Picture, the Painter is to take care
that nothing enter into it, which is not proper, or convenient to

1–2 Invention . . . Painter . . . Copier . . . Poet . . . Plagiary] *Invention . . . Painter
. . . Copier . . . Poet . . . Plagiary* Q.
2–3 Both . . . copy . . . translate . . . Authour] *Both . . . copy . . . translate . . .
Authour* Q.
3   you,] ~ˌ Q.   5   Poet] *Poet* Q.
5   men:] ~; Q.   8–9 ought; as] ~. As Q.
9–10 Copy . . . Original . . . Painter] *Copy . . . Original . . . Painter* Q.
11–12 Disposition of the Work] *Disposition of the Work* Q.
12–13 (to . . . harmony, . . . piece).] ˌ~ . . . ~; . . . ~ˌ. Q.
13–14 Compositions . . . Painter . . . Text . . . Ancient Authours] *Compositions
. . . Painter . . . Text . . . Ancient Authours* Q.
15–17 Poetry . . . Epique . . . Tragedy] *Poetry . . . Epique . . . Tragedy* Q.
19 represent:] ~. Q.   19 Rules . . . Drama] *Rules . . . Drama* Q.
26–63:3 Picture . . . Painter . . . Poet . . . Poem . . . Wenns . . . Excrescences]
Picture . . . Painter . . . Poet . . . Poem . . . Wenns . . . Excrescences Q.

the Subject; so likewise is the Poet to reject all incidents which
are foreign to his Poem, and are naturally no parts of it: they are
Wenns, and other Excrescences, which belong not to the Body,
but deform it: no person, no incident in the Piece, or in the
Play, but must be of use to carry on the main Design. All things
else are like six fingers to the hand; when Nature which is super-
fluous in nothing, can do her work with five. A Painter must
reject all trifling Ornaments, so must a Poet refuse all tedious,
and unnecessary Descriptions. A Robe which is too heavy, is
10 less an Ornament than a Burthen.

In Poetry *Horace* calls these things, *Versus inopes rerum, nug-*
æque canoræ; these are also the *lucus & ara Dianæ,* which he
mentions in the same *Art of Poetry.* But since there must be
Ornaments both in Painting and Poetry, if they are not neces-
sary, they must at least be decent: that is, in their due place, and
but moderately us'd. The Painter is not to take so much pains
about the Drapery as about the Face, where the principal resem-
blance lies: neither is the Poet who is working up a passion, to
make similes which will certainly make it languish. My *Monte-*
20 *zuma* dies with a fine one in his mouth: but it is ambitious and
out of season. When there are more Figures in a Picture than are
necessary, or at least ornamental, our Authour calls them *Figures*
to be lett: because the Picture has no use of them. So I have seen
in some modern Plays above twenty Actours; when the Action
has not requir'd half the number. In the principal Figures of a
Picture, the Painter is to employ the sinews of his Art, for in them
consists the principal beauty of his Work. Our Authour saves me
the comparison with Tragedy, for he says that herein he is to imi-
tate the Tragique Poet, who employs his utmost force in those

---

4   it:] ~. Q.
4–5   Piece . . . Play . . . main Design] *Piece . . . Play . . . main Design* Q.
7–8   Painter . . . Poet] *Painter . . . Poet* Q.
11   Poetry] *Poetry* Q.
14   Painting . . . Poetry] *Painting . . . Poetry* Q.
16–19   Painter . . . Poet . . . similes] *Painter . . . Poet . . . similes* Q.
22   Authour] *Authour* Q.
24   modern Plays . . . Actours] *modern Plays . . . Actours* Q.
26   Picture . . . Painter] *Picture . . . Painter* Q.
27–29   Our Authour . . . Tragedy . . . Tragique Poet] *Our Authour . . . Tragedy*
. . . Tragique Poet Q.

places wherein consists the height and beauty of the Action.

Du Fresnoy, whom I follow, makes Design or Drawing the second part of Painting: But the Rules which he gives concerning the Posture of the Figures, are almost wholly proper to that Art; and admit not any comparison, that I know, with Poetry. The Posture of a Poetique Figure is, as I conceive, the Description of his Heroes in the performance of such or such an Action: as of *Achilles* just in the act of killing *Hector:* or of *Æneas* who has *Turnus* under him. Both the Poet and the Painter vary the Pos-
10 tures according to the Action, or Passion which they represent of the same person: But all must be great and gracefull in them. The same *Æneas* must be drawn a Suppliant to *Dido,* with respect in his Gestures, and humility in his Eyes: But when he is forc'd in his own defence to kill *Lausus,* the Poet shows him compassionate, and tempering the severity of his looks with a reluctance to the Action, which he is going to perform. He has pity on his Beauty, and his Youth; and is loath to destroy such a Masterpiece of Nature. He considers *Lausus* rescuing his Father at the hazard of his own life, as an Image of himself when he took
20 *Anchises* on his Shoulders, and bore him safe through the rage of the Fire, and the opposition of his Enemies: And therefore in the posture of a retiring Man, who avoids the Combat, he stretches out his Arm in sign of peace, with his right Foot drawn a little back, and his Breast bending inward, more like an Oratour than a Souldier; and seems to disswade the Young man from pulling on his destiny, by attempting more than he was able to perform. Take the passage as I have thus translated it.

---

2 *Du] no paragraph break in Q.*
2–4 Design . . . Drawing . . . Painting . . . Posture of the Figures . . . that Art]
Design . . . Drawing . . . Painting . . . Posture of the Figures . . . that Art Q.
5 comparison, . . . know,] *comparison*ₐ . . . ~ₐ Q.
5 Poetry] *Poetry* Q.
6 Posture . . . [*to*] . . . Figure] *set in italics in Q.*
6 is,] ~ₐ Q.
6–7 Description . . . Heroes] *Description . . . Heroes* Q.
9–10 Poet . . . Painter . . . Postures] *Poet . . . Painter . . . Postures* Q.
11 person:] ~. Q.
12 *Dido,*] ~ₐ Q.
14 Poet] *Poet* Q.
19 life,] ~; Q.
21 Enemies:] ~. Q.
27 perform. Take] ~: take Q.

Shouts of Applause ran ringing through the Field,
To see the Son, the vanquish'd Father shield:
All, fir'd with noble Emulation, strive;
And with a storm of Darts to distance drive
The Trojan *Chief; who held at Bay, from far*
On his Vulcanian *Orb, sustain'd the War.*
Æneas *thus o'erwhelm'd on every side,*
Their first Assault undaunted did abide;
And thus to Lausus, *loud with friendly threatning cry'd,*
Why wilt thou rush to certain death, and rage
In rash attempts beyond thy tender Age,
Betray'd by pious love?

And afterwards.

He griev'd, he wept; the Sight an Image brought
Of his own Filial Love; a sadly pleasing thought.

But beside the Outlines of the Posture, the Design of the Picture comprehends in the next place the forms of Faces, which are to be different: and so in a Poem, or a Play, must the several Characters of the Persons be distinguish'd from each other. I knew a Poet, whom out of respect I will not name, who being too witty himself, cou'd draw nothing but Wits in a Comedy of his: even his Fools were infected with the Disease of their Authour. They overflow'd with smart Reperties, and were only distinguish'd from the intended Wits by being call'd *Coxcombs;* though they deserv'd not so scandalous a Name. Another, who had a great Genius for Tragedy, following the fury of his natural temper, made every Man, and Woman too, in his Plays stark raging mad: there was not a sober person to be had for love or money. All was tempestuous and blustering; Heaven and Earth were coming together at every word; a meer Hurrican from the be-

---

10–12   Why... [to] ... love?] *set in italics in* Q.
13   And afterwards.] *centered in* Q.   16   But] *no paragraph break in* Q.
16–17   Design ... Picture] *Design ... Picture* Q.
17   Faces,] ~_∧ Q.
18–19   Poem ... Play ... Characters] *Poem ... Play ... Characters* Q.
20–22   Poet ... Comedy ... their Authour] *Poet ... Comedy ... their Authour* Q.
26   Genius ... Tragedy] *Genius ... Tragedy* Q.
27   Man, ... too,] ~_∧ ... ~_∧ Q.   27   Plays] *Plays* Q.

ginning to the end, and every Actour seem'd to be hastning on
the Day of Judgment.

Let every Member be made for its own Head, says our Au-
thour; not a wither'd Hand to a young Face. So in the Persons of
a Play, whatsoever is said or done by any of them, must be consis-
tent with the manners which the Poet has given them distinctly:
and even the Habits must be proper to the degrees, and humours
of the Persons, as well as in a Picture. He who enter'd in the first
Act a Young man, like *Pericles* Prince of *Tyre,* must not be in
10 danger in the fifth Act, of committing Incest with his Daughter:
nor an Usurer, without great probability and causes of Repen-
tance, be turn'd into a *Cutting Moorcraft.*

I am not satisfy'd that the comparison betwixt the two Arts
in the last Paragraph is altogether so just as it might have been;
but I am sure of this which follows.

*The principal Figure of the Subject must appear in the midst
of the Picture, under the principal Light, to distinguish it from
the rest which are onely its attendants.* Thus in a Tragedy or an
Epique Poem, the Hero of the Piece must be advanc'd foremost
20 to the view of the Reader or Spectator; He must out-shine the
rest of all the Characters; He must appear the Prince of them,
like the Sun in the *Copernican* System, encompass'd with the
less noble Planets. Because the Hero is the Centre of the main
Action; all the Lines from the Circumference tend to him alone:
He is the chief object of Pity in the Drama, and of Admiration
in the Epique Poem.

As in a Picture, besides the principal Figures which compose
it, and are plac'd in the midst of it, there are less Grouppes or
Knots of Figures dispos'd at proper distances, which are parts

3–4 Authour;] *Authour,* Q.   5–6 Play ... Poet] *Play ... Poet* Q.
8   Persons,] ~ₐ Q.   8 Picture] *Picture* Q.
9   Act ... man,] ~, ... ~ₐ Q.
13–14 two Arts ... Paragraph] *two Arts ... Paragraph* Q.
17 *Light,*] ~ₐ Q.
18–23 Tragedy ... Epique Poem ... Hero ... Piece ... Reader ... Spectator
... Characters ... Prince ... Sun ... System ... Planets] *Tragedy ... Epique
Poem ... Hero ... Piece ... Reader ... Spectator ... Characters ... Prince ...
Sun ... System ... Planets* Q.
23–26 Hero ... Drama ... Admiration ... Epique Poem] *Hero ... Drama ...
Admiration ... Epique Poem* Q.
28 of it,] ~ ~; Q.

of the Piece, and seem to carry on the same Design in a more inferiour manner; so in Epique Poetry, there are Episodes, and a Chorus in Tragedy, which are Members of the Action, as growing out of it, not inserted into it. Such in the ninth Book of the *Æneids* is the Episode of *Nisus* and *Euryalus:* the adventure belongs to them alone; they alone are the Objects of Compassion and Admiration; but their business which they carry on, is the general Concernment of the *Trojan* Camp, then beleaguer'd by *Turnus* and the *Latines,* as the *Christians* were lately by the
10 *Turks.* They were to advertise the chief Hero of the Distresses of his Subjects occasion'd by his Absence, to crave his Succour, and sollicite him to hasten his Return.

The *Grecian* Tragedy was at first nothing but a Chorus of Singers; afterwards one Actor was introduc'd, which was the Poet himself, who entertain'd the people with a discourse in Verse, betwixt the Pauses of the Singing. This succeeding with the People, more Actors were added to make the variety the greater; and in process of time, the Chorus onely sung betwixt the Acts; and the Coryphæus, or Chief of them, spoke for the rest, as an
20 Actor concern'd in the business of the Play.

Thus Tragedy was perfected by degrees; and being arriv'd at that Perfection, the Painters might probably take the hint from thence, of adding Grouppes to their Pictures. But as a good Picture may be without a Grouppe; so a good Tragedy may subsist without a Chorus: notwithstanding any reasons which have been given by *Dacier* to the contrary.

Monsieur *Racine* has indeed us'd it in his *Esther,* but not that he found any necessity of it, as the *French* Critique would insinu-

---

2   manner; so] ∼. So Q.
2-3   Epique Poetry . . . Episodes . . . Chorus . . . Tragedy] *Epique Poetry* . . . *Episodes . . . Chorus . . . Tragedy* Q.
4   ninth Book] *ninth Book* Q.   5   *Æneids*] *Eneids* Q.
13   Chorus] *Chorus* Q.   14   Singers;] *Singers,* Q.
14   Actor . . . Poet] *Actor . . . Poet* Q.
17-19   Actors . . . Chorus . . . Acts . . . Coryphæus] *Actors . . . Chorus . . . Acts . . . Coriphæus* Q.
19   them,] ∼∧ Q.   20   Actor . . . Play] *Actor . . . Play* Q.
21   Tragedy] *Tragedy* Q.   21   degrees;] ∼, Q.
23   Pictures] *Pictures* Q.
23-25   Picture . . . Tragedy . . . Chorus] *Picture . . . Tragedy . . . Chorus* Q.
28   Critique] *Critique* Q.

ate. The Chorus at St. *Cyr,* was onely to give the young Ladies an
occasion of entertaining the King with vocal Musick, and of com-
mending their own Voices. The Play it self was never intended
for the publick Stage, nor, without disparagement to the learned
Author, could possibly have succeeded there; and much less the
Translation of it here. Mr. *Wicherly,* when we read it together,
was of my opinion in this, or rather I of his; for it becomes me
so to speak of so excellent a Poet, and so great a Judge. But since
I am in this place, as Virgil says, *Spatiis exclusus iniquis,* that is,
10 shorten'd in my time, I will give no other reason, than that it is
impracticable on our Stage. A new Theatre much more ample
and much deeper must be made for that purpose, besides the cost
of sometimes forty or fifty Habits, which is an expence too large,
to be supply'd by a Company of Actors. 'Tis true, I should not
be sorry to see a Chorus on a Theatre more than as large and as
deep again as ours, built and adorn'd at a King's Charges; and
on that condition, and another, which is, That my Hands were
not bound behind me, as now they are, I should not despair of
making such a Tragedy, as might be both instructive and de-
20 lightfull, according to the manner of the *Grecians.*

To make a Sketch, or a more perfect Model of a Picture, is in
the Language of Poets, to draw up the Scenary of a Play, and the
reason is the same for both; to guide the Undertaking, and to
preserve the Remembrance of such things, whose Natures are
difficult to retain.

To avoid Absurdities and Incongruities, is the same Law es-
tablish'd for both Arts. The Painter is not to paint a Cloud at
the Bottom of a Picture, but in the uppermost parts: nor the

1–2 Chorus ... King] *Chorus ... King* Q.
3–4 Play ... Stage] *Play ... Stage* Q.
5 Author] *Author* Q.
6 together,] ∼_∧ Q.
9 *iniquis,*] ∼; Q.
11 Stage] *Stage* Q.
11–14 Theatre ... Company of Actors] *Theatre ... Company of Actors* Q.
15 Chorus] *Chorus* Q.
16 King's] *King's* Q.
18 are,] ∼; Q.
21–22 Sketch ... Model ... Picture ... Poets ... Scenary ... Play] *Sketch ... Model ... Picture ... Poets ... Scenary ... Play* Q.
27 both Arts] *both Arts* Q.
28–69:2 Picture ... Poet ... Poem] *Picture ... Poet ... Poem* Q.

4 nor,] ∼_∧ Q.
5 there;] ∼, Q.
8 Poet ... Judge] *Poet ... Judge* Q.

15 Theatre] *Theatre,* Q.
16 Charges;] ∼, Q.
19 Tragedy] *Tragedy* Q.

Poet to place what is proper to the end or middle in the begin-
ning of a Poem. I might enlarge on this, but there are few Poets
or Painters, who can be suppos'd to sin so grosly against the Laws
of Nature, and of Art. I remember onely one Play, and for once
I will call it by its name, *The Slighted Maid,* where there is noth-
ing in the First Act, but what might have been said or done in
the Fifth; nor any thing in the Midst, which might not have been
plac'd as well in the Beginning or the End. To express the Pas-
sions which are seated in the Heart, by outward Signs, is one
great Precept of the Painters, and very difficult to perform. In
Poetry, the same Passions and Motions of the Mind are to be
express'd; and in this consists the principal Difficulty, as well as
the Excellency of that Art. This, says my Author, is the Gift of
Jupiter: and to speak in the same Heathen Language, we call
it the Gift of our *Apollo:* not to be obtain'd by Pains or Study, if
we are not born to it: For the Motions which are studied are
never so natural, as those which break out in the height of a
real Passion. Mr. *Otway* possess'd this part as thoroughly as any
of the Ancients or Moderns. I will not defend every thing in his
Venice Preserv'd; but I must bear this testimony to his Memory,
That the Passions are truly touch'd in it, though perhaps there is
somewhat to be desir'd both in the Grounds of them, and in the
Height and Elegance of Expression; but Nature is there, which
is the greatest Beauty.

In the Passions, says our Author, *we must have a very great
regard to the quality of the Persons who are actually possess'd
with them.* The Joy of a Monarch for the news of a Victory, must
not be express'd like the Ecstasy of a *Harlequin* on the Receipt

2–4 Poets . . . Painters . . . Nature . . . Art] *Poets . . . Painters . . . Nature . . .
Art* Q.
4 Play] *Play* Q.   5 *Maid,*] ∼: Q.
6–8 First Act . . . Fifth . . . Midst . . . Beginning . . . End] *First Act . . . Fifth . . .
Midst . . . Beginning . . . End* Q.
9 Heart,] ∼ₐ Q.   10 Painters] *Painters* Q.
11–13 Poetry . . . that Art] *Poetry . . . that Art* Q.
13–14 Author . . . Heathen Language] *Author . . . Heathen Language* Q.
16 it:] ∼. Q.
19 Ancients . . . Moderns] *Ancients . . . Moderns* Q.
20 *Preserv'd*] *preserv'd* Q.   21 Passions] *Passions* Q.
23 Nature] *Nature* Q.
27–70:2 Monarch . . . both the Arts . . . Comparison] *Monarch . . . both the
Arts . . . Comparison* Q.

of a Letter from his Mistress; this is so much the same in both the Arts, that it is no longer a Comparison. What he says of Face-painting, or the Portrait of any one particular Person (concerning the likeness) is also as applicable to Poetry. In the character of an Hero, as well as in an inferiour Figure, there is a better or worse likeness to be taken; the better is a Panegyrick if it be not false, and the worse is a Libel: *Sophocles,* says *Aristotle,* always drew men as they ought to be, that is, better than they were; another, whose name I have forgotten, drew them worse than naturally they were. *Euripides* alter'd nothing in the Character, but made them such as they were represented by History, Epique Poetry or Tradition. Of the three, the draught of *Sophocles* is most commended by *Aristotle.* I have follow'd it in that part of *Oedipus,* which I writ, though perhaps I have made him too good a man. But my Characters of *Antony* and *Cleopatra,* though they are favourable to them, have nothing of outrageous Panegyrick: their Passions were their own, and such as were given them by History; onely the deformities of them were cast into Shadows, that they might be Objects of Compassion: whereas if I had chosen a Noon-day Light for them, somewhat must have been discover'd, which would rather have mov'd our Hatred than our Pity.

The *Gothique* manner, and the barbarous Ornaments, which are to be avoided in a Picture, are just the same with those in an ill order'd Play. For example, our *English* Tragicomedy must be confess'd to be wholly *Gothique,* notwithstanding the Success

---

2–3 Face-painting] *Face-painting* Q.   3   Portrait] *Protrait* Q.
3–4   Person (concerning . . . likeness)] ~; ~ . . . ~ₐ Q.
4   Poetry] *Poetry* Q.
4–7   character . . . Hero . . . Panegyrick . . . Libel] *character . . . Hero . . . Panegyrick . . . Libel* Q.
7   *Sophocles,* . . . *Aristotle,*] ~ₐ . . . ~ₐ Q.
8   is,] ~ₐ Q.
11–12   History, Epique Poetry . . . Tradition] *History, Epique Poetry . . . Tradition* Q.
15   *Antony*] *Anthony* Q.   16–17   Panegyrick:] *Panegyrick,* Q.
18   History;] *History,* Q.   19   Shadows] *Shadows* Q.
19   Compassion:] ~; Q.
20   Noon-day Light] *Noon-day Light* Q.
24–25   Picture . . . Play] *Picture . . . Play* Q.
25–71:1   Tragicomedy . . . Theatre] *Tragicomedy . . . Theatre* Q.

which it has found upon our Theatre, and in the *Pastor Fido* of *Guarini;* even though *Corisca* and the Satyr contribute somewhat to the main Action. Neither can I defend my *Spanish Fryar,* as fond as otherwise I am of it, from this Imputation: for though the comical parts are diverting, and the serious moving, yet they are of an unnatural mingle. For Mirth and Gravity destroy each other, and are no more to be allow'd for decent, than a gay Widow laughing in a mourning Habit.

I had almost forgotten one considerable resemblance. *Du Fresnoy* tells us, *That the Figures of the Grouppes, must not be all on a side, that is, with their Face and Bodies all turn'd the same way; but must contrast each other by their several positions.* Thus in a Play, some characters must be rais'd to oppose others, and to set them off the better, according to the old Maxim, *Contraria juxta se posita, magis elucescunt.* Thus in the *Scornfull Lady,* the Usurer is set to confront the Prodigal. Thus in my *Tyrannique Love,* the Atheist *Maximin* is oppos'd to the character of St. *Catharine.*

I am now come, though with the omission of many Likenesses, to the third Part of Painting, which is call'd the *Cromatique* or *Colouring.* Expression, and all that belongs to words, is that in a Poem, which Colouring is in a Picture. The Colours well chosen in their proper places, together with the Lights and Shadows which belong to them, lighten the Design, and make it pleasing to the Eye. The Words, the Expressions, the Tropes and Figures, the Versification, and all the other Elegancies of Sound, as Cadences, Turns of Words upon the Thought, and many other things which are all parts of expression, perform exactly the same Office both in Dramatique and Epique Poetry. Our Author calls Colouring, *Lena Sororis;* in plain *English, The Bawd of her Sis-*

---

4   it,] ∼‸ Q.   9   resemblance] *resemblance* Q.
13 Play] *Play* Q.   13 others,] ∼; Q.
17 *Tyrannique*] *Tyrannicque* Q.
19–20 Likenesses ... Painting] *Likenesses ... Painting* Q.
21–22 Expression ... Poem ... Colouring ... Picture] *Expression ... Poem ... Colouring ... Picture* Q.
22 Colours] *Colours* Q.
29 Dramatique ... Epique Poetry ... Author] *Dramatique ... Epique Poetry ... Author* Q.
30 *Sororis;*] ∼, Q.   30 *English*] English Q.
30–72:1 *Sister,*] ∼‸ Q.

ter, the Design or Drawing: she cloaths, she dresses her up, she paints her, she makes her appear more lovely than naturally she is; she procures for the Design, and makes Lovers for her: For the Design of it self, is onely so many naked lines. Thus in Poetry, the Expression is that which charms the Reader, and beautifies the Design which is onely the Out-lines of the Fables. 'Tis true, the Design must of it self be good; if it be vicious or (in one word) unpleasing, the cost of Colouring is thrown away upon it. 'Tis an ugly woman in a rich Habit set out with Jewels, nothing

10 can become her: but granting the Design to be moderately good, 'tis like an excellent Complexion with indifferent Features; the white and red well mingled on the Face, make what was before but passable, appear beautifull. *Operum Colores* is the very word which *Horace* uses, to signify Words and elegant Expressions, of which he himself was so great a Master in his *Odes.* Amongst the Ancients, *Zeuxis* was most famous for his Colouring; amongst the Moderns, *Titian* and *Correggio.* Of the two Ancient Epique Poets, who have so far excell'd all the Moderns, the Invention and Design were the particular Talents of *Homer. Virgil* must

20 yield to him in both, for the Design of the *Latine* was borrowed from the *Grecian:* But the *dictio Virgiliana,* the expression of *Virgil,* his Colouring, was incomparably the better, and in that I have always endeavour'd to copy him. Most of the Pedants I know maintain the contrary, and will have *Homer* excell even in this part: But of all people, as they are the most ill manner'd, so they are the worst Judges. Even of words, which are their

---

1   Design . . . Drawing] *Design . . . Drawing* Q.
3   is;] ~, Q.   3   Design] *Design* Q.
3   her:] ~. Q.   4   Design] *Design* Q.
4–6   Poetry . . . Expression . . . Reader . . . Out-lines] *Poetry . . . Expression . . . Reader . . . Out-lines* Q.
7–8   Design . . . Colouring] *Design . . . Colouring* Q.
10   Design] *Design* Q.   16   Ancients] *Ancients* Q.
16   Colouring; amongst] *Colouring.* Amongst Q.
17   Moderns] *Moderns* Q.
17–19   Ancient Epique Poets . . . Moderns . . . Invention . . . Design] *Ancient Epique Poets . . . Moderns . . . Invention . . . Design* Q.
20   Design] *Design* Q.
22   *Virgil,* . . . Colouring,] ~; . . . *Colouring*ᴀ Q.
23   Pedants] *Pedants* Q.   25   part:] ~. Q.
26   Judges. Even . . . words,] ~; even . . . ~ᴀ Q.

Province, they seldom know more than the Grammatical con-
struction, unless they are born with a Poetical Genius; which is a
rare Portion amongst them. Yet some I know may stand ex-
cepted; and such I honour. *Virgil* is so exact in every word, that
none can be chang'd but for a worse: nor any one remov'd from
its place, but the harmony will be alter'd. He pretends some-
times to trip; but 'tis onely to make you think him in danger of
a fall, when he is most secure: Like a skilfull dancer on the Ropes
(if you will pardon the meanness of the similitude) who slips
10 willingly and makes a seeming stumble, that you may think him
in great hazard of breaking his neck; while at the same time he is
onely giving you a proof of his dexterity. My late Lord *Ros-
comon* was often pleas'd with this reflection, and with the ex-
amples of it in this admirable Author.

I have not leisure to run through the whole Comparison of
Lights and Shadows with Tropes and Figures; yet I cannot but
take notice of Metaphors, which like them have power to les-
sen or greaten any thing. Strong and glowing Colours are the
just resemblances of bold Metaphors, but both must be judi-
20 ciously apply'd; for there is a difference betwixt daring and fool-
hardiness. *Lucan* and *Statius* often ventur'd them too far, our
Virgil never. But the great defect of the *Pharsalia* and the
Thebais was in the Design; if that had been more perfect, we
might have forgiven many of their bold strokes in the Colour-
ing; or at least excus'd them: yet some of them are such as *De-
mosthenes* or *Cicero* could not have defended. *Virgil,* if he could
have seen the first Verses of the *Sylvæ,* would have thought *Statius*
mad in his fustian Description of the Statue on the brazen Horse.
But that Poet was always in a Foam at his setting out, even before
30 the Motion of the Race had warm'd him. The soberness of *Vir-*

1–2 Grammatical . . . Poetical Genius] *Grammatical . . . Poetical Genius* Q.
8 secure:] ~. Q.   14 Author] *Author* Q.
15–17 Comparison . . . Lights . . . Shadows . . . Tropes . . . Figures . . . Meta-
phors] *Comparison . . . Lights . . . Shadows . . . Tropes . . . Figures . . . Meta-
phors* Q.
18–19 Strong . . . glowing Colours . . . bold Metaphors] *Strong . . . glowing
Colours . . . bold Metaphors* Q.
23–25 Design . . . Colouring] *Design . . . Colouring* Q.
28 Statue . . . brazen Horse] *Statue . . . brazen Horse* Q.
29 that Poet] *that Poet* Q.

gil, whom he read it seems to little purpose, might have shown him the difference betwixt *Arma virumq; cano,* and *Magnanimum Æacidem, formidatamq; tonanti Progeniem.* But *Virgil* knew how to rise by degrees in his expressions: *Statius* was in his towring heights at the first stretch of his Pinions. The description of his running Horse just starting in the Funeral Games for *Archemorus,* though the Verses are wonderfully fine, are the true Image of their Author:

> *Stare adeo nescit, pereunt vestigia mille*
> *Ante fugam; absentemq; ferit gravis ungula campum;*

which would cost me an hour, if I had the leisure to translate them, there is so much of Beauty in the Original.

Virgil, as he better knew his Colours, so he knew better how and where to place them. In as much hast as I am, I cannot forbear giving one example. 'Tis said of him, That he read the Second, Fourth and Sixth Books of his *Æneids* to *Augustus Cæsar.* In the Sixth, (which we are sure he read, because we know *Octavia* was present, who rewarded him so bountifully for the twenty Verses which were made in honour of her deceas'd Son *Marcellus*) in this sixth Book, I say, the Poet speaking of *Misenus* the Trumpeter, says,

> ———*Quo non præstantior alter,*
> *Ære ciere viros,*———

and broke off in the Hemistick or midst of the Verse: but in the very reading, siez'd as it were with a divine Fury, he made up the latter part of the Hemistick, with these following words:

> ———*Martemq; accendere cantu.*

2 betwixt] ∼, Q.   8 Author:] ∼. Q.
10–11 *campum;* which] ∼. Which Q.   13 *Virgil*] *no paragraph break in* Q.
13 Colours] *Colours* Q.
16 Second, Fourth ... Sixth Books] *Second, Fourth ... Sixth Books* Q.
17 Sixth] *Sixth* Q.
20 Book,] ∼ₐ Q.   20 Poet] *Poet* Q.
24 and] And Q.   24 Hemistick] *Hemystick* Q.
25 reading,] ∼ₐ Q.   25 divine Fury] *divine Fury* Q.
26 Hemistick] *Hemystick* Q.   26 words:] ∼; Q.

How warm, nay how glowing a Colouring is this! In the begin-
ning of the Verse, the word *Æs,* or Brass, was taken for a Trum-
pet, because the Instrument was made of that Metal, which of
it self was fine; but in the latter end, which was made *ex tem-
pore,* you see three Metaphors, *Martemque,*————*accendere,*
————*cantu.* Good Heavens! how the plain sence is rais'd by the
Beauty of the words! But this was Happiness, the former might
be only Judgment: this was the *curiosa felicitas,* which *Petro-
nius* attributes to *Horace;* 'tis the Pencil thrown luckily full
10 upon the Horses mouth to express the Foam which the Painter
with all his skill could not perform without it. These hits of
words a true Poet often finds, as I may say, without seeking: but
he knows their value when he finds them, and is infinitely pleas'd.
A bad Poet may sometimes light on them, but he discerns not a
Diamond from a *Bristol*-stone; and would have been of the Cocks
mind in *Æsop,* a Grain of Barley would have pleas'd him better
than the Jewel. The Lights and Shadows which belong to Colour-
ing, put me in mind of that Verse in *Horace, Hoc amat obscurum,
vult hoc sub luce videri:* some parts of a Poem require to be
20 amply written, and with all the force and elegance of Words:
others must be cast into Shadows; that is, pass'd over in silence,
or but faintly touch'd. This belongs wholly to the Judgment of
the Poet and the Painter. The most beautifull parts of the Pic-
ture and the Poem must be the most finish'd, the Colours and
Words most chosen; many things in both which are not deserving
of this care, must be shifted off; content with vulgar expressions,
and those very short, and left, as in a shadow, to the imagination
of the Reader.

    We have the Proverb, *manum de tabulâ,* from the Painters;

1 warm ... glowing ... Colouring] *warm ... glowing ... Colouring* Q.
3 Instrument] Instument Q.   7 words!] ~. Q.
10 Painter] *Painter* Q.   12 Poet] *Poet* Q.
14–17 bad Poet ... Diamond ... *Bristol*-stone ... Cocks ... Grain of Barley ...
Jewel] *bad Poet ... Diamond ... Bristol-stone ... Cocks ... Grain of Barley ...
Jewel* Q.
17–18 Lights ... Shadows ... Colouring] *Lights ... Shadows ... Colouring* Q.
19 Poem] *Poem* Q.
23 Poet ... Painter] *Poet ... Painter* Q.
23–24 Picture ... Poem] *Picture ... Poem* Q.
26–27 expressions, ... left, ... shadow,] ~ʌ ... ~ʌ ... ~ʌ Q.
28 Reader] *Reader* Q.   29 Painters] *Painters* Q.

which signifies, to know when to give over, and to lay by the
Pencil. Both *Homer* and *Virgil* practis'd this Precept wonder-
fully well, but *Virgil* the better of the two. *Homer* knew that
when *Hector* was slain, *Troy* was as good as already taken; there-
fore he concludes his Action there. For what follows in the
Funerals of *Patroclus,* and the redemption of *Hector's* Body, is
not (properly speaking) a part of the main Action. But *Virgil*
concludes with the death of *Turnus:* for after that difficulty was
remov'd, *Æneas* might marry and establish the *Trojans* when
10 he pleas'd. This Rule I had before my Eyes in the conclusion
of the *Spanish Fryar,* when the discovery was made, that the
King was living, which was the knot of the Play unty'd; the rest
is shut up in the compass of some few lines, because nothing then
hinder'd the Happiness of *Torismond* and *Leonora.* The faults
of that Drama are in the kind of it, which is Tragi-comedy. But
it was given to the people; and I never writ any thing for my self
but *Antony and Cleopatra.*

This Remark I must acknowledge is not so proper for the
Colouring as the Design; but it will hold for both. As the words,
20 &c. are evidently shown to be the cloathing of the Thought, in
the same sense as Colours are the cloathing of the Design, so the
Painter and the Poet ought to judge exactly, when the Colouring
and Expressions are perfect, and then to think their work is truly
finish'd. *Apelles* said of *Protogenes, That he knew not when to
give over.* A work may be over-wrought as well as under-wrought:
too much Labour often takes away the Spirit by adding to the
polishing, so that there remains nothing but a dull correctness, a
piece without any considerable Faults, but with few Beauties;
for when the Spirits are drawn off, there is nothing but a *caput*
30 *mortuum. Statius* never thought an expression could be bold
enough; and if a bolder could be found he rejected the first.

---

2   Precept] *Precept* Q.
10–12   This Rule ... Play] *This Rule ... Play* Q.
12   unty'd;] ~, Q.
15   Drama ... Tragi-comedy] *Drama ... Tragi-comedy* Q.
17   *Antony and*] *Anthony* and Q.
18–19   This Remark ... Colouring ... Design] *This Remark ... Colouring ...
Design* Q.
22   Painter ... Poet] *Painter ... Poet* Q.
27   polishing,] ~; Q.

Virgil had Judgment enough to know daring was necessary; but he knew the difference betwixt a glowing Colour and a glaring: as when he compar'd the shocking of the Fleets at *Actium* to the justling of Islands rent from their Foundations, and meeting in the Ocean. He knew the comparison was forc'd beyond Nature and rais'd too high: he therefore softens the Metaphor with a *Credas.* You would almost believe, that Mountains or Islands rush'd against each other.

> ———*Credas innare revulsas*
> *Cycladas: aut montes concurrere montibus æquos.*

But here I must break off without finishing the Discourse.

Cynthius aurem vellit & admonuit, &c. The things which are behind are of too nice a consideration for an Essay, begun and ended in twelve Mornings, and perhaps the Judges of Painting and Poetry, when I tell them how short a time it cost me, may make me the same answer, which my late Lord *Rochester* made to one, who to commend a Tragedy, said it was written in three weeks; *How the Devil could he be so long about it?* For that Poem was infamously bad; and I doubt this Parallel is little better; and then the shortness of the time is so far from being a Commendation, that it is scarcely an Excuse. But if I have really drawn a Portrait to the Knees, or an half length with a tolerable Likeness, then I may plead with some Justice for my self, that the rest is left to the Imagination. Let some better Artist provide himself of a deeper Canvas, and taking these hints which I have given, set the Figure on its Legs, and finish it in the Invention, Design and Colouring.

2–5   glowing Colour . . . glaring . . . Islands . . . Ocean] *glowing Colour . . . glaring . . . Islands . . . Ocean* Q.
6   Metaphor] *Metaphor* Q.
12   &c. The] *&c.* the Q.
13–15   Essay . . . Judges . . . Painting . . . Poetry] *Essay . . . Judges . . . Painting . . . Poetry* Q.
15   them] ~, Q.
17   Tragedy] *Tragedy* Q.
18   *How . . . [to] . . . it] set in romans in* Q.
19   Poem . . . Parallel] *Poem . . . Parallel* Q.
26–27   Invention, Design . . . Colouring] *Invention, Design . . . Colouring* Q.

The Preface of the French Author

A MONG *all the beautiful and delightful Arts, that of Paint-
ing has always found the most Lovers; the number of
them almost including all Mankind. Of whom great mul-
titudes are daily found, who value themselves on the knowledge
of it; either because they keep company with Painters, or that
they have seen good Pieces; or lastly, because their Gusto is natu-
rally good. Which notwithstanding, that Knowledge of theirs (if
we may so call it) is so very superficial, and so ill grounded, that
it is impossible for them to describe in what consists the beauty*
10 *of those Works which they admire, or the faults which are in the
greatest part of those which they condemn: and truly 'tis not hard
to find, that this proceeds from no other cause, than that they are
not furnish'd with Rules by which to judge, nor have any solid
Foundations, which are as so many Lights set up to clear their
understanding and lead them to an entire and certain knowledge.
I think it superfluous to prove that this is necessary to the knowl-
edge of Painting. 'Tis sufficient, that Painting be acknowledg'd
for an Art; for that being granted it follows without dispute,
that no Arts are without their Precepts. I shall satisfy my self with*
20 *telling you, that this little Treatise will furnish you with in-
fallible Rules of judging truly: since they are not onely founded
upon right Reason but upon the best Pieces of the best Masters,
which our Author hath carefully examin'd during the space of
more than thirty years; and on which he has made all the reflec-
tions which are necessary to render this Treatise worthy of Pos-
terity: which though little in bulk, yet contains most judicious
Remarks, and suffers nothing to escape that is essential to the*

1–3 *Arts . . . Painting . . . Lovers . . . Mankind*] Arts . . . Painting . . . Lovers . . .
Mankind Q.
5–6 *Painters . . . Pieces . . . Gusto*] Painters . . . Pieces . . . Gusto Q.
7–13 *Knowledge . . . Rules*] Knowledge . . . Rules Q.
17 *Painting*] Painting Q.
17–19 *Painting . . . Art . . . Arts . . . Precepts*] Painting . . . Art . . . Arts . . . Pre-
cepts Q.
20–25 *Treatise . . . Reason . . . Pieces . . . Masters . . . Author . . . Treatise*] Treatise
. . . Reason . . . Pieces . . . Masters . . . Author . . . Treatise Q.

*Subject which it handles. If you will please to read it with atten-
tion, you will find it capable of giving the most nice and delicate
sort of Knowledge, not onely to the Lovers, but even to the Pro-
fessors of that Art.*

*It would be too long to tell you the particular advantages
which it has above all the Books which hath appear'd before it
in this kind: you need onely to read it, and that will convince you
of this truth. All that I will allow my self to say, is onely this,
That there is not a word in it, which carries not its weight;*
10 *whereas in all others, there are two considerable faults which lie
open to the sight, (viz.) That saying too much, they always say too
little. I assure my self, that the Reader will own 'tis a work of
general profit, to the Lovers of Painting, for their instruction
how to judge exactly, and with Knowledge of the Cause, which
they are to judge; and to the Painters themselves, by removing
their difficulties, that they may work with pleasure, because they
may be in some manner certain that their Productions are good.
'Tis to be used like Spirits and precious Liquours; the less you
drink of it at a time, 'tis with the greater pleasure: read it often,*
20 *and but little at once, that you may digest it better; and dwell
particularly on those passages which you find mark'd with an
Asterism*. For the observations which follow such a Note, will
give you a clearer Light, on the matter which is there treated.
You will find them by the Numbers which are on the side of
the Translation, from five to five Verses, by searching for the like
Number in the Remarks which are at the end of it, and which
are distinguish'd from each other by this note ¶. You will find in*

3–4   *Knowledge . . . Lovers . . . Professors . . . Art*] Knowledge . . . Lovers . . .
Professors . . . Art Q.
6   *Books*] Books Q.
11–12   *saying . . . [to] . . . little*] set in romans in Q.
12–13   *Reader . . . Lovers . . . Painting*] Readers . . . Lovers . . . Painting Q.
14–15   *exactly, . . . judge; and*] ~; . . . ~. And Q.
15   *Painters*] Painters Q.   16   *pleasure,*] ~; Q.
18   *Spirits . . . precious Liquours;*] Spirits . . . precious Liquours, Q.
19   *time,*] ~ₐ Q.
19–22   *read . . . Asterism*] read . . . Asterism Q.
22   *Note*] Note Q.
24–25   *Numbers . . . Translation*] Numbers . . . Translation Q.
25   *Verses,*] Verses; Q.
26–27   *Number . . . Remarks . . . note*] Number . . . Remarks . . . note Q.

the latter Pages of this Book, the Judgment of the Author on those Painters, who have acquir'd the greatest Reputation in the World: Amongst whom, he was not willing to comprehend those who are now living. They are undoubtedly his, as being found among his Papers written in his own hand.

As for the Prose Translation which you will find on the other side of the Latine *Poem, I must inform you on what occasion, and in what manner it was perform'd. The Love which I had for Painting, and the pleasure which I found in the Exercise of that*
10 *noble Art, at my leisure hours, gave me the desire of being acquainted with the late Mr.* du Fresnoy; *who was generally reputed to have a through knowledge of it. Our Acquaintance at length proceeded to that degree of Intimacy, that he intrusted me with his Poem, which he believ'd me capable both of understanding, and translating; and accordingly desir'd me to undertake it. The truth is, that we had convers'd so often on that Subject, and he had communicated his Thoughts of it so fully to me; that I had not the least remaining difficulty concerning it. I undertook therefore to translate it, and imploy'd my self in it*
20 *with Pleasure, Care, and Assiduity; after which, I put it into his hands, and he alter'd in it what he pleas'd, till at last it was wholly to his Mind. And then he gave his Consent that it should be publish'd: but his Death preventing that Design, I thought it a wrong to his Memory, to deprive Mankind any longer of this Translation, which I may safely affirm to be done according to the true sence of the Author, and to his liking: Since he himself has given great Testimonies of his Approbation to many of his Friends, and*

1–2 *Pages ... Book ... Judgment ... Author ... Painters*] Pages ... Book ... Judgment ... Author ... Painters Q.
3–4 *World: ... living.*] ~. .... ~: Q.   5 *Papers*] Papers Q.
6–7 *Prose Translation ... Poem*] Prose Translation ... Poem Q.
8–10 *Love ... Painting ... Exercise ... Art*] Love ... Painting ... Exercise ... Art Q.
11 Fresnoy] FRESNOY Q.   12 *knowledge*] knowledge Q.
12 *Acquaintance*] Acquaintance Q.   13 *Intimacy,*] Intimacy; Q.
14–15 *Poem ... understanding ... translating*] Poem ... understanding ... translating Q.
17 *Subject*] Subject Q.   19 *translate*] translate Q.
22–27 *Consent ... Death ... Design ... Memory ... Translation ... Author ... Testimonies ... Approbation*] Consent ... Death ... Design ... Memory ... Translation ... Author ... Testimonies ... Approbation Q.

they who were acquainted with him, know his humour to be such, that he wou'd never constrain himself so far, as to commend what he did not really approve. I thought my self oblig'd to say thus much, in vindication of the faithfulness of my Work, to those who understand not the Latine: *for as to those who are conversant in both the tongues, I leave them to make their own judgment of it.*

The Remarks which I have added to his work, are also wholly conformable to his opinions; and I am certain that he wou'd not
10 *have disapprov'd them. I have endeavour'd in them to explain some of the most obscure passages, and those which are most necessary to be understood; and I have done this according to the manner wherein he us'd to express himself, in many Conversations which we had together. I have confin'd them also to the narrowest compass I was able, that I might not tire the patience of the Reader, and that they might be read by all persons. But if it happens, that they are not to the tast of some Readers (as doubtless it will so fall out) I leave them entirely to their own discretion, and shall not be displeas'd that another hand*
20 *shou'd succeed better. I shall onely beg this favour from them, that in reading what I have written, they will bring no particular gusto along with them, or any prevention of mind, and that whatsoever judgment they make, it may be purely their own, whether it be in my favour, or in my condemnation.*

2–3   *commend . . . approve*] commend . . . approve Q.
4–7   *Work . . . tongues . . . judgment*] Work . . . tongues . . . judgment Q.
8–9   *Remarks . . . work . . . opinions*] Remarks . . . work . . . opinions Q.
10–14   *explain . . . obscure passages . . . necessary . . . understood . . . Conversations*] explain . . . obscure passages . . . necessary . . . understood . . . Conversations Q.
16   *Reader*] Reader Q.
17–19   *tast . . . Readers . . . another hand*] tast . . . Readers . . . another hand Q.
20–24   *favour . . . gusto . . . prevention . . . mind . . . judgment . . . favour . . . condemnation*] favour . . . gusto . . . prevention . . . mind . . . judgment . . . favour . . . condemnation Q.

A Table of the Precepts
Contain'd in This Treatise

---

to Nature ... Genius] to Nature ... Genius Q.
Figure,] ~∧ Q.
Ornaments] *Ornamens* Q.

---

ib. | *The Looking-glass*] ib_∧ | *The* Looking-glass Q.
natural.] ∼_∧ Q.

The Art of Painting

P AINTING* and Poesy are two Sisters, which are so like in all things, that they mutually lend to each other both their Name and Office. One is call'd a dumb Poesy, and the other a speaking Picture. [5.] The Poets have never said any thing but what they believ'd

would please the Ears. And it has been the constant endeavour of the Painters to give pleasure to the Eyes. In short, those things which the Poets have thought unworthy of their Pens, the Paint-
10 ers have judg'd to be unworthy of their Pencils. * For both of them, that they might contribute all within their power to the sacred Honours of Religion, [10.] have rais'd themselves to Heaven, and, having found a free admission into the Palace of *Jove* himself, have enjoy'd the sight and conversation of the Gods; whose Majesty they observe, and contemplate the wonders of their Discourse, in order to relate them to Mankind; whom at the same time they inspire with those Cœlestial Flames, which shine so gloriously in their Works. From Heaven they take their passage through the World; and are neither sparing of their
20 pains nor of their study [15.] to collect whatsoever they find worthy of them. They dive (as I may say) into all past Ages; and search their Histories, for Subjects which are proper for their use: with care avoiding to treat of any but those which, by their nobleness, or by some remarkable accident, have deserv'd to be consecrated to Eternity; whether on the Seas, or Earth, or in the Heavens. [20.] And by this their care and study it comes to pass, that the glory of Heroes is not extinguish'd with their lives: and that those admirable works, those prodigies of skill, which even

---

7 would] Q *(corrected form);* wou'd Q *(uncorrected form).*
16 Discourse,] ~; Q.
17 Flames] Q *(corrected form);* flames Q *(uncorrected form).*
19 World] Q *(corrected form);* world Q *(uncorrected form).*
21 They] *They Q.

yet are the objects of our admiration, are still preserv'd. * So
much these Divine Arts have been always honour'd: and such
authority they preserve amongst Mankind. [25.] It will not here
be necessary to implore the succour of *Apollo,* and the Muses,
for the gracefulness of the Discourse, or for the Cadence of the
Verses: which containing only Precepts, have not so much need
of Ornament, as of Perspicuity.

[30.] I pretend not in this Treatise to tye the hands of Artists,
whose skill consists only in a certain practice, or manner which
10 they have affected, and made of it as it were a Common Road.
Neither would I stifle the Genius by a jumbled heap of Rules:
nor extinguish the fire of a vein which is lively and abundant.
But rather to make this my business, that Art being strengthned
by the knowledge of things, may at length [35.] pass into Nature
by slow degrees; and so in process of time may be sublim'd into
a pure Genius which is capable of choosing judiciously what is
true, and of distinguishing betwixt the beauties of Nature, and
that which is low and mean in her; and that this Original Genius
by long exercise and customs, may perfectly possess all the Rules
20 and Secrets of that Art.

* The principal and most important part of   Precept I.
Painting, is to find out and thoroughly to un-   *Of what is*
derstand what Nature has made most beautifull,   *Beautifull.*
and most proper to this Art; * and that a choice of it may be
made according to the gust and manner of the Ancients, [40.]
* without which, all is nothing but a blind, and rash barbarity;
which rejects what is most beautifull, and seems with an au-
dacious insolence to despise an Art, of which it is wholly ig-
norant: which has occasion'd these words of the Ancients: *That*
30 *no man is so bold, so rash, and so overweening of his own works,*
as an ill Painter, and a bad Poet, who are not conscious to them-
selves of their own Ignorance.

[45.] * We love what we understand; we desire what we love;

4   Muses,] ~: Q.   10   affected,] ~; Q.
11   would] Q (*corrected form*); wou'd Q (*uncorrected form*).
17   true,] ~; Q.   26   which,] ~ₐ Q.
28–29   ignorant:] Q (*corrected form*); ~; Q (*uncorrected form*).

we pursue the enjoyment of those things which we desire; and arrive at last to the possession of what we have pursu'd, if we constantly persist in our Design. In the mean time, we ought not to expect that blind Fortune should infallibly throw into our hands those Beauties: For though we may light by chance on some which are true and natural, yet they may prove either not to be decent or not to be ornamental. Because it is not suffi-cient [50.] to imitate Nature in every circumstance, dully, and as it were literally, and meanly; but it becomes a Painter to take
10 what is most beautifull, * as being the Soveraign Judge of his own Art; and that by the progress which he has made, he may understand how to correct his errours, and * permit no transient Beauties to escape his observation.

    * In the same manner, that bare practice, [55.] destitute of the Lights of Art, is always subject to fall into a Precipice like a blind Traveller,   II.
Of Theory, and Practice.
without being able to produce any thing which contributes to a solid reputation, so the speculative part of Painting, without the assistance of manual operation, can never attain to that perfec-
20 tion which is its object, but sloathfully languishes as in a Prison: for it was not with his Tongue that *Apelles* perform'd his Noble Works. [60.] Therefore though there are many things in Painting, of which no precise rules are to be given (* because the greatest Beauties cannot always be express'd for want of terms) yet I shall not omit to give some Precepts which I have selected from among the most considerable which we have receiv'd from Nature, that exact School-mistress, after having examin'd her most secret recesses, as well as * those Master-pieces of Antiquity, which were the first Examples of this Art: And, 'tis by this means that the
30 mind, and the natural disposition [65.] are to be cultivated, and that Science perfects Genius, * and also moderates that fury of the fancy, which cannot contain it self within the bounds of Reason, but often carries a man into dangerous extremes: *For*

---

4 should] Q *(corrected form)*; shou'd Q *(uncorrected form)*.
16 Precipice] Q *(corrected form)*; precipice Q *(uncorrected form)*.
18 reputation, so] ∼: So Q.
20 object, but] ∼: But Q.
30–33 cultivated, . . . Reason,] ∼; . . . ∼; Q.

there is a mean in all things; and a certain measure, wherein the good and the beautifull consist; and out of which they never can depart.

This being premis'd, the next thing is to make choice of * a Subject beautifull and noble; [70.] which being of it self capable of all the charms

III.
*Concerning
the Subject.*

and graces, that Colours, and the elegance of Design can possibly give, shall afterwards afford, to a perfect and consummate Art, an ample field of matter wherein to expatiate it self; to exert all
10 its power, and to produce somewhat to the sight which is excellent, judicious, * and well season'd; and at the same time proper to instruct, and to enlighten the Understanding.

Thus at length I enter into the Subject-matter of my Discourse; and at first find only a bare strain'd Canvass, * on which the whole Machine (as it may be call'd) of the Picture is to be dispos'd, and the imagination of a powerfull, and easy Genius; [75.] * which is what we properly call *Invention.*

* Invention is a kind of Muse, which being possess'd of the other advantages common to her
20 Sisters, and being warm'd by the fire of *Apollo,*

*Invention the
first part of
Painting.*

is rais'd higher than the rest, and shines with a more glorious, and brighter flame.

* 'Tis the business of a Painter, in his choice of Postures, to foresee the effect, and harmony of the Lights and Shadows, with the Colours which are to enter into the whole; [80.] taking

IV.
*The Disposi-
tion or Oeco-
nomy of the
whole Work.*

from each of them, that which will most conduce to the production of a beautifull Effect.

* Let your Compositions be conformable to
30 the Text of Ancient Authours, to Customs, and to Times.

V.
*The faithful-
ness of the
Subject.*

* Take care that whatsoever makes nothing to your Subject, and is improper to it, be not admitted into your Work, or not possess [85.] the chief place in it. But on this occasion, imi-

VI.
*Whatsoever
palls the Sub-
ject to be re-
jected.*

14–16 Canvass, . . . dispos'd,] ∼: . . . ∼; Q.
18 Invention] INVENTION Q.
20 Sisters,] ∼; Q.

tate the Sister of Painting, Tragedy: which employs the whole
forces of her Art in the main Action.

　* This part of Painting, so rarely met with, and so difficult to
be found, is neither to be acquir'd by pains or study, nor by the
Precepts or Counsels of any Master. For they alone who have
been inspir'd at their birth with some portion of that Heavenly
fire * which was stollen by *Prometheus* [90.] are capable of re-
ceiving so divine a present; as the Proverb tells us, * *that it hap-
pens not to every one to see* Corinth.

10　Painting first appear'd in *Egypt,* but wholly different from the
truth, till having travell'd into *Greece,* and being cultivated by
the Study, and sublime Genius of that Nation, [95.] * it arriv'd
at length to that height of perfection, that it seem'd to surpass
even Original nature.

　Amongst the Academies, which were compos'd by the rare
Genius of those Great men, these four are reckon'd as the prin-
cipal: namely, the *Athenian* School, that of *Sicyon,* that of
Rhodes, and that of *Corinth.* These were little different from
each other, onely in the manner of their work; [100.] as it may be
20　seen by the Ancient Statues, which are the Rule of Beauty, and
to which succeeding Ages have nothing that is equal: * Though
they are not very much inferiour either in Science, or in the man-
ner of their Execution.

　* A Posture therefore must be chosen accord-
ing to their gusto: * The Parts of it must be
great * and large, * unequal in their position,
[105.] so that those which are before must con-
trast (or oppose) those others which are hindermost, and all of
them be equally balanc'd on their Centre.

VII.
*Design, the
second part of
Painting.*

30　* The Parts must have their out-lines in waves resembling
flames, or the gliding of a Snake upon the ground: They must
be smooth, they must be great, they must be almost impercep-
tible to the touch, and even, without either Eminences or Cavi-
ties. [110.] They must be drawn from far, and without breaks,

7–8　*Prometheus* ... present; as] ∼, ... ∼. As Q.
10　*Egypt,*] ∼: Q.　　　　　　　　17　School] *School* Q.
19–20　manner . . . Ancient Statues . . . Rule . . . Beauty] *manner . . . Ancient
Statues . . . Rule . . . Beauty* Q.

to avoid the multiplicity of lines. Let the Muscles be well in-
serted and bound together * according to the knowledge of them
which is given us by Anatomy. Let them be * design'd after the
manner of the *Græcians:* and let them appear but little, accord-
ing to what we see in the Ancient Figures. In fine, * let there be
a perfect relation betwixt the parts and the whole, that they may
be entirely of a piece.

[115.] Let the part which produces another part, be more
strong than that which it produces; and let the whole be seen by
one point of Sight.

* Though Perspective cannot be call'd a certain rule or a
finishing of the Picture, yet it is a great Succour and Relief to
Art, and facilitates the means of Execution; [120.] yet frequently
falling into Errors, and making us behold things under a false
Aspect, for Bodies are not always represented according to the
Geometrical Plane, but such as they appear to the Sight.

Neither the Shape of Faces, nor the Age, nor
the Colour ought to be alike in all Figures, any
more than the Hair: [125.] because Men are as
different from each other, as the Regions in which
they are born, are different.

VIII.
*Variety in the
Figures.*

* Let every Member be made for its own
head, and agree with it. And let all together
compose but one Body, with the Draperies
which are proper and suitable to it. And above
all, * let the Figures to which Art cannot give
a voice, imitate the Mutes in their Actions.

IX.
*The Members
and Drapery
of every Fig-
ure to be suit-
able to it.*
X.
*The Actions
of Mutes to
be imitated.*

* Let the principal Figure of the Subject
appear [130.] in the middle of the Piece under
the strongest Light, that it may have somewhat
to make it more remarkable than the rest, and
that the Figures which accompany it, may not steal it from our
Sight.

XI.
*Of the princi-
pal Figure of
the Subject.*

* Let the Members be combin'd in the same
manner as the Figures are, that is to say, coupled
and knit together. And let the Grouppes be

XII.
*Grouppes of
Figures.*

---

3   Anatomy] *Anatomy* Q.
5   Ancient Figures] *Ancient Figures* Q.

4   *Græcians*] *Grecians* Q.
15   Aspect,] ~; Q.

separated by a void space, to avoid a confus'd heap; which pro-
ceeding from parts that are dispers'd without any Regularity,
[135.] and entangled one within another, divides the Sight into
many Rays, and causes a disagreeable Confusion.

* The Figures in the Grouppes, ought not to
be like each other in their Motions, any more   XIII.
than in their Parts: nor to be all on the same   *The diversity*
side, but let them contrast each other: [140.]   *of Postures in*
                                                    the Grouppes.
bearing themselves on the one side, in Opposition to those which
10 are set against them on the other.

Amongst many Figures which show their foreparts, let there be
some one whose hinder parts may be seen; opposing the Shoul-
ders to the Stomach, and the right side to the left.

[145.] * One side of the Picture must not be   XIV.
void, while the other is fill'd to the Borders; but *Equality of*
let matters be so well dispos'd, that if one side of *the piece.*
the Piece be full, the Painter shall find some occasion to fill the
other, [150.] so that they shall appear in some sort equal, whether
there be many Figures in it, or but few.

20   * As a Play is very seldom good, in which
there are too many Actors, so 'tis very seldom   XV.
seen and almost impossible to perform, that a   *Of the num-*
                                                   ber of Fig-
Picture should be perfect in which there are too   *ures.*
great a number of Figures. And we cannot wonder that so few
Painters [155.] have succeeded who have introduc'd into their
works many Figures: Because indeed there are not many Painters
to be found, who have succeeded happily, when even they have
introduc'd but few. Many dispers'd Objects breed confusion, and
take away from the Picture that grave Majesty, that soft silence
30 and repose, which give beauty to the Piece, and satisfaction to
the sight. But if you are constrained by the subject, to admit of
many Figures, [160.] you must then conceive the whole to-
gether, and the effect of the work at one view; and not every
thing separately and in particular.

---

11   foreparts,] ~∧ Q.
18   other, . . . equal,] ~; . . . ~∧ Q.
26   Figures:] ~. Q.
32–33   together,] ~; Q.

* The extremities of the Joints must be sel-
dom hidden, and the extremities or end of the
Feet never.

XVI.
*Of the Joints
and Feet.*

* The Figures which are behind others, have
neither Grace nor Vigor, [165.] unless the Mo-
tions of the hands accompany those of the Head.

XVII.
*The motions of
the hands and
head must
agree.*

Avoid the views which are difficult to be
found, and are not natural, as also forc'd Ac-
tions and Motions. Show no parts which are
10 ungracious to the Sight, as all foreshortnings,
usually are.

XVIII.
*What must be
avoided in the
distribution
of the Figures.*

* Avoid also those Lines and Out-lines which are equal;
which make Parallels, or other sharp pointed [170.] and Geo-
metrical Figures; such as are Squares and Triangles: all which by
being too exact give to the Eye a certain displeasing Symmetry,
which produces no good effect. But as I have already told you,
the principal Lines ought to contrast each other: For which
reason in these out-lines, you ought to have a special regard
to [175.] the whole together: for 'tis from thence that the Beauty
20 and Force of the parts proceed.

* Be not so strictly ty'd to Nature, that you
allow nothing to study, and the bent of your
own Genius. But on the other side, believe not
that your Genius alone, and the Remembrance
of those things which you have seen, can afford
you wherewithall to furnish out a beautifull

XIX.
*That we must
not tie our
selves to Na-
ture, but ac-
commodate
her to our
Genius.*

Piece, without the Succour of that incomparable School-mistress,
Nature; [180.] * whom you must have always present as a wit-
ness to the Truth. We may make a thousand Errors of all kinds;
30 they are every-where to be found, and as thick set as Trees in
Forests; and amongst many ways which mislead a Traveller,
there is but one true one which conducts him surely to his
Journey's end; as also there are many several sorts of crooked
lines, but there is one only which is straight.

---

10   foreshortnings] fore shortnings Q.
21–23   Nature ... Genius] *Nature ... Genius* Q.
24–28   Genius ... Nature] *Genius ... Nature* Q.
31   Forests;] ∼, Q.
34   lines,] ∼; Q.

Our business is to imitate the Beauties of Na-
ture, as the Ancients have done before us, [185.]
and as the Object and Nature of the thing re-
quire from us. And for this reason we must be

XX.
Ancient Fig-
ures the rules
of imitating
Nature.

carefull in the search of Ancient Medals, Statues, Vases and Basso
Relievo's: * And of all other things which discover to us the
Thoughts and Inventions of the *Grӕcians;* because they furnish
us with great Ideas, and make our Productions wholly beau-
tifull. [190.] And in truth, after having well examin'd them,
we shall therein find so many Charms, that we shall pity the
Destiny of our present Age, without hope of ever arriving at
so high a point of Perfection.

* If you have but one single Figure to work
upon, you ought to make it perfectly finish'd
and diversify'd with many Colours.

XXI.
A single Fig-
ure, how to
be treated.

[195.] * Let the Draperies be nobly spread
upon the Body; let the Folds be large, * and let
them follow the order of the parts, that they may

XXII.
Of the Dra-
peries.

be seen underneath, by means of the Lights and Shadows; not-
withstanding that the parts should be often travers'd (or cross'd)
by the flowing of the Folds which loosely incompass them, [200.]
* without sitting too straight upon them; but let them mark the
parts which are under them, so as in some manner to distinguish
them, by the judicious ordering of the Lights and Shadows. * And
if the parts be too much distant from each other, so that there be
void spaces, which are deeply shadow'd, we are then to take
occasion to place in those voids some Fold to make a joining of
the parts. * And as the Beauty of the Limbs consists not in the
quantity and rising of the Muscles, but, on the contrary, [205.]
those which are less eminent have more of Majesty than the
others; in the same manner the beauty of the Draperies, consists
not in the multitude of the folds, but in their natural order,
and plain simplicity. The quality of the persons is also to be
consider'd in the Drapery. * As supposing them to be Magis-
trates, their Draperies ought to be large and ample: [210.] If

5–6 Ancient ... [*to*] ... Relievo's] *set in italics in* Q.
9–11 truth, ... Age,] ~ˬ ... ~ˬ Q.   13+–14+   *sidenote* *Figure,*] ~ˬ Q.
19–22 Shadows; ... them;] ~, ... ~, Q.
29 but,] ~ˬ Q.

Country Clowns or Slaves they ought to be course and short: * If Ladies or Damsels, light and soft. 'Tis sometimes requisite to draw out, as it were from the hollows and deep shadows, some Fold, and give it a Swelling, that receiving the Light, it may contribute to extend the clearness to those places where the Body requires it; and by this means we shall disburthen the piece of those hard Shadowings which are always ungracefull.

[215.] * The Marks or Ensigns of Vertues contribute not little, by their nobleness, to the Ornament of the Figures: Such, for example, as are the Decorations belonging to the Liberal Arts, to War or Sacrifices.

XXIII.
What things contribute to adorn the Picture.

* But let not the work be too much enrich'd with Gold or Jewels, because the rarest are ever the dearest and most precious; and those which serve only to increase the number, are of the common sort, and of little value.

XXIV.
Of precious Stones and Pearls for ornament.

* 'Tis very expedient to make a Model of those things, which we have not in our Sight, [220.] and whose Nature is difficult to be retain'd in the Memory.

XXV.
The Model.

* We are to consider the places, where we lay the scene of the Picture; the Countries where they were born whom we represent; the manner of their Actions, their Laws and Customs, and all that is properly belonging to them.

XXVI.
The Scene of the Picture.

* Let a nobleness and grace be remarkable through all your work. But to confess the truth, this is a most difficult undertaking; and a very rare Present which the Artist receives rather from the hand of Heaven, than from his own Industry and Studies.

XXVII.
The Graces and the Nobleness.

In all things you are to follow the order of Nature, [225.] for which reason you must beware of drawing or painting Clouds, Winds and Thunder towards the bottom of your Piece; and Hell, and Waters, in the uppermost parts of it: You are not

XXVIII.
Let every thing be set in its proper place.

---

9   little, ... nobleness,] ∼ₐ ... ∼ₐ Q.
10   Figures:] ∼. Q.   10   example,] ∼ₐ Q.
11–12   Liberal Arts ... War ... Sacrifices] *Liberal Arts ... War ... Sacrifices* Q.

to place a Stone Column on a foundation of Wood; but let every thing be set in its proper place.

[230.] Besides all this, you are to express the motions of the Spirits, and the affections or Passions whose Center is the Heart; in a word, to make the Soul visible, by the means of some few Colours: * this is that in which the greatest difficulty consists. Few there are whom *Jupiter* regards with a favourable eye in this Undertaking: So that it appertains only to those few, [235.] who participate some-
10 what of Divinity it self, to work these mighty Wonders. 'Tis the business of Rhetoricians, to treat the characters of the Passions: and I shall content my self with repeating what an excellent Master has formerly said on this Subject, That *the studied motions of the Soul, are never so natural as those, which are, as it were, struck out of it on the sudden by the heat and violence of a real Passion.*

XXIX.
Of the Passions.

[240.] We are to have no manner of relish for *Gothique* Ornaments, as being in effect so many Monsters, which barbarous Ages have produc'd;
20 during which, when Discord and Ambition caus'd by the too large extent of the *Roman* Empire, had pro-duc'd Wars, Plagues and Famine through the World, then I say, the stately Buildings fell to Ruin, and the nobleness of all beau-tifull Arts was totally extinguish'd: [245.] then it was that the admirable and almost supernatural Works of Painting were made Fuel for the Fire: But that this wonderfull Art might not wholly perish, * some Reliques of it took Sanctuary under ground, and thereby escap'd the common Destiny. And in the same profane age, the noble Sculpture was for a long time buried under the
30 same Ruines, with all its beautifull Productions and admirable Statues. The Empire in the mean time under the weight of its proper Crimes and undeserving to enjoy the day, [250.] was in-velop'd with a hideous night, which plung'd it into an Abyss of errors, and cover'd with a thick darkness of Ignorance those un-

XXX.
Gothique Or-
naments are
to be avoided.

5　Heart; in] ∼: In Q.
8　Undertaking:] ∼. Q.
14–15　*are, . . . were,*] ∼∧ . . . ∼∧ Q.
21　Empire] *Empire* Q.
25　Painting] *Painting* Q.

6　Colours:] ∼; Q.
11　Rhetoricians] *Rhetoricians* Q.
19　produc'd;] ∼: Q.
24　extinguish'd:] ∼; Q.

happy Ages, in just revenge of their Impieties: From hence it
comes to pass, that the works of those great *Græcians* are wanting
to us; nothing of their Painting and Colouring [255.] now re-
mains to assist our modern Artists, either in the Invention, or
the manner of those Ancients; neither is there any man who
is able to restore * the Chromatique part or   *Colouring the*
Colouring, or to renew it to that point of excel-   *third part of*
lency to which it had been carry'd by *Zeuxis:*   *Painting.*
who by this part which is so charming, so magical, and which
so admirably deceives the sight, made himself equal to the great
Apelles, that Prince of Painters; [260.] and deserv'd that height
of reputation which he still possesses in the World.

And as this part, which we may call the Soul of Painting and
its utmost perfection, is a deceiving Beauty, but withal soothing
and pleasing: So she has been accus'd of procuring Lovers for *
her Sister, and artfully ingaging us to admire her. But so little
have this Prostitution, these false Colours, and this Deceit, [265.]
dishonour'd Painting, that on the contrary, they have only serv'd
to set forth her Praise, and to make her merit farther known; and
therefore it will be profitable to us, to have a more clear under-
standing of what we call Colouring.

* The light produces all kinds of Colours, and the Shadow
gives us none. The more a Body is nearer to the Eyes, and the
more directly it is oppos'd to them, the more it is enlightn'd,
because the Light languishes and lessens the farther it removes
from its proper Sourse.

[270.] The nearer the Object is to the Eyes, and the more
directly it is oppos'd to them, the better it is seen, because the
Sight is weaken'd by distance.

'Tis therefore necessary that round Bodies,   **XXXI.**
which are seen one over against the other in a   *The conduct of*
right Angle, should be of a lively and strong   *the Tones of*
Colouring, and that the extremities turn, in los-   *Light and Shadows.*
ing themselves insensibly and confusedly, without precipitating

---

6–7 Chromatique...Colouring] CHROMATIQUE...COLOURING Q.
11 Prince of Painters] *Prince of Painters* Q.
13 part,] ~ʌ Q.
19 known;] ~, Q.
24–25 enlightn'd, because] ~. Because Q.

the Light all on the sudden into the Shadow; [275.] or the
Shadow into the Light. But the passage of one into the other
must be common and imperceptible, that is, by degrees of Lights
into Shadows and of Shadows into Lights. And it is in conformity
to these Principles that you ought to treat a whole Grouppe of
Figures, though it be compos'd of several parts, in the same
manner as you would do a single Head: [280.] or if your Com-
position requires, that you should have two Grouppes, or even
three (* which ought to be the most) in your Piece, take heed
10 that they may be detach'd, (that is, separated or distinguish'd
from each other by the Colours, the Lights and the Shadows,
which are so dextrously to be manag'd, * that you may make the
Bodies appear enlighten'd by the Shadows which bound the
sight; which permit it not suddenly to go farther; and which
cause it to repose for some space of time,) [285.] and that re-
ciprocally the Shadows may be made sensible by enlightning
your ground.
    The raising and roundness of a Body, ought to be given it * in
the same manner as we behold it in a Convex Mirrour, in which
20 we view the Figures and all other things which bear out with
more Life and strength than Nature it self. [290.] * And let
those which turn, be of broken Colours, as being less distin-
guish'd, and nearer to the borders.
    Thus the Painter and the Sculptor, are to work with one and
the same intention, and with one and the same conduct. For
what the Sculptor strikes off, and makes round with his instru-
ment of Steel, the Painter performs with his Pencil, casting be-
hind [295.] that which he makes less visible, by the Diminution
and breaking of his Colours; and drawing forward by his most
30 lively Colours and strongest Shadows, that which is directly
oppos'd to the Sight, as being more sensible, and more distin-
guish'd, and at last enriching the naked Canvass, with such
Colours as are borrow'd from Nature; [300.] in the midst of
which he seems to sit; and from thence with one glance of an

---

3   is,] ~∧ Q.
10–15   (that is, . . . time,)] ∧~~∧ . . . ~,∧ Q.
20   things] ~, Q.
27–28   Pencil, . . . behind . . . visible, . . . Diminution] ~; . . . ~, . . . ~∧ . . . ~, Q.

Eye and without removing his seat, he takes that part of her which she represents to his Sight, and turns as in a Machine about his work.

When solid Bodies, sensible to the feeling, and dark, are plac'd on Light, and transparent grounds, as for example, The Heavens, the Clouds and Waters, [305.] and every other thing which is in Motion, and void of different Objects, they ought to be more rough and more distinguishable than that with which
10 they are incompass'd, that being strengthen'd by the Lights and Shadows, or by the more sensible Colours, they may subsist and preserve their Solidity amongst those aereal and transparent Species, [310.] and that on the contrary those grounds (which are, as we have said, the Sky, the clouds and the Waters) being clearer and more united, may be thrown off from the Sight to a farther distance.

XXXII.
Of dark Bodies on light grounds.

We are never to admit two equal Lights in the same Picture; but the greater Light must strike forcibly on the middle, and there extend
20 its greatest clearness on those places of the Picture, [315.] where the principal Figures of it are, and where the strength of the action is perform'd, diminishing by degrees as it comes nearer and nearer to the Borders; and after the same manner that the Light of the Sun languishes insensibly in its spreading from the East, from whence it begins, towards the West where it decays and vanishes, so the Light of the Picture being distributed over all the Colours, [320.] will become less sensible the farther it is remov'd from its Original.

XXXIII.
That there must not be two equal Lights in a Picture.

The experience of this is evident in those Statues which we
30 see set up in the midst of Publique Places, whose upper parts are more enlighten'd than the lower; and therefore you are to imitate them in the distribution of your Lights.

Avoid strong Shadows on the middle of the Limbs; least the great quantity of black which composes those Shadows, should seem to enter into them and to cut them: [325.] Rather take care to place those shadowings round about them, thereby to heighten

the parts, and take so advantageous Lights, that after great
Lights, great Shadows may succeed. And therefore *Titian* said,
with reason, that he knew no better rule for the distribution of
the Lights and shadows, than his Observations drawn from a
* *Bunch of Grapes.*

[330.] * Pure or unmix'd white either draws
an object nearer, or carries it off to farther dis-
tance: It draws it nearer with black, and throws
it backward without it. * But as for pure black, there is nothing
10 which brings the object nearer to the Sight.

XXXIV.
Of White and
Black.

The light being alter'd by some Colour, never fails to com-
municate somewhat of that Colour to the Bodies on which it
strikes, and the same effect is perform'd by the Medium of Air,
through which it passes.

[335.] The Bodies which are close together,
receive from each other that Colour which is
opposite to them; and reflect on each other that
which is naturally and properly their own.

XXXV.
The reflection
of Colours.

'Tis also consonant to reason, that the great-
20 est part of those Bodies which are under a Light,
which is extended and distributed equally

XXXVI.
Union of Col-
ours.

through all, should participate of each others Colours. The
Venetian School having a great regard for that Maxim ([340.]
which the Ancients call'd *the Breaking of Colours*) in the quan-
tity of Figures with which they fill their Pictures, have always
endeavour'd the Union of Colours, for fear that being too differ-
ent, they should come to incumber the Sight by their confusion
with their quantity of Members separated by their Folds, which
are also in great number; [345.] and for this reason they have
30 painted their Draperies with Colours that are nearly related to
each other, and have scarce distinguish'd them any other way,
than by the Diminution of the Lights and Shadows joining the
contiguous Objects by the Participation of their Colours, and
thereby making a kind of Reconciliation or Friendship betwixt
the Lights and Shadows.

3   reason,] ~∧ Q.   13   Medium] *Medium* Q.
23 School] *School* Q.   24   *the*] the Q.
26 Union of Colours] *Union of Colours* Q.

[350.] The less aereal space which there is be-twixt us and the Object, and the more pure the Air is, by so much the more the Species are pre-serv'd and distinguish'd; and on the contrary the more space of Air there is, and the less it is pure, so much the more the Object is confus'd and embroyl'd.

Those objects which are plac'd foremost to the view, ought always to be more finish'd, than those which are cast behind; [355.] and ought to have dominion over those things which are confus'd and tran-sient. * But let this be done relatively, (*viz.*) one thing greater and stronger, casting the less behind and rendring it less sen-sible by its opposition.

Those things which are remov'd to a distant view, though they are many, yet ought to make but one Mass; as for example the Leaves on the Trees, and the Billows in the Sea.

Let not the Objects which ought to be con-tiguous be separated, and let those which ought to be separated be apparently so to us; [360.] but let this be done by a small and pleasing difference.

* Let two contrary extremities never touch each other, either in Colour or in Light, but let there always be a Medium partaking both of the one and of the other.

Let the Bodies every-where be of different Tones and Colours; that those which are be-hind may be ty'd in Friendship together, and that those which are foremost may be strong and lively.

[365.] * 'Tis labour in vain to paint a High-noon, or Mid-day light in your Picture, be-cause we have no Colours which can sufficiently express it, but 'tis better counsel, to choose a weaker light; such

---

25 Medium] *Medium* Q.

as is that of the Evening, with which the Fields are gilded by the Sun; or a Morning-light, whose whiteness is allay'd; or that which appears after a Shower of Rain, which the Sun gives us through the breaking of a Cloud: [370.] or during Thunder, when the Clouds hide him from our view, and make the light appear of a fiery colour.

Smooth bodies, such as Chrystals, polish'd Metals, Wood, Bones, and Stones; those which are cover'd with Hair, as Skins, the Beard, or 10 the Hair of the Head; as also Feathers, Silks, and the Eyes, which are of a watery nature; and those which are liquid, as Waters, [375.] and those corporeal species, which we see reflected by them; and in fine, all that which touches them, or is near them, ought to be much painted and unitedly on their lower parts, but touch'd boldly above by the light and shadows which are proper to them.

XLIV.
Of certain things relating to the practical part.

* Let the Field, or Ground of the Picture, be clean, free, transient, light, and well united with Colours which are of a friendly nature to each 20 other; [380.] and of such a mixture, as there may be something in it of every colour that composes your work, as it were the contents of your Palette. And let the bodies mutually partake of the colour of their ground.

XLV.
The field or ground of the Picture.

* Let your Colours be lively, and yet not look (according to the Painter's Proverb) as if they had been rubb'd or sprinkled with meal: that is to say, let them not be pale.

XLVI.
Of the vivacity of Colours.

* Let the parts which are nearest to us, and most rais'd, be strongly colour'd, and as it were sparkling; and let those parts 30 which are more remote from sight, and towards the borders, be more faintly touch'd.

[385.] * Let there be so much harmony, or consent, in the Masses of the Picture, that all the shadowings may appear as if they were but one.

XLVII.
Of Shadows.

* Let the whole Picture be made of one piece, and avoid as much as possibly you can, to paint drily.

XLVIII.
The Picture to be of one piece.

* The Looking-glass will instruct you in many Beauties, which you may observe from Nature: so will also those objects which are seen in an Evening in a large prospect.

XLIX.
The Looking-glass the Painter's best Master.

If you are to paint a half figure or a whole one, which is to be set before [390.] the other figures, it must be plac'd nearer to the view, and next the light. And if it is to be painted, in a great place, and at a distance from the Eyes; be sure on that 10 occasion not to be sparing of great lights, the most lively colours, nor the strongest shadows.

L.
An half figure, or a whole one, before others.

* As for a Portraict, or Pictures by the Life, you are to work precisely after Nature, and to express what she shows you, working at the same time [395.] on those parts which are resembling to each other: As for example, the Eyes, the Cheeks, the Nostrils and the Lips: so that you are to touch the one, as soon as you have given a stroke of the Pencil to the other, lest the interruption of time cause you to lose the Idea of one part, which Nature has produc'd to resemble the 20 other: and thus imitating Feature for Feature with a just and harmonious Composition of the lights and shadows, and of the colours, and giving to the Picture that liveliness which the freedom and force of the Pencil make appear, it may seem, the living hand of Nature.

LI.
A Portraict.

The works which are painted to be seen in little or narrow places, must be very tender and well united with tones, and colours; the degrees [400.] of which ought to be more different, more unequal, and more strong and vigorous, as the work is more distant: and if you 30 make great figures, let them be strongly colour'd, and in very spacious places.

LII.
The place of the Picture.

* You are to paint the most tenderly that possibly you can and endeavour to lose insensibly the * large lights in the shadows which succeed them, and incompass them about.

LIII.
Large Lights.

---

23 seem,] ~₋ Q.
33 can] ~; Q.

If the Picture be set in a place which is en-   LIV.
lighten'd, but with a little light, the colours   *What Lights*
must be very clear; [405.] as, on the contrary,   *are requisite.*
very brown, if the place be strongly enlighten'd, or in the
open Air.

Remember to avoid objects which are full   LV.
of hollows, broken in pieces, little, and which   *Things which*
are separated, or in parcels: shun also those   *are vicious in*
things which are barbarous, shocking to the   *painting to*
                                               be avoided.
10 Eye and party-colour'd, and all which is of an equal force
of light and shadow: [410.] as also all things which are ob-
scene, impudent, filthy, unseemly, cruel, fantastical, poor and
wretched; those things which are sharp and rough to the feeling:
In short, all things which corrupt their natural forms, by a con-
fusion of their parts which are intangled in each other: *For the*
Eyes have a horrour for those things which the Hands will not
condescend to touch.

But while you endeavour to avoid one vice,   LVI.
be cautious lest you fall into another: [415.] for   *The pruden-*
                                               tial part of a
20 *Vertue is plac'd betwixt two extreams, which*   *Painter.*
are on both sides equally blameable.

Those things which are beautifull in the ut-
most degree of Perfection, according to the   LVII.
                                               The Idea of
Axiom of ancient Painters, * ought to have   *a beautifull*
somewhat of greatness in them; and their out-   *piece.*
lines to be noble: they must be disintangled, pure and without
alteration, clean and knit together; compos'd of great parts, yet
those but few in number: [420.] In fine, distinguish'd by bold
Colours; but of such as are related, and friendly to each other.

30   And as it is a common saying, that *He who has*
                                               LVIII.
begun well, has already perform'd half his work;   *Advice to*
so * there is nothing more pernicious to a Youth,   *a young*
                                               Painter.
who is yet in the Elements of Painting, than to
engage himself under the discipline of an ignorant Master; who

depraves his taste, by an infinite number of mistakes, of which his wretched works are full, [425.] and thereby makes him drink the poyson, which infects him through all his future life.

Let him who is yet but a Beginner, not make so much haste to study after Nature, every thing which he intends to imitate, as not in the mean time to learn Proportions, the connexion of the parts, and their out-lines: [430.] And let him first have well examin'd the Excellent Originals, and have thoroughly studied all the sweet deceipts of his Art, which he must be rather taught 10 by a knowing Master, than by practice; and by seeing him perform, without being contented onely to hear him speak.

* Search whatsoever is aiding to your Art, and convenient, and avoid those things which are repugnant to it.

LIX.
Art must be subservient to the Painter.

* Bodies of divers natures which are aggroup'd (or combin'd) together, are agreeable and pleasant to the sight; [435.] * as also those things which appear to be perform'd with ease;

LX.
Diversity and facility are pleasing.

because they are ever full of Spirit, and seem animated with a 20 kind of Cœlestial fire: But we are not able to compass these things with facility, till we have for a long time weigh'd them in our judgment, and thoroughly consider'd them: By this means the Painter shall be enabled to conceal the pains and study which his Art and work have cost him, under a pleasing sort of deceipt: For the greatest secret which belongs to Art, is to hide it from the discovery of Spectatours.

[440.] Never give the least touch with your Pencil till you have well examin'd your Design, and have settled your out-lines, * nor till you 30 have present in your mind a perfect Idea of your work.

LXI.
The Original must be in the Head, and the Copy on the Cloth.

* Let the Eye be satisfy'd in the first place, even against and above all other reasons, which beget difficulties in your Art, which of it self suffers none; and let the compass be rather in your Eyes than in your Hands.

LXII.
The Compass to be in the Eyes.

---

1 mistakes,] ~; Q.
18–19 ease; because] ~. Because Q.

5 imitate,] ~; Q.
23 pains] ~, Q.

[445.] * Profit your self by the Counsels of
the knowing: And do not arrogantly disdain to
learn the opinion of every man concerning your
work. All men are blind as to their own produc-

LXIII.
Pride an
Enemy to
good Painting.

tions; and no man is capable of judging in his own cause: * but if
you have no knowing friend, to assist you with his advice, [450.]
yet length of time will never fail; 'tis but letting some weeks pass
over your Head, or at least some days, without looking on your
work; and that intermission will faithfully discover to you the
10 faults, and beauties: yet suffer not your self to be carried away by
the opinions of the Vulgar, who often speak without knowledge;
neither give up your self altogether to them, and abandon wholly
your own Genius, so as lightly to change that which you have
made: For he who has a windy Head, and flatters himself with
the empty hope of deserving the praise of the common people,
whose opinions are inconsiderate and changeable, does but in-
jure himself and pleases no man.

[455.] Since every Painter paints himself in
his own works (so much is Nature accustom'd
20 to produce her own likeness) 'tis advantageous

LXIV.
Know your
self.

to him to know himself, * to the end that he may cultivate those
Talents which make his Genius, and not unprofitably lose his
time in endeavouring to gain that which she has refus'd him. As
neither Fruits have the taste, [460.] nor Flowers the beauty which
is natural to them when they are transplanted in a foreign soil,
and are forc'd to bear before their season by an artificial heat:
so 'tis in vain for the Painter to sweat over his works in spight
of Nature and of Genius; for without them 'tis impossible for
him to succeed.

30   * While you meditate on these truths, and
observe them diligently, by making necessary
reflections on them; let the labour of the Hand
accompany the study of the Brain; let the for-
mer second and support the latter; [465.] yet

LXV.
Perpetually
practise, and
do easily what
you have con-
ceiv'd.

---

5   cause:] ∼; Q.
9   work;] ∼, Q.
10 beauties:] ∼; Q.
16 inconsiderate] ∼, Q.

without blunting the sharpness of your Genius, and abating of its vigour by too much assiduity.

* The Morning is the best, and most proper part of the day for your business; employ it therefore in the study and exercise of those things which require the greatest pains and application.

* Let no day pass over you without a line.

Observe as you walk the Streets, the Airs of
10 Heads; the natural Postures and Expressions; [470.] which are always the most free the less they seem to be observ'd.

*Be ready to put into your Table-book (which you must always carry about you) whatsoever you judge worthy of it; whether it be

upon the Earth, or in the Air, or upon the Waters, while the Species of them is yet fresh in your Imagination.

[475.] * Wine and good Cheer are no great Friends to painting, they serve only to recreate the Mind, when 'tis opprest and spent
20 with Labour; then indeed 'tis proper to renew your Vigour by the conversation of your Friends: Neither is a true Painter naturally pleas'd with the fatigue of business, and particularly of the Law, * but delights in the liberty which belongs to the Batchelour's Estate. * Painting naturally withdraws from Noise and Tumult, [480.] and pleases it self in the enjoyment of a Country Retirement: because Silence and Solitude set an edge upon the Genius, and cause a greater Application to work and study, and also serve to produce the Ideas, which, so conceiv'd, will be always present in the Mind, even to the finishing of the
30 work; the whole compass of which, the Painter can at that time more commodiously form to himself than at any other.

* Let not the covetous design of growing rich, induce you to ruin your reputation, [485.] but rather satisfy your self with a moderate fortune; and let your Thoughts be wholly taken up with acquiring to your self a glorious Name, which can never perish, but with the World; and make that the recompence of your worthy Labours.

---

1 Genius,] ~; Q.   36 World;] ~, Q.

Prose 1691–1698

* The qualities requisite to form an excellent Painter, are, a true discerning Judgment, a Mind which is docible, a noble Heart, a sublime Sense of things, and Fervour of Soul; after which follow, Health of Body, handsomeness, [490.] a convenient share of Fortune, Youth, Diligence, an affection for the Art, * and to be bred under the discipline of a knowing Master.

And remember, that whatsoever your Subject be, whether of your own Choice, or what chance or good fortune shall put into your hand, if you have not that Genius or natural Inclination, 10 which your Art requires, you shall never arrive to perfection in it, even with all those great advantages which I have mention'd; for the Wit, and the manual operation are things vastly distant from each other. 'Tis the Influence of your Stars, and the happiness of your Genius, to which you must be oblig'd for the greatest Beauties of your Art.

Nay, even your excellencies [495.] sometimes will not pass for such in the opinion of the learned, but only as things which have less of Error in them; for no man sees his own failings; * and Life is so short, that it is not sufficient for so long an Art. 20 Our strength fails us in our old Age, when we begin to know somewhat: Age oppresses us by the same degrees that it instructs us, and permits not that our mortal Members which are frozen with our years, should retain the Vigor and Spirits of our Youth.

[500.] *Take courage therefore, O ye Noble Youths! you legitimate Off-spring of *Minerva,* who are born under the influence of a happy Planet, and warm'd with a Celestial Fire, which attracts you to the Love of Science! exercise while you are young, your whole forces, and employ them with delight in an Art which 30 requires a whole Painter. Exercise them I say, while your boyling Youth supplies you with Strength, [505.] and furnishes you with Quickness and with Vigour; while your Mind, yet pure and void of Error, has not taken any ill habitude to vice; while yet

---

2 Judgment,] ~; Q.
18 them;] ~, Q.
27 happy Planet] *happy Planet* Q.
30 whole Painter] *whole Painter* Q.

6 * and] and Q.
25 Noble Youths] *Noble Youths* Q.
28 Science!] ~; Q.
33 vice;] ~, Q.

your Spirits are inflam'd with the Thirst of Novelties, and your Mind is fill'd with the first Species of things which present themselves to a young Imagination, which it gives in keeping to your Memory; and which your Memory retains for length of time, by reason of the moisture wherewith at that Age the Brain abounds.

* You will do well * to begin with Geometry, and after having made some progress in it, * set your self on designing [510.] after the Ancient
10 *Greeks,* * and cease not day or night from labour, till by your continual practice you have gain'd an easy habitude of imitating them in their invention, and in their manner. * And when afterwards your judgment shall grow stronger, and come to its maturity with years, it will be very necessary to see and examine one after the other, and part by part, [515.] those works which have given so great a Reputation to the Masters of the first form in pursuit of that Method, which we have taught you here above, and according to the Rules which we have given you; such are the *Romans,* the *Venetians,*
20 the *Parmesans,* and the *Bologneses.* Amongst those excellent Persons, *Raphael* had the Talent of Invention for his share, [520.] by which he made as many Miracles as he made Pictures: In which is observ'd * a certain Grace which was wholly natural and peculiar to him, and which none since him have been able to appropriate to themselves. *Michael Angelo* possess'd powerfully the part of Design, above all others. * *Julio Romano* (educated from his childhood among the Muses) has open'd to us the Treasures of *Parnassus:* and in the Poetry of Painting [525.] has discover'd to our Eyes the most sacred Mysteries of *Apollo,*
30 and all the rarest Ornaments which that God is capable of communicating to those works that he inspires; which we knew not

LXX.
The method of Studies for a young Painter.

6   abounds.] ~: Q.
7   * You] * you Q *(no paragraph break).*
7   Geometry] *Geometry* Q.
9   Ancient] *Ancient* Q.
22 Pictures:] ~. Q.
27 Muses] *Muses* Q.
30–31 communicating] commucating Q.
31 inspires;] ~, Q.

8   in it,] it it, Q.
21 Invention] *Invention* Q.
26 Design] *Design* Q.
30 God] *God* Q.

before, but only by the Recital that the Poets made of them: he
seems to have painted those famous Wars which Heroes have
wag'd, (and ended with Victory over crown'd Heads, whom they
have led in triumph;) and those other glorious Events which
Fortune has caus'd in all ages, even with more Magnificence and
Nobleness, than when they were acted in the World. *Correggio*
has made his Memory immortal by the Strength and Vigour he
has given to his Figures, [530.] and by sweetning his Lights and
Shadows, and melting them into each other so happily, that they
10 are even imperceptible. He is also almost single in the great
manner of his Painting, and the Facility he had in the managing
of his Colours. And *Titian* understood so well the Union of the
Masses, and the Bodies of Colours, the Harmony of the Tones,
and the Disposition of the whole together, that he has deserv'd
those Honours, and that wealth which were heap'd upon him,
together with that attribute of being surnam'd *the Divine
Painter.* [535.] The laborious and diligent *Annibal Carracci,* has
taken from all those great Persons already mention'd, whatso-
ever excellencies he found in them, and, as it were, converted
20 their Nourishment into his own Substance.

　　'Tis a great means of profiting your self to
copy diligently those excellent Pieces, and those
beautifull designs; But Nature which is present
before your Eyes, is yet a better Mistress: For
she augments [540.] the Force and Vigour of the Genius, and she
it is from whom Art derives her ultimate perfection by the means
of sure Experience. * I pass in silence many things which will be
more amply treated in the ensuing Commentary.

　　And now considering that all things are subject to the vicissi-
30 tude of Time, and that they are liable to Destruction by several
ways, I thought I might reasonably take the boldness * to in-

LXXI.
*Nature and
Experience
perfect Art.*

1　Poets] *Poets* Q.　　　　　　　　1　them:] ～; Q.
2　Heroes] *Heroes* Q.
3–4　(and ... triumph;)] ∧～ ... ～;∧ Q.
12–13　Union ... Masses] *Union ... Masses* Q.
16　*the*] the Q.
23–26　Nature ... Mistress ... Art] *Nature ... Mistress ... Art* Q.
27　Experience.] *Experience;* Q.　　　28　Commentary] *Commentary* Q.

trust to the Muses (those lovely and immortal Sisters of paint-
ing) these few Precepts which I have here made and collected of
that Art.

[545.] I employ'd my time in the study of this work at *Rome,*
while the honour of the *Bourbon* Family, and the just Avenger
of his injur'd Ancestors, the Victorious *Louis* was darting his
Thunder on the *Alpes,* and causing his Enemies to feel the force
of his unconquerable Arms, while he like another *Gallique Her-
cules,* born for the benefit and Honour of his Country, [549.] was
griping the *Spanish Geryon* by the Throat, and at the point of
strangling him.

---

6 *Louis*] *Lovis* Q.   9 Country] *Country* Q.

Observations on the Art of Painting of Charles Alphonse du Fresnoy

PAINTING *and Poesy are two Sisters,* &c. [¶ 1.]
'Tis a receiv'd truth, that the Arts have
a certain relation to each other. *There is
no Art* (said *Tertullian* in his *Treatise of Idola-
try*) *which is not either the Father or the near
Relation of another.* And *Cicero* in his Oration
for *Archias* the Poet, says, *That the Arts which
have respect to human life, have a kind of Alli-*

*The Number
at the head of
every Obser-
vation serves
to find in the
Text the par-
ticular Pas-
sage on which
the Observa-
tion was made.*

ance amongst themselves, and hold each other (as we may say) by
10 *the hand.* But those Arts which are the nearest related, and claim
the most ancient Kindred with each other, are Painting and
Poetry; and whosoever shall throughly examine them, will find
them so much resembling one another, that he cannot take them
for less than Sisters.

They both follow the same bent, and suffer themselves rather
to be carry'd away, than led by their secret Inclinations, which
are so many seeds of the Divinity. *There is a God within us* (says
Ovid in the beginning of his Sixth Book *de Fastis,* there speak-
ing of the Poets) *who by his Agitation warms us.* And *Suidas* says,
20 *That the famous Sculptor* Phidias, *and* Zeuxis *that incompa-
rable Painter, were both of them transported by the same En-
thusiasm, which gave life to all their works.* They both of them
aim at the same end, which is Imitation. Both of them excite
our Passions; and we suffer our selves willingly to be deceiv'd,
both by the one, and by the other; our Eyes and Souls are so fixt
to them, that we are ready to persuade our selves that the painted

---

3   *There*] "There Q.
3–7   *each printed italic line preceded by inverted double commas in Q.*
4–5   *Treatise of Idolatry*] *set in romans in Q.*
7   Poet] *Poet* Q.
8–10   *each printed italic line preceded by inverted double commas in Q.*
11–14   Painting . . . Poetry . . . Sisters] *Painting . . . Poetry . . . Sisters* Q.
17   *There*] "There Q.
17–22   *each printed italic line preceded by inverted double commas in Q.*

Bodies breath, and that the Fictions are Truths. Both of them are set on fire by the great Actions of Heroes; and both endeavour to eternize them: Both of them in short, are supported by the strength of their Imagination, and avail themselves of those licences, which *Apollo* has equally bestow'd on them, and with which their Genius has inspir'd them.

> ――――*Pictoribus atque Poetis*
> *Quidlibet audendi, semper fuit æqua potestas.*

> *Painters and Poets free from servile awe,*
> *May treat their Subjects, and their Objects draw.*

As *Horace* tells us in his *Art of Poetry.*

The advantage which Painting possesses above Poesie is this; That amongst so great a Diversity of Languages, she makes her self understood by all the Nations of the World; and that she is necessary to all other Arts, because of the need which they have of demonstrative Figures, which often give more Light to the Understanding than the clearest discourses we can make.

> *Segnius irritant animos demissa per aurem,*
> *Quam quæ sunt oculis commissa fidelibus.*

> *Hearing excites the Mind by slow degrees,*
> *The Man is warm'd at once by what he sees.*

Horace in the same *Art of Poetry.*

[¶ 9.] *For both of them that they might contribute,* &c. Poetry by its Hymns and Anthems, and Painting by its Statues, Altarpieces, and by all those Decorations which inspire Respect and Reverence for our Sacred Mysteries, have been serviceable to Religion. *Gregory* of *Nice,* after having made a long and beau-

---

6 Genius] *Genius* Q. 11 As] *indented in* Q.

11 *Art of Poetry*] Art of Poetry Q.

12–14 Painting . . . Poesie . . . Languages . . . understood . . . Nations of the World] *Painting . . . Poesie . . . Languages . . . understood . . . Nations of the World* Q.

22 *Horace*] *indented in* Q. 22 *Art of Poetry*] Art of Poetry Q.

23–27 Poetry . . . Hymns . . . Anthems . . . Painting . . . Statues, Altar-pieces . . . those Decorations . . . Sacred Mysteries . . . Religion] *Poetry . . . Hymns . . . Anthems . . . Painting . . . Statues, Altar-pieces . . . those Decorations . . . Sacred Mysteries . . . Religion* Q.

tifull Description of *Abraham* sacrificing his Son *Isaac,* says these words, *I have often cast my eyes upon a Picture, which represents this moving object, and could never withdraw them without Tears. So well did the Picture represent the thing it self, even as if the Action were then passing before my Sight.*

[¶ 24.] *So much these Divine Arts have been always honour'd,* &c. *The greatest Lords, whole Cities and their Magistrates of Old* (says *Pliny,* lib. 35.) *took it for an honour to obtain a Picture from the hands of those great Ancient Painters.* But this Honour is much fallen of late amongst the *French* Nobility: and if you will understand the cause of it, *Vitruvius* will tell you that it comes from their Ignorance of the charming Arts, *Propter ignorantiam Artis, virtutes obscurantur* (in the Preface to his Third Book.) Nay more, we should see this admirable Art fall into the last degree of Contempt, if our Mighty Monarch, who yields in nothing to the Magnanimity of *Alexander the Great,* had not shown as much Love for Painting as Valour in the Wars: we daily see him encouraging this noble Art, by the considerable Presents which he makes to his * chief Painter.

* Mr. Le Brun.

And he has also founded an Academy for the Progress and Perfectionating of Painting, which his * first Minister honours with his Protection,

* Mr. Colbert.

his care, and frequent Visits: insomuch that we might shortly see the age of *Apelles* reviving in our Country, together with all the beauteous Arts, if our generous Nobility, who follow our incomparable King with so much Ardour and Courage in those dangers to which he exposes his Sacred Person for the Greatness and Glory of his Kingdom, would imitate him in that wonderfull Affection which he bears to all who are excellent in this kind. Those Persons who were the most considerable in Ancient *Greece,* either for Birth or Merit, took a most particular care, for many ages, to be instructed in the Art of Painting: following that laudable and

2 *I*] "*I* Q.
2–5 *each printed italic line preceded by inverted double commas in* Q.
6 *So*] *no paragraph break in* Q.
8 *Pliny,*] ~ᴀ Q.   10 Nobility] *Nobility* Q.
12 Arts,] ~. Q.   13 *obscurantur*] ~: Q.
14 Third] Fifth Q.   16 the] the Q.
30–113:2 Ancient . . . Great . . . Design] *Ancient . . . Great . . . Design* Q.

profitable custom which was begun and establish'd by the Great *Alexander,* which was to learn how to Design. And *Pliny* who gives testimony to this in the tenth Chapter of his 35*th.* Book tells us farther (speaking of *Pamphilus* the Master of *Apelles*) *That it was by the authority of* Alexander, *that first at* Sicyon, *and afterwards thro' all* Greece, *the young Gentlemen learn'd before all other things to design upon Tablets of Boxen-wood; and that the first place among all the Liberal Arts was given to Painting.* And that which makes it evident, that they were very
10 knowing in this Art, is the love and esteem which they had for Painters. *Demetrius* gave high testimonies of this when he besieg'd the City of *Rhodes:* For he was pleas'd to employ some part of that time, which he ow'd to the care of his Arms, in visiting *Protogenes,* who was then drawing the Picture of *Jalisus. This* Jalisus, (says *Pliny) hinder'd King* Demetrius *from taking* Rhodes, *out of fear, lest he should burn the Pictures; and not being able to fire the Town on any other side, he was pleas'd rather to spare the Painting, than to take the Victory which was already in his hands. Protogenes* at that time had his Work-house
20 in a Garden out of the Town, and very near the Camp of the Enemies, where he was daily finishing those Pieces which he had already begun; the noise of Soldiers not being capable of interrupting his studies. But *Demetrius* causing him to be brought into his Presence, and asking him what made him so bold as to work in the midst of Enemies: He answer'd the King, *That he understood the War which he made, was against the* Rhodians *and not against the Arts.* This oblig'd *Demetrius* to appoint him Guards for his Security, being infinitely pleas'd that he could preserve that hand, which by this means he sav'd from the bar-
30 barity and insolence of Soldiers. *Alexander* had no greater pleasure, than when he was in the painting room of *Apelles,* where he commonly was found. And that Painter once receiv'd from him a sensible Testimony of Love and Esteem which that Monarch had for him: for having caus'd him to paint naked (by reason of her admirable beauty) one of his Concubines call'd *Campaspe,* who had the greatest share in his affections, and perceiving that *Apelles* was wounded with the same fatal dart of Beauty, he made a present of her to him. In that age so great a

deference was pay'd to Painting, that they who had any Mastery
in that Art, never painted on any thing but what was portable
from one place to another, and what could be secur'd from burn-
ing. They took a particular care, says *Pliny,* in the place above-
cited, not to paint any thing against a Wall, which could onely
belong to one Master, and must always remain in the same place;
and for that reason could not be remov'd in case of an acciden-
tal Fire. Men were not suffer'd to keep a Picture, as it were in
Prison, on the Walls: It dwelt in common in all Cities, and the
10 Painter himself was respected, as a Common Good to all the
World. See this Excellent Author, and you shall find that the
10*th.* Chapter of his 35*th.* Book is fill'd with the praises of this
Art, and with the Honours which were ascrib'd to it. You will
there find that it was not permitted to any but those of noble
Blood to profess it. *Francis the First,* as *Vasari* tells us, was in
love with Painting to that degree, that he allur'd out of *Italy*
all the best Masters, that this Art might flourish in his own
Kingdom: Amongst others *Leonardo da Vinci,* who after having
continued for some time in *France,* died at *Fontainbleau,* in the
20 Arms of that great King, who could not behold his death, with-
out shedding Tears over him. *Charles the Fifth* has adorn'd *Spain*
with the noblest Pictures which are now remaining in the World.
Ridolphi in his life of *Titian,* says, *that Emperor one day took
up a Pencil, which fell from the hand of that Artist, who was
then drawing his Picture, and upon the Compliment which*
Titian *made him on that occasion, he said these words,* "Titian
has deserv'd to be serv'd by Cæsar." And in the same life 'tis re-
markable, *That the Emperour valued himself not so much in
subjecting Kingdoms and Provinces, as that he had been thrice*
30 *made immortal by the hand of* Titian. If you will but take the
pains to read this famous life in *Ridolphi,* you will there see the
relation of all those honours which he receiv'd from *Charles the*

1 Painting] *Painting* Q.
10–11 Painter . . . Common Good to all the World] *Painter . . . Common Good
to all the World* Q.
11 Excellent Author] *Excellent Author* Q.
12–13 praises . . . [*to*] . . . it] *set in italics in* Q.
18 Kingdom:] ~. Q.
25 *and*] *aud* Q.
26–27 "Titian . . . Cæsar."] ∧~ . . . ~·∧ Q.

Fifth. It would take up too much time here to recount all the particulars: I will onely observe that the greatest Lords who compos'd the Court of that Emperour, not being able to refrain from some marks of Jealousy, upon the preference which he made of the Person, and Conversation of *Titian,* to that of all his other Courtiers; he freely told them, *That he could never want a Court or Courtiers, but he could not have* Titian *always with him.* Accordingly he heap'd Riches on him, and whensoever he sent him Money, which, ordinarily speaking, was a great
10 Summ, he always did it with this obliging Testimony, *That his design was not to pay him the value of his Pictures, because they were above any price.* After the example of the Worthies of Antiquity, who bought the rarest Pictures with Bushels of Gold, without counting the weight or the number of the pieces, *In nummo aureo, mensurâ accepit, non numero,* says *Pliny,* speaking of *Apelles. Quinctilian* inferrs from hence, *that there is nothing more noble than the Art of Painting,* because other things for the most part are Merchandice, and bought at certain Rates; most things for this very reason, (says he) are vile because they
20 have a price, *Pleraque hoc ipso possunt videri vilia, quod pretium habent:* see the 34*th.,* 35*th.* and 36*th.* Books of *Pliny.* Many great persons have lov'd it with an extream Passion, and have exercis'd themselves in it with delight. Amongst others, *Lelius Fabius,* one of those famous *Romans,* who, as *Cicero* relates, after he had tasted painting and had practis'd it, would be call'd *Fabius Pictor:* as also *Turpilius,* a *Roman* Knight; *Labeo,* Prætor & Consul; *Quintus Pedius;* the Poets *Ennius* and *Pacuvius; Socrates, Plato, Metrodorus, Pyrrho, Commodus, Nero, Vespasian, Alexander Severus, Antoninus,* and many other Kings and Em-
30 perours, who thought it not below their Majesty to employ some part of their time in this honourable Art.

[¶ 37.] *The principal and most important part of Painting, is to find out and thoroughly to understand what Nature hath made most beautifull and most proper to this Art,* &c. Observe here the rock on which the greatest part of the *Flemish* Painters

---

have split: most of that Nation know how to imitate Nature, at
least as well as the Painters of other Countries, but they make a
bad choice in Nature it self; whether it be, that they have not
seen the Ancient pieces to find those beauties; or that a happy
Genius, and the beautifull Nature is not of the growth of their
Country. And to confess the truth, that which is naturally beau-
tifull is so very rare, that it is discover'd by few persons; 'tis dif-
ficult to make a choice of it, and to form to our selves such an
Idea of it, as may serve us for a Model.

10   [¶ 39.] *And that a choice of it may be made according to the
gust and manner of the Ancients,* &c. That is to say, according
to the Statues, the Basso Relievo's, and the other Ancient Pieces,
as well of the *Græcians* as of the *Romans;* Ancient (or Antique)
is that which has been made from the time of *Alexander the
Great,* till that of *Phocas;* during whose Empire the Arts were
ruin'd by War. These Ancient works from their beginning have
been the rule of Beauty; and in effect, the Authors of them have
been so carefull to give them that perfection, which is still to be
observ'd in them, that they made use not onely of one single

20   Body, whereby they form'd them, but of many, from which they
took the most regular parts to compose from them a beautifull
whole. *The Sculptors,* says *Maximus Tyrius* in his 7th. Disserta-
tion, *with admirable Artifice chose out of many Bodies those
parts which appear'd to them the most beautifull, and out of
that diversity made but one Statue: But this mixture is made
with so much prudence and propriety, that they seem to have
taken but one onely perfect Beauty. And let us not imagine
that we can ever find one natural Beauty which can dispute with
Statues, that Art which has always somewhat more perfect than*

30   *Nature.* 'Tis also to be presum'd, that in the choice which they
made of those parts, they follow'd the opinion of the Physicians,
who at that time were very capable of instructing them in the

---

12–13 Statues . . . Basso Relievo's . . . Ancient Pieces . . . Ancient . . . Antique]
Statues . . . Basso Relievo's . . . Ancient Pieces . . . Ancient . . . Antique Q.
16–17 Ancient works . . . rule of Beauty . . . Authors] *Ancient works . . . rule of
Beauty . . . Authors* Q.
22 The] "*The* Q.
22–30 *each printed italic line preceded by inverted double commas in* Q.
31 Physicians] *Physicians* Q.

rules of Beauty: Since Beauty and Health ordinarily follow each other. *For Beauty,* says *Galen, is nothing else but a just Accord and mutual Harmony of the Members, animated by a healthfull constitution. And men,* said the same Author, *commend a certain Statue of* Polycletus, *which they call the rule, and which deserves that name for having so perfect an agreement in all its parts, and a proportion so exact, that it is not possible to find a fault in it.* From what I have quoted, we may conclude, that the Ancient Pieces are truly beautifull, because they resemble the Beauties of Nature; and that Nature will ever be beautifull which resembles those Beauties of Antiquity. 'Tis now evident upon what account none have presum'd to contest the proportion of those Ancient Pieces, and that on the contrary, they have always been quoted as Models of the most perfect Beauty. *Ovid in the* 12*th. Book of his Metamorphoses,* where he describes *Cyllarus,* the most beautifull of all the *Centaures,* says, *That he had so great a Vivacity in his Countenance, his Neck, his Shoulders, his Hands and Stomach were so fair, that it is certain the manly part of him was as beautifull as the most celebrated Statues.* And *Philostratus* in his *Heroiques,* speaking of *Protesilaus* and praising the beauty of his face, says, *That the form of his Nose was square, as if it had been of a Statue;* and in another place speaking of *Euphorbus,* he says, *That his beauty had gain'd the affections of all the* Greeks, *and that it resembled so nearly the beauty of a Statue, that one might have taken him for* Apollo. Afterwards also speaking of the Beauty of *Neoptolemus,* and of his likeness to his Father *Achilles,* he says, *That in beauty, his Father had the same advantage over him, as Statues have over the beauty of living Men.*

This ought to be understood of the fairest Statues, for amongst the multitude of Sculptors which were in *Greece* and *Italy,* 'tis

2-8 each printed italic line preceded by inverted double commas in Q.
15 *Metamorphoses*] *Metamorphosis* Q.
20 *Heroiques*] *Heroiqnes* Q.
21-22 each printed italic line preceded by inverted double commas in Q.
23 *That*] "*That* Q.
23-25 each printed italic line preceded by inverted double commas in Q.
27 *That*] "*That* Q.
27-29 each printed italic line preceded by inverted double commas in Q.
30 fairest Statues] *fairest Statues* Q.

impossible but some of them must have been bad work-men,
or rather less good: for though their works were much inferiour
to the Artists of the first form, yet somewhat of greatness is to
be seen in them, and somewhat of harmonious in the distribu-
tion of their parts, which makes it evident, that at this time
they wrought on Common Principles, and that every one of them
avail'd himself of those Principles according to his Capacity and
Genius. Those Statues were the greatest Ornaments of *Greece;*
we need onely open the Book of *Pausanias* to find the prodigious
10 quantity of them, whether within or without their Temples, or
in the crossing of Streets, or in the Squares and publique Places,
or even the Fields, or on the Tombs. Statues were erected to the
Muses, to the Nymphs, to Heroes, to great Captains, to Magis-
trates, Philosophers and Poets: In short, they were set up to all
those who had made themselves eminent either in defence of
their Country, or for any noble action which deserv'd a recom-
pence; for it was the most ordinary and most authentique way,
both amongst the *Greeks* and *Romans,* thus to testifie their grati-
tude. The *Romans* when they had conquer'd *Græcia,* transported
20 from thence, not onely their most admirable Statues, but also
brought along with them the most excellent of their Sculptors,
who instructed others in their Art, and have left to posterity the
immortal Examples of their knowledge, which we see confirm'd
by those curious Statues, those Vases, those Basso-Relievo's, and
those beautifull Columns call'd by the names of *Trajan* and
Antonine: They are those Beauties which our Author proposes
to us for our Models, and as the true Fountains of Science, out of
which both Painters and Statuaries are bound to draw for their
own use, without amusing themselves with dipping in streams
30 which are often muddy, at least troubled; I mean the manner
of their Masters, after whom they creep, and from whom they

5   evident,] ~; Q.
13–14 Muses . . . Nymphs . . . Heroes . . . Captains . . . Magistrates, Philosophers
. . . Poets] *Muses . . . Nymphs . . . Heroes . . . Captains . . . Magistrates, Philoso-
phers . . . Poets* Q.
24–25 Statues . . . Vases . . . Basso-Relievo's . . . Columns] *Statues . . . Vases . . .
Basso-Relievo's . . . Columns* Q.
26 our] out Q.   27 Models, and] *Models.* And Q.
28 Painters . . . Statuaries] *Painters . . . Statuaries* Q.

are unwilling to depart, either through negligence, or through the meanness of their Genius. *It belongs onely to heavy minds, says* Cicero, *to spend their time on streams, without searching for the Springs from whence their materials flow in all manner of abundance.*

[¶ 40.] *Without which all is nothing, but a blind and rash barbarity,* &c. All that has nothing of the Ancient gust, is call'd a barbarous or *Gothique* manner, which is not conducted by any rule, but onely follows a wretched fancy, which has nothing in
10 it that is noble: we are here to observe, that Painters are not oblig'd to follow the Antique as exactly as the Sculptors, for then their Picture would favour too strongly of the Statue, and would seem to be without Motion. Many Painters, and some of the ablest amongst them, believing they do well, and taking that Precept in too literal a Sence, have fallen thereby into great inconveniencies; it therefore becomes the Painters to make use of those Ancient Patterns with discretion, and to accommodate the Nature to them in such a manner, that their Figures which must seem to live, may rather appear to be Models for the Antique,
20 than the Antique a Model for their figures.

It appears that *Raphael* made a perfect use of this conduct, and that the *Lombard* School have not precisely search'd into this Precept, any further than to learn from thence how to make a good choice of the Nature, and to give a certain grace and nobleness to all their works, by the general and confus'd Idea, which they had of what is beautifull; as for the rest, they are sufficiently licentious, excepting onely *Titian,* who, of all the *Lombards* has preserv'd the greatest purity in his works. This barbarous manner of which I spoke, has been in great vogue
30 from the year 611 to 1450. They who have restor'd Painting in *Germany,* (not having seen any of those fair Reliques of Antiquity) have retain'd much of that barbarous manner. Amongst

---

2 *It]* "*It* Q.
2–5 *each printed italic line preceded by inverted double commas in* Q.
8–12 barbarous ... Painters ... Antique ... Sculptors ... Statue] *barbarous ... Painters ... Antique ... Sculptors ... Statue* Q.
19–20 Models ... [*to*] ... figures] *set in italics in* Q.
22 School] *School* Q.

others *Lucas van Leyden,* a very laborious man, who with his
Scholars has infected almost all *Europe* with his designs for
Tapestry, which by the ignorant are call'd Ancient Hangings,
(a greater honour than they deserve:) these I say are esteem'd
beautifull by the greatest part of the World. I must acknowledge
that I am amaz'd at so gross a stupidity, and that we of the *French*
Nation should have so barbarous a Tast, as to take for beautifull
those flat, childish and insipid Tapestries. *Albert Durer,* that
famous *German,* who was contemporary to that *Lucas,* has had
10 the like misfortune to fall into that absurd manner, because he
had never seen any thing that was beautifull. Observe what
Vasari tells us in the life of *Marc Antonio* (*Raphael's* Graver)
having first commended *Albert* for his skill in graving, and his
other Talents: *And in truth,* says he, *if this, so excellent, so exact,*
and so universal a Man, had been born in Tuscany, *as he was in*
Germany, *and had form'd his studies according to those beauti-*
full pieces which are seen at Rome, *as the rest of us have done,*
he had prov'd the best Painter of all Italy, *as he was the greatest*
Genius, and the most accomplish'd which Germany *ever bore.*
20 [¶ 45.] *We love what we understand,* &c. This period informs
us, that though our inventions are never so good, though we are
furnish'd by Nature with a noble Genius, and though we follow
the impulse of it, yet this is not enough, if we learn not to under-
stand what is perfect and beautifull in Nature, to the end that
having found it, we may be able to imitate it, and by this
instruction we may be capacitated to observe those errors which
she her self has made, and to avoid them, so as not to copy her
in all sorts of subjects; such as she appears to us, without choice
or distinction.
30 [¶ 50.] *As being the Sovereign Judge of his own Art,* &c. This
word of *Sovereign Judge* or *Arbiter of his own Art,* presupposes
a painter to be fully instructed in all the parts of Painting; so that

---

2–3 designs for Tapestry . . . Ancient Hangings] *designs for Tapestry . . . Ancient*
Hangings Q.
7 Nation] *Nation* Q.
14–19 *each printed italic line preceded by inverted double commas in* Q.
22 Nature . . . Genius] *Nature . . . Genius* Q.
28 us,] ~∧ Q.

being set as it were above his Art, he may be the Master and Sovereign of it, which is no easie matter. Those of that profession are so seldom endow'd with that supreme Capacity, that few of them arrive to be good Judges of Painting: and I should many times make more account of their judgment, who are men of Sence, and yet have never touch'd a Pencil, than of the opinion which is given by the greatest part of Painters. All Painters therefore may be call'd *Arbiters of their own Art*, but to be *Sovereign Arbiters* belongs onely to knowing Painters.

10   [¶ 52.] *And permit no transient Beauties to escape his observation*, &c. Those fugitive or transient Beauties are no other than such as we observe in Nature with a short and transient view, and which remain not long in their subjects. Such are the Passions of the Soul. There are of these sort of Beauties which last but for a moment; as the different Aires of an Assembly, upon the Sight of an unexpected and uncommon Object, some particularity of a violent Passion, some gracefull Action, a Smile, a Glance of an Eye, a disdainfull Look, a Look of Gravity, and a thousand other such like things; we may also place in the
20 Catalogue of these flying Beauties, fine Clouds, such as ordinarily follow Thunder or a Shower of Rain.

    [¶ 54.] *In the same manner that bare practice destitute of the Lights of Art*, &c. We find in *Quinctilian*, that *Pythagoras* said, *The Theory is nothing without the practice. And what means* (says the younger *Pliny*) *have we to retain what has been taught us, if we put it not in practice?* We would not allow that Man to be an Orator who had the best thoughts imaginable, and who knew all the rules of Rhetorique if he had not acquir'd by exer-
cise the Art of using them, and of composing an excellent Dis-
30 course. Painting is a long Pilgrimage; what avails it to make all the necessary preparatives for our Voyage, or to inform our selves of all the difficulties in the rode? if we do not actually begin the journey, and travel at a round rate, we shall never arrive at

1–2   Master . . . Sovereign] *Master . . . Sovereign* Q.
7–9   All Painters . . . knowing Painters] *All Painters . . . knowing Painters* Q.
10   no] no⸺ Q.   24   *The*] "The Q.
24–26   *each printed italic line preceded by inverted double commas in* Q.
26   *practice?* We] ~: we Q.   32   rode?] ~, Q.

the end of it. And as it would be ridiculous to grow old in the
study of every necessary thing, in an Art which comprehends so
many several parts; so on the other hand to begin the practice
without knowing the rules, or at least with a light Tincture of
them, is to expose our selves to the scorn of those who can judge
of Painting, and to make it apparent to the World that we have
no care of our reputation. Many are of opinion, that we need
onely work and mind the practical part to become skilfull and
able Painters; and that the Theory onely incumbers the mind,
10 and tyes the hand: Such Men do just like the Squirrel, who is
perpetually turning the Wheel in her Cage; she runs apace and
wearies her self with her continual Motion, and yet gets no
ground. *'Tis not enough for doing well to walk apace,* says
Quinctilian, but it is enough for walking apace to do well. 'Tis
a bad excuse to say, *I was but a little while about it.* That grace-
full Easiness, that celestial Fire which animates the work, pro-
ceeds not so much from having often done the like, as from
having well understood what we have done. See what I shall
farther say, in the 6o*th.* Rule, which concerns easiness. Others
20 there are who believe the Precepts and Speculation, to be of
absolute necessity, but as they were ill instructed, and what
they knew rather entangl'd than clear'd their understanding,
so they oftentimes stop short; and if they perform a work, 'tis
not without Anxiety and Pain. And in truth, they are so much
the more worthy of Compassion because their intentions are
right, and if they advance not in knowledge as far as others, and
are sometimes cast behind, yet they are grounded upon some sort
of reason; for 'tis belonging to good sence, not to go over fast
when we apprehend our selves to be out of the way, or even where
30 we doubt which way we ought to take. Others on the contrary,
being well instructed in good Maximes, and in the rules of Art,
after having done fine things, yet spoil them all by endeavouring
to make them better, which is a kind of over-doing, and are so

---

5   them,] ~ᴀ Q.
10   Such Men . . . Squirrel] *Such Men . . . Squirrel* Q.
14   *Quinctilian*] Quinctilian Q.
15   *I* . . . [*to*] . . . *it.] set in romans in* Q (it:).
19   6o*th.] errata page in* Q; 51st. Q.
19   Rule] *errata page in* Q; *Rule* Q.   32   things,] ~ᴀ Q.

intoxicated with their work and with an earnest desire of being above all others, that they suffer themselves to be deceiv'd with the appearance of an imaginary good. Apelles *one day admiring the prodigious Labour which he saw in a Picture of* Protogenes, *and knowing how much*   Pliny, 35.10. *sweat it must have cost him, said, That* Protogenes *and himself were of equal strength; nay, that he yielded to him in some parts of Painting, but in this he surpass'd him, that* Protogenes *never knew when he had done well, and could never hold his hand; he*

10 *also added in the nature of a Precept, that he wish'd all Painters would imprint this lesson deeply in their Memory, that with over-straining and earnestness of finishing their Pieces they often did them more harm than good. There are some*   10.3. *(says* Quinctilian) *who never satisfie themselves, never are contented with their first Notions and Expressions, but are continually changing all, till nothing remains of their first Ideas. Others there are* (continues he,) *who dare never trust themselves, nor resolve on any thing, and who being as it were intangl'd in their own Genius, imagine it to be a laudable correct-*

20 *ness, when they form difficulties to themselves in their own work. And to speak the truth, 'tis hard to discern whether of the two is in the greatest Error; he who is enamour'd of all he does, or he whom nothing of his own can please. For it has happen'd to young Men, and often even to those of the greatest Wit, to waste their Spirits, and to consume themselves with Anxiety and Pain of their own giving, so far as even to doze upon their work with too much eagerness of doing well; I will now tell you how a reasonable man ought to carry himself on this occasion: 'Tis certain that we ought to use our best endeavour to give the last Perfec-*

30 *tion to our works; yet it is always to be understood, that we attempt no more than what is in the compass of our Genius, and according to our Vein: for to make a true Progress, I grant that diligence and study are both requisite, but this study ought to have no mixture, either of Self-opinion, Obstinacy, or Anxiety; for which reason, if it blows a happy Gale we must set up all our Sails (though in so doing it sometimes happens that we follow*

4+ *sidenote* Pliny,] ∼ₐ Q.   14 says *Quinctilian] says* Quinctilian Q.
36–124:2 *Sails (though ... correctness)*] ∼, ∼ ... ∼, Q.

those Motions where our natural heat is more powerfull than our care and our correctness) provided we abuse not this licence, and suffer not our selves to be deceiv'd by it; for all our productions cannot fail to please us at the moment of their Birth, as being new to us.

[¶ 61.] *Because the greatest Beauties cannot always be express'd for want of terms,* &c. I have learn'd from the mouth of Monsieur *du Fresnoy,* that he had oftentimes heard *Guido* say, *That no man could give a rule of the greatest Beauties, and that* 10 *the knowledge of them was so abstruse, that there was no manner of speaking which could express them.* This comes just to what *Quinctilian* says, *That things incredible wanted words to express them: for some of them are too* Declam. 19. *great and too much elevated to be comprehended by human discourse.* From hence it proceeds that the best Judges when they admire a noble Picture, seem to be fasten'd to it; and when they come to themselves you would say they had lost the use of Speech.

Pausiacâ torpes, insane, Tabellâ, says **Horace,* and †*Symmachus* says, *that the greatness of* * Lib.2.Sat.7. 20 *astonishment hinders men from giving a just* † Lib. 10.Ep. *applause.* The *Italians* say *Opera da stupire,* when a thing is 22. wonderfully good.

[¶ 63.] *Those Master-pieces of Antiquity, which were the first Examples of this Art,* &c. He means the most knowing and best Painters of Antiquity, that is to say, from the last two Ages to our times.

[¶ 66.] *And also moderates that fury of the Fancy,* &c. There is in the *Latine* Text, *which produces onely Monsters,* that is to say, things out of all probable resemblance: Such things as are 30 often found in the works of *Pietro Testa. It often happens,* says *Dionysius Longinus,* a grave Author, *That some men imagining themselves to be possess'd with a divine Fury; far from being carry'd into the rage of* Bacchanalians, *often fall into toys and trifles which are only Puerilities.*

[¶ 69.] *A subject beautifull and noble,* &c. Painting is not

---

3 *it;*] ~, Q.
28 *Latine*] Latine Q.
29–30 resemblance: ... *Testa.*] ~....~: Q.

onely pleasing and divertising, but is also a kind of Memorial of those things which Antiquity has had the most beautifull and noble in their kinds, re-placing the History before our Eyes; as if the thing at that time were effectually in Action, even so far that beholding the Pictures wherein those noble deeds are represented, we find our selves stung with a desire of endeavouring somewhat which is like that Action there express'd, as if we were reading it in the History. The Beauty of the subject inspires us with Love and Admiration for the Pictures: As the
10 fair mixture causes us to enter into the subject which it imitates and imprints it the more deeply into our Imagination and our Memory. These are two Chains which are interlink'd, which contain, and are at the same time contain'd, and whose matter is equally precious and estimable.

[¶ 72.] *And well season'd,* &c. *Aliquid salis,* somewhat that is ingenious, fine and picquant, extraordinary, of a high relish, proper to instruct and to clear the Understanding. *The Painters ought to do like the Orators,* says *Cicero. Let them instruct, let them divertise, and let them*   De Opt. Gen. Orat.
20 *move us;* this is what is properly meant by the word *Salt.*

[¶ 74.] *On which the whole Machine (as it may be call'd) of the Picture is to be dispos'd,* &c. 'Tis not without reason, nor by chance, that our Author uses the word *Machine.* A Machine is a just assembling or Combination of many pieces to produce one and the same effect. And the Disposition in a Picture is nothing else but an Assembling of many parts, of which we are to foresee the agreement with each other, and the justness to produce a beautifull effect, as you shall see in the fourth Precept, which is
30 concerning the Oeconomy. This is also call'd the *Composition,* by which is meant the distribution and orderly placing of things, both in general and in particular.

9–12 Pictures: ... Memory. These] ~....~: these Q.
16 extraordinary,] ~ᴧ Q.   17 *The*] The Q.
18 *ought* ... [*to*] ... *the*] *set in romans in Q.*
18–20 *Let* ... [*to*] ... *us*] *set in romans in Q.*
22 *as* ... [*to*] ... *call'd*] *set in romans in Q.*
24 Machine] *Machine* Q.
26 Disposition in a Picture] *Disposition in a Picture* Q.
28 other, and] ~: And Q.   30 Oeconomy] *Oeconomy* Q.

[¶ 75.] *Which is what we properly call Invention,* &c. Our
Author establishes three parts of Painting, the Invention, the
Design or Drawing, and the Colouring, which in some places he
also calls the *Cromatique.* Many Authors who have written of
Painting, multiply the parts according to their pleasure; and
without giving you or my self the trouble of discussing this mat-
ter, I will onely tell you, that all the parts of Painting which
others have nam'd, are reducible into these three which are
mention'd by our Author.

10   For which reason, I esteem this division to be the justest: and
as these three parts are Essential to Painting, so no man can be
truly call'd a Painter who does not possess them all together:
In the same manner that we cannot give the name of *Man* to any
Creature which is not compos'd of Body, Soul and Reason, which
are the three parts necessarily constituent of a Man. How there-
fore can they pretend to the Quality of Painters, who can onely
copy and purloyn the works of others who therein employ their
whole industry, and with that onely Talent would pass for able
Painters? And do not tell me that many great Artists have done

20 this; for I can easily answer you that it had been their better
course, to have abstain'd from so doing; that they have not
thereby done themselves much honour, and that copying was
not the best part of their reputation. Let us then conclude that
all Painters ought to acquire this part of Excellence; not to do
it, is to want courage and not dare to shew themselves. 'Tis to
creep and grovel on the ground, 'tis to deserve this just reproach,
O imitatores servum pecus! 'Tis with Painters, in reference to
their productions, as it is with Orators. A good beginning is al-
ways costly to both: much sweat and labour is requir'd, but 'tis

30 better to expose our works and leave them liable to censure for
fifteen years, than to blush for them at the end of fifty. On this

---

2–4 Invention . . . Design . . . Drawing . . . Colouring . . . *Cromatique*] IN-
VENTION . . . DESIGN . . . DRAWING . . . COLOURING . . . CROMA-
TIQUE Q.
11–15 three parts . . . Essential . . . Painting . . . Painter . . . Body, Soul . . .
Reason . . . Man] *three parts . . . Essential . . . Painting . . . Painter . . . Body, Soul
. . . Reason . . . Man* Q.
19 Painters?] ~. Q.   21 so doing] *so doing* Q.
27 *pecus!*] ~: Q.
27–28 Painters . . . Orators] *Painters . . . Orators* Q.

account 'tis necessary for a Painter to begin early to do somewhat of his own, and to accustom himself to it by continual exercise; for so long as endeavouring to raise himself, he fears falling, he shall be always on the ground. See the following observation.

[¶ 76.] *Invention is a kind of Muse, which being possess'd of the other advantages common to her Sisters, &c.* The Attributes of the Muses are often taken for the Muses themselves; and it is in this sence, that Invention is here call'd a *Muse.* Authors ascribe to each of them in particular the Sciences which they have (say
10 they) invented; and in general the *belle-lettre,* because they contain almost all the others. These Sciences are those advantages of which our Author speaks, and with which he would have a Painter furnish himself sufficiently: and in truth, there is no man, though his understanding be very mean, who knows not and who finds not of himself how much Learning is necessary to animate his Genius, and to compleat it. And the reason of this is, that they who have studied, have not onely seen and learn'd many excellent things in their course of studies, but that also they have acquir'd by that exercise a great Facility of profiting
20 themselves by reading good Authors. They who will make profession of Painting, must heap up treasures out of their reading and there will find many wonderfull means of raising themselves above others, who can onely creep upon the ground, or if they elevate themselves, 'tis onely to fall from a higher place, because they serve themselves of other Men's Wings, neither understanding their Use nor Vertue: 'Tis true that it is not the present Mode for a Painter to be so knowing: and if any of them in these times be found to have either a great Wit or much Learning, the multitude would not fail to say, that it was great pity, and
30 that the Youth might have come to somewhat in the practical part, or it may be in the Exchequer, or in the Families of some Noble-men. So wretch'd is the Destiny of Painting in these later ages. By Learning 'tis not so much the knowledge of the *Greek*

7–8 Muses . . . Muses . . . Invention] *Muses . . . Muses . . . Invention* Q.
10 *belle-lettre] belle lettere* Q.   14 mean,] ~ₐ Q.
31 Exchequer] *Exchequer* Q.
33–128:3 knowledge . . . Tongue . . . reading . . . good Authors . . . Translations
. . . best Authors] *knowledge . . . Tongue . . . reading . . . good Authors . . .*
Translations . . . best Authors Q.

and *Latine* Tongue, which is here to be understood as the reading of good Authors, and understanding those things of which they treat: for Translations being made of the best Authors, there is not any Painter who is not capable in some sort of understanding those Books of Humanity, which are comprehended under the name of the *belle-lettre*. In my opinion the Books which are of the most advantage to those of the Profession, are these which follow.

The *Bible*.

10   The History of *Josephus*.

The *Roman* History of *Coeffeteau*, (for those who understand the *French*,) and that of *Titus Livius*, translated by *Vigenere*, with the Notes which are both curious and profitable. They are in two Volumes.

Homer, whom *Pliny* calls the Fountain-head of Invention and noble thoughts.

Virgil, and in him, particularly his *Æneids*.

The Ecclesiastical History of *Godeau*, or the Abridgement of *Baronius*.

20   *Ovid*'s *Metamorphoses*, translated into *French* by *Du Rier*, and in *English* by *Sandys*.

The * Pictures of *Philostratus*.   * Tableaux.

Plutarch's *Lives*, translated from the *Greek* by several hands, in 5 Volumes.

Pausanias, though I doubt whether that Author be translated. He is wonderfull for giving of great Ideas; and chiefly, for such as are to be plac'd at a distance, (or cast behind) and for the combining of Figures. This Author, in conjunction with *Homer*, make a good mingle of what is pleasing and what is perfect.

30   *The Religion of the Ancient Romans*, by *Du Choul;* and in *English, Godwin*'s *Roman Antiquities*.

Trajan's Pillar, with the discourse which explains the Figures on it, and instructs a Painter in those things with which he is

---

6   *belle-lettre*] belle lettere Q.   20   *Ovid's*] Ovid's Q.
22   The *Pictures] *~ˬ~ Q.
25   Author ... translated] *Author ... translated* Q.
28   Author,] *Author*ˬ Q.
30   *The ... [to] ... the*] set in romans in Q.
32   Pillar] *Pillar* Q.

undispensibly to be acquainted. This is one of the most prin-
cipal and most learned Books, which we have for the Modes, the
Customs, the Arms, and the Religion of the *Romans*. *Julio
Romano* made his chief studies on the Marble it self.

The Books of Medals.

The *Bass-Reliefs* of *Perrier* and others, with their Explana-
tions at the bottom of the Pages, which give a perfect under-
standing of them.

Horace's *Art of Poetry*, by the Earl of *Roscomon*, because of
10 the relation which there is betwixt the Rules of Poetry and those
of Painting.

And other Books of the like Nature, the reading of which are
profitable to warm the Imagination: such as in *English*, are
Spencer's *Fairy Queen;* The *Paradise lost* of *Milton; Tasso* trans-
lated by *Fairfax;* and the History of *Polybius*, by Sir *Henry
Shere*.

Some Romances also are very capable of entertaining the Ge-
nius, and of strengthening it by the noble Ideas which they give
of things; but there is this danger in them, that they almost
20 always corrupt the truth of History.

There are also other Books which a Painter may use upon
some particular occasions and onely when he wants them: Such
are,

The Mythology of the Gods.

The Images of the Gods.

The Iconology.

The *Fables* of *Hyginus*.

The practical Perspective.

And some others not here mention'd.

30 Thus it is necessary, that they who are desirous of a name in
Painting, should read at leisure times these Books with diligence,
and make their observations of such things as they find for their

---

2–3 Modes . . . Customs . . . Arms . . . Religion] *Modes . . . Customs . . . Arms . . .
Religion* Q.
5 Medals] *Medals* Q.
10–11 Poetry . . . Painting] *Poetry . . . Painting* Q.
24–26 Mythology . . . Images . . . Iconology] *Mythology . . . Images . . . Ico-
nology* Q.
27 *Fables*] Tables Q.

purpose in them, and of which they believe they may sometime
or other have occasion; let the Imagination be employ'd in this
reading, and let them make Sketches and light Touches of those
Ideas which that reading forms in their Imagination. *Quinc-
tilian, Tacitus,* or whoever was the Author of that Dialogue
which is call'd in *Latine De causis corruptæ eloquentiæ,* says,
*That Painting resembles Fire which is fed by the Fuel, inflam'd
by Motion, and gathers strength by burning: For the power of
the Genius is onely augmented by the abundance of matter to*
10 *supply it; and 'tis impossible to make a great and magnificent
work, if that matter be wanting or not dispos'd rightly.* And
therefore a Painter who has a Genius, gets nothing by long think-
ing and taking all imaginable care to make a noble Composition
if he be not assisted by those studies which I have mention'd. All
that he can gain by it, is onely to weary his Imagination, and to
travel over many vast Countries without dwelling on any one
thing, which can give him satisfaction.

All the Books which I have named may be serviceable to all
sorts of Persons as well as to Painters. As for those Books which
20 were of particular use to them, they were unfortunately lost in
those Ages which were before the Invention of Printing, the
Copyers neglecting, probably out of ignorance, to transcribe
them, as not finding themselves capable of mak-
ing the *demonstrative Figures. In the mean   * *That is to*
time, 'tis evidently known by the relation of   *the Eye by*
                                                      Diagrams
Authors, that we have lost fifty Volumes of them   *and Sketches,*
at the least. See *Pliny* in his 35*th.* Book; and   &c.
Franc. Junius in his 3*d.* Chapter of the 2*d.* Book
of the *Painting of the Ancients.* Many Moderns have written of
30 it with small success, taking a large compass without coming
directly to the point, and talking much without saying any thing:
yet some of them have acquitted themselves successfully enough:
Amongst others *Leonardo da Vinci* (though without method;)
Paulo Lomazzo, whose Book is good for the greatest part, but

---

6 *Latine*] Latine Q.   21 Printing,] ~. Q.
21–22 the Copyers neglecting,] *errata page in* Q (The Copiers neglecting∧); Ne-
glecting the Copyers∧ Q.   22 ignorance,] ~∧ Q.
25 relation] *errata page in* Q; reltaion Q.
32–131:1 enough: ... tiresome;] ~.....~. Q.

whose discourse is too diffusive and very tiresome; *John Baptist Armenini, Franciscus Junius,* Monsieur *de Cambray,* to whose Preface I rather invite you than to his Book; we are not to forget what Monsieur *Felebien* has written of the Picture of *Alexander* by the hand of Monsieur *Le Brun:* besides that the work it self is very eloquent, the Foundations which he establishes for the making of a good Picture are wonderfully solid. Thus I have given you very near the Library of a Painter, and a Catalogue of such Books as he ought either to read himself or have read to
10 him, at least if he will not satisfie himself with possessing Painting as the most sordid of all Trades and not as the noblest of all Arts.

[¶ 78.] *'Tis the business of a Painter in his choice of Postures,* &c. See here the most important Precept of all those which relate to Painting. It belongs properly to a Painter alone, and all the rest are borrow'd either from Learning, or from Physick, or from the Mathematicks, or in short, from other Arts; for it is sufficient to have a natural Wit and Learning to make that which we call in Painting a good Invention: for the design we must have some
20 insight into Anatomy; to make Buildings, and other things in Perspective, we must have knowledge in the Mathematicks; and other Arts, will bring in their Quota's to furnish out the matter of a good Picture; but for the Oeconomy or ordering of the whole together, none but onely the Painter can understand it, because the end of the Artist is pleasingly to deceive the Eyes, which he can never accomplish if this part be wanting to him. A Picture may make an ill effect, though the Invention of it be truly understood, the Design of it correct and the Colours of it the most

2   Monsieur] *Monsieur* Q.
8   Library of a Painter] *Library of a Painter* Q.
13   78] 77 Q.
14–15   most important Precept . . . Painting] *most important Precept . . . Painting* Q.
15–17   Painter alone . . . Learning . . . Physick . . . Mathematicks . . . other] *Painter alone . . . Learning . . . Physick . . . Mathematicks . . . other* Q.
17   Arts;] *Arts,* Q.   19   Invention:] ~, Q.
20   Anatomy;] *Anatomy,* Q.   21   Perspective] *Perspective* Q.
21   Mathematicks;] *Mathematicks,* Q.   22   other Arts] *other Arts* Q.
22   Quota's] *Quota's* Q.   23   Oeconomy] *Oeconomy* Q.
27–28   Invention . . . Design] *Invention . . . Design* Q.

beautifull and fine that can be employ'd in it. And on the contrary we may behold other Pictures ill invented, ill design'd and painted with the most common Colours, which shall make a very good effect, and which shall more pleasingly   *In Oecono-* deceive; *Nothing pleases a man so much as or-*   mico. *der,* says *Xenophon:* And *Horace,* in his *Art of Poetry,*

Singula quæque locum teneant sortita decenter.

Set all things in their own peculiar place,
And know that Order is the greatest Grace.

10   This Precept is properly the use and application of all the rest; for which reason it requires much judgment. You are therefore, in such manner to foresee things, that your Picture may be painted in your Head: *i. e.* before it come upon the Canvas. *When* Menander (says a celebrated Authour)
                                             Comm.vetus.
had order'd the Scenes of his Comedy, he held it
to be, in a manner, already made; though he had not begun the
first Verse of it. 'Tis an undoubted truth, that they who are endu'd with this foresight, work with incredible pleasure and facility; others on the contrary are perpetually changing and re-
20 changing their work, which when it is ended leaves them but anxiety for all their pains. It seems to me that these sorts of Pictures remind us of those old *Gothique* Castles, made at several times, and which hold together onely as it were by Rags and Patches.

    It may be inferr'd from that which I have said, that the Invention and the Disposition are two several and distinct parts in effect; though the last of them depends upon the first, and that commonly 'tis comprehended under it: yet we are to take great care that we do not confound them. The Invention simply finds
30 out the subjects, and makes a choice of them suitable to the History which we treat; and the Disposition distributes those things which are thus found each to its proper place, and ac-

---

4+   *sidenote   In*] In Q.   6   *Poetry,*] ~. Q.
25–26   Invention ... Disposition] *Invention ... Disposition* Q.
27   effect;] ~, Q.
29–133:4   Invention ... Disposition ... Oeconomy ... to the Eyes ... Consort of
Musick ... Ears] *Invention ... Disposition ... Oeconomy ... to the Eyes ...*
Consort of Musick ... Ears Q.

commodates the Figures and the Grouppes in particular, and the *Tout Ensemble* (or whole together) of the Picture in general: so that this Oeconomy produces the same effect in relation to the Eyes, as a Consort of Musick to the Ears.

There is one thing of great consequence to be observ'd in the Oeconomy of the whole work, which is, that at the first Sight we may be given to understand the quality of the subject: and that the Picture at the first Glance of the Eye, may inspire us with the principal passion of it: for Example, if the subject which
10 you have undertaken to treat be of joy, 'tis necessary that every thing which enters into your Picture should contribute to that Passion, so that the Beholders shall immediately be mov'd with it. If the Subject be mournfull, let every thing in it have a stroke of sadness; and so of the other Passions and Qualities of the Subjects.

[¶ 81.] *Let your Compositions be conformable to the Text of Ancient Authors,* &c. Take care that the Licences of Painters be rather to adorn the History, than to corrupt it.
And though *Horace* gives permission to Paint-   *Art of Poetry.*
20 ers and Poets to dare every thing, yet he encourages neither of them, to make things out of nature or verisimility; for he adds immediately after,

> But let the Bounds of Licences be fix'd,
> Not things of disagreeing Natures mix'd;
> Not Sweet with Sowre, nor Birds with Serpents joyn'd,
> Nor the fierce Lyon with the fearfull Hind.

The Thoughts of a Man endued with good Sence are not of kin to visionary madness; Men in Feavers are onely capable of such Dreams. Treat then the Subjects of your Pictures with all
30 possible faithfulness, and use your Licences with a becoming boldness, provided they be ingenious, and not immoderate and extravagant.

[¶ 83.] *Take care that whatsoever makes nothing to your Subject,* &c. Nothing deadens so much the Composition of a Picture,

---

6–9 Oeconomy ... for Example] *Oeconomy ... for Example* Q.
19–20 Painters ... Poets] *Painters ... Poets* Q.
23 *be*] *he* Q.

as Figures which are not appertaining to the Subject: We may
call them pleasantly enough, *Figures to be let.*

[¶ 87.] *This part of Painting so rarely met with, and so dif-
ficult to be found,* &c. That is to say, Invention.

[¶ 89.] *Which was stollen by* Prometheus, *&c.* The Poets feign
that *Prometheus* form'd out of Clay, so fair a Statue, that *Mi-
nerva* one day having long admir'd it, said to the workman, that
if he thought there was any thing in Heaven which could add to
its perfection, he might ask it of her; but he being ignorant of
10 what might be most beautifull in the Habitation of the Gods,
desir'd leave that he might be carry'd thither, and being there to
make his choice. The Goddess bore him thither upon her Shield,
and so soon as he had perceiv'd that all Celestial things were
animated with Fire, he stole a Parcel of it, which he carry'd down
to Earth, and applying it to the stomach of his Statue enliven'd
the whole Body.

[¶ 92.] *That it happens not to every one to see* Corinth, &c.
This is an Ancient Proverb which signifies, that every man has
not the Genius nor the Disposition that is necessary for the
20 Sciences, neither yet a Capacity fit for the undertaking of things
which are great and difficult. *Corinth* was heretofore the Centre
of all Arts, and the place whither they sent all
those whom they would render capable of any   * Pro lege
thing. **Cicero* calls it *the Light of all* Græcia.   Man.

[¶ 95.] *It arriv'd at length to that height of perfection,* &c.
This was in the time of *Alexander the Great,* and lasted even to
Augustus; under whose reign Painting fell to great decay. But
under the Emperors, *Domitian, Nerva* and *Trajan,* it appear'd
in its primitive lustre, which lasted to the time of *Phocas* the
30 Emperor, when vices prevailing over the Arts, and War being
kindled through all *Europe,* and especially in *Lombardy,* (oc-
casion'd by the irruption of the *Hunns,*) Painting was totally
extinguish'd. And if some few in the succeeding Ages strain'd
themselves to revive it, it was rather in finding out the most glar-
ing, gawdy and costly Colours, than in imitating the harmonious

---

2 *Figures to be let*] Figures to be let **Q.**
4 Invention] *Invention* **Q.**
24 *the* ... [*to*] ... Græcia] *italics and romans reversed in* **Q.**

Simplicity of those illustrious Painters who preceded them. At length, in the fourteenth Century, some there were who began to set it again on foot. And it may truly be said, that about the end of the fifteenth Age, and the beginning of our Sixteenth it appear'd in much Splendor by means of many knowing Men in all parts of *Italy,* who were in perfect possession of it. Since those happy times which were so fruitfull of the noble Arts, we have also had some knowing Painters but very few in number, because of the little inclination which Sovereign Princes have
10 had for Painting: but thanks to the zeal of our Great Monarch, and to the care of his first Minister, Monsieur *Colbert,* we may shortly behold it more flourishing than ever.

[¶ 102.] *Though they are not very much inferior,* &c. Our Author means this of *Michael Angelo,* and other able Sculptors of that time.

[¶ 103.] *A Posture therefore must be chosen according to their gusto,* &c. This is the second part of Painting, which is call'd Design or Drawing; as the Ancients have sought as much as possible whatsoever contributes to the making of a perfect Body,
20 so they have diligently examin'd in what consists the beauty of good postures, as their works sufficiently inform us.

[¶ 104.] *The parts of it must be great,* &c. Yet not so great as to exceed a just proportion. But he means that in a noble posture, the greatest parts of the Body ought to appear foremost rather than the less, for which reason in another passage he vehemently forbids the foreshortnings, because they make the parts appear little, though of themselves they are great.

[¶ 104.] *Large or ample,* &c. To avoid the dry manner, such as is most commonly the Nature which *Lucas van Leyden* and
30 *Albert Durer* have imitated.

[¶ 105.] *Unequal in their Position, so that those which are before must contrast or oppose those others which are hindermost, and all of them be equally balanc'd on their Centre,* &c. The Motions are never natural, when the Members are not equally balanc'd on their Centre: and these Members cannot be balanc'd on their Centre in an equality of weight, but they must

---

18   Design . . . Drawing] *Design . . . Drawing* Q.
29   Nature] *Nature* Q.

contrast each other. A Man who dances on the Rope, makes a manifest Demonstration of this Truth. The Body is a weight balanc'd on its Feet, as upon two Pivots. And though one of the Feet most commonly bears the weight, yet we see that the whole weight rests Centrally upon it; insomuch, that if, for Example, one Arm is stretched out, it must of necessity be either that the other Arm, or the Leg be cast backward, or the Body somewhat bow'd on the opposite Side, so as to make an Equilibrium, and be in a Situation which is unforc'd. It may be, though seldom
10 (if it be not in old Men) that the Feet bear equally; and for that time half the weight is equally distributed on each Foot. You ought to make use of the same Prudence, if one Foot bears three parts in four of the Burthen, and that the other Foot bore the remaining part. This in general is what may be said of the Balance, and the Libration of the Body. In particular, there may many things be said which are very usefull and curious, of which you may satisfie your selves in *Leonardo da Vinci.* He has done wonderfully well on that subject, and one may truly say that the Ponderation, is the best and soundest part of all his Book of
20 Painting. It begins at the 181st. Chapter, and concludes at the 273d. I would also advise you to read *Paulo Lomazzo* in his 6th. Book, Chapter 4th., *Del moto del Corpo humano,* that is, the motion of a human Body. You will there find many things of great profit; for what concerns the Contrast, I will onely say in general, that nothing gives so much grace and life to Figures. See the 13th. Precept, and what I say upon it in the Remarks.

[¶ 107.] *The parts must have their out-lines in Waves resembling Flames, or the gliding of a Snake upon the ground,* &c. The reason of this proceeds from the action of the Muscles,
30 which are as so many Well-buckets; when one of them acts and draws, 'tis necessary that the other must obey; so that the Muscles which act, drawing always towards their principle, and those which obey, stretching in length and on the side of their inser-

3 Pivots] *Pivots* Q.   5 Centrally] *Centrally* Q.
5 it; insomuch] ~. Insomuch Q.   8 Equilibrium] *Equilibrium* Q.
19–20 Ponderation . . . Book of Painting] *Ponderation . . . Book of Painting* Q.
22 Book, Chapter 4th.,] *Book, Chapter 4th.*‸ Q.
26 13th. Precept] *errata page in Q;* 43d. Precept Q.
33 obey,] ~‸ Q.

tion, it must needs follow that the parts must be design'd in Waves: but beware lest in giving this form to the parts you do not break the Bones which sustain them, and which always must make them appear firm.

This Maxim is not altogether so general, but that actions may be found where the masses of the Muscles are situate one over against another, but this is not very common. The out-lines which are in waves, give not only a grace to the Parts, but also to the whole Body, when it is only supported on one Leg; as we

10 see in the Figures of *Antinous, Meleager,* the *Venus* of *Medicis,* that of the *Vatican,* the two others of *Borghese,* and that of *Flora,* of the Goddess *Vesta,* the two *Bacchus's* of *Borghese,* and that of *Ludovisio,* and in fine of the greatest number of the Ancient Figures, which are standing, and which always rest more upon one Foot than the other. Besides, that the Figures and their Parts, ought almost always to have a serpentine and flaming form naturally, these sorts of out-lines have, I know not what of life and seeming motion in them, which very much resembles the activity of the Flame, and of the Serpent.

20 [¶ 112.] *According to the knowledge of them, which is given us by Anatomy,* &c. This part is nothing known at present amongst our modern Painters. I have shewn the profit and even the necessity of it in the Preface of a little Epitome which I have made, and which Monsieur *Tortebat* has publish'd. I know there are some who think this Science a kind of Monster, and believe it to be of no Advantage, either because they are mean spirited, or that they have not consider'd the want which they have of it; nor reflected as they ought, on its importance: contenting themselves with a certain track, to which they have been us'd. But

30 certain it is, that whoever is capable of such a thought, will never be capable of becoming a great Designer.

[¶ 113.] *Design'd after the manner of the* Græcians, &c. That

---

5   Maxim] *Maxim* Q.
9   Leg; as] ~. As Q.
10   *Medicis*] *Medices* Q.
12   *Bacchus's*] *Bacchus's* Q.
13–14   Ancient Figures] *Ancient Figures* Q.
24   *Tortebat*] *Torrebat* Q.
32   Græcians, &c.] *Græcians,* &c. Q.
32   That] that Q.

is to say, according to the Ancient Statues, which for the most part come from *Greece.*

[¶ 114.] *Let there be a perfect relation betwixt the parts and the whole,* &c. or let them agree well together, which is the same thing. His meaning in this place, is to speak of the justness of proportions; and of the harmony which they make with one another. Many famous Authours have thoroughly treated this matter; amongst others *Paulo Lomazzo,* whose first Book speaks of nothing else: But there are so many subdivisions, that a Reader
10 must have a good Brain, not to be turn'd with them. See those which our Author has remark'd in general, on the most beautifull Statues of the Ancients. I believe them to be so much the better, as they are more conformable to those, which *Vitruvius* gives us, in the first Chapter of his third Book: And which he tells us, that he learn'd from the Artists themselves: because in the Preface to his seventh Book, he makes his boast to have had them from others, and particularly from Architects and Painters.

The Measures of a Humane Body.

The Ancients have commonly allow'd eight Heads to their
20 Figures; though some of them have but seven. But we ordinarily divide the Figure into *ten Faces: that is to say, from the Crown of the Head to the Sole of the Foot in the following manner.

    From the Crown of the Head to the Forehead, is the third part of a Face.

    The Face begins, at the root of the lowest Hairs, which are upon the Forehead; and ends at the bottom of the Chin.

    The Face is divided into three proportionable parts; the first
30 contains the Forehead, the second the Nose, and the third the Mouth and the Chin.

* *This depends on the Age & Quality of the persons. The* Apollo *and* Venus *of Medicis have more than ten Faces.*

---

1   Ancient Statues] *Ancient Statues* Q.
8   matter; amongst] ~. Amongst Q.
12 Statues of the Ancients] *Statues of the Ancients* Q.
14 first ... [*to*] ... Book] *set in italics in* Q.
16–17 seventh Book ... Architects ... Painters] *seventh Book ... Architects ... Painters* Q.
19 Ancients] *Ancients* Q.
24+–25+ *sidenote* Medicis] Medices Q.

From the Chin, to the pit betwixt the Collar-bones are two lengths of a Nose.

From the pit betwixt the Collar-bones, to the bottom of the Breast, one Face.

* From the bottom of the Breasts, to the Navel, one Face.

* From the Navel to the Genitories, one Face.

From the Genitories to the upper part of the Knee, two Faces.

10   The Knee contains half a Face.

From the lower part of the Knee to the Anckle, two Faces.

From the Anckle to the Sole of the Foot, half a Face.

The Apollo *has a Nose more.*

The Apollo *has half a Nose more: and the upper half of the* Venus de Medicis *is to the lower part of the Belly, and not to the Privy parts.*

A Man, when his Arms are stretch'd out, is, from the longest Finger of his Right hand, to the longest of his left, as broad as he is long.

From one side of the Breasts to the other, two Faces.

The bone of the Arm call'd *Humerus* is the length of two
20 Faces, from the Shoulder to the Elbow.

From the end of the Elbow to the root of the little Finger, the bone call'd *Cubitus,* with part of the Hand, contains two Faces.

From the box of the Shoulder-blade, to the pit betwixt the Collar-bones, one Face.

If you would be satisfy'd in the Measures of breadth, from the extremity of one Finger to the other, so that this breadth shou'd be equal to the length of the Body, you must observe that the boxes of the Elbows with the Humerus, and of the Humerus
30 with the Shoulder-blade, bear the proportion of half a Face, when the Arms are stretch'd out.

The Sole of the Foot is the sixth part of the Figure.

The Hand is the length of a Face.

The Thumb contains a Nose.

The inside of the Arm, from the place where the Muscle dis-

---

4   Breast,] ~, Q.
10+–11+   *sidenote*   Medicis] Medices Q.
29   Humerus ... Humerus] *Humerus ... Humerus* Q.

5–6   Navel,] ~, Q.
27   other,] ~; Q.

appears, which makes the Breast, call'd the *Pectoral Muscle,* to the middle of the Arm, four Noses.

From the middle of the Arm to the beginning of the Hand, five Noses.

The longest Toe, is a Nose long.

The two utmost parts of the Teats, and the pit betwixt the Collar-bones of a Woman make an equilateral triangle.

For the breadth of the Limbs no precise measures can be given; because the measures themselves are changeable accord-
10 ing to the quality of the persons; and according to the movement of the Muscles.

If you wou'd know the Proportions more particularly, you may see them in *Paulo Lomazzo:* 'tis good to read them, once at least, and to make Remarks on them; every man according to his own judgment, and according to the occasion which he has for them.

[¶ 117.] *Though Perspective cannot be call'd a certain Rule,* &c. That is to say, purely of it self, without prudence, and discretion. The greatest part of those, who understand it, desiring
20 to practice it too regularly, often make such things as shock the sight, though they are within the Rules. If all those great Painters, who have left us such fair Platforms, had rigorously observ'd it in their Figures, they had not wholly found their account in it. They had indeed made things more regularly true, but withall very unpleasing. There is great appearance that the Architects, and Statuaries of former times, have not found it to their purpose always; nor have follow'd the Geometrical part so exactly as Perspective ordains. For He who wou'd imitate the Frontispiece of the Rotunda according to Perspective, wou'd be grosly
30 deceiv'd; since the Columns which are at the extremities have more diameter, than those which are in the middle. The Cornish of the *Palazzo Farnese,* which makes so beautifull an effect below, when view'd more nearly, will be found not to have its just measures. In the Pillar of *Trajan,* we see that the highest Figures are greater than those below; and make an effect quite contrary

1   *Pectoral Muscle*] Pectoral Muscle Q.
25–26   Architects ... Statuaries] *Architects ... Statuaries* Q.
29   Rotunda] *Rotunda* Q.   34   Pillar] *Pillar* Q.

to Perspective, increasing according to the measure of their distance. I know there is a Rule which teaches a way of making them in that manner; and which though 'tis to be found in some Books of Perspective, yet notwithstanding is no rule of Perspective: Because 'tis never made use of, but onely when we find it for our purpose; for if (for example) the Figures which are at the top of *Trajan*'s Pillar, were but as great as those which are at the bottom, they wou'd not be for all that against Perspective: and thus we may say, with more reason, that it is a rule of De-
10 corum in Perspective to ease the sight, and to render objects more agreeable. 'Tis on this general observation, that we may establish in Perspective, the rules of Decorum (or convenience) whensoever occasion shall offer. We may also see another Example in the base of the *Farnesian Hercules;* which is not upon the level, but on an easie declivity on the advanc'd part, that the feet of the Figure may not be hidden from the sight, to the end that it may appear more pleasing: which the noble Authors of these things have done, not in contempt of Geometry and Perspective, but for the satisfaction of the Eyes, which was the end they pro-
20 pos'd to themselves in all their works.

We must therefore understand Perspective, as a Science which is absolutely necessary; and which a Painter must not want: Yet without subjecting our selves so wholly to it, as to become slaves of it. We are to follow it, when it leads us in a pleasing way, and that it shows us pleasing things; but for some time to forsake it, if it lead us through mire, or to a precipice. Endeavour after that which is aiding to your Art, and convenient, but avoid whatsoever is repugnant to it; as the 59*th.* rule teaches.

[¶ 126.] *Let every Member be made for its own Head,* &c.
30 That is to say, you ought not to set the Head of a Young man on the Body of an Old one; nor make a white Hand for a wither'd Body. Not to habit a *Hercules* in Taffeta; nor an *Apollo* in course stuff: Queens and persons of the first quality, whom you wou'd make appear Majestical, are not to be too negligently dress'd, or

---

4–5   rule . . . Perspective:] *rule . . . Perspective.* Q.
6–10   for example . . . Pillar . . . rule . . . Decorum] *for example . . . Pillar . . . rule . . . Decorum* Q.
11   agreeable.] ~: Q.   12   Decorum] *Decorum* Q.
21   Perspective] *Perspective* Q.   28   59*th.* rule] 59th∧ *rule* Q.

en dishabillee, no more than Old men: The Nymphs are not to be overcharg'd with drapery: In fine, let all that which accompanies your Figures, make them known for what effectively they are.

[¶ 128.] *Let the Figures to which Art cannot give a Voice, imitate the Mutes in their Actions,* &c. Mutes having no other way of speaking (or expressing their thoughts) but onely by their gestures and their actions, 'tis certain that they do it in a manner more expressive than those who have the use of Speech, for which reason the Picture which is mute ought to imitate them, so as to make it self understood.

[¶ 129.] *Let the principal Figure of the Subject,* &c. 'Tis one of the greatest blemishes of a Picture, not to give knowledge, at the first Sight, of the Subject which it represents. And truly nothing is more perplexing, than to extinguish, as it were, the principal Figure by the opposition of some others, which present themselves to us at the first view, and which carry a greater lustre. An Orator, who had undertaken to make a Panegyrick on *Alexander the Great,* and who had employ'd the strongest Figures of his Rhetorique in the praise of *Bucephalus,* would do quite the contrary to that which was expected from him; Because it would be believ'd that he rather took the Horse for his Subject than the Master. A Painter is like an Orator in this. He must dispose his matter in such sort, that all things may give place to his principal Subject. And if the other Figures, which accompany it, and are onely as Accessaries there, take up the chief place, and make themselves most remarkable, either by the Beauty of their Colours, or by the Splendour of the Light, which strikes upon them, they will catch the Sight, they will stop it short, and not suffer it to go further than themselves, till after some considerable space of time, to find out that which was not

---

1   *en dishabillee*] *errata page in* Q; indishabile Q.
6   Mutes] *paragraph break in* Q.
13–14   knowledge,... Sight,] ∼ʌ ... ∼ʌ Q.
15   extinguish,] ∼ʌ Q.
18–20   Panegyrick ... Rhetorique] *Panegyrick ... Rhetorique* Q.
23   Painter ... Orator] *Painter ... Orator* Q.
31   time,] ∼ʌ Q.

discern'd at first. The principal Figure in a Picture is like a King among his Courtiers, whom we ought to know at the first Glance, and who ought to dim the Lustre of all his Attendants. Those Painters who proceed otherwise, do just like those who in the relation of a story ingage themselves so foolishly in long digressions, that they are forc'd to conclude quite another way than they began.

[¶ 132.] *Let the Members be combin'd in the same manner as the Figures are,* &c. I cannot better compare a Grouppe of Figures, than to a Consort of Voices, which supporting themselves all together by their different parts make a Harmony, which pleasingly fills the Ears and flatters them; but if you come to separate them, and that all the parts are equally heard as loud as one another, they will stun you to that degree, that you would fancy your Ears were torn in pieces. 'Tis the same of Figures; if you so assemble them, that some of them sustain the others, and make them appear; and that all together they make but one entire Whole, then your Eyes will be fully satisfied: But if on the contrary, you divide them, your Eyes will suffer by seeing them all together dispers'd, or each of them in particular: All together, because the visual Rays are multiply'd by the Multiplicity of Objects; each of them in particular, because, if you fix your Sight on one, those which are about it will strike you and attract your Eyes to them, which extremely Pains them in this sort of Separation and Diversity of Objects. The Eye, for example, is satisfied with the Sight of one single Grape, and is distracted, if it carries it self at one view, to look upon many several Grapes which lie scatter'd on a Table: we must have the same regard for the Members; they aggrouppe and contrast each other in the same manner as the Figures do. Few Painters have observ'd this Precept as they ought, which is a most solid Foundation for the Harmony of a Picture.

9–11 Grouppe of Figures ... Consort of Voices ... Harmony] *Grouppe of Figures ... Consort of Voices ... Harmony* Q.
20 all together ... in particular:] *all together ... in particular.* Q.
20–21 All together] *All together* Q.
22 Objects; each of them in particular,] ~. *Each of them in particular;* Q.
28 Table:] ~, Q.

[¶ 137.] *The Figures in the Grouppes ought not to be like each other in their Motions,* &c. Take heed in this contrast to do nothing that is extravagant, and let your Postures be always natural. The Draperies, and all things that accompany the Figures, may enter into the contrast with the Members, and with the Figures themselves: And this is what our Poet means in these words of his Verses, *Cætera frangant.*

[¶ 145.] *One side of the Picture must not be void, while the other is fill'd,* &c. This sort of Symmetry, when it appears not affected, fills the Picture pleasingly; keeps it in a kind of balance; and infinitely delights the Eyes, which thereby contemplate the Work with more repose.

[¶ 152.] *As a Play is very seldom good, in which there are too many Actors,* &c. *Annibal Caracci* did not believe that a Picture cou'd be good, in which there were above twelve Figures. It was *Albano* who told our Authour this, and from his mouth I had it. The Reasons which he gave were, first, That he believ'd there ought not be above three great Grouppes of Figures in any Picture: And secondly, That Silence and Majesty were of necessity to be there, to render it beautifull; and neither the one nor the other cou'd possibly be in a multitude and crowd of Figures. But nevertheless, if you are constrain'd by the Subject; (As for Example, If you painted the Day of Judgment, the Massacre of the Innocents, a Battel, *&c.*) on such occasions you are to dispose things by great masses of Lights and Shadows, and union of Colours, without troubling your self to finish every thing in particular, independently one of the other, as is usual with Painters of a little Genius; and whose Souls are uncapable of embracing a great Design, or a great Composition.

> *Æmylium circa ludum, Faber imus & ungues*
> *Exprimet, & molles imitabitur ære capillos;*
> *Infelix Operis Summâ, quia ponere totum*
> *Nesciet.*

---

13   is very] is Q.
16   our Authour] our *Authour* Q.
22–24   As for Example . . . Day of Judgment . . . Massacre of the Innocents . . . Battel, *&c.*] *As for Example . . . Day of Judgment . . . Massacre of the Innocents . . . Battel,* &c. Q.
24   on] On Q.

The meanest Sculptor in th' Emylian Square,
Can imitate in Brass, the Nails and Hair;
Expert in Trifles, and a cunning Fool,
Able t' express the Parts, but not dispose the whole.

Says *Horace* in his *Art of Poetry.*

[¶ 162.] *The Extremities of the Joints must be seldom hidden,* *and the Extremities or End of the Feet never,* &c. These Extremities of the Joints are as it were the Hafts or Handles of the Members; for example, the Shoulders, the Elbows, the Thighs, and the Knees. And if a Drapery should be found on these ends of the Joints, 'tis the duty of Science and of Decorum, to mark them by Folds, but with great discretion; for what concerns the Feet, though they should be hidden by some part of the Drapery; nevertheless, if they are mark'd by Folds, and their shape be distinguish'd, they are suppos'd to be seen. The word *never,* is not here to be taken in the strictest Sense; he means but this, *so rarely* that it may seem we should avoid all occasions of dispensing with the Rule.

[¶ 164.] *The Figures which are behind others, have neither* *Grace nor Vigour,* &c. *Raphael* and *Julio Romano,* have perfectly observ'd this Maxime, and *Raphael* especially in his last Works.

[¶ 169.] *Avoid also those Lines and Contours which are equal,* *which make Parallels,* &c. He means principally to speak of the Postures so order'd, that they make together those Geometrical Figures which he condemns.

[¶ 176.] *Be not so strictly tied to Nature,* &c. This Precept is against two sorts of Painters; first against those who are so scrupulously tied to Nature, that they can do nothing without her, who copy her just as they believe they see her, without adding or retrenching any thing, though never so little, either for the Nudities or for the Draperies: And secondly, against those who Paint every thing by Practice, without being able to subject

---

5 Says] *indented in Q.*   5   *Art of Poetry*] Art of Poetry Q.
9 Members; for example] ~. *For example* Q.
17 *rarely*] ~, Q.   27   Precept] *Precept* Q.
32 Draperies:] ~. Q.

themselves to retouch any thing, or to examine by the Nature.
These last, properly speaking, are the Libertines of Painting,
as there are Libertines of Religion; who have no other Law
but the vehemence of their Inclinations which they are resolv'd
not to overcome: and in the same manner the Libertines of
Painting, have no other Model but a Rhodomontado Genius,
and very irregular, which violently hurries them away. Though
these two sorts of Painters, are both of them in vicious Extremes,
yet nevertheless the former sort seems to be the more support-
10 able; because though they do not imitate Nature as she is ac-
company'd by all her Beauties, and her Graces, yet at least they
imitate that Nature, which we know and daily see. Instead of
which the others show us a wild or salvage Nature, which is
not of our acquaintance, and which seems to be of a quite new
Creation.

[¶ 178.] *Whom you must have always present as a witness to
the truth,* &c. This passage seems to be wonderfully well said.
The nearer a Picture approaches to the truth, the better it is; and
though the Painter, who is its Author, be the first Judge of
20 the Beauties which are in it, he is nevertheless oblig'd not to
pronounce it, till he has first consulted Nature, who is an irre-
proachable evidence, and who will frankly, but withall truly,
tell you its Defects and Beauties, if you compare it with her
Work.

[¶ 188.] *And of all other things which discover to us the
Thoughts and Inventions of the* Græcians, *&c.* As good Books,
such as are *Homer* and *Pausanias:* the prints which we see of the
Antiquities, may extremely contribute to form our Genius, and
to give us great Ideas; in the same manner as the Writings of
30 good Authors, are capable of forming a good Style in those who
are desirous of writing well.

[¶ 193.] *If you have but one single Figure to work upon,* &c.
The reason of this is, That there being nothing to attract the
Sight but this onely Figure, the visual Rays will not be too

2–6 Libertines . . . Painting . . . Libertines . . . Religion . . . Libertines . . . Paint-
ing . . . Rhodomontado Genius] *Libertines . . . Painting . . . Libertines . . . Re-
ligion . . . Libertines . . . Painting . . . Rhodomontado Genius* Q.
8   vicious Extremes] *vicious Extremes* Q.
22   truly,] ~∧ Q.   27   *Pausanias:*] ~; Q.

much divided by the Diversity of Colours and Draperies; but onely take heed to put in nothing, which shall appear too sharp or too hard; and be mindfull of the 41*st*. Precept, which says, that two Extremities are never to touch each other either in Colour or in Light; but that there must be a mean, partaking of the one and of the other.

[¶ 195.] *Let the Draperies be nobly spread upon the Body; let the Folds be large,* &c. As *Raphael* practis'd, after he had for-saken the manner of *Pietro Perugino,* and principally in his 10 latter Works.

[¶ 196.] *And let them follow the order of the parts,* &c. As the fairest pieces of Antiquity will show us: And take heed, that the folds do not only follow the order of the parts, but that they also mark the most considerable Muscles; because that those Figures, where the drapery and the naked part are seen both together, are much more gracefull than the other.

[¶ 200.] *Without sitting too streight upon them,* &c. Painters ought not to imitate the Ancients in this circumstance; the an-cient Statuaries made their Draperies of wet Linen, on purpose 20 to make them sit close and streight to the parts of their Figures, for doing which they had great reason; and in following which the Painters would be much in the wrong: and you shall see upon what grounds those great Genius's of Antiquity, finding that it was impossible to imitate with Marble the fineness of stuffs or garments (which is not to be discern'd but by the Colours, the Reflexes, and more especially by the Lights and Shadows,) finding it, I say, out of their power to dispose of those things, thought they could not do better nor more prudentially, than to make use of such Draperies, as hinder'd not from seeing, 30 through their Folds, the delicacy of the Flesh, and the purity of the Out-lines; things which, truly speaking, they possest in the last perfection, and which in all appearance were the subject of their chief study. But Painters, on the contrary, who are to

3   41*st*.] *errata page in Q; 4th.* Q.   7   *Draperies*] *Drapery* Q.
12   us:] ~. Q.
25–27   (which ... Shadows,)] ∧~ ... ~,∧ Q.
27   it,... say,] ~∧ ... ~∧ Q.
29   Draperies,... seeing,] ~∧ ... ~∧ Q.
31   which,... speaking,] ~∧ ... ~∧ Q.

deceive the Sight, quite otherwise than Statuaries, are bound to
imitate the different sorts of Garments, such as they naturally
seem; and such as Colours, Reflexes, Lights and Shadows (of all
which they are Masters) can make them appear: Thus we see
that those who have made the nearest imitations of Nature,
have made use of such Stuffs (or Garments) which are familiar to
our Sight, and these they have imitated with so much Art that
in beholding them we are pleas'd that they deceive us; such were
Titian, Paul Veronese, Tintoret, Rubens, Van Dyck, and the
10 rest of the good Colourists, who have come nearest to the truth
of Nature: Instead of which, others who have scrupulously tied
themselves to the practice of the Ancients, in their Draperies,
have made their works crude and dry: and by this means have
found out the lamentable secret how to make their Figures
harder than even the Marble it self; as *Andrea Mantegna,* and
Pietro Perugino have done, and *Raphael* also had much of that
way in his first Works, in which we behold many small foldings
often repleated, which look like so many Whipcords. 'Tis true
these repetitions are seen in the Ancient Statues, and they are
20 very proper there: Because they who made use of wet Linen, and
close Draperies, to make their Figures look more tender, rea-
sonably foresaw that the Members would be too naked, if they
left not more than two or three Folds scarce appearing, such as
those sorts of Draperies afford the Sight, and therefore have us'd
those Repetitions of many Folds, yet in such a manner that the
Figures are always soft and tender, and thereby seem opposite
to the hardness of Marble. Add to this, that in Sculpture, 'tis
almost impossible that a Figure cloath'd with course Draperies,
can make a good effect on all the sides; and that in Painting the
30 Draperies of what kind soever they be, are of great advantage,
either to unite the Colours and the Grouppes, or to give such a
ground as one would wish to unite or to separate, or farther, to
produce such reflections as set off, or for filling void spaces, or
in short for many other advantages, which help to deceive the

---

Sight, and which are no ways necessary to Sculptors, since their Work is always of Relievo.

Three things may be inferr'd from what I have said concerning the rule of Draperies: First, that the Ancient Sculptors had reason to cloath their Figures as we see them; secondly, that Painters ought to imitate them in the order of their Folds, but not in their quality nor in their number; thirdly, That Sculptors are oblig'd to follow them as much as they can, without desiring to imitate unprofitably or improperly the manners of the Paint-

10 ers, and to make many ample Folds, which are insufferable hardnesses, and more like a Rock than a natural Garment. See the 211*th*. Remark, about the middle of it.

[¶ 202.] *And if the parts be too much distant from each other,* &c. 'Tis with intent to hinder (as we have said in the rule of Grouppes) the visual Rays, from being too much divided, and that the Eyes may not suffer by looking on so many objects, which are separated. *Guido* was very exact in this observation. See in the Text the end of the Rule which relates to Draperies.

[¶ 204.] *And as the Beauty of the Limbs consists not in the*

20 *quantity and rising of the Muscles,* &c. *Raphael* in the beginning of his Painting, has somewhat too much multiply'd the Folds; because being with reason charm'd with the graces of the Ancients, he imitated their Beauties somewhat too regularly; but having afterwards found that this quantity of Folds glitter'd too much upon the Limbs, and took off that Repose and Silence which in Painting are so friendly to the Eyes, he made use of a contrary conduct in the works which he painted afterwards, which was at that time when he began to understand the effect of Lights, of Grouppes, and the oppositions of the Lights and

30 Shadows, so that he wholly chang'd his manner, (this was about eight years before his death) and though he always gave a Grace to whatsoever he painted, yet he made appear in his latter works,

---

1-2 Sculptors . . . Relievo] *Sculptors . . . Relievo* Q.
4 Draperies:] ∼. Q.
4 Ancient Sculptors] *Ancient Sculptors* Q.
5 them; secondly] ∼. Secondly Q.   6 Painters] *Painters* Q.
7 number; thirdly] ∼. Thirdly Q.
7 Sculptors] *Sculptors* Q.   12 Remark,] *Remark*∧ Q.
18 Rule] *Rule* Q.   26 Eyes,] ∼; Q.

a Greatness, a Majesty, and a Harmony quite other than what
we see in his first manner: And this he did by lessening the num-
ber of his Folds, making them more large and more opposing
them, and by making the Masses of the Lights and Shadows
greater and more disentangl'd. Take the pains to examine these
his different manners in the Prints which we see of that Great
Man.

[¶ 210.] *As supposing them to be Magistrates, their Draperies
ought to be large,* &c. Yet make not your Draperies so large that
they may be big enough to cloath four or five Figures, as some
there are who follow that method. And take heed that the fold-
ing be natural and so dispos'd, that the Eye may be directed to
discover the Folds from the beginning of them to the end. By
Magistrates, he means all great and grave Persons, and such as
are advanc'd in age.

[¶ 211.] *If Ladies or Damsels, light and soft,* &c. By this name
of *Ladies, Maids,* or *Damsels,* he means all young persons, slen-
der, finely shap'd, aery and delicate; such as are Nymphs, and
Naiades, and Fountains. Angels are also comprehended under
this head, whose Drapery should be of pleasing Colours, and re-
sembling those which are seen in the Heavens, and chiefly when
they are suspended in the Air. They are only such sorts of light
habits as are subject to be ruffl'd by the Winds, which can bear
many Folds; yet so that they may be freed from any hardnesses.
'Tis easie for every one to judge that betwixt the Draperies of
Magistrates, and those of young Maids, there must be some me-
diocrity of Folds, such as are most commonly seen and observ'd,
as in the Draperies of a *Christ,* of a *Madonna,* of a King, a Queen,
or a Dutchess, and of other persons of Consideration and Maj-
esty; and those also who are of a middle age, with this distinc-
tion, that the Habits must be made more or less rich, according

4 Shadows] ∼, Q.
6–7 Great Man] *Great Man* Q.
18 delicate; such] ∼. Such Q.
18–19 Nymphs . . . Naiades . . . Fountains] *Nymphs . . . Naiades . . . Fountains* Q.
19 Angels] *Angels* Q.
26 Magistrates . . . young Maids,] *Magistrates . . . young Maids;* Q.
28–29 King . . . Queen . . . Dutchess] *King . . . Queen . . . Dutchess* Q.
30 age,] ∼ₐ Q.

to the dignity of the Persons; and that Cloth Garments may be distinguish'd from those of Silk, Sattin from Velvets, Brocard from Embroidery, and that, in one word, the Eye may be deceiv'd by the truth and the difference of the Stuffs. Take notice, if you please, that the light and tender Draperies having been onely given to the Female Sex, the Ancient Sculptors have avoided as much as they could to cloath the Figures of Men, because they thought, (as we have formerly said) that in Sculpture, Garments could not be well imitated, and that great Folds made a very bad effect. There are almost as many examples of this truth, as amongst the Ancients there are Statues of naked men. I will name only that of *Laocoon,* which according to all probability ought to have been cloath'd: And in effect what likelihood can there be, that the Son of a King, and the Priest of *Apollo* should appear naked in the actual Ceremony of Sacrifice? For the Serpents pass'd from the Isle of *Tenedos* to the *Trojan* Shore, and surpriz'd *Laocoon* and his Sons while they were sacrificing to *Neptune* on the Sea Shore, as *Virgil* witnesses in the second of his *Æneids.* Notwithstanding which, the *Sculptors who were Authors of this noble work had well consider'd, that they could not give Vestments suitable to the quality of the Persons represented, without making as it were a heap of Stones, whose Mass would rather be like a Rock, than those three admirable Figures, which will ever be the Admiration of all Ages. And for this reason of two inconveniences, they judg'd that of Draperies to be greater, than that which was against the truth it self.

* Polydorus, Athenodorus, *and* Agesander, *all* Rhodians.

This observation well confirms what I have said in the 200*th.* Remark. It seems to me, that it deserves you should make some reflection on it; and to establish it the better in your mind, I

1–3 Cloth Garments . . . Silk, Sattin . . . Velvets, Brocard . . . Embroidery] *Cloth Garments . . . Silk, Sattin . . . Velvets, Brocard . . . Embroidery* Q.
3 that, . . . word,] ~ₐ . . . ~ₐ Q.   4 notice,] ~ₐ Q.
6 Ancient Sculptors] *Ancient Sculptors* Q.
8 Sculpture,] ~ₐ Q.   15–16 Sacrifice?] ~. Q.
18 Sea Shore] *Sea Shore* Q.   19 Æneids] *Eneids* Q.
30 Remark] *Remark* Q.

will tell you, that *Michael Angelo,* following this Maxim, has
given the Prophets which he painted in the Chappel of the
Pope, such Draperies whose Folds are large, and whose Garments
are course; instead of which the *Moses,* which he has made in
Sculpture, is habited with a Drapery much more close to the
parts and holding more of the Ancients. Nevertheless he is a
Prophet as well as those in the Chappel, a man of the same
quality, and to whom *Michael Angelo* ought to have given the
same Draperies, if he had not been hinder'd by those very reasons
10 which have been given you.

[¶ 215.] *The Marks or Ensigns of Vertues,* &c. That is to say,
of the Sciences and Arts. The *Italians* call a man a *Vertuoso,* who
loves the noble Arts, and is a Critick in them. And amongst our
French Painters, the word *Vertueux,* is understood in the same
Signification.

[¶ 217.] *But let not the work be too much enrich'd with Gold
or Jewels,* &c. *Clemens Alexandrinus* relates, *That* Apelles *hav-
ing seen a* Helena, *which a young Scholar of
his had made and adorn'd with a great quantity*   Lib.2.*Pædag.*
20 *of Golden Ornaments and Jewels, said to him,*   cap.12.
"*My good Friend, though thou couldst not make her beautifull,
at least thou hast made her rich.*" Besides, that these glittering
things in Painting, as precious Stones prodigally strew'd over the
habits, are destructive to each other, because they draw the Sight
to several places at the same time, and that they hinder round
Bodies from turning and making their due effect; 'tis the very
quantity which often makes us judge that they are false. And
besides, it is to be presum'd, that precious things
are always rare. *Corinna,* that learned *Theban*   Plutarch.
30 Lady, reproach'd *Pindar,* whom she had five times overcome in

1–3 this Maxim . . . Prophets . . . Chappel . . . Pope] *this Maxim . . . Prophets
. . . Chappel . . . Pope* Q.
4   course;] ~, Q.
5–6 Sculpture . . . Ancients] *Sculpture . . . Ancients* Q.
7   Prophet . . . Chappel] *Prophet . . . Chappel* Q.
11   say,] ~ₐ Q.   17 *That* Apelles] That *Apelles* Q.
18+ *sidenote Pædag.*] Pædag. Q.   21–22 "*My . . . rich.*"] ₐ~ . . . ~·ₐ Q.
22 Besides, that] ~ₐ ~, Q.   24 habits,] ~ₐ Q.
28 besides,] ~ₐ Q.

Poetry, that he scatter'd through all his works the Flowers of *Parnassus* too prodigally, saying to him, *That men sow'd with the Hand, and not with the Sack:* for which reason a Painter ought to adorn his Vestments with great discretion. And precious Stones look exceedingly well, when they are set in those places which we would make to come out of the Picture; as for example, on a Shoulder, or an Arm, to tie some Drapery, which of it self is of no strong colouring. They do also perfectly well with white and other light Colours, which are us'd in bringing the Parts or
10 Bodies forward, because Jewels make a show and glitter through the opposition of the great Lights in the deep brown, which meet together.

[¶ 220.] *'Tis very expedient to make a model of those things which we have not in our Sight, and whose nature is difficult to be retain'd in the Memory,* &c. As for example, the Grouppes of many Figures, the Postures difficult to be long kept, the Figures in the Air, in Ceilings, or much rais'd above the Sight; and even of Animals, which are not easily to be dispos'd.

By this rule we plainly see how necessary it is for a Painter
20 to know how to model, and to have many Models of soft Wax. *Paul Veronese* had so good store of them, with so great a quantity of different sorts, that he would paint a whole historical Composition on a perspective Plan, how great and how diversified soever it were. *Tintoret* practis'd the same, and *Michael Angelo* (as *Giovan. Bapt. Armenini* relates) made use of it, for all the Figures of his *day of Judgment.* 'Tis not that I would advise any one who would make any very considerable work, to finish after these sorts of Models, but they will be of vast use and advantage to see the Masses of great Lights, and great Shad-
30 ows, and the effect of the whole together. For what remains, you are to have a *Lay-man almost as big as the life, for every Figure in particular, besides the nat- ural Figure before you, on which you must also look, and call it for a witness, which must first

* *A Figure made of wood or cork, turn- ing upon joints.*

---

6 as for example] *as for example* Q.   7 Arm,] ~ₐ Q.
15 As for example] *As for example* Q.
20 model] *model* Q.

confirm the thing to you, and afterwards to the Spectators as it is in reality.

You may make use of these Models with delight, if you set them on a Perspective Plan, which will be in the manner of a Table made on purpose. You may either raise or let it down according to your convenience; and if you look on your Figures through a hole so contriv'd, that it may be mov'd up and down, it will serve you for a point of Sight and a point of Distance, when you have once fix'd it.

10   The same hole will further serve you, to set your Figures in the Ceiling, and dispos'd upon a Grate of Iron-wire, or supported in the Air, by little Strings rais'd at discretion, or by both ways together.

You may joyn to your Figures what you see fitting, provided that the whole be proportion'd to them; and in short what you your self may judge to be of no greater bigness than theirs. Thus, in whatsoever you do there will be more of truth seen, your work it self will give you infinite delight, and you will avoid many doubts and difficulties which often hinder you, and chiefly for
20 what relates to lineal perspective, which you will there infallibly find, provided that you remember to proportion all things to the greatness of your Figures and especially the points of Sight and of Distance; but for what belongs to aerial perspective, that not being found, the judgment must supply it. *Tintoret,* as *Ridolphi* tells us in his *Life,* had made Chambers of Board and Past-board, proportion'd to his Models, with Doors and Windows, through which he distributed on his Figures artificial Lights, as much as he thought reasonable, and often pass'd some part of the night to consider and observe the effect of his Compositions.
30 His Models were of two Foot high.

[¶ 221.] *We are to consider the places where we lay the Scene of the Picture,* &c. This is what Monsieur *de Chambray,* calls, to

4   Perspective Plan] *Perspective Plan* Q.
10–12   you, . . . Ceiling, . . . Air,] ~∧ . . . ~∧ . . . ~∧ Q.
20–23   lineal perspective . . . aerial perspective] *lineal perspective . . . aerial perspective* Q.
25   *Life*] life Q.
26   Models,] ~∧ Q.
30   Models] *Models* Q.

do things according to Decorum. See what he says of it, in the Interpretation of that word in his Book of the *Perfection of Painting*. 'Tis not sufficient that in the Picture there be nothing found which is contrary to the place, where the action which is represented, passes; but we ought besides, to mark out the place and make it known to the Spectator by some particular Address, that his mind may not be put to the pains of discovering it, as whether it be *Italy*, or *Spain*, or *Greece*, or *France*; whether it be near the Sea shore, or the Banks of some River,
10 whether it be the *Rhine*, or the *Loyre*; the *Po*, or the *Tyber*; and so of other things, if they are essential to the History. Nealces, *a man of Wit and an ingenious Paint-*   Lib. 35.12.
er, as *Pliny* tells us, *being to paint a Naval Fight betwixt the* Egyptians *and the* Persians, *and being willing to make it known that the Battle was given upon the* Nile, *whose waters are of the same Colour with the Sea, drew an Ass drinking on the Banks of the River, and a Crocodile endeavouring to surprize him.*

[¶ 222.] *Let a Nobleness and Grace*, &c. It is difficult enough
20 to say what this Grace of Painting is; 'tis to be conceiv'd and understood much more easily than to be explain'd by words. It proceeds from the illuminations of an excellent Mind, which cannot be acquir'd, by which we give a certain turn to things which makes them pleasing. A Figure may be design'd with all its proportions, and have all its parts regular, which notwithstanding all this, shall not be pleasing, if all those parts are not put together in a certain manner, which attracts the Eye to them, and holds it fix'd upon them: For which reason there is a difference to be made betwixt Grace and Beauty. And it seems
30 that *Ovid* had a mind to distinguish them, when he said (speaking of *Venus*)

---

1 Decorum] *Decorum* Q.
2 Interpretation . . . that word . . . Book] *Interpretation . . . that word . . . Book* Q.
12 Nealces] "Nealces Q.
12–18 *each printed italic line preceded by inverted double commas in* Q.
12+ *sidenote* 35] 25 Q.
13 as *Pliny* tells us] *as* Pliny *tells us* Q.
20 Grace of Painting] *Grace of Painting* Q.

Multaque cum formâ gratia mista fuit.

A matchless Grace was with her Beauty mix'd.

And *Suetonius* speaking of *Nero,* says, he was rather beautifull than gracefull, *Vultu pulchro, magis quam venusto.* How many fair women do we see, who please us much less than others, who have not such beautifull Features? 'Tis by this grace that *Raphael* has made himself the most renown'd of all the *Italians,* as *Apelles* by the same means carry'd it above all the *Greeks.*

[¶ 233.] *This is that in which the greatest difficulty consists,*
10 &c. For two reasons, both because great study is to be made as well upon the ancient Beauties and on noble Pictures, as upon nature it self: and also because that part depends entirely on the Genius, and seems to be purely the gift of Heaven, which we have receiv'd at our Birth, upon which account our Author adds, *Undoubtedly we see but few, whom in this particular,* Jupiter *has regarded with a gracious Eye, so that it belongs only to those elevated Souls, who partake somewhat of Divinity to work such mighty wonders.* Though they who have not altogether receiv'd from Heaven this precious Gift, cannot acquire
20 it without great Labour, nevertheless 'tis needfull in my opinion, that both the one and the other should perfectly learn the character of every Passion.

All the Actions of the sensitive Appetite are in Painting call'd *Passions,* because the Soul is agitated by them, and because the Body suffers through them, and is sensibly alter'd. They are those divers Agitations and different Motions of the Body in general, and of every one of its parts in particular, that our excellent Painter ought to understand, on which he ought to make his study, and to form to himself a perfect Idea of them. But
30 it will be proper for us to know in the first place, that the Philosophers admit eleven, Love, Hatred, Desire, Shunning, Joy, Sadness, Hope, Despair, Boldness, Fear and Anger. The

---

4 gracefull,] ~. Q.   13 Genius] *Genius* Q.
23 sensitive Appetite] *sensitive Appetite* Q.
31–32 Love ... [*to*] ... Fear] *set in italics in* Q.
32 Anger] *Anger* Q.

Painters have multiply'd them not onely by their different De-
grees, but also by their different Species, for they will make, for
example, six persons in the same degree of Fear, who shall ex-
press that Passion all of them differently. And 'tis that diversity
of Species which distinguishes those Painters who are able Art-
ists, from those whom we may call *Mannerists,* and who repeat
five or six times over in the same Picture the same Airs of a
Head. There are a vast number of other Passions, which are as
the Branches of those which we have nam'd; we might for exam-
10 ple, under the Notion of Love, comprehend Grace, Gentleness
and Civility; Caresses, Embraces, and Kisses, Tranquillity and
Sweetness; and without examining whether all these things
which Painters comprize under the name of *Passions,* can be
reduc'd to those of the Philosophers, I am of opinion that every
one may use them at his pleasure, and that he may study them
after his own manner; the name makes nothing. One may even
make Passions of Majesty, fierceness, Dissatisfaction, Care, Ava-
rice, Sloathfulness, Envy, and many other things like these. These
Passions (as I have said,) ought to be learnt from the life it self,
20 or to be studied on the Ancient Statues and excellent Pictures:
we ought to see, for example, all things which belong to Sadness,
or serve to express it, to design them carefully, and to imprint
in our Memories after such a manner, as we may distinctly un-
derstand seven or eight kinds of them more or less, and imme-
diately after draw them upon Paper without any other Original
than the Image which we have conceiv'd of them. We must be

1–3 Degrees . . . Species . . . for example . . . Fear] *Degrees . . . Species . . . for
example . . . Fear* Q.
5–6 Species . . . able Artists] *Species . . . able Artists* Q.
7 Airs] Hairs Q.
10–14 Grace, Gentleness . . . Civility; Caresses, Embraces . . . Kisses, Tranquillity
. . . Sweetness . . . Philosophers] *Grace, Gentleness . . . Civility; Caresses, Embraces
. . . Kisses, Tranquillity . . . Sweetness . . . Philosophers* Q.
17–18 Majesty . . . [to] . . . Envy] *set in italics in* Q.
18 these] *these* Q.
19–21 Passions . . . Ancient Statues . . . excellent Pictures . . . for example . . .
Sadness] *Passions . . . Ancient Statues . . . excellent Pictures . . . for example . . .
Sadness* Q.
22 it,] ~∧ Q.
25–26 Original . . . Image] *Original . . . Image* Q.

perfect Masters of them: but above all, we must make sure of possessing them throughly. We are to know that it is such or such a stroke, or such a Shadow stronger or weaker, which make such or such a Passion in this or that degree. And thus, if any one should ask you, what makes in Painting the Majesty of a King, the Gravity of a Hero, the Love of a *Christ,* the Grief of a *Madonna,* the Hope of the *good Thief,* the Despair of the *bad One,* the Grace and Beauty of a *Venus,* and in fine the Character of any Passion whatsoever, you may answer positively, on
10 the spot, and with assurance, that it is such a Posture or such lines in the parts of the Face, form'd of such or such a fashion, or even the one and the other both together: for the parts of the Body separately, make known the Passions of the Soul or else conjoyntly one with the other. But of all the parts the Head is that which gives the most of Life, and the most of Grace to the Passion, and which alone contributes more to it, than all the rest together. The others separately can onely express some certain Passions, but the Head expresses all of them; nevertheless there are some which are more particular to it; as, for example, Hu-
20 mility, which it expresses by the stooping or bending of the Head; Arrogance, when it is lifted, or as we say, toss'd up; Languishment, when we hang it on one side, or lean it upon one Shoulder; Obstinacy (or as the *French* calls it *Opiniatreté,*) with a certain stubborn, unruly, barbarous Humour, when 'tis held upright, stiff, and poiz'd betwixt the Shoulders. And of the rest,

4 Passion] *Passion* Q.
5–9 Majesty . . . King . . . Gravity . . . Hero . . . Love . . . Grief . . . Hope . . . Despair . . . Grace . . . Beauty . . . Character . . . Passion] *Majesty . . . King . . . Gravity . . . Hero . . . Love . . . Grief . . . Hope . . . Despair . . . Grace . . . Beauty . . . Character . . . Passion* Q.
10–11 such a Posture . . . such lines . . . Face . . . such . . . such a fashion] *such a Posture . . . such lines . . . Face . . . such . . . such a fashion* Q.
13 Passions . . . Soul] *Passions . . . Soul* Q.
14–16 parts . . . Head . . . Life . . . Grace . . . Passion] *parts . . . Head . . . Life . . . Grace . . . Passion* Q.
17–18 others separately . . . Passions . . . Head . . . all of them] *others separately . . . Passions . . . Head . . . all of them* Q.
19–20 for example, Humility] *for example, Humility* Q.
21 Head;] *Head.* Q.   21 Arrogance] *Arrogance* Q.
21 up;] ~. Q.
21–22 Languishment] *Languishment* Q.
23 Shoulder;] ~. Q.   23 Obstinacy] *Obstinacy* Q.

there are many marks more easily conceiv'd than they can be express'd; as, Bashfulness, Admiration, Indignation, and Doubt. 'Tis by the Head that we make known more visibly our Supplications, our Threatnings, our Mildness, our Haughtiness, our Love, our Hatred, our Joy, our Sadness, our Humility; in fine, 'tis enough to see the Face, and to understand the Mind at half a word. Blushing and Paleness speak to us, as also the mixture of them both.

10 The parts of the Face do all of them contribute to expose the Thoughts of our Hearts; but above the rest, the Eyes, which are as it were the two Windows through which the Soul looks out and shows it self. The Passions which they more particularly express, are Pleasure, Languishment, Disdain, Severity, Sweetness, Admiration and Anger. Joy and Sadness may bear their parts, if they did not more especially proceed from the Eye-brows and the Mouth. And the two parts last nam'd agree more particularly in the expression of those two Passions; nevertheless if you joyn the Eyes as a third, you will have the Product of a wonderfull Harmony for all the Passions of the Soul.

20 The Nose has no Passion which is particular to it, it onely lends its assistance to the others before nam'd, by the stretching of the Nostrils, which is as much mark'd in Joy, as it is in Sadness. And yet it seems that Scorn makes us wrinkle up the Nose and stretch the Nostrils also, at the same time drawing up the

---

2 Bashfulness, Admiration, Indignation . . . Doubt] *Bashfulness, Admiration, Indignation . . . Doubt* Q.
3–6 Head . . . Supplications . . . Threatnings . . . Mildness . . . Haughtiness . . . Love . . . Hatred . . . Joy . . . Sadness . . . Humility . . . Face . . . Mind] *Head . . . Supplications . . . Threatnings . . . Mildness . . . Haughtiness . . . Love . . . Hatred . . . Joy . . . Sadness . . . Humility . . . Face . . . Mind* Q.
7 Blushing and Paleness] *Blushing and Paleness* Q.
9–10 Face . . . Hearts . . . Eyes] *Face . . . Hearts . . . Eyes* Q.
12 Passions] *Passions* Q.
13–14 Pleasure . . . [to] . . . Admiration] *set in italics in* Q.
14 Anger] *Anger* Q.
14–16 Joy . . . Sadness . . . Eye-brows . . . Mouth] *Joy . . . Sadness . . . Eyebrows . . . Mouth* Q.
17–19 Passions . . . Eyes . . . Passions . . . Soul] *Passions . . . Eyes . . . Passions . . . Soul* Q.
20–23 Nose . . . Nostrils . . . Joy . . . Sadness] *Nose . . . Nostrils . . . Joy . . . Sadness* Q.
23–24 Scorn . . . Nose . . . Nostrils] *Scorn . . . Nose . . . Nostrils* Q.
24 time] ~, Q.

upper Lip to the place which is near the corners of the Mouth.
The Ancients made the Nose the seat of Derision; *eum subdolæ
irrisioni dicaverunt,* says *Pliny;* that is, *they dedicated the Nose
to a cunning sort of Mockery.* We read in the 3d. Satyre of *Per-
sius, Disce, sed ira cadat Naso, rugosaque sanna; Learn, but let
your Anger fall from your Nose and the sneering Wrinkles be
dismounted.* And *Philostratus* in the Picture of *Pan* whom the
Nymphs had bound, and scornfully insulted over, says of that
God; *that before this, he was accustom'd to sleep with a peace-*
10 *able Nose, softning in his slumbers the Wrinkles of it, and the
Anger which commonly mounted to that part; but now his
Nostrils were widen'd to the last degree of Fury.* For my own
part, I should rather believe that the Nose was the seat of Wrath
in Beasts than in Mankind, and that it was unbecoming of any
God but onely *Pan,* who had very much of the Beast in him, to
wrinkle up his Nose in Anger, like other Animals. The moving
of the Lips ought to be but moderate, if it be in Conversation,
because we speak much more by the Tongue than by the Lips:
And if you make the Mouth very open, 'tis onely when you are
20 to express the violence of Passion, and more properly of Anger.
    For what concerns the Hands, they are the Servants of the
Head, they are his Weapons and his Auxiliaries; without them
the action is weak, languishing, and half dead; their Motions
which are almost infinite, make innumerable expressions: Is it
not by them, that we desire, that we hope, that we promise, that

---

1   upper Lip ... Mouth] *upper Lip ... Mouth* Q.
2   Ancients ... Nose ... Derision] *Ancients ... Nose ... Derision* Q.
3–4   they ... [to] ... Mockery] *set in romans in* Q.
4   Satyre] *Satyre* Q.
5–7   Learn ... [to] ... dismounted] *set in romans in* Q.
8   Nymphs] *Nymphs* Q.
9–12   *each printed italic line preceded by inverted double commas in* Q.
13–16   Nose . . . Wrath . . . Nose . . . Anger] *Nose . . . Wrath . . . Nose . . .
Anger* Q.
17–20   Lips . . . Conversation . . . Tongue . . . Lips . . . Mouth . . . Passion . . .
Anger] *Lips . . . Conversation . . . Tongue . . . Lips . . . Mouth . . . Passion . . .
Anger* Q.
21–22   Hands ... Head] *Hands ... Head* Q.
23   dead;] ∼, Q.
25–161:1   them . . . desire . . . hope . . . promise . . . call towards us . . . reject]
them ... desire ... hope ... promise ... call towards us ... reject Q.

we call towards us, and that we reject? besides, they are the in-
struments of our Threats, of our Petitions, of the Horror which
we show for things, and of the Praises which we give them: By
them we fear, we ask Questions, we approve, and we refuse, we
show our Joy and our Sadness, our Doubts, and our Lamenta-
tions, our Concernments of Pity, and our Admirations. In short,
it may be said, that they are the Language of the Dumb, that they
contribute not a little to the speaking of the universal Tongue,
common to all the World, which is that of Painting.

10   Now to tell you how these parts are to be dispos'd, so as to
express the different Passions, is impossible; no precise Rules can
be given of it, both because the task it self is infinite, and also
because every one is left to the Conduct of his own Genius, and
to the Fruit of his former Studies; onely remember to be care-
full, that all the actions of your Figures must be natural. *It seems
to me, says Quinctilian, speaking of the Passions, That this part
which is so noble and so great, is not altogether unaccessible, and
that an easie way may be found to it; 'tis to consider nature and
to copy her, for the Spectators are satisfied, when in artificial*
20 *things they can discern that nature which they are accustom'd to
behold.* This passage of *Quinctilian* is perfectly explain'd by the
words of an excellent Master which our Author proposes to us
for a rule: they are these which follow, *That the studied Motions
of the Soul, are never so natural as those which we see in the
transport of a true passion.* These Motions will better be ex-
press'd, and be much more natural, if we enter into the same
thoughts, become of the same piece, and imagine our selves to
be in the same circumstances with those whom we would repre-

1–3 they ... Threats ... Petitions ... Horror ... Praises] *they ... Threats ...
Petitions ... Horror ... Praises* Q.
4–6 fear ... ask Questions ... approve ... refuse ... Joy ... Sadness ... Doubts
... Lamentations ... Concernments of Pity ... Admirations] *fear ... ask Ques-
tions ... approve ... refuse ... Joy ... Sadness ... Doubts ... Lamentations
... Concernments of Pity ... Admirations* Q.
7–9 Language ... Dumb ... universal Tongue ... Painting] *Language ...
Dumb ... universal Tongue ... Painting* Q.
11–13 Passions ... Rules ... Genius] *Passions ... Rules ... Genius* Q.
15 It] "*It* Q.
15–21 *each printed italic line preceded by inverted double commas in* Q.
23 follow,] ~. Q.

sent. *For Nature,* says *Horace* in his *Art of Poetry, disposes the
inside of Mankind to all sorts of Fortunes, sometimes she makes
us contented, sometimes she drives us into Choler, and some-
times she so oppresses us with Grief, that she seems to tread us
down and plunge us into mortal Anxieties; and on all these occa-
sions, she drives outwards the Motions of the Heart by the
Tongue which is her Interpreter.* Now instead of the Tongue,
let the Painter say by the Actions, which are her Interpreters.
What means have we, (says *Quinctilian,*) *to give a Colour to a*
10 *thing if we have not the same Colour? 'tis necessary that we our
selves should first be touch'd with a Passion before we endeavour
to move others with it. And how,* continues he, *can we be touch'd,
since the Passions are not in our power? This is the way, in my
opinion; We must form to our selves the Visions and Images of
absent things, as if they were in reality before our Eyes; and he
who conceives these Images with the greatest strength of Imagi-
nation, shall possess that part of the Passions with the most ad-
vantage and the greatest ease.* But we must take care, as I have
already said, that in these visions, the Motions may be natural,
20 for there are some who imagine they have given abundance of
Light to their Figures, when they have made them do violent
and extravagant Actions, which we may more reasonably call
the Convulsions or Contorsions of the Body, than the Passions
of the Mind; and by this means often put themselves to much
pains, to find a strong Passion, where no Passion is requir'd.
Add to all that I have said concerning the Passions, that we are
to have a very serious regard to the quality of the Persons who

---

1 *For*] *"For* Q.
1–7 *each printed italic line preceded by inverted double commas in* Q.
1 *Art of Poetry*] Art of Poetry Q.
7–8 Tongue . . . Actions] *Tongue . . . Actions* Q.
9 *What*] *"What* Q.
9–18 *each printed italic line preceded by inverted double commas in* Q.
10 *Colour?*] ~; Q.
13 *way,*] ~ₐ Q.
21–24 violent . . . extravagant Actions . . . Convulsions . . . Contorsions of the
Body . . . Passions of the Mind] *violent . . . extravagant Actions . . . Convulsions
. . . Contorsions of the Body . . . Passions of the Mind* Q.

are to be express'd in Passions. The Joy of a King ought not to
resemble that of a Serving-man. And the Fierceness of a private
Soldier must not be like that of an Officer. In these differences
consists all the Fineness and Delicacy of the Passions. *Paulo
Lomazzo* has written at large on every Passion in particular, in
his second Book, but beware you dwell not too long upon it,
and endeavour not to force your Genius.

[¶ 247.] *Some Reliques of it took Sanctuary under ground,*
&c. All the ancient Painting that was in *Italy* perish'd in the In-
10 vasion of the *Hunns* and *Goths,* excepting those works which
were hidden under ground or there painted, which, by reason
they had not been much expos'd to view, were preserv'd from
the insolence of those Barbarians.

[¶ 256.] *The Cromatique part or Colouring,* &c. The third
and last part of Painting, is call'd the *Cromatique* or *Colouring.*
Its object is Colour, for which reason, Lights and Shadows are
therein also comprehended, which are nothing else but white
and brown (or dark,) and by consequence have their place among
the Colours. *Philostratus* says in his life of *Apollonius, That
20 it may be truly call'd Painting which is made only with two
Colours, provided the Lights and Shadows be observ'd in it:
for there we behold the true resemblance of things with their
Beauties; we also see the Passions, though without other Colours:
so much of life may be also express'd in it, that we may perceive
even the very Bloud: the Colour of the Hair and of the Beard,
are likewise to be discern'd, and we can distinguish without
confusion, the fair from the black, and the young from the old,
the differences betwixt the white and the flaxen hair; we dis-
tinguish with ease betwixt the* Moors *and the* Indians; *not onely*

1 Passions] *Passions* Q.
1–2 Joy ... King ... Serving-man] *Joy ... King ... Serving-man* Q.
2–3 Fierceness ... private Soldier ... Officer] *Fierceness ... private Soldier ...
Officer* Q.
4 Fineness ... Delicacy ... Passions] *Fineness ... Delicacy ... Passions* Q.
5–6 Passion ... second Book] *Passion ... second Book* Q.
11 which,] ~_∧ Q.   13 Barbarians] *Barbarians* Q.
15 *Colouring*] Colouring Q.
16–19 Colour ... Colours] *Colour ... Colours* Q.
19 *That*] "*That* Q.
19–164:3 *each printed italic line preceded by inverted double commas in Q.*

*by the Camus Noses of the Blacks, their woolly Hair and their
high Jaws, but also by that black Colour which is natural to
them.* We may add to what *Philostratus* has said, that with two
onely Colours, the Light and the Dark, there is no sort of Stuff
or Habit but may be imitated. We say then, that the colouring
makes its observations on the Masses or Bodies of the Colours,
accompany'd with Lights and Shadows more or less evident by
degrees of diminution, according to the Accidents: First of a
luminous Body, as for example, the Sun or a Torch; Secondly,
10 of a diaphanous or transparent Body, which is betwixt us and the
object, as the Air either pure or thick, or a red Glass, *&c.;*
Thirdly, of a solid Body illuminated, as a Statue of white Mar-
ble, a green Tree, a black Horse, *&c.;* Fourthly, from his part,
who regards the Body illuminated, as beholding it either near or
at a distance, directly in a right Angle, or aside in an obtuse
Angle, from the top to the bottom, or from the bottom to the
top. This part, in the knowledge which it has of the vertue of
Colours, and the Friendship which they have with each other,
and also their Antipathies, comprehends the Strength, the Re-
20 lievo, the Briskness, and the Delicacy which are observ'd in good
Pictures; the management of Colours, and the labour depend
also on this last part.

[¶ 263.] *Her Sister,* &c. That is to say, the Design or Drawing,
which is the second part of Painting, which consisting onely of
Lines, stands altogether in need of the Colouring to appear. 'Tis
for this reason, that our Author calls this part her Sisters Pro-
curer, that is, the Colouring shows us the Design, and makes us
fall in love with it.

[¶ 267.] *The Light produces all kinds of Colours,* &c. Here
30 are three Theorems successively following, which our Author

1   *Camus*] Camus Q.   5   imitated. We] ~; we Q.
8   Accidents:] ~. Q.   9   Body,] ~; Q.
9   Torch;] ~. Q.   11–13   *&c.;* . . . *&c.;*] &c.ʌ . . . &c.ʌ Q.
17   part,] ~ʌ Q.
19   comprehends] *errata page in Q;* it comprehends Q.
21   Pictures;] ~, Q.
21   Colours] *Colours* Q.
23–25   Design . . . Drawing . . . second part . . . Painting . . . Colouring] *Design
. . . Drawing . . . second part . . . Painting . . . Colouring* Q.
26–27   Procurer . . . Colouring] *Procurer . . . Colouring* Q.
30   Theorems] *Theorems* Q.

proposes to us, that from thence we may draw some conclusions. You may likewise find others, which are in the nature of so many Propositions to which we ought to agree, that from thence we may draw the Precepts contain'd in the following part of this Treatise; they are all founded on the Sense of Seeing.

[¶ 280.] *Which ought to be the most,* &c. See the Remark of number 152.

[¶ 283.] *That you may make the Bodies appear enlightned by the shadows which bound your Sight,* &c. That is properly
10 to say, that after the great Lights, there must be great Shadows, which we call *reposes:* because in reality the Sight would be tired, if it were attracted by a Continuity of glittering objects. The Lights may serve for a repose to the Darks, and the Darks to the Lights. I have said in another place, that a Grouppe of Figures ought to be consider'd, as a Choir of Musick, in which the Bases support the Trebles, and make them to be heard with greater pleasure. These reposes are made two several ways, one of which is Natural, the other Artificial. The Natural is made by an extent of Lights or of Shadows; which naturally and neces-
20 sarily follow solid Bodies, or the Masses of solid Bodies ag-groupp'd when the Light strikes upon them. And the Artificial consists in the Bodies of Colours, which the Painter gives to certain things, such as pleases him; and composes them in such a manner, that they do no injury to the objects which are near them. A Drapery, for example, which is made yellow or red on some certain place, in another place may be brown, and will be more suitable to it, to produce the effect requir'd. We are to take occasion as much as possibly we can, to make use of the first manner, and to find the repose of which we speak, by the
30 Light and by the Shadow, which naturally accompany solid

3–5 Propositions . . . Precepts . . . Treatise . . . Seeing] *Propositions . . . Precepts . . . Treatise . . . Seeing* Q.
6–7 Remark of number] *Remark of number* Q.
11 *reposes*] reposes Q.
14–16 Grouppe of Figures . . . Choir of Musick . . . Bases . . . Trebles] *Grouppe of Figures . . . Choir of Musick . . . Bases . . . Trebles* Q.
18 Natural . . . Artificial] *Natural . . . Artificial* Q.
18 Natural] *Natural* Q.
21 Artificial] *Artificial* Q.
25 for example] *for example* Q.

Bodies. But since the Subjects on which we work are not always favourable to dispose the Bodies as we desire, a Painter in such a case may take his advantage by the Bodies of Colours, and put into such places as ought to be darken'd, Draperies or other things which we may suppose to be naturally brown and sully'd, which will produce the same effect and give him the same reposes as the Shadows would which could not be caus'd by the disposition of the objects.

Thus, an understanding Painter will make his advantages
10 both of the one manner and the other. And if he makes a design to be grav'd, he is to remember that the Gravers dispose not their Colours as the Painters do; and that by consequence he must take occasion to find the reason of his Design, in the natural Shadows of the Figures, which he has dispos'd to cause the effect. *Rubens* has given us a full information of this in those prints of his which he caus'd to be engrav'd; and I believe that nothing was ever seen more beautifull in that kind: the whole knowledge of Grouppes, of the Lights and Shadows, and of those Masses which *Titian* calls a *Bunch of Grapes,* is there expos'd so
20 clearly to the Sight, that the view of those Prints and the carefull observation of them, might very much contribute to the forming of an able Painter. The best and fairest of them are graven by *Vorsterman, Pontius,* and *Bolsvert,* all of them admirable Gravers, whose works *Rubens* himself took care to oversee, and which without doubt you will find to be excellent if you examine them. But expect not there the Elegance of Design, nor the Correctness of the Out-lines.

'Tis not but the Gravers can, and ought to imitate the Bodies of the Colours by the degrees of the Lights and Shadows, as much
30 as they shall judge that this imitation may produce a good effect: on the contrary, 'tis impossible in my opinion to give much strength to what they grave, after the works of the School, and of all those who have had the knowledge of Colours and of the Contrast of the Lights and Shadows, without imitating in some

---

11–13 Gravers . . . Painters . . . Design] *Gravers . . . Painters . . . Design* Q.
20–22 Prints . . . able Painter] *Prints . . . able Painter* Q.
24 Gravers] *Gravers* Q.
26–27 Elegance . . . Design . . . Correctness . . . Out-lines] *Elegance . . . Design . . . Correctness . . . Out-lines* Q.

sort the Colour of the Objects, according to the relation which
they have to the degrees of white and black. We see certain
Prints of good Gravers different in their kinds, where these
things are observ'd, and which have a wonderfull strength. And
there appears in publick of late years, a Gallery of Arch-duke
Leopold, which though very ill graven, yet shows some part of
the Beauty of its Originals, because the Gravers who have exe-
cuted it, though otherwise they were sufficiently ignorant, have
observ'd in almost the greatest parts of their Prints, the Bodies
10 of Colours in the relation which they have to the degrees of the
Lights and Shadows. I could wish the Gravers would make some
reflection upon this whole Remark, 'tis of wonderfull conse-
quence to them; for when they have attain'd to the knowledge of
these reposes, they will easily resolve those difficulties which
many times perplex them: And then chiefly when they are to
engrave after a Picture, where neither the Lights and Shadows,
nor the Bodies of the Colours are skilfully observ'd, though in
its other parts the Picture may be well perform'd.

[¶ 286.] *In the same manner as we behold it in a Convex*
20 *Mirror,* &c. A Convex Mirror alters the objects which are in the
middle, so that it seems to make them come out from the Super-
ficies. The Painter must do in the same manner in respect of the
Lights and Shadows of his Figures, to give them more Relievo
and more Strength.

[¶ 290.] *And let those which turn be of broken Colours, as
being less distinguish'd and nearer to the borders,* &c. 'Tis the
duty of a Painter, even in this also, to imitate the Convex Mirror,
and to place nothing which glares either in Colour or in Light
at the borders of his Picture; for which, there are two reasons,
30 the first is, that the Eye at the first view directs it self to the midst
of the object, which is presented to it, and by consequence, must
there necessarily find the principal object, in order to its satis-
faction. And the other reason is, that the sides or borders, being

3 Gravers] *Gravers* Q.
5–7 Gallery ... Originals] *Gallery ... Originals* Q.
11–12 Gravers ... whole Remark] *Gravers ... whole Remark* Q.
20–22 Convex Mirror ... Superficies] *Convex Mirror ... Superficies* Q.
27 Painter ... Convex Mirror] *Painter ... Convex Mirror* Q.
33–168:1 borders, ... work,] ~∧ ... ~∧ Q.

overcharg'd with a strong and glittering work, attract the Eyes thither, which are in a kind of Pain, not to behold a continuity of that work, which is on the sudden interrupted, by the borders of the Picture; instead of which the borders being lighten'd and eas'd of so much work, the Eye continues fixt on the Center of the Picture, and beholds it with greater pleasure. 'Tis for the same reason, that in a great composition of Figures, those which coming most forward, are cut off by the bottom of the Picture, will always make an ill effect.

10   [¶ 329.] *A bunch of Grapes,* &c. 'Tis sufficiently manifest, that *Titian* by this judicious and familiar comparison, means that a Painter ought to collect the objects, and to dispose them in such a manner, as to compose one whole; the several contiguous parts of which, may be enlighten'd, many shadow'd, and others of broken Colours to be in the turnings; as on a Bunch of Grapes, many Grapes, which are the parts of it, are in the Light, many in the Shadow, and the rest faintly colour'd to make them go farther back. *Titian* once told *Tintoret, That in his greatest works, a Bunch of Grapes had been his principal rule*
20 *and his surest guide.*

      [¶ 330.] *Pure or unmix'd white, either draws an object nearer or carries it off to farther distance. It draws it nearer with black, and throws it backward without it,* &c. All agree that white can subsist on the fore-ground of the Picture, and there be us'd without mixture; the question therefore is to know, if it can equally subsist and be plac'd in the same manner, upon that which is backward, the Light being universal and the Figures suppos'd in a Campaign and open Field.

      Our Author concludes affirmatively, and the reason on which
30 he establishes his rule is this, That there being nothing which partakes more of the Light than Whiteness, and the Light being capable of subsisting well in remoteness (or at a long distance, as we daily see in the rising and setting of the Sun) it follows that white may subsist in the same manner. In Painting, the Light and a white Colour are but one and the same thing. Add to this,

---

14–15 enlighten'd, . . . shadow'd, . . . turnings;] enlighten'd; . . . shadow'd‸ . . .
~, Q.
29 Author] *Author* Q.

that we have no Colour, which more resembles the Air than white, and by consequence no Colour which is lighter, from whence it comes that we commonly say, the Air is heavy, when we see the Heavens cover'd with black Clouds, or when a thick fog takes from us that clearness, which makes the Lightness or Serenity of the Air. *Titian, Tintoret, Paul Veronese,* and all those who best understood Lights, have observ'd it in this manner, and no man can go against this Precept, at least without renouncing any skill in Landtschape, which is an undoubted
10 confirmation of this truth. And we see that all the great Masters of Landtschape, have follow'd *Titian* in this, who has always employ'd brown and earthly Colours upon the fore-part, and has reserv'd his greatest Lights for remotenesses and the back parts of his Landtschapes.

It may be objected against this opinion, that white cannot maintain it self in remotenesses, because it is ordinarily us'd to bring the Objects nearer, on the advanc'd part. 'Tis true, that so it is us'd, and that to very good purpose, to render the Objects more sensible, by the opposition of the Dark, which must accom-
20 pany it; and which retains it, as it were, by force, whether the Dark serves it for a ground, or whether it be combin'd to it. For example, If you wou'd make a white Horse on the fore-ground of your Picture, 'tis of absolute Necessity, that the ground must be of a mixt brown, and large enough, or that the Furniture must be of very sensible Colours; or lastly, that some Figure must be set upon it, whose Shadows and the Colour may bring it forward.

But it seems (say you) that blue is the most flying or transient Colour, because the Heavens and Mountains, which are at the greatest distance, are of that Colour. 'Tis very true that blue is
30 one of the lightest and sweetest Colours: But it is also true, that it possesses these qualities so much the more, because the white is mingled in it, as the example of the distances demonstrate to us. But if the Light of your Picture be not universal, and that you suppose your Figures in a Chamber, then recall to your

---

10–14 Masters of Landtschape . . . Landtschapes] *Masters of Landtschape . . . Landtschapes* Q.
20 were,] ~∧ Q.
21–22 For example . . . white Horse] *For example . . . white Horse* Q.

Memory that Theorem which tells you that the nearer a Body
is to the Light, and the more directly 'tis oppos'd to us, so much
the more it is enlighten'd, because the Light grows languishing,
the farther it removes from its original.

You may also extinguish your white, if you suppose the Air to
be somewhat thicker, and if you foresee that this supposition
will make a good effect in the Oeconomy of the whole work; but
let not this proceed so far, as to make your Figures so brown,
that they may seem as it were in a filthy Fog, or that they may
10 appear to be part of the ground. See the following Remark.

[¶ 332.] *But as for pure black, there is nothing that brings the
Object nearer to the Sight,* &c. Because black is the heaviest of
all Colours, the most earthly, and the most sensible: This is
clearly understood by the qualities of white, which is oppos'd
to it, and which is, as we have said, the lightest of all Colours.
There are few who are not of this opinion; and yet I have
known some, who have told me, that the black being on the
advanc'd part, makes nothing but holes. To this there is little
else to be answer'd, but that black always makes a good effect,
20 being set forward, provided it be plac'd there with Prudence.
You are therefore so to dispose the Bodies of your Pictures
which you intend to be on the fore-ground, that those sorts of
holes may not be perceiv'd, and that the blacks may be there by
Masses, and insensibly confus'd. See the *47th.* Rule.

That which gives the Relievo to a Bowl, (may some say to me)
is the quick Light, or the white, which appears to be on the
side, which is nearest to us, and the black by consequence dis-
tances the Object: we are here to beware, not to confound the
turnings with the distances: the question is onely in respect of
30 Bodies, which are separated by some distance of a backward
Position, and not of round Bodies, which are of the same Con-
tinuity: the brown which is mingled in the turnings of the Bowl,
makes them go off, rather in confounding them, as we may say,
than in blackning them. And do you not see, that the reflects are
an Artifice of the Painter, to make the turnings seem more
Light, and that by this means the greatest blackness remains

---

1 Theorem] *Theorem* Q.   13 sensible:] ~. Q.
14 white,] ~ʌ Q.   32–171:1 Bowl ... Bowl] *Bowl ... Bowl* Q.

towards the middle of the Bowl, to sustain the white, and make it deceive us with more pleasure.

This Rule of White and Black is of so great consequence, that unless it be exactly practis'd, 'tis impossible for a Picture to make any great effect, that the Masses can be disentangl'd, and the different distances may be observ'd at the first Glance of the Eye without trouble.

It may be inferr'd from this Precept, that the Masses of other Colours, will be so much the more sensible, and approach so much the nearer to the Sight the more brown they bear; provided this be amongst other Colours which are of the same Species. For example, A yellow brown shall draw nearer to the Sight, than another which is less yellow. I said provided it be amongst other Colours, which are of the same Species, because there are simple Colours, which naturally are strong and sensible, though they are clear, as Vermillion; there are others also, which notwithstanding that they are brown, yet cease not to be soft and faint, as the blue of Ultramarine. The effect of a Picture comes not onely therefore from the Lights and Shadows, but also from the nature of the Colours. I thought it was not from the purpose in this place to give you the qualities of those Colours which are most in use, and which are call'd *Capital,* because they serve to make the composition of all the rest, whose number is almost infinite.

Red Oker is one of the most heavy Colours.

Yellow Oker is not so heavy, because 'tis clearer.

And the Masticot is very Light, because it is a very clear yellow, and very near to white.

Ultramarine or Azure, is very light and a very sweet Colour.

Vermillion is wholly opposite to Ultramarine.

3 Rule ... White ... Black] *Rule ... White ... Black* Q.
8 Precept] *Precept* Q.
12 For example] *For example* Q.
16–18 Vermillion ... Ultramarine] *Vermillion ... Ultramarine* Q.
22 *Capital*] Capital Q.
25 Red Oker] *Red Oker* Q.
26 Yellow Oker] *Yellow Oker* Q.
27 Masticot] *Masticot* Q.
29 Ultramarine ... Azure] *Ultramarine ... Azure* Q.
30 Vermillion ... Ultramarine] *Vermillion ... Ultramarine* Q.

Lake is a middle Colour betwixt Ultramarine and Vermillion, yet it is rather more sweet than harsh.

Brown Red is one of the most earthy and most sensible Colours.

Pinck is in its nature an indifferent Colour, (that is) very susceptible of the other Colours by the mixture: if you mix brown-red with it, you will make it a very earthy Colour; but on the contrary, if you joyn it with white or blue, you shall have one of the most faint and tender Colours.

10   Terre Verte (or green Earth) is light; 'tis a mean betwixt yellow Oker and Ultramarine.

Umbre is very sensible and earthy; there is nothing but pure black which can dispute with it.

Of all Blacks, that is the most earthly, which is most remote from Blue. According to the Principle which we have establish'd of white and black, you will make every one of these Colours before-nam'd more earthy and more heavy, the more black you mingle with them, and they will be light the more white you joyn with them.

20   For what concerns broken or compound Colours, we are to make a judgment of their strength by the Force of those Colours which compose them. All who have thoroughly understood the agreement of Colours, have not employ'd them wholly pure and simple in their Draperies, unless in some Figure upon the foreground of the Picture; but they have us'd broken and compound Colours, of which they made a Harmony for the Eyes, by mixing those which have some kind of Sympathy with each other, to

---

1   Lake ... Ultramarine ... Vermillion] *Lake ... Ultramarine ... Vermillion* Q.
3   Brown Red] *Brown Red* Q.
5–8   Pinck . . . brown-red . . . white . . . blue] *Pinck . . . brown-red . . . white ... blue* Q.
10–11   Terre Verte . . . yellow Oker . . . Ultramarine] *Terre Verte . . . yellow Oker ... Ultramarine* Q.
12–13   Umbre ... pure black] *Umbre ... pure black* Q.
14–15   Blacks ... Blue] *Blacks ... Blue* Q.
15–19   Principle . . . white . . . black . . . black . . . white] *Principle . . . white ... black ... black ... white* Q.
20   broken ... compound Colours] *broken ... compound Colours* Q.
25–173:1   broken ... compound Colours ... Whole] *broken ... compound Colours ... Whole* Q.

make a Whole, which has an Union with the Colours which are
neighbouring to it. The Painter who perfectly understands the
force and power of his Colours, will use them most suitably
to his present purpose, and according to his own Discretion.

[¶ 355.] *But let this be done relatively,* &c. One Body must
make another Body fly off in such a manner that it self may be
chas'd by those Bodies which are advanc'd before it. *We are to
take care and use great attention,* says *Quinctilian, not onely of
one separate thing, but of many which follow each other, and
by a certain relation which they have with each other, are as it
were continued, in the same manner as if, in a straight Street,
we cast our Eyes from one end of it to the other, we discover at
once those different things which are presented to the Sight, so
that we not onely see the last, but whatsoever is relating to
the last.*

[¶ 361.] *Let two contrary extremities never touch each other,*
&c. The Sense of seeing has this in common with all the rest of
the Senses, that it abhorrs the contrary Extremities. And in the
same manner as our hands, when they are very cold feel a griev-
ous pain, when on the sudden we hold them near the Fire, so
the Eyes which find an extreme white next to an extreme black,
or a fair cool Azure next to a hot Vermillion, cannot behold
these extremities without Pain, though they are always attracted
by the Glareing of two contraries.

This rule obliges us to know those Colours which have a
Friendship with each other, and those which are incompatible,
which we may easily discover in mixing together those Colours
of which we would make trial.

And if by this mixture, they make a gracious and sweet Colour,
which is pleasing to the Sight, 'tis a Sign that there is an Union
and a Sympathy betwixt them: but if, on the contrary, that
Colour which is produc'd by the mixture of the two be harsh
to the Sight, we are to conclude, that there is a Contrariety and

---

7   *We*] "*We* Q.
7   *each printed italic line preceded by inverted double commas in* Q.
8   *Quinctilian*] Quinctilian Q.
9–11   *other, ... continued, ... manner ... if,*] ~: ... ~ₐ ... ~, ... ~ₐ Q.
21   white] ~, Q.

Antipathy betwixt these two Colours. Green, for example, is a pleasing Colour, which may come from a blue and a yellow mix'd together, and by consequence blue and yellow are two Colours which sympathize: and on the contrary, the mixture of Blue with Vermillion, produces a sharp, harsh, and unpleasant Colour; conclude then that Blue and Vermillion are of a contrary Nature. And the same may be said of other Colours of which you make the experiment. And to clear that matter once for all, (see the Conclusion of the 332d. Remark, where I have

10 taken occasion to speak of the force and quality of every Capital Colour,) yet you may neglect this Precept, when your Piece consists but of one or two Figures, and when amongst a great number you would make some *one* Figure more remarkable than the rest; *One,* I say, which is one of the most considerable of the Subject, which otherwise you cannot distinguish from the rest. *Titian* in his *Triumph of* Bacchus, having plac'd *Ariadne* on one of the Borders of the Picture, and not being able for that reason to make her remarkable by the brightness of Light, which he was to keep in the middle of his Picture, gave her a Scarf of a

20 Vermillion Colour, upon a blue Drapery, as well to loosen her from his ground, which was a blue Sea, as because she is one of the principal Figures of his Subject, upon which he desir'd to attract the Eye. *Paul Veronese,* in his *Marriage of* Cana, because *Christ* who is the principal Figure of the Subject, is carry'd somewhat into the depth of the Picture, and that he cou'd not make him distinguishable by the strength of the Lights and Shadows, has cloath'd him with Vermillion and Blue, thereby to conduct the Sight to that Figure.

1–4 Green . . . blue . . . yellow . . . blue . . . yellow . . . sympathize] *Green* . . . *blue* . . . *yellow* . . . *blue* . . . *yellow* . . . *sympathize* Q.
5–6 Blue . . . Vermillion . . . Blue . . . Vermillion] *Blue* . . . *Vermillion* . . . *Blue* . . . *Vermillion* Q.
9 Remark] *Remark* Q.
14 rest;] ~. Q.
14 *One,*] ~ᴧ Q.
16 *Triumph of* Bacchus] triumph of *Bacchus* Q.
20–21 Vermillion . . . blue . . . blue Sea] *Vermillion* . . . *blue* . . . *blue Sea* Q.
23 *Paul*] *Paulo* Q.
23 *Marriage of* Cana] Marriage of *Canaa* Q.
27 Vermillion . . . Blue] *Vermillion* . . . *Blue* Q.

The hostile Colours may be so much the more ally'd to each other, the more you mix them with other Colours, which mutually sympathize; and which agree with those Colours, which you desire to reconcile.

[¶ 365.] *'Tis labour in vain to paint a High-noon,* &c. He said in another place, Endeavour after that which aids your Art, and is suitable to it, and shun whatsoever is repugnant: 'tis the 59*th.* Precept. If the Painter wou'd arrive to the end he has propos'd, which is to deceive the sight, he must make choice of such a
10 Nature, as agrees with the weakness of his Colours; because his Colours cannot accommodate themselves to every sort of Nature. This Rule is particularly to be observ'd, and well consider'd, by those who paint Landtschapes.

[¶ 378.] *Let the Field or Ground of the Picture,* &c. The reason of it is, that we are to avoid the meeting of those Colours, which have an Antipathy to each other, because they offend the Sight, so that this Rule is prov'd sufficiently by the 41*st.* which tells us, that two contrary Extremities are never to touch each other, whether it be in Colour, or in Light, but that there ought
20 to be a mean betwixt them, which partakes of both.

[¶ 382.] *Let your Colours be lively, and yet not look (according to the Painters Proverb) as if they had been sprinkled with Meal,* &c. *Donner dans la farine,* is a Phrase amongst Painters, which perfectly expresses what it means, which is to paint with clear, or bright Colours, and dull Colours together; for being so mingled, they give no more life to the Figures, than if they had been rubb'd with Meal. They who make their flesh Colours very white, and their Shadows grey or inclining to green, fall into this inconvenience. Red Colours in the Shadows of the most
30 delicate or finest Flesh, contribute wonderfully to make them lively, shining and natural; but they are to be us'd with the same discretion, that *Titian, Paul Veronese, Rubens* and *Van Dyck,* have taught us by their example.

To preserve the Colours fresh, we must paint by putting in more Colours, and not by rubbing them in, after they are once laid; and if it could be done, they should be laid just in their

---

1   hostile Colours] *hostile Colours* Q.   7–8   59*th.* Precept] 59th. *Precept* Q.
13   Landtschapes] *Landtschapes* Q.   16   Antipathy] *Antipathy* Q.

proper places, and not be any more touch'd, when they are once so plac'd; it would be yet better, because the Freshness of the Colours is tarnish'd and lost, by vexing them with the continual Drudgery of Daubing.

All they who have colour'd well, have had yet another Maxim to maintain their Colours fresh and flourishing, which was to make use of white Grounds, upon which they painted, and oftentimes at the first Stroke, without retouching any thing, and without employing new Colours. *Rubens* always us'd this way,
10 and I have seen Pictures from the hand of that Great Person, painted up at once, which were of a wonderfull Vivacity.

The reason why they made use of those kind of Grounds, is, because white as well preserves a Brightness, under the Transparency of Colours, which hinders the Air from altering the whiteness of the Ground, as that it likewise repairs the injuries which they receive from the Air, so that the Ground and the Colours assist and preserve each other. 'Tis for this reason that glaz'd Colours have a Vivacity which can never be imitated by the most lively and most brillant Colours, because according to
20 the common way, the different Teints are simply laid on each in its place one after another. So true it is, that white with other strong Colours, with which we paint at once that which we intend to glaze, are as it were, the Life, the Spirit, and the Lustre of it. The Ancients most certainly have found, that white Grounds were much the best, because, notwithstanding that inconvenience, which their Eyes receiv'd from that Colour, yet they did not forbear the use of it; as *Galen* testifies in his tenth Book *Of the use of the parts. Painters,* says he, *when they work upon their white Grounds, place before them dark Colours, and*
30 *others mixt with blue and green, to recreate their Eyes, because white is a glareing Colour, which wearies and pains the Sight more than any other.* I know not the reason why the use of it is left off at present, if it be not that in our days there are few Painters who are curious in their Colouring, or that the first Strokes which are begun upon white, are not seen soon enough,

7   white Grounds] *white Grounds* Q.   10   Person,] ~∧ Q.
27–28   tenth Book Of] *tenth Book of* Q.   28   *Painters*] "*Painters* Q.
28–32   *each printed italic line preceded by inverted double commas in Q.*

and that a more than *French* Patience is requir'd to wait till it be accomplish'd; and the Ground, which by its whiteness tarnishes the Lustre of the other Colours, must be entirely cover'd, to make the whole work appear pleasingly.

[¶ 383.] *Let the parts which are nearest to us and most rais'd,* &c. The reason of this is, that upon a flat superficies, and as much united as a Cloth can be, when it is strain'd, the least Body is very appearing, and gives a heightning to the place which it possesses; do not therefore load those places with Colours, which 10 you would make to turn; but let those be well loaded, which you would have come out of the Canvass.

[¶ 385.] *Let there be so much Harmony or Consent in the Masses of the Picture, that all the shadowings may appear as if they were but one,* &c. He has said in another place, that after great Lights, great Shadows are necessary, which he calls *Reposes.* What he means by the present Rule is this, That whatsoever is found in those great Shadows, should partake of the Colours of one another, so that the different Colours which are well distinguish'd in the Lights seem to be but one in the Shadows, by 20 their great Union.

[¶ 386.] *Let the whole Picture be made of one Piece,* &c. That is to say, of one and the same Continuity of Work, and as if the Picture had been painted up all at once; the *Latine* says, *all of one Pallet.*

[¶ 387.] *The Looking-Glass will instruct you,* &c. The Painter must have a principal Respect to the Masses, and to the Effect of the whole together. The Looking-Glass distances the Objects, and by consequence gives us onely to see the Masses, in which all the little parts are confounded. The Evening, when the Night 30 approaches, will make you better understand this observation, but not so commodiously, for the proper time to make it, lasts but a quarter of an hour, and the Looking-Glass may be usefull all the day.

3   cover'd,] ~∧ Q.
13   *Picture*] *Pictures* Q.
16   Rule] *Rule* Q.
23   *Latine*] Latin Q.
23–24   says, *all of one Pallet*] ~∧ all of one Pallet Q.
27–32   Looking-Glass . . . Looking-Glass] *Looking-Glass . . . Looking-Glass* Q.

Since the Mirror is the rule and Master of all Painters, as
showing them their faults by distancing the Objects, we may
conclude that the Picture which makes not a good effect at a
distance cannot be well done; and a Painter must never finish
his Picture, before he has examin'd it at some reasonable dis-
tance, or with a Looking-Glass, whether the Masses of the Lights
and Shadows, and the Bodies of the Colours be well distributed.
Giorgione and *Correggio* have made use of this method.

[¶ 393.] *As for a Portrait, or Pictures by the Life,* &c. The end
10 of Portraits is not so precisely as some have imagin'd, to give a
smiling and pleasing Air together with the resemblance; this is
indeed somewhat, but not enough. It consists in expressing the
true temper of those persons which it represents, and to make
known their Physiognomy. If the Person whom you draw, for
example, be naturally sad, you are to beware of giving him any
Gayety, which would always be a thing which is foreign to his
Countenance. If he or she be merry, you are to make that good
Humour appear by the expressing of those parts where it acts,
and where it shows it self. If the Person be grave and majestical,
20 the Smiles or Laughing, which is too sensible, will take off from
that Majesty and make it look childish and undecent. In short,
the Painter, who has a good Genius must make a true Discern-
ment of all these things, and if he understands Physiognomy, it
will be more easie to him, and he will succeed better than
another. *Pliny* tells us, *That* Apelles *made his Pictures so very
like, that a certain Physiognomist and Fortune-teller,* (as it is
related by *Appion* the Grammarian) *foretold by looking on
them the very time of their Deaths, whom those Pictures repre-
sented, or at what time their Death happen'd, if such persons*
30 *were already dead.*

[¶ 403.] *You are to paint the most tenderly that possibly you
can,* &c. Not so as to make your Colours die by force of torment-
ing them, but that you should mix them as hastily as you can,

---

1 Mirror] *Mirror* Q.   6 Looking-Glass] *Looking-Glass* Q.
10 Portraits] *Portraits* Q.   14 Physiognomy] *Physiognomy* Q.
14–15 for example] *for example* Q.
22–23 Genius ... Physiognomy] *Genius ... Physiognomy* Q.
25 That] "*That* Q.
25–30 *each printed italic line preceded by inverted double commas in* Q.

and not retouch the same place, if conveniently you can avoid it.

[¶ 403.] *Large Lights,* &c. 'Tis in vain to take pains if you cannot preserve large Lights, because without them, your work will never make a good effect at a distance; and also because little Lights are confus'd and effac'd, proportionably, as you are at a distance from the Picture. This was the perpetual Maxim of *Correggio.*

[¶ 417.] *Ought to have somewhat of Greatness in them, and their Out-lines to be noble,* &c. As the Pieces of Antiquity
10 will evidently show us.

[¶ 422.] *There is nothing more pernicious to a Youth,* &c. 'Tis common to place our selves under the Discipline of a Master of whom we have a good opinion, and whose manner we are apt to embrace with ease, which takes root more deeply in us, and augments the more we see him work, and the more we copy after him. This happens oftentimes to that degree, and makes so great an Impression in the Mind of the Scholar, that he cannot give his approbation to any other manner whatsoever, and believes there is no man under the Cope of Heaven, who is so
20 knowing as his Master.

But what is most remarkable in this point is, that nature appears to us always like that manner which we love, and in which we have been taught, which is just like a Glass through which we behold Objects, and which communicates its Colour to them without our perceiving it. After I have said this, you may see of what consequence is the choice of a good Master, and of following in our beginning the manner of those who have come nearest to Nature. And how much injury do you think have the ill manners which have been in *France,* done to the Painters of
30 that Nation, and what hindrance have they been to the knowledge of what is well done, or of arriving to what is so when once we know it? The *Italians* say to those whom they see infected

---

6 Maxim] *Maxim* Q.
9 Antiquity] *Antiquity* Q.
12–13 Master] *Master* Q.
20 his Master] *his Master* Q.
21 remarkable] remarakble Q.
26–28 good Master ... Nature] *good Master ... Nature* Q.
32 it?] ~. Q.

with an ill manner, which they are not able to forsake, *If you knew just nothing, you would soon learn something.*

[¶ 433.] *Search whatsoever is aiding to your Art and convenient, and avoid those things which are repugnant to it,* &c. This is an admirable Rule; a Painter ought to have it perpetually present in his Mind and Memory. It resolves those difficulties which the Rules beget; it loosens his hands, and assists his understanding. In short, this is the Rule which sets the Painter at liberty, because it teaches him that he ought not to
10 subject himself servilely, and be bound like an Apprentice to the Rules of his Art; but that the Rules of his Art ought to be Subject to him, and not hinder him from following the Dictates of his Genius, which is superior to them.

[¶ 434.] *Bodies of diverse Natures which are aggroupp'd or combin'd together are agreeable and pleasant to the Sight,* &c. As Flowers, Fruits, Animals, Skins, Sattins, Velvets, beautifull Flesh, Works of Silver, Armors, Instruments of Musick, Ornaments of Ancient Sacrifices, and many other pleasing Diversities which may present themselves to the Painters imagination. 'Tis
20 most certain that the diversity of Objects recreates the Sight, when they are without confusion; and when they diminish nothing of the Subject on which we work. Experience teaches us, that the Eye grows weary with poring perpetually on the same thing, not onely on Pictures, but even on Nature it self. For who is he who would not be tir'd in the Walks of a long Forest, or with beholding a large plain which is naked of Trees, or in the Sight of a Ridge of Mountains, which instead of Pleasure, give us onely the view of Heights and Bottoms. Thus to content and fill the Eye of the Understanding, the best Authors
30 have had the Address to sprinkle their Works with pleasing Digressions, with which they recreate the Minds of Readers. Discretion, in this as in all other things is the surest Guide: and as

---

1   *If*] "*If* Q.
1–2   *each printed italic line preceded by inverted double commas in* Q.
5   Rule] *Rule* Q.
7   Rules] *Rules* Q.
8–13   Rule . . . Rules . . . Rules . . . Genius] *Rule . . . Rules . . . Rules . . . Genius* Q.
16–18   Flowers . . . [*to*] . . . Sacrifices] *set in italics in* Q.

tedious Digressions, which wander from their Subject, are im-
pertinent, so the Painter who under Pretence of diverting the
Eyes, would fill his Picture with such varieties as alter the truth
of the History, would make a ridiculous Piece of Painting, and
a mere Gallimaufry of his Work.

[¶ 435.] *As also those things which appear to be perform'd
with ease,* &c. This ease attracts our Eyes, and Spirits so much
the more, because it is to be presum'd that a noble work, which
appears so easie to us, is the product of a skilfull Hand which is
10 Master of its Art. It was in this part, that *Apelles* found himself
superior to *Protogenes,* when he blam'd him, for not knowing
when to lay down his Pencil and (as I may almost say) to make
an end of finishing his Piece. And it was on this account he
plainly said, *That nothing was more prejudicial to Painters than
too much exactness; and that the greatest part of them knew not
when they had done enough:* as we have likewise a Proverb,
which says, *An* Englishman *never knows when he is well.* 'Tis
true, that the word *enough* is very difficult to understand. What
you have to do, is to consider your Subject thoroughly, and in
20 what manner you intend to treat it according to your rules, and
the Force of your Genius; after this you are to work with all the
ease and all the speed you can, without breaking your head so
very much, and being so very industrious in starting Scruples
to your self, and creating difficulties in your work. But 'tis im-
possible to have this Facility without possessing perfectly all the
Precepts of the Art, and to have made it habitual to you. For
ease consists in making precisely that work which you ought to
make, and to set every thing in its proper place with speed and
Readiness, which cannot be done without the Rules, for they
30 are the assur'd means of conducting you to the end that you
design with Pleasure. 'Tis then most certain, (though against
the opinion of many,) that the Rules give Facility, Quiet of
Mind, and readiness of Hand to the slowest Genius, and that the

4 History] *History* Q.   12 and (as] (and as Q.
14 *That*] "*That* Q.
14–16 *each printed italic line preceded by inverted double commas in* Q.
17 Englishman] *Englishman* Q.   21 Genius] *Genius* Q.
26 Precepts ... Art] *Precepts ... Art* Q.
32–182:1 Rules ... Rules] *Rules ... Rules* Q.

same Rules increase, and guide that ease in those who have already receiv'd it at their Birth from the happy influence of their Stars.

From whence it follows that we may consider Facility two several ways, either simply, as Diligence and a readiness of Mind and of the Hand; or as a Disposition in the Mind, to remove readily all those difficulties which can arise in the work. The first proceeds from an active temper full of Fire; and the second from a true knowledge and full possession of infallible Rules:
10 the first is pleasing, but it is not always without Anxiety, because it often leads us astray; and on the contrary, the last makes us act with a Repose of Mind, and wonderfull Tranquillity, because it ascertains us of the goodness of our work. 'Tis a great advantage to possess the first, but 'tis the height of perfection to have both in that manner which *Rubens* and *Van Dyck* possessed them, excepting the part of Design or Drawing, which both too much neglected.

Those who say that the Rules are so far from giving us this Facility, that on the contrary they puzzle and perplex the Mind
20 and tie the hand, are generally such people who have pass'd half their lives in an ill practice of Painting, the habit of which is grown so inveterate in them, that to change it by the Rules, is to take as it were thier Pencils out of their hands, and to put them out of condition of doing any thing; in the same manner as we make a Country-man dumb whom we will not allow to speak but by the Rules of Grammar.

Observe, if you please, that the Facility and Diligence of which I spoke, consists not in that which we call bold strokes and a free handling of the Pencil, if it makes not a great effect at a distance.
30 That sort of Freedom belongs rather to a Writing-Master than a Painter. I say yet further, that 'tis almost impossible that things which are painted should appear true and natural, where we observe these sorts of bold strokes. And all those who have come

---

4–6 Facility . . . Diligence . . . readiness of Mind . . . the Hand . . . Disposition in the Mind] *Facility . . . Diligence . . . readiness of Mind . . . the Hand . . . Disposition in the Mind* Q.
9 Rules:] ~; Q.   11 astray;] ~, Q.
12 Tranquillity,] ~; Q.   25 speak] ~, Q.

nearest to nature, have never us'd that manner of Painting;
those tender Hairs, and those hatching strokes of the Pencil,
which make a kind of minced meat in Painting, are very fine I
must confess, but they are never able to deceive the Sight.

[¶ 442.] *Nor till you have present in your Mind a perfect Idea*
of your work, &c. If you will have pleasure in Painting, you
ought to have so well consider'd the œconomy of your work, that
it may be entirely made and dispos'd in your head before it be
begun upon the Cloath. You must I say, foresee the effect of
10 the Grouppes, the ground, and the Lights and Shadows of every
thing, the Harmony of the Colours, and the intelligence of all
the Subject, in such a manner, that whatsoever you shall put
upon the Cloth, may be onely a Copy of what is in your Mind.
If you make use of this Conduct, you will not be put to the
trouble of so often changing and rechanging.

[¶ 443.] *Let the Eye be satisfied in the first place, even against*
and above all other Reasons, &c. This passage has a respect to
some particular Licences which a Painter ought to take: And
as I despair not to treat this matter more at large; I adjourn
20 the Reader to the first opportunity which I can get for his farther
satisfaction on this point to the best of my Ability: but in general
he may hold for certain, that those Licences are good which
contribute to deceive the Sight, without corrupting the truth
of the Subject on which the Painter is to work.

[¶ 445.] *Profit your self by the Counsels of the knowing,* &c.
Parrhasius and *Cliton* thought themselves much oblig'd to *Soc-*
rates for the knowledge which he gave them of the Passions. See
their Dialogue in *Xenophon* towards the end of the third Book
of *Memoirs: They who the most willingly bear*
30 *reproof,* says *Pliny* the Younger, *are the very*   8.20.
men in whom we find more to commend than in other people.
Lysippus was extremely pleas'd when *Apelles* told him his opin-

---

1   Painting;] ~, Q.   10   ground,] ~ₐ Q.
20   Reader] *Reader* Q.   27   Passions] *Passions* Q.
28–29   third Book of] *third Book of* Q.
29+   8.20.]   *sidenote erroneously placed in Q, indicating a location in Xenophon*
(*rather than in Pliny*).
29–31   *each printed italic line preceded by inverted double commas in Q.*

ion; and *Apelles* as much, when *Lysippus* told him his. That which *Praxiteles* said of *Nicias* in *Pliny*, shows the Soul of an accomplish'd and an humble man. 35.2.

Praxiteles *being ask'd which of all his Works he valued most? Those, says he, which* Nicias *has retouch'd.* So much account he made of his Criticisms and his opinions. You know the common practice of *Apelles;* when he had finish'd any work, he expos'd it to the Sight of all Passengers, and conceal'd himself to hear the Censure of his faults, with the Prospect of making his advantage

10 of the Informations which unknowingly they gave him, being sensible that the people would examine his works more rigorously than himself, and would not forgive the least mistake.

The Opinions and Counsels of many together are always preferable to the advice of one single person. And *Cicero* wonders that any are besotted on their own Productions, and say to one another, *Very good, if your* Tuscul.lib.5. *works please you, mine are not unpleasing to me.* In effect there are many who through Presumption or out of Shame to be reprehended, never let their works be seen. But there is nothing can be

20 of worse consequence; *for the disease is nourish'd and increases,* says *Virgil, while it is con-* Georg.3. *ceal'd.* There are none but Fools, says *Horace,* who out of Shamefac'dness hide their Ulcers, which if shown might easily be heal'd. *Stultorum incurata malus pudor ulcera celat:* L.I.Ep.16. There are others who have not altogether so much of this foolish Bashfulness, and who ask every ones opinion with Prayers and Earnestness; but if you freely and ingenuously give them notice of their Faults, they never fail to make some pitifull excuse for them, or which is worse, they take in ill

30 part the Service which you thought you did them, which they but seemingly desir'd of you, and out of an establish'd Custom amongst the greatest part of Painters. If you desire to get your self any honour, and acquire a Reputation by your works, there

---

2+ *sidenote* 35.2.] 5.8. Q.   4 Praxiteles] "Praxiteles Q.
4–5 *each printed italic line preceded by inverted double commas in Q.*
7 *Apelles;*] ~, Q.   10 him, being] ~. Being Q.
20+ *sidenote* 3.] 3.l.5. Q.   24+ *sidenote* L.I.Ep.] Ep. Q.

is no surer way than to show them to persons of good Sense, and chiefly to those who are Criticks in the Art; and to take their Counsel with the same Mildness and the same Sincerity, as you desir'd them to give it you. You must also be industrous to discover the opinion of your Enemies, which is commonly the truest, for you may be assur'd, that they will give you no quarter, and allow nothing to complaisance.

[¶ 449.] *But if you have no knowing Friend,* &c. *Quinctilian* gives the reason of this, when he says, *That the best means to*
10 *correct our faults, is doubtless this, To remove our designs out of Sight, for some space of time, and not to look upon our Pictures, to the end, that after this interval, we may look on them as it were with other Eyes, and as a new work which was of another hand, and not our own.* Our own Productions do but too much flatter us; they are always too pleasing, and 'tis impossible not to be fond of them at the moment of their Conception. They are Children of a tender age, which are not capable of drawing our Hatred on them. 'Tis said, That Apes, as soon as they have brought their Young into the World, keep their
20 Eyes continually fasten'd on them, and are never weary of admiring their Beauty: so amorous is Nature of whatsoever she produces.

[¶ 458.] *To the end that he may cultivate those Talents which make his Genius,* &c.

Qui sua metitur pondera, ferre potest.

That we may undertake nothing beyond our forces, we must endeavour to know them. On this Prudence our reputation depends. *Cicero* calls it *a good Grace,* because it makes a man seen in his greatest Lustre. *'Tis,* (says he) *a becoming* 1 Off.
30 *Grace, which we shall easily make appear, if we are carefull to cultivate that which Nature has given us in pro-*

9 *That*] "That Q.
10–14 *each printed italic line preceded by inverted double commas in Q.*
25 *Qui ...* [*to*] *... potest*] *set in romans in Q.*
26–27 *each printed italic line preceded by inverted double commas in Q.*
26 *forces, we*] *forces,* Offic. B.I. / *we* Q.   29 *'Tis*] "'Tis Q.
29–186:33 *each printed italic line preceded by inverted double commas in Q.*

priety, and made our own, provided it be no Vice or Imperfec-
tion: we ought to undertake nothing which is repugnant to Na-
ture in general; and when we have paid her this duty, we are
bound so religiously to follow our own Nature, that though many
things which are more serious and more important, present them-
selves to us, yet we are always to conform our Studies and our
Exercises to our natural Inclinations. It avails nothing to dispute
against Nature, and think to obtain what she refuses; for then
we eternally follow what we can never reach; for, as the Proverb
10 *says, There is nothing can please, nothing can be gracefull which*
we enterprize in spight of Minerva; *that is to say, in spight of*
Nature. When we have consider'd all these things attentively, it
will then be necessary, that every man should regard that in par-
ticular which Nature has made his portion, and that he should
cultivate it with care; 'tis not his business to give himself the
trouble of trying whether it will become him to put on the
Nature of another man; or as one would say, to act the person
of another: there is nothing which can more become us, than
what is properly the Gift of Nature. Let every one therefore
20 *endeavour to understand his own Talent, and without flattering*
himself, let him make a true judgment of his own Vertues, and
his own Defects and Vices; that he may not appear to have less
judgment than the Comedians, who do not always chuse the best
Plays, but those which are best for them; that is, those which
are most in the compass of their acting. Thus we are to fix on
those things for which we have the strongest Inclination. And
if it sometimes happen that we are forc'd by necessity to apply
our selves to such other things to which we are no ways inclin'd;
we must bring it so about by our Care and Industry, that if we
30 *perform them not very well, at least we may not do them so very*
ill as to be sham'd by them: we are not so much to strain our
selves to make those Vertues appear in us which really we have
not, as to avoid those Imperfections which may dishonour us.
These are the Thoughts and the Words of *Cicero*, which I have
translated, retrenching onely such things as were of no concern-

---

ment to my Subject: I was not of opinion to add any thing, and the Reader I doubt not will find his satisfaction in them.

[¶ 464.] *While you meditate on these Truths, and observe them diligently,* &c. There is a great Connexion betwixt this Precept and that other, which tells you, That *you are to pass no day without drawing a line.* 'Tis impossible to become an able Artist, without making your Art habitual to you: and 'tis impossible to gain an exact Habitude, without an infinite number of Acts, and without perpetual Practice. In all Arts the
10 Rules of them are learn'd in little time; but the perfection is not acquir'd without a long Practice and a severe Diligence. *We never saw that Laziness produc'd any thing which was excellent,* says *Maximus Tyrius:* and *Quinctilian* tells us, That *the Arts draw their beginning* Diss. 34. *from Nature;* the want we often have of them causes us to search the means of becoming able in them, and exercise makes us entirely Masters of them.

[¶ 466.] *The morning is the best and most proper part of the day,* &c. Because then the Imagination is not clouded with the
20 Vapours of Meat, nor distracted by Visits which are not usually made in the morning. And the Mind by the Sleep of the foregoing Night, is refresh'd and recreated from the Toyls of former Studies. *Malherbe* says well to this purpose.

Le plus beau de nos jours, est dans leur matinée.

The sprightly Morn is the best part of Day.

[¶ 468.] *Let no day pass over you without drawing a line,* &c. That is to say, without working, without giving some strokes of the Pencil or the Crayon. This was the Precept of *Apelles;* and 'tis of so much the more necessity, because Painting is an Art
30 of much length and time, and is not to be learn'd without great Practice. *Michael Angelo* at the Age of fourscore years, said, That he *learn'd something every day.*

[¶ 473.] *Be ready to put into your Table-book,* &c. As it was

---

4–5 this Precept ... other] *this Precept ... other* Q.
24 *matinée*] *matinee* Q.   32 he] *he* Q.

the custom of *Titian* and the *Carraches;* there are yet remaining in the hands of some who are curious in Painting, many thoughts and observations which those great Men have made on Paper, and in their Table-books which they carry'd continually about them.

[¶ 475.] *Wine and good Cheer are no great Friends to Painting, they serve onely to recreate the Mind when it is oppress'd and spent with Labour,* &c. During the time, says *Pliny, that* Protogenes *was drawing the Pic-* 35.10.
10 *ture of* Jalysus, *which was the best of all his Works, he took no other nourishment than Lupines mix'd with a little water, which serv'd him both for Meat and Drink, for fear of clogging his Imagination by the Luxury of his Food.* Michael Angelo, while he was drawing his *Day of Judgment,* fed onely on Bread and Wine at Dinner. And *Vasari* observes in his life, that he was so sober that he slept but little, and that he often rose in the Night to work, as being not disturb'd by the Vapours of his thin Repasts.

[¶ 478.] *But delights in the liberty which belongs to the*
20 *Batchelors Estate,* &c. We never see large and beautifull and well-tasted Fruits proceeding from a Tree which is incompass'd round, and choak'd with Thorns and Bryars. Marriage draws a world of business on our hands, subjects us to Law-suits, and loads us with multitudes of domestick Cares, which are as so many Thorns that encompass a Painter, and hinder him from producing his works in that perfection of which otherwise he is capable. *Raphael, Michael Angelo,* and *Annibal Carracci* were never marry'd: and amongst the Ancient Painters we find none recorded for being marry'd, but onely *Apelles,* to whom *Alex-*
30 *ander the Great* made a present of his own Mistress *Campaspe;* which yet I would have understood without offence to the Institution of Marriage, for that calls down many Blessings upon Families, by the Carefulness of a vertuous Wife. If Marriage be in general a remedy against Concupiscence, 'tis doubly so in

---

2 Painting,] ~; Q.   8 *During*] "During Q.
9–13 *each printed italic line preceded by inverted double commas in* Q.
14 *Day of Judgment*] day of Judgment Q.
27 *Annibal*] *Hannibal* Q.

respect of Painters; who are more frequently under the occa-
sions of Sin than other Men; because they are under a frequent
necessity of seeing Nature bare-fac'd. Let every one examine his
own strength upon this point: but let him preferr the interest
of his Soul to that of his Art and of his Fortune.

[¶ 480.] *Painting naturally withdraws from noise and tumult,*
&c. I have said at the end of the first Remark, that both Poetry
and Painting were upheld by the strength of Imagination. Now
there is nothing which warms it more than Repose and Solitude:
10 Because in that estate, the Mind being freed from all sorts of
business, and in a kind of Sanctuary undisturb'd by vexatious
Visits, is more capable of forming noble Thoughts and of Ap-
plication to its Studies.

> *Carmina secessum scribentis & otia quærunt.*
>
> *Good Verse, Recess and Solitude requires:*
> *And Ease from Cares, and undisturb'd Desires.*

We may properly say the same of Painting, by reason of its con-
formity with Poetry, as I have shown in the first Remark.

[¶ 484.] *Let not the covetous design of growing rich,* &c. **We**
20 read in *Pliny,* that *Nicias* refus'd Sixty Talents
from King *Attalus,* and rather chose to make a   *7500 l.*
free Gift of his Picture to his Country. *I enquir'd of a pru-*
dent man, (says a grave Author) in what times
those noble Pictures were made which now we   Petron. Arbiter.
see; and desir'd him to explain to me some of their Subjects,
which I did not well understand. I ask'd him likewise the reason
of that great negligence which is now visible amongst Painters:
And from whence it proceeded, that the most beautifull Arts were
now bury'd in Oblivion, and principally Painting, a faint Shadow
30 *of which is at present remaining to us. To which he thus reply'd,*
That the immoderate desire of Riches had produc'd this change:
For of old, when naked Vertue had her Charms, the noble Arts
then flourish'd in their Vigour: and if there was any contest
amongst men, it was onely who should be the first Discoverer of
what might be of advantage to posterity. Lysippus and Myron,

---

5 Soul . . . Art . . . Fortune] *Soul . . . Art . . . Fortune* Q.
22–190:9 *each printed italic line preceded by inverted double commas in* Q.

those renown'd Sculptors, who could give a Soul to Brass, left no
Heirs, no Inheritance behind them, because they were more
carefull of acquiring Fame than Riches. But as for us of this pres-
ent Age, it seems by the manner of our Conduct, that we upbraid
Antiquity for being as covetous of Vertue as we are of Vice:
wonder not so much therefore, if Painting has lost its Strength
and Vigour, because many are now of opinion, that a heap of
Gold is much more beautifull than all the Pictures and Statues
of Apelles *and* Phidias, *and all the noble Performances of* Greece.

10   I would not exact so great an act of Abstinence from our mod-
ern Painters, for I am not ignorant that the hope of gain is a
wonderfull sharp spur in Arts, and that it gives industry to the
Artist; from whence it was that *Juvenal* said even of the *Greeks*
themselves, who were the Inventors of Painting, and who first
understood all the Graces of it and its whole perfection,

> *Græculus esuriens, in Cælum, jusseris, ibit.*

> *A hungry* Greek, *if bidden, scales the Skies.*

But I could heartily wish, that the same hope which flatters them
did not also corrupt them: and did not snatch out of their hands
20   a lame, imperfect Piece, rudely daub'd over with too little Re-
flection and too much haste.

[¶ 487.] *The qualities requisite to form an excellent Painter,*
&c. 'Tis to be confess'd that very few Painters have those quali-
ties which are requir'd by our Author, because there are very
few, who are *able* Painters. There was a time when onely they
who were of noble Blood, were permitted to exercise this Art;
because it is to be presum'd, that all these Ingredients of a good
Painter, are not ordinarily found in men of vulgar Birth. And
in all appearance, we may hope that though there be no Edict in
30   *France* which takes away the Liberty of Painting from those to
whom Nature has refus'd the Honour of being born Gentlemen,
yet at least that the *Royal Academy* will admit hence-forward
onely such who being endu'd with all the good Qualities and

---

the Talents which are requir'd for Painting, those endowments may be to them instead of an honourable Birth. 'Tis certain, that which debases Painting, and makes it descend to the vilest and most despicable kind of Trade, is the great multitude of Painters who have neither noble Souls nor any Talent for the Art, nor even so much as common Sence. The Origin of this great Evil, is that there have always been admitted into the Schools of Painting all sorts of Children promiscuously, without Examination of them, and without observing for some conve-
10 nient space of time, if they were conducted to this Art by their inward Disposition, and all necessary Talents, rather than by a foolish Inclination of their own, or by the Avarice of their Relations, who put them to Painting, as a Trade which they believe to be somewhat more gainfull than another. The qualities properly requir'd, are these following:

A good Judgment, That they may do nothing against Reason and Verisimility.

A docible Mind, That they may profit by instructions, and receive without Arrogance the opinion of every one, and prin-
20 cipally of knowing Men.

A noble Heart, That they may propose Glory to themselves, and Reputation rather than Riches.

A Sublimity, and Reach of Thought, To conceive readily, to produce beautifull Ideas, and to work on their Subjects nobly and after a lofty manner, wherein we may observe somewhat that is delicate, ingenious and uncommon.

A warm and vigorous Fancy, To arrive at least to some degree of Perfection, without being tir'd with the Pains and Study which are requir'd in Painting.

30 Health, To resist the dissipation of Spirits, which are apt to be consum'd by Pains-taking.

Youth, Because Painting requires a great Experience and a long Practice.

---

15 following:] ~. Q.   16 A good Judgment] *A good Judgment* Q.
18 A docible Mind] *A docible Mind* Q.
21 A noble Heart] *A noble Heart* Q.
23 A ... [to] ... Thought] *set in italics in* Q.
27 A ... [to] ... Fancy] *set in italics in* Q.
30 Health] *Health* Q.   32 Youth] *Youth* Q.

Beauty or Handsomeness, Because a Painter paints himself in all his Pictures, and Nature loves to produce her own Likeness.

A convenient Fortune, That he may give his whole time to study, and may work chearfully, without being haunted with the dreadfull Image of Poverty, ever present to his Mind.

Labour, Because the Speculation is nothing without the Practice.

A Love for his Art, We suffer nothing in the Labour which is pleasing to us: or if it happen that we suffer, we are pleas'd
10 with the Pain.

And to be under the Discipline of a knowing Master, Because all depends on the Beginnings, and because commonly they take the manner of their Master, and are form'd according to his Gusto: See Verse 422, and the Remark upon it. All these good qualities are insignificant and unprofitable to the Painter, if some outward dispositions are wanting to him. By which I mean favourable times, such as are times of Peace, which is the Nurse of all noble Arts; there must also some fair occasion offer to make their Skill manifest by the performance of some considerable
20 Work within their power: and a Protector, who must be a Person of Authority, one who takes upon himself the care of their Fortune, at least in some measure, and knows how to speak well of them in time and place convenient. *'Tis of much importance,* says the Younger *Pliny, in what times Vertue appears. And there is no Wit, howsoever excellent it may be, which can make it self immediately known. Time and Opportunity are necessary to it, and a person who can assist us with his favour and be a* Mæcenas *to us.*

[¶ 496.] *And Life is so short, that it is not sufficient for so long*
30 *an Art,* &c. Not onely Painting but all other Arts, consider'd in

1   Beauty ... Handsomeness] *Beauty ... Handsomeness* Q.
3   A convenient Fortune] *A convenient Fortune* Q.
6   Labour] *Labour* Q.
8   A ... [*to*] ... Art] *set in italics in* Q.
11   And ... [*to*] ... knowing] *set in italics in* Q.
11   Master,] *Master,* &.c. Q.
14   Verse ... Remark] *Verse ... Remark* Q.
17   Peace] *Peace* Q.   21   the ... their] their ... the Q.
22   measure,] ~; Q.   28   Mæcenas] *Mœcenas* Q.
30–193:1   Arts, ... themselves,] ~ʌ ... ~ʌ Q.

themselves, require almost an infinite time to possess them perfectly. 'Tis in this Sense that *Hippocrates* begins his *Aphorisms* with this saying, *That Art is long and Life is short*. But if we consider Arts as they are in us, and according to a certain degree of Perfection, sufficient enough to make it known that we possess them above the common sort, and are comparatively better than most others, we shall not find that Life is too short on that account, provided our time be well employ'd. 'Tis true, that Painting is an Art which is difficult and a great undertaking. But they
10 who are endu'd with the qualities that are necessary to it, have no reason to be discourag'd by that apprehension. *Labour always appears difficult before 'tis try'd*. The passages by Sea, and the Knowledge Veget. de re Milit. lib. 2. of the Stars, have been thought impossible, which notwithstanding have been found and compass'd, and that with ease by those who endeavour'd after them. *'Tis a shamefull thing*, says *Cicero*, *to be weary of Enquiry, when* Lib. 1. de fin. *what we search is excellent*. That which causes us to lose most of our time, is the repugnance which we naturally have to La-
20 bour, and the Ignorance, the Malice, and the Negligence of our Masters: we waste much of our time in walking and talking to no manner of purpose, in making and receiving idle Visits, in Play and other Pleasures which we indulge, without reckoning those hours which we lose in the too great care of our Bodies, and in Sleep, which we often lengthen out till the day is far advanc'd: and thus we pass that Life which we reckon to be short, because we count by the years which we have liv'd, rather than by those which we have employ'd in study. 'Tis evident that they who liv'd before us, have pass'd through all those difficulties to arrive
30 at that Perfection which we discover in their Works, though they wanted some of the Advantages which we possess, and that none had labour'd for them as they have done for us. For 'tis certain that those Ancient Masters, and those of the last preceding Ages, have left such beautifull Patterns to us, that a better and more happy Age can never be than ours; and chiefly under the Reign of our present King, who encourages all the noble Arts, and

2 *Aphorisms*] Aphorisms Q.   4 Arts] ~, Q.
5 enough] ~, Q.   24 Bodies,] ~; Q.

spares nothing to give them the share of that Felicity of which
he is so bountifull to his Kingdom: and to conduct them with all
manner of advantages to that supreme Degree of Excellence,
which may be worthy of such a Master, and of that Sovereign
Love which he has for them. Let us therefore put our hands to
the work, without being discourag'd by the length of time, which
is requisite for our Studies; but let us seriously contrive how to
proceed with the best Order, and to follow a ready, diligent, and
well understood Method.

10   [¶ 500.] *Take Courage therefore, O ye noble Youths! you
legitimate Offspring of* Minerva, *who are born under the influ-
ence of a happy Planet,* &c. Our Author intends not here to sow
in a barren, ungratefull Ground, where his Precepts can bear
no Fruit: He speaks to young Painters, but to such onely who
are born under the Influence of a happy Star; that is to say, those
who have receiv'd from Nature the necessary dispositions of be-
coming great in the Art of Painting: and not to those who follow
that Study through Caprice or by a sottish Inclination, or for
Lucre, who are either incapable of receiving the Precepts, or
20 will make a bad use of them when receiv'd.

[¶ 509.] *You will do well,* &c. Our Author speaks not here of
the first Rudiments of Design; as for example, The management
of the Pencil, the just relation which the Copy ought to have
to the Original, *&c.* He supposes, that before he begins his
Studies, one ought to have a Facility of Hand to imitate the best
Designs, the noblest Pictures and Statues, that in few words he
should have made himself a Key, wherewith to open the Closet
of *Minerva,* and to enter into that Sacred Place, where those fair
Treasures are to be found in all abundance, and even offer them-
30 selves to us, to make our advantage of them by our Care and
Genius.

[¶ 509.] *You are to begin with Geometry,* &c. Because that is
the Ground of Perspective, without which nothing is to be done
in Painting: besides, Geometry is of great use in Architecture,
and in all things which are of its dependence; 'tis particularly
necessary for Sculptors.

33–36 Perspective . . . Geometry . . . Architecture . . . Sculptors] *Perspective* . . .
Geometry . . . *Architecture* . . . *Sculptors* Q.

[¶ 510.] *Set your self on designing after the Ancient* Greeks, *&c.* Because they are the Rule of Beauty, and give us a good Gusto; for which reason 'tis very proper to tie our selves to them, I mean generally speaking, but the particular Fruit which we gather from them, is what follows: To learn by heart four several Ayres of Heads; of a Man, a Woman, a Child, and an Old Man. I mean those which have the most general Approbation; for example those of the *Apollo,* of the *Venus de Medicis,* of the little *Nero,* (that is, when he was a Child,) and of the God *Tiber.*
10 It would be a good means of learning them, if when you have design'd one after the Statue it self, you design it immediately after from your own Imagination, without seeing it; and afterwards examine, if your own work be conformable to the first Design. Thus exercising your self on the same Head, and turning it on ten or twelve sides; you must do the same to the Feet, to the Hands, to the whole Figure. But to understand the Beauty of these Figures, and the justness of their Outlines, it will be necessary to learn Anatomy. When I speak of four Heads and four Figures, I pretend not to hinder any one from designing
20 many others after this first Study, but my meaning is onely to show by this, that a great Variety of things undertaken at the same time, dissipates the Imagination, and hinders all the Profit; in the same manner as too many sorts of Meat are not easily digested, but corrupt in the Stomach instead of nourishing the parts.

[¶ 511.] *And cease not Day or Night from Labour, till by your continual Practice,* &c. In the first Principles, the Students have not so much need of Precepts as of Practice: And the Antique Statues being the rule of Beauty, you may exercise your selves
30 in imitating them without apprehending any consequence of ill Habits and bad Ideas, which can be form'd in the Soul of a young Beginner. 'Tis not as in the School of a Master, whose Manner and whose Gust are ill, and under whose Discipline the Scholar spoils himself the more he exercises.

1-2 Greeks, *&c.*] *Greeks,* &c. Q.   3 Gusto; for] ~: For Q.
4 speaking,] ~; Q.   5 follows:] ~. Q.
6 Heads;] ~: Q.   8 *Medicis*] *Medices* Q.
18 Anatomy. When] *Anatomy:* when Q.
32 not] ~, Q.

[¶ 514.] *And when afterwards your Judgment shall grow stronger,* &c. 'Tis necessary to have the Soul well form'd, and to have a right Judgment to make the Application of his rules upon good Pictures, and to take nothing but the good. For there are some who imagine, that whatsoever they find in the Picture of a Master, who has acquir'd Reputation, must of necessity be excellent; and these kind of people never fail when they copy to follow the bad as well as the good things; and to observe them so much the more, because they seem to be extraordinary and out of the common road of others, so that at last they come to make a Law and Precept of them. You ought not also to imitate what is truly good in a crude and gross Manner, so that it may be found out in your works, that whatsoever Beauties there are in them, come from such or such a Master. But in this imitate the Bees, who pick from every Flower that which they find most proper in it to make Honey. In the same manner a young Painter should collect from many Pictures what he finds to be the most beautifull, and from his several Collections form that Manner which thereby he makes his own.

[¶ 520.] *A certain Grace which was wholly natural and peculiar to him,* &c. *Raphael* in this may be compar'd to *Apelles,* who in praising the Works of other Painters, said That Gracefulness was wanting to them: and that without Vanity he might say, it was his own peculiar portion. See the Remark on the 218*th.* Verse.

[¶ 522.] Julio Romano, *(educated from his Childhood in the Country of the Muses,)* &c. He means in the Studies of the *belle-lettre,* and above all in Poesy, which he infinitely lov'd. It appears, that he form'd his Ideas and made his Gust from reading *Homer;* and in that imitated *Zeuxis* and *Polignotus,* who, as *Maximus Tyrius* relates, treated their Subjects in their Pictures, as *Homer* did in his Poetry.

To these Remarks I have annex'd the Opinions of our Author upon the best and chiefest Painters of the two foregoing Ages.

22–24   That . . . [*to*] . . . portion] *set in italics in* Q.
24   Remark on the] *Remark on the* Q.
25   Verse] *Verse* Q.   27–28   *belle-lettre*] *belle lettere* Q.
28   Poesy] *Poesy* Q.   31   *Maximus Tyrius*] *Tyrius Maximus* Q.

He tells you candidly and briefly what were their Excellencies, and what their Failings.

[¶ 541.] *I pass in Silence many things which will be more amply treated in the ensuing Commentary.* 'Tis evident by this, how much we lose, and what damage we have sustain'd by our Authors death, since those Commentaries had undoubtedly contain'd things of high Value and of great instruction.

[¶ 544.] *To intrust with the Muses,* &c. That is to say, to write in Verse, Poetry being under their Protection, and consecrated to them.

---

4 *the ensuing*] the ensuing Q.
9 Poetry] *Poetry* Q.

The Judgment of Charles Alphonse du Fresnoy
On the Works of the Principal and Best
Painters of the Two Last Ages

P AINTING *was in its Perfection amongst the* Greeks. *The
principal Schools were at* Sycion, *afterwards at* Rhodes,
at Athens, *and at* Corinth, *and at last in* Rome. *Wars and
Luxury having overthrown the* Roman *Empire, it was totally ex-
tinguish'd, together with all the noble Arts, the Studies of Hu-
manity, and the other Sciences.*

    *It began to appear again in the Year 1450 amongst some Paint-
ers of* Florence, *of which* Domenico Ghirlandaio *was one, who
was Master to* Michael Angelo, *and had some kind of Reputation,*
10 *though his manner was* Gothique *and very dry.*

    Michael Angelo *his Scholar, flourish'd in the times of* Julius
the Second, Leo the Tenth, Paul the Third, *and of eight succes-
sive Popes. He was a Painter, a Sculptor, and an Architect, both
Civil and Military. The Choice which he made of his Postures
was not always beautifull or pleasing: His Gust of Designing was
not the finest, nor his Out-lines the most elegant: The Folds
of his Draperies, and the Ornaments of his Habits, were neither
noble nor gracefull. He was not a little fantastical and extrava-
gant in his Compositions; he was bold even to Rashness, in tak-
20 ing Liberties against the Rules of Perspective. His Colouring
is not over true or very pleasant. He knew not the Artifice of the
Lights and Shadows: But he design'd more learnedly, and better
understood all the Knittings of the Bones, with the Office and
Situation of the Muscles, than any of the modern Painters. There
appears a certain Air of Greatness and Severity in his Figures,
in both which he has oftentimes succeeded: But above the rest
of his Excellencies, was his wonderfull skill in Architecture,*

7   *1450*] 1450 Q.
8 Domenico Ghirlandaio] DOMENICO GHIRLANDAIO Q.
11   Michael Angelo] MICHAEL ANGELO Q.
12 the Second . . . the Tenth . . . the Third] *the second . . . the tenth . . . the
third* Q.
13 *Painter . . . Sculptor . . . Architect*] Painter . . . Sculptor . . . Architect Q.

wherein he has not onely surpass'd all the Moderns, but even the Ancients also: The St. Peter's *of* Rome, *the St.* John's *of* Florence, *the* Capitol, *the* Palazzo Farnese, *and his own House, are sufficient Testimonies of it. His Scholars were* Marcello Venusto, Andrea de Vaterra, Il Rosso, Georgio Vasari, Fra. Bastiano, *(who commonly painted for him) and many other* Florentines.

Pietro Perugino *design'd with sufficient knowledge of Nature, but he is dry and his manner little.*

10   *His Scholar was* Raphael Santio, *who was born on* Good Friday, *in the Year 1483; and died on* Good Friday, *in the Year 1520: So that he liv'd onely 37 years compleat. He surpass'd all modern Painters, because he possess'd more of the excellent parts of Painting than any other; and 'tis believ'd, that he equall'd the Ancients, excepting onely that he design'd not naked Bodies with so much Learning, as* Michael Angelo: *But his Gust of Designing is purer and much better. He painted not with so good, so full, and so gracefull a manner as* Correggio; *nor has he any thing of the Contrast of the Lights and Shadows,*
20   *or so strong and free a Colouring, as* Titian; *but he had a better disposition in his Pieces, without comparison, than either* Titian, Correggio, Michael Angelo, *or all the rest of the succeeding Painters to our days. His Choice of Postures, of Heads, of Ornaments, the Suitableness of his Drapery, his manner of Designing, his Varieties, his Contrasts, his Expressions, were beautifull in Perfection; but above all, he possess'd the Graces in so advantageous a manner, that he has never since been equall'd by any other. There are Portraits (or single Figures of his) which are finish'd Pieces. He was an admirable Architect. He was hand-*
30   *some, well made, and tall of Stature, civil, and well-natur'd, never refusing to teach another what he knew himself. He had many Scholars, amongst others,* Julio Romano, Polydore, Gaud-

---

3   *House*] House Q.
8   Pietro Perugino] PIETRO PERUGINO Q.
10   *His*] *no paragraph break in* Q.
10   Raphael Santio] RAPHAEL SANTIO Q (*paragraph break at* "RAPHAEL").
10–11   Good Friday] *Good Friday* Q.   11   *1483*] 1483 Q.
11   Good Friday] *Good Friday* Q.   12   *1520 ... 37*] 1520 ... 37 Q.
21   *Pieces,*] ~∧ Q.   28   *Portraits*] *Protraits* Q.

ens, Giovanni d'Udine, *and* Michael Coxis. *His Graver was* Marc
Antonio, *whose Prints are admirable for the correctness of their
Out-lines.*

   Julio Romano *was the most excellent of all* Raphael's *Scholars;
he had Conceptions which were more extraordinary, more pro-
found, and more elevated, than even his Master himself. He was
also a great Architect, his Gust was pure and exquisite. He was
a great Imitator of the Ancients, giving a clear Testimony in all
his Productions, that he was desirous to restore to Practice the*
10 *same Forms and Fabricks which were ancient. He had the good
Fortune to find great persons who committed to him the care of
Edifices, Vestibules and Portico's, all Tetrastyles, Xistes, Thea-
tres, and such other places as are not now in use. He was wonder-
full in his Choice of Postures. His manner was drier and harder
than any of* Raphael's *School. He did not exactly understand the
Lights and Shadows or the Colours. He is frequently harsh and
ungracefull: The Folds of his Draperies are neither beautifull
nor great, easie nor natural, but all extravagant and too like the
Habits of fantastical Comedians. He was very knowing in hu-*
20 *mane Learning. His Scholars were* Pirro Ligorio, *(who was ad-
mirable for Ancient Buildings, as for Towns, Temples, Tombs,
and Trophies, and the Situation of Ancient Edifices)* Æneas Vico,
Bonasone, Georgio Mantuano, *and others.*

   Polydore, *Scholar to* Raphael, *design'd admirably well, as to
the practical part, having a particular Genius for Freezes, as we
may see by those of white and black, which he has painted at*
Rome. *He imitated the Ancients, but his manner was greater
than that of* Julio Romano: *Nevertheless* Julio *seems to be the
truer. Some admirable Grouppes are seen in his Works, and such*
30 *as are not elsewhere to be found. He colour'd very seldom, and
made Landtschapes of a reasonable good Gusto.*

   Gio. Bellino, *one of the first who was of any consideration at*
Venice, *painted very drily according to the manner of his time.
He was very knowing both in Architecture and Perspective. He*

---

4   Julio Romano] JULIO ROMANO Q.
12–13   *Edifices, Vestibules . . . Portico's . . . Tetrastyles, Xistes, Theatres*] Edifices,
Vestibules . . . Portico's . . . Tetrastyles, Xistes, Theatres Q.
24   Polydore] POLYDORE Q.
32   Gio. Bellino] GIO. BELLINO Q.

was Titian's *first Master, which may easily be observ'd in the first Painting of that noble Scholar; in which we may remark that Propriety of Colours which his Master has observ'd.*

About this time Georgione, *the Contemporary of* Titian, *came to excell in Portraits or Face-painting, and also in great Works. He first began to make choice of Glowing and Agreeable Colours; the Perfection and entire Harmony of which were afterwards to be found in* Titian's *Pictures. He dress'd his Figures wonderfully well: And it may be truly said, that but for him,*
10 Titian *had never arriv'd to that height of Perfection, which proceeded from the Rivalship and Jealousy of Honour betwixt those two.*

Titian *was one of the greatest Colourists, who was ever known; he design'd with much more Ease and Practice than* Georgione. *There are to be seen Women and Children of his hand, which are admirable both for the Design and Colouring: the Gust of them is delicate, charming and noble, with a certain pleasing Negligence of the Head-dresses, the Draperies and Ornaments of Habits, which are wholly peculiar to him. As for the Figures*
20 *of Men, he has design'd them but moderately well. There are even some of his Draperies, which are mean and savour of a little gust. His painting is wonderfully glowing, sweet and delicate. He made Portraicts, which were extremely noble; the Postures of them being very gracefull, grave, diversify'd, and adorn'd after a very becoming fashion. No man ever painted Landtschape, with so great a manner, so good a colouring, and with such a resemblance of Nature. For eight or ten years space, he copy'd with great labour and exactness whatsoever he undertook; thereby to make himself an easy way, and to establish some*
30 *general maximes for his future conduct. Besides the excellent gust which he had of Colours, in which he excell'd all Mortal Men, he perfectly understood how to give every thing the touches which were most suitable, and proper to them; such as distinguish'd them from each other, and which gave the greatest Spirit, and the most of Truth. The Pictures which he made in his be-*

---

2   *Scholar;*] ∼, Q.
4   Georgione, ... Titian,] GEORGIONE∧ ... ∼∧ Q.
13   Titian] TITIAN Q.   33–34   *them; ... other,*] ∼, ... ∼; Q.

*ginning, and in the declension of his Age, are of a dry, and mean
manner. He liv'd ninety nine years. His Scholars were* Paul
Veronese, Giacomo Tintoret, Giacomo da Ponte, Bassano, *and
his Brothers.*

Paul Veronese *was wonderfully graceful in his Airs of Women:
with great variety of shining Draperies; and incredible vivacity,
and ease. Nevertheless his Composition is sometimes improper;
and his Design is uncorrect. But his colouring, and whatsoever
depends on it, is so very charming in his Pictures, that it surprizes*
10 *at the first sight, and makes us totally forget those other qualities
which are wanting in him.*

Tintoret *was Scholar to* Titian, *great in the practical part of
Designing; but sometimes also sufficiently extravagant. He had
an admirable Genius for Painting, if he had had as great an
affection to his Art, and as much patience in undergoing the
difficulties of it, as he had fire and vivacity of Nature: He has
made Pictures, not inferiour in beauty to those of* Titian: *his
Composition and his Dresses, are for the most part improper;
and his Out-lines are not correct: But his Colouring, and the*
20 *dependencies of it, like that of his Master, are most admirable.*

The Bassans *had a more mean and poorer gust in Painting
than* Tintoret; *and their Designs were also less correct than his.
They had indeed an excellent gust of Colours; and have touch'd
all kinds of Animals with an admirable manner: But were no-
toriously imperfect in the Composition and Design.*

Correggio *painted at* Parma *two large Cupolo's in Fresco, and
some Altar-pieces. This Artist, found out certain natural and
unaffected Graces, for his* Madonna's, *his Saints, and little Chil-
dren, which were particular to him. His Manner is exceeding*
30 *great, both for the design and for the work, but withall is very
uncorrect. His Pencil was both easie and delightfull, and 'tis to
be acknowledg'd, that he painted with great Strength, great
Heightning, great Sweetness, and liveliness of Colours, in which
none surpass'd him.*

2 Paul] Paulo Q.   4 *Brothers*] Q; *Sons* Q (*errata page*).
5 Paul Veronese] PAULO VERONESE Q.
12 Tintoret] TINTORET Q.   21 Bassans] BASSANS Q.
26 Correggio] CORREGGIO Q.   28 Madonna's] Madonnas' Q.
28–29 *Saints . . . little Children*] Saints . . . little Children Q.

He understood how to distribute his Lights in such a manner
as was wholly peculiar to himself, which gave a great force and
great roundness to his Figures. This manner consists in extend-
ing a large Light, and then making it lose it self insensibly in the
dark shadowings, which he plac'd out of the Masses. And those
give them this great roundness, without our being able to per-
ceive from whence proceeds so much of force, and so vast a
pleasure to the Sight. 'Tis probable, that in this part the rest of
the Lombard School copied him. He had no great choice of
10 gracefull Postures, nor of distribution for beautifull Grouppes:
his Design oftentimes appears lame, and the Positions are not
much observ'd in them. The Aspects of his Figures are many
times unpleasing; but his manner of designing Heads, Hands,
Feet, and other parts, is very great, and well deserves our imita-
tion. In the conduct and finishing of a Picture, he has done won-
ders; for he painted with so much Union, that his greatest Works
seem'd to have been finish'd in the compass of one day; and
appear, as if we saw them from a Looking-glass. His Landtschape
is equally beautifull with his Figures.

20   At the same time with Correggio, liv'd and flourish'd Par-
megiano; who besides his great manner of well Colouring, ex-
cell'd also both in Invention and Design, with a Genius full of
gentileness and of spirit, having nothing that was ungracefull
in his choice of Postures and in the dresses of his Figures, which
we cannot say of Correggio: there are Pieces of his to be seen,
which are both beautifull and correct.

These two Painters last mention'd, had very good Scholars, but
they are known onely to those of their own Province; and be-
sides there is little to be credited of what his Country-men say,
30 for Painting is wholly extinguish'd amongst them.

I say nothing of Leonardo da Vinci, because I have seen but

9   *School*] School Q.   9   *him. He*] ~: *he* Q.
18 *Looking-glass*] Looking-glass Q.
18–19 *Landtschape ... Figures*] Landtschape ... Figures Q.
20–21 Parmegiano] PARMEGIANO Q.
22 *Genius*] Genius Q.
23 *gentileness*] *errata page in Q* (gentileness); *gentleness* Q.
27 *These*] *no paragraph break in Q.*   29 *Country-men*] Country-men Q.
31 Leonardo ... Vinci] LEONARDO ... VINCI Q.

little of his, though he restor'd the Arts at Milan, *and had many Scholars there.*

Ludovico Carracci, *Uncle to* Hannibal *and* Augustine, *studied at* Parma *after* Correggio; *and excell'd in Design and Colouring, with such a Gracefulness, and so much Candour, that* Guido, *the Scholar of* Hannibal, *did afterwards imitate him with great success. There are some of his Pictures to be seen, which are very beautifull, and well understood. He made his ordinary residence at* Bologna, *and it was He, who put the Pencil into the hands of*
10 Hannibal *his Nephew.*

Hannibal *in a little time excell'd his Master, in all parts of Painting: He imitated* Correggio, Titian, *and* Raphael, *in their different manners as he pleas'd, excepting onely that you see not in his Pictures, the Nobleness, the Graces, and the Charms of* Raphael, *and that his Out-lines are neither so pure, nor so elegant as his. In all other things, he is wonderfully accomplish'd, and of an Universal Genius.*

Augustine, *Brother to* Hannibal, *was also a very good Painter, and an admirable Graver. He had a Natural Son, call'd* Antonio,
20 *who dyed at the age of 35, and who according to the general opinion, wou'd have surpass'd his Uncle* Hannibal: *for by what he left behind him, it appears that he was of a more lofty Genius.*

Guido *chiefly imitated* Ludovico Carracci, *yet retain'd always somewhat of the manner which his Master* Lawrence *the* Flemming *taught him. This* Lawrence *liv'd at* Bologna, *and was Competitor and Rival to* Ludovico Carracci: Guido *made the same use of* Albert Durer, *as* Virgil *did of old* Ennius: *borrow'd what pleas'd him, and made it afterwards his own: that is, he accommodated what was good in* Albert *to his own manner:*
30 *which he executed with so much gracefulness and beauty, that He alone got more Money, and more Reputation in his time, than his own Masters, and all the Scholars of the* Carraccis,

---

3   Ludovico Carracci] LUDOVICO CARRACCI Q.
5   Guido,] ~∧ Q.
11 Hannibal] HANNIBAL Q.
17 *Universal Genius*] Universal Genius Q.
18 Augustine] AUGUSTINO Q.
19 Antonio] ANTONIO Q.   20   *35*] 35 Q.
23 Guido] GUIDO Q.   32   Carraccis] Carraches Q.

though they were of greater capacity than himself. His Heads yield no manner of precedence to those of Raphael.

Sisto Badolocchi *design'd the best of all his Scholars: but he dy'd young.*

Domenichino *was a very knowing Painter, and very laborious, but otherwise of no great Natural Endowments: 'tis true, he was profoundly skill'd in all the parts of Painting, but wanting Genius, as I said, he had less of nobleness in his Works than all the rest who studied in the School of the* Carraccis.

10   Albani *was excellent in all that belong'd to Painting, and adorn'd with variety of Learning.*

John Lanfranc, *a Man of a great and sprightly wit, supported his Reputation for a long time with an extraordinary gust of Design and Colouring. But his foundation being onely on the practical part, he at length lost ground in point of correctness: so that many of his Pieces appear extravagant and fantastical. And after his Decease, the School of the* Carraccis *went dayly to decay in all the parts of Painting.*

Gio. Viola *was very old before he learn'd Landtschape, the*
20   *knowledge of which was imparted to him by* Hannibal Carracci, *who took pleasure to instruct him, so that he painted many of that kind which are wonderfully fine and well colour'd.*

If we cast our eyes towards Germany *and the* Low-Countries, *we may there behold* Albert Durer, Lucas Van Leyden, Holbein, Aldegrave, *and* Isbin, *who were all Contemporaries. Amongst these,* Albert Durer *and* Holbein, *were both of them wonderfully knowing and had certainly been of the first form of Painters, had they travell'd into* Italy: *For nothing can be laid to their charge, but onely that they had a* Gothique *Gust. As for* Holbein,

---

3   Sisto Badolocchi] SISTO BADOLOCCHI Q.
5   Domenichino] DOMENICHINO Q.
8   *Genius*] Genius Q.
9   Carraccis] Carraches Q.
10   Albani] ALBANO Q.
12   John Lanfranc] JOHN LANFRANC Q.
17   Carraccis] Carraches Q.
19   Gio. Viola] GIO. VIOLA Q.
20   Carracci] Carracche Q.
24–25   Albert Durer, Lucas Van Leyden, Holbein, Aldegrave . . . Isbin] ALBERT DURER, LUCAS VAN LEYDEN, HOLBEIN, ALDEGRAVE . . . ISBIN Q.

he perform'd yet better than Raphael; *and I have seen a Portrait of his Painting, with which one of* Titian's *could not come in Competition.*

Amongst the Flemmings, *we had* Rubens, *who deriv'd from his Birth, a lively, free, noble and universal Genius; a Genius which was capable not onely of raising him to the rank of the Ancient Painters, but also to the highest employment in the Service of his Country: so that he was chosen for one of the most important Embassies of our Age. His Gusto of Designing savours*
10 *somewhat more of the* Flemming *than of the Beauty of the Antique, because he stay'd not long at* Rome. *And though we cannot but observe in all his Paintings, somewhat of great and noble; yet it must be confess'd, that generally speaking, he design'd not correctly: But for all the other parts of Painting, he was as absolute a Master of them, and possess'd them all as throughly as any of his Predecessors in that noble Art. His principal Studies were made in* Lombardy, *after the Works of* Titian, Paul Veronese *and* Tintoret; *whose Cream he has skimm'd (if you will allow the Phrase) and extracted from their several Beauties*
20 *many general Maxims and infallible Rules, which he always follow'd, and by which he has acquir'd in his Works, a greater Facility than that of* Titian; *more of Purity, Truth and Science, than* Paul Veronese; *and more of Majesty, Repose and Moderation, than* Tintoret. *To conclude, His manner is so solid, so knowing, and so ready, that it may seem, this rare accomplish'd Genius was sent from Heaven to instruct Mankind in the Art of Painting.*

His School was full of admirable Scholars, amongst whom Van Dyck *was he who best comprehended all the Rules and general*
30 *Maxims of his Master; and who has even excell'd him in the delicacy of his Colouring and in his Cabinet Pieces; but his Gust in the designing Part, was nothing better than that of* Rubens.

---

1 *Portrait*] Portrait Q.   4 **Rubens**] RUBENS Q.
5 *Genius; a Genius*] Genius. *A* Genius Q.
7 *Ancient Painters*] Ancient Painters Q.
9 *Embassies*] Embassies Q.
28–29 Van Dyck] VAN DYCK Q.
29 *he*] ∼, Q.

FRONTISPIECE OF *The Works of Lucian* (1711)

ENGRAVED TITLE OF THE FIRST EDITION

THE
WORKS
OF
LUCIAN,

Tranflated from the G R E E K,
by feveral Eminent Hands.

𝕿𝖍𝖊 𝕱𝖎𝖗𝖘𝖙 𝖁𝖔𝖑𝖚𝖒𝖊.

W I T H

The Life of *Lucian,*
A
Difcourfe on his WRITINGS,
A N D
A CHARACTER of fome of the prefent
Tranflators.

Written by JOHN DRYDEN, *Efq;*

L O N D O N,
Printed for SAM. BRISCOE, and fold by *J. Wood-
ward* in *Scalding-Alley* againft *Stocks-Market,* and
J. Morphew near *Stationers-Hall.* 1711.

TITLE PAGE OF THE FIRST EDITION (MACDONALD 141)

The Life of Lucian
Written by John Dryden, Esq;
Poet Laureate and Historiographer
to King Charles II and James II

THE Writing a Life is at all Times, and in all Circumstances the most difficult Task of an Historian; and notwithstanding the numerous Tribe of Biographers, we can scarce find one, except *Plutarch,* who deserves our Perusal, or can invite a second View. But if the Difficulty be so great, where the Materials are plentiful, and the Incidents extraordinary; what must it be when the Person that affords the Subject, denies Matter enough for a Page? The Learned seldom abound with Action, and it is Action only, that furnishes the Historian with
10 Things agreeable and instructive. 'Tis true, that *Diogenes Laertius,* and our learned Country-man Mr. *Stanley,* have both written the Lives of the Philosophers; but we are more obliged to the various Principles of their several Sects, than to any thing remarkable, that they did, for our Entertainment.

But *Lucian,* as pleasing and useful as he was in his Writings, in the opinion of the most candid Judges, has left so little of his own Affairs on Record, that there is scarce sufficient to fill a Page from his Birth to his Death.

There were many of the Name of *Lucian* among the Antients,
20 eminent in several Ways, and whose Names have reach'd Posterity with Honour and Applause. *Suidas* mentions one, as a Man of singular Probity, who having discharg'd the Administration of the Chief Prefect of the Oriental Empire, under *Arcadius,* with extraordinary Justice and Praise of the People, drew on himself the Envy and Hate of the Courtiers (the constant Attendant of eminent Virtue and Merit) and the Anger of the Emperor himself; and was at last murder'd by *Rufinus.*

---

3   Biographers] *Biographers* O.   9   Action ... Action] *Action ... Action* O.
14   Entertainment] O *(corrected form?)*; Entertainmeut O *(uncorrected form?).*
15   useful] ∼, O.   24   People,] ∼; O.
27   *Rufinus*] *Rafiany* O.

Among those, who were Eminent for their Learning, were some Divines, and Philosophers. Of the former we find one in St. *Cyprian,* to whom the fourth and seventeenth Epistles are ascrib'd. There was another, Priest of the Church of *Antioch,* who, as *Suidas* assures us, reviewed, corrected and restored, to its primitive Purity, the *Hebrew* Bible; and afterward suffer'd Martyrdom at *Nicomedia,* under *Maximinian.* A third was a Priest of *Jerusalem,* who not only made a Figure among the Learned of his own Age, but, as *Gesnerus* observes, convey'd
10 his Reputation to Posterity by the remains of his Writings.

But none of this Name has met with the general Applause of so many Ages, as *Lucian* the Philosopher, and eminent Sophist, who was Author of the following Dialogues; of whose Birth, Life, and Death, I shall give you all I could collect of any certain and historical Credit.

He had not the good Fortune to be born of illustrious or wealthy Parents, which give a Man a very advantagious Rise on his first Appearance in the World; but the Father of our *Lucian* labour'd under so great a straitness of Estate, that he was fain to
20 put his Son Apprentice to a Statuary, whose Genius for the finer Studies was so extraordinary and so rare; because he hoped from that Business not only a speedy supply to his own Wants, but was secure, that his Education, in that Art, would be much less Expensive to him.

He was born in *Samosata,* a City of *Syria,* not far from the River *Euphrates;* and for this reason he calls himself more than once an *Assyrian,* and a *Syrian;* but he was deriv'd from a *Greek* Original, his Forefathers having been Citizens of *Patras* in *Achaia.*

30 We have nothing certain as to the exact Time of his Birth. *Suidas* confirms his flourishing under the Emperor *Trajan;* but then he was likewise before him: Some mention the Reign of *Adrian;* but it cannot be fix'd to any Year, or Consulate.

The Person he was bound to was his Uncle; a Man of a severe and morose Temper; of whom he was to learn the Statuaries and

3 fourth...seventeenth] Fourth...Seventeenth O.
13 Dialogues; of] ~. Of O.   27 but] But O.
28 *Patras*] *Patra* O.

Stone-cutters Art: For his Father observing our *Lucian,* now a
Boy, of his own Head, and without any Instructor, make various
Figures in Wax, he persuaded himself, that if he had a good
Master, he could not but arrive to an uncommon Excellence in it.

But it happen'd, in the very beginning of his Time, he broke
a Model, and was very severely call'd to account for it by his
Master. He not liking this Treatment, and having a Soul and
Genius above any Mechanic Trade, run away Home.

After which, in his Sleep, there appear'd to him two young
10 Women, or rather the tutelar Goddesses of the Statuary Art, and
of the Liberal Sciences, hotly disputing of their Preference to
each other: and on a full Hearing of both Sides, he bids adieu to
Statuary, and entirely surrenders himself to the conduct of Vir-
tue, and Learning. And as his Desires of Improvement were
great, and the Instructions he had very good, the Progress he
made was as considerable; till by the maturity of his Age and
his Study, he made his Appearance in the World.

Tho' it is not to be suppos'd, that there is any thing of reality
in this Dream or Vision of *Lucian,* which he treats of in his
20 Works; yet this may be gather'd from it, that, *Lucian* himself
having consulted his Genius, and the nature of the Study his
Father had allotted him and that to which he found a Propensity
in himself, he quitted the former and pursued the latter, choos-
ing rather to form the Minds of Men, than their Statues.

In his Youth he taught Rhetoric in *Gaul,* and in several other
Places. He pleaded likewise at the Bar in *Antioch,* the Capital
of *Syria;* but the Noise of the Bar disgusting, and his ill Success
in Causes disheart'ning him, he quitted the Practice of Rhetoric,
and the Law, and applied himself to Writing.

30 He was forty Years old when he first took to Philosophy. Hav-
ing a mind to make himself known in *Macedon,* he took the
Opportunity of Speaking in the publick Assembly of all that
Region. In his old Age he was receiv'd into the Imperial Family,
and had the Place of Intendant of *Egypt,* after he had travell'd

---

1   Art:] ~. O.
2   Head] O (*corrected form?*); head O (*uncorrected form?*).
3   Wax,] ~; O.   20–22   that, . . . him] ~ₐ . . . ~, O.
23   latter,] O (*corrected form?*); ~; O (*uncorrected form?*).
33   Imperial Family] *Imperial Family* O.

through almost all the known Countries of that Age, to improve
his Knowledge in Men, Manners and Arts: For some Writers
make this particular Observation on his Travel into *Gaul* and
Residence in that Country, That he gain'd there the greatest
part of his knowledge in Rhetoric; that Region being in his
Age, and also before it, a Nursery of Eloquence and Oratory,
as *Juvenal, Martial,* and others, sufficiently witness.

The manner of his Death is obscure to us, tho' 'tis most prob-
able he died of the Gout. *Suidas* alone tells a Story of his being
10 worry'd to death, and devour'd by Dogs, returning from a Feast;
which being so uncommon a Death, so very improbable, and
attested only by one Author, has found little Credit with Pos-
terity. If it be true, that he was once a *Christian,* and afterwards
became a Renegade to our Belief, perhaps some Zealots may
have invented this Tale of his Death, as a just and signal Punish-
ment for his Apostacy. All Men are willing to have the Miracle,
or at least the wonderful Providence, go on their Side; and will
be teaching *God Almighty* what he ought to do in this World,
as well as in the next: as if they were proper Judges of his De-
20 crees, and for what end he prospers some, or punishes others in
this Life. *Ablancourt,* and our learned Countryman Dr. *Mayne,*
look on the Story, as a Fiction: and for my part, I can see no
reason either to believe he ever profess'd *Christianity;* or if he
did, why he must not more probably die in his Bed at so great an
Age, as Fourscore, and Ten, than be torn in Pieces and devour'd
by Dogs, when he was too feeble to defend himself. *So early
began the want of Charity, the presumption of meddling with
God's Government, and the Spirit of Calumny, amongst the
primitive Believers.*

30 Of his Posterity we know nothing more, than that he left a
Son behind him, who was as much in Favour with the Emperor
Julian, as his Father had been with *Aurelius* the Philosopher.
This Son became in time a famous Sophist; and among the
Works of *Julian* we find an Epistle of that great Person to him.

---

2 Arts:] ~. O.   5 Rhetoric;] ~: O.
6 Oratory,] ~; O.   12 Author] *Author* O.
16 Apostacy] *Apostacy* O.   21 *Ablancourt*] *Ablancour* O.
21 *Mayne*] *Mayn* O.

I find that I have mingled, before I was aware, some things which are doubtful with some which are certain; forc'd indeed by the narrowness of the Subject, which affords very little of undisputed Truth: Yet I find myself oblig'd to do Right to Monsieur *d'Ablancourt,* who is not positively of opinion, that *Suidas* was the Author of this Fable; but rather, that it descended to him by the Tradition of former Times, yet without any certain ground of Truth. He concludes it however to be a Calumny; perhaps a charitable kind of Lye, to deter others from Satyrizing the new Dogma's of *Christianity,* by the Judgment shown on *Lucian.* We find nothing in his Writings which gives any hint of his professing our Belief: But being naturally Curious, and living not only amongst *Christians,* but in the Neighbourhood of *Judea,* he might reasonably be suppos'd to be knowing in our Points of Faith, without believing them. He ran a muck, and laid about him on all Sides, with more Fury on the Heathens, whose Religion he profess'd; he struck at ours but casually, as it came in his way, rather than, as he sought it; he contemn'd it too much to write in earnest against it.

We have indeed the highest Probabilities for our reveal'd Religion; Arguments which will preponderate with a reasonable Man, upon a long, and careful Disquisition; but I have always been of Opinion, that we can demonstrate nothing, because the Subject-matter is not capable of a Demonstration. 'Tis the particular Grace of God, that any Man believes the Mysteries of our Faith; which I think a conclusive Argument against the Doctrine of Persecution in any Church. And tho' I am absolutely convinc'd, as I heartily thank God I am, not only of the general Principles of *Christianity,* but of all Truths necessary to Salvation in the *Roman* Church; yet I cannot but detest our Inquisition as it is practis'd in some foreign Parts, particularly in *Spain,* and in the *Indies.*

Those Reasons which are cogent to me, may not prevail with others, who bear the Denomination of *Christians;* and those

---

5   *d'Ablancourt*] *d'Ablancour* O.
5   *Suidas*] O *(corrected form?); Suidas* O *(uncorrected form?).*
10   *Christianity,*] ∼‸ O.   16   Heathens] *Heathens* O.
20   We] *no paragraph break in* O.

which are prevalent with all *Christians,* in regard of their Birth and Education, may find no Force when they are used against *Mahometans* or Heathens. To instruct, is a charitable Duty; to compel, by Threatnings and Punishment, is the Office of a Hangman, and the Principle of a Tyrant.

But my Zeal in a good Cause (as I believe) has transported me beyond the Limits of my Subject. I was endeavouring to prove that *Lucian* had never been a Member of the *Christian* Church; and methinks it makes for my Opinion, that in relating the Death
10 of *Peregrinus,* who being born a Pagan, pretended afterwards to turn *Christian,* and turned himself publickly at the *Olympic* Games, at his Death professing himself a Cynic Philosopher; it seems, I say, to me, that *Lucian* wou'd not have so severely declaim'd against this *Proteus,* (which was another of *Peregrinus* his Names) if he himself had been guilty of that Apostacy.

I know not that this Passage has been observ'd by any Man before me. And yet in this very place it is that this Author has more severely handled our Belief, and more at large, than in any other part of all his Writings, excepting only the Dialogue
20 of *Triephon* and *Critias,* wherein he lashes his own false Gods with more severity than the true; and where the first *Christians,* with their cropt Hair, their whining Voices, melancholy Faces, mournful Discourses, nasty Habits, are describ'd with a greater air of *Calvinists* or *Quakers,* than of *Roman Catholicks,* or *Church of England Men.*

After all, what if this Discourse last mention'd, and the rest of the Dialogues, wherein the *Christians* are Satyriz'd, were none of *Lucian's?* The learned and ingenious Dr. *Mayne,* whom I have before cited, is of this Opinion; and confirms it by the
30 attestation of *Philander, Obsopæus, Micyllus* and *Cognatus;* whom, since I have not read, or two of them but very super-

---

3   Heathens] *Heathens* O.
4   of a] of O.
10 Pagan] *Pagan* O.
12 Cynic] *Cynic* O.
18 Belief] *Belief* O.
26 Discourse] ∼, O.
29 before cited] before-cited O.
30 *Micyllus*] *Mycillus* O.

10 *Peregrinus*] *Perigrinus* O.
12 Death] ∼, O.
12 Philosopher; it] ∼. It O.
25 *England Men*] England Men O.
28 *Mayne*] *Mayn* O.
30 *Obsopæus,*] ∼∧ O.
30 *Cognatus*] *Copnatus* O.

ficially, I refer you, for the faith of his Quotation, to the Authors themselves.

The next Supposition concerning *Lucian*'s Religion, is, that he was of none at all. I doubt not but the same People, who broach'd the Story of his being once a *Christian,* follow'd their blow upon him, in this second Accusation.

There are several sorts of *Christians* at this Day reigning in the World, who will not allow any Man to believe in the Son of God, whose other Articles of Faith are not in all things con-
10 formable to theirs. Some of these exercise this rigid, and severe kind of Charity, with a good Intent of reducing several Sects into one common Church. But this Spirit of others is evidently seen by their detraction, their Malice, their spitting Venom, their raising false Reports of those, who are not of their Communion. I wish the Antientness of these censorious Principles may be prov'd by better Arguments, than by any near resemblance, they have with the primitive Believers. But till I am convinc'd, that *Lucian* has been charg'd with Atheism of Old, I shall be apt to think, that this Accusation is very modern.
20   One of *Lucian*'s Translators pleads in his Defence, that it was very improbable, a Man, who has laugh'd Paganism out of Doors, should believe no God; that he who cou'd point to the Sepulchre of *Jupiter* in *Crete,* as well as our *Tertullian,* shou'd be an Atheist. But this Argument, I confess, is of little weight to prove him a Deist, only because he was no Polytheist. He might as well believe in none, as in many Gods. And on the other side, he might believe in many, as *Julian* did, and not in one. For my own part, I think it is not prov'd, that either of them were Apostates; though one of them, in hopes of an Empire, might
30 temporize, while *Christianity* was the Mode at Court. Neither is our Author clear'd any thing the more because his Writings have serv'd in the times of the Heathens, to destroy that vain, unreasonable and impious Religion: that was an oblique Service, which *Lucian* never intended us; for his Business, like that of some modern Polemiques, was rather to pull down every

---

22 God] GOD O.   25 Polytheist] *Polythiest* O.
30 Mode at Court.] *Mode at Court:* O.   33 Religion:] ∼, O.
34 us; for] ∼. For O.   35 Polemiques] *Polemiqus* O.

thing, than to set up any thing. With what show of probability can I urge in his defence, that one of the greatest among the Fathers has drawn whole Homilies from our Author's Dialogues, since I know that *Lucian* made them not for that purpose? The occasional good which he has done, is not to be imputed to him; St. *Chrysostom,* St. *Augustin,* and many others, have apply'd his Arguments on better Motives, than their Author propos'd to himself in framing them.

These Reasons therefore, as they make nothing against his
10 being an Atheist, so they prove nothing of his believing One God; but only leave him as they found him, and leave us in as great an Obscurity concerning his Religion, as before. I may be as much mistaken in my Opinion, as these great Men have been before me; and this is very probable, because I know less of him, than they; yet I have read him over more than once, and therefore will presume to say, that I think him either one of the Elective School, or else a Sceptic: I mean, that he either form'd a Body of Philosophy for his own use, out of the Opinions, and Dogma's of several Heathen Philosophers, disagreeing amongst
20 themselves; or that he doubted of every thing; weigh'd all Opinions, and adher'd to none of them; only us'd them, as they serv'd his occasion for the present Dialogue; and perhaps rejected them in the next. And indeed, this last opinion is the more probable of the two, if we consider the Genius of the Man, whose Image we may clearly see in the Glass, which he holds before us of his Writings, which reflects him to our sight.

Not to dwell on Examples, with which his Works are amply furnish'd, I will only mention two. In one *Socrates* convinces his Friend *Chærephon* of the Power of the Gods in Transforma-
30 tions, and of a supream Providence, which accompanies that Power in the administration of the World. In another, he confutes *Jupiter,* and pulls him down from Heaven to Earth by his own *Homerical* Chain, and makes him only a subservient Slave

---

11   in] ~, O.
13   be] ~, O.
15   more] ~, O.
17   Elective ... Sceptic] *Elective ... Sceptic* O.
31   In] *paragraph break in O.*

to blind eternal Fate. I might add, that he is, in one half of his Book, a Stoic, in the other an *Epicurean,* never constant to himself in any Scheme of Divinity, unless it be in despising his Gentile Gods: And this derision, as it shows the Man himself, so it gives us an Idea of the Age in which he liv'd; for if that had been devout, or ignorant, his scoffing Humour wou'd either have been restrain'd, or had not pass'd unpunish'd: all knowing Ages being naturally Sceptic, and not at all bigotted; which, if I am not much deceiv'd, is the proper Character of our own.

To conclude this Article, he was too fantastical, too giddy, too irresolute, either to be any thing at all, or any thing long; and in this view, I cannot think he was either a steady Atheist, or a Deist, but a Doubter, a Sceptic, as he plainly declares himself to be in the Dialogue (when he puts himself under the Name of *Hermotimus* the Stoic) call'd the *Dialogue of the Sects.*

As for his Morals, they are spoken of as variously as his Opinions. Some are for decrying him more, than he deserves; his Defenders themselves dare not set him up for a Pattern of severe Vertue. No Man is so profligate, as openly to profess Vice; and therefore it is no wonder if under the Reign of *Nerva, Trajan, Hadrian,* and the two *Antonines,* of which the last was his Patron and Benefactor, he liv'd not so much a Libertine as he had it to be in his Nature. He is more accus'd for his Love of Boys, than of Women. Not that we have any particular Story to convince us of this detestable Passion in him; but his own Writings bear this record against him, that he speaks often of it, and I know not, that ever he condemns it. Repeated Expressions, as well as repeated Actions, witness some secret Pleasure in the Deed, or at least, some secret Inclination to it. He seems to insinuate, in his *Dialogue of Loves,* that *Socrates* was given to this Vice; but we find not that he blames him for it, which if he had been wholly innocent himself, it became a Philosopher to have done.

---

2   Stoic] *Stoic* O.   2   *Epicurean*] *Epicuræan* O.
3–4   Gentile] *Gentile* O.   8   Sceptic] *Sceptic* O.
13   Sceptic,] *Sceptic*ᴧ O.
14–15   Dialogue (when ... Stoic)] ~, ~ ... *Stoic;* O.
15   *Dialogue of the Sects*] Dialogue of the Sects O.
21   *Antonines*] *Antonins* O.
30   *Dialogue of*] Diologue of O.

But as we pass over a foul way, as hastily, as we can, so I will leave this abominable Subject, which strikes me with Horrour when I name it.

If there be any, who are guilty of this Sin, we may assure our selves they will never stop at any other; for when they have over-leapt the Bounds of Nature, they run so fast to all other Immoralities, that the Grace of God, without a Miracle, can never overtake them.

Lucian is accus'd likewise for his writing too lusciously in his
10 *Dialogue of the Harlots.* It has been the common Fault of all Satyrists, to make Vice too amiable, while they expose it. But of all Men living, I am the most unfit to accuse *Lucian,* who am so little able to defend my self from the same Objection. We find not, however, that *Lucian* was charg'd with the Wantonness of his Dialogues, in his own Life-time. If he had been, he wou'd certainly have answered for himself, as he did to those, who accus'd him for exposing *Socrates, Plato, Diogenes,* and other great Philosophers, to the laughter of the People, when *Jupiter* sold them by an inch of Candle. But, to confess the Truth, I
20 am of their Opinion, who think, that Answer of his not over ingenuous, (*viz.*) that he only attack'd the false Philosophers of their Sects, in their Persons whom he honour'd; so I am persuaded, that he cou'd not have alledg'd more in his excuse, for these Dialogues, than that, as he taught Harlots to deceive, so, at the same time, he discover'd their Deceits to the knowledge of young Men, and thereby warn'd them to avoid the Snare.

I find him not charg'd with any other Faults, than what I have already mention'd. He was otherwise of a Life, as unblameable, as any Man, for ought we find to the contrary. And I
30 have this probable Inducement to believe it, because he had so honourable an Employment under *Marcus Aurelius,* an Emperour, as clear sighted, as he was truly vertuous; for both which Qualities, we need not quote *Lucian,* who was so much oblig'd to him, but may securely appeal to *Herodian,* and to all the Historians, who have written of him (besides the Testimony of

10   *Dialogue of the Harlots*] Dialogue of the Harlots O.
10   It] *paragraph break in O.*   11   amiable] aimable O.
22   Persons] ~, O .   32   vertuous; for] ~. For O.
35–218:2   (besides . . . Learned)] ∧~ . . . ~∧ O.

his own admirable Works; which are yet in the Hands of all the Learned).

As for those, who condemn our Author for the too much Gall, and Virulency of his Satires; 'tis to be suspected, says Dr. *Mayne,* that they themselves are guilty of those Hypocrisies, Crimes, and Follies, which he so sharply exposes, and at the same time endeavours to reform. I may add, that for the most part, he rather laughs like *Horace,* than bites like *Juvenal.* Indeed his Genius was of kin to both; but more nearly related to the former. Some
10 Diseases are curable by Lenitives; to others Corrosives are necessary. Can a Man inveigh too sharply against the Cruelty of Tyrants, the Pride and Vanity of the Great, the Covetousness of the Rich, the Baseness of the Sophists, and particularly of the Cyniques (who while they Preach Poverty to others, are heaping up Riches, and living in Gluttony), besides the Wrangling of the Sects amongst themselves, about Supream Happiness, which he describes at a Drunken Feast, and calls it the Battel of the *Lapithæ?*

Excepting what already is excepted, he seems to me, to be an
20 Enemy to nothing but to Vice, and Folly. The Pictures which he draws of *Nigrinus* and of *Demonax,* are, as fair, as that of Vertue her self; if, as the Philosopher said, she could wear a Body. And if we oppose to them the Lives of *Alexander* the false Prophet, and of *Peregrinus,* how pleasingly, and with how much Profit, does the Deformity of the last, set off the Beauty of the first!

Some of his Censurers accuse him of Flatness and want of Wit, in many places. These I suppose have read him in some *Latin* Translations, which I confess, are generally dull; and this
30 is the only Excuse I can make for them. Otherwise they accuse themselves too manifestly for want of Tast, or Understanding. Of this number is the wretched Author of the *Lucien en belle*

4   *Mayne*] *Mayn* O.
13–14   Sophists ... Cyniques] *Sophists ... Cyniques,* O.
14–15   (who ... Gluttony)] ₐ~ ... ~ₐ O.   16   Happiness,] ~; O.
18   *Lapithæ?*] ~. O.   25   Deformity] Deformity O.
26   first!] ~. O.   27   Some] *no paragraph break in O.*
28   These] *paragraph break in O.*   29   dull; and] ~. And O.

Humeur, who being himself as insipid as a *Dutch* Poet, yet ar-
raigns *Lucian* for his own Fault; introduces the Ghost of *Ablan-
court,* confessing his Coldness in many places, the poorness of
his Thoughts, and his want of Humour; represents his Readers
tir'd and yawning at his ill Buffoonry, and false Mirth, and
sleeping over his melancholick Stories, which are every where
stuff'd with Improbabilities. He cou'd have said no worse of a
Leyden Slip.

10 The best on't is, the Jaundice is only in his own Eyes, which
makes *Lucian* look yellow to him. All Mankind will exclaim
against him for Preaching this Doctrine; and be of Opinion
when they read his *Lucian,* that he look'd in a Glass, when he
drew his Picture. I wish I had the liberty to lash this *Frog-land*
Wit as he deserves: But when a Speech is not seconded in Parlia-
ment, it falls of course; and this Author has the whole Senate of
the Learned to pull him down: *Incipient Omnes pro Cicerone
loqui.*

'Tis to be acknowledged, that his best Translator, *Ablancourt,*
thinks him not a profound Master in any sort of Philosophy; but
20 only that he skimm'd enough from every Sect to serve his turn
in Rhetorick, which was his Profession. This he gathers from
his superficial way of Arguing. But why may not another Man
reply in his Defence, that he made choice of those kinds of
Reasons, which were most capable of being made to shine in
his facetious way of Arguing? and those undoubtedly were not
the most knotty, nor the deepest, but the most diverting, by
the sharpness of the Raillery. Dr. *Mayne,* so often prais'd, has
another opinion of *Lucian's* Learning, and the strength of his
witty Arguments, concluding on that Subject in these Words,
30 or near them: *For my part, I know not to whose Writings we*

---

1 *Humeur,* ... himself ... insipid] ~; ... ~, ... ~, O.
2 introduces] Introduces O.
5 at his ... and false] and his ... at false O.
6 Stories,] ~; O.   14 Wit] *Wit* O.
15 Senate] *Senate* O.   16 down:] ~. O.
18 Translator,] ~ₐ O.   25 Arguing?] ~; O.
27 *Mayne*] *Mayn* O.   30 them:] ~. O.
30 *For*] For O (*paragraph break*).
30–220:1 *my* ... [*to*] ... *our*] *set in romans in O.*

owe more our Christianity *(where the true God has succeeded a multitude of false), whether to the grave confutation of* Clemens Alexandrinus, Arnobius, Justin Martyr, *St.* Augustin, Lactantius, *&c. or the facetious Wit of* Lucian. I cannot doubt but the Treacherous Translatour wou'd have given his hand to what the *Englishman* has said of their common Author. The Success has justify'd his Opinion in the sight of all the World. *Lucian*'s manner of convincing, was certainly more pleasant, than that of the *Christian* Writers; and we know the Effect was full as powerful;
10 so easily can the Eternal Wisdom draw Good out of Evil, and make his Enemy subservient to the Establishment of his Faith.

I will not enlarge on the Praises of his Oratory: If we compare his Style with the *Greek* Historians his contemporaries, or near his time, we shall find it much more pure, than that of *Plutarch, Dion,* or *Appian;* though not so grave, because his Subjects and theirs, requir'd to be treated after a different manner. It was not of an uniform Webb, says *Mayne,* like *Thucydides, Polybius,* and some others, whom he names; but was somewhat peculiar to himself; his Words well chosen, his Periods round, the parts of
20 his Sentences harmoniously divided, a full Flood or even a Torrent of perswasion, without inequalities or swellings; such as might be put in equal comparison with the best Orations of *Demosthenes* or *Isocrates;* not so dry, as the first, nor so flowery, as the last. His Wit, says *Ablancourt,* was full of Urbanity, that *Attic* salt, which the *French* call fine Raillery; not obscene, not gross, not rude, but Facetious, well Manner'd, and well bred: Only he will not allow his Love the Quality last mention'd, but thinks it rustical, and according either to his own Genius, or that of the Age in which he liv'd.

---

1   Christianity] *Christianity,* O.
1–2   *(where ... false)]* ∧where ... false∧ O.
1–2   *the ... [to] ... of]* set in romans in O.
2–4   *whether ... [to] ...* Lucian] romans and italics reversed in O.
7   World.] ∼∧ O.
7–8   manner] mannner O.   13   *Greek*] Greek O.
17   *Mayne*] *Mayn* O.   20   Sentences] ∼, O.
20   harmoniously] harminously O.   20   Flood] ∼, O .
21   perswasion,] ∼; O.   21   swellings;] ∼, O.
22   put] pust O.   26   bred:] ∼. O.

If Wit consists in the Propriety of Thoughts and Words, (which I imagin'd I had first found out; but since am pleasingly convinc'd, that *Aristotle* has made the same Definition in other Terms) then *Lucian's* Thoughts and Words, are always proper to his Characters, and to his Subject. If the pleasure arising from Comedy and Satyr, be either Laughter, or some nobler sort of Delight, which is above it; no Man is so great a Master of Irony, as our Author: That Figure is not only a keen, but a shining Weapon in his Hand; it glitters in the Eyes of those it kills; his own God's, his greatest Enemies, are not butchered by him, but fairly slain: they must acknowledge the Heroe in the stroke; and take the comfort which *Virgil* gives to a dying Captain: *Æneæ magni dextrâ cadis.*

I know not whom *Lucian* imitated, unless it might be *Aristophanes* (for you never find him mentioning any *Roman* Wit, so much the *Grecians* thought themselves superior to their Conquerours:) But he who has best imitated him in *Latin,* is *Erasmus,* and in *French, Fontenelle,* in his *Dialogues of the Dead;* which I never read but with a new Pleasure.

Any one may see, that our Author's chief Design, was to disnest Heaven of so many immoral and debauch'd Deities: His next, to expose the Mock-Philosophers; and his last, to give us Examples of a good Life in the Persons of the true.

The rest of his Discourses are on mix'd Subjects, less for profit, than delight; and some of them too Libertine.

The way which *Lucian* chose of delivering these profitable, and pleasing Truths, was that of Dialogue: A Choice worthy of the Author, happily follow'd, as I said above, by *Erasmus* and *Fontenelle* particularly; to whom I may justly add a Triumvir of our own, the Reverend, Ingenious, and Learned Dr. *Echard,* who by using the same Method, and the same Ingredients of Raillery, and Reason, has more baffled the Philosopher of *Malms-*

---

1   Propriety . . . Thoughts] ~, . . . ~, O.
10   kills;] ~, O.   10   God's,] God's‸ O.
13   Captain] *Captain* O.   13   *Æneæ*] *Æneæ* O.
17   *Latin*] Latin O.   18   *French,*] French‸ O.
18   *Dialogues . . . [to] . . . Dead*] set in romans in O.
30   own, the] ~. The O.

bury, than those who assaulted him with blunt, heavy Arguments, drawn from Orthodox Divinity: For *Hobbs* foresaw where those strokes wou'd fall, and leapt aside before they cou'd descend; but he cou'd not avoid those nimble Passes, which were made on him, by a Wit more active, than his own, and which were within his Body, before he cou'd provide for his Defence.

I will not here take notice of the several kinds of Dialogue, and the whole Art of it, which wou'd ask an entire Volume to perform. This has been a Work long wanted, and much desir'd,
10 of which the Ancients have not sufficiently inform'd us; and I question whether any Man, now living, can treat it accurately. *Lucian,* it seems, was very sensible of the difficult Task which he undertook in writing Dialogues; as appears in his discourse, against one who had call'd him *Prometheus:* He owns himself, in this particular, to be like him to whom he was resembled, to be the Inventor of a new Work, attempted in a new manner; the Model of which he had from none before him; but adds withall, that if he cou'd not give it the Graces which belong to so happy an Invention, he deserves to be torn by twelve Vulturs,
20 instead of one, which preys upon the Heart of that first Man-Potter. For, to quit the beaten Road of the Ancients, and take a Path of his own choosing, he acknowledges to be a bold and ridiculous Attempt, if it succeed not. The Mirth of Dialogue and Comedy in my Work, says he, is not enough to make it pleasing; because the Union of two contraries, may as well produce a Monster as a Miracle; as a Centaur results from the joint Natures of a Horse and Man. 'Tis not but that from two excellent Beings, a third may arise of perfect Beauty; but 'tis what I dare not promise to my self: for Dialogue being a solemn
30 Entertainment of grave Discourse, and Comedy the Wit and Fooling of a Theatre, I fear that through the Corruption of two good Things, I have made one bad. But whatever the Child be, 'tis my own at least; I beg not with another's Brat upon my Back. From which of the Ancients shou'd I have stol'n or borrowed it? My *Chimæras* have no other Being than my own

7 I] *no paragraph break in* O.   9 This] *paragraph break in* O.
20 one,... Heart] ~∧ ... ~, O.   27 'Tis] *paragraph break in* O.

Imagination; let every Man produce who can; and whether this be a lawful Birth, or a mishappen Mass, is left for the present Age, and for Posterity to judge.

This is the Sense of my Author's Words, contracted in a narrow compass: For, if you will believe *Ablancourt,* and others, his greatest Fault is, that he exhausts his Argument; like *Ovid,* knows not when to give over, but is perpetually gallopping beyond his Stage.

10 But tho' I cannot pursue our Authour any farther, I find my self oblig'd to say something of those Translators of the following Dialogues, whom I have the honour to know, as well as of some other Translations of this Author, and a word, or two of Translation it self.

As for the Translators, all of them, that I know, are Men of establish'd Reputation, both for Wit, and Learning, at least sufficiently known to be so, among all the finer Spirits of the Age. Sir *Henry Sheers,* has given many Proofs of his Excellence in this kind; for while we, by his admirable Address, enjoy *Polybius* in our Mother Tongue, we can never forget the Hand, that 20 bestow'd the Benefit. The Learning and Judgment above his Age, which every one discovers in Mr. *Moyle,* are proofs of those Abilities he has shown in his Country's Service, when he was chose to serve it in the Senate, as his Father had done. The Wit of Mr. *Blount,* and his other Performances, need no Recommendation from me, they have made too much noise in the World, to need a Herald. There are some other Persons concerned in this Work, whose Names deserve a place among the foremost, but that they have not thought fit to be known, either out of a bashful Diffidence of their own Performance, or out of 30 Apprehension of the Censure of an ill-natur'd, and ill-judging Age. For Criticism is now become mere Hang-man's Work, and meddles only with the Faults of Authors; nay, the Critick is disgusted less with their Absurdities, than Excellence, and you can't displease him more, than in leaving him little room for

4   This] *no paragraph break in O.*   6–7   Argument; ... over,] ~, ... ~; O.
18   Address] Adress O.   29   Performance,] ~; O.
31   Age.] ~‸ O.   31   Criticism] *Criticism,* O.

his Malice in your Correctness and Perfection; tho' that indeed is what he never allows any Man; for like the Bed of *Procrustes,* they stretch, or cut off an Author to its length. These spoilers of *Parnassus,* are a just excuse for concealing the Name, since most of their Malice is levell'd more at the Person, than the thing; and as a sure mark of their Judgment, they will extoll to the Skys, the Anonymous work of a Person they will not allow to write common Sense.

　　But this Consideration, of our Modern Criticks, has led me
10 astray, and made me insensibly deviate from the Subject before me; the Modesty, or Caution of the Anonymous Translators of the following Work. Whatever the Motive of concealing their Names may be, I shall not determine; but it is certain, nothing cou'd more contribute to make a perfect Version of *Lucian,* than a confederacy of many Men of Parts and Learning to do him Justice. It seems a Task too hard for any one Man to undertake; the Burden wou'd indeed be insupportable, unless we did what the *French* have done in some of their Translations, allow twenty Years to perfect the Work, and bestow all the brightest
20 Intervals, the most sprightly hours, to polish and finish the Work.

　　But this has not been the fate of our Author hitherto; for *Lucian,* that is the sincere Example of *Attique* Eloquence, as *Grævius* says of him, is only a mass of Solecism, and mere Vulgarisms in Mr. *Spence.* I do not think it worth my while, to rake into the filth of so scandalous a Version; nor had I vouchsaf'd so much as to take notice of it, had it not been so gross an Affront to the Memory of *Lucian,* and so great a scandal to our Nation. *D'Ablancourt* has taken a great deal of pains to furnish this
30 Intruder into Print with *Lucian,* in a Language more known to him than *Greek;* nay, he has left him not one crabbed Idiotism to study for, since he has admirably cloath'd him in a Garb, more familiar to the Moderns, still keeping the Sense of his Author in view. But in spight of all these helps, these Leading-strings were not sufficient to keep Mr. *Spence* from falling to the

---

ground, ev'ry step he made; while he makes him speak in the Stile and Language of a *Jack-Pudding,* not a Master of Eloquence, admir'd for it through all the Ages since he wrote. But too much of this Trifler.

I have said enough already of the Version of the Learned Dr. *Mayne,* to shew my Approbation of it, but it is only a select parcel of *Lucian's* Dialogues, which pleas'd him most, but far from the whole. As for any other Translator, if there be any such in our Language, it is what I never saw, and suppose it 10 must be antiquated, or of so inferior a degree, as not even to rival *Spence.*

The present Translation, as far as I can Judge by what I have seen, is no way inferiour to *Ablancourt's,* and in many things is superiour. It has indeed the Advantage of appearing in a Language more strong and expressive, than *French,* and by the Hands of Gentlemen, who perfectly understand him, and their own Language.

This has brought me to say a word or two about Translation in general: In which no Nation might more excell, than the 20 *English,* tho' as Matters are now manag'd, we come so far short of the *French.* There may indeed, be a Reason assign'd, which bears a very great probability; and that is, that here the Booksellers are the Undertakers of Works of this nature, and they are Persons more devoted to their own Gain, than the publick Honour. They are very parcimonious in Rewarding the wretched Scribblers they employ; and care not how the Business is done, so that it be but done. They live by selling Titles, not Books, and if that carry off one Impression, they have their Ends, and value not the Curses they and their Authors meet 30 with from the bubbled Chapmen. While Translations are thus at the disposal of the Booksellers, and have no better Judges, or Rewarders of the Performance, it is impossible, that we should make any Progress, in an Art so very useful to an enquiring

1   ev'ry] e'ry O.
6   *Mayne*] *Mayn* O.
22–23   Booksellers] *Booksellers* O.
26   Scribblers] *Scribblers* O.
31   Booksellers] *Booksellers* O .

1   made; while] ~. While O.
21   *French.* There] ~; there O.

People, and for the Improvement and spreading of Knowledge, which is none of the worst preservatives against Slavery.

It must be confess'd, that when the Bookseller has Interest with Gentlemen of Genius and Quality, above the Mercenary Prospects of little Writers, as in that of *Plutarch's* Live's, and this of *Lucian,* the Reader may satisfy himself, that he shall have the Author's Spirit and Soul in the Traduction. These Gentlemen know very well that they are not to creep after the Words of their Author in so servile a Manner, as some have done; for that must infallibly throw them on a Necessity of introducing a new Mode of Diction and Phraseology, with which we are not at all acquainted, and wou'd incur that Censure which my Lord *Dorset* made formerly on those of Mr. *Spence,* viz. *that he was so cunning a Translator, that a Man must Consult the Original to understand the Version.* For every Language has a Propriety and Idiom peculiar to it self, which cannot be convey'd to another without perpetual Absurditys.

The Qualification of a Translator worth Reading must be a Mastery of the Language he Translates out of, and that he Translates into; but if a deficience be to be allow'd in either, it is in the Original, since if he be but Master enough of the Tongue of his Author, as to be Master of his Sense, it is possible for him to express that Sense, with Eloquence, in his own, if he have a through Command of that. But without the Latter, he can never Arive at the Useful and the Delightful; without which, Reading is a Penance and Fatigue.

'Tis true, that there will be a great many Beautys, which in every Tongue depend on the Diction, that will be lost in the Version of a Man, not skill'd in the Original Language of the Author: But then on the other side, First it is impossible to render all those little Ornaments of Speech in any two Languages; and if he have a Mastery in the Sense and Spirit of his Author, and in his own Language have a Stile and Happiness of

9–10 done; for] ~. For O.   13 viz.] viz‚ O.
23 own,] ~‚ O.
24–25 Latter, . . . Useful . . . Delightful; . . . which,] ~‚ . . . ~, . . . ~, . . .
~‚ O.
28 lost] left O.   30 Author:] ~. O.

Expression, he will easily supply all that is lost by that defect.

A Translator, that wou'd write with any Force or Spirit of an Original, must never dwell on the Words of his Author: He ought to possess himself entirely, and perfectly comprehend the Genius and Sense of his Author, the Nature of the Subject, and the Terms of the Art or Subject treated of; and then he will express himself as justly, and with as much Life, as if he wrote an Original: Whereas, he who Copies Word for Word, loses all the Spirit in the tedious Transfusion.

10 I wou'd not be understood, that he should be at liberty to give such a Turn, as Mr. *Spence* has in some of his, where for the fine Raillery, and *Attique* Salt of *Lucian,* we find the gross Expressions of *Billings-Gate,* or *More-Fields* and *Bartholomew* Fair. For I write not to such Translators, but to Men capacious of the Soul and Genius of their Authors, without which, all their Labour will be of no use, but to disgrace themselves, and injure the Author that falls into their Slaughter-House.

I believe, I need give no other Rules to the Reader than the following Version, where Example will be stronger than Pre-
20 cept, to which I now refer them; in which a Man justly Qualifi'd for a Translator will Discover many Rules, extreamly useful to that End. But to a Man who wants these Natural Qualifications which are necessary for such an Undertaking, all particular Precepts are of no other Use than to make him a more Remarkable Coxcomb.

---

6 of; and] off. And O.
18 Reader] READER O.
20 them; in] ~. In O.
22 to a] a O.
22 Qualifications] Qualification O.

The WORKS of
C. CORNELIVS
TACITVS

Engraved Title of the First Edition

THE
ANNALS and *HISTORY*
OF
Cornelius Tacitus:
His Account of the
ANTIENT GERMANS,
AND THE
LIFE of AGRICOLA.

Made English by several Hands.

WITH THE
POLITICAL REFLECTIONS
AND
HISTORICAL NOTES
OF
Monsieur Amelot *De La Houssay*, and the Learned Sir Henry Savile.

In Three Volumes.

VOL. I.

LONDON:
Printed for *Matthew Gillyflower* at the Spread-Eagle in *Westminster-Hall*, MDCXCVIII.

TITLE PAGE OF THE FIRST EDITION (MACDONALD 140A)

The Annals of Cornelius Tacitus, Book I

R OME was govern'd at the first by *Kings. *Liberty[†] and
the Consulship were introduc'd by *Lucius Brutus:* the
Dictatorship* was granted, but *as necessity requir'd,* and
for some time: And the Authority of the Decemvirate* con-
tinu'd only for two Years[†]. The Consular Power of the Military
Tribunes* remain'd in force but for a little space[†]. Neither was
the *Arbitrary* Dominion of *Cinna,* or that of *Sylla,* of any long
continuance[†]. The Power of *Pompey* and *Crassus,* were soon
transferr'd to *Julius Cæsar;* and the Arms of *Marc Antony* and
10 *Lepidus,* gave place to those of *his Successor, Augustus.* Then
it was, that the Civil Wars having exhausted the Forces of the
Common-wealth, *Augustus Cæsar* assum'd the Government[†], un-
der the *Modest* Title of Prince[†] of the Senate*.

   But all the good or adverse Fortune, which happen'd to the
Ancient Republique of the *Romans,* has already been related,
by great Authors[†]. Neither were there wanting Famous Wits to
transfer the Actions of *Augustus* to *future Ages,* till they were
hinder'd by the Growth of Flattery[†]. During the Reigns of
Tiberius, Caligula, Claudius, and *Nero;* their several Actions
20 were falsify'd through fear, while they were yet living; and
after their Decease, were traduc'd through the recent hate *of
their Historians*[†]. For which reason, I shall only give you here
a Summary Account of those Actions which were perform'd by
Augustus in the latter part of his Life; and afterwards the His-
tory of *Tiberius,* and of the three succeeding Emperors: the
whole without Partiality or Prejudice; to neither of which I
can have a Motive[†].

   [II] After the Death of *Cassius* and *Brutus**, when there were
none remaining to take up Arms for Liberty, the Younger *Pom-*

---

3 Dictatorship*] cDictatorship O.   4 Decemvirate*] dDecemvirate O.
5–6 Military Tribunes*] eMilitary Tribunes O.
9 *Antony*] *Anthony* O.   15 *Romans*] Romans O.
22 For] *paragraph break in O.*   28 *Brutus**] *Brutus*ʌ O.
29 Liberty,] ~; O.   29–231:1 *Pompey**] *Pompey*ʌ O.

*pey** being defeated in *Sicily, Lepidus** dispossess'd of his Command, and that *Marc Antony** had lost his Life together with his Power, *Augustus,* the only Survivor of the three Competitors, and Heir of *Cæsar,* laying down the Title of *Triumvir*[†]*, took up the *less invidious* Name of *Consul;* and pretended to satisfy himself with the Tribunitial Power, thereby to protect the People[†] in their Rights and Privileges; but when he had once gain'd the Soldiery to his Interest, by rewards[†], the People by *Donatives* and plenty of Provisions[†], and allur'd all in general,
10 by the Mildness of his Government, he began by degrees to incroach upon them, and to draw into his own hands, the Authority of the Senate, of the Magistrates, and Laws; none daring to oppose him, the most violent of his Enemies being either slain in Battle, or cut off by Proscriptions, and the remaining Nobility, the more ready they were to enter into Servitude, the more sure of Honours and Preferment: Besides, that they who found their account in the Change of Government, were more willing to embrace the Present Slavery, with an assur'd prospect of Ease and Quiet, than to run the Hazard of new Dangers
20 for the recovery of their Ancient Freedom[†]. Neither were the Provinces any ways unwilling to admit these Alterations, as being weary'd out with the continual dissentions of the Senators among themselves, and the Covetousness of their Magistrates, against whom it was in vain to seek the Protection of the Laws: Which either through Force, or Cabals, or Bribery, were become of no effect.

[III] As for the rest, *Augustus* to strengthen his Authority, advanc'd *Claudius Marcellus,* the Son of his Sister, and yet very Young, to the Dignity of the Pontificat, and that of *Edile*:* And
30 also honour'd with two Successive Consulships *Marcus Agrippa,* a Man of mean Parentage[†], but an expert Soldier, and the Companion of his Victories; and not long after, *Marcellus* being dead he Marry'd him to his Daughter *Julia.* He also gave *Tiberius Nero,* and *Claudius Drusus,* the Command of Armies, though

---

1   *Lepidus**] *Lepidus*ᴧ O.
4   *Triumvir*] Triumvir O.
10 Government, he] ~; He O.
16 Preferment:] ~. O.

2   *Antony**] *Anthony*ᴧ O.
5   *Consul*] Consul O.
12 Laws;] ~: O.
29 *Edile*:*] *Edile*ᵍ. O.

but the Sons of his Wife *Livia,* and that his own Family was yet flourishing with Heirs. For he had already adopted into the *Julian* Family *Cajus* and *Lucius,* his Grandsons by *Agrippa* and his Daughter: And had earnestly desir'd, though with a seeming repugnance†, that they should be made Princes of the Youth, and design'd Consuls, while yet they wore the Pretext Robe*. In a short time after *Agrippa's* Death, his Sons follow'd him, either through the Force of an immature destiny, or through the Treachery of their Mother-in-Law *Livia*†: One of them as he was going into *Spain,* to command the Armies there; and the other as he was returning from *Armenia,* and ill of a Wound, *which he had receiv'd.* And as *Drusus* was not long e'er this deceas'd, *Tiberius* only was remaining: Who from thence-forward, was regarded as Successor to the Sovereignty. *Augustus* adopted him*; and made him his Collegue in the Empire, and the Tribunitial Power: He sent him also to make his Publick Appearance in all the Armies, that he might be known to the Soldiers; and all this at the open Sollicitations of *Livia,* who now no longer manag'd her affairs by Intrigues and secret Artifices, as formerly she had done. For she had gain'd so great an Ascendant over her Husband, now in his declining Age†, that to satisfie her desires he had banish'd *Agrippa Posthumus,* his only remaining Grandson, into the Island of *Planasia.* This Youth, 'tis to be confess'd, had been ill Educated, was of a rude Behaviour, and valu'd himself too brutally on his strength of Body: but otherwise, was free from any apparent Vice. The Emperor had also plac'd *Germanicus,* the Son of *Drusus,* at the Head of Eight Legions, which were quarter'd towards the *Rhine*†, and had commanded *Tiberius* to adopt him for his Son; that he might thereby strengthen the Succession†; tho' *Tiberius* at that time, had a Son also of his own, then of Age, and capable of Publick Business.

He had now no other War upon his hands, but that of *Germany,* which he continu'd rather to blot out the Ignominy which he had receiv'd, by the Defeat of *Quintilius Varus,* than to extend the Bounds of the *Roman* Empire: or for any other important Interest. All things at *Rome* being in a settled Peace; the

Magistrates still retain'd their former names†: The Youth being
born after the Battle of *Actium,* and the Elder sort, during the
Civil War, few were now remaining of those which had seen
the times of Liberty.

[IV] All things had another face. Nothing of the Form or
Force of the Ancient Government was left. Equality and Free-
dom were at once distinguish'd; the Common Interest was to
obey and serve the Prince, at least, before he grew subject to
the Decays of Age, and cou'd attend with Vigour to the Cares of
10 Government, and to the Fortunes of his Family. But when he
was infeebled with Years and Sickness, and his end was visibly
approaching; the Minds of Men were alter'd by the prospect of
a Change. Some few cry'd up the Advantage of Publick Freedom:
Many were fearful of an impending War, which was earnestly
desir'd by others. But the greater Part employ'd their time in
various Discourses of future Masters†.

Agrippa, they said, *was fierce by Nature, and exasperated by*
the Disgraces which he suffer'd†; besides, that he was wholly
unacquainted with Affairs, and incapable of sustaining so great
20 *a Weight.* Tiberius *was indeed mature in Years, and experienc'd*
in Warfare; but had inherent in him, the Severity and Pride of
the Claudian *Family, which he cou'd not so perfectly dissem-*
ble, but that some signs of Cruelty might be observ'd in his
Nature and his Actions. What was there to be expected from
a Man, bred from his Infancy*, in the Imperial House, and
amidst Arbitrary Power, *loaded with Honours and Triumphs*
in his Youth†, and during his retreat at Rhodes, *which was, in*
effect, but a specious Exile, feeding his thoughts with the hopes
of Vengeance, forming himself to the Practice of Dissimulation,
30 *and consuming the rest of his time in Luxury†: His Mother of a*

1   names†:] ~ₐ:¹ O.   4   Liberty.] ~; O.
5   All] *no paragraph break in O.*
16   Masters] Matters O.
17   Agrippa] *Agrippa* O.
17–234:4   *each printed line preceded by inverted double commas in O.*
17–22   *was* … [*to*] … *the*] *italics and romans reversed in O.*
22–28   *Family* … [*to*] … *specious*] *italics and romans reversed in O.*
28   *Exile,*] Exile; O.
28–30   *feeding* … [*to*] … *in*] *set in romans in O* (Vegeance).
30   *Luxury†:*] Luxury². O.
30–234:4   *His* … [*to*] … *Decease*] *set in romans in O.*

Violent and Imperious Nature, according to the Sex themselves,
subjected to the Slavery of a Woman; besides, two Youths, who
at present were chargeable to the Common-Wealth, and wou'd
tear it piece-meal after the Emperor's Decease.

[V] While these things were in agitation, the Health of *Augustus* was impairing daily; and there wanted not some, who suspected the Impiety of his Wife by *Poison*†. For, some Months before, there had been spread a Rumour, that *Augustus,* attended by some of his most trusty Servants, and accompany'd
10 only by *Fabius Maximus* his Friend and Confident, had made a Secret Voyage to the Island of *Planasia,* there to visit Young *Agrippa;* that many tears had been mutually shed, with reciprocal testimonies of tenderness*; from which it might be gather'd, that there were yet some hopes of his being restor'd into the Family of his Grandfather†. *It was farther reported,* that *Fabius* had reveal'd this Secret to his Wife *Marcia*†, and she to *Livia*†, who complain'd of it to *Augustus:* these things being come at length to the notice of the Emperor, and shortly after, *Maximus* being dead, ('tis doubtful whether by a Voluntary
20 Death, or not,) *Marcia* was heard at his Funeral amidst her sorrows to accuse her self, as the Cause of her Husband's Destiny†. But however it was, *Tiberius* was scarcely enter'd into *Illyria;* when he was speedily recall'd by Letters from his Mother; and it is not known for certain, whether or no he found *Augustus* yet living* when he arriv'd at *Nola.* For *Livia* had order'd the *Corps du Guard* to be all under Arms at every Avenue of the Palace and the Town, and caus'd reports to be hourly spread of the Emperor's amendment, till having all things in a readiness, which the present Conjunction cou'd require. She declar'd at
30 once the Death of *Augustus**, and the Accession of *Tiberius* to the Empire*.

THE REIGN OF TIBERIUS:

Beginning in the Year of *Rome,* 767.

[VI] The first Action of the New Reign, was the Murder of *Agrippa Posthumus*†; who unarm'd as he was, and wholly Ig-

32   THE REIGN OF TIBERIUS] The Reign of *TIBERIUS* O.

norant of the design, was not without some difficulty slain, by a
Centurion hardned in blood. *Tiberius* was silent of this matter
in the Senate, feigning a Command from his Father *Augustus,*
wherein he had order'd the Officer of the Guard to murther the
Young Man, immediately after his own decease. 'Tis undoubted
that *Augustus* had often, and that with bitterness, complain'd
in the Senate, of his Manners; and had also exacted a Decree
from them to authorize his Banishment. Yet he had never pro-
ceeded to so much cruelty, as to compass the Death of any of his
10 Relations. Nor is it credible that he would command his Grand-
son to be murder'd, to secure the safety of his Son-in-Law. The
suspicion fell more naturally on *Tiberius* and *Livia,* for hastning
the Death of a Young Man, obnoxious to the hatred of the first
through fear of a Competitor*, and of the last, through the
inbred malice of a Step-mother. When the Centurion, according
to Military Custom, told *Tiberius* that he had perform'd his
orders; his answer was, that he had given him no such Commis-
sion†; that the Officer should be answerable to the Senate for
his offence, which coming to the knowledge of *Sallustius Crispus,*
20 who was the confident of all his Secrets, and who had issued out
those orders to the Centurion, He fearing that the Murther
would be charg'd on him, and knowing that it was equally
dangerous in his case, *either to confess the Truth, or divulge the
Secret,* to approve himself, either Innocent or Guilty†; advis'd
Livia, that care should be taken not to expose the Secrets of the
Imperial House, or the Counsels of Ministers†, or the Names of
the Soldiers, whom he privately employ'd to execute his orders.
For *Tiberius* would certainly weaken the Government, if he
permitted his actions to be scan'd in the Senate†: Arbitrary Do-
30 minion being of that nature, that the Performance of a Com-
mand, from a single Person, can be accountable but to him
alone*.

II. [VII] In the mean time, at *Rome* the Consuls, Senators,
and Knights, endeavour'd to out-strip each other in the race to
Servitude. And they who were the most Noble and Illustrious,
made the greatest speed; using so specious a behaviour, that

without shewing any exterior gladness for the Death of their late Emperor, or any discontent, for the Succession of the New*, their Mourning was mingled with their Joy, and their Tears with expressions of Flattery. *Sextus Pompeius* and *Sextus Apuleius,* then Consuls, were the first who took the Oath of Fidelity to *Tiberius,* and gave it afterwards in his name, to *Sejus Strabo,* Captain of the Pretorian-Guard, and to *Cajus Turranius,* Commissary-General of the Publick Provisions: after these, to the Senate, to the Forces, and to the People. For *Tiberius* affected
10 to begin all publick Functions from the Consuls†, as in the ancient Common-Wealth, and as if he were yet doubtful, whether or no, he would assume the Government. Even the Edict it self by which he summon'd the Senate to the Court, was short and modest, declaring, that he exercis'd this Right but only in vertue of the Tribunitial Power*, which was vested in him by *Augustus†;* and in order to deliberate on those funeral Honours, which were to be paid to his Father, whose Corps, in the mean time, he would not forsake*, and that all the part to which he pretended in the Publick Administration, was no more than what
20 was reducible to that Edict*. Yet after the Death of *Augustus,* it was his Custom to give the word to the Prætorian Cohorts, to be attended by Soldiers, and no part of the State belonging to an Emperor, was wanting to him. Whether he walk'd the Streets, or went to the Senate, his Guards follow'd him. He had also written to the Armies in the style of Emperour and Successor, and all without the least Ambiguity or Hesitation, unless it were when he spoke in Senate†. The principal Cause of his dissimulation† was, that he fear'd *Germanicus* who commanded so many Legions, assur'd of succour from all the Allies and lov'd
30 even to Idolatry by the *Roman* People, would rather chuse to enjoy the Empire in present, than to attend it *from his Death.* Neither was there wanting a mixture of Vain-Glory, in these proceedings, for he affected to have it thought, that he was Elected by the Common-Wealth†, rather than introduc'd by the Artifices of a Woman†, and the adoption of an old doting Man. It was afterwards discover'd also, that this Irresolution which he

25   and] O *(some copies);* and and O *(some copies).*
29–30   Allies . . . Idolatry] ~, . . . ~, O.   30   *Roman*] Roman O.

shew'd, tended to sound the Affections of the Great towards him; for he study'd their Countenance, and their Words, to make them guilty afterwards, whom he purpos'd to destroy.

III. [VIII] The first time he came into the Senate, he would permit no other business to come on, than only what related to the Funeral of his Father†; whose Testament was brought thither by the Vestals. By it *Tiberius* and *Livia* were declar'd his Heirs. *Livia* was adopted also into the *Julian* Family, and honour'd with the Title of *Augusta**. In the second Degree were
10 rank'd his Grand-Children, and their Descendants; in the third, the Greatest of the *Romans,* not out of Affection, for he hated most of them, but out of Ostentation†, to be admir'd by Posterity*. His Legacies exceeded not the common Rules, only he bequeath'd to the People four hundred Thousand great Sesterces; to the most Inferior sort thirty five Thousand great Sesterces; to each of the Prætorian Soldiers (or Guards) a Thousand small Sesterces, and three hundred to every Legionary. After this, they spoke of the Honours which were to be render'd to the Dead: and the Chief on which they insisted, were, that
20 the Funeral State should pass through the Triumphal Gate, which was first advis'd by *Gallus Asinius;* that the Titles of the Laws which had been Instituted by him, and the names of the Nations which he had vanquish'd, should be carried before the Body, which was propos'd by *Lucius Arruntius.* But *Messala Valerius* adding, that the Oath of Fidelity to *Tiberius,* should be annually renew'd; *Tiberius (interrupting him on the sudden)* ask'd, if it were by his Order, that he had thus spoken? And *Messala* replying, that it was of his own head, adjoin'd farther, that in all things which concern'd the Publick Good, he would
30 never take any Man's opinion but his own, though in so doing he should make *Cæsar* himself his Enemy. This was the only remaining kind of Flattery. The Senators with a General Cry, demanded, that the Imperial Corps should be carried to the Pile on their Shoulders only. But *Tiberius* dispens'd with that Office rather out of Vanity, and to do himself honour in the

---

8 *Julian*] Julian O.   11 *Romans*] Romans O.
19 Dead:] ∼; O.   21 *Asinius;* that] ∼. That O.

refusal, than out of real Modesty. After this he publish'd an
Edict to the People, warning them not to disturb these Funerals,
as they had done those of *Julius Cæsar*, with their excess of Zeal,
and not obstinately to persist in their desire, that the Body
should be burn'd in the Market-place, and not in the Field of
Mars, which was the place decreed *for that Ceremony*.

On the day of the Funeral Solemnity, the Soldiers were or-
der'd to be under Arms: Those who had either seen themselves,
or had heard from their Fathers of that day, whereon *Julius*
10 *Cæsar* the Dictator had been slain, when the sharpness of their
Slavery was yet fresh upon them, and their Liberty, with an ill
Omen just restor'd, much deriding the superfluous care now
us'd by *Tiberius* on this occasion; for even at that time, as there
were some who judg'd his Death an impious action, so there
were others* who extoll'd it as a glorious Justice†. But in the
present case, here was an old Emperor, *quietly* gone out of
the World, who had been settled in a long course of Sovereignty
of 44 years*, and who had establish'd the Succession against the
Common-Wealth, by a large Provision of Heirs, and those in
20 power; he, it seems, must have a Guard of Soldiers about his dead
body, to secure it from disturbance at his Funeral.

IV. [IX] This afforded no small occasion of discourse con-
cerning *Augustus* himself. The greater part of the Assistants
vainly admiring, that he should happen to die on the same day
on which he first assum'd the Empire*: that he died at *Nola*,
in the same House and Chamber, wherein his Father *Octavius**
had finish'd his Life. The number of his Consulships was ex-
toll'd likewise, which equall'd those of *Valerius Corvinus*, and
*Caius Marius**, both together, that had enjoy'd the Tribunitial
30 Power, without Intermission, 37 Years; had been saluted Em-
peror* one and twenty times: Besides, a multitude of other
Honours which had been heap'd upon him, or invented for him.
But the Politicians examin'd the conduct of his Life, after
another manner. Some said, that his filial Piety to *Cæsar*, the
necessity of Affairs, and the importance of the Laws had hurry'd

---

7 On] *no paragraph break in O.*   8   Arms:] ~. O.

him into a Civil War[†] (which cou'd not possibly be manag'd
with the Forms of Justice) though the Cause was honest; that
he had consented to many violent proceedings of *Antony* and
*Lepidus[†], because he had need of their assistance, to revenge
the Murther of his Father; that *Lepidus* being grown Effeminate
by the Sloath of a Private Life, *Antony* drown'd in his de-
bauches, and the Common-Wealth torn in pieces by the Discord
of her Citizens, there was no other Remedy left in Nature, but
the Government of a single Person (which notwithstanding,
10 *Augustus* had never taken up the Title* of King[†], or of Dic-
tator[†], but contented himself to be call'd Prince of the Senate);
that the Empire was owing to him, for being surrounded by the
Ocean*, and remote Rivers[†]; that the Provinces, the Legions,
and the Naval Force, were well united, the Citizens obedient
to the Laws, the Allies in terms of dutiful respect, and the
Town adorn'd with stately Buildings; that it was to be ac-
knowledg'd he sometimes made use of Severity and Force, but
very rarely, and always for preservation of the Publick Safety.
[X] On the other side it was alledg'd, that the boasted Piety of
20 a Son to a Father, and the Necessities of a Common-Wealth*,
were only his pretext[†]; that through an insatiable desire of reign-
ing, he being then a Youth, and of a private Fortune, had cor-
rupted the Veteran Troops with Bribes and Donatives, had rais'd
an Army, and debauch'd the Legions of *Decimus Brutus* then
Consul, under colour of reconciliation with *Pompey*'s party;
that after he had extorted from the Senate, the Ornaments and
Authority of a Prætor, and seiz'd on the Troops which had been
commanded by *Hirtius* and *Pansa*, newly slain*, either by the
Enemy, or by the Treason of this young *Cæsar*, (for *Pansa* was
30 thought to have been brought to his end by an envenom'd
Plaister apply'd to his wound, and *Hirtius* was slain by the hands
of his own Soldiers,) he caused himself to be created Consul in

---

1–2 War[†] (which ... Justice)] ∼¹; ∼ ... ∼; O.
2 honest; that] ∼. That O.   3 *Antony*] *Anthony* O.
5 Father; that] ∼. That O.   6 *Antony*] *Anthony* O.
9–12 Person (which ... Senate); that] ∼; ∼ ... ∼; That O.
13 that] That O.   14–15 united, ... Laws,] ∼; ... ∼; O.
20 Common-Wealth*] Common-Wealth∧ O.

spight of the Senate, and had turn'd those arms against the Com-
mon-Wealth, which he had taken up against *Antony:* The Pro-
scription of so many Citizens was charg'd on him; and the divi-
sion of the Lands* disapprov'd even by those to whom they fell.
The Death of *Cassius* and the two *Bruti**, must indeed be own'd
for a just Vengeance on the Murderers of his Father*; though
still it had been more glorious for him, to have sacrific'd his
private hatred, to the Publick Interest: But the younger *Pompey*
had been unworthily betray'd under the shadow of a pretended
10 Peace; and *Lepidus* by a dissembled Friendship: *Antony* sooth'd
and lull'd asleep, by the Treaties of *Tarentum,* and *Brundusium,*
and by his Marriage with the Sister of *Augustus,* had paid with
his Life the forfeit of that fraudulent Alliance. After this a Peace
was of necessity to ensue, but it was a bloody Peace; and in-
famous for the punishment of the *Varro's,* the *Egnatti**, and the
Julii of *Rome;* to which succeeded the Defeats of *Lollius** and
Varus* in *Germany.*
    Neither did they spare his private Life in their discourses.
They reproach'd him for having forcibly taken from her Hus-
20 band a Woman then with Child; and for having made a Scoff of
Religion, by demanding of the Priests if it were lawful for him
to espouse her before she was deliver'd[t]. They allow'd him to
have suffer'd the Luxury of *Quintus Atedius,* and *Vedius Pollio*[t],
his *Minions,* and also of having given himself up to be govern'd
by *Livia*[t], a heavy Burden to the Common-Wealth, and a worse
Step-mother to the Family of the *Cæsars;* that he had made him-
self a Fellow to the Gods, commanding Temples to be dedicated
to him as to a Deity, with the Pomp of Images, Priests, and Sac-
rifices; that for the rest, he had appointed *Tiberius* to succeed
30 him[t], not out of any Affection which he bore him, nor out of any
Consideration for the Publick Good, but only to add a Lustre
to his own Glory, by the Foyl of that Comparison; as having a
perfect Insight into his Nature, and knowing him at the bottom
to be Proud* and Cruel[t]. For not many Years before, *Augustus*

2, 10 *Antony*] *Anthony* O.   17 *Germany.*] ~: O.
18 Neither] *no paragraph break in O.*   24 *Minions*] *Minors* O.
26 that] That O.   28–29 Sacrifices; that] ~. That O.
34 Cruel[t]] [11]Cruel O.

requesting the Senate once more to confer the Tribunitial Power on *Tiberius**, had cast out some Words concerning his Humour, and the Oddness of his Manners, which seeming to Excuse, did in effect Reproach them†.

V. The Funerals of *Augustus* being ended, there was a Temple and Divine Worship decreed for him; [XI] and that being done, earnest Supplications were address'd to *Tiberius;* who, on his side, spoke ambiguously concerning the Greatness of the Empire, and the Diffidence he had of his own Abilities: Saying,

10 *That nothing but the Soul and Genius of* Augustus *could support so great a Burden of Affairs†; and that having sustain'd some part of them during the Life of the Emperour†, he was sensible by his own Experience, how difficult and dangerous it was to charge his Shoulders with the Weight of Government; that in a City, which abounded with the Choice of great and able Persons, all Things ought not to be intrusted to the Management of one, since Publick Functions were better exercis'd, when many join'd their Cares and Labours†.* But there was more of Ostentation, than of upright Meaning, in these Discourses.

20 And besides, if *Tiberius,* whether by Nature, or by Custom, spoke obscurely even on those Subjects, where he had no occasion to dissemble, his Words at this time became more intricate and doubtful, when he studied altogether to disguise his Thoughts. Then the Senators, who were all equally afraid of seeming to divine his Meaning, broke out into Tears, Complaints and Vows; holding out their Hands to the Gods, and to the Image of *Augustus,* and embracing the Knees of *Tiberius,* till he commanded a Register* to be brought written by the Hand of *Augustus†,* and containing a Particular of the Publick

30 Revenues, with a Roll of the Names of Citizens and Allies, which serv'd in the Armies, of the Tributary Kingdoms, of the Conquer'd Provinces, of the Naval Strength, of the Imposts, and

---

10–14 *That . . .* [*to*] *. . . of*] *italics and romans reversed in O* ("That).
10–18 *each printed line preceded by inverted double commas in O.*
14–15 *Government; that*] Government. That O.
15–17 *in . . .* [*to*] *. . . of*] *set in romans in O.*
17 *one,*] one; O.
17–18 *since . . .* [*to*] *. . . Labours*] *set in romans in O.*

all the Pensions and Expences which were charg'd on the Com-
monwealth: To which, *Augustus,* whether out of Fear for the
Empire, which had receiv'd so great a Blow in *Germany,* or
out of Jealousie, lest some of his Successors should have the
Glory of extending the *Roman* Conquests farther than himself,
added the Advice of Restraining the Empire within the present
Limits†.

    VI. [XII] In the mean time, the Senate still descending to the
most abject Supplications, it happen'd that *Tiberius* said un-
10 warily, He found himself uncapable of Governing the whole
Empire, but if it pleas'd them to commit some part of it to his
Administration, whatsoever it were, he would accept it. Then
Asinius Gallus laying hold of the Word, *And what part of it,
O Tiberius,* said he, *wouldst thou undertake?* He not expecting
such a Question, and not having his Answer in a readiness, for
a while stood silent†: But having recover'd the use of his Rea-
son, answer'd, *That it was unbecoming of his Modesty to choose
a Share of it, when he had rather discharge himself altogether of
the Burden*†. *Asinius,* who discover'd in his Countenance, that
20 he had stung him, replied, *That the Demand which he had made,
tended not to the sharing of that Power, which could not be
divided, but to draw this Acknowledgment from his own Mouth,
that the Commonwealth, being but one Body, could only be gov-
ern'd by one Soul.* Then, after he had prais'd *Augustus,* he de-
sired *Tiberius* to remember his own Victories in War, and his
excellent Actions in Peace, during the space of so many Years,
wherein he had the Management of Affairs. But all this was not
sufficient to make him well with the Emperour†, who bore him
an ancient Grudge, suspecting him for having espous'd *Vipsania,*
30 the Daughter of *Marcus Agrippa,* and formerly the Wife of *Ti-
berius**, as if by that Marriage he design'd to raise himself above
the Condition of a private Life†, and inherited the imperious
Humour of *Asinius Pollio* his Father.

    VII. [XIII] After this Speech, *Lucius Arruntius* likewise of-

---

1–2 Commonwealth:] ∼. O.
17–19 *That ... [to] ... Burden*] set in romans in O ("That).
17–19 *each printed line preceded by inverted double commas in O.*
34 *Arruntius*] *Aruncius* O.

fended him by another, almost of the same Tenour: For though *Tiberius* had not any old Animosity against him, yet he hated him for his Riches, for the Excellency of his Natural Endowments, and Moral Perfections; and for the Reputation which they had gain'd him with the People, which was not inferiour to his Merit[†]. Besides, that *Augustus* in one of the last Discourses which he held, speaking of those, who would refuse the Empire, though capable of Ruling it; or who would be Ambitious of it, though uncapable of Governing; or who at once
10 would be capable of Governing, and desirous of the Government; said, *That* Lepidus *would be worthy of it, without wishing for it; that* Asinius *would be desirous of it, without deserving it; that* Arruntius *neither was unworthy of it, nor would fail to lay hold of the first Occasion[†], to seize it[†]*. Concerning the two first of these, 'tis agreed on all Hands; but some, in stead of *Arruntius,* have nam'd *Cneius Piso.* Certain it is, that all of them, excepting *Lepidus,* perish'd afterwards, by *Tiberius,* under the supposition of several Crimes.

Quintus Haterius, and *Mamercus Scaurus,* incurr'd likewise
20 the Displeasure of that suspicious Soul: The first, for asking him, *How long, O* Cæsar, *wilt thou suffer the Commonwealth to be without a Head[†]?* The other, for saying, *It was to be hop'd, that the Suit of the Senate would not be unprofitable, because when the Consuls propos'd him to them for Emperour, he interpos'd not his Tribunitial Power to resist the Motion.* He reprehended *Haterius* on the spot, but he said not a Word in reply to *Scaurus,* against whom he was more deeply *offended[†]. At length being tir'd with hearing the general Complaints and Murmurs, and the Remonstrances of each Man in particular,
30 he unbent somewhat of his Stiffness; not to the degree of declaring, that he would accept the Empire; but only as he said, to put an end to their Requests[†], and his Refusals. 'Tis undoubted, that *Haterius* going to the Palace to ask his Pardon, wanted but little of being slain by the Soldiers of the Guard, as he was embracing the Knees of *Tiberius,* who slipping at that instant, happen'd to fall as he was going forward[†]; whether by chance, or having his Legs entangled with the Hands of *Ha-*

---

21   Cæsar] *Cæsar* O.

terius: But the Risque, which so great a Personage had run, abated nothing of his Resentment. *Haterius* continued still obnoxious to his Anger, till the Empress, whose Protection he had sought, interceding in his Favour, by force of Prayers obtain'd his Pardon.

VIII. [XIV] The Flatteries of the Senate were yet more excessive, in relation to *Livia:* Some of them voting her the Title of *Mother**, by *way of Excellence and Distinction:* Others, that of *Mother of her Country;* and many of them were likewise for
10 passing a Decree, that to the Name of *Cæsar*, should be added *the Son of Julia.* But *Tiberius* replied to all these, *That they ought not to confer Honours on Women too lavishly*[†]: *That for himself, he would use the same Moderation in those which were propos'd for him*[†]; which he said out of Envy to his Mother, whose Elevation he regarded as a Lessening to his own Authority. He would not, that even a Lictour* should be decreed for her, and hindred the erecting of an Altar, in memory of her Adoption into the *Julian* Family; and forbad them to ascribe to her any other Honour of the like Nature. But he ask'd the Proconsular
20 Power for *Germanicus,* and sent him the Decree by some of the Senate; who were also commission'd to comfort him for the Death of *Augustus*[†]. The Reason why he requir'd not the same Honours for his Son *Drusus,* was because he was then in *Rome,* and besides was design'd Consul. He afterwards nam'd twelve Pretors, which was the Number establish'd by *Augustus*[†]; and the Senate requesting him to create more[†], he took a Solemn Oath, never to exceed that Number.

IX. [XV] It was now, that the Assembly* for electing Magistrates, was for the first time transferr'd from the Field of *Mars*
30 to the Senate: For though formerly the Emperour had manag'd all Affairs of Consequence according to his Pleasure, yet some Things were still permitted to be done, by the Intrigues and Suffrages* of the Tribes[†]: For which loss of Privileges, the People shewed no other Resentment, but by insignificant Complaints and Murmurs. And the Senate, for their part, were well satisfied, that thereby they were discharg'd from the shameful

7   *Livia:*] ∼. O.   9   *Country;* and] ∼: And O.
11   *the*] the O.   14   *him*[†]; which] ∼[2]. Which O.

Necessity of bribing and supplicating the Commons[†], to favour their Election: And this the more, for that *Tiberius* reserv'd to himself but the Naming[†] of four Candidates*, who were to be admitted without Caballing, or any Contradiction. At the same time, the Tribunes of the People demanded the Permission, to celebrate at their own Charges those Plays in Honour of *Augustus*[†], which in their Calendars* were call'd by the Name of *Augustales*. But it was order'd, that the Publick should be at the Expence, and that the Tribunes should wear the Triumphal
10 Robe* in the *Circus;* where, nevertheless, it was not allow'd them to be born in Chariots. And the Annual Celebration was thenceforward committed to that particular Prætor, to whose Lot it should fall, to judge the Differences arising betwixt Citizens and Strangers.

X. [XVI] This was the face of Affairs at *Rome,* when a Sedition arose, of the Legions in *Pannonia*. They had no new occasion of Disturbance; only the change of an Emperour inspir'd them with Boldness to make some Disturbance, in hope to better their Condition by a Civil War[†]. Three Legions were quarter'd to-
20 gether in the same Camp, under the Command of *Junius Blæsus,* who having heard of the Death of *Augustus,* and the Succession of *Tiberius,* had interrupted the daily Exercises of the Soldiers, either in Token of Mourning*, or of Joy. This Disport began to give a Loathing to the Army of their Labour, and Military Discipline, and infuse into them a Propensity of Idleness and Pleasure. It furnish'd them with Occasions of frequent Quarrels with one another; and of lending an Ear to the mutinous Discourses of the most dissolute amongst them. There was in the Camp a Fellow called *Percennius,* formerly Head of a Faction among
30 the Stage-Players[†]; afterwards a private Soldier: Insolent in his Speech, and who had learn'd to raise Sedition, by his Practice, in the Playhouse. This Man haunting the Conversation of the most Ignorant, and Silly, who were very inquisitive to know what their Condition was like to be under their new Emperour, debauch'd them by his Nightly Conversations with them, or at least when it grew late in the Evening; and when the more sober Party were

---

2 Election:] ~. O.   12 Prætor] *Prætor* O.
23 Disport] Dispute O.

withdrawn to Rest, assembled the Band of Mutineers. [XVII] At length many others, who were Promoters of Sedition, being associated with him, he question'd them, like a General who Harangues his Army, on these following Propositions.

XI. *Why they paid a Slavish Obedience to a small number of Centurions, and a less of *Tribunes*†? *When would they have the Courage to expose their Grievances, and require a Remedy, if not now, in the unsettled Condition of a new Emperour*†, *with whom they safely might Expostulate, or,* if need were, *demand*
10 *Redress by force of Arms? They had in their own Wrong been already silent for the space of many Years, when would they be weary of so tame a Patience? Not the least Account was made of thirty or forty Years of Service, without mentioning the Infirmities of Age; the greatest part of them had their Bodies mangl'd, and their Limbs disabl'd with their Wounds. That even they who were exempted from their daily Duties, yet saw no end of their Sufferings; being still retain'd under their Colours, they still endur'd the same Miseries, without other Advantage, than that of a more honourable Name*. If some amongst them*
20 *surviv'd so many Misadventures, they were sent into remote Countries, where, under the specious Title of* Rewards, *they had Fens allotted them to drain, or barren Hills to cultivate: That the Trade of Warfare was of it self Laborious and Unprofitable; that they earn'd a hard Livelihood of Eight Pence a Day*, or little more, out of which they were to supply themselves with Clothing, Tents and Arms; and pay their exacting Centurions for their Exemption from Military Duties*†: *That the Blows of their Officers, their Mayms, the Severity of the Winter, the insufferable Toyls of Summer*, a bloody War, and a barren*
30 *Peace, were endless Evils; for which, there was no other Remedy, than not to list themselves for Soldiers under the Daily Pay of a* Roman *Penny (or* Denarius**); covenanting also to be discharg'd from Service, at the end of Sixteen Years; to be sent to their respective Homes, to receive their Pay in Silver, and in the Camp where they had serv'd; shall then the Prætorian Soldiers receive each of them a double Sallary to ours, and be dismissed*

---

14   *Age;*] ~, O.   21   Rewards] *Rewards* O.
27   *Duties*†:] ~³. O.   35   *Prætorian*] Prætorian O.

after Sixteen Years of Warfare? Are their Actions, or Sufferings to be compar'd with ours? I speak not this, either out of Envy, or Contempt; but at least we may say for our Reputation, that being in the midst of barbarous and fierce Nations, we have our Enemies in view, even from our Tents.

XII. [XVIII] The whole Company receiv'd his Oration with a general applause; though from different motives: some of them shew'd the Marks of the Civil Blows which their Officers had given them; Others their hoary Hair, and many bar'd their

10 Flesh, ill cover'd, with old and tatter'd Cloaths. In short, they were inflam'd to that heighth of rage, that they propos'd the Uniting the three Legions into one*; but their jealousy put a stop to that, every Man pretending to the chief Honour for his own Legion. They bethought themselves of another Expedition, which was for mixing the three Eagles confusedly, with the Ensigns of the Cohorts; which having done, they rais'd a Tribunal on sods of Grass, that the Seat might be the farther seen. *Blæsus* arriving thereupon, took those by the Arm whom he met in his Passage, and reproach'd them with great Severity†.

20 *Rather dip your Hands,* said he to the Mutineers, *in the live Blood of your General; it will be a less Crime for you to murder me, than to revolt against your Emperor: I will either restrain you within your due Obedience, if you suffer me to live, or I will hasten your Repentance by my Death*.*

XIII. [XIX] In the mean time they proceeded with their Work, which they had already rais'd to the height of their Shoulders; when at length their Obstinacy being conquer'd by his Courage, they gave it over. *Blæsus*, who was a Master of Well-speaking†, represented to them, That their Demands ought not

30 to be carri'd to the Emperour, by way of Sedition†; that their Predecessors had never offer'd any thing of that Nature to former Generals; nor they themselves, to the Divine *Augustus;* that they had ill tim'd their Purpose, to give new Troubles to a Prince, oppress'd with the weight of his Affairs now in the beginning of his Reign†; that if, notwithstanding, they would make such Demands in the midst of Peace, which the conquering Side in a Civil War had never presum'd to ask from their Com-

---

18, 28 *Blæsus*] *Blesus* O.

mander; yet why would they transgress the Limits of Respect, and violate Discipline by taking Arms? Why nam'd they not their Deputies, for whom they might draw up their Instructions in his Presence? At these Words they answer'd with a general Cry, That the Son of *Blæsus,* who was one of the Tribunes, was the most proper Man to take upon him that Commission; and to require a Discharge for all, when their sixteen Years[†] of Service should be expir'd; and that they would send him fresh Instructions, when that first Article was accorded. When young
10 *Blæsus* was set forward on his Journey, they were somewhat calm: But the Soldiers grew more haughty, on the account of that Deputation; which shew'd, that they had carried that by Violence, which by other Methods they could never have obtain'd.

XIV. [XX] In the mean time, those Bands of Soldiers*, who, before the Sedition, had been sent to *Nauportum** to repair the Ways and Bridges, and for other Occasions, receiving Notice of what had pass'd in the Camp, laid hold on the Ensigns, plunder'd the Neighbourhood, and *Nauportum* it self, which was in
20 the nature of a Municipal Town*, contemn'd, revil'd, and even beat their Centurions, who endeavour'd to restrain their Madness. Their Rage was chiefly bent against *Aufidienus Rufus,* who, from a private Soldier, had been rais'd to a Centurion, and from thence to a Prefect, or *Mareschal de Camp*[†]. They pull'd him from his Chariot, they loaded him with Baggage, and made him march at the Head of a Battalion, asking him in scorn, If he were not pleas'd to carry such a Burden, and to travel so far on Foot? For *Rufus* was an indefatigable Man, who restor'd to use the strictness of the ancient Discipline[†], and who spar'd their
30 Labour so much the less, because he had undergone himself what he had impos'd on others.

XV. [XXI] The arrival of these Mutineers renew'd the Tumult, and roaming lawlesly round the Country, they made Waste of all Things in their way. *Blæsus* caus'd some of them, who return'd loaden with their Plunder, to be beaten, and made Prisoners, thereby to imprint a greater Terror in the rest: (For

5, 10 *Blæsus*] Blesus O.   21 endeavour'd] endeavonr'd O.
34 *Blæsus*] Blesus O.

the Centurions, and the sober part of the Soldiers, still con-
tinu'd in their Duty.) The Pillagers thereupon resist those who
force them to Prison, embrace the Knees of their Camerades,
implore their Succour; either, in particular, by their Names;
or, in general, the Company, the Cohort, or the Legion, in which
they serv'd; crying out, Their own Turn must be next in the
same Usage. They pour out a thousand Reproaches against their
General, and call the Gods to witness his Injustice. In short,
they omit nothing to move Compassion, to raise Envy and Fear,
10 and to foment Sedition. The Soldiers run in heaps to their
Relief, break open the Prisons, deliver their Companions, and
strengthen their Party with Deserters, and Criminals condemn'd
to Death.

XVI. [XXII] From thence, the Mutiny grew more outragious,
and the Numbers of their Heads increas'd. One *Vibulenus*, a
private Soldier[†], being hoisted on the Backs of his Companions,
was carried, as it were, in *Triumph*, before the Tribunal of the
General, and the Soldiers big with expectation of his Speech,
and thronging to hear him, thus began, *'Tis true, Companions,*
20 *you have restor'd to Life and Liberty our innocent Fellow-
Soldiers; but who shall give me back my Brother, who, being
Commission'd to you from the Army now in* Germany, *for our
common Interests, has this Night been butcher'd by the Gladia-
tors, who are purposely entertain'd by* Blæsus, *for our General
Massacre? Tell me,* Blæsus, *where thou hast thrown this mur-
der'd Body? Even Enemies refuse not Burial to the Slain. When
I have satisfied my Grief with Tears and Kisses, command me
to be murder'd; and I consent to my own Death, provided thou
wilt order us to be laid in one common Grave, like Brothers, who*
30 *suffer'd Death, not for the Guilt of any Crime, but only for de-
fending the Cause of the *Legions[†].*

XVII. [XXIII] He animated this Discourse with Sobs and
Groans, and with the Blows which he gave himself on his Face
and Breast; then getting loose from those who had carried him
on their Shoulders, he threw himself hastily at the Feet of the
Assistants, and mov'd them so much to Compassion and Re-

---

19 began,] ∼. O.
25 *Massacre?*] ∼. O.

24 Blæsus] Blesus O.
25 Blæsus] Blesus O .

venge†, that one part of the Soldiers seiz'd on the Gladiators of
Blæsus, another secur'd his Menial Servants, whilst many of them
ran searching here and there for the Body of their slain Com-
panion. And if, by good Fortune, it had not been immediately
discover'd, that *Vibulenus* never had a Brother, that there was
no such Body to be found, and that the Slaves of *Blæsus,* being
put to the Torture, persisted to deny the Murder; the General
was in immediate danger of Assassination. In the mean time,
they forc'd the Tribunes, and the Præfect of the Camp, to fly
10 for their Safety; they plunder'd their Baggage, and kill'd *Lucilius*
the Centurion, to whom they had given the Nick-name of *Cedo*
alteram; because when he had broken his Baton* on the Back
of any Soldier, he was wont to call for another, to *continue the*
Correction. The rest of the Centurions absconded, excepting
only *Julius Clemens,* who was sav'd; as being one, who, for his
ready Wit, was thought a proper Man to execute the Commis-
sions of the Soldiers†. There were two of the Legions, the Eighth
and the Fifteenth, who were ready to come to Blows with one
another concerning one *Sirpicus* a Centurion; the Eighth de-
20 manding him to be produc'd and put to Death, the other de-
fending him: If the Ninth had not interpos'd, and partly with
Prayers, partly with Threatnings, brought them to Reason on
either side.

XVIII. [XXIV] These Things coming to the knowledge of
Tiberius, constrain'd him, as expert as he was in dissembling
his Temper, and concealing all ill News†, to send away his Son
with all speed to *Pannonia,* without other Instructions, than
only to act according to the present Necessity, and as the junc-
ture of Affairs† requir'd. He gave for his Attendants two Præ-
30 torian Cohorts, reinforc'd with a Recruit of select Soldiers, with
a great part of his Cavalry, and the Choice of his *German* Guards;
sent in his Company the principal Men of *Rome,* and appointed
for the Governor of his Person *Elius Sejanus,* his Favourite†,
then Præfect of the *Prætorium*,* and Collegue to his Father
Strabo, in that Office: Employ'd particularly, on this Occasion,
to promise Rewards to those who should submit, and threaten
Punishments to such as should persist in their Rebellion. On

2, 6 *Blæsus*] Blesus O.

the approach of *Drusus* to the Army, the Legions drew out,
to meet him on the way, and do him Honour; not with chearful
Countenances, as was the Custom, nor with shining Arms and
Ensigns*, but in a mean and ragged Equipage, and with sad and
sullen Looks, which shew'd more of Contumacy, than of Re-
pentance.

XIX. [XXV] When he was enter'd into the Camp, they plac'd
Sentinels at the Gates, and Corps de Guard in several Parts; the
main Body of them gather'd round the Tribunal of *Drusus*, who
10 was standing, and held out his Hand, as desiring their Attention.
As often as the Mutineers cast round their Eyes, and consider'd
their own Multitude, they fill'd the Air with Shouts and Threat-
nings†, but when they turn'd their Sight towards *Drusus*, they
shook for fear†. To this confus'd Noise, and these insolent Clam-
ours, succeeded a profound Silence; and by their different Mo-
tions they gave, and took Terror in their turns. At length, the
Tumult being ceas'd, *Drusus* read to them the Letters of his
Father; which contain'd in effect, That he would take a par-
ticular Care of those valiant Legions which had assisted him in
20 sustaining several Wars†; That so soon as his Grief for the Death
of *Augustus* would give him leave, he would propose their De-
mands to the Senate; That, in the interim, he had sent his Son
to them, with full Power, and without the least Delay, to grant
them all that was possible to be done for them on the sudden:
And what requir'd more Leisure, should pass through the Hands
of the Senate; it being unjust to take from them the Glory of
Rewarding, or the Power of Punishing.

XX. [XXVI] To this, the Assembly return'd Answer, That
Julius Clemens was intrusted by them to make known their De-
30 sires. He then began, with their Pretension, to be discharg'd
from Service at the end of sixteen Years, with a Recompence in
Silver; that their daily Pay should be a *Roman Denarius*; and
that the Veterans should no longer be detain'd under their En-
signs. *Drusus*, alledging that the Cognizance of these Matters
belong'd to the Senate and his Father†, was interrupted by their

8 Corps de Guard] Corps-de-Guard O.
33 Veterans] *Veterans* O.
34–35 *Drusus,* alledging ... Father†,] ~ʌ ~, ... ~¹; O.

Clamours. *What Business has he here,* they cry'd, *since he is not impower'd, either to augment the Soldiers Pay, or to redress their Grievances, while in the mean time they are expos'd to be beaten and slain at the Pleasure of their Officers? We remember since* Tiberius *has evaded our Petitions, by remitting us to Augustus, and has he sent his Son on the same Errand? Shall we always have to deal with Children, who come to us in their Fathers Name? Is it not a strange manner of Proceeding, that the Emperour refers nothing to the Senate, but what concerns*
10 *the Rewarding of his Soldiers*†*! Why does he not also consult the Senate, when he is to give a Battle, or punish us with Death? Is it reasonable, that Recompences should not be given, but by the Consent of so many Masters? And that, on the contrary, every Officer has right to punish us at his own Pleasure, and without Comptrol from any Man?*

XXI. [XXVII] At this, they flung from the Tribunal, threatning all they met of the Prince's Guard, or of his Friends, and seeking an occasion of Quarrel and Revenge. Their Malice was chiefly bent at *Cneius Lentulus,* because that being elder, and
20 of greater Reputation in War than any of the other Officers: He was thought the Man, who most despis'd the Danger of the Mutineers, and render'd *Drusus* inflexible† to their Demands. And shortly after, when departing from *Drusus,* to shun the Danger which he foresaw, he took his way to the Winter Quarters; they inclos'd him in the midst of them, and ask'd him, Whither he was going, and if he was returning to *Rome,* in order to oppose the Interest of the Legions? And they were already beginning to stone him, if the Troops which *Drusus* had brought along with him had not rescu'd him from their Hands
30 all over bloody as he was.

XXII. [XXVIII] The Night threaten'd some horrible Attempt, but an Accident unforeseen turn'd all to Quiet. The Moon in a calm and serene Night, on the sudden, was eclips'd; and the Soldiers, who were wholly ignorant of Astronomy, drew from thence an Augury, for the present Juncture of Affairs; and

---

1   *What*] 'What O.
1–15   *Business . . .* [to] *. . . Man*] italics and romans reversed in O.
1–15   *each printed line preceded by an inverted comma in O.*

comparing the defect of Light in the Moon to their own Labours, interpreted, that all would go well with them, if the eclips'd Goddess recover'd Light. Therefore, they beat on brazen Instruments, sounded their Trumpets, and rais'd confus'd Clamours; and as she appear'd more bright, or became more dusky, they vary'd their Sadness, and their Joy. But when the Sky grew cloudy, and took her wholly from their Sight, so that they believ'd her lost in Darkness, as Minds once strucken* with Amazement†, are prone to Superstition, so they imagin'd a Perpetuity of Labours was portended to them, and lamented, that the Gods were averse to their impious Attempt. *Drusus* thought it Wisdom†, to lay hold on the Occasion which their Fear administer'd, and order'd some to go into their Tents. He made choice of *Clemens,* and others, who, by their Merit, had acquir'd Credit with the common sort. These mixing with the Centries, and those who went the Rounds, or watched about the Gates, redoubl'd their Apprehensions, and withal, awak'd their Hopes. *How long,* said they, *shall we continue to besiege the Son of* Cæsar? *Shall we take the Oath of Fidelity to* Percennius, *and to* Vibulenus? *Will they give us the Pay and Rewards which we pretend? In a word, Shall they Usurp the Empire of the* Nero's, *and the* Drusi? *Why should not we be the first to repent us, as we have been the last to be seduc'd*? The Demands which are made in common, are ever slowly granted, and late received; on the contrary, the Reward comes speedily to their Hands, who will each* deserve it singly†.* These Words having once shaken their Resolution†, and cast a Distrust into them of each other, the Love of their Prince re-enter'd into them by degrees, the Legions separate, and the new Soldiers divide from the Veterans: They forsake the Gates, and replace their Eagles by themselves, which they had shuffl'd together in the beginning of the Mutiny.

XXIII. [XXIX] At break of Day, *Drusus* calls the General Assembly and (though he had not the Gift of Speaking well, yet his Discourse had in it a certain Air of Greatness, inborn to those

18 *How*] 'How O.
18–23 *each printed line preceded by an inverted comma in O.*
18–26 *long . . . [to] . . . singly] italics and romans reversed in O.*
29 Veterans] *Veterans* O.
33–254:1 Assembly . . . (though . . . Blood†)] ~; . . . ∧~ . . . ~¹; O.

of Noble Blood†) highly condemns the past Proceedings, and extols the present. He tells them, he is not capable of Fear, and that, by consequence, he is not to be mov'd with Threatnings†; that if he finds in them due Repentance, and Respect, he will write to his Father in their behalf, and incline him to receive their Petition, and graciously to answer it. Accordingly, at their Request, the fore-mention'd *Blæsus, Lucius Apronius* a *Roman* Knight, of the Cohort of *Drusus*, and *Justus Catonius* Captain of the first Century*, are sent to *Tiberius.* After this, a Council
10 of War was held, where their Judgments were divided: Some were of Opinion, that the Soldiers should be mildly Treated, till the return of their Deputies; others thought it more adviseable to use Rigour, there being no Moderation to be expected from a Multitude†, which makes it self formidable when it fears nothing, and which may safely be despis'd when timorous: That Terrour was to be imprinted in them, while they were yet fill'd with Superstition; and that they were to be made sensible they had a Master, by the Punishment of those who were Authors of the Mutiny†.
20   XXIV. *Drusus,* whose Nature inclin'd him to Severity†, caus'd *Vibulenus* and *Percennius* to be brought before him, and commanded them to be put to Death†. Many relate, that they were slain, and buried in his Tent†, to keep the Execution secret; others say, that their Bodies were cast out of the Camp, to serve for an Example, and remain a Spectacle to their Companions. [XXX] Enquiry was made afterwards for the other Promoters of the Sedition, and many flying here and there for shelter, were discover'd and kill'd by Centurions, and Soldiers of the Guard; some of them were deliver'd up by their own Comerades, as a
30 Pledge of their Fidelity. The Disquiets of the Mutineers were yet more augmented by an over-early Winter, with continual Rains, and Storms so furious, that they durst not stir out of their Tents to meet in Assemblies; and hardly were they able to keep their Colours, which the fierceness of the Winds threatned every moment to bear away. Add to this, That they were still in apprehension of the Wrath of Heaven; and their guilty Minds

7 *Blæsus*] *Blesus* O.   7 *Roman*] Roman O.
14 formidable] formidale O.

suggested to them, that the Planets were not eclips'd in vain, or that the Tempests roul'd without Presage over the Heads of Rebels†; that there was no other Remedy remaining for their present Evils, but to abandon a profan'd Camp, an unfortunate Abode, and to return to their Garisons, after they had expiated their Crime. The eighth Legion remov'd first, and was soon followed by the fifteenth. The ninth oppos'd themselves to this Departure, crying out, The Answer of *Tiberius* was to be attended there; but being surpriz'd with Fear, as being left alone,
10 they prevented the Necessity of being forc'd to Obedience. So that all Things being compos'd in a settl'd Calm, *Drusus* went immediately for *Rome,* without longer waiting for the return of the Deputies.

XXV. [XXXI] Almost at the same time, and for the same Reasons, the Legions in *Germany* rebell'd†; and their Mutiny had in it the more of Insolence, because they were in greater Numbers; and all of them concluded, that *Germanicus* would never submit to the Government of another, but that, to prevent Subjection, he would Head those Legions†; by whose means, he
20 might put himself in a condition of reducing all others to his Party. There were two Armies encamp'd on the Banks of the *Rhine;* that on the upper part was commanded by *Gaius Silius,* in Quality of Lieutenant-General; that on the nether, by *Aulus Cecina.* Their common General was *Germanicus,* who, at that time, was busied in *Gaul* about gathering the Tributes. But those who were under *Silius,* protracted the time of declaring themselves, till they saw what Fortune would befal the Army of *Cecina†,* where the Sedition began from the Twenty first and Fifth Legions, which also drew into their Party the Twentieth,
30 and the First; for they were quartered together on the Frontiers of the *Ubians*,* living in Idleness†, or, at least, with small Employment. When the Death of *Augustus* was known amongst them, the Soldiers of the new Recruits, accustom'd to the Softnesses of Life at *Rome,* and, consequently, Enemies to the Toyls of War, began to broach amongst those who were Simple and Credulous, That now the Time was come for the Veterans to demand a quick Discharge; for the new-rais'd Troops to have

31 *Ubians*] *Ubiens* O.   36 Veterans] *Veterans* O.

their Pay enlarg'd; for both Parties to require an end of their
Sufferings; and to revenge themselves on the Cruelty of their
Centurions. It was not any single Person, (as *Percennius* was
amongst the *Pannonian* Legions,) who declaim'd in this man-
ner: Neither did the Soldiers tremble at the sight of another
Army more powerful than their own, and which were Witnesses
of what they said and did; but many Mouths which cry'd in Con-
cert, That the *Roman* Empire was in their Hands, to *dispose
of as they pleas'd;* that they had inlarg'd it by their Victories;
10 and that the Cæsars* held it for an Honour, to bear the Sirname
of *Germanicus.*

XXVI. [XXXII] *Cecina* durst not oppose this, either by Word
or Action, their Multitude having over-master'd his Resolution.
The Seditious, being seiz'd with one common Fury, fell with
their drawn Swords on their Centurions, (ever the Object of
their Hate, and the first Sacrifice which they offer'd to their
Vengeance;) they pull'd them down, and beat them afterwards
to Death with Cudgels; Sixty of them at once assaulting one, to
equal the Number of the Centurions, which were Sixty to every
20 Legion. To conclude, they cast them out of the Camp half dead,
or threw their Bodies into the *Rhine.* One of them call'd *Sep-
timius,* who had refug'd himself in the Tribunal of *Cecina,* and
had embrac'd his Knees, was demanded with so much Obstinacy,
that the General was forc'd to deliver him up to their Fury.
Cassius Chærea, an intrepid Youth, the same who afterwards
eterniz'd his Memory by the Death of *Caligula*[†], open'd himself
a Passage with his Sword through a Crowd of Arm'd Soldiers,
who endeavour'd to have seiz'd him. From that moment, neither
the Tribunes, nor the *Mareschals de Camp,* were any more
30 obey'd. The Mutineers themselves plac'd the Sentinels and the
Corps de Guard, and order'd all Things which their present
Needs requir'd. Those who pierc'd into the depth of that Affair,
drew from thence a certain Augury, that the Sedition would be
of a long Continuance; because they acted not with any separate
Interest, or, by the Instigation of any particular Men among

10   Cæsars] *Cæsars* O.
14   Seditious, . . . seiz'd . . . Fury,] ∼_∧ . . . ∼, . . . ∼_∧ O.
29   *Mareschals de Camp*] Mareschals de Camp O.

them; they rais'd their Clamours all at once, and at once they ceas'd them; with so much Equality, and so good an Understanding amongst themselves, that it might have been reasonably believ'd, they were under the Government of one Head.

XXVII. [XXXIII] While *Germanicus,* as we have said, was detain'd in *Gaul* to collect the Tributes, he receiv'd the News of *Augustus*'s Death, whose Grand-daughter he had marry'd. He was the Son of *Drusus,* Nephew to *Tiberius,* and Grand-son to *Livia;* But the secret Hatred of his Uncle, and his Grand-mother,
10 gave him great Inquietude, knowing that their Aversion was so much the more to be fear'd, because their Motives to it were unjust[†]. For the Memory of *Drusus* was in high Veneration amongst the *Romans;* it being the general Opinion, That if he had come to possess the Empire[†], he would have restor'd their Liberty to the People: From thence, their Favour was deriv'd to *Germanicus,* and their Hopes of him the same: For *Germanicus* was of a soft, pleasing Humour, affable in Conversation, and his Behaviour wholly different from the sullen Reservedness and Arrogance[†] of *Tiberius.* The Quarrels betwixt the Women con-
20 tributed not a little to this Enmity; For *Livia* behav'd herself with the Loftiness of a Mother-in-Law to *Agrippina,* and *Agrippina* carry'd it somewhat too resentingly towards *Livia;* but her known Chastity, and the Love she bore her Husband, to whom she had born many Children, wrought so far upon her Soul, that, though naturally haughty and inflexible, she contain'd herself within the Bounds of what was Virtuous and Laudable.

XXVIII. [XXXIV] But *Germanicus,* the nearer he approach'd to the height of Sovereignty, the more eagerly he strove to maintain *Tiberius* in Possession[†]; he caus'd him to be recogniz'd by
30 the Neighbouring Provinces[*] of the *Sequani* and *Belgæ;* and when he was inform'd, that the Legions were tumultuously up in Arms, he made all possible Expedition in his Journey to them. They met him without the Camp with dejected Eyes, as in sign of their Repentance. But as soon as he was enter'd, the Camp resounded with confus'd and jarring Clamours. Some of them taking his Hand, as it were, to kiss it, put his Fingers into their Mouths, to make him sensible that they had lost their Teeth. Others shew'd him their decrepid Limbs, and Shoulders bending

under the weight of Age. As they were all mingled in a Crowd, and without Order, he commanded them to draw up in their several Companies, under pretence that they might with more convenience hear his Answer, and to separate their Colours, that he might distinguish every Cohort by its proper Ensign. They obey'd him but as slowly as possibly they could†. Then beginning his Oration with the Praises of *Augustus*†, he descended to those of *Tiberius*, but above all enlarging on those Exploits, which he had perform'd with them in *Germany*. He set before
10 them the Universal Consent of *Italy*, the Fidelity of the *Gauls*, and the Concord of all the other Provinces of the Empire. [XXXV] And thus far he was heard with a respectful Silence, or, at least, with little or no Disturbance.

XXIX. But when he came to ask them, what was become of their Obedience, and of their ancient Discipline, where were their Tribunes, and what they had done with their Centurions? They stripp'd themselves naked, to shew him, by way of Reproach, the Scars of the Wounds, and the Bruises of those Blows which they had receiv'd from their Officers; and afterwards
20 speaking all at once, they complain'd of their scanty Pay, and the intolerable Price with which they were forc'd to purchase their Exemption from Duties; and the Miseries they suffered in† labouring Night and Day on their Retrenchments, in providing Forage for their Horses and Beasts of Burden, and heaps of Faggots, (or Fascines;) and what other Employments are invented to keep the Soldiers in exercise, when no Enemy is near. A fierce Clamour of the Veterans arose, who having serv'd the space of 30 or 40 Years, besought *Germanicus* to take Pity on them, and not suffer them to die in the Hardships of Warfare, but to give
30 them their Discharge, and wherewithal to subsist afterwards in their Age†. Some amongst them also demanded the Legacies of Money, which were left them by *Augustus*, not without loud Acclamations to *Germanicus*, and engaging to serve him, if he would accept the Empire*. But he, as if he fear'd there had been Infection in their Crime, leap'd precipitately down from his Tribunal†, and was departing from the Camp, till they held him by the Arm, and turning the Points of their Swords against

25   Fascines] *Fascines* O.   27   Veterans] *Veterans* O.

him, threaten'd to kill him if he refus'd to mount his Seat. He protesting, he would rather die, than be wanting to his Duty, drew his Sword, and raising his Arm, was plunging it into his Breast, if those who were nearest him had not stop'd his Hand. They who stood farmost in the Crowd press'd nearer, and some of them (what is almost incredible to relate) singling themselves from the rest, came up to him, and exhorted him to strike as he had threaten'd; And a certain Soldier, called *Calusidius*, offer'd him his naked Sword, assuring him, that the Point was sharper*
10 than his own. But this appear'd of bad Example, and even execrable to those who were mad themselves; so that there was Time given for his Friends to draw him off into his Tent.

XXX. [XXXVI] There a Council was call'd, in order to appease the Mutiny; for Notice had been given, that the Seditious had propos'd to send Deputies to the Army of *Silius*, and to ingage them in their Revolt†; that they had resolv'd to plunder the City of the *Ubians*†; and that if once they had tasted the Sweets of Rapine, they would soon be tempted onwards, to make a Prey of *Gaul*. It was also apprehended, that the *Germans*, who were
20 not ignorant of what had pass'd, should make an Irruption into the *Roman* Province, in case the Legions should withdraw from the *Rhine:* And that, on the other side, if they should arm the Allies and the Auxiliaries* against the Legions, to hinder their departure, that was in effect to kindle a Civil War. That Severity expos'd *Germanicus* to Danger, and Mildness to *Contempt†; that whether all Things should be granted, or all refus'd to the Mutineers, was of equal Hazard to the common Good. In fine, all Reasons, both on the one and the other side, being duly weigh'd, it was resolv'd to counterfeit Letters as from *Tiberius*, by which
30 he gave a free Discharge to all such as had serv'd for the space of Twenty Years†; and declar'd those for Voluntiers who had serv'd Sixteen, retaining them under a particular Ensign, exempted from all sorts of Duty*, excepting only to repulse the Enemy; and ordaining them to be paid double the Legacy which had been left them by *Augustus*.

XXXI. [XXXVII] The Soldiers suspecting the Design†, requir'd that all this should be immediately perform'd. And the

22   *Rhine:*] ~. O.

Tribunes expedited the Discharge; but the Payment being post-
pon'd till they were in Winter-Quarters, the Fifth and the
Twenty first Legions refus'd to return into their Garisons: And
Germanicus was forc'd to pay them out of the Money[†] which he
brought with him to defray his Voyage, and out of what he could
borrow from his Friends. *Cecina* brought back to the *Ubians*
the First and the Twentieth Legions; and it was indeed a shame-
ful March, to see carried, *as it were, in Triumph,* the Silver*,
which they had extorted from their General, amongst the Eagles
10 and the Ensigns. In the mean time, *Germanicus* being gone to
visit the Army on the *Upper Rhine,* the Second, the Thirteenth,
and the Sixteenth Legion took the Oath of Fidelity without the
least demurr; and the Fourteenth having paus'd a little on the
Matter, he offer'd them the Money, and their Discharge, without
their once demanding it[†].

XXXII. [XXXVIII] But the Sedition was again renewing in
the Country of the *Chauci*, through the Malice of those Re-
bellious Veterans, who were there in Garison, if a timely Stop
had not been put to the Beginnings by the Execution of two
20 Soldiers, whom *Mennius,* the *Mareschal de Camp,* caus'd to be
suddenly put to Death: A daring Action, and of good Example,
rather than of true[†] Justice*. Notwithstanding which, the Mu-
tiny still gathering to a greater Head, he took flight, and hid
himself; but being discover'd, he call'd his Courage to his Suc-
cour. *This Violence,* said he, *is not offer'd to me, but to* Ger-
manicus, *your General; and to* Tiberius, *your lawful Emperour*[†].
Saying this, and seeing them amaz'd, he snatch'd their Ensign*,
and turning directly towards the *Rhine,* he cried out, that *he
held him for a Deserter who forsook his Rank*[†]; insomuch, that
30 they all return'd to their Winter-Quarters much discontented,
and without daring to proceed in their Attempt.

XXXIII. [XXXIX] In the mean time, *Germanicus* being al-
ready on his return from the *Upper Germany,* the Deputies of
the Senate, found him at the Altar of the *Ubians*, where the
First and the Twentieth Legions, together with the Veterans,

---

9   extorted . . . [*to*] . . . General] *set in italics in* O.
18   Veterans] *Veterans* O.
20   *Mareschal de Camp*] Mareschal-de-Camp O.
35   Veterans] *Veterans* O.

who were discharg'd, had their Winter Quarters, and were still
retain'd under their Ensigns. A terrible Affright suddenly seiz'd
those Soldiers, who felt the Stings of Conscience for the Crime
they had committed. They suspected, that those Deputies had
Orders to revoke the Grants, which they had extorted by their
Mutiny. And as it is the common Practice of the Multitude to
accuse one wrongfully, they make *Munatius Plancus,* a Consular
Man, and Chief of the Deputation, the Author of this Decree
of the Senate[t]. Towards Midnight they came to a Resolution
among themselves to demand the Standard, which was kept in
the Lodgings of *Germanicus**. Accordingly they ran thither in
a Crowd, broke open the Doors, and dragging the Prince[t] out
of his Bed, they threaten'd him with Death, and constrain'd him
to deliver up the Ensign[t]. Then running through the Camp,
they met the Legats, who hearing the Uproar, were hastening to
Germanicus; they resolve to murder them, and particularly
Plancus, whom regard of his Character[t] would not permit to
escape by flight; and therefore, having no other Refuge, he cast
himself into the Quarter of the First Legion, and made Religion
his Buckler, by embracing the Eagle and the Ensigns*: Which
notwithstanding, the *Roman* Camp, and even the Altars of the
Gods, were in danger of being profan'd by the Blood of a *Roman*
Ambassador, (an unusual Crime even among our Enemies) if
Calpurnius, who was Eagle-bearer*, had not prevented the Blow
by his Resistance. When it was Day-light, and Men and Actions
could be discern'd, *Germanicus* entring the Camp, caus'd *Plan-
cus* to be brought before him, and seated him by his Side on his
Tribunal; then reproaching them with their mad Behaviour,
and exclaiming against their fatal Disobedience, which he chose
to attribute to the Anger of the Gods[t], rather than the Fury of
the Soldiers, he openly declar'd the Occasion of that Embassy,
and eloquently deplor'd the cruel Outrage done to *Plancus*
without cause, and the Infamy which the Legion had incurr'd,
by violating in his Person the sacred Character of Ambassadors[t].
After this Harangue, which rather astonish'd the Multitude,

than appeas'd them, he licens'd the Deputies to depart, and caus'd
them to be convoy'd by the Auxiliary Troops.

XXXIV. [XL] During this Consternation, *Germanicus* was
generally blam'd, that he repair'd not to the Army on the *Upper
Rhine,* where he might have found both Obedience and Aid
against the Rebels. *Germanicus* (said they) *has discover'd his
Weakness, and his Fear, in rewarding the Revolters[t]. If he re-
garded not his own Safety, yet why should he abandon his Infant
Son[t], and his Wife with Child, to the Fury of those Mutineers,*
10 *to whom nothing is inviolable? He ought, at least, to have re-
stor'd those Pledges to* Tiberius, *and to the Commonwealth.*
After long Consideration, he embrac'd his Wife and Son with
many Tears, and order'd their departure: And though *Agrip-
pina,* to avoid that mournful Separation, said, That the Grand-
daughter of *Augustus* had too much Courage to fear Danger[t],
yet at length she submitted to the Journey. It was a sad Spectacle,
to see the Wife of a General, in the Equipage of a Fugitive,
carrying a helpless Infant in her Arms, encompass'd with a
Troop of other Women, all in Tears; and those who stay'd be-
20 hind, as much afflicted, as those who went.

XXXV. [XLI] These lamentable Outcries, which one would
have thought had rather come from a sack'd City, than from the
Camp of *Germanicus,* at that time in a flourishing Condition,
excited the Curiosity of the Soldiers. They came forth from their
Tents to learn the Cause. There they beheld so many Ladies of
Illustrious Birth, without any Convoy or Guard to attend them;
Agrippina, without her ordinary Train, or any one remaining
Sign to distinguish the Wife of their General from other Women:
And informing themselves, that she was going for *Treves,* there
30 to seek a Sanctuary among Strangers, they were equally mov'd
with Shame and Pity, by the dear Remembrance of her Father
Agrippa, of her Grand-father *Augustus,* and of her Father-in-
Law *Drusus;* by the Honour of her Fruitfulness, and her in-
violable Chastity; and more particularly, by their Regret they
had to see her carry away, in a manner so unworthy of her, her
Infant Son who was born within their Camp, nurs'd, as it were,
in the Bosom of the Legions, and call'd *Caligula,* because he
wore the common Boots* of Soldiers, to gain their Affections in

his very Childhood. But nothing was more grievous to them, than the Envy of that Honour, which was done to those of *Treves*. Some of them ran after her, and besought her to stay among them; others went to *Germanicus,* and importun'd him for her Return. But, as he was yet in the first Ferment of his Grief and Choler, he answer'd them in this manner.

XXXVI. [XLII] *Believe not, that my Wife and Son are dearer to me than the Emperour, and the Empire*[†]*. For my Father, his own Fortune will defend him; and the Empire*[†] *wants not other*
10 *Armies, without this, for its Support. As I would freely sacrifice my Wife and Children for your Honour, so I remove them not at present from you, but to hinder you from becoming yet more guilty, by the Murder of* Augustus*'s Grand-daughter, and the Grand-son of* Tiberius; *and to expiate by my Blood alone, the Crime which your Fury is about to perpetrate. For what is it you have not dar'd to Enterprize of late? What is there so Sacred, which you have not presum'd to violate? By what Name can I call you,* Soldiers? *You who have besieg'd the Son of your Emperour, or* Roman Citizens, *who have, with so much Insolence,*
20 *contemn'd the Authority of the Senate? You have profan'd even the sacred Laws of Nations, even the inviolable Persons of Ambassadors*[†]*, even the common Rights observ'd by Enemies. The Divine* Julius *stifled a Sedition by one single Word, when he call'd his Soldiers (who were deserting his Service*)* Rabble[†]*. The Divine* Augustus *made his* Actian-*Legions* tremble only with a Look. And though I am unworthy to be nam'd with them, yet having the Honour to be descended from their Loins*[†]*, I should think it strange, and even unjust, that the Armies of* Spain *and* Syria *should despise me: But what shall I say! they*
30 *are the Fifth and the Twentieth Legion which have revolted!*

---

7   *Believe*] 'Believe O.
7–17   *not* ... [*to*] ... *to*] *italics and romans reversed in* O.
7–264:34   *each printed line preceded by an inverted comma in* O.
17   *violate?*] violate. O.
17–18   *By* ... [*to*] ... *you*] *set in romans in* O.
18–19   *You* ... [*to*] ... *or*] *set in romans in* O.
19   Roman] *Roman* O.
19–25   *who* ... [*to*] ... *his*] *italics and romans reversed in* O (*Rabble*ᴧ.).
25   Actian-*Legions*] Actian-Legions O.
25–264:7   *tremble* ... [*to*] ... *well the*] *italics and romans reversed in* O.

the one of them, *inroll'd by the Hand of* Tiberius *himself; and
the other, the constant Companion of his Victories, and enrich'd
by his Bounties! And, to do you Right, you have both made him
in return, a wonderful Acknowledgment of his Favours. Shall I
be the Bearer of such News to him, who receives none but happy
Tidings from all the other Provinces? Shall I tell him, that his
Soldiers, as well the Veterans, as the new Recruits, are not to be
quieted, either by their Discharge, or by their Pay? That 'tis
here they kill Centurions; drive away Tribunes; imprison Leg-*
10 *ates: That the Camp and Rivers are overflow'd with Blood;
and that his Son is at the Mercy of as many Enemies, as he has
Soldiers?* [XLIII] *Ah, my once dear Fellow-Soldiers! why did
you snatch away that Sword, which I was plunging into my
Body? He, of your Number, was my best Friend, who presented
me his own. I had now been dead; I had not been a Witness of
so many Crimes, with which you have stain'd your Honour since
that Day! You had chosen another General, who would have left
my Death unpunish'd, but in return, would have reveng'd the
Massacre of* Varus, *and his three Legions. For I should be sorry,*
20 *(for your Honour) that the* Belgæ, *who make offer of their Ser-
vice, should have the Glory of reducing the* Germans *to Obedi-
ence, and restoring the Reputation of the* Romans. *Oh! that thy
Soul, Divine* Augustus, *now in Heaven, and thou, Oh my Father*
Drusus! *whose Resemblance I behold in these Ensigns! Oh that
the Remembrance of these Actions may inspire these very Sol-
diers, who now begin to feel the Stings of Shame, and Spurs of
Glory, with a Resolution of blotting out that foul Disgrace, and
of turning their Swords against our Enemies! And you, in whose
alter'd Countenances I read another Heart, in sign, that you*
30 *will pay your Emperour the Obedience which you owe to him;
and to the Senate, to their Ambassadors, to your General, to his
Wife, and to his Son; separate your selves from the Company of
these Mutineers, as a Pledge of your Fidelity, and an authen-
tick Testimony of your sincere Repentance.*

7–12   *as the* ... [*to*] ... *why*] set in romans in O.
12   *did*] did did O.
13–34   *you* ... [*to*] ... *Repentance*] italics and romans reversed in O.

XXXVII. [XLIV] At this, they threw themselves before his Feet; and confessing, that his Reproaches were all deserv'd and just, they besought him to punish the Offenders; to pardon those, who had only err'd through Frailty; and to lead them on to Battle: As also, to recal his Wife, and not to give in Hostage to the *Gauls* the Nursling of the Legions. He excus'd himself as to what regarded *Agrippina,* by her being so near her Time of Childbed, and by the approach of Winter; as for his Son, he consented to recal him; adding, that he left them to finish what 10 remain'd. From that moment they began to seize on the most Seditious, and brought them bound in Fetters to *Caius Cetronius,* who commanded the first Legion*; and he caus'd immediate Justice to be done on them in this manner: The Legions encompass'd his Tribunal with their naked Swords; A Tribune* from above shew'd the Soldier who was accus'd, to those below; if the Assembly pronounc'd him guilty, he was immediately cast down, in order to be executed; and every one took pleasure in killing his Camerade, as if thereby he clear'd his own Innocence*. *Germanicus* was silent while this was passing; so that 20 nothing being done by his Command, the whole Hatred of the Massacre fell upon the Actors. The Veterans follow'd this Example, and soon after were commanded into *Rhetia,* under colour of defending that Province from the Incursions of the *Suevæ,* but in reality, to remove them from a Camp, the very sight of which rais'd Horrour in them, because it set the Image of their late Revolt before their Eyes. Then *Germanicus* made a strict Enquiry into the Conduct of the Centurions: He examin'd them one by one; each of them was oblig'd to tell his Name; his Country; what Company* he commanded; how long 30 he had serv'd; what Actions he had done in War; and they, who had been honour'd with any Military Presents, shew'd them. In short, if any Legion, or any Tribune, gave a good Account of their Probity and Diligence, they were continued in their Stations; and, on the contrary, he degraded those who were accus'd by common Fame, either of Covetousness, or of Cruelty: [XLV] And in this manner the Sedition was appeas'd.

XXXVIII. But what was yet remaining on his Hands, in refer-

---

21 Veterans] *Veterans* O. 29 Company*] cCompany O.

ence to the Fifth and Twenty-first Legion, was not of less Importance. Those Legions had their Winter Quarters Sixty Miles from thence, in a Place call'd *Vetera**. The Sedition was begun by them; there was no Crime so heinous, which they had not committed; and, to compleat their Villany, they were still for pushing on their Fury to the utmost; nothing frighted with the Punishment of some; nothing mov'd with Remorse, or with the Penitence of others. *Germanicus* therefore gave his Orders to prepare Vessels on the *Rhine;* resolving to terrifie them into
10   Duty, in case they persisted in their Disobedience.

XXXIX. [XLVI] The News of this Revolt amongst the Legions being come to *Rome,* before the Event of the other in *Pannonia* was known, the City, struck with Fear, began to murmur against *Tiberius;* accusing him, that while he by his artificial Delays and Dissimulations was still imposing on the People and the Senate, which were both of them unarm'd, and without Power, in the mean time the Soldiers were raising a Rebellion: They said, that the two young Princes, for want of Knowledge and Authority, could not hold the Armies in Obedience; it was
20   his Duty to go in Person thither, and oppose the Majesty of the Empire to the Mutineers, who would never dare to make Head against a Prince, of consummate Wisdom and Experience, and who alone had their Life and Death at his Dispose; that *Augustus,* in his declining Age, and languishing with Sickness, had taken many Journeys into *Germany;* and that *Tiberius,* now in the Vigour of his Years, led a sedentary Life at *Rome,* and employ'd his Time in cavilling at the Expressions of the Senators; that he very sufficiently provided for domestick Slavery; that it was now incumbent on him, to restrain the License of the Sol-
30   diers, and teach them how to behave themselves in Peace[†].

XL. [XLVII] *Tiberius* was unmov'd at these *Discourses[†]; having fix'd his Resolutions, not to leave the Seat of Empire[†], or put to hazard his own Life, or the Safety of the Commonwealth. His Mind was perplex'd with many Cares, and contrary Thoughts. The *German* Army was the stronger, and the *Pannonian* nearer *Rome;* one was supported by the *Gauls,* and the

---

19–22   Obedience; it ... Mutineers, ... Experience,] ~: It ... ~; ... ~; O.

other had an easie Passage into *Italy**. To which of these should he go first? For the Legions, which were last visited, would take Offence, and think themselves neglected. On the other side, by sending his two Sons, both Armies might be at once contented, and the Majesty of the Supream Power preserved, which is always most respected at a distance. Besides that, *Germanicus* and *Drusus* might be held excus'd, if they sent extravagant Demands from the Legions to their Father, who would still be in condition either to appease, or punish the Rebellious, when ever they
10 should transgress the Limits of Respect to the young Princes; but if they should once despise the Person of the Emperour, what other Remedy remain'd? In the mean time, he neglected not to prepare a Fleet to provide his Equipage, and set on foot an Army of choice Soldiers, as if they were to follow him to the Wars, and he just upon the March. But sometimes he excus'd his Journey by the approach of Winter, and at other Times by the multiplicity of Business† which interven'd: By which Pretences he at first impos'd on the most Intelligent, then on the Vulgar, and for a long time kept the Provinces in suspence*.

20 XLI. [XLVIII] But *Germanicus,* though he had assembled his Forces, and was in a condition to punish the Offenders, yet thought it more expedient to give them leisure to Repent, and make Trial, if, by the Example of the two other Legions, they would prevent his Vengeance. In order to this, he wrote first to *Cecina,* and gave him notice, that he was already on his march with a powerful Army, fully determin'd to put all the Rebels to the Sword, without sparing the Life of any one, if they themselves did not Justice on the Criminals before his arrival. *Cecina* read these Letters privately to the Chief Commanders*, and to
30 some others, who had no Hand in the Sedition, at the same time adjuring them to preserve themselves from Death, and save their Companions from the Infamy of that Punishment which attended them: Representing also to them, that Reason might be heard in Times of Peace, but in War the Innocent perish'd with the Guilty. Upon this, the Officers sound the Intentions of those Soldiers whom they thought most proper for the Execution of their Design, and finding that the greater Number still con-

---

6   Besides that,] ∼, ∼ₐ O.   33   them:] ∼. O.

tinu'd Loyal, they agree with *Cecina,* on a Time appointed, to put to Death the most Seditious. The Signal being given, they fall at once upon the Factious, and execute them in their Tents, none but the Contrivers, and Assistants in the Action, knowing from whence began the Slaughter, nor when it would conclude.

XLII. [XLIX] Of all the Civil Wars which ever were, none resembled this. It was not in Battle, nor by the Hands of Enemies, that this Massacre was made; but by Men, who the same Day convers'd familiarly, and eat in Company, and at Night
10 were lodg'd together in one Bed*. On the sudden they are divided into Parties opposite; nothing but Outcries and Bloodshed, the rest was govern'd by blind Chance, and the cause of Enmity unknown by those who perish'd. Many fell who deserv'd not Death; for the Guilty had taken Arms in their own Defence, when once they found on whom the Slaughter was design'd. Neither *Cecina,* nor the Tribunes, gave themselves the Trouble to stop their Fury; the common Soldiers had all manner of Freedom to exercise their Vengeance, till they were tir'd with killing. *Germanicus* soon after enter'd the Camp, and beholding so
20 many Corps extended on the Ground, said with many Tears, That this was not a Remedy, nor the breathing of a Vein, but a Butchery; and commanded the Bodies to be burn'd. While their Minds were in this Ferment, the Soldiers cried out to be led against the Enemy, as if the *Manes* of those, whom they had slain, were to be appeas'd no other way, than by exposing their impious Breasts to honest Wounds. *Germanicus* gratifies their Desire, and having laid a Bridge across the *Rhine,* passes over Twelve thousand Legionary Soldiers, Twenty six Cohorts of the Allies, and Eight Regiments of Horse, all of try'd Valour, and of
30 Proof against Sedition.

XLIII. [L] The *Germans,* who were not far distant, pass'd their Time secure in Pleasure, while the War seem'd to sleep about them; and a Cessation of Arms ensu'd of course, from the Death of *Augustus,* and a Civil Discord amongst our selves. The *Romans,* by speedy Marches, cross'd the Forest of *Cesia*,* and posted their Forces on a Rampart, which *Tiberius* had begun to raise in the time of *Augustus;* there they fortifi'd themselves, both before and behind, with a strong Palisade: Both their

Wings were cover'd by huge Trunks of Trees which they had fell'd, and which serv'd them for a Barricade. From thence, traversing thick Forests, they held a Council, which way they should bend their March: The shortest, and most frequented; or that which was farthest about, and more difficult to pass, but where they thought the Enemy would not attend them. The Reasons for the longer Way prevail'd, but all the rest was perform'd with haste; for their Scouts brought back Intelligence, that the *Germans* solemniz'd a Feast that Night with publick
10 Rejoycing. *Cecina* was commanded to advance with the Cohorts without their Baggage, and to free a Passage through the Forest, by cutting down and removing all Incumbrances. The Legions follow'd at some distance; the Night was clear and calm, and favourable to the March. They enter'd the Village of the *Marsi,* which they encompass'd with Corps de Guard. They found the *Germans,* either asleep in Bed, or laid along by their Tables sides, without Sentinels, or the least suspicion of an Enemy; so great was their Confidence, or their Neglect. They thought themselves secure of War, yet it was not properly a state of Peace,
20 but rather a stupid Debauch, and a Lethargick Rest.

XLIV. [LI] To make the Waste yet greater, *Germanicus* divided his Forces into four Battalions, who breath'd nothing but Revenge*, setting the Country on Fire for fifty Miles about, and putting all the Inhabitants to the Sword, neither sparing Age or Sex, or Sacred Places or Profane. The famous Temple call'd *Tanfane*, was raz'd to the Foundations; and all this perform'd by ours, without receiving any Wound, having met no opposition; no Enemies, but Men half asleep, disarm'd, or wandring about the Fields. This Massacre awaken'd the *Bructeri*, the
30 *Tubantes*, and the *Usipetes*, who incamp'd themselves in certain Forests, through which the Army, in their return, was of necessity to pass. The Auxiliary Cohorts, and one half of the Horse, compos'd the Van: The First Legion march'd after them, inclosing the Baggage in the midst; the Twenty first Legion march'd on the Left Wing; the Fifth on the Right; and the Twentieth in the Rear, with the rest of the Allies. The Enemy

---

5 pass,] ~; O.
15 Corps de Guard] Corps-de-Guard O.

mov'd not, till they saw the main Body enter'd into the Wood; then they began a light Skirmish on the Front and Wings, pouring with their Gross upon the Rear. The Cohorts, who were all Light-Horsemen, already bent before the closs Body of the *Germans,* not being able to sustain the Charge, when *Germanicus* spurring his Horse at speed, came up with the Twentieth Legion, and cry'd aloud, That now was the Time for them to wash away the Stain of their late Sedition; bid them haste to redeem their Honour, and turn their Offence into Merit, their Infamy to
10 Glory. At these Words, their Courage was kindl'd to that height, that at the first Charge they broke the Enemy, drove them headlong back into the Plain, and there made a terrible Execution. At the same time, the Van-Guard got clear of the Forest, and hasted to Retrench. After this, the Way was free, and the Soldiers went into their Winter Quarters, highly pleas'd with their Expedition, and putting all that was past into Oblivion.

XLV. [LII] When *Tiberius* had Intelligence of this, it fill'd him with excess of Joy; but the Pleasure was not so sincere, as not to be mix'd with great Disturbance. He rejoyc'd that the
20 Sedition was wholly quench'd, but it stung him that *Germanicus* had the Glory of it†; and more, that he had entirely gain'd the Affections of the Soldiers by his Bounty†; and above all, by giving them their Discharge so soon. Yet he was not wanting to relate to the Senate his Exploits, and to give large Commendations to his Valour; but in Terms too much affected and labour'd, to be thought sincere*. He spoke more sparingly of *Drusus,* and of the Success of his Voyage into *Illyria;* but it was with more Frankness, and more Love; and besides, he order'd the same Conditions to be made for the Legions in *Pannonia,*
30 which *Germanicus* had granted to his own.

XLVI. [LIII] In the same Year died *Julia,* the Daughter of *Augustus*,* whom, for her Incontinence, he had formerly confin'd to the Isle of *Pandataria*,* and afterwards to *Rhegium,* near the Coast of *Sicily.* During the Life of *Caius,* and *Lucius Agrippa,* her Sons, she had been given in second Marriage to *Tiberius,* whom she despis'd, as a Man below her Quality†; and this was the principal Occasion of the Retirement of *Tiberius* to *Rhodes.* But when he succeeded to the Empire, not content to behold

her banish'd, dishonour'd, and, by the Death of *Agrippa Post-humus,* depriv'd not only of all Hopes, but of all Support, he caus'd her to die in Want and Misery; imagining, that the distance of the Place to which she was banish'd would hide the manner of her Death. *Sempronius Gracchus* was likewise slain on her Account. *Gracchus,* who was of a ready Wit and Eloquent, with Cunning and Insinuation had debauch'd *Julia,* during her Marriage with *Agrippa;* and his Gallantry with that Lady ended not with her first Husband's Death, for he con-
10 tinu'd her perpetual Adulterer even after her Marriage with *Tiberius.* He was continually provoking her against her Husband, and encourag'd her to Disobedience. It was also thought, that he was the Author of those Letters, which she writ to her Father against *Tiberius,* and which occasion'd his Disgrace. For these Reasons, he was confin'd to an *African* Island, call'd *Cercina,* where he remain'd in Exile 14 Years. He was found by the Soldiers, who were sent to kill him, on a Prominence at a little distance from the Shore; and presaging no Good from their Arrival. He desir'd some little Time to write his Last Will to his
20 Wife *Alliaria,* after which, he freely offer'd them his Head: A Constancy, not unworthy of the *Sempronian* Name, though he had degenerated from it by the Voluptuousness of his Life[t]. Some have written, that those Soldiers were not sent from *Rome,* but from *Lucius Asprenas,* Proconsul of *Africa,* on whom *Tiberius* thought, in vain, to have cast the Odium of that Murder[t].

XLVII. [LIV] This Year was also made Remarkable by the Institution of new Ceremonies; for there was establish'd at this time a College of Priests in Honour of *Augustus,* in imitation of the *Titian* Priests, formerly instituted by *Titus Tatius**, to
30 preserve the Religion of the *Sabines.* Twenty one of the Principal Men among the *Romans* were drawn by Lot, of which Number were *Tiberius, Drusus, Claudius,* and *Germanicus*[t]. Then it was that the *Augustinian* Games began to be disturb'd by the Contention of the Stage-Players, and different Factions arose concerning the Preference of this or that Actor*. *Augustus* himself had been much addicted to these Divertisements, out of his Complaisance to *Mæcenas,* who was desperately in love with the

---

20 Head:] ~. O.

Pantomime *Bathyllus:* Besides, that he was himself no Enemy
to those Entertainments, and knew it was becoming of a Gracious
Prince, to enter into the Pleasures[†] of his People*. *Tiberius* was
of a Temper wholly different, but he durst not yet subject a
Multitude[†] to more rigid Customs, which had so long been ac-
custom'd to a soft, voluptuous way of Living.

The Year of *Rome,* 768.

XLVIII. [LV] Under the Consulship of *Drusus* and *Norbanus,*
a Triumph for *Germanicus* was decreed, though the War was
10 yet in being. And though he had made great Preparations for
the Summer following, yet he anticipated the Time, by a sudden
Irruption in the beginning of the Spring into the Country of the
Catti: For there were Grounds of Hope, that Factions would
arise among them, some taking part with *Arminius,* others with
Segestes; both of them very considerable to the *Romans,* one by
his breach of Faith, the other by his Constancy. *Arminius* had
disturb'd the Peace of *Germanicus,* and kindl'd the War against
the *Romans: Segestes* had openly declar'd in the last solemn
Festivals, and many times before they rose in Arms, that a Con-
20 spiracy was hatching to Revolt; at the same time advising *Varus*[†]
to secure *Arminius* and himself, and all the Leading Men of the
Germans; the People not being in any capacity of Rebelling,
when they were unfurnish'd of Commanders. And this once
done, *Varus* would have sufficient Leisure, to distinguish after-
wards betwixt the Guilty and the Innocent[†]. But *Varus* perish'd
by his Destiny[†], and by the Valour of [†]*Arminius*. For *Segestes,*
though he was drawn into the War by the general Consent of his
Country-men, yet he liv'd in perpetual Discord with *Arminius;*
and the bad Understanding betwixt them was increas'd by a
30 particular Offence; for *Arminius* had taken away by force his
Daughter *Thusnelda,* betroth'd already to another. Thus the
Father-in-Law, and Son, were equally hateful to each other; and
those mutual Ties, which commonly beget Friendship, were now
the Provocations to the most bitter Enmity[†].

XLIX. [LVI] *Germanicus,* on this Account, commanded out

1 Pantomime] *Pantomine* O.   3 Pleasures[†] 2Pleasures O.
7 The Year of *Rome,*] *The Year of* Rome∧ O.   15 *Romans,*] ∼. O.

Cecina with Four Legions, Five thousand Auxiliary Soldiers, and some Companies of *Germans* rais'd in haste from some Places on this side the *Rhine.* He himself conducted a like Number of Legions, but double the Number of Allies; and having built a Fortress on the old Foundations, which his Father had laid, and which were yet standing, he march'd with great speed against the *Catti,* leaving behind him *Lucius Apronius,* with Order to take care, that if the Rivers should overflow by any sudden fall of Rains, yet the Ways might be kept in repair, and
10 continue passable: For in setting forward, he found the Waters so very low, and the Ways so dry, (a Thing uncommon in that Climate,) that he found no difficulty in his March; but he feared in his return it might be otherwise. He came so suddenly upon the *Catti,* that the old Men, the Women, and the Children, were either kill'd at first, or taken Prisoners, and the young Men forc'd to swim the River of *Adrana*;* who attempting afterwards to obstruct the *Romans* in the building of a Bridge over it, were repuls'd by their Arrows, and their Engines. These Hopes failing, and their Propositions for Peace being also rejected, some
20 of them came over, and submitted to *Germanicus;* the rest forsaking their Cantons, retir'd into the Fastnesses of their Woods. *Germanicus* having burn'd *Martium*,* their Capital Town, ravag'd all the Low-lands, and took his March backwards to the *Rhine;* the Enemy not daring to attack his Rear, as their Custom is when they feign to fly, rather through Stratagem, than Fear. The *Cherusci** were desirous to have succour'd their Friends the *Catti,* but they were apprehensive of *Cecina,* who carry'd far and near the Terrour of his Arms. On the contrary, the *Marsi,* having presum'd to charge him, were vigorously repuls'd, and entirely
30 routed.

    L. [LVII] Some time afterwards, there came Deputies from *Segestes,* to desire his Assistance against his Country-men who had besieg'd him, for *Arminius* had there the stronger Party, because he had advis'd the War[†]; it being the common Practice of Barbarians, only to love and esteem those Persons who are Fierce and Daring, and more especially in unquiet Times. *Se-*

gestes had added to the Deputies his Son *Segimond*, though the
Mind of the young Man was wholly averse to that Employment[†];
for the Year, in which all *Germany* revolted, being created Priest
of the Altar of the *Ubian*, he tore in pieces his Sacred Fillets*,
and went over to the Party of the Rebels. Nevertheless, confiding
in the Clemency of the *Romans*, he undertook the Commission
enjoyn'd him by his Father, and was well received[†]; and sent
afterward under Guard to the Confines of the *Gauls*. Germanicus
lost not his Labour by this Return, for after some Encounters,
10 he disingag'd *Segestes* from the Hands of his Enemies, with many
of his Relations and his Vassals. There were also some Ladies of
Quality, and, among the rest, the Daughter of *Segestes*, who
shew'd by her Countenance, that she had more of her Husband's
Courage, than of her Father's Temper[†]. She walk'd with her
Hands folded on her Bosom, and seem'd to look downward on
the Fruit of her Body, with which she was now big, without
shedding one Tear, or saying one single Word, or doing one
Action which had any thing of a Suppliant. There were also
carried, the Spoils which the Enemies had taken at the Defeat of
20 *Varus*, and which had been shar'd by many of those who were
now Prisoners. At last appear'd *Segestes*, of a Stature higher
than any of the rest, with an assur'd Countenance, as having been
always in the *Roman* Interest: [XLVIII] And accordingly he
bespoke them in these Terms.

LI. *This Day, O* Romans, *is not the first, wherein I have begun
to give you the Proofs of an inviolable Faith. Since the time that
the Divine* Augustus *made me Citizen of* Rome, *I have had
neither Friends nor Enemies, but yours*[†]; *neither have I steer'd
this Course out of any Hatred to my Country, (for Traitors are*
30 *odious, even to them whose Cause they have espous'd*,) but only
because I preferr'd Peace to War*[†], *and was convinc'd, that Peace
was the common Interest of both Nations. On this Account it
was, that I accus'd* Arminius *to* Varus, *who then commanded the*
Roman *Army;* Arminius, *I say, the Ravisher of my Daughter,
and Infringer of the Alliance made with you*[†]. *Tir'd with the
Delays and Irresolutions of your General*[†], *and beside, despair-*

_____

3–4 Priest of the Altar of the] *Priest of the Altar of the* O.
13 she had] he shad O.

ing of Protection from the Laws, I desir'd of Varus *to make me
Prisoner, together with* Arminius *and his Accomplices. I call that
Night to witness of this Truth, which I wish to Heaven had been
my last. What since has happen'd, may be Deplor'd better than
Excus'd. For what remains, I have formerly detain'd* Arminius
*in Fetters, and he and his Faction in their Turn have given me
the same Treatment. Ever since, I have had the Opportunity of
making my Addresses to you, O* Cæsar, *I have constantly retain'd
my old Inclinations, and I preferr'd Repose to Trouble: And*
10 *this not in prospect of any Recompence which I pretend, but to
clear my Innocence from Suspicion of Perjury; and to put my
self the better in condition to make Terms with* Rome *for my
Compatriots, when ever they consult their Safety by Repentance.
I implore your Clemency in my Son's behalf, desiring that his
Youth may excuse his Error. I confess, my Daughter is brought
hither against her Consent; I leave it to your Judgment, whether
you will consider her as the Wife of* Arminius, *or as the Daugh-
ter of* Segestes.

LII. To this, *Germanicus* graciously answer'd, *That his Chil-*
20 *dren and Relations had no cause of Fear; that for himself, he
had provided an honourable Retreat in an ancient* Roman *Prov-
ince, where he might live secure from Danger.* This Affair being
thus ended, he brought back his Army, and receiv'd the Title of
Imperator by the Command of *Tiberius.* The Wife of *Arminius*
was deliver'd of a Son, who had his Breeding at *Ravenna.* What
contumelious Usage he receiv'd when he was grown to Age[†],
shall be related in due place.

LIII. [LIX] The News of the good Entertainment given to
Segestes, was diversly received; by some with Pleasure, by others
30 with Regret; as they either fear'd, or wish'd the War. *Arminius,*
besides the Violence of his Nature, being inflam'd with the Out-
rage done to him in the Person of his Wife, whom his Enemies
had seiz'd, and of his Child unborn, yet already destin'd for a
Slave, took a rapid Course through the Country of the *Cherusci,*
solliciting that People to rise in Arms against *Germanicus,* and
sparing no opprobrious Language against *Segestes. Behold,* said

36   *Behold*] 'Behold O.
36–276:10   said ... [*to*] ... *Country;*] *italics and romans reversed in O.*

he, *a pious Father in* Segestes! *Behold a doughty Warriour in*
Germanicus! *A wonderful Exploit, for a whole Army to take a*
Woman Prisoner! I, on the other side, have destroy'd three Le-
gions of theirs, and three Lieutenant-Generals. The Wars I
make are without Surprize, or Treachery; I fight fairly, and in
the open Field; not with Women big with Child, but with Arm'd
Soldiers. There are yet to be seen, in our Sacred Woods, the
Roman *Eagles, and their Ensigns, which I have hung in Tri-*
umph on the Altars of our Gods. Let Segestes *please himself*
10 *with his secure Abode in a conquer'd Country; let him restore*
to his Son the Priesthood of the Ubians; *the* Germans *never can*
forgive him, for having brought betwixt the Elb *and the* Rhine
the Consulary Fasces, and Axes of the Romans, *with all other*
the Marks of their Dominion. The rest of the Nations, who are
free from their Subjection, know not yet the Names of Punish-
ment *and* Taxes. *After having shaken off the Yoke, and made*
vain the Attempts of that Augustus, *to whom they have given the*
Title of a God; *and of that* Tiberius, *whom they have chosen in*
his stead, to inslave our Country; shall we fear a Boy, a Novice
20 *in the War, and an Army made up of Mutineers? If then you have*
more Affection for your Native Country, your Families, and your
ancient Laws, than for Tyrants and new Colonies, rather follow
Arminius, *the Defender of your Freedom and your Honour,*
than the infamous Segestes, *who would betray you into Slavery.*

LIV. [LX] Not only the *Cherusci,* but all the Neighbouring
Nations, were set on fire by this Oration. He also drew *Inguiomer*
into his Party, who was his Uncle by the Father's side, and of
great Reputation among the *Romans;* which increas'd the Trou-
ble of *Germanicus,* who apprehended, lest with their United
30 Forces they should come pouring upon him. To make some
Diversion*, he sent *Cecina* with Forty *Roman* Cohorts through
the Country of the *Bructerians; Pedo* led the Cavalry by the Con-
fines of *Frisia,* and he himself embarking with Four Legions,

---

pass'd the Lakes; the Foot, the Horse, and his Navy, arriving at
the same time on the Banks of *Amisia**, which was the Place
appointed for the Rendevous. The *Cauci,* who had offer'd their
Assistance, were receiv'd as Companions of the War. The *Bruc-
terians,* who had set fire on all their open Towns, were defeated
by *Lucius Stertinius,* whom *Germanicus* had sent forth with some
Troops of Light-Horsemen to encounter them. Amidst the Dead,
and amongst the Spoils, he found the Eagle of the Nineteenth
Legion, which was lost at the Overthrow of *Varus**. Our Army
10 thereupon advanc'd to the farmost Limits of the *Bructerian*
Country, wasting all Things in their way, betwixt the Rivers
of *Amisia* and *Lippa**.

LV. The Army being now within a small march of the Forest
of *Teutburg,* where it was told *Germanicus,* that the Bones of
the Legions, which were slain with *Varus,* lay yet unbury'd*,
[LXI] he was seiz'd with a violent Desire of rendring their last
Dues to those sad Relicks. The whole Army approv'd their Gen-
eral's Design, whether mov'd with Pity for their Friends and
Relations, or by a Natural Reflection on the Chance of War,
20 and the wretched Condition of Mankind. *Cecina* was sent before
to discover the Fastnesses of the Woods, prepare Bridges, and
lay Causeways, where the Footing was unsure, and the Ground
treacherous, by reason of the Bogs*. Entring into these mourn-
ful Places, which were dreadful to their Sight, and irksom to
their Remembrance, the first Object presented to their view,
was the Camp of *Varus,* remarkable by its large Compass, and
by the three Voids*, which separated the three Legions. A little
farther might be seen, the Retrenchments half in Ruine, inclos'd
with a Ditch, now choak'd up, and almost fill'd; in which it was
30 believ'd, that the shatter'd Remnants of the Army had been
rally'd for their last Refuge. The middle of the Field was strew'd
with Carcasses, and white dry Bones, some scatter'd here and
there, and others pil'd on heaps; by which might be observ'd,
whether they receiv'd their Death in flight, or fell together in
manly Resistance to the last. Every where were found their
broken Pikes, and Javelins; the Limbs of Horses, and their Jaw-
bones; and the Heads of Men, which were fix'd to the Trunks,
or hung on the Branches of the Trees. In the Woods about the

Field were seen the Altars, where those Barbarians had executed
the Tribunes and Captains of the first Orders*. They who had
escap'd from this Battel, or afterwards from their Captivity,
related many Particulars of that dreadful Day. On this Place,
said they, were slain the Commanders of the Legions; and there
it was we lost our Eagles. Here *Varus* receiv'd his first Wound,
and a little farther he fell upon his Sword, and perish'd by his
own unhappy Hand. Behold the Eminence from whence *Ar-
minius* harangu'd his Soldiers; and yonder he rais'd Gibbets for
the Prisoners, or sunk Ditches*, to behead and bury them ac-
cording to the *Roman* Fashion: While the Proud Conquerour
forgot not to drag along the Ground, with Scorn, our Ensigns
and our Eagles.

LVI. [LXII] In this manner, the *Roman* Army, six Years after
the Defeat, interr'd the Bones of the three Legions, it being
impossible for any Man to distinguish those of his Relations
from the rest: Every one performing his Duty to all in general,
as to so many Friends and Brothers, with Hearts equally divided
betwixt Sorrow, and desire of Vengeance. *Germanicus* partaking
in their Grief, laid the first Turf on the common Sepulchre*:
But this pious Office to the Slain was nothing pleasing to *Ti-
berius;* whether he took in the worst sense all the Actions of
Germanicus†, or that he thought, so sad a Spectacle as that was,
of unbury'd Bodies, would slacken the Courage of his Soldiers†,
and make their Enemies appear more formidable; besides, that
the General of any Army vested with the Augural Priesthood,
and design'd for the Ministry of Religious Rites, ought not to
have put his Hand to Ceremonies belonging to the Dead.

LVII. [LXIII] In the mean time, *Germanicus* pursu'd *Ar-
minius,* who retir'd into Places unfrequented, and inaccessible;
when at length he had join'd the Enemy, he commanded his
Cavalry to advance, and dislodge him from the Post he had pos-
sess'd. *Arminius*, with his Forces drawn up in close Order,
march'd along the Forest, and suddenly wheeling, fac'd the *Ro-
mans,* giving the Signal to those Soldiers, whom he had laid in

Ambush in the Wood. The *Roman* Horse, amaz'd at the sight of
these new Enemies, was put into disorder; and the Cohorts com-
ing up to their Assistance, being incumber'd with a Croud of
those who fled from the *Germans,* and press'd upon their Ranks,
were forc'd to open as they could, and make a Passage for them:
In this Confusion, and general Affright, the Enemy, who knew
the Country, were driving our Men headlong on the Morass,
from whence it was impossible to disingage themselves, if *Ger-
manicus* had not with timely foresight drawn up the Legions in
10 Battalia: This gave Terrour to the *Germans,* and restor'd the
Courage of our Soldiers, so that both Sides retir'd without Ad-
vantage. Soon after this, *Germanicus* march'd back his Army to
the *Amisia,* where he embark'd the Legions, to return in the
same manner as they came. One part of the Cavalry were order'd
to draw towards the *Rhine,* still coasting the Ocean in their
March. *Cecina,* who led back his Cohorts, was advis'd, That
though he was well acquainted with the Way which he had
taken, yet he should make all imaginable Haste to get over the
long Bridges*. That way is narrow, inclos'd on either hand with
20 Marshes, over which these Bridges, or rather Causeways, were
formerly laid by *Lucius Domitius.* The rest is all either miry
Ground, or glewy Clay, cumbersom to the Feet, or uncertain,
with scattering Rivulets; round about are rising Woods, which,
with a gentle Descent, reach even to the Plain. In this place,
Arminius had lodg'd a great Number of his Soldiers, having by
long Marches, and by shorter Ways, got before our Men, who
were loaden with their Arms and Baggage. *Cecina,* not knowing
how to repair the Causway, now decay'd, and at the same time
to repulse the Enemy, took a Resolution to incamp in the same
30 place; that while one part of his Army was employ'd in repairing
the ruin'd Passage, the other might be in a readiness to fight.
　　LVIII. [LXIV] The Barbarians made a strong Effort to push
our Corps de Garde, and afterwards to have pour'd upon the
Workmen; they charg'd our Men, sometimes on one side, and
sometimes on the other, harassing them with continual Attempts,
and endeavouring to break in upon them. The Cries of those

10　Battalia] *Battalia* O.　　　　　12–13　to the] to O.
32　Barbarians] *Barbarians* O.　　　33　Corps de Garde] Corps-de-Garde O.

who were employ'd in working, were confusedly mix'd with
theirs who fought: All Things conspir'd against the *Romans,*
the depth of the Morass, the slipperiness of the Ground, on
which they could neither march, nor scarcely set a Foot, without
danger of falling; the weight of their Armour; and the height
of the Waters, which diminish'd their force in lanching their
Javelins. On the other side, the *Cherusci* were accustom'd to
engage in marshy Ground, where the height of their Stature
gave them a manifest Advantage, as also their long Pikes, with
10　which they push'd to a great distance. The Night alone was the
apparent Safety of our Legions, which began already to give
Ground before the Enemy. But the *Germans,* by their good For-
tune made indefatigable*, without allowing themselves the least
Repose, cut a Passage through the Mountains, round about, for
the Waters to descend on the *Roman* Camp, thereby to float the
Works they had already made, and increase the Difficulties of
their new Labours. *Cecina,* who for the space of Forty Years had
exercis'd the Trade of War, either as a private Soldier, or a
Leader, had made Trial both of prosperous and adverse For-
20　tune†, and by Experience was become intrepid, considering all
which might possibly arrive, could find no other Expedient, than
to shut up the Enemy in their Woods, till he had pass'd over,
his Baggage, and his wounded Men. For betwixt the Hilly
Ground, and the Morass, there was a narrow Plain, only capable
of receiving a small Army. He therefore gave the Right Wing
to the Fifth Legion; the Left to the Twenty first; the Van to the
First Legion; and the Rear to the Twentieth.

　　LIX. [LXV] The Night pass'd without Repose on either side;
for the Barbarians, who were in debauch, made the Valleys and
30　the Woods resound, sometimes with the Noise of their Drunken
Songs, and otherwhile with Shouts and Outcries, rais'd on pur-
pose to terrifie the *Romans.* On the contrary, there was a deep
sad Silence among our Troops, unless sometimes interrupted
by casual Words; our Fires were languishing; some of our Sol-
diers leaning on the Palisade; others walking round the Tents,
rather like People wanting Sleep, than quite awake. The Gen-
eral himself had a dreadful dream: It seem'd to him that he be-

29　Barbarians] *Barbarians* O.

held *Quintilius Varus* arising from the bottom of those Marshes, and cover'd over with his Blood; who holding forth his Hand to him[†], implor'd his Assistance[*]; but that he, far from answering his Request, had push'd him backward. At break of Day, the Legions plac'd on the Wings, forsook their Post, whether through Fear, or Disobedience, is uncertain, and precipitately rang'd themselves in Battel beyond the Morass. *Arminius* did not immediately charge them, though nothing hinder'd; but when he saw their Baggage fasten'd in the Mire, and sticking in the Ditches, the Soldiers out of their Ranks, and only sollicitous how to save themselves, (as commonly it happens on such Occasions, when the Commanders are ill obey'd;) he encourag'd the *Germans* to the Charge, calling to them with repeated Cries: *Behold* Varus *and his Legions, who are offering themselves to be once more vanquish'd.* Having said this, he forc'd through our Battalions with the flower of his Troops, and charg'd impetuously on our Horse; who sliding on their own Blood, and floundring in the Mud of the Morass; cast their Riders to the Ground; and then running furiously through the Ranks, crush'd those to Death who were already fallen, and threw down others whom they met. That which gave us the greatest Trouble, was the defence of our Eagles, which could not be carried into the Combat, because of the multitude of Darts, which were continually lanc'd against the Bearers; nor yet fasten'd in the Ground, by reason of the Marshes. While *Cecina* with great Courage sustain'd this unequal Fight, his Horse was kill'd under him, and himself upon the point of being taken, if the First Legion had not hasten'd to his Succour. On the other side, the Enemy was so greedy of the Spoil, that they intermitted the Slaughter, to seize the Prey. This Covetousness of theirs, was the safety of the Legions; for it gave them the opportunity of making their Retreat[†], at the close of Day, into a Plain, where the Footing was firm, and the Ground solid. But the end of their Miseries was not yet come. They were of necessity to make new Palisades,

7 Morass] *Morats* O.   14 *Behold*] "Behold O.
14–15 Varus ... [to] ... *vanquish'd*] *italics and romans reversed in* O.
14–15 *each printed line preceded by inverted double commas in* O.
18 Morass] *Morats* O.

and new Retrenchments, though they had lost the greatest part
of their Instruments, which were to be employ'd in casting up
the Earth, and cutting of the Turfs. They wanted Tents to re-
ceive the weary Soldiers, and Salves to dress the Wounded. Their
Food, which they divided into Portions, was soak'd in Mire and
Blood; and they deplor'd that fatal Night, which only hid them
till the approach of Day, which was to be the last to so many
Thousands of valiant Men[†].

LX. [LXVI] By chance a Horse, who was broken loose from
10 his Standing, and terrifi'd with the Cries of his Pursuers, bore
down those whom he encounter'd in his way. The whole Camp
possess'd with a panick Fear, took the Alarm; every one believ-
ing, that the *Germans*[†] were breaking in upon them, they rush
together to the Gates, and chiefly to the Decumane* which was
the farthest from the Enemy, and consequently the most secure.
Cecina found it was a false Alarm; but not being able to retain
the Soldiers, either by Authority, or Prayer[†], though he took hold
upon their Arms to stop them, he laid himself across the Gate,
and block'd up the Issue[†], through the Horrour which they had
20 to pass over the Body of their General*: And at the same time,
the Tribunes made it evident to them, that their Fear was
groundless.

LXI. [LXVII] After this, being assembled in the Place of
Arms*, *Cecina* desir'd them to hear him with Silence and Atten-
tion, and to consider well the present Juncture of Affairs. He
told them, there was no other Hope of Safety remaining, but in
their Courage, which also they were oblig'd to manage with
Prudence; that their Safety was to continue in their Camp, till
the *Germans* should approach near it, being allur'd with the
30 hope of Victory; then all at once to sally out upon them from
every Side: This Onset, said he, will open you a Passage to the
Rhine; whereas if you should fly, you have to cross many other
Forests, and to pass over many Morasses, more deep than these;
and, after all, remain expos'd to the Fury of your Enemies:
When on the other side, if you are Victorious in the Battle, you

---

14   Decumane*] *Decumaneu,* O.
23–24   Place of Arms] *set in italics in O.*
25   Affairs.] ∼ᴧ O(?).

shall not only assure your Safety, but obtain Immortal Honour. In fine, he set before their Eyes whatsoever they held dearest in the World, their present Friends, their absent Relations, and the Reputation they had gain'd in Arms; but pass'd over in silence the Miseries they had already suffer'd, and those which they were yet to suffer. After this, he distributed amongst the bravest Soldiers, without Partiality, the Horses of the Tribunes and Lieutenants, and amongst the rest, his own; with Order to those Horsemen to begin the Charge, and for the Infantry to sus-
10 tain them.

LXII. [LXVIII] Neither were the *Germans* less unquiet, betwixt their Hopes of Victory, and their Desire of Booty; they were also divided in their Councils[†]: For *Arminius* was of Opinion, to leave the Passage open to the *Romans,* that marching thence, they might oppress them afterwards in other Marshes which lay before them, and involve them yet in greater Difficulties. *Inguiomer,* on the other side, advis'd to besiege them in their present Camp, which they should be able to force suddenly, and with ease; that they should take more Prisoners, and
20 lose nothing of the Plunder: And this Advice, as the more daring, was most to the humour of the Barbarians[†]. At break of Day they issued out of their Forests, and being arriv'd at the *Roman* Camp, they cast Faggots into the Ditch, and throw in Earth upon them to facilitate their Passage to the Rampart; then attack the Palisade[*], where there appear'd but few Defendants, as if our Soldiers had been seiz'd with Fear. But when the *Germans* were just upon the Rampart, *Cecina* gave the Signal, and sounded to the Charge: The *Romans* sally'd out with a dreadful Clamour, and attack'd the *Germans;* crying out, They had them
30 now without their Woods, and on stable Ground, unprotected by their Marshes; that the Gods would do Justice to their Valour, by giving them an equal Field of Combat, for the decision of their Quarrel. The Enemies, who expected an easie Conquest over a handful of Men, and those too half disarm'd, and quite dishearten'd, were terrifi'd with the sound of Trumpets, and the clattering of Arms, and slain almost without Resistance[†], wanting Moderation in their good Fortune, and Courage in their

---

21 Barbarians] *Barbarians* O.

bad. *Arminius* and *Inguiomer* retir'd out of the Battle, the first
untouch'd, the last desperately wounded. The Slaughter lasted
all the Day, and, at the shutting of Evening, the Legions return'd
into their Camp, many of them being hurt, and all without
Victuals, yet well contented, finding in their Victory, Health
and Vigour, and large Provision of whatsoever they desir'd.

LXIII. [LXIX] In the mean time, a Report was spread, that
the *Romans* were defeated, and that the *Germans* were descend-
ing upon *Gaul:* And they were on the point of breaking down
the Bridge upon the *Rhine,* if *Agrippina* had not oppos'd her
Courage, to the Cowardise of those who had advis'd so infamous
an Action. During the time of that Consternation, she discharg'd
all Duties of a General*; she reliev'd the poor Soldiers, she
supply'd the Sick with Remedies†, and provided Clothes for those
who were perishing with Cold. *Caius Plinius,* who has written
the History of these Wars, says, That she stood on the entry of
the Bridge to praise and thank the Legions, as they pass'd along.
All which Proceedings made a deep Impression of Discontent
and Melancholy on the Soul of *Tiberius.* He strongly suspected,
that this Over-Diligence and Care could not possibly be inno-
cent† at the bottom; that it was not against Foreigners, that
Agrippina thus fortifi'd herself with the Favour of the Soldiers;
that the Generals might now securely take their Ease, when a
Woman could perform their Office, take Reviews of the Le-
gions, march amidst the *Roman* Ensigns and their Eagles, and
make Donatives to the Soldiers. How could it be without Design,
that her little Son was carried round the Camp in the plain
habit of a private Soldier; that she caus'd him to be Sirnam'd
Caligula; that she had already more Authority in the Army
than all the Generals†, since she had appeas'd a Mutiny, where
the Name of the Emperour had been of no Consideration†.
Sejanus, who was well acquainted with the suspicious Temper
of *Tiberius*†, was not wanting to foment these Discontents†, but
bury'd the Seeds of them deep under Ground†, and remov'd
from sight, that they might shoot up in their appointed time,
and produce the Fruits which he desir'd.

LXIV. [LXX] *Germanicus,* who was embark'd already with

29 *Caligula;* that] ∼: That O.

his Legions, intrusted *Publius Vitellius* with the Command of
the Second and the Fourteenth, that he might bring them back
by Land, thereby to lighten his Transport Vessels, lest they
should knock upon the Sands, or lie a-Ground, the Water dur-
ing the Ebbs, being extreamly sholy upon those Seas. At the
beginning, *Vitellius,* who coasted the Shores, found no Incon-
venience in his March, because the Soil was dry, and the Tide
moderate. But after the Breeze began to blow, and the Sun
was in the Equinox[t], (at which time the Seas begin to swell, and
10 grow tempestuous,) all the Campaign was floated on the sud-
den, and the two Legions in apparent danger of being lost. The
Sea and Land bore the same Figure; the firm Earth was not to
be distinguish'd from the moving Sands, nor the fordable Pas-
sages from the Deep. The Billows bore away the Soldiers, and
devour'd them; dead Bodies of Men, and Horses, were seen
floating confusedly with the Baggage on the Waves. The Bri-
gades were mix'd with one another; some of the Soldiers were
wading up to the Waste in Water; others to their Shoulders;
and always one or other, their Footing failing, were carried to
20 the bottom. Their Cries, and mutual Encouragements, avail'd
them nothing against the Fury of the Waves, which suck'd them
in, and swallow'd them; no distinction was to be found betwixt
the Cowards and the Brave, the Prudent and the Fools, the Cau-
tious and the Bold; all were equally overpower'd by the violence
of the Seas and Winds. At length, *Vitellius* having sav'd himself
on a rising Ground, shew'd the way of Safety to the remains of
his wreck'd Legions. They pass'd the following Night without
Fires, without Provisions, and without Tents, the greatest part
of them all bruis'd and naked, and more miserable than those
30 who are surrounded by their Enemies, because their Death was
without Honour; whereas the others were in a capacity of selling
their Lives at a dear Rate, and dying not ingloriously. The re-
turn of Day restor'd them to dry Land, and afforded them the
means of retiring to the *Rhine*,* whither *Germanicus* had al-
ready brought his Forces. The two Legions reimbark'd with him,
while the Rumour yet continu'd, that they were lost; which was

---

19   other,] ~ₐ O.

obstinately believ'd, till all the World had seen the return of
Germanicus with his Army.

    LXV. [LXXI] During this Interval, *Stertinius* was gone to
receive *Segimer,* the Brother of *Segestes,* and brought him, to-
gether with his Son, into the City of the *Ubians.* A Pardon was
granted to both of them; to the Father without any difficulty,
because he had surrender'd himself of his own free motion; but
more hardly to his Son, because he was accus'd to have insulted
the dead Body of *Varus.* As for the rest, *Spain, Gaul,* and *Italy,*
10 seem'd to vye with each other, in sending Horses, Arms, and
Silver, to *Germanicus,* to repair the Losses which his Army had
sustain'd. But he, with high Praises of their Zeal, accepted only
of the Arms and Horses, which he wanted to carry on the War,
being resolved to supply the Soldiers with his own Money. And
to efface wholly from their Memory, the Thoughts of their late
Suffering by his Kindness, he visited the Wounded, desir'd to
see their Hurts, commended every one in particular, according
to the Merits of his Service[†]; some he inflam'd with desire of
Honour, others with the hopes of Riches. In short, whether by
20 his Affability, or the Care which he took of them, he won them
all to be at his Devotion, and ready to follow him in any Danger.

    LXVI. [LXXII] In the same Year, the Triumphal Ornaments
were decreed to his Lieutenants, *Aulus Cecina, Lucius Apronius,*
and *Caius Silius. Tiberius* refus'd the Title of *Father of his
Country*,* which the People were often desirous to have given
him; nor even would permit, that they should take their Oaths
upon his [†]Acts*, many times repeating these words, *That there
was nothing stable in this Life; and that the more he was exalted,
the more in danger of a Fall[†]:* But this affected Modesty of his,
30 gain'd him not a better Opinion with the People; for he had
lately revived the Law of High-Treason for Offences committed
against the Person or Dignity of the Prince; which 'tis granted
had the same Name in the Times of our Fore-Fathers, but was
not of the same Extent[†]. If any one had betray'd his General in
War, or rais'd Sedition, or dishonour'd the Majesty of the *Roman*

27–29   *That . . . [to] . . . a] set in romans in* O.
29   *Fall*[†]:] Fall2, O.

People in the publick Exercises of his Function, he was attainted
for a Crime of State. Actions were punishable, but Words were
free. *Augustus* was the first, who comprehended Libels within
the Cognizance of the Law; being provok'd by the Petulancy of
Cassius Severus, who had defam'd, in his Writing, Men and
Women of the highest Quality[†]. *Tiberius* afterwards had an-
swer'd the Prætor *Pompeius Macer,* who had consulted him con-
cerning this very Law, That his Pleasure was, it should be
observ'd; being piqu'd himself likewise by certain Verses of
10 conceal'd Authors, which had reproach'd him for his Cruelty,
his Pride, and his Ingratitude[*] to his Mother[†].

LXVII. [LXXIII] 'Tis not from the purpose, in this place, to
relate the Accusations which were carry'd on against *Falanius*
and *Rubrius,* two *Roman* Knights, but both of very moderate
Estates, to shew the Birth and Rise of that pernicious Invention,
and with what Cunning *Tiberius* fomented it: How the Growth
of it was stopp'd for a certain time, and how afterwards it was
renew'd, and increas'd so much in Strength, that it set the whole
Empire in a Flame. He who inform'd against *Falanius,* accus'd
20 him to have admitted into the Society of those, who were the
Adorers of *Augustus,* and were divided into several Fraternities,
a certain Buffoon[†], call'd *Cassius,* who had prostituted his Body;
and that he had sold, together with his Gardens, a Statue of that
Emperour, which was erected there. *Rubrius,* in like manner,
was accus'd for violating the Divinity of *Augustus* by Perjury.
Tiberius, having Information of these Procedures, writ to the
Consuls thus concerning them: That Heaven had not been de-
creed to his Father, with intention that his Worship should serve
for a Pretence, to the Ruine of *Roman* Citizens[†]; That *Cassius*
30 had been accustom'd to assist with those of his Profession at the
Plays, which *Livia* had consecrated to the Memory of *Augustus;*
That to leave his Images, with those of other Gods, in Houses
and Gardens which were sold, had not the least reference to
Religion; That the Perjury of *Rubrius* ought not to be held a
more enormous Crime, than that of Forswearing himself by the
Name of *Jupiter*[†].

---

21 Fraternities,] ~ₐ O.

LXVIII. [LXXIV] Shortly after, *Granius Marcellus,* Prætor
of *Bithynia,* was accus'd of High-Treason by *Cœpio Crispinus,*
his Treasurer, with the corroborating Evidence of *Romanus
Hispo.* This *Hispo,* who was of an unquiet Spirit, had taken up
a kind of Life, which the Iniquity of the Times, and the Wicked-
ness of Men, turn'd afterwards into a common Practice†; for
from a poor, unknown, and despicable Fellow†, as he was, he
accommodated himself so well to the Cruelty of *Tiberius,* at first
by secret Memoirs which he gave him, and afterwards by open
10 Accusations, which he brought against the greatest Men of
Rome, that becoming as powerful with the Prince, as hated by
the People, he serv'd for an Example to many others; who, like
him, rising from Poverty to Riches, and from Contempt to
formidable Greatness, split at length upon that Rock to which
they had driven others. He accus'd *Marcellus* to have spoken
with too great License of *Tiberius.* An inevitable Crime! be-
cause the Informer picking out all the infamous Actions of the
Prince, the Person accus'd was believ'd guilty of saying that,
which was notoriously true. He added, That a Statue of *Marcel-*
20 *lus* had been plac'd higher than any of the Cæsars; and that he
had taken off the Head from an Image of *Augustus,* and plac'd
in the room of it the Effigies of *Tiberius*†. At these Words, *Ti-
berius,* without breaking into Choler, cried aloud, That he
would deliver his Opinion in open Senate concerning this Affair,
and that with a solemn Obtestation* of *Jupiter,* to oblige the
rest to the same Sentence†. As there were yet some small Re-
mainders of the ancient Liberty, tho now expiring, *Cneius Piso*
demanded of him, In what Place he would give his Suffrage?
For if you speak first, (added he) *I have no more to do, than to*
30 *follow your Sentence; but if you deliver your Opinion last of*
all, my Vote by misfortune may have been opposite to yours.
Tiberius amaz'd at this unexpected Boldness, and suddenly mol-
lified, out of shame to have been surpriz'd in that Transport of
his Passion, suffer'd the Accus'd to be acquitted from the Charge

---

1 *Granius*] *Grænius* O.
20 Cæsars] *Cæsars* O.
29 *For if you speak first*] set in romans in O.
29–31 *I ...* [*to*] *... yours*] set in romans in O.

of High-Treason†, and remitted him to the common Magistrates to be try'd, for his Management of the publick Treasure.

LXIX. [LXXV] Not satisfi'd to assist only at the Judiciary Proceedings of the Senate, he frequented also the Inferior Court*, where he sate on one side of the Tribunal†, because he would not displace the Judge from the Seat of Justice; and occasion'd by his Presence, that many good Regulations were made concerning the Partial Recommendations of the Great. But while he kept so strict a Hand on Justice, he extinguish'd Liberty. About this

10 time it was, that *Pius Aurelius,* a Senator, petition'd the Senate to be consider'd for the Loss he had sustain'd in the Ruine of his House, which was demolish'd for the Convenience of Publick Ways, and the Structure of Aqueducts. *Tiberius,* who was always pleas'd to exercise his Liberality in those Things which might do him Honour, (a Virtue which he retain'd a long time after he had divested himself of all the rest,) order'd, That the Price of his House should be refunded to him: though the Prætors, who were at that time Commissioners of the Treasury, were against the Grant. *Propertius Celer,* who had formerly

20 been Prætor, and who desir'd Leave to lay down the Dignity of a Senator, because of his Poverty†, receiv'd a Thousand great Sesterces*, to *support his Quality; Tiberius* being given to understand, that his Father had left him much in Debt. Some others endeavour'd to obtain the same Favour from *Tiberius,* but he order'd them to address to the Senate†, affecting to be thought severe, and hard†, even in those very Things which were but Acts of Justice: Which was the cause, that all the rest sate down content with silent Poverty, rather than endure the Shame of owning it unprofitably†.

30 LXX. [LXXVI] The same Year, the *Tiber* being swell'd by the continual fall of Rains, overflow'd the nether Parts of the Town, and carried off both Houses and Men in its Retreat. *Asinius Gallus* propos'd in Senate to consult the Sibils* Books; which *Tiberius* withstood†; who was as careful to conceal the Mysteries of Religion, as those of State. But the care of restraining those Inundations, was committed to *Ateius Capito,* and *Lucius Arruntius.* On occasion of Complaints, which were made by

---

27 Justice:] ~. O.

Greece and *Macedonia*, it was order'd, That they should be dis-
charg'd, at present†, from the Government of Proconsuls, and
rul'd by the Emperour*. *Drusus*, in the Name of *Germanicus*,
and in his own, gave the Spectacle of Gladiators, at which him-
self presided, taking, as was thought, too great a Pleasure in the
sight of Bloodshed, though it was only the Blood of Inferiour
Men. And his Father, as it was reported, gave him a severe
Reprehension for it, because it had given the People an Occa-
sion to murmur, who were apprehensive of his Cruelty, when it
10 should be his Turn to Reign. It was diversly interpreted, why
Tiberius refrain'd from that Spectacle. Some conjectur'd, that
he lov'd not great Assemblies; others, that being of a sullen and
melancholick Humour, he fear'd that an odious Comparison
would be made betwixt him and *Augustus*†, who was always
present at these publick Entertainments, behaving himself with
great Familiarity and Complaisance†. I cannot think, that it was
to put his Son into the ill Opinion of the People†, by shewing
his Cruel and Sanguinary Temper, though there were some of
that Belief.
20   LXXI. [LXXVII] The License of the Theatre, which began
the Year before, was now grown excessive. Many Murders were
committed, not only on Men of common Rank, but even on some
Soldiers, and one Centurion, who would have restrain'd the
Quarrels of the Populace, and repress'd the Insults, which they
made on the Persons of the Magistrates: And the Tribune of
a Prætorian Cohort was also wounded. A Decree of Senate being
made, which impower'd the Prætor, to cause the Actors of those
Farces to be scourg'd; *Haterius Agrippa*, Tribune of the People,
oppos'd this Order; and *Gallus Asinius* sharply reproving him,
30 *Tiberius* did not interrupt him†; for he was willing to sooth the
Senate with that vain appearance of their Power, and publick
Liberty. Nevertheless, the Opposition had the wish'd Effect, be-
cause *Augustus* had declar'd the Farcers to be exempt from the
servile Punishment of the Whip; and *Tiberius* seem'd very
scrupulous, in breaking any of his Edicts†. Many other Ordi-
nances were made concerning the Stipends of Comedians*, and
against the License of their Favourers*; and the most Remark-
able are these: That the Senators should return no Visits to the

Pantomimes*; That the *Roman* Knights should not accompany
them in the Streets; That those Farcers should not be permitted
to Play, unless only on the Theatres; And that, for the future,
the Prætors should have Power to send into Banishment those
Spectators, who behav'd themselves with Insolence.

LXXII. [LXXVIII] *Spain* had leave to build a Temple to
Augustus Cæsar, in the Colony of *Terragona;* and this serv'd for
an Example to all the Provinces. The People desiring to be dis-
charg'd from the Impost laid on the Hundredth part of[†] the
10 *Gains by Commerce, Tiberius* declar'd, the Fund for War* sub-
sisted chiefly by that Income; and also, that the whole Revenue
of the Commonwealth would not satisfie for the Payment of the
Forces, if the Veterans were dismiss'd before they had serv'd the
term of 20 Years: By which, the Promise made for their Dis-
charge at the end of 16 Years was *virtually* revok'd, which the
Seditious Legions had extorted[†] from *Germanicus* and *Drusus*
not long before.

LXXIII. [LXXIX] *Arruntius* and *Capito* consulted the Senate,
concerning the Inundations of the *Tiber,* whether they thought
20 fitting to have them stopp'd, by diverting the Course of the
Lakes and Rivers, which discharg'd themselves into it. But be-
fore the Debate pass'd farther, they were to hear the Reasons
which were offer'd by the Towns and Colonies, which were
interess'd in that Affair. It was remonstrated by those of *Flor-
ence,* that their Country was lost, if the *Clane* should disburthen
it self into the *Arn:* The *Interamnates** alledg'd, that the most
fruitful Parts of *Italy* would be turn'd to marish Ground, if the
Nar should be sluc'd out into many Rivulets, which they were
ready to have done. The *Reatines* would not consent, that the
30 Passage should be stopp'd, by which the Lake *Velinus* runs into
the *Nar;* declaring, That it would overflow the Neighbouring
Country; That Nature had made the best Provision, for the Con-
venience of Mankind, in disposing the Course of Rivers, ordain-
ing their Outlets, and their Bounds, as she had appointed, where
their Springs should rise; That they ought to have regard to the

1 Pantomimes] *Pantomimes* O.   13 Veterans] *Veterans* O.
14 Years:] ∼. O.   18 *Arruntius*] *Aruntius* O.
21 themselves] themselve O.

Religion of their Allies, who had consecrated Woods, and Altars, and Priests, to the Rivers of their Country; That even the *Tiber** would creep along, diminish'd of his Glory, if he were robb'd of the Income, which was paid him by his Tributary Rivers. At length, whether deterr'd by Superstition, or yielding to the Request of the Colonies, or forc'd by the difficulty of the Undertaking, they decreed, That no Alteration should be made, as *Piso* from the beginning had advis'd.

LXXIV. [LXXX] *Poppeius Sabinus* was continu'd in the Gov-
10 ernment of *Mesia,* to which were added, *Achaia* and *Macedonia.* For it was a Maxim of *Tiberius,* To let the Governours grow old in the Provinces which they commanded, and many of them died[†] in the Possession of those Places they held, whether Military or Civil*. Various Reasons are assign'd for this: Some affirm, That, to spare himself the Care and Trouble of a second Choice, he kept constant to the first; Others say, That it was to advance as few as possible he could[†]. Some have believ'd, that as he had a quick and piercing Wit, so his Judgment was always in suspence; for as he could not suffer the Extremities of Vice, so
20 neither did he love extraordinary and shining Virtues: Being jealous of his Authority, he fear'd great Men[†]; and as he was jealous of his own Reputation, and of the publick Honour, he rejected those who pass'd for Scandalous, or Insufficient*. In short, his Irresolution was so great, that he gave Governments to some such Persons, as he had absolutely determin'd, should never leave the Town to take possession of them.

LXXV. [LXXXI] As to the Assemblies which were held for the Election of Consuls, I have nothing to affirm for certain, either in the time of *Tiberius,* or after it: So great is the Differ-
30 ence which is found, not only in the Relations of Historians, but also in his own Speeches. Sometimes, without naming the Candidates for the Consulship, he describ'd them by their Birth; by their Manners, and by the number of Years which they had serv'd in War. Sometimes, omitting even those Descriptions, he desir'd the Pretenders not to trouble the Assemblies with their Intrigues, promising his own particular Care in their Concerns. And sometimes he said, That no Competitors had presented

2   Country;] ∼. O.   29   it:] ∼. O.

themselves to him, but only they, whose Names he had deliver'd to the Consuls; yet that others were not debarr'd* from pretending to that Dignity, who either confided in their own Merits, or in the Favour of the Senate. Specious Words†, but either void of Meaning, or full of Cunning; and couch'd under a flattering shew of Freedom, to break out afterwards with greater danger of a worse Servitude.

COMMENTARY

List of Abbreviated References

Amelot: *Tacite avec des Notes Politiques et Historiques,* trans. Abraham Nicolas Amelot de la Houssaye, The Hague, 1692

BH: Samuel Johnson, *Lives of the English Poets,* ed. George Birkbeck Hill, Oxford, 1905

BIHR: Bulletin of the Institute of Historical Research

Bourdelot: Λουκιανου . . . *Luciani Samosatensis Philosophi Opera,* ed. Joannes Bourdelotius, Paris, 1615

Casaubon: Πολυβιου . . . *Polybii Lycortæ F. Megalopolitani Historiarum Libri qui Supersunt, interprete Isaaco Casaubono: Jacobus Gronovius recensuit,* II, 2d pagination, Amsterdam, 1670

CL: Comparative Literature

CP: Classical Philology

CSPD: Calendar of State Papers, Domestic Series

D'Ablancourt: *Lucien,* trans. Nicholas Perrot, Sieur d'Ablancourt, Paris, 1688

Des Maizeaux: *The Works of Monsieur de St. Evremond, Made English,* ed. and trans. Pierre Des Maizeaux, 2d ed., 1728

DNB: Dictionary of National Biography

ELH: A Journal of English Literary History

Hagstrum: Jean H. Hagstrum, *The Sister Arts,* Chicago, 1958

HLQ: Huntington Library Quarterly

HMC: Historical Manuscripts Commission

JHI: Journal of the History of Ideas

JWCI: Journal of the Warburg and Courtauld Institutes

Kinsley: *The Poems of John Dryden,* ed. James Kinsley, Oxford, 1958

L'Art de Peinture: Charles Alphonse Dufresnoy, *L'Art de Peinture . . . Traduit en François* [by Roger de Piles], *avec des Remarques* [by de Piles], Paris, 1668

Lucian: Λουκιανου Απαντα: *Luciani Samosatensis Opera,* Basle, 1563

Luttrell: Narcissus Luttrell, *A Brief Historical Relation of State Affairs 1678–1714,* Oxford, 1857

Macdonald: Hugh Macdonald, *John Dryden: A Bibliography of Early Editions and of Drydeniana,* Oxford, 1939

Malone: *Critical and Miscellaneous Prose Works of John Dryden,* ed. Edmond Malone, 1800

Mayne: *Part of Lucian Made English . . . By Jasper Mayne, . . . To which are adjoyned those other Dialogues of Lucian as they were formerly translated by Mr Francis Hicks,* Oxford, 1663

MP: Modern Philology

N&Q: Notes and Queries

Noyes: *Poetical Works of Dryden,* ed. George R. Noyes, 2d ed., Cambridge, Mass., 1950

OED: Oxford English Dictionary

Osborn: James M. Osborn, *John Dryden: Some Biographical Facts and Problems,* rev. ed., Gainesville, Fla., 1965

Pauly-Wissowa: Paulys *Real-Encyclopädie der Classischen Altertumswissenschaft,* ed. Georg Wissowa et al., Stuttgart, 1894–1981
PBSA: Papers of the Bibliographical Society of America
Pichon: *C. Cornelii Taciti Opera,* ed. Julianus Pichon Abbas, Paris, 1682–1687
PMLA: Publications of the Modern Language Association of America
PQ: Philological Quarterly
RES: Review of English Studies
Saint-Evremond: *Miscellaneous Essays: By Monsieur St. Euremont,* 1692
Sheeres: *The History of Polybius,* trans. Sir Henry Sheeres, 1693
SP: Studies in Philology
Spence: *Lucian's Works,* trans. Ferrand Spence, 1684–1685
Spingarn: *Critical Essays of the Seventeenth Century,* ed. J. E. Spingarn, reissue, Bloomington, Ind., 1957
S-S: *The Works of John Dryden,* ed. Sir Walter Scott and George Saintsbury, Edinburgh, 1882–1893
Ternois: Saint-Evremond, *Oeuvres en Prose,* ed. René Ternois, Paris, 1962–1969
Tilley: M. P. Tilley, *A Dictionary of the Proverbs in England in the Sixteenth and Seventeenth Centuries,* Ann Arbor, 1950
Van Lennep: *The London Stage, 1660–1800,* Part I: 1660–1700, ed. William Van Lennep, with Critical Introduction by Emmett L. Avery and Arthur H. Scouten, Carbondale, Ill., 1965
Ward, *Letters: The Letters of John Dryden,* ed. Charles E. Ward, Durham, N.C., 1942
Ward, *Life:* Charles E. Ward, *The Life of John Dryden,* Chapel Hill, N.C., 1961
Watson: *John Dryden: Of Dramatic Poesy and Other Critical Essays,* ed. George Watson, 1962
Works: Dryden's works in the present edition
Works of Lucian: The Works of Lucian, Translated from the Greek, 1710–1711

Preface to A Dialogue Concerning Women

Dryden arranged for the publication of *A Dialogue Concerning Women* and supplied a preface out of friendship for its author, William Walsh (1662–1708). Slight in itself and seemingly innocuous, the preface nonetheless excited the suspicion and contempt of an anonymous lampooner, whose verses circulated in manuscript some time after Walsh's dialogue was advertised in the *London Gazette* for 16–20 April 1691. Rather than the defense of women proclaimed on the title page, Walsh's dialogue was construed by the lampooner as an attack upon them, and Dryden was charged with controlling Walsh and masterminding the attack. But the story underlying the dialogue involved more than another case of would-be praise interpreted as actual satire, and to understand Dryden's involvement in the composition, publication, and reception of the dialogue, we need to retrace the steps of his friendship with Walsh. That story has been told before,[1] but it merits repetition, even though (or perhaps because) it seems to offer little more than centuries-old gossip. There are, moreover, fresh inferences to be drawn from some of the story's details.

While patchy records have left the origin of the friendship obscure, sufficient correspondence survives to show that Walsh, more than thirty years Dryden's junior, probably initiated the relationship. He drafted a letter to Dryden in 1686 requesting a judgment on some of his "Compositions," even though the two had not met.[2] Walsh never sent the letter, at any rate as drafted; so much can be inferred from a letter by Dryden commending some of Walsh's verses, expressing pleased surprise at learning that Walsh was a poet, and making plain that the two had already met, probably at Will's coffeehouse.[3] Dryden's letter, though undated, may be provisionally assigned to 1690, because a letter from Walsh takes note of the "favourable opinion . . . of yᵉ songs" and goes on to ask, among other things, for Dryden's additional "opinion" of a work that was evidently to become *A Dialogue Concerning Women*,[4] which was published, we have seen, late in April 1691.

Dryden gave his opinion early enough for incorporation in the published work. He recommended such stylistic changes as avoidance of contractions and prepositions at the end of sentences, as well as maintenance of a distinction between "who" and "that." Dryden also praised the work for its "disposition" and "thoughts," its adaptation of the Ciceronian dialogue, and its gallant apostrophes,[5] which were addressed as asides to the lady for whom the work was created. Properly grateful for what must have been a swift response, Walsh asked Dryden, when he could, "to look it over

---

[1] See Osborn, pp. 226–233, and, for a more authoritative account, Phyllis Freeman, "William Walsh and Dryden: Recently Recovered Letters," *RES*, XXIV (1948), 195–202.

[2] Ward, *Letters*, p. 25.   [3] *Ibid.*, pp. 30–31.

[4] *Ibid.*, pp. 31–32.   [5] *Ibid.*, pp. 33–34, 36.

again." [6] For Walsh had high stakes in this work, as is evident from a subsequent letter, also written early in 1691, where he addressed himself to "plaguing" Dryden for a preface. Declaring that he lacked "confidence . . . to print [the dialogue] in [his] own name," yet fearing that something completely anonymous might "perhaps never come to bee read," Walsh hoped that "some little preface" by Dryden would be "a very great means to recommend it to ye World." [7] More particularly, Walsh hoped that his dialogue would come to the attention of two women in such a way that they might be able to identify its author.

The first of these women was the Eugenia addressed in the dialogue, who had "commanded" its composition. [8] Eugenia, Walsh confided to Dryden, had "playd [him] some scurvy tricks for which" he might "come to fall out publickly with her," and, if he did so, he hoped that a published defense of women, known to be his, would "engage" him "a party amongst" women and persuade at least some of them away from support of Eugenia. [9] We now know that Eugenia was the Countess of Kingston, [10] widowed on 17 September 1690, [11] pursued by Walsh and rival lovers even before her husband's death, and known by London gossips in April 1691 for an intrigue with Walsh. [12] Walsh, indeed, had hoped to marry her, only to learn before April 1691 of a rumored, secret remarriage. [13] She had, in fact, remarried on 3 March 1691, [14] although it seems unlikely that the remarriage constituted all the "scurvy tricks" that Walsh thought Lady Kingston had played upon him. After the dialogue appeared, town gossips started a rumor that it would be followed by a second edition containing all Lady Kingston's letters to Walsh. She herself apparently believed the rumor, and Walsh wrote to reassure her that he "never had any such design," and instead contemplated a different form of publication, evidently by word of mouth: he thought of "clearing" himself "by publishing ye History of all ye Amours between" them. [15] Walsh, we must suppose, thought he had to clear himself of more, say, than a rumor of his disappointment at Lady Kingston's remarriage. Indeed, the alternative methods of exposure outlined by Walsh suggest that he was responding to gossip started by her which represented him as a vain pretender to her fortune and affections without any encouragement on her side.

A dialogue written to flatter and impress Lady Kingston was, then, to be

---

6 *Ibid.,* p. 36.

7 *Ibid.,* pp. 38–39.

8 *Ibid.,* pp. 32, 38; Walsh, *A Dialogue Concerning Women,* pp. 1–2.

9 Ward, *Letters,* p. 38.

10 Born Anne Greville, elder daughter of Robert, 4th Baron Brooke (see Joseph Edmondson, *An Historical and Genealogical Account of the Noble Family of Greville* [1766], p. 95; and *The Complete Peerage,* ed. Vicary Gibbs [1929], VII, 306).

11 Her husband, William Pierrepont, Earl of Kingston-upon-Hull, died of apoplexy (*ibid.*).

12 Freeman, *RES,* XXIV, 198–199.

13 *Ibid.,* p. 199.

14 Her late husband's cousin, another William Pierrepont (see HMC, *Finch,* III, 28 and n; Luttrell, II, 221; Gibbs, VII, 306).

15 Freeman, *RES,* XXIV, 199.

published as the first step in a campaign to discredit her. But Walsh saw a further use in publication. He now wished, he assured Dryden, to impress "another Mistress, who is resolved to confer favour upon none but Merit; & as shee is a person of sense, so shee . . . is a great friend to Witt & Learning."[16] Publication of the dialogue, he trusted, would display his parts to this lady, who was almost certainly Jane Leveson-Gower, as emerges from subsequent events. We have no reason to suppose that Dryden at once identified Walsh's new mistress, although he had known Jane Leveson-Gower for some months at least and had already commended in print both her "Charms" and her literary "Judgment."[17]

However genuine Walsh's feelings at the time, his involved calculations might strike us as more than a little absurd. But we should remember that he belonged to a limited social group devoted to gossip, assignation, and intrigue, to the keeping and breaking of secrets, and to the damaging of reputations by murmured scandal or circulated lampoon. This world is reflected in, not invented by, the comedy of the time,[18] and if Walsh sounds in his letters to Dryden as though inventing a plot for such a comedy, he could also offer in his dialogue a social judgment whose literary applications no one familiar with Restoration drama can fail to see: "it is only the Half Wit that is intolerable, and a true Fool, is next a true Wit the best Company in the World."[19] Walsh obviously thought himself a true wit and, much like a master intriguer from the contemporary stage, he sought to ensure the success of his plans by asking several things of Dryden. He asked for a preface that would preserve anonymity while making it clear that Dryden knew the author: "tho' I will not venture to put my Name, yet except it is known to bee mine, it will not answer ye Ends for wch I design'd it."[20] He noted, evidently as an objection to be dealt with by Dryden in the preface, that he had spoken favorably of Dryden in the dialogue, and a prefatory commendation by Dryden might therefore seem no more than French praise of "one friend . . . for another." Walsh further suggested topics for Dryden's praise, most of which Dryden had already taken up in correspondence: the "manner" of the dialogue, the "Gallantry of ye Apostrophes," the "reading shewn in it."[21] In the light of Walsh's letter, Dryden's preface reads almost as if written to order. Walsh had one more favor to ask: "I will send you the Copy, wch you may dispose of with ye same freedom as if it were yor own, reserving mee as sufficient number of Printed ones to disperse among my friends."[22] Walsh plainly intended to ensure that his authorship did not go unknown—friends with author's

---

16 Ward, *Letters,* p. 38.

17 See the dedication of *Amphitryon* (to her father) in *Works,* XV, 225:26–30. *Amphitryon* was advertised in the *London Gazette* for 30 October–3 November 1690.

18 See Maximillian E. Novak, "Love, Scandal, and the Moral Milieu of Congreve's Comedies," in *Congreve Consider'd* (1971), pp. 23–50.

19 Walsh, *Dialogue,* p. 63. Walsh here failed to correct his prose in accordance with Dryden's injunction: "*That,* ought alwayes to signify a thing; *who* a person" (Ward, *Letters,* p. 34).

20 Ward, *Letters,* p. 40.

21 *Ibid.,* pp. 33, 36, 39.   22 *Ibid.,* p. 40.

copies can be relied upon for discreet disclosures—and, just as plainly, he relied upon Dryden to arrange publication. Dryden evidently obliged: Walsh's dialogue was published by Dryden's then regular bookseller, Jacob Tonson, and by his sometime bookseller, Richard Bentley.[23]

In a Restoration comedy the true wit's stratagems would have succeeded, if with some fourth-act obstacles to overcome and some fifth-act disclosures that would redefine his plans. Walsh, alas, carried his plot only into the opening scene of the fifth act, and fourth-act obstacles proved rather too much for him. Surviving records show only that Lady Kingston and her friends supplied vigorous opposition in Walsh's fourth act to which Walsh made indecisive rejoinder. He succeeded, to be sure, in impressing Jane Leveson-Gower, but this little drama never ran its course to song, dance, and anticipated nuptials; fifth-act disclosures assigned Walsh's plans to oblivion. Dryden was involved in both acts.

On 25 July 1691, three months after publication of *A Dialogue Concerning Women,* Walsh drafted a letter to the woman who had sent him a copy of a lampoon upon it.[24] Two extant manuscripts of the lampoon show us what he saw and explain his reaction to a set of verses entitled "On the Author of a Dialogue concerning Women, pretended to be writ in Defence of the Sex."[25] The lampoon ends by identifying Walsh as author of the dialogue, but takes the occasion of the preface to attack Dryden:

> To these a mighty Bard is Holder-forth,
> He molds their Parts, and dubs them Men of Worth,
> A Turncoat-Poet, Proteus of the Quill,
> Prostitute Scribler, true to nought but Ill,
> Who, with the false Light of his glittering Style,
> Th'unwary Judgment cheats, and does beguile;
> To any Subject he his Lyre can string,
> And can the Villain for the Heroe sing,
> With forc'd Encomium smut great Waller's Muse,
> But ne'r his Noble Cause or Theme cou'd chuse.
> Now to the witling Club at Will's he's Guide
> As Brother Hodge was to the Levite Tribe;
> Where he in Numbers trains admiring Fop,
> And with his Hind and Panther brings him up.

Dryden is further accused of masterminding the dialogue:

> He that but strictly marks the whole Design
> May trace the Prefacer in every Line;
> And thô he does not own the wanton Ape,
> He nurs'd the Cub, and lick'd him into Shape.

Probably by early September 1691 Walsh was writing apologetically to Dryden: "I am sorry y[t] I have brought you into such ill circumstances"

---

[23] Bentley co-published with M. Magnes *Oedipus* (1679) and *The Kind Keeper* (1680); with Tonson he co-published *The Duke of Guise* (1683).

[24] Freeman, *RES,* XXIV, 201.

[25] Folger MS x. d. 194 and BL Harleian MS 7319 (fols. 366*b*–368*b*). We quote from the Folger MS, which differs in some particulars from the Harleian and seems a slightly more finished version of a strikingly bad poem.

with society women; "A Lady sent mee down a Copy of Verses . . . ag^t my self. But they had brought in you & my Lady Dorchester by y^e by as Friends of mine. If you have not seen it it is not worth ye sending you."[26]

In the letter of 25 July to a woman who sent him the lampoon, Walsh assumed its author to be a rival, probably a (still unidentified) "Mr. T——, & hee corrected by" Lady Kingston. "Certainly," Walsh goes on, "they had some hand in it, or else shee woud rather have been put in" than Lady Dorchester.[27] After jeering at Walsh for "holding-forth" at the coffeehouse, the lampooner claimed that Walsh

> Thence goes to Miss of Abdicated James,
> And at her tainted Beautyes lights his Flames.
> To all rich Fortunes he makes vain Pretence,
> And will jointure 'em with his great Stock of Sense,
> Which others think an Irish Confidence.

The initial couplet identifies Katherine Sedley, Countess of Dorchester, the mistress of James both before and during his reign, who was celebrated for her wit and her ugliness; she must, Charles II reportedly said, have been imposed upon James by his confessor for a penance.[28] The triplet, though, may have stung more than the couplet, because the triplet probably glosses those "scurvy trickes" that Walsh thought Lady Kingston had played upon him, cheapening his reputation, it may be, both by questioning his "Sense" and by representing him as a fortune hunter. In the letter of 25 July Walsh certainly thought himself "extremely obliged" to the lampooner "for favouring" him with Dryden's "style" and Lady Dorchester's "conversation. If hee takes y^t for an affront I dare answer for him, y^t his Verses were never corrected by Mr. Dryden, nor his Company very agreeable to my Ld[y]. D."[29]

The following year Walsh dared to answer by printing a version of the lampoon in his *Letters and Poems, Amorous and Gallant*.[30] Walsh's text differs from the manuscript texts in some particulars, but chiefly in the omission of twenty-seven lines, among them those attacking Dryden (although not the couplets crediting him with supervising the dialogue) and those associating Walsh with Lady Dorchester and representing him as a fortune hunter.[31] Walsh accompanied the lampoon with a prose epistle

---

[26] Freeman, *RES*, XXIV, 197.

[27] *Ibid.*, p. 201.

[28] She herself reportedly said, when puzzling over what attracted James to her and to his other mistresses: "We are none of us handsome, and if we had wit, he has not enough to discover it." For Katherine Sedley see *DNB* and V. De Sola Pinto, *Sir Charles Sedley* (1927), esp. pp. 132–140, and 156–164. In the spring of 1691, from late April to late June, gossip associated her with Jacobite intrigue (she was also thought a government agent or a double agent), and her case was investigated, although there proved insufficient evidence to convict her of treason (see HMC, *Finch*, III, 47, 128, 313, 321, 325–326; HMC, *Portland*, III, 465). By the end of 1691 she stood "very well at Court" (*CSPD, 1691–1692*, p. 41).

[29] Freeman, *RES*, XXIV, 201.

[30] *Letters and Poems* (1692), pp. 47–50. Walsh's volume was advertised in the *London Gazette* for 13–16 June 1692 and reviewed in the *Gentleman's Journal* (June 1692), pp. 24–25.

[31] In the fifty-six lines that Walsh's text has in common with the manuscripts, it corresponds more closely with the Folger than with the Harleian. Another

"To a Lady who sent him the foregoing Verses in the Country," who was presumably the woman addressed by Walsh on 25 July 1691. The published epistle offers a critique of the lampoon's inanities and triumphantly concludes with a thrust first made privately the preceding July. The lampooner, Walsh remarks, "has maliciously insinuated, That Mr. Dryden writes for me, and that I am covetous of M.L.D.'s Company, yet I must do him the justice to declare, I do not in the least believe Mr. Dryden has any hand in his Works, or that he ever found any great Satisfaction in the Conversation of M.L.D."[32] Since Walsh omitted from the printed text of the lampoon the couplet associating him with Lady Dorchester, his second charge must have puzzled the uninitiated.[33] His published epistle, moreover, makes no allusion to Lady Kingston, who must, as far as we can tell, be credited with outmaneuvering Walsh.

Walsh's other plan for the dialogue seemed likely to succeed at first. Jane Leveson-Gower was sufficiently impressed with the dialogue to translate it into French along with Dryden's preface. By the end of the summer in 1691 she and Walsh were using Dryden as intermediary to transmit their compositions to each other, although both laid injunctions upon Dryden (which he properly ignored) to conceal their authorship.[34] In this way, Walsh transmitted to "ye fair Lady" a "Song" he had made, presumably for her entertainment.[35] In return, Walsh received from Dryden by way of "the French Booksellers" in the Strand a copy of "ye fair Ladys Book," which, a subsequent letter makes clear, was a translation (not "extraordinarily well done," Walsh ungallantly observed to Dryden) of "a little treatise of [Walsh's] into French."[36] Walsh's letters concerning the song and translation date to September 1691, and in 1691 Jacques (i.e., James) Partridge of Charing Cross published a *Defense du Beau Sexe Addressée à Eugenie, Dialogue: Ecrit en Anglois par une Personne de Qualité, Et Traduit en François par une Dame Angloise*. Although the translator has hitherto been unidentified, there seems no reason to doubt that she was Jane Leveson-Gower.

---

manuscript, BL Add. MS 5947 (fols. 146a–149b), agrees substantively with Walsh's version, except that it inadvertently omits one line; it was probably copied from the printed text.

[32] *Letters and Poems* (1692), p. 58.

[33] It puzzled Freeman (*RES*, XXIV, 201), who worked only from the printed text together with those few of the additional lines in the Folger MS which were printed by Ward, *Letters*, pp. 158–159; Ward did not include the Dorchester couplet.

[34] Freeman, *RES*, XXIV, 197.

[35] *Ibid*. The poem cannot be identified with assurance, but it could perhaps have been "To his Mistress: Against Marriage" (*Letters and Poems*, pp. 102–103), whose opening stanza runs:

> Yes, all the World must sure agree,
> He who's secur'd of having thee,
>   Will be entirely blest;
> But 'twere in me too great a Wrong,
> To make one who has been so long
>   My Queen, my Slave at last.

[36] Freeman, *RES*, XXIV, 197–198.

But even before the exchange of compositions, the affair had become clouded, at least for Walsh. He wrote on 13 August asking whether Dryden had "heard out of Staff," where the Leveson-Gowers had their seat, Trentham Hall. Walsh himself "had a letter from London wch told [him] ye young Lady was just going to be marryd to a young L^d whose name they coud not tell. That is not fair play methinkes to take so considerable place, w^thout proclaiming War."[37] Two or three weeks later, Walsh was still asking "who is ye Lord pray y^t was talkt of for ye fair Lady?"[38] But by the time he was arranging for transmission of "ye fair Ladys Book," Walsh had learned the identity of his successful rival and had composed himself into nonchalance:

> They tell mee there is a Match made between her & my
> Ld. Hyde, who is in Flanders wth ye Kg. However Marryd
> or Unmarryd I do not apprehend any danger from a fair
> Ladyes knowing I love her; w^tever some Women [Lady
> Kingston?] may think of mee. No Woman I take it is
> angry at a Mans loving her, how little soever shee may
> care for him.[39]

Jane Leveson-Gower married Henry, Lord Hyde, heir to the Earl of Rochester, on 3 March 1692, a year to the day after Lady Kingston had remarried.[40]

Walsh continued his friendship with Dryden, perhaps to the end of Dryden's life. As late as 1697 Dryden was commending Walsh as "the best Critick of our Nation,"[41] although Walsh published nothing to justify the praise. Dryden no doubt had in mind their correspondence and conversation, for in surviving letters Walsh outlined to Dryden his plans for further treatises. There was to be one concerning "ye Nature of Love,"[42] planned while Walsh was pursuing Jane Leveson-Gower, but this remained "only an Embryo in ye Brain."[43] Later, Walsh promised to supply a preface to Dryden's *Love Triumphant*,[44] but when Walsh communicated his plans, Dryden judged his "Critique" to be too "large for a preface" and accordingly offered to arrange for its separate publication as a treatise by Walsh defending modern dramatic practice against the ancient.[45] No such treatise ever appeared, and perhaps it, too, remained "only an Embryo in ye Brain."

Walsh, indeed, had little sense of an ending, whether to affairs of the

37 Ward, *Letters*, p. 44.   38 *Ibid.*, p. 45.
39 Freeman, *RES*, XXIV, 197.
40 For the date see Lady Theresa Lewis, *Lives of the Friends and Contemporaries of Lord Chancellor Clarendon* (1852), III, 412; and Luttrell, II, 374. It was expected on 1 March (HMC, *Portland*, III, 490). Two months later, in the dedication of *Cleomenes* to her father-in-law (1692, sig. A3r–v; S-S, VIII, 216–217), Dryden once more praised her beauty and acknowledged the part she played in persuading the Lord Chamberlain to lift a ban on the performance of *Cleomenes*.
41 *Works*, VI, 809. A few months later Dryden solicited Walsh's opinion of verses by Lady Mary Chudleigh commending Dryden's Virgil (Ward, *Letters*, p. 98; for the verses see Appendix B in *Works*, VI, 1188–1190).
42 See Ward, *Letters*, pp. 41–48, for Walsh's outline.
43 Freeman, *RES*, XXIV, 198.
44 Ward, *Letters*, p. 54.   45 *Ibid.*, pp. 61–62.

heart or projects of the head. Even his dialogue does not conclude as promised.[46] But Dryden evidently valued his friendship, holding him in both affection and esteem,[47] respecting his learning, and entering with interest into his literary projects. Even the brief preface to Walsh's dialogue shows that interest, for Dryden, after fulfilling the obligations of friendship by treating the topics Walsh suggested, proceeds to underwrite Walsh's defense of women, recommending Ariosto's "sharp Satyr" on the "envy" of men, through which "the Vertue and great Actions of Women are purposely conceal'd."[48] Dryden's own defense of women is both chivalric and feminist: he has been their "Servant," just as Walsh is their "new Champion;" but, invoking Ariosto, he also finds "at this time particularly . . . more Heroines than Heroes."[49] Both attitudes can be found elsewhere in his work. In *Eleonora*, a year after the preface, the lady bore "Love and Obedience to her Lord" (l. 176), but the "Good of both Sexes" ennobled England.[50] Earlier, St. Catherine confessed, even at the height of her intellectual and spiritual supremacy, that "My Sex is weak,"[51] but St. Cecilia outdid Orpheus in art.[52] In sum, then, Dryden's brief preface has interest by affording us another glimpse of his views on women, and in context—the context of Walsh's dialogue, its preparation and reception, and Walsh's hopes for it—the preface carries us once again into the fascinating world of late seventeenth-century life and letters.

P. 3, ll. 3–4 *one so young.* Walsh was about twenty-nine.

3:5–6 *Ingenious.* See Ward, *Letters*, p. 30.

3:6 *improv'd . . . Travelling.* In the *Dialogue* Walsh indicates a visitor's knowledge of a ruined palace outside Naples (p. 34, n. 2), has Philogynes refer to "my stay at Venice" (p. 95) and to conversation with Queen Christina of Sweden (p. 97), although without saying whether at Rome or Paris, and has Misogynes recall mountebanks in Naples (p. 13).

3:10–11 *so much . . . Authors.* More than 130 ancients and moderns

---

[46] Walsh's so-called dialogue in fact takes the form of a debate in the park between Misogynes and Philogynes. They are accompanied by gentlemen who are to determine the victor, with the loser, if Misogynes, to be "in Love by to morrow morning," or, if Philogynes, "to be out of Love by the same time" (p. 7). Misogynes then puts the case against women, arguing from examples, and Philogynes follows with the case for them, also arguing from examples, and concluding with the present Queen Mary, an instance so "Illustrious" (p. 134) that there is no more to say, so much so that we never learn the gentlemen's judgment.

[47] As did the young Pope afterwards (see the praise of Walsh in *Essay on Criticism*, ll. 729–737). For the probability that Walsh was also the friend of Addison and the possibility that, partly because of Walsh's unsuccessful courtship of the widow, Catherine Bovey, in 1696, he provided Addison with hints for the character of Sir Roger de Coverley see Phyllis Freeman, "Who Was Sir Roger De Coverley?" *Quarterly Review*, CCLXXXV (1947), 592–604.

[48] See 4:13–15 above.

[49] See 4:18, 21–23 above. See also note to 4:20–22.

[50] *Works*, III, 234:18.

[51] *Tyrannick Love*, IV, i, 521 (*Works*, X, 163).

[52] *A Song for St. Cecilia's Day, 1687*, ll. 48–51 (*Works*, III, 203).

(about half and half) supply example and argument throughout the *Dialogue*. Moreover, the *Dialogue* is annotated: footnotes supply the numerous sources from which Walsh drew the examples described by Misogynes and Philogynes. Walsh's *Dialogue*, however, is not the most encyclopedic contemporary gathering of allusions to women. See, e.g., *The Wonders of the Female World, Or a General History of Women. Wherein By many hundreds of Examples is shewed what Woman hath been from the first Ages of the World to these Times . . . To which is added, a Plesant Discourse of Female Pre-eminence, Or The Dignity and Excellency Of that Sex above the Male* (1683).

3:14–18 *It puts . . . heard of him.* Malone (III, 54–55n) and Scott (S-S, XVIII, 6n) question Dryden's memory, citing Anthony à Wood (*Athenae Oxoniensis* [1692], II, 302) to suggest that the remark was not said of Waller, but by Waller of Denham in 1641 on the publication of the latter's *The Sophy:* "Waller . . . said of the author that he broke out like the Irish rebellion, threescore thousand strong, when no body was aware, or in the least suspected it." But Clarendon wrote that "at the Age when other Men used to give over writing Verses" Waller "surprised the Town with two or three Pieces" (*The Life of Edward Earl of Clarendon . . . Written by Himself* [Oxford, 1761], I, 47–48). Waller's eighteenth-century editors (notably Elijah Fenton and Percival Stockdale) persisted in acclaiming his first poetic efforts as exceptionally impressive. In the absence of controverting evidence, however, Dryden's memory here seems in question. Clarendon's chronology in his *Life* is, as Dr. Johnson (BH, I, 279–283) early noted, unreliable (B. H. G. Wormald, *Clarendon: Politics, History & Religion, 1640–1660* [1951], p. xi). And while Wood is the only source for attributing the remark to Waller, he remains, so far, unchallenged, though he is not significantly informative. For, as Brendan O. Hehir ("The Early Acquaintance of Denham and Waller," *N&Q*, CCXI [1966], 19–23) properly points out, the date and occasion of Waller's alleged remark remain "involved in impenetrable obscurity."

3:15–16 *the Father . . . Numbers.* Dryden often acknowledges Waller's achievement in versification. See the dedication of *The Rival Ladies* (1664), *Works*, VIII, 100:14–18; *Defence of the Epilogue* (1672), *Works*, XI, 210: 5–6; Dryden's touch in *The Art of Poetry* (1683), *Works*, II, 128:131–142; *Discourse of Satire* (1693), *Works*, IV, 14:34, 84:21. See also note to 3:21.

3:19 *Apostrophe's.* Walsh's term (Ward, *Letters*, pp. 36, 39) for his asides to Eugenia in the *Dialogue*, which introduce and then interrupt the debate between Misogynes and Philogynes, and which are always set off in italics and are often enclosed in parentheses.

3:20–23 *Waller . . . cou'd Write.* For this praise Dryden was attacked by the lampoon quoted in the headnote, p. 302.

3:21 *on all occasions.* Besides lauding Waller's influence on English versification (see note to 3:15–16), Dryden often noted instructive aspects of Waller's poetic art: his harmonious prosody, in *Of Dramatick Poesie* (*Works*, XVII, 14:4–5) and *The Conquest of Granada* (*Works*, XI, 212:22–23); his development of English versification, in the preface to *Fables* (1700, sigs. A, B2v; Watson, II, 270–271, 281); his sensitive flexibility as translator, in the preface to *Ovid's Epistles* (*Works*, I, 114:28–32) and in the dedication of *Aeneis* (*Works*, V, 325); his capacity as a judge of writing, in the dedication of *Examen Poeticum* (*Works*, IV, 374:19–21); and his sense of the English language and its prosody, in Ward, *Letters*, p. 34.

3:29 *Beaux Endroits.* A critical term for fine or striking passages used, e.g., by René Rapin when speaking about natural description in Lucretius (*Réflexions sur la Poétique d'Aristote* [Paris, 1674], p. 89). See also such phrases as "endroits heureux" and "endroits brillans & agreables" (*ibid.*, pp. 90, 165).

3:30–31 *because . . . me.* Just twice, in fact: Walsh refers in an aside to Eugenia to Dryden's forthcoming translation of Juvenal (p. 18), and his Philogynes (pp. 74–75) praises the handling of passions in *Aureng-Zebe*.

4:9–17 *I thought . . . Malice.* See *Orlando Furioso*, XXXVII, i–xxiii. In the *Dialogue* (p. 119), Walsh refers (through Philogynes) only to the story of Bradamante in Canto XXXII. For Dryden's other use of Ariosto, mainly in critical discussion of epic or heroic drama, see *Of Heroique Playes* (1672; *Works*, XI, 10:8–17); *Prologue to the University of Oxford, 1681* (ll. 1–8; *Works*, II, 183); *Discourse of Satire* (1693; *Works*, IV, 13:10–14, 17:14–18:7); and the note on *Aeneis*, IX, 1094–1095 (1697; *Works*, VI, 828–829).

4:18–19 *have never . . . against them.* In the *Prologue to the University of Oxford* (1680; *Works*, I, 164) Dryden in fact caustically ridicules certain actresses, but no more so than actors like them who have deserted the King's Company to play in Edinburgh. Some eighteen months after writing the preface to Walsh's *Dialogue*, Dryden published a translation of Juvenal's sixth Satire, a celebrated indictment of women. Walsh was already anticipating Dryden's translation in his *Dialogue* (p. 18). In an extended "Argument of the Sixth Satire" (more than twice the length of his prefatory arguments to the other four of Juvenal's satires which he translated), Dryden takes pains to dissociate himself from Juvenal's antifeminism (see *Works*, IV, 145–147). Unimpressed by these disclaimers, Felicity A. Nussbaum accuses Dryden of an intent to commit misogyny (see *The Brink of All We Hate: English Satires on Women, 1660–1750* [1984], pp. 78–85).

4:20–22 *in this Age . . . than Heroes.* Bearing out his claim are his celebrations of women in the years just before and after 1691: *To Mrs Anne Killigrew* (1686; *Works*, III, 109–115), *A Song for St. Cecilia's Day, 1687* (*ibid.*, pp. 201–203), *On the Marriage of Mrs Anastasia Stafford* (possibly 1687; *ibid.*, pp. 204–207, 467), *Epitaph on the Lady Whitmore* (1690?; *ibid.*, p. 229), *Eleonora* (1692; *ibid.*, pp. 231–248), *The Monument Of A Fair Maiden Lady* (printed in 1700), *To Her Grace The Dutchess of Ormond* (1700), and *Lines to Mrs. Creed* (date unknown).

Character of Saint-Evremond

An English translation of *Miscellaneous Essays* by Saint-Evremond was entered in the *Stationers' Register* on 18 February 1692 and advertised for sale in the *London Gazette* for 21–25 April of the same year. The translation, capitalizing on the popularity of Saint-Evremond,[1] an exile in England

---

[1] In the preceding decade or so, at least four volumes of English translations of various of Saint-Evremond's works had appeared: *Judgment on Alexander and*

since 1662,[2] was prefaced by a *Character* of Saint-Evremond, begun by "A Person of Honour" and "continued" by Dryden. Early in the next century Des Maizeaux, himself a translator and biographer of Saint-Evremond, identified the "Person of Honour" as Knightly Chetwood, but Des Maizeaux' reliability has been seriously questioned,[3] and authorship of the *Character's* opening paragraphs is uncertain.

Dryden continued a character of Saint-Evremond which seems, from the phrasing on the title page, not merely begun, but done by the Person of Honour. That information is all we have to go on concerning the arrangements that led Dryden to write his part, although the "continued" suggests that Dryden may have read the Person of Honour's contribution before writing his own.

Read together, the two parts reveal very different conceptions of Saint-Evremond and his work. The Person of Honour in his section (up to the rule, p. 8)[4] finds Saint-Evremond as man and writer exemplary, flawless, resembling the ancient Augustans in universality of comprehension and

---

Caesar (1672); *Reflections upon Tragedies, Comedies and Operas* (1684); *Mixt Essays* (1685); and *Miscellanea, Or Various Discourses* (1686). After 1692 came *Miscellany Essays* (1694–1695) and *The Works of Mr de St. Evremont* (1700). The then authoritative translation, *The Works of Monsieur de St. Evremont, Made English from the French Original: With the Life of the Author; By Mr. Des Maizeaux*, in three volumes, appeared in 1714; a second revised edition, herein used for citation, in 1728. Besides translations an exceptional number of French editions were published in London between 1705 and 1725 (see A. F. B. Clark, *Boileau and the French Classical Critics in England (1660–1830)* [1925], p. 289). Happily announcing the *Miscellaneous Essays* of 1692, Pierre Motteux, in the *Gentleman's Journal* (March 1692), pp. 9–10, expressed typical eagerness for work by Saint-Evremond: "Whatever comes from his Pen is so nice and well writ, that all the Ingenious are fond of publishing any thing of his, when his Manuscripts fall into their hands."

2 Until his death in 1703, except between 1665 and 1670. See Des Maizeaux, I, liv–lxxii; Violet Barbour, *Henry Bennet, Earl of Arlington, Secretary of State to Charles II* (1914), p. 103; Ternois, I, xxxv, n. 2; Francis J. Crowley, "Saint-Evremond in Exile," *Revue de Littérature Comparée*, XLI (1967), 583–585; Saint-Evremond, *Sir Politick Would-Be*, ed. Robert Finch and Eugène Joliat (1978), pp. 5–6 and n. 27; and D. C. Potts, rev. of this work in *French Studies*, XXXIII (1979), 444.

3 For Des Maizeaux' identification, see I, "The Preface," p. 2. For the questioning of his reliability, see note to 8:23–26. (In his 1714 edition of *The Works*, III, 203, Des Maizeaux had designated the "Person of Honour" as "Dr. N———" as had the 1700 English translation cited above in note 1. But this was an anonymous attribution, as Clark, *Boileau*, p. 289, points out.) Dryden scholars have accepted Des Maizeaux (Macdonald, p. 173; Kinsley, IV, 2039–2040) or have noted his identification, but with varying degrees of doubt (Malone, III, 65; S-S, XVIII, 11–12; Watson, II, 56). Knightly Chetwood had served with Dryden on the 1683 Plutarch project (*Works*, XVII, 430, n. 3), had gained Dryden's warm praise as "the Learned, and every way Excellent Mr. *Chetwood*" (*Works*, VI, 814:10–11), would write both a preface to the *Pastorals* (Ward, *Letters*, p. 98) and a life of Virgil for Dryden's Virgil. Such facts make for probability but not certainty.

4 See textual headnote, p. 409. The Yale (Hfc35.148) and the Newberry (Y762. S1352) show the rule and the notation. Malone (III, 65) worked from a copy containing them and was perplexed by the latter.

appeal. But when we cross the rule, we leave a mind warm with unreserved commendation and enter one warily at work, offering praise undercut by qualification or reproof enclosed within courtesy de rigueur. The final ambiguity, intensifying the ambiguity of the whole, comes in the last paragraph. Dryden protests that what he has done in his part of the *Character* has had to be so "contracted" that it does not convey the "true Character" of Saint-Evremond. Dryden's readers of 1692 were left to infer the true character.

If Dryden's first readers inferred correctly, they did so because they knew details that we do not have about the publication arrangements and about the nature of the relationship between Dryden and Saint-Evremond, historical particulars which were part of the substance and meaning of Dryden's literature.[5] They may have known the answers to the questions raised by the one datum on the title page: Why are there two writers for the *Character*? Why did one begin it? Was he not finished? Why did Dryden "continue" it? Did the two writers confer? Were they or others back of this publication venture at odds? Who initiated the thought that the form of the preface should be a character?

As we have no answers, we are tempted by the cryptic in Dryden's part of the *Character* to suspect a view of Saint-Evremond that was qualified— to an undetermined degree. Several other matters suggest reservations on Dryden's part. For one thing, scholarship has already demonstrated that Dryden derived no critical ideas from Saint-Evremond, owed him no debts.[6] Further, Dryden's comments on Saint-Evremond elsewhere than in the *Character* on balance suggest cool distance and critical disagreement. In his *Life of Plutarch* (1683) Dryden at one point clearly accepts Saint-Evremond's judgment,[7] but he counterbalances that approbation at other points, once with disapproval, exceedingly respectful, and again, with a trace of reservation.[8] In the dedication of *Aeneis* (1697), where he does not name Saint-Evremond, now a favorite of the Whig court, Dryden ranges from shielding or mock shielding him[9] to contemptuous dismissal,[10] to bitter scorning of him as one of the "wretched Critics"[11] of Virgil's characterization of Aeneas. A possible inference, therefore, from an overview of Dryden's allusions to Saint-Evremond might be that Dryden saw no advantage ever to challenging a very popular foreign critic, perhaps not fluent in English, and clearly on friendly terms with Dryden's taunters in both Charles II's and William's court. Hence, when he named him he maintained the keenest circumspection; when he referred anonymously to him, he showed his feelings.

No evidence beyond Dryden's own remarks in the *Character* has so far appeared to establish whether or not Dryden and Saint-Evremond met.

---

[5] A solid and eloquent statement of the connection between history and meaning in Dryden's work is John Barnard, "Dryden: History and 'The Mighty Government of the Nine,'" *University of Leeds Review*, XXIV (1981), 13–42.

[6] John M. Aden, "Dryden and St. Evremond," *CL*, VI (1954), 232–239.

[7] *Works*, XVII, 286:18–19.

[8] *Works*, XVII, 281:30–282:32, 285:7–12.

[9] *Works*, V, 307:15–17.

[10] *Works*, V, 277:17–18.

[11] *Works*, V, 292:8–17.

What we do have is speculation. It has been much wondered whether two of the most eminent literary figures of the day could have lived in London for nearly forty years, traversing the same crossroads—court, playhouse, coffeehouse—without meeting. Commentary has affirmed and denied encounter, with no decisive proof.[12] Literature, criticism, satire, eclectic intellect, such mutually respected acquaintances as Waller, Cowley, the Duke of Ormonde, and even Saint-Evremond's personal physician, Henry Morelli[13] —all, one would think, should have brought them together. Other circumstances could have kept them apart. Saint-Evremond's closest friends in London were English residents who, unlike Dryden, had lived or roamed in France and between most of whom and Dryden some source of actual or potential irritation had developed: Buckingham,[14] Arlington,[15] Sunderland,[16] and, of course, William III. Saint-Evremond conceivably hit sore spots: he paired Shadwell with Jonson as a significant English comic playwright, joked about Bayes, and collaborated with Buckingham in *Sir Politick Would-Be*.[17] Whether either could or could not speak the other's tongue fluently has not been established.[18] Whether Saint-Evremond could speak English at all remains unsettled.[19] Temperament, like Dryden's "natural bashfulness,"[20] might have forestalled an encounter. But after all is said, Dryden's remark "Had [Saint-Evremond's] Conversation in the Town been more general, he had certainly received other Idea's on that Subject"

---

[12] *Œuvres Complètes de H. Rigault*, ed. Saint-Marc Girardin (Paris, 1859), I, 302–303; Walter Melville Daniels, *Saint-Evremond En Angleterre* (1907), pp. 33, 103; Trusten Wheeler Russell, *Voltaire, Dryden & Heroic Tragedy* (1946), p. 25; George Gordon, "St. Evremond," in *The Lives of Authors* (1950), pp. 122–124; Watson, II, 56; Paul Krüger, *Studier i komparativ Litteratur* (1968), p. 26; Toivo David Rosvall, *The Mazarine Legacy: The Life of Hortense Mancini* (1969), p. 187; Edward Valentine Geist, Jr., "Temple, Dryden and Saint-Evremond: A Study in Libertine Aesthetic and Moral Values" (Ph.D. diss., University of Virginia, Charlottesville, 1971), p. 145; Aden, "Dryden and St. Evremond," pp. 232–239.

[13] For Morelli see *Works*, V, 324:22 and note.

[14] Buckingham, with others, burlesqued Dryden's heroic dramas in *The Rehearsal* (1672) and poked fun at his person in the character of Bayes. Dryden satirized Buckingham's ineptitude and instability in *Absalom and Achitophel*, ll. 544–568 (*Works*, II, 21–22).

[15] In the summer of 1682 Dryden had to appear before Arlington, the Lord Chamberlain, to defend *The Duke of Guise* against Whig protests. He came with Davila, his source, in hand. The play was temporarily banned, pending a decision. See Ward, *Life*, p. 184.

[16] See *Works*, XIII, 501, n. 20. Although with high respect Dryden had dedicated *Troilus and Cressida* (1679) to Sunderland, in *The Hind and the Panther* (1687) he regarded him as one of James II's rash Catholic advisers (see *Works*, III, 421, 423, 425).

[17] For Shadwell and Jonson, see Des Maizeaux, II, 171, "Of English Comedy." For Bayes, see Ternois, IV, 429–430.

[18] For publication Dryden could translate French rapidly. See the *Parallel betwixt Painting and Poetry*, 39:26–28 above.

[19] See Des Maizeaux, I, xl; *The Letters of Saint Evremond*, ed. John Hayward (1930), p. lxi; George McFadden, *Dryden the Public Writer, 1660–1685* (1978), p. 172; *Sir Politick Would-Be*, ed. Finch and Joliat, pp. 8–9; D. C. Potts, rev. in *French Studies*, XXXIII (1979), 443–444.

[20] *Works*, IX, 8:3–5; Ward, *Letters*, p. 86.

strongly suggests that heretofore they had not met, for Dryden would certainly have supplied Saint-Evremond with some of the "other Idea's." If indeed they never met, one fair inference could be that they had never wished to meet.

Finally, the form of Dryden's commentary on Saint-Evremond may contain clues to Dryden's view of him. In his last paragraph it is clear from the way his entire exposition turns finally on the two words "true Character" that he has done his assignment in the form that was presumably requested of him, but that he has accepted and used the character as a kind of intellectual balancing act.

The development of the character into one of the most vigorous popular literary forms in the seventeenth century has been well documented.[21] Although not as frequently as other social types, writers were on occasion the subject of characters. So it is with *A Character of the True Blue Protestant Poet: or, the Pretended Author of the Character of a Popish Successor* (1682), which defines its subject as a despicable coward. To elaborate that definition, various elements are juxtaposed: background information, revelatory incidents, evaluative comment, a focusing metaphor, and a vituperative ironic tone throughout. Occasionally, rather than the writer, the writing will be the focus of a character, as in Cleveland's *The Character Of A London-Diurnall*, which defines the quality of diurnal writing by reductive metaphors ("A Diurnal is a punie Chronicle, scarce pin-feather'd with the wings of time") and a generally disapproving tone.[22]

Within this extension of character writing to a writer and his works, Dryden had shown, early in *Of Dramatick Poesie* and later elsewhere, what entered his mind as constituents for his own "Character of [an] Authour,"[23] first Ben Jonson. He has a leading idea about Jonson: "the most learned and judicious Writer which any Theater ever had." Dryden elaborates that idea with information, example, analysis, comparison, and metaphor: "He invades Authours like a Monarch, and what would be theft in other Poets, is onely victory in him."[24] Dryden similarly elsewhere treated writers and works in embryonic characters. In the *Discourse of Satire* he applies the term "character" by allusion to Jonson's verses on Shakespeare prefixed to the first folio and by panegyric to Dorset, to his "Person" and his "Writings."

---

21 For studies of the character and its permutations, see Anna Janney De-Armond, "Some Aspects of Character-Writing in the Period of the Restoration," *Delaware Notes*, 16th ser. (1943), 55–89; Benjamin Boyce, *The Theophrastan Character in England to 1642* (1947); Benjamin Boyce, *The Polemic Character 1640–1661: A Chapter in English Literary History* (1955); David Nichol Smith, *Characters from the Histories & Memoirs of the Seventeenth Century* (1920); and Mark Van Doren, *John Dryden: A Study of His Poetry* (3d ed., 1946), pp. 149–169, where a brief account of the character is followed by a survey of Dryden's use of the form in his poetry, translations, and post-Revolution plays. See also Gerald P. Tyson, "Dryden's Dramatic Essay," *Ariel*, 4 (1973), 72–86; and Paul J. Korshin, "Probability and Character in the Eighteenth Century," in *Probability, Time, and Space in Eighteenth-Century Literature*, ed. Paula R. Backscheider (1979), pp. 63–77.
22 *The Character of a London-Diurnall* (1647), sig. A2.
23 *Works*, XVII, 55:11–12.
24 *Works*, XVII, 57:10–58:16.

The passage shows the impress of the well-traveled paths of argument and the intellectual anatomy of the character.[25]

The two ends of the character are to define the thing under consideration and to show the aptness of the definition. To the Person of Honour these two ends were simply served: excellence defines Saint-Evremond; and principally a straightforward catalogue of excellences demonstrates the definition. For Dryden, who from all appearances had a ticklish task, an inviting delineation of a popular critic about whom he had somewhat more than mild reservations, the job was not so easy. But the character helped him out, especially in suggesting the way to convey his view of Saint-Evremond and his work. Its flexibility allowed him to maneuver. He could place, however he chose, varying constructs of praise, reproof, courtesy, ambiguity, allusion, example, enigma. He could also rely on the Person of Honour's unqualified praise to temper the force of his own reservations, and he could end with ambiguity. After all, not only have Dryden's "contracted ... Thoughts" fallen "short of the true Character of *Monsieur St. Evremont* and his Writings," but the translator of Saint-Evremond's essays has also, he conceded, failed to "come up to the Original." We are left with a meager testimonial to an intellect whose actual vigor is occasionally asserted, never demonstrated, and perhaps questioned.

P. 8, ll. 22–31 *Yet the Example . . . against it.* Bouhours in *Pensées Ingénieuses Des Anciens Et Des Modernes* (Lyon, 1693; 1st ed., 1689) cites Saint-Evremond four times (pp. 4, 58 [without naming him], 109, 454). He gives Dryden the hint for the successful test of Saint-Evremond's merit—its survival through disgrace and disfavor in France—when he points out that Saint-Evremond is the exception to his policy in *Pensées Ingénieuses* not to name living authors ("Avertissement," sigs. ã5v–ã6): "Je ne nomme point les Auteurs vivans hors un seul, qui étant disgracié & hors du Royaume depuis plusieurs années, peut en quelque sorte être compté parmi les morts; quoyque les nouvelles choses que nous voyons de lui tous les jours, nous répondent bien qu'il vit encore, & ne nous laissent pas même croire qu'il ait vieilli." For further discussion of Bouhours, see *Works*, XVIII, 443–446; XIX, 472–473, 483–490.

8:23–26 *Had not Monsieur . . . Banishment.* Charles de Marquetel de Saint-Denis-le-Guast, seigneur de Saint-Evremond (1613 or 1614–1703) rose to high position in the army, being much favored by the Prince of Condé, entrusted to discuss details of the siege of Dunkirk with Cardinal Mazarin and attached to the peace delegation that was assigned to draw up the Treaty of the Pyrenees (see Des Maizeaux, III, xxi, xxiv. For evaluation of Des Maizeaux and his collaborator Silvestre as sources for Saint-Evremond's life, see Ternois, I, viii–xi, xlvi–lxvii; for mixed reactions, see J. H. Broome,

25 *Works*, IV, 6:10–7:25. See also preface to *Sylvæ* (1685), *Works*, III, 5:31, 6:17, 7:17–18 and 34, 16:27; *Discourse of Satire* (1693), *Works*, IV, 77:34; dedication of *Examen Poeticum* (1693), *Works*, IV, 370:10. For another contemporary use of "Character" applied to a writer's works, see Thomas Sprat, *An Account of the Life and Writings of Mr. Abraham Cowley: Written to Mr. M. Clifford*, in Spingarn, II, 128 and 146, where he refers to his entire effort as "a Character of Mr. Cowley."

"Pierre Desmaizeaux, Journaliste," *Revue de Littérature Comparée* [1955], pp. 184, 185, 195, 204; George Gordon, "St. Evremond," in *The Lives of Authors* [1950], p. 120. For details of the collaboration of Des Maizeaux and Silvestre, see Des Maizeaux, III, x–xiv. For Saint-Evremond's birthdate, see René Ternois, "Saint-Evremond: Gentilhomme normand," *Annales de Normandie*, X [October 1960], 235.) In the very involved negotiations between France and Spain over the Treaty of the Pyrenees, Saint-Evremond saw through Cardinal Mazarin and Don Luis de Haro, each of whom wanted peace but for different reasons. In a famous letter of 1659 to the Marquis de Créqui, he unmasked Mazarin the negotiator with ingenious irony (cf. Des Maizeaux, I, xxii–xxxv; III, xxiv). When it came to light, this letter soon blew up his life in France (*ibid.*, III, xxv–xxvii). With it in 1661 Le Tellier and Colbert thoroughly disgraced him in the eyes of Louis XIV (*ibid.*, III, xxvii; I, xxxvii). Fearing the Bastille, Saint-Evremond left France in 1661 and, after staying briefly in the Low Countries, arrived in England the following year.

8:32–9:4 *but also . . . Petronius*. Cf. Dryden's earlier remark: Saint-Evremond "has well observ'd [that Seneca's Latin] has nothing in it of the purity, and elegance of *Augustus* his times"; thereafter Dryden follows Saint-Evremond's lead to Petronius, who found Seneca and "his imitators" incompetent and insincere (see *Works*, XVII, 286:18–30, and notes).

9:6–8 *our Author . . . Reason*. According to Saint-Evremond (p. 337), Epicurus regarded ideal pleasure not as, say, single gratification of the senses or of the intellect, but as varying with time and place: "I'm of Opinion, That Epicurus was a very wise Philosopher, who, according to the time and occasions, loved Pleasure in Repose, or Pleasure in Motion." Further, Epicurus, in Saint-Evremond's explanation of his morality, looked upon ideal pleasure not as immediate gratification indifferent to painful precedent act or thought or to painful consequences, but as continuous long-range satisfaction (*ibid.*, pp. 340–341): "if he loved the Enjoyment of [Leontium and Ternissa] as a voluptuous Person, he managed himself as a prudent Man; and being indulgent to the Motions of Nature, contrary to Efforts, not always reckoning Chastity for a Vertue, always accounting Luxury a Vice, he would have Sobriety to be a Dispensation of the Appetite, and that the Feasts which were made, should never hurt those that were to be."

9:8–9 *I am a Religious Admirer of Virgil*. Admiration for Virgil runs through Dryden's works (see the discussion in *Works*, V, 849–853).

9:9–10 *I cou'd wish . . . Nakedness*. See Genesis 9:20–27.

9:10–11 *we must confess . . . Hero's*. See the attack by Saint-Evremond (pp. 174–188) on Virgil's characterization of Aeneas in "Reflections Upon The French Translators," written originally in 1669 (Ternois, III, 96–98) and triggered by Segrais' argument supporting Virgil's characterization in *Traduction de L'Eneïde de Virgile* (Paris, 1668), I, 35–45. Saint-Evremond saw "little merit [in] the good Æneas," whom Virgil rendered contemptible rather than valorous: "as Italy was promised to this Trojan by the Gods, 'tis with Reason, that Virgil has given him a great Compliance to their Wills; but when he describes him to us so devout, he ought to attribute to him a Devotion full of Confidence, which agrees with the Constitution of Heroes, not a scrupulous Sentiment of Religion, which never subsists with a true Valour. . . . [Ought] the Son of Venus, assured by Jupiter, of his Prosperity, and future Glory, to have Piety only to fear Danger, and to distrust the Success of every Undertaking? . . . I know how much the intervention of the Gods is necessary to an Epick Poem: but that doth not hinder, that one ought to leave more things to the Valour of the Heroe; for if the Heroe is too confident, who in contempt of the Gods, will found all upon himself; the God is too favourable, who, to perform all, quite takes off from the Merit of the Heroe" (pp. 179, 180, 184). See also notes to 10: 23–25, 10:25.

9:14–16 *Nay more . . . in his Defence.* See *Iliad,* V, 297–342.

9:20–28 *Since therefore . . . Augustus Cæsar.* Dryden's view of Aeneas, built on piety and designed to celebrate Augustus, is sharpened in the dedication of *Aeneis* (1697). There, expressly using Segrais' conception of Aeneas rather than Saint-Evremond's, he carries the argument about piety versus valor a step further than here by subsuming the latter under the former: "What follows is Translated literally from *Segrais.* . . . A Man may be very Valiant, and yet Impious and Vicious. But the same cannot be said of Piety; which excludes all ill Qualities, and comprehends even Valour it self, with all other Qualities which are good" (*Works,* V, 288:11–12, 28–31; cf. Segrais, *Traduction de L'Eneïde,* I, 37). For Dryden's then indebtedness to Segrais, his elaborated sense of correspondences between Aeneas and Augustus, and his view of the significance of piety, see *Works,* V, 281:11–288:37; see also *A Parallel betwixt Painting and Poetry* (49:14–50:25 above), where his completed argument of the 1697 dedication is essentially in place.

9:23–24 *'Tis true . . . the former.* Saint-Evremond (p. 187) accumulates examples of valor in such Homeric heroes as Achilles, Ajax, and Diomedes.

9:24–26 *it intitled . . . undertakings.* Cf. Saint-Evremond (p. 179), arguing that valor appealed to the gods, and Dryden, arguing in the dedication of the *Aeneis* (*Works,* V, 288:13–21) for piety as a comprehensive virtue in Aeneas.

9:27–29 *nearer . . . Relations.* Augustus' desire to be remembered for an almost preternatural piety is well known (see, e.g., *Res Gestae Divi Augusti: The Achievements of the Divine Augustus,* ed. P. A. Brunt and J. M. Moore [1967], pp. 27–29). Dryden could have seen this wish in a life of Augustus contained in Sir Thomas North, *The Lives of the Noble Grecians & Romans* (1676), p. 972, one of his sources for *The Life of Plutarch* (*Works,* XVII, 432–433 and nn. 14–17). In Dryden's translation of the *Aeneid* (I, 521–524), Aeneas identifies himself as "Good," as acting with "pious Care" (*Works,* V, 360).

9:27–28 *his Patron Augustus Cæsar.* Augustus himself had grown to know and encourage Virgil. Dryden and his times knew Virgil to be "one of [Augustus'] most familiar friends" (North, p. 975); see also Suetonius' life of Virgil.

9:29–32 *that very . . . Antony.* See, e.g., Suetonius, *Augustus,* X, XIII, XV, XVII.

9:30–31 *his Uncle Julius.* I.e., his great-uncle, Julius Caesar. Augustus was reared by his mother, who was the niece of Julius Caesar.

9:32–33 *As for Personal . . . pushing.* Dryden's low opinion of Augustus' valor accords with that in historians whom he knew well (e.g., Suetonius, *Augustus,* XX, and Plutarch, *Antony,* XXII). See also the life of Augustus

by S. G. S. included by North in his translation of Plutarch: "As for . . .
exercises, [Augustus] left Arms and Horses immediately after the Civill
Wars: for he was never any great Souldier" (p. 960). See also *All for Love*,
II, i, 112–122 and notes (*Works*, XIII, 43, 420–421). Instances of Augustus'
courage are not unknown to twentieth-century inquiry (see Bernard M.
Allen, *Augustus Caesar* [1937], pp. 49–50, 106–107).

10:5 *Agrippa*. Marcus Vipsanius Agrippa (63–12 B.C.), one of Augustus'
most devoted friends, won for him all the crucial wars that secured and
consolidated his reign. Dio Cassius, whom Dryden had studied (along with
Plutarch and Appian) to draw "the character of *Antony* as favourably as
[those historians] wou'd give me leave" (*Works*, XIII, 10:14–16), stresses
the point that Agrippa "devoted all the . . . valour he himself possessed to
the highest interests of Augustus" (Loeb trans.: *Roman History*, LIV, 29, 2).

10:6–7 *to make . . . a Cloud*. I.e., as the wounded Aeneas escaped death
at the hands of the Greeks when he fell from the wounded Aphrodite's
arms, only to be taken up by Phoebus Apollo, who concealed him in a dark
cloud. See *Iliad*, V, 343–345.

10:8–13 *Bossu . . . Gods*. See René Le Bossu, *Traité du Poëme Epique*
(Paris, 1675), pp. 66–67, 69–71.

10:8–9 *the Roman . . . Monarchy*. Dryden (and Le Bossu) have in mind
Augustus' position in the Roman Empire between 29 and 19 B.C., when
Virgil was working on the *Aeneid*. To Dryden and contemporary readers,
the defeat of Antony at Actium in 31 B.C. signaled "the beginning of the
Monarchy of Caesar" (North, p. 965).

10:18–22 *Quicquid . . . prior*. See *Aeneid*, XI, 288–292 (Loeb trans.: "In
all our tarrying before the walls of stubborn Troy, it was by the hand of
Hector and Aeneas that the Greeks' victory was halted and withdrew its
advent till the tenth year. Both were renowned for courage, both eminent
in arms; Aeneas was first in piety"); cf. Dryden's *Aeneis*, XI, 443–448 (*Works*,
VI, 736).

10:23–25 *As for . . . Tempest*. See Saint-Evremond, p. 180.

10:25 *Extemplo . . . membra*. See *Aeneid*, I, 92 (Loeb trans.: "Straightway
Aeneas' limbs weaken with chilling dread"); see also Dryden's translation,
I, 135 (*Works*, V, 347).

11:5 *His Examination . . . Alexandre*. See "A Discourse Upon the Great
Alexander," Saint-Evremond, pp. 216–232.

11:7 *his Observations . . . Theatre*. Saint-Evremond commented on
English drama in three pieces: "Sur Les Tragédies," "De La Comedie
Angloise," and "A Messieurs de***," which is part of "Défense de Quelques
Pièces de M. Corneille," written respectively in 1668 or 1669 (Ternois, III,
21), 1666–1667 (Ternois, III, 55), and 1677 (Ternois, IV, 428). These items
are not included in the volume that Dryden was introducing, but he could
have seen translations of the first two in *Mixt Essays* (1685); the third did
not appear in known print until 1705 (the edition followed by Ternois,
IV, 423).

11:8 *had he . . . Eyes*. Saint-Evremond in fact claimed to have been inside
the English theatre, however briefly. See "Sur Les Opéra," written about
1669–1670 (Ternois, III, 139): "J'ai vû des Comédies en Angleterre où il y
avoit beaucoup de Musique; mais pour en parler discretement, je n'ai pû
m'accoûtumer au chant des Anglois. Je suis venu trop tard en leur Pays pour

pouvoir prendre un goût si different de tout autre" (*ibid.*, III, 158). But a charge like Dryden's had on another occasion been made: attributed to Armand Jean du Plessis, Duc de Richelieu, cited by John Hayward, ed., *The Letters of Saint Evremond* (1930), p. lxi, it accused Saint-Evremond of "discussing the opera which he ha[d] never seen, and the English and Italian Comedy without knowing either English or Italian."

11:9–10 *conversing . . . Court.* After 1675 Saint-Evremond hovered about the household of Hortense Mancini, Duchess of Mazarin, for twenty-five years (see Hester W. Chapman, *Privileged Persons: Four Seventeenth-Century Studies* [1966], pp. 227–228, 230–243). In this court enclave Saint-Evremond, his best friend, Lord D'Aubigny, and the Duke of Buckingham "were," if we can credit Des Maizeaux (I, xl), "together almost every day, and their conversation was often upon Theatrical performances."

11:10–12 *he has . . . home.* Presumably because Saint-Evremond linked Shadwell's *Epsom-Wells* with Jonson's *Bartholomew Fair* as good examples of English comedy (Des Maizeaux, II, 171).

11:12–14 *Had his . . . Subject.* A year after the *Character* (c. November 1693; see *Works,* IV, 742), Dryden in *To my Dear Friend Mr. Congreve* showed whom he regarded as the great English playwrights: Fletcher, Jonson, Etherege, Southerne, Wycherley, Shakespeare, and Congreve.

11:21 *the Translator.* The *Stationers' Register* (III, 398) attributes the translation to "F. M. Gent.," possibly meaning Francis Manning. Malone (III, 65) asserts, without giving grounds, that "Dr. [Knightly] Chetwood . . . was doubtless the translator." Des Maizeaux names none but lists the translators of the second volume, which appeared in 1694, as "Dr. DRAKE, Mr. BROWN, Mr. SAVAGE, Mr. MANNING [most likely James Drake (1667–1707), Thomas Brown (1663–1704), John Savage (1673–1747), and Francis Manning (fl. 1700)], and some others, who did not think fit to let their Names be known" (I, 5).

The Character of Polybius and His Writings

At least as early as April of 1692, a very busy year for him, Dryden was jotting down minor corrections on a manuscript of Sir Henry Sheeres's English translation of Polybius.[1] Peter Motteux, favored by Dryden to see it, optimistically announced that before long it would be in press.[2] In his preface to *Cleomenes,* performed in April 1692[3] and advertised in the *London Gazette* of 2–5 May 1692, Dryden alluded to Polybius, who "*is . . . made* English, *and will shortly be publish'd for the Common Benefit.*"[4] In September 1692 the world was told that the Sheeres Polybius was in press.[5] In October 1692, happily promising the imminent appearance of the English Polybius, Peter Motteux announced that Dryden "doth the

---

1 See 13:18–21 above.
2 *Gentleman's Journal* (April 1692), p. 22.
3 Van Lennep, pp. 407–408.
4 *Cleomenes* (1692, sig. a; S-S, VIII, 226).
5 *Gentleman's Journal* (September 1692), p. 16.

Character of Polybius."[6] Finally, the first edition of *The History of Polybius . . . Translated by Sir H. S. To which is added, a Character of Polybius and His Writings: By Mr. Dryden* appeared in 1693, probably in January.[7]

Just when Dryden put together *The Character of Polybius and His Writings*, maybe rapidly in between other big projects, is conjectural. Until March 1692 he was fashioning an exacting poem, *Eleonora*.[8] *Cleomenes*, the licensing process of which dragged on from October 1691 until mid-April 1692 because of suspected seditious or insulting parallels, held his mind until May.[9] The translation of Juvenal and Persius with the lengthy *Discourse of Satire* was not published until fall 1692, probably October.[10] Perhaps, if not in spring and summer, then between late August and November (depending on when the text was ready for licensing), Dryden wrote his *Character*, probably with little time for review. Unsurprisingly, he had the Sheeres manuscript around for many months.[11]

Although Sheeres's translation of Polybius occasioned Dryden's *Character of Polybius and His Writings*, the connections elude us. Whether Sheeres requested the essay remains uncertain; extolling Polybius' life and writings in his preface, Sheeres breaks off to say, "But I should intrench on the Province of a much abler Undertaker, should I further prosecute this Subject; The character of Polybius being as I am told undertaken by one who of all others is best able to do him justice."[12] Dryden seems similarly uninformed about the contents of Sheeres's preface: "He, I suppose, will acquaint you with his own purpose in the Preface, which I hear he intends to prefix before *Polybius*" (33:19–21).

We can discern the genesis of Sheeres's translation of Polybius. He did it, as he says, "to comply with the injunctions of a Great Man, and a Friend, whose commands to me while he liv'd were Sacred, as his Memory must be now he is remov'd from among us."[13] Sheeres names no one, but evidence, including avoidance of identification, points to George Legge, first Baron of Dartmouth (1648–1691). He had served James when Duke of York and king, most recently commanding the fleet sent in 1688 to intercept the mission of William of Orange. Though unfailingly loyal to James II during his last days as king, Dartmouth had reproved him for unconstitutional behavior. But the new regime, unimpressed, deprived Dartmouth of his command on 10 January 1689, charged him with treason, accusing him, wrongly as evidence shows, of scheming to promote a French invasion of England, and committed him to the Tower, where, disgraced, suspected,

---

6 *Ibid.* (October 1692), p. 20.

7 *Ibid.* (January 1692), p. 27, refers to the favorable reception of the work. The imprimatur is dated 25 November 1692.

8 See *Works*, III, 491–495; Ward, *Life*, pp. 252–253.

9 Ward, *Life*, pp. 253–255 and n. 9.

10 Dryden dated the *Discourse* 18 August 1692 (*Works*, IV, 90).

11 Sheeres, "The Preface Of The Translator," I, sig. a3*v*, remarked that the translation, "rather a Diversion than a Task, help[ed] me to while away a few long Winter Hours," possibly in 1691–92. On Sir Henry Sheeres, see note to 13:1; *The Life of Lucian*, 223:14–20; *Works*, XV, 421; and Dryden's note to his translation of Virgil's fourth Georgic in *Works*, VI, 815:7–17.

12 Sheeres, "Preface," I, sig. a7.

13 *Ibid.*, I, sig. a1*v*.

and tortured by the conviction of his innocence, he died on 25 October 1691.[14] Sheeres had associated closely with Dartmouth since at least 1683 in Tangier, through the Monmouth uprising, and during the 1688–89 revolution, when he counseled his superior. Like Dartmouth, Sheeres had been imprisoned (twice) after 1688–89 as a Jacobite even though, like Dartmouth, he had deplored James's unconstitutional acts.[15] Unsurprisingly, Sheeres leaves his hero unnamed in the atmosphere of the early 1690s.

However Dryden became author of the *Character*, he was short on time and materials. "I want leisure," he remarks when limiting his examples (30:3), and he confesses to "the weakness of my own Performance" (14:27), which he bolsters with the "helps I ingenuously profess to have receiv'd from" sources (14:24–25).

⚬∽⚭∽⚬

About two-thirds of *The Character of Polybius and His Writings* derive from Isaac Casaubon's edition of Polybius with some small accessions from Julien Pichon's edition of Tacitus.[16] The remaining third of the *Character* is original with Dryden. Although the derivative part predominates and the nonderivative is only intermittent, the entire work is a coherent, original flow of mind, for a number of reasons.

First, the material translated by Dryden from sources frequently displays his own stylistic preferences. Sometimes he follows Casaubon detail for detail, but he will freely turn, for example, exclamatory Latin into understated English: *Cicero, Strabo, Josephus, Plutarchus, Deus bone, qui quantique viri!* becomes "*Cicero, Strabo, Josephus,* and *Plutarch;* and in what rank of Writers they are plac'd, none of the Learned need to be inform'd."[17] Elsewhere, Dryden attaches a dependent clause to qualify Casaubon's laudatory tone, so that *T. Livius, ille Romanæ longe princeps historiæ* becomes "*Livy,* commonly esteem'd the Prince of the *Roman* History. . . . Tho the *Latin* Historian is not to be excus'd, for not mentioning the man to whom he had been so much oblig'd."[18] Sometimes Dryden modifies Casaubon to change tone, replacing, for example, lamentation with mathematics: *Nunc, proh dolor! solos quinque primos libros, quales auctor reliquerat habemus: cætera varia manu interpolata ad nos pervenerunt*[19] becomes "and amongst the rest, some of these remaining fragments of Polybius [were rescued after the fall of Constantinople]: the body of this History, as he left it finish'd,

---

14 *Ibid.,* sigs. a1v–a2v; HMC, *Dartmouth,* I, 275, 276, 289, 290; Luttrell, II, 298.

15 HMC, *Dartmouth,* I, 102, 112–114, 126, 128, 236; III, 133, 134; Sheeres, I, sigs. a1v–a2, a3v–a4.

16 Casaubon's edition of Polybius was first published at Paris, 1609, and subsequently at Frankfurt, 1610 and 1619. We use the edition of Casaubon's Polybius by Jakob Gronovius (Amsterdam, 1670). The Abbé Pichon published the Delphin Tacitus at Paris, 1682–1687. Dryden drew material for the *Character of Polybius* from Casaubon's dedication and Pichon's preface. Although Dryden chose Casaubon as his principal source, he used only about a third of that writer's material.

17 Casaubon, p. 24; 18:1–2 above.

18 Casaubon, p. 24; 18:3–6 above.

19 Casaubon, p. 49. (What a shame, alas, it is that now we have only the first five books intact as the author left them, whereas the rest has come down to us interpolated by various hands.)

was consisting of forty Books, of which the eighth part is only remaining to us, entire." [20] On another occasion Dryden announces that "I will select but some few instances, because I want leisure to expatiate on many"; but he is in fact "selecting" from Casaubon's selection.[21] Sometimes he borrows from both Pichon and Casaubon, as when he compares Tacitus and Polybius in order to illustrate the character of Polybius and his writings. Indeed, nothing better displays Dryden's transmuting of his sources according to his lights than his correction of Casaubon's criticism, not of Polybius, but of Tacitus. Thus, Dryden summons evidence to redress Casaubon's "usual partiality," but he knows just when to call a digression a digression to keep the central matter clear: "it is not my business to defend *Tacitus;* neither dare I decide the preference betwixt him and our *Polybius.*" [22]

Second, the original matter, interspersed among the derivative, contains the issues that most exercised Dryden, and to sample just three of some twenty instances of original comment reveals the quality of his thought. Two brisk rebukes to Livy for appropriating Polybius without credit "in whole Books" and for filling his accounts with superstitions[23] show that Dryden believed historical study must be a discipline for instructive or corrective truth. His admiration for Polybius' meticulous explanation of causes[24] suggested to him that progress toward the meaning of history was possible. His uncompromising application to Polybius of Polybius' own criterion of uncompromising truth[25] reveals his readiness to turn this principle to the behavior and assumptions of anyone, including himself.

Third, the character, very familiar to seventeenth-century readers, directed their understanding of Polybius and his work. With his title, *The Character of Polybius and His Writings,* Dryden had from the start prepared them to follow his argument. As in his essay on Saint-Evremond, the character—simultaneously analytic and narrative—suggested detail and shaped thought.[26] Dryden early gives the central conception of this character of a writer and his writings. Polybius is the most instructive historian, disciplined by liberal studies[27] and by experience with political figures, local and world; his writings are "plain and unaffected," but comprehend the fifty-three-year rise of the Roman Empire and interrelated actions.[28] Beginning at " 'Tis now time to enter into the particular Praises of *Polybius,* which I have given you before in gross" (18:24–25), Dryden particularizes the central conception of Polybius and his writings according to the conventions of the character. Polybius' political skill, for example, is depicted by discursive modes: examples, definition, narrative, reiteration, and transition. Polybius' central teaching that "Truth is the foundation of all Knowl-

[20] 15:3–6 above.

[21] 30:2–3 above; Casaubon, pp. 40–41.

[22] See 34:24–35:26 above and notes.

[23] See 18:3–7 above and note, 28:3–7 above, and note to 28:1–6.

[24] See 29:34–30:3 above and note.

[25] See 31:23–32:13 above and notes.

[26] For relevant history of the character, Dryden's use of it in criticizing writers and their writing, and its operation in his *Character of Saint-Evremond,* see pp. 312–313 above.

[27] See 13:14–15, 16:13–19 above.

[28] See 13:17, 15:16–31 above.

edge, and the cement of all Societies" (23:7–9) is implanted in the *Character* by allusion, catalogue, and citation. Dryden ends the character with a conventional device, comparison.[29] Also in this conclusion he exploits a structural potential of the character—self-revelation: Polybius displays himself and his work through his own description of the consummate historian.[30]

༺◦ⵣ◦༻

Although scanning his sources with precise purpose, Dryden also swept through them with risky haste. Truth suffers twice. Dryden mistook the Constantine in Casaubon for Constantine the Great (*c.* 274–337), thinking him an admirer of Polybius and a preserver of some of his writings.[31] He did not realize that Constantine Porphyrogenitus (*c.* 905–959) was meant,[32] because the name appears only as Constantine in material through which Dryden sifted for the *Character,* although the full name is given in passages not used. Then, too, each reference to "Aratus" in the *Character* is somewhat inaccurate, failing to distinguish properly among the three men of that name who are mentioned by Polybius.[33] Although Polybius makes the distinctions only sparingly, Dryden himself contributed to the confusion, partly by an inexact translation of one source and partly, it may be, by faulty memory or undue haste.

Haste in Dryden's *Character* is evident, but so, too, is the depth of his thought. First, as one of two works on historians,[34] it gives Dryden's ideas about history as a form of writing and as a view of human destiny. On history as writing he remarks, for one thing, on the essential qualifications of the historian. The historian has to acquire comprehensive knowledge; and he can do so through the study of the arts, science, philosophy, politics, the arts of war and peace as well as through firsthand acquaintance with major figures, as exemplified by Polybius' friendship with Scipio Africanus during the demolition of Carthage.[35] Further, in order to determine the causes of events so as to find truth, historical method involves procedures all demonstrated by Polybius: participation in events, consultation with eyewitnesses, the study of documents, and the cross-checking of histories of eras beyond the historian's lifetime.[36] The historian, moreover, cannot compromise truth in the use of sources and, when "settl'd certainty" is unattainable, has to rely on "the methods at least of probability."[37] Both determining and resulting from these qualifications and this method is the design of historical writing: history is a thesis grasped in accumulated and then arranged detail, like Polybius' accounting for the fifty-three-year rise

---

29 See 34:24–35:26 above.
30 See 33:22–34:7 above.
31 See 15:9–15, 16:3, 18:17–19, 18:22, 33:14–16 above. Cf. Casaubon, pp. 15, 17, 18, 24, 49.
32 See note to 15:6–15.
33 See 16:21–22, 24:31–26:8, 32:21 above, and notes.
34 For Dryden's view of history in his *Life of Plutarch* (1683), see *Works,* XVII, 435–440. See also, concerning Dryden, history, and translation, *Works,* XVIII, 428–434.
35 See 16:15–18, 16:22–24 above.
36 See 23:7–9, 15:30–31, 23:31–24:6, 23:27–31 above.
37 See 24:27–30, 29:9–10 above.

of Rome to world dominance.[38] Finally, Dryden reiterates the conventional uses of history: it provides political instruction for kings, ministers of state, and youthful understudies; and it also instructs all who wish a safe and beneficent world.[39]

Concerning history as a view of human destiny, some conceptions always in Dryden are here as well. He implicitly locates the origin of history in the mind: Scipio, "sent to demolish *Carthage*," has a conception of what he must do, and Polybius, his counselor, helps him plan.[40] Dryden saw talented, determined figures, like the Scipios, at the center of affairs as a major force shaping history.[41] The revolution of 1688, which displaced Dryden's favored powerful men, did not weaken this view, though it made him desire the powerful figure who, rather than directing events by action, might affect or transform them through vision: the "one vertuous Man in a whole Nation . . . worth the buying; as one Diamond is worth the search, in a heap of Rubbish." [42] As to agents other than man affecting the course of history, Dryden, sympathetically following Polybius, dismisses chance, because "Providence" in the sense of "Prudence," or intelligent human foresight, renders it meaningless.[43] Dryden gave centrality to providence in the theological sense, as is evident when he refutes Casaubon's effort to kidnap Polybius for "us Christians, [who believe that] God administer'd all humane Actions and Affairs" and when he remarks that, although Polybius discredited his contemporaries' notions of the gods, he could not see what really constituted a divine force in history because he lacked Revelation.[44] Elsewhere, for Dryden, providence is secondary; here it predominates as an enclosing conception,[45] but not an excluding one. For together with a providential view of history, Dryden allows some place to the Polybian view of history as an inexorable cycle.[46] Three forms of government, each fol-

---

[38] See 30:3–8, 15:16–29 above.

[39] See 22:33–23:1, 19:7–8, 21:19–20 above. See *Works*, XVII, 439, and nn. 31 and 32.

[40] See 20:33–35 above. Dryden's was a view held widely in the sixteenth and seventeenth centuries. Thus, Sir Thomas More, according to Ascham, scanned "the inward disposition of the mind" (*The Whole Works of Roger Ascham*, ed. J. A. Giles [1864], III, 6); Bodin saw the source of history mainly in "the will of mankind" (Jean Bodin, *Method for the Easy Comprehension of History*, trans. Beatrice Reynolds [1945], p. 17); and Bacon called "the wits of men" "the shops wherein all actions are forged" (*The Works of Francis Bacon*, ed. James Spedding, Robert Ellis, and Douglas Heath [1860], XI, 36). See also *The English Works of Thomas Hobbes*, ed. Sir William Molesworth (1839–1845), III, 71; Clarendon, *History of the Rebellion*, ed. W. D. Macray (1888), I, 4.

[41] Cf. Lisideius' remark that "in the management of all affairs . . . some one will be superiour to the rest" (*Works*, XVII, 38:20–22).

[42] 22:1–3 above.

[43] See notes to 30:23, 31:1.

[44] See 31:5–6, 31:17–21 above.

[45] See *Works*, XVII, 436.

[46] Generally in the extant five books of Polybius, but particularly in the fragmentary sixth. Sheeres did not translate the sixth book for the 1693 edition. But Dryden need not have gained his knowledge of Polybius there; as he points out in the *Character* (18:27–19:4), he knew the available Polybius from the age of ten on. See also 13:9–10 and note, and note to 18:27–28.

lowed by its corruption, succeeded one another: monarchy, the original instinctual form, then its corruption, tyranny; aristocracy, then oligarchy; democracy, then mob rule; and then repetition of the cycle. Awareness of this cycle, or anacyclosis, as Polybius called it, permits one to identify the current condition of a state and to predict the form into which it will eventually evolve, although not the precise moment at which the evolution will be complete.[47] Polybius predicted the eventual, because inevitable, decline of Rome but implied that it would be long delayed, and did so by dwelling on the achievment of Lycurgus. To slow the destructive cycle, Lycurgus instituted a mixed government for Sparta, which accordingly enjoyed a longer liberty than that of any other state. For Polybius, the Rome of his time has achieved the same thing pragmatically instead of by institution.[48]

Dryden's awareness of Polybius' theory is evident from allusions to the constitutions of Sparta and Rome and to the course followed by Rome "from a Common-wealth, to an absolute Monarchy."[49] He saw Scipio the Younger accelerate the cycle by channeling power into the Senate, then into his own hands, thereby drawing on "those fatal Consequences, which not only ruin'd the Republick, but also, in process of time, the Monarchy it self."[50]

◦◦◦

After citing Polybius' capacity to give readers an immediate sense of "the greatest Heroes, and most prudent Men of the greatest Age, in the *Roman* Common-wealth,"[51] Dryden "cannot hold from breaking out with *Montaign*, into this expression: *'Tis just, says he, for every honest man to be content with the Government, and Laws of his native Country, without endeavouring to alter or subvert them: but if I were to choose where I would have been born, it shou'd have been in a Commonwealth.*"[52] And at the end of his *Character of Polybius*, Dryden, adapting his source, finds Polybius "profitable, and instructive . . . to those who live in a Republick."[53] Such statements might suggest that Dryden had abandoned monarchy for commonwealth, especially since there is no doubting at all his admiration for Polybius. But Dryden nowhere recommends Polybius' depiction of the Roman republic as a model for England in the 1690s. Instead, he offers general propositions about government possibly applicable to contemporary England, and to see how Dryden's readers might have made such an application we need to recall one of the ways in which seventeenth-century men read and used history.

---

[47] VI, IX, 10–12.

[48] VI, X, 1–14.

[49] See 34:20–23, 31:28–29 above.

[50] 31:29–32:10 above. The view expressed by Dryden of Scipio's ultimately "fatal" effect on the Roman polity can still be found among the interpretations of modern scholars (see e.g. H. H. Scullard, "Scipio Aemilianus and Roman Politics," *Journal Of Roman Studies*, L (1960), 59–74; A. E. Astin, *Scipio Aemilianus* [1967], pp. 282–293).

[51] 34:11–12 above.

[52] 34:14–19 above.

[53] 35:20–23 above. See note to 35:21–23.

They preferred a discourse couched in terms of "examples," particular men, that is, and particular acts. These examples prompted moral and political generalizations, or "precepts." Together, precept and example allowed men who read correctly to regulate their own conduct and to apply one set of particulars from the past to the different particulars of the present by way of the general precept common to both. Twenty years before writing the *Character of Polybius* Dryden reiterated the commonplace by declaring that "the dead vertue animates the living . . . [because] the World is govern'd by precept and Example."[54] Dryden's readers, if they chose, could find exemplary the character of Polybius himself, a Greek historian who sought to understand the success of his Roman conquerors and who admired the mixed constitution of the Spartan and Roman republics. Dryden, moreover, supplied his readers with precepts.

Many of these precepts are lodged in a long passage where Dryden adapts Casaubon with considerable freedom.[55] First, a historian must present truth unconditionally. Polybius showed his subscription to the precept when he applied it to his father and when he found bad in good figures and good in bad ones; and Dryden endorsed the precept when he himself applied it twice to Polybius.[56] Second, "Truth," which "is the foundation of all Knowledge, and the cement of all Societies,"[57] must be the sole guide of princes. Supporting precepts follow: "tricking, [and] cunning" are unconscionable and disastrous in a government, whether it be a monarchy or commonwealth;[58] occasional supersession of the law by the governor is justifiable only on rare occasions, and only if sanctioned by the majority and essential to "Publick safety."[59] Third, Polybius' history is useful to those living in a commonwealth, whereas Tacitus' history is useful to those born under a monarchy.[60] Fourth, a monarch who rules to serve his own interest, who does not love his people, will be deserted at the first opportunity; at best he will be endured on an impersonal basis and will have it made clear to him "that Prerogatives are given, but Priviledges are inherent."[61]

Dryden's precepts could be applied to contemporary history as well by Whigs as by Tories. True, we lack evidence of contemporary reactions to Dryden's *Character of Polybius*. But it is not difficult to see that absolutist Stuarts and parliamentary Williamites could have read the precepts to one another. James II's Declaration of Indulgence and William III's re-

---

[54] *Works*, XI, 3:10–11. See also John M. Wallace, " 'Examples Are Best Precepts': Readers and Meanings in Seventeenth-Century Poetry," *Critical Inquiry*, I (1974), 273–290; *Works*, XVIII, 428–434.

[55] See 21:25–22:31 above.

[56] See 30:29–31:25, 32:10–12 above and note.

[57] 23:7–9 above.

[58] See 22:11–14 above. To compare Casaubon's commentary and Dryden's transformation, see 22:11–16 and note. Dryden has turned Casaubon's general *Politicis* into "Soveraigns" and "Commonwealths," terms designating the two types of government locked in mortal struggle in the Civil War and in continuing philosophical and political conflict in the Restoration.

[59] See 22:18–29 above.

[60] See 35:21–23 above.

[61] See 22:10–11 above.

sistance to a triennial act could have seemed justifiable or unconstitutional. Trickery and cunning could have been "King-craft"[62] in James or in William as they could have been "reason of State [not only] in Commonwealths"[63] but in the Glorious Revolution of 1688.

Dryden himself nowhere made any of these applications in the *Character of Polybius*. Nor is his unmistakable admiration for Polybius implicit endorsement of the Revolution of 1688 or necessarily a hint of softening toward the Whig establishment. No decisive evidence has come to light indicating that he had abandoned his Jacobite sympathies or that he had ceased to question William. His political position in the *Character of Polybius*, however, is not entirely elusive, for, although he makes no applications, he has altered a precept that he had enunciated in 1684. In the Postscript to *The History of the League*, Dryden had declared prerogative to be "inherent in" the king: he governs by law, and "what the Laws are silent in, I think I may conclude to be part of his Prerogative."[64] The king, for his part, "swears . . . to maintain the several Orders of Men under him, in their lawful priviledges," but, should he fail to do so, he is not answerable to his subjects.[65] Now, in the *Character of Polybius*, Dryden asserts that "Prerogatives are given, but Priviledges are inherent."[66] He did not concede to William III an inherent prerogative. The prerogative was now permitted or given, presumably by the nation's laws. However repugnant Dryden may have found the need even to give prerogative to William, he fell back on another precept he had consistently followed in his works from the poem on Cromwell to 1693. It was best to support settled government and order: " *'Tis just . . . for every honest man to be content with the Government, and Laws of his native Country, without endeavouring to alter or subvert them.*"[67]

What can one say finally about Dryden's *Character of Polybius and His Writings*? How much value has a work that confuses Constantine the Great with Constantine Porphyrogenitus through inattentiveness, contains more flawed sentences than one can confidently blame a printer for,[68] has not interested Polybius scholarship,[69] has drawn few and short remarks from Dryden commentators,[70] and without protest heretofore has been called "largely hack-work"?[71]

Because of Dryden's heavy dependence upon Casaubon, the *Character*

---

[62] 22:12 above.
[63] 22:12–13 above.
[64] *Works*, XVIII, 394:15–17.
[65] *Ibid.*, 393:15–21.
[66] 22:10–11 above.
[67] 34:15–17 above.
[68] See 17:27–28, 19:24, 20:35–21:6, 28:12 above.
[69] See note to 13:24–25.
[70] Significant topics have come up—history, boyhood reading, candor about sources, astrology, translation of Juvenal—but they have not inspired much inquiry. See Watson, II, 65; L. R. M. Strachan, "Dryden's 'Character of Polybius,' " *N&Q*, CXXIX (1914), 104; S-S, XVIII, 22; Alan Roper, *Dryden's Poetic Kingdoms* (1965), p. 29. One commentator, William Myers (*Dryden* [1973], p. 134) finds the work "alive with the tensions of political duty and natural wisdom under an unlawful government."
[71] Watson, II, 65.

lets us observe once more his skill as a translator. It comments flexibly and
dispassionately upon forms of government, a subject so often treated in
everyday politics with reductive partisanship. It contains major compon-
ents of his view of history, and it supplies an interesting adaptation and
extension of the seventeenth-century character. It exemplifies Dryden's
power, even when hurried, to instruct, by encouraging his countrymen—
whether exponents of monarchy or commonwealth, whether Jacobites or
Whigs—to apply Polybius' principle of disinterested scrutiny and thereby
to know the good and the bad in themselves.

P. 13, l. 1 *The worthy . . . Translation.* Sir Henry Sheeres (d. 1710).
Dryden's spelling was "Shere," but other forms, most of them ending in
"s," persisted in the period: Shear, Sheere, Sheers, Sheres, Shiers, Shires,
and Sheeres. For a sketch of his life, see headnote, pp. 318–319; 13:14–16
and notes; *Works*, XV, 421.

13:1–2 *who is . . . Friend.* Cf. Dryden's note on l. 27 of his translation of
Virgil's fourth Georgic (*Works*, VI, 815:7–17): "My most Ingenious Friend
Sir *Henry Shere. . . .*" In the *Life of Lucian* Dryden referred to Sheeres as
one of the "finer Spirits of the Age" (see 223:16 above). Sheeres may have
written the "Prologue, Sent to the Authour by an unknown hand" for
Don Sebastian (1690). The prologue was too unabashedly Jacobite to be
used. See *Works*, XV, 75–77, 420–421.

13:2–3 *for many Months together.* See headnote, pp. 317–318.

13:9–10 *'Tis true . . . English Dress.* Polybius had appeared in English,
not in one earlier translation, as Dryden thinks, but in two: that of Chris-
topher Watson in 1568 and of Edward Grimestone in 1633. Watson (II, 65,
n. 2) reasonably states that Dryden here "condemns" Grimestone's transla-
tion.

13:13–15 *that esteem . . . Historians.* See 17:31–18:1 and note.

13:24–25 *I doubt . . . Judgment.* See the *Gentleman's Journal* (January
1693), p. 27: "That part of Polybius's Works lately english'd, was so well
received, that a Person of Quality intends to oblige the World with a
Translation of the Embassies of that famous Historian." After Dryden's
times such enthusiasm for Sheeres's work was wanting; see Malone, III,
230n; S-S, XVIII, 21; Watson, II, 65, 66 n. 1; *The Histories of Polybius*,
ed. and trans. Evelyn S. Shuckburgh (1889), I, xii. Twentieth-century Poly-
bius scholars ignore it.

13:28 *who has . . . kinds.* Polybius had been adviser to Scipio the
Younger, fleet commander, geographer, and diplomat (20:27–21:3, 32:20–
24); Sheeres had been a military engineer, adviser to Lord Dartmouth,
diplomat with the Earl of Sandwich, and artillery strategist against Mon-
mouth.

13:28–14:1 *has Travell'd . . . History.* Both had been to Spain, Africa,
and the Mediterranean.

14:3–6 *perfectly . . . Country.* Sheeres applied his mathematics to build-
ing and demolishing a masterwork of engineering genius, the Mole at
Tangier (HMC, *Dartmouth*, I, 102). Recommending a successor to Sir
Jonas Moore, the mathematician and Surveyor-general of the Ordnance,
Pepys automatically had thought of Sir Henry Sheeres, for during the early

1680s Pepys had been fully aware of his "universality of knowledge in all useful learning, particularly mathematics, and of them those parts especially which relate to gunnery and fortifications" (*Letters and the Second Diary of Samuel Pepys,* ed. R. G. Howarth [1932], p. 145). Pepys continued to respect Sheeres's engineering genius (see Edwin Chappell, *The Tangier Papers of Samuel Pepys* [1935], index, *sub* Sheres, esp. p. 150).

14:28–15:3 *The taking . . . possess.* Casaubon (pp. 19–20) reminded Dryden of the fall of Constantinople on 29 May 1453 to Turkish forces led by Mohammed II.

14:29–31 *Pope Nicholas . . . in others.* For cues to Dryden's characterization here and at 16:7–13, see Casaubon, pp. 20, 60. Pope from 1447 to 1455, Nicholas V employed many people to copy and translate ancient Greek authors into Latin, leaving a library of 807 Latin and 353 Greek manuscripts (*New Catholic Encyclopedia*).

15:3–6 *amongst . . . entire.* See headnote, pp. 319–320 and note 19. The first five books of Polybius' *History* remain; books 6 through 40 are in fragments. For texts, see Pauly-Wissowa, XXI, 1572–1578. For the genesis and scope of Polybius' history, see F. W. Walbank, *Polybius* (1972), esp. chap. i.

15:6–15 *As for . . . with them.* Cues for Dryden are at Casaubon, pp. 24, 49. Dryden wrongly thought Constantine the Great was meant. Neither contemporaries of Constantine the Great (e.g., Eusebius Pamphili, Bishop of Caesarea, in *De Vita Constantini*) nor modern scholars (e.g., H. A. Drake, *In Praise of Constantine* [1976]) ever mention Polybius in connection with him. Constantine Porphyrogenitus, however, took to Polybius because of interests in diplomacy and politics (see Pauly-Wissowa, IV, 1038, John M. Moore, *The Manuscript Tradition of Polybius* [1965], pp. 127–129).

15:16–16:5 *Polybius . . . concerning it.* Dryden conflates details from Casaubon's preface and Sheeres's translation (see e.g., Casaubon, pp. 23, 36, 40, 46–47, 48–49, Sheeres, I, 2–5).

15:28–29 *three and fifty Years.* Polybius in fact deals with events from 264 to 146 B.C., although he indicates an intention to trace only the fifty-three-year rise of Rome to world supremacy between 220 and 168 B.C. (I, i, 5–6).

16:3–4 *It appears . . . already noted.* Malone (III, 238) notes that "Caesar Bryennius is supposed to have had a perfect copy of Polybius in the beginning of the twelfth century." On Constantine, see headnote, p. 321, and note to 15:6–15.

16:7–13 *the same Pope . . . them all.* See note to 14:29–31.

16:13–17:16 *This is . . . afforded.* Dryden follows Casaubon, pp. 21–22, omitting or adding a detail, generally condensing, and changing syntax.

16:15 *Institution.* Training, education (*OED*).

16:18–19 *his Education . . . Lycortas.* Extant sources are silent on Polybius' general education. Dryden's context suggests that he alludes to education in statecraft provided Polybius by his father. Dryden did not find the detail in Casaubon, though he might have inferred it from the fact that Lycortas was an important statesman. Modern scholarship makes such an inference (Walbank, *Polybius*, p. 7).

16:19–21 *Lycortas . . . Commonwealth.* Neither Casaubon nor extant sources say Lycortas resigned supreme power in Megalopolis. Dryden correctly places Lycortas among the leaders of the Achaean League, whereas

Casaubon (p.21) makes him the sole leader: *Reipublicæ Achæorum . . . Lycortas diu princeps præfuit.*

16:21-22 *under . . . Aratus.* Three Aratuses appear in Polybius' history. Aratus of Sicyon (271-213/2 B.C., according to F. W. Walbank, *Aratos of Sicyon* [1933], pp. 156-157, 174-175), an able statesman, spearheaded the Achaean League or Confederacy—or "Commonwealth," as Dryden calls it— its military operations and its negotiations, especially between 245 B.C. and his death, which Polybius attributed to poisoning by Philip of Macedon (Polybius, *Histories*, VIII, xii, 2). Polybius' history—mainly Books I, II, and IV—depict this Aratus. The second Aratus was son to the first. His dates are unknown, but events in his life are recorded by Polybius, especially in Books IV and V. Dead by at least 198 B.C. (see Livy, XXXII, xxi, 23), and probably earlier (see Walbank, *Aratos*, p. 157), according to Plutarch (*Aratus*, XLIX, 1; LIV, 1) and Livy (XXVII, xxxi, 8; XXXII, xxi, 24) he went mad upon learning that Philip of Macedon had seduced his wife. About 181 B.C., Lycortas, his son Polybius, and a third Aratus, alluded to as the son of Aratus of Sicyon (see Polybius, *Histories*, XXIV, vi, 3; XXIV, viii, 8), were appointed envoys for an aborted embassy to King Ptolemy. Modern scholars propose either that this third Aratus was son to the second and grandson to Aratus of Sicyon (Pauly-Wissowa, II, 391) or that he was an unspecified member of the Aratus clan (R. M. Errington, *Philopoemen* [1969], p. 7). Although Dryden lacked the dates known to modern scholarship, he had enough in Polybius, Livy, and Plutarch to see that Aratus the Sicyonian and his son were most likely dead when Lycortas helped guide the Achaean Confederacy and that they were certainly dead during Polybius' lifetime. See headnote, p. 321, and 24:31, 32:21, and notes.

16:22-24 *friendship . . . Counsellour.* Publius Cornelius Scipio Aemilianus Africanus Numantius, known as Scipio Africanus Minor or Scipio the Younger (185/4-129 B.C.). In 146 B.C., accompanied by Polybius, he oversaw the destruction of Carthage.

16:28-17:7 *This Authour . . . on him.* Dryden condenses Casaubon, pp. 21-22.

17:3-5 *a person . . . into Latin.* Niccolò Perotti (1492-1480). He is not identified in Casaubon's dedication, which Dryden follows, but in the prefatory "De Prioribus Polybii Interpretibus et Nova Hac Versione" ("Concerning Previous Translators of Polybius and This New Version"), immediately following the dedication on pp. 70-79. Perotti was probably brought to Pope Nicholas V's attention by Giovanni Tortelli, a papal secretary. By 1454 he had completed a Latin translation of the first five books of Polybius, published in 1472 in Rome, which was the standard until Casaubon's. See Revilo Pendleton Oliver, *Niccolò Perotti's Version of the Enchiridion of Epictetus* (1954), pp. 6, 9 and n. 40, 15 and n. 61, 137-166.

17:10-16 *neither did . . . Age afforded.* Perotti's contemporaries admired his Polybius, but subsequent scholars blamed and praised it (see Oliver, *Niccolò Perotti's Version*, p. 16).

17:13-14 *one-eyed . . . Blind.* Proverbial (see Tilley, E240).

17:17-21 *And this . . . Learning.* Casaubon eludes us if he so remarks. Dryden seems to be inferring from Casaubon, pp. 21-23.

17:21 *Some.* Casaubon (p. 23) does not identify but alludes to "some" European scholars.

17:24–29 *no man . . . Scholars.* Dryden pays his respect to Casaubon's accomplishment by distilling Casaubon's own account of it (see p. 23).

17:24–25 *the first Translation.* Dryden (via Casaubon) regards Perotti as the first Latin translator of Polybius. As to whether Leonardo Bruni (1369–1444) might have preceded him, see John Edwin Sandys, *A History of Classical Scholarship* (1906–1908; repr. 1967), II, 45–46; Oliver, *Niccolò Perotti's Version,* p. 16 n. 67.

17:31–18:7 *Our Author . . . another.* See headnote, p. 320.

17:31–18:1 *Our Author . . . Plutarch.* Cf. Cicero, *Republic,* I, xxi, II, xiv; Strabo, *Geography,* I, ii, 1, VI, i, 11, IX, iii, 11, and *passim;* Josephus, *Jewish Antiquities,* XII, 134–137, 358–359; Plutarch, *Aratus,* XXXVIII, 7, *Pelopidas,* XVII, 2, *Pelopidas and Marcellus,* I, 4, *Aemilius Paulus,* XIX, 2, and *Tiberius Gracchus,* IV, 3, in *Lives.*

18:3–7 *he is copied . . . of another.* Here and at 28:3–6, Dryden rebukes Livy. In fact, Livy explicitly cites Polybius as authority at least six times, twice describing him favorably (XXXIII, x, 10; XXX, xlv, 5; for Livy's other acknowledgments of Polybius, see XXXIV, 1, 6; XLV, xliv, 19). Livy's references to Polybius recur in large tracts of his history. Also, nineteenth- and twentieth-century scholars have not yet charted the complex nature of Livy's derivations from Polybius and others. For example, it is not always clear whether Livy used Polybius or Roman annalists who used Polybius. For the scope of this "Quellenfrage," see Heinrich Nissen, *Kritische Untersuchungen über die Quellen der vierten und fünften Dekade des Livius* (Berlin, 1863; repr. 1975); P. G. Walsh, *Livy: His Historical Aims and Methods* (1961), esp. pp. 124–135; John Briscoe, *A Commentary on Livy Books XXXI–XXXIII* (1973), pp. 1–12; Hermann Tränkle, *Livius und Polybios* (1977), esp. pp. 13–19.

18:7–13 *Marcus . . . deserv'd.* Brutus had been expected by contemporaries, when Pompey and Caesar battled for empire, to join Caesar, since Pompey had caused his father's death. But Brutus went over to Pompey, thinking him closer to justice. Dryden gets his allusion to Marcus Brutus' "Compendium," or Epitome, from Casaubon, p. 24; he might also have recalled Casaubon, pp. 14, 49. See also Plutarch, *Brutus,* IV, 4.

18:14–15 *He . . . Tully.* In a letter to Atticus, Brutus, seeing Cicero intimidated by Antony, declares *Ego vero iam iis artibus nihil tribuo, quibus Ciceronem scio instructissimum esse* (Cicero, *Epistulae ad Brutum,* XVII, 5; Loeb trans.: "For my part I no longer pay any homage to those arts in which I know that Cicero is a virtuoso").

18:16–21 *It was . . . his abilities.* See headnote, p. 321; note to 15:6–15.

18:21–22 *a Prince . . . Constantine.* Dryden accepted the legend that Constantine was of English extraction (see *Britannia Rediviva,* l. 89 and note in *Works,* III, 213, 477): it depicted Constantine as the son of Constantius, a Roman legate, and of St. Helena, daughter of Coel, a shadowy British king who ruled the land jointly with Constantius. For sources of the myth, see Ernest Cushing Richardson, trans. and ed., Eusebius' *Life of Constantine* in *A Select Library of Nicene and Post-Nicene Fathers of the Christian Church,* ed. Henry Wace and Philip Schaff (1890), I, 441–442. Modern scholarship yields no evidence that Constantine was of British extraction; he was born, probably in 272 or 273, in Naissus, son of Constantius and of Helena, who came from Drepanum in Bithynia (Timothy D. Barnes, *Constantine and Eusebius* [1981], pp. 3, 221). For contrary speculation and particularly for conjecture on how British patriotism might early have come to claim Constantine, see John Holland Smith, *Constantine the Great* (1971), pp. 17–19.

18:27–28 *I had . . . of Age.* Dryden probably read Polybius before entering Westminster School (Ward, *Life*, pp. 8–9). For English versions of Polybius see note to 13:9–10.

19:1–4 *by reading . . . to him.* For the scope of Dryden's knowledge of historians and his interest in them, see A. E. Wallace Maurer, "Dryden's Knowledge of Historians, Ancient and Modern," *N&Q*, CCIV (1959), 264–266.

19:4 *Tacitus . . . to him.* See the comparison of Polybius and Tacitus at 34:24–35:23.

19:5–21:25 *'Tis wonderful . . . obligement.* Dryden uses Casaubon, pp. 28–30.

20:3–9 *But the . . . the Senate.* Polybius was one of a thousand Achaean hostages who in 167 B.C. suffered imprisonment in Italian towns without trial upon the defeat of Macedonia; the survivors gained release sixteen years later (Polybius, XXX, xiii, 1–11; xxxii, 1–12; Pausanius, X, xi–xii; Livy, XLV, xxxi). Polybius was permitted to stay in Rome, where he and Scipio the Younger became close friends (see note to 31:35–32:3).

20:12–13 *Cato, the Censor.* Marcus Porcius Cato "Censorius" (234–149 B.C.).

20:13–14 *Scipio Emilianus . . . Carthage.* I.e., Scipio the Younger (see note to 16:22–24).

20:29 *Scipio and Lelius.* For Scipio the Younger see note to 16:22–24. His closest friend was Gaius Laelius Minor (called Sapiens), who as Scipio's legate led the attack on Carthage. Along with his chief, Laelius is a central figure in Cicero's *De Republica* and *De Amicitia*.

21:6 *Pausanius has written.* Dryden repeats Casaubon's correct allusion at p. 29. See Pausanius, VIII, xxx, 8–9; xxxvii, 2; xliv, 5; xlviii, 8.

21:20–21 *This Philanthropy . . . to express.* Early seventeenth-century "philanthropia," a loanword from Greek or later Latin, had become the English "philanthropy" by 1650, although "philanthropia" continued to be used (*OED*). Dryden translates Casaubon's "bonitas" at p. 30.

21:23 *Scipio.* I.e., the Younger.

21:27–22:11 *This is . . . inherent.* Cf. Casaubon, p. 30: *Fidem, candorem, integritatem in dictis factisque, passim commendans, qui iis utantur, viros bonos pronuntiat; versutos, veteratores, vafros, & dolorum architectos, nusquam non abominatur* (Everywhere eulogizing good faith, candor, integrity displayed in word and deed, he salutes their practitioners as good men; and he never fails to cry down the crafty, the sly foxes, the cunning rascals, and the architects of trouble). Dryden transforms Casaubon's references to mischievous politicians censured by Polybius into general precepts applicable to contemporary examples (see headnote, pp. 323–326; notes to 22:11–16 and 22:16–31).

22:10–11 *Prerogatives . . . inherent.* With this cf. the absolutist formulas of the postscript to *The History of the League* (*Works*, XVIII, 393:9–394: 17), especially, a king swears "to maintain the several Orders of Men under him, in their lawful priviledges; and those Orders swear Allegiance and Fidelity to him, but with this distinction, that the failure of the People is punishable by the King, that of the King is only punishable by the King of Kings. . . . [The King] Governs as he has promis'd by explicit Laws; and what the Laws are silent in, I think I may conclude to be part of his Prerogative; for what the King has not granted away, is inherent in him."

22:11–16 *As for tricking . . . Publick*. Cf. Casaubon, p. 30: *Malitiam astutam, quæ fere Politicis hominibus prudentia dicitur, tanta severitate, tot locis, tam serio insectatur, κακοπραγμοσύνην vera appellatione indigetans, ut vel eo dumtaxat nomine bonorum omnium amore, studio, ac lectione jugi, sit unus omnium historicorum dignissimus* (As for astute malice, which by politicians is generally hailed as "prudence," he chastises it with such severity, so often, and so earnestly, invoking it by its true name of "wrongdoing," that at least on this account he, among all historians, is the most worthy of love, study, and incessant perusal). See notes to 21:27–22:11, 22: 16–31; headnote, pp. 324–325.

22:12 *King-craft*. The term, as the *OED* shows, was ambivalently used in the period to denote "the art of ruling as a king" and also to suggest "the use of clever or crafty diplomacy in dealing with subjects." As a vivid example of the latter, see Milton, *Eikonoklastes*, ed. William Haller, in *The Works of John Milton*, ed. Frank Allen Patterson (1932), V, 181. For Dryden's use of the term here, see headnote, p. 325, and cf. the obviously analogous "Priest-craft" in the opening line of *Absalom and Achitophel* (*Works*, II, 5).

22:16–31 *He commends . . . suddain Necessities*. The following sentence in Casaubon (p. 30) is to Dryden a bare, inadequate hint for the advice he elaborates for future English political conduct: *Neque, tamen is est Polybius, qui supercilium quoddam Stoïcum, aut rusticam simplicitatem, ad judicandum de actionibus hominum Politicorum afferat* (Yet Polybius is not one to bring into play a sort of Stoic superciliousness or a rustic simplemindedness in judging the behavior of politicians). See notes to 21: 27–22:11, 22:11–16; headnote, pp. 323–326.

22:21 *artificial*. Made up, feigned (*OED*).

22:31–23:4 *From hence . . . Tyranny*. Dryden condenses and translates Casaubon (p. 31) very freely: *ut in nostris Commentariis diligenter exposuimus. Discant igitur ab hoc doctore juvenes studii politici candidati, veram prudentiam & ejus leges; non ab illo Etrusco, in opprobrium religionis Christianae nato; cui probitas, fides, integritas, atque adeo in Deum pietas; ô seculi dedecus: inania sunt sine re nomina; prudentia, ars fallendi; Politica doctrina, instrumentum inhumanæ tyrannidis* (as in our Commentaries we have carefully set forth, the candidates for political advancement should therefore learn from this teacher true wisdom and the laws thereof; not from that Etruscan, born to the reproach of the Christian religion, for whom honesty, good faith, integrity, and indeed reverence for God—O disgrace of his age!—are words without any substance; wisdom is the art of deceiving; political doctrine, the instrument of inhuman tyranny).

23:3 *Machiavel*. This is Dryden's only known explicit reference to Machiavelli. Casaubon's allusion is oblique: that Etruscan (see preceding note).

23:4–9 *Farther-more . . . Societies.* Between "Farther-more" and "Knowl-edge" Dryden translates Casaubon closely. His next six words translate nineteen of Casaubon's (see Casaubon, p. 31).

23:14–17 *none but . . . another Party.* Both Polybius and Commines were firsthand witnesses, analysts of events, and spokesmen for history as basic advice to governors and citizens. With his early entry into politics, Polybius followed Philopoemen, the Achaean statesman, whose ashes he carried in 183 B.C. and on whom he wrote a panegyric; after deportation to Rome he accompanied Scipio the Younger, whom he befriended and under whose patronage he wrote his history of the rise of Rome. But he never re-nounced his Greek sympathies. Dryden might have recalled passages in Commines showing on-the-spot analysis of his master, Louis XI (*The History of Comines: Englished by Thomas Dannett*, 1596 [repr. 1967, p. 23]). In 1472 Commines (c. 1447–1511) abandoned Charles the Bold of Bur-gundy (to whom he had been made squire in 1464) for Louis XI, who rewarded him lavishly. (Recent research has generally vindicated his change in allegiance; see *The Memoirs of Philippe de Commynes,* ed. Samuel Kinser and trans. Isabelle Cazeaux [1969–1973], I, 10–11; William J. Bouwsma, "The Politics of Commynes," *Journal of Modern History,* XXIII [1951], esp. 316–317). Except for the reservation about his loyalty, Dryden's respect for Commines was firm and consistent: in *The Life of Plutarch* (1683), he had linked Commines and Polybius as exemplary practitioners of "*History* properly so call'd" (*Works,* XVII, 272–273), and in the postscript to *The History of the League* (1684), he confidently cited him as a source, albeit with incorrect details (see *Works,* XVIII, 410:23–28 and n).

23:18–19 *since Truth . . . a Well.* Diogenes Laertius in his life of Pyrrho (IX, 72) attributes the remark to Democritus.

24:1–10 *He also . . . Wars.* Dryden closely follows Casaubon, p. 33.

24:10–26 *He who . . . falshood.* After skipping a sentence, Dryden re-sumes close translation of both commentary and quotation from Casaubon, p. 33.

24:15 *What . . . transcribe.* See 18:7–13 and note.

24:26–30 *This sincerity . . . to Truth.* This passage typifies condensation by Dryden. His first sentence (with thirteen words) collapses Casaubon's praise (in sixty-two Latin words) for Polybius' pursuit of truth. His second sentence (forty-one words) translates only part of Casaubon's version of Polybius (sixty-one Latin words). See Casaubon, p. 34.

24:31–25:12 *Aratus the Sicyonian . . . by our Polybius.* The ultimate source of this character of Aratus is Polybius, Book IV (see Sheeres, II [2d pag.], 13–17). But Dryden follows Casaubon's recapitulation of Poly-bius at p. 34.

24:31 *in the . . . Author.* See headnote, p. 321, and notes to 16:21–22 and 32:21 for the chronological confusion, here created through mistrans-lation of Casaubon's phrase *paulo ante hujus ætatum* (p. 34): a little before his time.

25:10–11 *tedious . . . deliberations.* Not taken from Casaubon. Cf. Sir George Savile to Sir William Temple, on 4 April 1666: "a Spanish Council I imagine to be as slow an Assembly as a House of Commons" (H. C. Fox-croft, *The Life And Letters of Sir George Savile* [1898], I, 44).

25:12–14 *as they . . . this History*. Dryden himself recalls Plutarch, *Aratus*, X, 2–3, and *Philopoemen*, VIII, 4.

25:14–28 *In plain . . . Grecians*. Following Casaubon, pp. 34–35.

25:25 *chapters*. Reproves, takes to task (*OED*, citing Dryden's use), and especially with the sense of drawing up a list (of faults), as in the now obsolete sense of "capitulates."

25:28–28:3 *attributing . . . impossibilities*. Dryden follows Casaubon, pp. 35–38, at times loosely, at others closely.

25:33–26:2 *On this . . . commended*. Dryden is translating, not Polybius, but Casaubon's redaction of Polybius at p. 35.

26:6–8 *Is it . . . Aratus*. A loose rather than a close translation of Casaubon, pp. 35–36.

26:19–20 *148th. Olympiad*. I.e., 188/7–185/4 B.C.

27:6 *I rather believe*. Dryden's "I" is Casaubon's first person in *arbitrer* at p. 37.

28:1–6 *You hear . . . Wars*. With Dryden's reproof of Livy cf. "The Translators Preface" in the anonymous translation of *The Roman History of Livy* (1686), sig. A2: "I confess his over-frequent Stories of Prodigies and their Expiations, cannot but be somewhat nauseous to a judicious Christian Reader, but we must consider him as he was an Heathen, and then we can scarce blame him for shewing so much respect to those feigned Deities, which were all he knew" (see also *Works*, XVIII, 183). Modern scholarship finds that Livy "regarded attention given to prodigies as historically important . . . [and] he was aware that many could be explained in non-religious ways" (Briscoe, *Commentary on Livy*, p. 88). Livy expressed outright skepticism toward prodigies at, e.g., XXI, lxii, 1; XXIV, x, 6 (see Briscoe, *Commentary*, p. 88).

28:6–10 *than our . . . Events*. Although he was seriously interested all his life in judicial astrology (see William Bradford Gardner, "John Dryden's Interest in Judicial Astrology," *SP*, XLVII [1950], 506–521), Dryden ridiculed generalized prophecy by such popular astrologers as William Lilly (1602–1681). See, e.g., Dryden's epilogue to *Sir Martin Mar-all*, ll. 13–16 (*Works*, IX, 209), and the discussion in *Works*, I, 232, 258; II, 253; IX, 369; X, 471, 473; XV, 371–372. With Dryden's "seldom" cf. Lilly's published almanac for 1677 (sig. A8), which had predicted a comet for before or after 1682; one appeared in December 1680 (*Elias Ashmole*, ed. C. H. Josten [1966], I, 239; IV, 1677).

28:10–17 *If you . . . approaches*. The two examples are from Casaubon (p. 38), but the satiric touches "journey-work" and "drudgery" are Dryden's. The "other Authors" are only one: namely, Livy (see note to 28:1–6), who reports the miracles involving Hannibal and Scipio (Livy, XXI, xxii, 5–9; XXVI, xlv, 7–9); Casaubon knew it (p. 38).

28:12–15 *Scipio . . . New Carthage*. Publius Cornelius Scipio Africanus Major (236–184/3 B.C.), or Scipio the Elder. In 209 B.C. he seized New Carthage in Spain, and in 202 B.C. he defeated Hannibal in Africa at the battle of Zama.

28:17–26 *Polybius . . . deliverance*. Though Dryden sounds as if he comes from a fresh reading of Polybius, he is translating Casaubon closely, but his touch is seen in phrases like "bungle up" and "into a plunge" ("a critical situation": *OED*). Cf. Casaubon, p. 38.

28:26–29:10 *'Tis a . . . certainty.* Dryden condenses Casaubon, p. 38, taking the barest hints from two spots in the passage to make his own point: he sympathizes strongly with Polybius' criterion of "probability," to him and to Polybius a proper substitute for unthinking superstition.

29:11–30:2 *He was . . . explains.* Dryden follows Casaubon, pp. 38–39.

29:20 *Scipio.* I.e., the Elder (see note to 28:12–15).

29:27–28 *the best . . . Scipio.* Gaius Laelius Major, the close friend of Scipio the Elder, led the fleet during Scipio's Spanish campaign of 209 B.C. and met Polybius in 160 B.C., more than two decades after Scipio's death.

30:2–9 *Of which . . . Legions.* Dryden selects from Casaubon, who gives examples from six books (pp. 40–41).

30:10–13 *When also . . . Republick.* Condensed from Casaubon, p. 41.

30:10–11 *the three great Battels.* At the river Ticinus and at the river Trebia in 218 B.C., and at Lake Trasimene in 217 B.C.

30:12 *Cannæ.* In 216 B.C.

30:13–15 *he gives . . . side.* Dryden does not get the causes from Casaubon. See Polybius, III, in Sheeres's translation, II, 156–157 (which includes the phrase "choice of Ground"), 220, and 130–141.

30:15–20 *After . . . World.* Condensed from Casaubon, p. 41.

30:20–28 *In these . . . understood.* Cf. Casaubon, p. 41, on Polybius' view of causation.

30:23 *Providence.* The word is not used in its theological sense of divine intervention in human affairs for immediate or eternal good. It is here equivalent to Casaubon's "Prudentia" at p. 41: "Prudence," as Dryden calls it later. I.e., calculation by human beings, not "Fortune," shapes history. But see also note to 31:1.

30:23 Συμβαινόντων . . . φαῦλον. Casaubon, p. 41, has τῶν συμβαινόντων τύχην αἰτιᾶσθαι, φαῦλον (to blame things on fortune is a foul idea).

30:31–32 *his partiality . . . forgotten.* See Dryden's *Discourse of Satire* (1693), in *Works*, IV, 50–57, esp. 50:28–29.

30:33–31:6 *Because . . . Affairs.* See Casaubon, pp. 41–43. The issue is at the heart of Polybius' and Dryden's views of history (see headnote, pp. 323–326).

31:1 *believ'd a Providence.* An idiom used into the eighteenth century (see *OED*, believe, 8). Here (cf. 30:23 and note) Dryden uses "Providence" in its theological sense (31:5–6) to refute Casaubon, who has tried to make Polybius a Christian.

31:3 *Suidas.* Casaubon as well as Dryden took Suidas (as many did until recently) to be an author. See *Works*, XVII, 446–447.

31:6–33:21 *But our . . . Polybius.* Except for allusions traced below, these pages do not derive from Dryden's sources.

31:7 *reclaims to.* Probably, protests at or exclaims against (*OED*).

31:25 *his own Maxim.* I.e., as presented at 24:27–30.

31:29–32 *He who . . . from them.* Having himself reviewed Sheeres's translation, Dryden could have recalled such a passage as that at II, 58: "what was the issue of such and such Actions, what was contemporary and principally the Causes of Events . . . is that which animates the Body of History." See also Sheeres, II, 56.

31:35–32:3 *that great . . . Consulship.* In 147 B.C. Scipio the Younger, then thirty-seven or thirty-eight, became consul when he was probably below the age limit and had certainly not held the necessary qualifying offices. The exact age limit for consulship at that time is still in dispute among scholars (see A. E. Astin, *The Lex Annalis before Sulla* in *Collection Latomus,* XXXII [1958]), but it was probably forty-two (*ibid.,* pp. 41, 46). Dryden refers to the tribunes' one-year repeal of the law establishing age limits in response to popular demand for Scipio's election; the events are described by Appian, *Roman History,* CXII, and are alluded to by Livy, LI. In both accounts Scipio emerges as less active in his election than Dryden suggests (see also A. E. Astin, *Scipio Aemilianus* [1967], pp. 61–69). A year after the *Character of Polybius,* in his poem, "To my Dear Friend Mr. Congreve," ll. 35–38 (*Works,* IV, 433), Dryden confused the election of Scipio the Elder as consul with that of the Younger (see Alan Roper's discussion of this passage in *Dryden's Poetic Kingdoms* [1965], pp. 176–178). In the *Character* itself the two Scipios are not confused (*pace* Roper, p. 204).

32:3–6 *by making . . . Souldiery.* Scipio was assigned the African province, and therefore the conduct of the Punic war, by popular demand and election instead of by lot (see Appian, *Roman History,* CXII; see also Astin, *Scipio Aemelianus,* pp. 68–70).

32:10–12 *But the . . . Reader.* The "other Reasons" might be those catalogued by Polybius at VI, 57. They include quarrelsomeness, ambition, extravagance, pride, covetousness, fury, and disobedience: qualities which work to make the state an ochlocracy in fact, even if it retains the name of a democracy.

32:21 *the Younger Aratus.* Translating Casaubon's *Arato Arati F(ilio)* (Aratus the son of Aratus) at p. 44. In fact, a third Aratus, not the son of Aratus of Sicyon, must have been involved in the projected embassy to Egypt in *c.* 181 B.C. (see note to 16:21–22 and headnote, p. 321).

32:29–30 *Preparations . . . large.* The first two books, which Sheeres (I, 6) "thought . . . necessary . . . to conceive and digest . . . into a form of Preface to the main Work."

33:12–16 *I will say . . . Great.* I.e., the last two of three parts described by Casaubon, p. 49, as making up his edition: after the five intact books of Polybius comes the body of excerpts, thought by Casaubon to be the epitome by Brutus, described by Plutarch (*Brutus,* IV), and the collection of excerpts commanded by Emperor Constantine (Porphyrogenitus, not the Great). Dryden's cautionary "as *Casaubon* thinks" anticipates the inability of modern scholarship (e.g., Moore, *Manuscript Tradition of Polybius,* p. 55) to determine the authorship of the *Excerpta Antiqua.* (Malone [III, 264, n. 4] has evidence to reject Casaubon's attribution.) On Marcus Brutus' "Epitome," see 18:7–13 and note. On Constantine, see headnote, p. 321, and 15:6–15.

33:19–21 *He . . . Polybius.* See headnote, p. 318.

34:8–12 *When we hear . . . Common-wealth.* Cf. Pinchon (I, ĩ): *Cum audis Polybium, crede mihi, loquuntur Scipiones, Lælii, Massinissæ* (Believe me, when you hear Polybius, it is the Scipios speaking, the Laeliuses, the Massinissas).

34:9 *Cato, the Censor.* See 20:12–13 and note.

34:10 *Lelius.* For the two men of this name see 20:29, 29:27–28, and notes.

34:10 *Massinissa.* Masinissa (*c.* 240–148 B.C.), powerful Carthaginian ally won over to the Romans by Scipio Africanus Major (236–184/3 B.C.) and thereafter, as master of Numidia, a powerful Roman ally.

34:14–19 *I cannot . . . Venice.* Dryden seems to have in mind Montaigne's essay *De L'Amitié,* in which Montaigne says, not of himself, but of his friend Etienne de la Boétie (1530–1563), that "s'il eut eu à choisir, il eut mieux aimé estre nay à Venise qu'à Sarlac: et avec raison" (*Les Essais de Michel de Montaigne,* ed. Pierre Villey [1922–1923], I, 250). In the same essay, Montaigne attributes to La Boétie "un' autre maxime souverainement [besides his passion for liberty] empreinte en son ame, d'obeyr et de se soubmettre tres-religieusement aux loix sous lesquelles il estoit nay" (*Les Essais,* ed. Villey, I, 250–251). For Dryden's subsequent allusion to Montaigne and Venice see *Works,* V, 281:2–10.

34:19–20 *which . . . wish.* By the end of the sixteenth century and on to about 1640, Venice had the reputation in England, regardless of political differences, of a republic superior even to the Roman commonwealth. The Civil War changed that: royalists rejected the Venetian republic whereas parliamentarians favored it as a modern counterpart of their antique republican models, Sparta and Rome. From the end of the Interregnum, as the Protectorate faltered, into the Restoration and through the Exclusion Crisis, royalists found, as contemporary polemic shows, much to attack: what they saw was the inglorious beginning of Venice, the forced analogy between the Senate of Rome and the Grand Council of Venice, the predominance of popery and whoredom in Venice, its character as a tyrannical oligarchy, its decay as a republic, the irresolution and wickedness of the Venetian Senate, the manning of the Venetian government by more fools than wise men, liquidation of the gifted and of the partisans of the people, dissolute private lives, and debauched insolent youth (see Z. S. Fink, *The Classical Republicans: An Essay in the Recovery of a Pattern of Thought in Seventeenth-Century England,* 2d ed. [1962], pp. 41–43, 45, 88, 119–135, 142–143). Although he nowhere specified his reservations about Venice, Dryden might very well have been influenced by these charges.

34:20–23 *Rome . . . Preference.* See Polybius, *The Histories,* VI, 50 (Loeb trans.: "the Laconian constitution is defective, while that of Rome is superior and better framed for the attainment of power"). Sheeres did not translate the fragmentary sixth book (a version by "another Hand" was added in the 2d ed.); Dryden presumably remembered his earlier reading of Polybius.

34:24–28 *I will . . . thoughts.* Visible is a trace of Casaubon (p. 55), who is reluctant to compare Tacitus and Polybius (*Nam quid simile, quid ulla ex parte comparandum?* [What can you find to match this? What is there worthy to be compared with it in any way?]) and who alludes in passing to the pithy eloquence of Tacitus.

34:28–30 *The manner . . . Cicero.* Cf. Casaubon, pp. 64–65: *Equidem hoc loco . . . si orator [essem], enthymemata Demosthenis, aut opulentiam Tulli* (Indeed at this point, if I were an orator, I should crave the enthymemes of Demosthenes or the opulence of Tully); Casaubon is not comparing Tacitus and Polybius. A remoter echo might be Pichon, I, sig. ũ: *Non habuit certè Tacitus eloquentiam Tullii* (To be sure, Tacitus did not have the eloquence of Cicero).

34:31–32 *Amongst . . . Herodotus.* The hint for the comparison might have come from a lengthy passage in Casaubon, pp. 52–53. A direct suggestion exists in Pichon, I, sig. ũv (see also I, sig. ũ4): *Certe brevis, abscissus, & velut abruptus à se ipso est Tacitus, præcipuè in concionibus, æmulatione Thucydidis* (Assuredly Tacitus is compact, concise, and, as one might say, abrupt, especially so in the speeches, by way of imitating Thucydides).

35:7–13 *Casaubon . . . sence.* Casaubon, p. 56.

35:11–18 *'Tis not his fault . . . turn.* Dryden expands upon Pichon, I, sig. õv–õ2.

35:21–23 *Tacitus . . . Republick.* Dryden gets the substance from Pichon, I, sig. ĩv: *Nam quod præscivit, quod vidit Polybius in statu populi & principum, seu optimatum; hoc idem Tacitus in Imperio unius. Quod Polybius in Aristocratia Rom. temperata nempe ex potestate Consulum, Senatûs, & plebis seu tribunorum; hoc Tacitus in Monarchia scivit, vidit, providit* (What Polybius foreknew and beheld in the political status of the people and the leading men or optimates, the same thing Tacitus beheld in the imperial rule of one man. What Polybius saw in the Roman aristocracy, tempered to be sure by the power of the consuls, the Senate, and the plebeians or tribunes, that was what Tacitus knew, saw, and foresaw in the monarchy).

De Arte Graphica

Sometime before midsummer 1694 Dryden agreed to the request of several painters that he translate Charles Alphonse Dufresnoy's Latin poem, *De Arte Graphica*.[1] When he did so, he may already have begun negotiating with Tonson to translate the works of Virgil. On 15 June 1694 Dryden entered into formal contract with Tonson, tying himself exclusively to Virgil until the translation should be completed, except for the writing of short occasional pieces and the discharge of two commitments, one of them the translation of "a little French Booke of Painting which he hath engag'd to perform for Some Gentlemen Vertuoso's and Painters."[2] That "little French Booke" ran to some 180 octavo pages in the first edition, although 56 of them offered, on facing pages, Dufresnoy's poem and an

---

1 Dufresnoy (1611–1665) was born in Paris, where he studied painting with François Perrier and Simon Vouet. Between 1633 and 1656 he lived in Italy, most of the time in Rome, where he befriended Pierre Mignard, the painter, studied ancient art, painted, and composed *De Arte Graphica*. He returned to Paris in 1656.

2 *Works,* VI, 1179.

anonymous translation of it into French prose supplied by one Roger de Piles,[3] who also contributed extensive remarks explaining and elaborating upon Dufresnoy's points. De Piles added a brief preface setting out, among other things, his relationship with Dufresnoy, who had died in 1665, three years before de Piles brought out the first edition. The edition opened with a Latin dedication of the poem, signed by Dufresnoy, and closed with his observations in French on some modern painters. In fulfilling his obligation to the painters, Dryden substituted for Dufresnoy's dedication a critical preface of his own, *A Parallel betwixt Painting and Poetry*, which was followed by the remaining contents of the 1668 edition in their original order, including a prose translation of *De Arte Graphica* faithful, it was later revealed, to de Piles' French rather than Dufresnoy's Latin. Dryden completed his work sometime before 21 June 1695, when the book was advertised in *A Collection for the Improvement of Husbandry and Trade*.[4] The English book concluded with a "Short Account" of ancient and modern painters contributed "By another Hand," which was later identified as Richard Graham's.

During the year that elapsed between first mention and eventual publication of *De Arte Graphica* Dryden was preoccupied with Virgil, and records of his activities at that time are too fragmentary for us to determine precisely which part or parts of the year he devoted to *De Arte Graphica*. But Dryden has told us how much of the year he borrowed from translating Virgil, and a few dates and reasonable suppositions help us to form an hypothesis. The translation, Dryden tells us early in his preface,[5] occupied two months, and the preface itself, we learn from its final paragraph, was "begun and ended in twelve Mornings." During the year in question Dryden also completed translations of Virgil's *Eclogues* and *Georgics,* the first four Aeneids, and probably the fifth and at least part of the sixth.[6] Dryden was to receive by his contract with Tonson £50 in copy money on completion of the *Eclogues* and *Georgics* and a further £50 on completion of each block of four Aeneids. We may suppose, although we do not certainly know, that, once embarked upon a segment of the Virgil, Dryden moved without interruption to complete it so as to receive his copy money from Tonson. When he signed the contract with Tonson, Dryden had already made and was soon to see published a translation of the third Georgic; he might also have started on the *Eclogues* and other Georgics. We may hypothesize that Dryden completed at least the first segment of the Virgil translation before turning to *De Arte Graphica*. William Rogers, its publisher, secured a license for it on 27 October 1694, as he later recorded when entering it in the *Stationers' Register*. Dryden, then, may have completed his translation of the *Eclogues* and *Georgics* in fall 1694, received his copy money from Tonson, and perhaps informed Rogers he was ready to start on *De Arte Graphica*. Rogers then secured a license and with it the copy-

[3] De Piles (1635–1709) was a painter, engraver, writer, diplomat, and theorist of art, as well as the editor and, he claimed, the friend of Dufresnoy.
[4] See also the *London Gazette* for 27 June–1 July 1695.
[5] 39:26–28 above.
[6] For fuller discussion of Dryden's progress when translating Virgil see *Works,* VI, 843–844.

right.[7] But Rogers did not enter the book in the *Stationers' Register* until 10 April 1695, nearly six months after licensing. During those six months Dryden also translated the first four Aeneids, each of them, to judge from later indications of his progress, occupying him for about a month. He announced their completion in a letter to Tonson, which has been dated to April 1695.[8] If we accept the traditional date, we ought to assign the two months of November and December 1694, immediately following its licensing, to the translated portions of *De Arte Graphica,* thus placing Dryden's work between the first two segments of the Virgil translation. Why then did Rogers delay entry in the *Stationers' Register* for four months and publication for a further two?

An alternative and perhaps more winning hypothesis requires that we date the letter announcing completion of the fourth Aeneid some two months earlier than it has traditionally been dated and place Dryden's work on *De Arte Graphica* in February and March 1695. Rogers' entry in the *Stationers' Register* would then have come soon after Dryden completed the translation. His copy, however, did not go immediately to Rogers: as Dryden indicates in his preface, the translation was first checked by some or some one of the painters who asked that he make it, in order to ensure that technical terms were translated into their proper English equivalents.[9] Perhaps during that process of revision the painters decided to ask Dryden—they "importun'd" him—to supply a preface in which he might "say something farther" of painting by way of paralleling it with poetry.[10] This second request, for such it seems to have been, would have come when Dryden had already returned to Virgil. On 8 June 1695 Dryden wrote to Tonson that it was "now high time . . . to think of my second Subscriptions,"[11] and Dryden had contracted to complete the first six Aeneids before advertising a second subscription, the profits from which were to go entirely to him. However we date the earlier letter announcing completion of the fourth Aeneid, Dryden must have devoted most of April and May to the fifth and sixth. But in the letter of 8 June Dryden also remarked that he had "now been idle just a fortnight" and, since he was addressing Tonson, presumably meant only that he had translated no Virgil for a fortnight. That fortnight, then, may correspond to the twelve mornings he assigned to the *Parallel betwixt Painting and Poetry.* Although he would have interrupted his work on Virgil to do so and thus delayed receipt of copy money for *Aeneid,* V–VIII, with the sixth Aeneid nearing completion he could look forward to additional income from the

---

[7] The Licensing Act originally served the purpose of establishing ways to screen and, if necessary, to censor works intended for publication. But by 1694 licensing had become pro forma and publishers used it principally as a way of establishing copyright (see John P. Feather, "From Censorship to Copyright: Aspects of the Government's Role in the English Book Trade, 1695–1775," in *Books and Society in History,* ed. Kenneth E. Carpenter [1983], p. 187). Rogers may have been required to submit no more than the Latin and French original of *De Arte Graphica* and could have done so before Dryden made his translation.

[8] Ward, *Letters,* pp. 74, 170.

[9] See 39:4–12 above.

[10] See 40:4–5 above.

[11] Ward, *Letters,* p. 76.

second subscribers, each of whom was to pay one guinea in advance and a second on publication.

Dryden, then, most probably translated *De Arte Graphica* either in November-December 1694 or in February-March 1695. He seems to have deferred composition of his prefatory *Parallel betwixt Painting and Poetry* for some weeks or months after completing the translation, perhaps to late May —early June 1695. The precise indications of time spent—two months, twelve mornings—are unusual for Dryden and, although addressed to all readers of *De Arte Graphica*, seem particularly meant for Tonson and for subscribers to the Virgil by way of assurance that Dryden had their concerns in mind. He underlined that assurance by occasional references in his preface to his work on Virgil and perhaps also by the frequency of his quotations from the *Aeneid*.

⟨⟩W⟨⟩

When Dryden made his translation of Dufresnoy and de Piles, several editions of the original were available, principally those published as *L'Art de Peinture* at Paris in 1668, 1673, and 1684,[12] the last two being slightly augmented editions of the first. Numerous variants between the first edition and those derived from it suffice to show that Dryden used a copy of the first when making his translation.[13] The painter or painters who reviewed Dryden's work to ensure correct terminology used a copy of the third edition, at one point introducing a reading that appears only in 1684 and at another fashioning a clumsy translation of a remark that de Piles added in the editions of 1673 and 1684.[14] But he or they never made an attempt, as far as we can tell, to adjust Dryden's translation away from de Piles' French prose and toward Dufresnoy's Latin verse.

We must assume that Dryden elected to offer a prose version of a poem because there already existed a more easily translatable version in French prose. That decision in the winter of 1694-95 shaped the subsequent history of Dryden's work. By the end of the eighteenth century four competitors had offered translations of Dufresnoy's poem into English verse and Dry-

---

[12] There were also a separate edition of the Latin poem unaccompanied by a prose translation but with a few notes by Pierre Mignard (Paris, 1668) and what appears to be a piracy (Paris, 1688) of the de Piles editions which lacks the Latin poem, most of de Piles' preface, and all his "remarques." Clearly, neither of these could have served as Dryden's original.

[13] There are 41 variants between the editions of 1668 and 1673, involving choice of word or phrase, syntax, wording of sidenotes or citation within them. In all instances Dryden's version corresponds to the 1668 reading. The 1684 edition accepts the 41 variants from 1673 and adds a further 25. In all but two of those 25 Dryden's version again corresponds to the 1668 reading.

[14] Q's citation of Pliny as "5.8" for the sidenote to 184:2 corresponds to the citation in 1684; 1668 and 1673 have "35.2." The additional observation occurs at 183:16-24. De Piles also enlarged another remark for the editions of 1673 and 1684. The additional passage is absent from Dryden's translation (it would have occurred at 140:17-18), as it is from the 1668 edition. Dryden's friends may have thought this addition unimportant because it constituted an enlargement rather than a wholly new remark. The text of Dufresnoy's poem in the 1695 quarto was set from the 1684 edition of *L'Art de Peinture*, as emerges from errors in lining and some accidentals common to both but absent from 1668.

den's own prose had been revised to accord with Dufresnoy's Latin rather than with de Piles' French. Despite an expressed wish late in the nineteenth century to return to Dryden's own text and a lament early in the twentieth that the wish remained unfulfilled,[15] the eighteenth-century revision supplied a text transmitted to subsequent editions, so that the present edition is the first to return to the 1695 quarto for a text of Dryden's translation.

The story begins with the reviser's work. In 1716 Bernard Lintott issued a second edition in octavo of *The Art of Painting,* as he called it, dropping the initial Latin title of the first edition. The other hand that contributed an account of ancient and modern painters is now identified as Richard Graham's.[16] Graham also added a dedication to the octavo in which he noted that Dryden, trusting de Piles' fidelity to Dufresnoy's poem, had supplied a version that in places misrepresented the Latin. Those places, Graham informs us, had been corrected for the second edition by Charles Jervas, the painter, his changes being enclosed within quotation marks.[17] Of nearly forty such changes most indeed offer readings that are closer to the sense of the Latin, although a few are merely stylistic. There are also some fifty additional changes not set off in quotation marks, nearly half of them reflecting the Latin sense, the remainder adjusting the style. Graham credited Jervas only with correcting the version that Dryden offered of Dufresnoy's poem, but the 1716 edition also revises, mostly on stylistic grounds, Dryden's translation of de Piles' remarks and Dufresnoy's comments on painters. The second edition also offers an edited version of Dryden's preface. Changes are once more stylistic and only a few have been accepted into editions published after the eighteenth century. But during the eighteenth century the 1716 edition supplied copy for editions of the complete work in 1750 and 1769 and for a reprinting in 1783 of Dufresnoy's comments and Dryden's preface, which William Mason appended to his new verse translation of *De Arte Graphica* with notes, replacing de Piles' remarks, by Mason and by Sir Joshua Reynolds. The 1716 text of the *Parallel betwixt Painting and Poetry* was not displaced until Malone returned in 1800 to the 1695 quarto for his copy. A few years later Scott followed Malone in preferring the first to the second edition for Dryden's preface but accepted the second edition when establishing his text of the

15 The wish was Saintsbury's (see S-S, XVII, 284; XVIII, 322). The lament was Edmund Gosse's (see the *Athenæum* for 12 August 1905, pp. 208–209).

16 He was also the Mr. Graham who assisted Dryden in the accounting with Tonson for the Virgil translation (see John Taylor, "Drydeniana," *N&Q,* LV [1877], 386; John Barnard, "Dryden, Tonson, and Subscriptions for the 1697 *Virgil,*" *PBSA,* LVII [1963], 132n). Richard Graham was a two-guinea subscriber to the Virgil (*Works,* V, 69) and may well have been among the "Gentlemen Vertuoso's" who helped prevail upon Dryden to translate Dufresnoy. In 1697 he served as steward of the St. Luke's Club for painters (see William T. Whitley, *Artists and Their Friends in England, 1700–1799* [1928], II, 243) and knew well the painter John Closterman, who was certainly associated with Dryden in those years (see "Vertue Note Books, V," *Walpole Society,* XXVI [1937–1938], 61; HMC, *Fifteenth Report, Appendix, Pt. VII,* p. 205).

17 Sig. A4v–5. Jervas, or Jarvis (1675?–1739), specialized in portrait painting. He studied under Kneller, eventually succeeding him as principal painter to George I. Jervas taught Pope to paint in 1713–14 and was the addressee of Pope's epistolary poem in the 1716 edition.

translated matter,[18] which Malone, according to his practice, had not included. In our subsequent annotations we include only those readings from 1716 which adjust the sense toward Dufresnoy's Latin and omit those which reflect stylistic editing.

A copy of the 1695 quarto now in the Folger Shakespeare Library supplies a curious footnote to the history of the first two editions.[19] This copy contains handwritten marginalia that correspond, aside from minor variants, to those changes introduced into the second edition which were enclosed in quotation marks. The same early eighteenth-century hand wrote out Pope's epistle to Jervas (first published in the 1716 edition of *De Arte Graphica*) on the blank leaves at the end of the book and was probably responsible for noting on the title page that the copy came "Ex dono J: C: Pictor" (or "Pictore"). A claim that the marginalia are in Dryden's hand, the poem in Pope's, is incorrect, and the proposal that the initials on the title page are those of Charles Jervas reversed is unconvincing. The initials may represent John Closterman, who painted the portrait of Dryden reproduced as the frontispiece to this volume,[20] who helped collect subscriptions to Dryden's Virgil,[21] and who was most probably one of the painters who prevailed upon Dryden to translate *De Arte Graphica*. Closterman died in 1711 and could not have been responsible for the marginalia in the Folger copy, which were obviously taken from the second edition, along with Pope's epistle to Jervas, by an owner concerned to emend his copy of the first edition, received from J. C., Pictor, so as to show the readings of the second. (Had the Folger quarto once served as compositor's copy for the second edition, it would have included, as it does not, the silent as well as the marked emendations.)[22] The Folger copy, then, has no bibliographical or canonical significance, but its existence testifies, like the 1716 edition, to an interest in Dufresnoy's poem which took precedence over Dryden's secondhand translation of it.

Such an interest shows also in four eighteenth-century attempts, of which Mason's was the third, to translate Dufresnoy into English verse. The first is the most curious. It appeared in 1720, four years after the second edition of Dryden's prose rendering, and announced itself as *The Compleat Art of Painting: A Poem Translated from the French of M. du Fresnoy: By D. F.*

---

[18] Scott did so because he assumed the 1716 edition to be more accurate than the 1695 quarto in the use of technical terms, a matter he was not competent to judge (S-S, XVII, 283). Earlier, Johnson had used the 1695 quarto for the numerous citations that appear in his *Dictionary* (W. K. Wimsatt, Jr., "Samuel Johnson and Dryden's *Du Fresnoy*," *SP*, XLVIII [1951], 27n).

[19] The copy was once part of Percy Dobell's collection.

[20] For an account of Closterman (1660–1711) see Malcolm Rogers, "John and John Baptist Closterman: A Catalogue of Their Works," *Walpole Society*, XLIX (1983), 224–279.

[21] Ward, *Letters*, p. 77. Closterman was a five-guinea subscriber to Dryden's Virgil (*Works*, V, 68).

[22] Two of the silent emendations are in fact included among the marginalia, but both are easily seen. The marginalia also contain some dozen minor variants from the 1716 readings (addition or omission of articles or scattered words, a reversal of adjectives) and at one point offer an abbreviated version of a footnote that appears in full in 1716.

Gent. The poem has been attributed to Defoe, but Defoe's most recent bibliographer, while noting that the initials are Defoe's and that the poem was issued by one of his publishers, finds no other evidence of his hand in the work.[23] As puzzling as its claim to be a verse translation from Dufresnoy's "French" is the absence of any preface or other material justifying its existence, even though it was competing with a recent reissue of Dryden's text. Indeed, its stilted couplets read at times like a versification of Dryden's English prose.[24] No such oddity attaches to the appearance in 1754 of James Wills's *De Arte Graphica; Or, The Art of Painting. Translated from the Original Latin.* Wills offers a blank-verse translation facing the Latin original together with some explanatory footnotes and a preface citing Graham's reference to Dryden's inexactitude and insisting that there were still other departures from the Latin sense left uncorrected by Jervas (pp. i–ii). Whereas Wills emphasized that his version competed with Dryden's, Mason, thirty years later, touched upon the matter deferentially in an introductory epistle to Reynolds redolent of the age of sensibility (p. v):

> When Dryden, worn with sickness, bow'd with years,
> Was doom'd (my Friend let Pity warm thy tears)
> The galling pang of penury to feel,
> For ill-plac'd Loyalty, and courtly Zeal,
> To see that Laurel, which his brows o'erspread,
> Transplanted droop on Shadwell's barren head,
> The Bard oppress'd, yet not subdu'd by Fate,
> For very bread descended to translate:
> And He, whose Fancy, copious as his Phrase,
> Could light at will Expression's brightest blaze,
> On Fresnoy's Lay employ'd his studious hour;
> But niggard there of that melodious power,
> His pen in haste the hireling task to close,
> Transform'd the studied strain to careless prose,
> Which, fondly lending faith to French pretence,
> Mistook its meaning, or obscur'd its sense.

Mason followed these verses with a preface to his own translation in which he expressed the hope that his epistle to Reynolds had "obviated . . . every suspicion of arrogance in attempting this work after Mr. Dryden. The single consideration that his Version was in Prose were in itself sufficient." As for competing translations in verse, Mason was apparently unacquainted with the work of D. F., Gent., and claimed it unnecessary to apologize "for undertaking it after Mr. Wills, who . . . published a Translation of it in Metre without Rhyme," which could not properly be called "Blank Verse, because it was devoid of all harmony of numbers" (pp. xii–xiii). Like D. F., Gent., Mason preferred couplets. In 1789, six years after Mason's version appeared, Walter Churchey published by subscription his *Poems and Imitations of the British Poets,* including in it a new translation of *De Arte*

---

[23] Maximillian E. Novak in *The New Cambridge Bibliography of English Literature,* ed. George Watson, II (1971), 901.

[24] As noted by Lawrence Lipking, *The Ordering of the Arts in Eighteenth-Century England* (1970), 38–65, esp. p. 47. In this chapter Lipking compares Dryden's and the four eighteenth-century verse translations.

Graphica into heroic quatrains, together with a brief preface to the transla-
tion, which also has a verse dedication to George III. Churchey mentions
Mason's version with Reynolds' notes in both the preface to the translation
and the dedication to the king. He refers neither to Dryden nor to other
earlier translators but followed his version with an abridgment of de Piles'
observations as translated by Dryden, which Churchey credits to Richard
Graham. The observations are given to Graham in none of the four
editions of Dryden's work, but by the time of the last, in 1769, Graham's
name had achieved equal prominence with Dryden's on the title page, and
Churchey may have mistakenly assumed that Dryden was responsible only
for the translation of Dufresnoy's poem, and for the prefatory *Parallel
betwixt Painting and Poetry*. The story of Dufresnoy in English translation
ends with Churchey's mistake and the obliteration of Dryden's name.[25]

This continued interest in Dufresnoy's poem,[26] which was paralleled on
the Continent but which waned after the eighteenth century,[27] helps us to
understand the eagerness of those "Gentlemen Vertuoso's and Painters"
who, probably early in 1694, laid upon Dryden the "honourable task" of
turning Dufresnoy into English. Dryden leaves his taskmasters unnamed,
but, as scholars have assumed, they most probably included John Closter-
man and Sir Godfrey Kneller.[28] Like Closterman, Kneller soon became
involved in collecting subscriptions to Dryden's Virgil.[29] He painted several
portraits of Dryden; the most famous, a three-quarter portrait, has been
dated to 1695. When Dryden contracted to translate Virgil, he was soon to
see published in the *Annual Miscellany* his verse epistle to Kneller, a copy
of which Kneller no doubt received as soon as it was written. We do not
know when Dryden wrote the epistle but may suppose he did so after pub-
lication of *Examen Poeticum* in June 1693, in which it would presumably

---

[25] One apparently phantom translation should be mentioned. Paul Vitry, *De
C. A. Dufresnoy Pictoris Poemate quod "De Arte graphica" inscribitur* (1901),
lists in his bibliography (p. 109) a translation by J. Wright published in 1728.
Hagstrum (p. 175) also refers in passing to this translation, perhaps relying on
Vitry. But nothing resembling the work is traceable in other bibliographies or in
catalogues of the major collections, and Lipking notes (*Ordering of the Arts*,
p. 49n) that one James Wright translated Dufresnoy's prose observations on
modern painters in his *Country Conversations* (1694), pp. 56[59]–75. Lipking
remarks that "according to Vitry . . . Wright also translated *De arte graphica*."
But the James Wright of *Country Conversations* died in 1713, fifteen years before
the supposed publication of the mysterious work attributed to J. Wright by
Vitry and Hagstrum.

[26] For another account of this interest, stressing Dufresnoy's significance for
Shaftesbury, Pope, Gray, and Reynolds, as well as Dryden, see Wladyslaw Folkier-
ski, "*Ut Pictura Poesis* ou l'étrange fortune du *De Arte Graphica* de Du Fresnoy
en Angleterre," *Revue de Littérature Comparée*, XXVII (1953), 385–402.

[27] The poem was frequently reprinted and was translated into French, Dutch,
German, and Italian, as well as English (see bibliography in Vitry, *De C. A.
Dufresnoy*, pp. 108–109).

[28] See, e.g., Malone, I, 251–252; Ward, *Letters*, p. 172.

[29] Ward, *Letters*, p. 77. Like Closterman, Kneller was a five-guinea subscriber
to the Virgil (*Works*, V, 68).

have been included had it been available. The epistle to Kneller offers a progress of painting and a running parallel between painting and poetry. Whatever its own occasion, the epistle appears to have contributed to the occasion of *De Arte Graphica* by reminding Kneller, were it necessary, that Dryden was the obvious person to turn Dufresnoy into English.

Kneller and Closterman, then, may well have urged Dryden to undertake the task but, if so, they spoke for more than themselves, for, as Dryden remarks at the beginning of his preface, "Many of our most Skillfull Painters, and other Artists, were pleas'd to recommend this Authour to me." It seems most likely that the decision to approach Dryden was reached at a meeting of the St. Luke's Club, of which Kneller and Closterman were members. The club had been founded by Van Dyck and took its name from his practice of inviting artists and connoisseurs to his home and feasting them every 18 October, St. Luke's Day. The club became dormant with Van Dyck's death in 1641 but was revived after the Restoration by Lely, who continued the tradition until his own death in 1680. Thereafter, the meetings lapsed once more until their reinstitution with a difference in 1689, when

> several of the most considerable Virtuosi, emulated and encouraged by Mr. Riley the King's Principal Painter, met at a public tavern, and remembering the inconvenience of so many persons meeting at a private house (besides the freedom) they resolved to meet in former manner, but at a tavern, one evening in the week during the winter and once a month in the summer.[30]

With the feast of 18 October 1689 Closterman became the first annual steward (Riley having fallen ill), and the practice of selecting annual stewards continued until 1735. In 1696 the steward was "Mr. Henry Cooke, History Painter," who was presumably the H. Cooke who designed the frontispiece to Dryden's *De Arte Graphica*.[31]

༄

Kneller may have been reminded by Dryden's epistle that Dryden possessed an easy familiarity with the terms and techniques of painting together with an ability to run them into prose or verse discourse. But the epistle displayed no freshly acquired knowledge, for throughout his career Dryden drew upon painting for tropes illustrative of literary practice. His poems so often feature people doing things, his dramatic criticism so often addresses the proper representation of character and action, that it is perhaps unsurprising he should seek analogies in portraiture and in what his age called history painting; only the frequency of such reference and the precision of his analogizing seem not to be inevitable. To be sure, when analogizing he sought to catch what two objects had in common, and perhaps for that reason he very rarely referred to particular paintings, although there were also only limited opportunities to see continental art in late

---

[30] Quoted in William T. Whitley (*Artists and Their Friends in England, 1700–1799* [1928], I, 74), who also gives (pp. 74–75) an account of the club's origins and early activities.

[31] *Ibid.*, II, 243. Cooke was a two-guinea subscriber to Dryden's Virgil (*Works*, V, 69).

seventeenth-century England, as Dryden himself notes.[32] Before *De Arte Graphica* he mentioned only a few paintings: Titian's "famous Table of the Altar piece" in the dedication of *The History of the League*,[33] Anne Killigrew's portraits of James II and Mary of Modena,[34] and, in the epistle to Kneller, a portrait of Shakespeare copied from the Chandos painting which Kneller had presented to Dryden.[35] Even in *A Parallel betwixt Painting and Poetry* Dryden specifies only two more pieces: a Poussin *Cena* and Annibale Carracci's frescoes in the palace of Cardinal Odoardo Farnese, particularly the *Choice of Hercules,* although for an account of the latter he relied upon Bellori and for the former either upon an engraving or a published description of the original.[36] In *A Parallel betwixt Painting and Poetry* Dryden also displays some familiarity with the subjects of paintings but specifies no actual examples of those subjects.[37]

If Dryden specifies little, modern scholars have specified much. They have found that *Annus Mirabilis* reflects paintings by Rubens, Titian, and Veronese; they have found Rubens again in *Britannia Rediviva* and *To Her Grace the Dutchess of Ormond;* Roelandt Savery in the translation of Virgil's third Eclogue (ll. 69–70).[38] They have argued for the influence of baroque paintings upon *Threnodia Augustalis,* the ode to Anne Killigrew, *Britannia Rediviva,* and the two odes for St. Cecilia's Day.[39] They have placed *Absalom and Achitophel* within a pictorialist tradition and have found the influence of Poussin upon landscape description in Dryden's Virgil.[40] *All for Love,* we learn, displays picturesque tendencies because it draws upon the topos of the choice of Hercules, which had served as subject for paintings by such as Rubens as well as Annibale Carracci.[41]

Closer to the surface of Dryden's work we find numerous remarks and allusions that display a ready knowledge of the different kinds of painting. He accepted a hierarchy among those kinds which corresponded to a hierarchy of literary kinds, and he equated, for example, history painting with epic, genre painting with comedy.[42] Part of Dryden's subject in the ode to Anne Killigrew involved him in discourse upon landscape and portrait painting in themselves.[43] But most often the kinds of painting served

[32] 38:18–20 above.
[33] The "Votive Portrait of the Vendramin Family" (*Works,* XVIII, 7:14–16, 480).
[34] In the ode to Anne Killigrew, ll. 127–140 (*Works,* III, 113); her portrait of James II is reproduced as the frontispiece to *Works,* III.
[35] L. 73 (*Works,* IV, 463, and 750–751).
[36] See 54:22–29 and 52:16–21 above and notes.
[37] See 53:3–16 above.
[38] See Jeffrey B. Spencer, *Heroic Nature: Ideal Landscape in English Poetry from Marvell to Thomson* (1973), pp. 139, 141–142, 162, 177–178.
[39] Hagstrum, pp. 197–209; Henry V. S. and Margaret S. Ogden, *English Taste in Landscape in the Seventeenth Century* (1955), p. 102; Spencer, *Heroic Nature,* p. 179.
[40] For *Absalom and Achitophel* see Hagstrum, p. 181; Ruth Wallerstein, "To Madness Near Allied: Shaftesbury and His Place in the Design and Thought of *Absalom and Achitophel,*" *HLQ,* VI (1943), 448–449. For Dryden's Virgil see Spencer, *Heroic Nature,* pp. 168, 172–174.
[41] Hagstrum, pp. 190–197.
[42] *Works,* I, 274–276.
[43] Ll. 106–141.

Dryden as analogues for verbal representation. So, in the *Life of Plutarch* portrait and history painting illustrate the difference between biography and history "properly so call'd." [44] Portraiture also supplies analogies for the literary representation of character, whether in a play, poem, or dedication. [45] Failure to achieve a true likeness may be attributed to the artist's incompetence. But when the artist deliberately distorts the likeness, he shuns nature, produces the grotesque in painting, [46] libel, farce, or hypercriticism in writing, and everywhere monsters, those *lusus naturae*, freaks or sports of nature. [47] Some of Dryden's references to the graphic arts occur in his poems, especially when the subject required their inclusion, as in *The Medall*, the ode to Anne Killigrew, and the epistle to Kneller. They can also be found in other poems, as in the complimentary verses to Lee and Congreve on plays they had written. But the majority of the most extended references occur in the prose, whether dedication, preface, or essay. Seen in one way, these references take their place with the many other analogies that troop through Dryden's discourse, analogies drawn from architecture and music, trade and the law, hunting and fighting. They display, that is, Dryden's homogeneous sense of society, by which writing, whether in verse or prose, both occurs within and reflects the unity and diversity of civilization.

Dryden's friends and acquaintances from the St. Luke's Club no doubt felt exclusive concern for the graphic arts and could have found throughout his works, not only similes uniting literary kinds and kinds of painting, but also allusions to the techniques of painting which serve to illustrate human acts or literary endeavors. Thus, Cromwell's character displays a perfect, unshaded portrait drawn by heaven, and the same visual effect of rounding corresponds, we learn, to the aural effect of rhyme. [48] Dryden conveyed the graduated sequence of events which led to the restoration of Charles II by, among other tropes, an artist's sweetening of the colors, a blending of them "so / That by degrees they from each other go," and the same technique serves to place Trimmers on the political spectrum in *The Vindication of The Duke of Guise*. [49] An awkward stiffness in Statius' representation of character finds an analogue in a clumsy overapplication of paint which obscures the lines of a face, [50] and throughout his criticism, in verse as well as prose, Dryden likened the challenges confronting a

---

44 *Works*, XVII, 272:18, 274:20–34.

45 For dramatic character see, e.g., the dedication of *Tyrannick Love* (*Works*, X, 110:13–18). For poetic character see the prefatory epistle to *The Medall* (*Works*, II, 38:13–21). For the character of a dedicatee see the dedication of *Plutarchs Lives* (*Works*, XVII, 236:10–15).

46 *Works*, XVII, 236:15–18.

47 For libel see *The Hind and the Panther*, III, 1040–1050 (*Works*, III, 192). For farce see 55:14–24 above. For hypercriticism see the dedication of *Examen Poeticum* (*Works*, IV, 365:14–17, 366:11–17). For monsters see the preface to *Fables* (1700, sig. *A2v; Watson, II, 275).

48 *Heroique Stanzas*, ll. 59–60 (*Works*, I, 13, 199–200); *Of Dramatick Poesie* (*Works*, XVII, 76:34–77:8).

49 *Astraea Redux*, ll. 125–130 (*Works*, I, 25); *Vindication* (1683, p. 26; S-S, VII, 182).

50 *To Sir Robert Howard*, ll. 71–76 (*Works*, I, 19).

writer to those confronting a painter. Thus, as early as the prologue to *Secret Love* in 1668 Dryden associated an artist's laying of dead colors upon a canvas, the application, that is, of the first layer of paint, with a dramatist's preliminary observance of the unities and the liaison des scènes.[51] As late as the preface to *Fables* in 1700 Dryden found the same artistic practice useful when explaining the conduct of an essay.[52] In between, in the preface to *Sylvæ* (1685), translation becomes

> a kind of Drawing after the Life; where every one will
> acknowledge there is a double sort of likeness, a good
> one and a bad. 'Tis one thing to draw the Out-lines true,
> the Features like, the Proportions exact, the Colouring it
> self perhaps tolerable, and another thing to make all these
> graceful, by the posture, the shadowings, and chiefly by
> the Spirit which animates the whole.[53]

Dryden, then, filled his works with analogies between the products of pen and pencil, most often to show that the writer's pen should obey the same aesthetic laws as the artist's pencil. Tropes of design, proportion, and perspective abound in Dryden's literary criticism, and his accounts of deeds and motives run easily to the picturesque, to the posing of men as in a painting. Thus, when dedicating *Plutarchs Lives* to the Duke of Ormonde, Dryden celebrated Ormonde's loyalty to Charles II by juxtaposing Ormonde with the rebellious sons of other loyalists and finding them too "sad an object" to dwell upon:

> Let this part of the Landschape be cast into shadows, that
> the heightnings of the other may appear more beautiful.
> For as Contraries the nearer they are plac'd are brighter,
> and the *Venus* is illustrated by the Neighbourhood of the
> *Lazar,* so the unblemish'd Loyalty of your Grace, will shine
> more clearly, when set in competition with their stains.[54]

Perhaps the clearest indication of Dryden's lifelong interest in painting comes in the dedication of the music to *The Prophetess,* which Dryden drafted for Purcell's signature in 1691. Dryden begins by associating "All arts and Sciences" in their common need of patronage and quickly asserts a closer relationship between music and poetry, which "have ever been acknowledgd Sisters," for, "As poetry is the harmony of words, so musick is that of notes." But Dryden soon moves to a more congenial topic—"Painting is, indeed, another Sister"—and thereupon offers a compact comparison between music and poetry on one side and painting on the other. The comparison has no obvious relevance to a discourse on music and perhaps for that reason was omitted from the published form of the dedication.[55] But its presence in the draft once more reveals Dryden's bent: again and again he drew upon the other arts, especially painting,

51 *Works,* IX, 119.
52 1700, sig. *A2; Watson, II, 273.
53 *Works,* III, 4:18–24.
54 *Works,* XVII, 233:29–34.
55 *Works,* XVII, 324:5–325:12. For a comparison of this piece with *A Parallel betwixt Painting and Poetry* see Roswell G. Ham, "Dryden's Dedication for *The Music of the Prophetesse,* 1691," *PMLA,* L (1935), 1065–1075.

to illustrate the technical challenges confronting a writer; he rarely reversed the flow to illustrate from writing the challenges confronting practitioners of other arts. As rarely, too, Dryden dwelt upon the other arts in themselves. Unsurprisingly, therefore, the epigraph to *De Arte Graphica*, taken, perhaps, from the first line of Dufresnoy's poem but ultimately from Horace, directs attention less to the thoughts of Dufresnoy and de Piles on the art of painting itself than to Dryden's prefatory parallel between painting and poetry: *ut pictura poesis erit.*[56]

Horace, it seems, intended no analogy between the goals and the techniques of the two arts, instead concerning himself with the comparable reception of different products of the two. For Horace the arts are alike in that one kind of poem or painting pleases more when closely scrutinized, whereas another kind pleases more when seen from a distance, the appeal lying presumably in the composition of the whole rather than in the careful crafting of detail.[57] But Horace's simile easily lost its context and frequently became yoked, as it is in Dufresnoy's opening lines, with the maxim of Simonides that painting is mute poetry, poetry a speaking picture.[58] In such a form the simile inspired centuries of analogizing that has continued to our own day.[59]

Dufresnoy himself pursued the analogy for only thirty lines and only in general terms, perhaps by way of offering an exordium in which he could show himself self-consciously aware of writing about painting in a poem instead of in a prose treatise. Thereafter he discoursed on painting in itself with no more than brief, scattered references to poetry.[60] To be sure, Dufresnoy probably knew that the analogy between the arts included the assumption that both could be described in terms developed for the practice of rhetoric. He certainly adopted those terms for his discourse about painting, using them to organize part of the discourse into sections, so that he proceeds, as in rhetoric, from invention, the finding or choice of subject, to disposition, the arrangement of the subject to best effect, to coloring, the use of colors appropriate to the subject and arrangement.[61] The third stage

[56] For Horace, Dufresnoy, and the form of the maxim with *erit* see note to the epigraph.

[57] For discussion of the simile in the context of *Ars Poetica* see Wesley Trimpi, "The Meaning of Horace's *Ut Pictura Poesis*," *JWCI*, XXXVI (1973), 1–34.

[58] The maxim was recorded by Plutarch, *Moralia*, 346F. It served from time to time as a gloss on *Ars Poetica*, l. 361, in annotated editions of Horace (e.g., those by John Bond [1670], p. 261, and Ludovicus Desprez [Paris, 1691], p. 904).

[59] For scholarly surveys see Rensselaer W. Lee, "*Ut Pictura Poesis*: The Humanistic Theory of Painting," *Art Bulletin*, XXII (1940), 197–269; William Guild Howard, "*Ut Pictura Poesis*," *PMLA*, XXIV (1909), 40–123. Howard devotes considerable space to Dufresnoy and de Piles, with some reference to Dryden, who is more prominently featured by Dean T. Mace, "*Ut Pictura Poesis*: Dryden, Poussin and the Parallel of Poetry and Painting in the Seventeenth Century," in *Encounters: Essays on Literature and the Visual Arts*, ed. John Dixon Hunt (1971), pp. 58–81.

[60] See above, 87:35–88:2, 90:20–24.

[61] Cf. Lodovico Dolce's division of the three stages of painting into "invenzione,

of rhetoric, that making of a persuasive speech, was in fact *elocutio*, the use of appropriate diction, and it could be adopted without change as the third stage of any rhetorically based theory of poetic composition, such as we find in Dryden's prefatory epistle to *Annus Mirabilis*.[62] For painting, the orator's *elocutio* necessitated adaptation rather than adoption, and there was to hand an ancient trope that represented diction itself as stylistic colors or coloring: *colores* or χρώματα, as is evident from Greek and Latin dictionaries.

Dryden carried across into his prefatory parallel the rhetorical triad that he found in Dufresnoy's poem or de Piles' prose translation and used it to organize the later stages of his own discourse,[63] making the terms work for poetry as well as for painting. He also supplied poetic analogues for some of Dufresnoy's examples of painterly practice. (Such correspondences are recorded in the annotations that follow.) Beyond these things Dryden offered a discourse, occupying most of the first two-thirds of his preface, on the artist's relation to nature. The subject had also interested Dufresnoy, but he advanced no systematic argument and instead took largely for granted that the artist should imitate what is best in nature. Dufresnoy, that is, adopted a cautious and uninquiring Aristotelianism. Although engaging in no open disagreement with Dufresnoy, Dryden evidently felt some dissatisfaction with Dufresnoy's terms. In their place Dryden offered a Neoplatonic view of the artist's relation to nature, insisting that the artist represents not so much what is in nature as an idea of what is best, which cannot be found fully formed in nature itself. Such a view accords well with Dryden's earlier practice in the heroic play; indeed, his unstated dissent from Dufresnoy's Aristotelianism finds a counterpart in his avowed dissent in *Of Heroique Playes* from Davenant's Aristotelianism and his substitution of a Neoplatonic heightening of character beyond what may be found in nature.[64] The view also accords with Dryden's panegyric practice, wherein the person praised is shown as an ideal exemplar rather than represented as he is.[65]

Those who read Dryden's prefatory parallel without reference to the work it introduces can easily be disconcerted by the long, early quotation from the Neoplatonizing Bellori.[66] But the quotation in fact serves several purposes. The first must occur even to a reader who does not proceed to the translated matter that follows the preface. Taking part of his argument

---

disegno e colorito" (*Dialogo Della Pittura: Intitolato L'Aretino* [1557], in *Trattati D'Arte Del Cinquecento*, ed. Paola Barocchi [1960], I, 164). For Dufresnoy's use of the terms see above, 87:18, 87:23 *sidenote*, and 95:6 *sidenote*.

[62] *Works*, I, 53:23–30.

[63] See 61:16–17, 62:11–12, 71:19–21 above.

[64] *Works*, XI, 10:21–11:8.

[65] See James Kinsley, "Dryden and the Art of Praise," in *Essential Articles for the Study of John Dryden*, ed. H. T. Swedenberg, Jr. (1966), pp. 541–550.

[66] Dryden quotes from the Neoplatonic passages of Bellori's treatise. Bellori in fact adumbrates a more Aristotelian theory of imitation by proposing that the artist achieved an idea of excellence, not a priori, but by combining the partial and scattered excellences he had observed in nature (see discussion by Lee, "*Ut Pictura Poesis*," pp. 208–209).

from Bellori evidently involved Dryden in expending less of the limited time he felt able to devote to the essay than would have the fashioning of his own discourse from, as was his practice elsewhere, a variety of authors. Beyond that obvious fact, quoting Bellori enabled Dryden to shift the philosophical basis of the inquiry from what he found in Dufresnoy. It further enabled Dryden to offer his alternative view through a third person and thus to gain such support and authority as an independent voice could provide. Quoting Bellori also allowed Dryden to differ from Dufresnoy without drawing attention to the fact of dissent. We cannot suppose that the artists who asked Dryden to translate Dufresnoy and to preface his translation with thoughts on the analogy between the arts would have included a request that Dryden draw attention to whatever he found deficient in Dufresnoy's thought.

If we keep in mind the nature as well as the decorum of Dryden's occasion, we will not only see the several purposes that inform his long quotation from Bellori; we will also see *De Arte Graphica*, its preface and translation, within the context of those busy years for Dryden between 1694 and 1697. Dryden produced the whole book in the shadow of his work on Virgil, and his awareness of that shadow evidently accounts for some of the decisions that went into the making of *De Arte Graphica:* to translate de Piles' prose rather than Dufresnoy's verse, or to order part of his preface with some of Dufresnoy's topics and examples. Beyond these things we should also see why, when presented with an opportunity to expatiate upon the text of *ut pictura poesis,* Dryden offered no digested treatise on aesthetics.[67] Such a treatise may have been beyond him, but time and Virgil in any case conspired to elicit from him one more expression of a long-settled habit. For years Dryden had used painting to illustrate the challenges confronting a writer. In the *Parallel betwixt Painting and Poetry* Dryden made some effort to redress the balance by showing how poetry might reciprocally illustrate painting. But the preface is still principally read for its literary criticism rather than its aesthetic analysis, for what Dryden tells us about his own work and that of some contemporaries. It should also be read as an extensive expression, almost a summing up, of a lifelong habit. Dufresnoy began his poem by remarking that poetry will be like painting and painting should be like poetry. Dryden could obviously assent to both propositions, but he had far more to say about the first than the second.

Finally, time and Virgil prevailed. In addition to those intermittent reminders that Dryden should be fulfilling his contract with Tonson, in addition to the use of Virgil as a principal exemplary author, we can see how much Dryden was thinking of Virgil if we read on in his career to the consummation of the Virgil project in 1697. Topics in the *Parallel betwixt Painting and Poetry* recur in the dedication of *Aeneis* as if, or because, Dryden used the occasion of *De Arte Graphica* to work out his ideas on epic and tragedy or the place of the Dido episode within Virgil's poem.

---

67 Thus Lipking, *Ordering of the Arts,* p. 49: Dryden offers "a literal-minded point by point comparison, not an aesthetic inquiry into the common sources of painting and poetry" (see also Lee, "*Ut Pictura Poesis,*" p. 259).

Time also prevailed. The essay is put together in a way that would understandably anger the editor of a modern scholarly journal. Aside from the fact that it generates very little argumentative logic of its own, the preface displays, if intermittently, an old man's self-absorbed loquaciousness, which recurs in the second by-product of the Virgil years, the *Life of Lucian*. We should always remember in reading any work of Dryden's the circumstances in which it was written. In the *Parallel betwixt Painting and Poetry* Dryden made the circumstances more obviously a part of the discourse than he had done or was to do in any other work, except, perhaps, the postscript to his translation of Virgil. The interest of the essay accordingly lies not only in the way it seems to sum up a habit of drawing analogies between the arts, not only in the way it offers many remarks about literary principles and practice which have often been taken out of context for application elsewhere, but also in the way it so emphatically reminds us that Dryden's works exist as facts in a busy life at the same time as they make contributions to criticism, drama, or poetry.

ENGRAVED TITLE

Facing p. 38. Thus described by Edmund Gosse in the *Athenæum* for 12 August 1905, p. 208: "a symbolical frontispiece of Minerva directing the Infant Arts, designed by Henry Cooke (or Cook), and engraved by Simon Gribelin. (These two artists had been engaged together on the Cartoons of Raffaelle.)"

TITLE PAGE

Epigraph. *Ut Pictura Poesis erit.* I.e., poetry will be like painting: the opening clause of Dufresnoy's *De Arte Graphica* (for which see Appendix A) but presumably offered here as a quotation from Horace's *Ars Poetica*, l. 361, to which Dufresnoy alludes. Horace's simile is now usually quoted as *ut pictura poesis,* with *erit* assigned, by means of punctuation, to the clauses that follow. Thus the Loeb text has

> *Ut pictura poesis: erit quae, si propius stes,*
> *te capiat magis, et quaedam, si longius abstes.*

(As painting, so poetry: there will be one that takes you more if you stand closer and another if you stand farther off.) Many early texts of Horace, established, like modern texts, from unpunctuated manuscripts, insert punctuation that assigns *erit* to what precedes rather than to what follows it. Hagstrum (pp. 59–60) discusses the alternative punctuation, listing five editions, published between 1483 and 1579, which punctuate so as to assign *erit* to what precedes it and six others, published between 1567 and 1711, which assign *erit* to what follows. Hagstrum includes no editions published between 1587 and 1690 and none later than 1579 which assigns *erit* to what precedes it. He accordingly notes that Dufresnoy's opening line and Dryden's epigraph are "punctuated in the manner of the early Renaissance" (p. 174). An edition by John Bond (1670), although providing no punctuation immediately before or after *erit,* makes clear by the gloss that *erit* is to be construed with what follows rather than what precedes it (p. 261). But four other seventeenth-century editions punctuate the line so as to construe *erit* with *poesis* rather than with *quae.* Thus the edition of

Daniel Heinsius (Leyden, 1629), to which Dryden refers in the dedication of *Aeneis* (*Works*, V, 275:5–7) offers this text (p. 236):

> *Ut pictura, poesis erit, quae, si propius stes,*
> *Te capiet magis, & quædam, si longius abstes.*

Precisely the same punctuation occurs in editions published by Robert Stephanus (Paris, 1613), p. 224, and by the Imprimerie Royale (Paris, 1642), p. 316, and much the same occurs in the Delphin Horace, ed. Ludovicus Desprez (Paris, 1691): *Ut pictura poesis erit; quae, si propius stes, | Te capiet magis* (p. 904). Moreover, in 1711 Addison still favored the form with *erit* for his epigraph to *Spectator* no. 58. We need, then, to modify Hagstrum's conclusion by saying that, at least until the early eighteenth century, there was no preferred punctuation of Horace's line and that his simile was as likely to be quoted in the prescriptive form it takes in Dryden's epigraph as in the descriptive form familiar to modern scholars. (Dryden had earlier quoted Horace in the prescriptive form: see *A Defence of an Essay* in *Works*, IX, 6:26.) We have no certain evidence that Dryden himself selected the epigraph, but it seems probable that he did so for this as well as for his other works: in the dedication of *Aeneis* he claimed the epigraph to his Virgil as "my Motto in the Title Page" (*Works*, V, 328:22).

A PARALLEL BETWIXT PAINTING AND POETRY

P. 38, ll. 19–26 *the best . . . and others.* Charles I's collection of more than 1,300 paintings, containing many by Raphael and other Italians, had been sold, largely to continental buyers, by 1653, and the Duke of Buckingham's collection had also passed out of England during the Commonwealth (see Henry G. Hewlett, "Charles II as a Picture Collector," *Nineteenth Century*, XXVIII [1890], 201–217). Charles II assembled a collection, less distinguished than his father's, of more than 1,000 paintings, which was augmented by James II, chiefly in the Dutch school. The royal collection was dispersed through the palaces of Whitehall, St. James's, Hampton Court, and Windsor.

38:21–22 *one . . . History-painting.* I.e., Rubens.

39:3 *the Original . . . Authour.* Dryden presumably distinguishes here between Dufresnoy's Latin poem and de Piles' (anonymous) translation of it into French prose as well as his remarks. Later in his own preface Dryden several times refers to Dufresnoy by name and he translated de Piles' preface as the "Preface of the French Authour." But elsewhere in the preface Dryden uses "our Authour" to refer either to Dufresnoy's poem (in de Piles' anonymous French translation) or to de Piles' (anonymous) observations on the poem.

39:18 *The Prose . . . Poem.* Presumably Dryden's English rather than de Piles' French version.

39:26–28 *When I . . . two months.* See headnote, pp. 337–340.

40:6–7 *Poetry, its Sister.* For the sixteenth-century origins of the idea that painting is of equal stature with poetry see, e.g., Nadia Tscherny, "Domenico Corvi's *Allegory of Painting*: An Image of Love," *Marsyas*, XIX (1977–78), 23–24 and pl. XV. By the eighteenth century painting, music, sculpture, architecture, and poetry had achieved equivalence as the "fine arts" or "beaux arts" (see Paul Oskar Kristeller, "The Modern System of the Arts: A Study in the History of Aesthetics," *JHI*, XII [1951], 496–527; XIII [1952], 17–46).

40:7–45:23 *I copy . . . for himself.* Dryden translates and condenses "L'Idea del Pittore, dello Scultore, e dell' Architetto," which Giovanni Pietro Bellori (1613–1696) prefixed to his *Le Vite de' Pittori, Scultori et Architetti Moderni* (Rome, 1672). We have not undertaken to annotate Bellori's citations, transmitted by Dryden, except when they are misleading. For Aristotelianism and Bellori's Neoplatonism see headnote, pp. 350–351.

41:17–27 *Zeuxis . . . parts.* The story is in Cicero's *De Inventione*, II, 1–3, not his *Orator.*

41:28–31 *Maximus . . . Statues.* The reference is to sculptors rather than painters. De Piles quoted the relevant passage in a remark on Dufresnoy's poem (see 116:22–30 above).

42:6 *and most . . . Painters.* Not in Bellori.

42:7–9 *Lysippus . . . to be.* According to Pliny, *Natural History*, XXXIV, xix, 61, 65, Lysippus in fact strove for realistic detail.

42:9–10 *he made . . . Painters.* Not a precept of Aristotle's, although in *Poetics*, II, Aristotle observes that men may be painted or poetically represented as better or worse than they are, or just as they are.

43:24–25 *and to . . . Comparison.* Not in Bellori.

44:6–7 *Si . . . Aquis.* The now accepted reading of the first line (*Ars Amatoria*, III, 401) is *Si Venerem Cous nusquam posuisset Apelles* (if Coan Apelles had never fashioned Venus). Dryden's text of this line (if Apelles had never painted Venus for the Coans) is taken from Bellori, p. 7, and can also be found in Renaissance editions of Ovid, e.g., an Aldine *Vita . . . ex ipsius libris excerpta* (Venice, 1515), p. 145, and (with *pinxisse*) another *Vita ex ipsius libris excerpta* (Florence, 1528), p. 143. An edition of Ovid by Gregorius Bersmanus (1655–1656) has *pinxisset* and *Cous*, but notes *Cois* as a variant (I, 231).

44:28–45:1 *In this . . . shewn you.* Not in Bellori.

45:19–23 *I must . . . for himself.* Elaborating upon Bellori's "io però quì manco nel dire, e taccio" (p. 13: but further words fail me and I fall silent).

45:27–28 *Plato . . . Homer.* See Longinus, *On the Sublime*, XIII, 3–4, and Dryden's preface to *Troilus and Cressida* in *Works*, XIII, 228:21–32 and note.

46:2–47:5 *What . . . Pictures.* From the proem to the *Imagines* of Philostratus the Younger. Dryden makes English the Italian version of just this portion of the proem which Bellori included among the prefatory material to his *Vite de' Pittori.*

47:3–4 *by the . . . Shadows.* Dryden's elaboration.

47:6–7 *as . . . Merchants.* Perhaps alluding, as Scott notes (S-S, XVII, 299), to William III's deployment of the fleet in the war against France instead of assigning it to protect merchant vessels; the unprotected Smyrna convoy of 1693 suffered heavy losses from privateers (see Julian S. Corbett, *England in the Mediterranean* [1917], II, 422–424). James Anderson Winn, *John Dryden and His World* (1987), p. 480, also draws attention to Luttrell's reports (III, 291, 294, 298) of the taking of the *Berkeley Castle*, a merchantman, in April 1694.

48:2–8 *The perfection . . . Mankind.* Based upon Aristotle, *Poetics*, II.

48:10–11 *draw . . . Eyes.* See Pliny, *Natural History*, XXXV, xxxvi, 90.
48:13–24 *'Tis . . . requited.* Based upon Aristotle, *Poetics*, XIII.
48:27 *my own St. Catharine.* The heroine of *Tyrannick Love* (*Works*, X).
49:6–9 *In Comedy . . . Aristotle.* See *Poetics*, V, 1–2.
49:14–18 *The Heroes . . . undergo.* Cf. *Character of Saint-Evremond*, 9:8–10:32 above, and dedication of *Aeneis* in *Works*, V, 288:1–5, 291:16–292:23.
49:19–20 *Son . . . Jerusalem.* Luke 19:41.
49:20–21 *Lentulus . . . laughing.* See Montague Rhodes James, *The Apocryphal New Testament* (1926), p. 478.
49:23–27 *I will . . . to him.* For the first of many statements about decorum by Dufresnoy and de Piles see 87:23–28 and 133:5–15 above.
50:2–12 *Homer's . . . intention.* Cf. dedication of *Aeneis* in *Works*, V, 271:5–12.
50:5 *tax'd . . . bad.* See *Republic*, II, xvii–III, v.
50:11–13 *the moral . . . Poet.* Cf. the preface to *Troilus and Cressida* in *Works*, XIII, 234:18–24 and notes.
50:21 *the Marquess . . . ne'er knew.* See John Sheffield, Earl of Mulgrave and Marquis of Normanby, *An Essay upon Poetry*, (1682), p. 15; the line should end with "saw," not "knew."
51:3–6 *the Authour . . . Mind.* See 84:5–8 above.
51:12–17 *the means . . . Fiction.* The doctrine of artistic deception was already current for Plutarch, *Moralia*, 15 C–D, and was as contemporary with Dryden as André Dacier, *La Poëtique d'Aristote* (Paris, 1692), p. 280. Painterly deception gained special authority from Pliny's anecdotes in *Natural History*, XXXV, and the general doctrine was summarized in a passage Dryden had already quoted in his preface from the proem of Philostratus the Younger (see 46:17–21 above).
51:17–19 *as all . . . Picture.* Cf. 84:8–10, 111:1–2 above.
51:19–21 *The Subjects . . . it self.* See 85:17–18, 102:6–17 above.
51:21 *wave.* I.e., waive.
51:22–25 *Catullus . . . holy.* See Catullus, XVI; Ovid, *Tristia*, II, 353–356. Dryden had earlier instanced the epigram of Catullus when responding to charges of indecency in *The Kind Keeper* (1680, sig. A3*v*; S-S, VI, 9).
51:27 *Vita proba est.* Martial, *Epigrams*, I, iv, 8, with *est* added (the life is honorable).
52:2–4 *the Adventure . . . at it.* See *Aeneid*, IV, 160–172; Dryden's ll. 231–250. Cf. dedication of *Aeneis* in *Works*, V, 302:21–24.
52:14–16 *Altar-Pieces . . . Poetry.* Cf. 84:10–13, 111:23–27 above.
52:16–21 *Farnesian . . . Bellori.* See Bellori's *Vite de' Pittori* (Rome, 1672), pp. 33–35, 44–66. Cf. de Piles' reference to Caracci and the gallery, 140:31–34, 141:13–18 above.
52:24–25 *our Author . . . noble.* See 84:23–26, 87:4–5, 102:22–29 above; cf. 124:35–125:14 above.
53:3 *Cloth.* Canvas (*OED*).
53:3–4 *Anger . . . Iphigenia.* For lists of the many paintings on these subjects see A. Pigler, *Barockthemen: Eine Auswahl von Verzeichnissen zur Ikonographie des 17. und 18. Jahrhunderts* (1956), II, 266–280, 307–310.
53:9–10 *History . . . Poet.* Cf. 84:21–26 above.
53:10–17 *Curtius . . . History.* See Livy, VII, vi; VIII, ix–x; X, xxviii;

XXVI, 1. For lists of the many paintings on these subjects see Pigler, *Barockthemen*, II, 368–370, 404–409.

53:21–54:3 *Homer took . . . Turnus.* See Le Bossu, *Traité du poëme épique* (Paris, 1675), II, 268–271. Le Bossu computed the duration of the *Aeneid*'s action at rather less than seven years because he included the events narrated by Aeneas to Dido. Dryden discussed the duration of epic action more extensively in the dedication of *Aeneis* (*Works*, V, 309:20–313:7).

54:22–29 *Thus . . . Table.* Although Poussin made several paintings of the Last Supper, Dryden seems to describe the one reproduced as pl. 159 in Anthony Blunt, *Nicolas Poussin* (1967). It is in the second of Poussin's two series depicting the seven sacraments, a series owned in Dryden's time by Paul Fréart de Chantelou which did not come to England until it was bought by the Duke of Bridgewater in 1798 (see Anthony Blunt, *The Paintings of Nicolas Poussin* [1966], pp. 76–77). Roland Fréart de Chambray described the painting in *Idee de la Perfection de la Peinture* (Le Mans, 1662), pp. 128–134; see also the translation by John Evelyn, *An Idea of the Perfection of Painting* (1668), pp. 131–136. But Dryden may have seen, or perhaps owned, engravings of the Chantelou series made by Jean Pesne (1623–1700), for which see A.-P.-F. Robert-Dumesnil, *Le Peintre-Graveur Français* (1838), III, 130–141.

55:9 *Kermis.* A fair or carnival.

55:9–10 *Snick or Snee.* "The practice of fighting with cut-and-thrust knives" (*OED*).

55:12 *Such . . . Venus.* Cf. *Works*, I, 56:13–17 and note.

55:15–16 *Farce is . . . unnatural.* See Leo Hughes, "Attitudes of Some Restoration Dramatists toward Farce," *PQ*, XIX (1940), 268–287.

55:19–23 *Horace . . . Laughter.* In *Ars Poetica*, ll. 1–8, the human head is a woman's; Dryden corrected the allusion in the dedication of *Aeneis* (*Works*, V, 273:1–2).

55:25 *propriety.* Distinctive characteristic (*OED*).

56:17–20 *Davenant . . . chearfully.* A free paraphrase of Davenant's remarks (see Spingarn, II, 47).

56:28–57:12 *Hippocrates . . . impossible.* See Dacier, preface to *Poëtique d'Aristote*, p. viii.

57:18–20 *Nature . . . her self.* Dacier repeated this commonplace in the sentence preceding his quotation from Hippocrates.

57:21–22 *Philostratus for Painting.* Both Philostrati devoted their Εἰκόνες to rhetorical descriptions of paintings and neither could be construed as a rule giver. Dryden seems to have in mind the proem of the younger Philostratus, which Dryden had quoted earlier, where brief reference is made to the laws of painting and the common subjects of painting and poetry (see 46:21–47:5 above).

58:3–5 *they have . . . ruine.* Cf. 116:11–16 above.

58:12–27 *The greatest . . . uncertain.* Cf. 134:25–135:12 above.

58:20–21 *Leo . . . First.* De Piles, whom Dryden here follows, refers only to "the end of the fifteenth Age, and the beginning of our Sixteenth" (135:3–4 above). Leo X was Pope, 1513–1521; Charles V was Holy Roman Emperor, 1519–1556; Francis I was King of France, 1515–1547.

58:23 *in revenge.* In return; Malone (III, 321) notes the Gallicism (from *en revanche* or *revenche*).

58:27–59:2 *by what . . . Europe.* Dryden updates de Piles' reference in 1668 to Louis XIV's patronage to include Louis' six-year war with the Dutch in the 1670s and the war against William III which began in 1689 and did not conclude until 1697 with the Treaty of Ryswick.

59:2–4 *our Author . . . Attempts.* Dufresnoy counseled that honor, not riches, should be the painter's goal (105:32–37 above). But de Piles, after exemplifying the precept, added that "hope of gain is a wonderfull sharp spur in Arts" (190:11–12 above).

59:11–13 *Bossu . . . upon him.* For Le Bossu and Dacier see above, 53: 21–54:3, 56:28–57:12, and notes.

59:17–19 *The principal . . . Art.* See 85:21–24 above.

60:10–13 *Aristotle . . . Original.* See *Poetics,* IV. Aristotle is in fact concerned only with the pleasure that comes from contemplating accurate—not from detecting inaccurate—representation. From what Dryden goes on to say (61:3), it seems likely that the citation of Aristotle formed part of the "Remark" on imitation contributed by Walter Moyle to Dryden's preface.

61:4 *Walter Moyle.* See *Life of Lucian,* 223:20–23 above and note.

61:16 *The principal . . . follow.* For the rhetorical divisions employed see headnote, pp. 349–350 above.

61:16–17 *Invention . . . part.* See above, 87:18 *sidenote.*

61:22–23 *How to . . . teach us.* For de Piles' list, augmented with English titles by Dryden, see 128:9–131:12 above.

61:25 *Tu . . . Minervâ.* Horace, *Ars Poetica,* l. 385 (Loeb trans.: "But *you* will say nothing and do nothing against Minerva's will").

62:4–5 *Imitatours . . . Poet.* Horace, *Epistles,* I, xix, 19. De Piles had quoted Horace's Latin (see 126:27 above) and Dryden recalled the stricture in the dedication of *Aeneis* (*Works,* V, 305:16–18).

62:11–12 *the Disposition of the Work.* See above 87:23 *sidenote.*

62:12–15 *to put . . . Times.* See 87:24–31 above.

62:19–21 *Not . . . Masters.* See *El Arte Nuevo de Hacer Comedias en este Tiempo,* ed. Juana de José Prades (1971). Lope de Vega rejected the rules and examples of the ancients and aimed to please the vulgar (ll. 9–10, 42–48); he defended tragicomedy (ll. 174–180) and violation of the unity of time (ll. 188–210).

62:26–63:2 *As in . . . of it.* Cf. 87:32–88:2 above.

63:7–10 *A Painter . . . Burthen.* Cf. 152:16–25 above.

63:11–13 *Horace . . . Poetry.* See ll. 322 and 16 (Loeb trans.: "verses void of thought, and sonorous trifles"; "Diana's grove and altar").

63:18–19 *neither . . . languish.* Cf. the dedication of *Aeneis* (*Works,* V, 307:28–30).

63:19–21 *Montezuma . . . season.* See *The Indian Emperour,* V, ii, 248–249 (*Works,* IX, 106). Cf. the preface to *Troilus and Cressida* (*Works,* XIII, 243:20–244:5).

63:22–23 *Our Authour . . . lett.* The author is de Piles (see 133:34–134:2 above).

63:23–25 *I have . . . number.* Dryden's mind may still be running on his own plays and to the practice of filling the stage at climactic moments of serious drama (see stage direction in the penultimate scene of *The Spanish Fryar:* "*Enter* Gomez, Elvira, Dominic, *with Officers, to make the Stage as full as possible"* [1681, p. 77; S-S, VI, 513]). The practice was satirized in *The Rehearsal* (see *Works*, XI, 548).

63:27–64:1 *Our Authour . . . Action.* The author is here Dufresnoy (see 87:35–88:2 above).

64:2–3 *Du Fresnoy . . . Painting.* See 88:24 *sidenote* above.

64:8 *Achilles . . . Hector.* See *Iliad*, XXII, 289–336.

64:8–9 *Æneas . . . him.* See *Aeneid*, XII, 938–952.

64:12–13 *Æneas . . . Eyes.* See *Aeneid*, I, 594–602; but the description corresponds less closely to Virgil's than to Dryden's in the translation he may well have recently completed (see *Aeneis*, I, 833–845, in *Works*, V, 369).

64:13–27 *when he . . . to perform.* See *Aeneid*, X, 794–830.

64:27–65:15 *Take . . . thought.* As translated for *The entire Episode of Mezentius and Lausus* (in *Sylvæ*, 1685), ll. 65–70, 77–82, 97–98 (*Works*, III, 36–37), except that Dryden here substitutes *"Their first Assault"* for the *Sylvæ* reading, "The Storm of darts," probably because, by collapsing his translation, Dryden would otherwise have repeated the phrase within five lines, whereas in *Sylvæ* ten lines intervene. Dryden restored the *Sylvæ* reading for the 1697 Virgil and also changed *"noble Emulation"* to "gen-'rous Indignation." Thus modified in 1697, these lines became *Aeneis*, X, 1134–1139, 1146–1151, 1166–1167 (*Works*, VI, 713–714).

65:16–18 *Design . . . different.* See 89:17–18 above.

65:19–25 *I knew . . . Name.* Quoted in a letter to Congreve by Dennis in 1721. Dennis remarked that Dryden "in this Passage doth certainly reflect upon Mr. Wycherley, and particularly upon his *Plain-dealer*" (*Critical Works*, ed. Edward Niles Hooker [1939, 1943], II, 231). Malone (III, 331) insists that Dryden's "words—'I *knew*,' clearly denote a *dead* poet, and consequently will exclude Wycherley," as well as Congreve, whose candidacy Malone also considers. Malone proposes Etherege, Dryden's friend until his death in 1691, and cites a couplet from Dryden's epilogue to *The Man of Mode*, ll. 7–8: "Sir *Fopling* is a Fool so nicely writ, / The Ladies wou'd mistake him for a Wit" (*Works*, I, 154). Etherege would indeed seem more likely than Wycherley, whom Dryden names a few pages later not only with respect but in terms that denote close friendship between the two (68:6–8 above).

65:25–66:2 *Another . . . Judgment.* Always, and with reason, taken to be Nathaniel Lee, whom Dryden had known through collaboration upon *Oedipus* and *The Duke of Guise,* and who was committed to Bedlam from 1684 to 1688. Contemporary explanations of Lee's insanity included excessive drinking and undue straining after the poetical sublime (see *Works*, ed. Thomas B. Stroup and Arthur L. Cooke [1954; reprint 1968], I, 16). For a particular speech answering to Dryden's description of Lee's style see the often parodied conclusion to the fourth act of *Oedipus* (*Works*, XIII, 196–197). Lee died in 1692.

66:3–4 *Let . . . Face.* Dryden first quotes in italics his own translation of Dufresnoy's precept and then adapts the illustration that he found in de Piles' observation (see above, 89:22–23, 141:30–32).

66:8–10 *He who . . . Daughter.* Dryden thought *Pericles* an early and therefore imperfect work of Shakespeare's (see his epilogue to an unknown play, ll. 16–19 [*Works*, I, 158]).

66:11–12 *nor . . . Moorcraft.* See *Works*, XI, 492–493.

66:16–18 *The principal . . . attendants.* See 89:28–33 above.

66:27–67:2 *As in . . . manner.* Cf. 89:34–90:10 above.

67:4–12 *Such . . . Return.* See *Aeneid*, IX, 176–449. Dryden had trans-
lated the episode for *Sylvæ* (*Works*, III, 22–34); in the 1697 Virgil it makes
up, with many changes from the *Sylvæ* version, *Aeneis*, IX, 217–600 (*Works*,
VI, 648–659).

67:9–10 *as the . . . Turks.* For several years the war between the Hapsburg
and Ottoman empires had produced only inconclusive campaigning, and
Dryden probably refers to the event that precipitated the war: the two-
month siege of Vienna by the Turks in the summer of 1683 which was
eventually raised by allied forces under the command of Sobieski (see, e.g.,
the foreign dispatches recorded by Luttrell, I, 269, 272, 275, 280).

67:10 *advertise.* Inform.

67:13–20 *The Grecian . . . Play.* See Aristotle, *Poetics*, IV.

67:24–68:3 *a good . . . Voices.* In the dedication of *Examen Poeticum*
(1693) Dryden had dismissed Rymer's claim in *A Short View of Tragedy*
(1692) that the chorus "is certainly always the most necessary part of
Tragedy" (see *Works*, IV, 367:28–32; Rymer, *Critical Works*, p. 84). Ry-
mer's claim had already been challenged more extensively by Dennis in
The Impartial Critick, with particular reference to Racine's *Esther* (1689).
Racine, Dennis notes, conceded in his preface to *Esther* that he had been
asked to write a tragedy with chorus "by those who had the Superintendency
of the House of St. Cyr. . . . So that what Mr. R—— calls a necessity, was
but at the best a conveniency. . . . [to ensure that] the cloister'd Beauties of
that blooming Society, had a favourable occasion of shewing their Parts in
a Religious way, to the French Court" (*Critical Works*, ed. Hooker, I, 31).
Dacier commended Racine's experiment in *Poëtique d'Aristote*, p. xvi,
arguing that "il faut rétablir le Chœur," because in antiquity it was the
principal agent of instruction, the chief end of tragedy. Although debate
over the chorus was especially lively in the 1690s, it began earlier and
continued into the next century (see the useful summary by Hooker in
Dennis, *Critical Works*, I, 437).

68:6–8 *Wicherly . . . Judge.* As early as 1677, in the *Author's Apology*
prefixed to *The State of Innocence,* Dryden declared himself "*proud to call*
[Wycherley] *my Friend*" (1677, sig. b2v; S-S, V, 115). In the 1690s Dryden
frequently referred to Wycherley with no diminution of respect (see Ward,
Letters, pp. 54, 73; *To Mr. Southern*, ll. 26–31, in *Works*, III, 227–228;
Discourse of Satire in *Works*, IV, 57:26–27; *To My Dear Friend Mr. Con-
greve*, l. 30, in *Works*, IV, 432).

68:9 *Spatiis exclusus iniquis.* See *Georgics*, IV, 147 (Loeb trans.: "barred
by these narrow bounds").

68:15–16 *a Theatre . . . Charges.* Perhaps glancing at William III's ne-
glect of the public theatre in England and continued support of it in
Holland (see Nesca A. Robb, *William of Orange: A Personal Portrait* [1962–
1966], II, 228–229). Cf. Dryden's *Prologue to The Prophetess*, ll. 1–12, whose
double reference to the company's costly preparations for the opera and
William III's costly preparations for the Irish campaign resulted in the
prologue's prohibition (*Works*, III, 255, 508–509).

68:17–20 *That my . . . delightfull.* Malone (III, 336) took this as a refer-
ence to the translation of Virgil. But Scott (S-S, XVII, 324) seems right to

construe it more generally as alluding once more to Dryden's circumstances after the Glorious Revolution: "curb'd in my Genius," as he put it in the postscript to the Virgil, "lyable to be misconstrued in all I write" (*Works*, VI, 807:4–5). Any serious play by Dryden at this time could easily have prompted unfavorable application to government policies, and Scott pertinently notes the temporary prohibition of *Cleomenes* in 1692, the suppression of the *Prologue to The Prophetess* in 1690, and Dryden's lament in the prologue to *Amphitryon* (1690), ll. 10–11: "*How can he show his Manhood, if you bind him | To box, like Boys, with one Hand ty'd behind him?*" (*Works*, XV, 227).

68:21–25 *To make . . . retain.* See 93:17–20 above.

68:22 *Scenary.* "The disposition and consecution of the scenes of a play" (*OED*); the word was later replaced by "scenario." Cf. *The Vindication* of *The Duke of Guise* (1683, p. 42; S-S, VII, 203).

68:27–28 *The Painter . . . parts.* See 93:32–34 above.

69:4–8 *I remember . . . End.* Sir Robert Stapylton's play (1663), which Dryden had already criticized for this fault in the preface to *Troilus and Cressida* (*Works*, XIII, 230:32–34). Cf. Dryden's epilogue to an unknown play, l. 15 (*Works*, I, 158).

69:8–18 *To express . . . real Passion.* See 94:3–16 above.

69:18–24 *Otway . . . Beauty.* Dryden's remarks helped determine the tone and topics of critical comment on Otway during the eighteenth century (see A. M. Taylor, *Next to Shakespeare* [1950], pp. 249–255).

69:25–27 *In the . . . with them.* The author here is de Piles (see 162:26–163:1 above).

70:2–6 *What . . . taken.* Although both discuss portraiture, neither Dufresnoy nor de Piles employs Dryden's distinction (see 101:12–24, 178:9–25 above).

70:7–13 *Sophocles, says . . . by Aristotle.* See *Poetics*, XXV, where only Sophocles and Euripides are specified in Dryden's terms and the third poet, Xenophanes, represents something very different from what Dryden ascribes to him. Dryden may be conflating Chapter XXV with Chapter II, where Aristotle distinguishes between representation of superior, normal, and inferior men, specifying painters and poets who exemplify each kind of representation. Although Aristotle's preference for Sophocles may be inferred from the *Poetics*, Aristotle makes no particular commendation in Dryden's terms.

70:13–14 *that part . . . writ.* I.e., the first and third acts, the remainder being written by Lee (see *Works*, XIII, 443).

70:15–22 *my Characters . . . Pity.* Cf. the preface to *All for Love* (*Works*, XIII, 10:8–21).

70:23–24 *The Gothique . . . Picture.* See 94:17–19 above.

70:25–71:8 *our English . . . Habit.* For a useful collection of Dryden's fluctuating views on tragicomedy see John M. Aden, *The Critical Opinions of John Dryden* (1963), pp. 252–253.

71:1–3 *Pastor . . . Action.* Cf. *Works*, IV, 79:19–24; see also *Works*, XV, 363.

71:9–12 *Du Fresnoy . . . positions.* See 90:5–10 above.

71:14–15 *Contraria . . . elucescunt.* For source and translation see *Works,* XVII, 378.

71:15–16 *Thus . . . Prodigal.* Cf. 66:11–12 above; see also *Works,* XI, 492–493.

71:16–18 *in my . . . Catharine.* Cf. *Works,* X, 110:7–9.

71:19–21 *I am . . . Colouring.* See 95:6–7 above.

71:27 *Turns . . . Thought.* Cf. *Discourse of Satire* in *Works,* IV, 84: 14–86:15.

71:29–30, 72:3 *Our . . . Sororis | she procures . . . for her.* Dryden seems to be retranslating from de Piles' remark: "nostre Autheur appelle cette derniere Partie, *Lena Sororis.* . . . On l'accusoit de produire sa Sœur, & de nous engager adroitement à l'aimer" (*L'Art de Peinture,* p. 121). Dufresnoy's *Lena Sororis* (l. 263) is made French by de Piles in his translation of the poem and then English by Dryden, who also makes English the phrase when translating de Piles' remark (see 95:15–16, 164:25–28 above).

72:13 *Operum Colores.* See *Ars Poetica,* l. 86 (Loeb trans.: "shades of poetic forms").

72:15–16 *Amongst . . . Colouring.* Cf. 95:8–12 above.

72:17–73:6 *Of the two . . . alter'd.* Dryden consistently preferred Homer's invention and design to Virgil's, summing up his opinion in the preface to *Fables* (1700, sig. *A2v; Watson, II, 274–276). In that place he also found Virgil's "Expression . . . at least equal to" Homer's, although in the unpublished *Heads of an Answer to Rymer* he noted that "*Homer* excels *Virgil*" in diction (*Works,* XVII, 190:27–28). Elsewhere Dryden had highest praise for Virgil's diction—e.g., in the preface to *Sylvæ* (*Works,* III, 8:33–9:6)—and in the dedication of *Aeneis,* in a passage alluding to *A Parallel betwixt Painting and Poetry,* he repeated that he had "endeavour'd to form [his] Stile by imitating" Virgil (*Works,* V, 326:17–18). By pedants of a contrary persuasion Dryden seems to mean commentators on Homer, but he may have been recalling (as he did in the passage already cited from the preface to *Fables*) Hobbes's preface to his translation of Homer, where Hobbes, finding Homer and Virgil equal in propriety of diction, preferred Homer over Virgil in "clearness of Images, or Descriptions" (Spingarn, II, 72–73).

73:12–14 *My late . . . Author.* See Roscommon's *Essay on Translated Verse* (1684), p. 21:

> When Virgil, seems to Trifle in a Line,
> 'Tis like a Warning-Piece, which gives the Sign
> To Wake your Fancy, and prepare your Sight,
> To reach the noble Height of some unusual Flight.

73:15–16 *the whole . . . Figures.* Cf. *The Author's Apology* prefixed to *The State of Innocence* (1677, b3v; S-S, V, 117).

73:26–28 *Virgil . . . Horse.* Dryden had quoted the opening line of *Sylvæ* in his dedication of *The Spanish Fryar* (1681, sig. A3; S-S, VI, 407) in order to contrast Virgil's "*Majesty of a lawfull Prince*" with Statius' "*blustring of a Tyrant.*"

74:2–3 *Magnanimum . . . Progeniem.* See *Achilleid,* I, 1–2 (Loeb trans.: "of great-hearted Aeacides and of the progeny that the Thunderer feared").

74:9–10 *Stare . . . campum.* Presumably to make the verses a "true Image of their Author," Dryden substituted *nescit* (he knows not) for *miserum est* (it is a wretched thing) (see *Thebaid*, VI, 400–401; Loeb trans.: he does not know how "to stand still[;] a thousand steps are lost ere they start, and, on the absent plain, their hooves ring loud").

74:15–27 '*Tis said . . . cantu.* See Suetonius, *Virgil,* XXXIV. In Dryden's day the life was either attributed to Donatus or considered anonymous; it was included in the prefatory material of the Delphin Virgil, ed. Carolus Ruaeus, which was Dryden's principal text for the translation of Virgil. Dryden repeated the story of Virgil's extemporizing the hemistich on Misenus while reading to Augustus in the dedication of *Aeneis* (*Works,* V, 333:1–7).

74:22–23, 27 *Quo . . . viros | Martemq; . . . cantu.* See *Aeneid,* VI, 164–165 (Loeb trans.: "surpassed by none in stirring men with his bugle's blare, and in kindling with his clang the god of war"). Cf. Dryden's ll. 243–246 (*Works,* V, 534).

75:5–6 *you see . . . cantu.* Because *accendere* literally means to set on fire and figuratively to incite, and because *Martem* literally means the god and is also a metonym for the war over which Mars presides. Dryden probably thought that *cantu* literally meant music produced by voice (in Elyot's *Dictionary, cantus* is glossed simply as "a songe") and that when applied, as here, to music produced by instrument, the usage was metaphorical. But by Virgil's time *cantus* had so often signified either vocal or instrumental harmony that any metaphor in the latter usage would have been faded.

75:8–9 *curiosa . . . Horace.* See *Satyricon,* 118. The phrase comes lamely into English as "studied felicity," since *felicitas* means good fortune unsought for and, with *curiosa,* forms an oxymoron.

75:9–11 '*tis the . . . without it.* See Pliny, *Natural History,* XXXV, xxxvi, 104.

75:15 *Bristol-stone.* A "kind of transparent rock-crystal found in the Clifton limestone near Bristol, resembling the diamond in brilliancy" (*OED*). Cf. the preface to *Troilus and Cressida* (*Works,* XIII, 247:3–4).

75:15–17 *the Cocks . . . Jewel.* The first fable in most Renaissance collections, e.g., L'Estrange's (1692).

75:18–22 *that Verse . . . touch'd.* For the line, illustrating the proposition that *ut pictura poesis,* see *Ars Poetica,* l. 363: *haec amat obscurum, volet haec sub luce videri* (Loeb trans.: "This courts the shade, that will wish to be seen in the light"). Horace is distinguishing between different kinds of poems and paintings, not different parts of the same piece.

75:29–76:2 *We have . . . Pencil.* See Pliny, *Natural History,* XXXV, xxxvi, 80. Apelles criticized Protogenes for excessive care, for not knowing when to take his hand from the canvas. See 123:3–9, 181:10–13 above.

76:17 *Antony and Cleopatra.* I.e., *All for Love.*

76:24–25 *Apelles . . . over.* See above, note to 75:29–76:2.

76:29–30 *caput mortuum.* Worthless residue after distillation.

77:9–10 *Credas . . . æquos.* Dryden substitutes *æquos* for *altos* in *Aeneid,* VIII, 691–692. His version of the Latin runs in English, "you would think that the Cyclades were torn up and floating, or that mountains rushed against mountains of equal height."

77:12 *Cynthius . . . admonuit.* Virgil, *Eclogue* VI, 3–4 (Cynthian Apollo plucked my ear and warned me).

77:13 *behind.* "Not yet brought forward or mentioned" (*OED*).

THE PREFACE OF THE FRENCH AUTHOR

P. 79, l. 24 *on the side.* The numbers are set in the margins of Q, but are embedded within our text.

80:12 *through.* I.e., thorough.

80:26, 80:27–81:1 *Since | and they.* Understanding another "since" between "and" and "they" clarifies the English syntax and brings it closer to the French: "puisque . . . & que ceux" (*L'Art de Peinture*, sig. ã3).

81:22 *prevention of mind.* Prepossession, prejudice, a Gallicism from *L'Art de Peinture*, sig. a3v: "prevention d'esprit."

A TABLE OF THE PRECEPTS

P. 82, ll. 5–6 [col. a] *Invention . . . Painting.* Dryden's addition.

82:13–14 [col. a] *Design . . . Painting.* Substituted for "Attitude" or "Posture," as Dryden translated it in *The Art of Painting* (88:24 above).

82:27–28 [col. b] *Colouring . . . Painting.* Dryden's addition.

THE ART OF PAINTING

P. 84, ll. 19–20 *are neither . . . study to.* For the 2d ed. Jervas substituted "with concurring Studies" (p. 5).

84:21 *They.* Preceded by an asterisk in Q to signal an observation; there is no asterisk in the French editions and no subsequent observation in them or in Q.

85:9–10 *whose . . . Road.* For the 2d ed. Jervas substituted "whom Practice only directs" (p. 7).

87:13–16 *Thus . . . Genius.* For the 2d ed. Jervas substituted "At length I come to the Work itself, and at first find only a bare strain'd Canvas, on which the Sketch is to be disposed by the Strength of a happy Imagination" (p. 13).

87:24 *Postures.* Dryden seems to have glanced from the French—"Attitudes" (*L'Art de Peinture*, p. 11)—to the Latin: *Posituras* (l. 78). Jervas substituted "Attitudes" for the 2d ed. (p. 15).

87:29 *your Compositions be.* For the 2d ed. Jervas substituted "there be a genuine and lively Expression of the Subject" (p. 15).

87:32–35 *Take . . . occasion.* For the 2d ed. Jervas substituted "Whatever is trivial, foreign, or improper, ought by no means to take up the principal Part of the Picture. But herein" (p. 15).

87:32–33 *whatsoever makes nothing to.* A Gallicism; cf. *L'Art de Peinture*, p. 11: "ce qui ne fait rien."

88:3–4 *and so . . . found.* Omitted from the 2d ed. (p. 15), although de Piles' "& si difficile" (*L'Art de Peinture*, p. 11) answers to Dufresnoy's *Ardua* (l. 88).

88:10–11 *Painting . . . travell'd.* For the 2d ed. Jervas substituted "Painting in Egypt was at first rude and imperfect, till being brought" (p. 15).

88:20 *Beauty.* For the 2d ed. Jervas added "and Gracefulness" (p. 17) to make the phrase correspond to the Latin: *formæ atque decoris* (l. 100); the French has only "la Beauté" (*L'Art de Peinture*, p. 12).

88:21–22 *Though . . . or.* For the 2d ed. Jervas correctly changed the disjunctive into a conjunctive clause by substituting "Or indeed that is not very much inferiour, both in Science, and" (p. 17). Cf. the Latin (l. 102) and the French: "quoy qu'on ne s'en soit pas si fort éloigné, tant" (*L'Art de Peinture*, p. 12).

88:24 *Posture.* Cf. the Latin, *Positura* (l. 103) and the French, "Attitude" (*L'Art de Peinture*, p. 12); Jervas substituted "Attitude" in the 2d ed. (p. 17).

88:26–29 *unequal . . . Centre.* For the 2d ed. Jervas substituted "contrasted by contrary Motions, the most noble Parts foremost in sight, and each Figure carefully poised on its own Centre" (p. 17).

88:30–89:5 *must have . . . Figures.* For the 2d ed. Jervas substituted "must be drawn with flowing glideing Outlines, large and smooth, rising gradually, not swelling suddenly, but which may be just felt in the Statues, or cause a little Relievo in Painting. Let the Muscles have their Origin and Insertion according to the Rules of Anatomy; let them not be subdivided into small Sections, but kept as entire as possible, in imitation of the Greek Forms, and expressing only the principal Muscles" (pp. 17, 19).

89:11–12 *or a . . . Picture.* For the 2d ed. Jervas substituted "for designing" (p. 19).

89:34–36 *Members . . . together.* For the 2d ed. Jervas substituted "Parts be brought together, and the Figures dispos'd in Grouppes" (p. 21).

90:5 *sidenote of Postures.* Cf. the Latin, *Positurarum* (l. 138 *sidenote*), and the French, "d'Attitudes" (p. 16); Jervas substituted "Attitudes" in the 2d ed. (p. 21).

90:6–13 *be like . . . the left.* For the 2d ed. Jervas substituted (p. 21):
have the same Inflections of the Body, nor the same Motions; nor should they lean all one way, but break the Symmetry, by proper Oppositions and Contrastes.
To several Figures seen in Front oppose others with the Back toward the Spectator, that is, the Shoulders of some oppos'd to the Breasts of others and right Limbs to left, whether the Piece consists of many Figures or but of few.

90:16–18 *if one . . . other.* For the 2d ed. Jervas substituted "if any thing rises high on one side of the Piece, you may raise something to answer it on the other" (pp. 21, 23).

90:18–19 *whether . . . few.* Omitted from the 2d ed. (p. 23).

90:24–28 *And we . . . few.* For the 2d ed. Jervas substituted "How should they excel in putting several Figures together, who can scarce excel in a single one?" (p. 23).

91:7–8 *the views . . . as also.* For the 2d ed. Jervas substituted "all odd Aspects or Positions, and all ungraceful or" (p. 25).

91:29–31 *We may . . . Forests.* For the 2d ed. Jervas substituted "Errors are infinite" (pp. 25, 27), but the trope is in Dufresnoy (l. 180), as well as in de Piles (*L'Art de Peinture*, p. 19).

92:5 *Vases.* For the 2d ed. Jervas added "Gems" before "Vases" and "Paintings" after it (p. 27).

92:22 *straight.* I.e., strait in the sense of "tight-fitting" (*OED*).

92:23 *distinguish.* Make conspicuous (*OED*).

92:28–31 *the Beauty . . . others.* For the 2d ed. Jervas substituted "those Limbs and Members which are exprest by few and large Muscles, excell in Majesty and Beauty" (p. 29).

93:14–16 *because . . . value.* For the 2d ed. Jervas substituted "for the abundance of them makes them look cheap, their Value arising from the Scarcity" (p. 31).

94:1 *Wood.* For the 2d ed. Jervas substituted "Reeds" (p. 33).

94:13–16 *the studied . . . Passion.* For the 2d ed. Jervas substituted "a true and lively Expression of the Passions, is rather the Work of Genius than of Labour and Study" (p. 33).

94:27 *under ground.* For the 2d ed. Jervas then added "in Sepulchres and Catacombs" (p. 35).

95:30–33 *round . . . Colouring.* For the 2d ed. Jervas substituted "those Parts of round Bodies which are seen directly opposite to the Spectator, should have the Light entire" (p. 39).

96:7–23 *if your . . . borders.* Extensively revised by Jervas for the 2d ed. (pp. 39, 41):

> if the Wideness of the Space or Largeness of the Composition requires that you should have two Grouppes or three (which should be the most) let the Lights and Shadows be so discreetly manag'd, that light Bodies may have a sufficient Mass or Breadth of Shadow to sustain 'em, and that dark Bodies may have a sudden Light behind to detach them from the Ground.
>
> As in a Convex Mirrour the collected Rays strike stronger and brighter in the middle than upon the natural Object, and the Vivacity of the Colours is increas'd in the Parts full in your Sight; while the goings off are more and more broken and faint as they approach to the Extremities, in the same Manner Bodies are to be rais'd and rounded.

96:20 *bear out.* Translating "avancent" (*L'Art de Peinture,* p. 31) and perhaps meaning "to 'come out' effectively or with some effect" as used of colors in painting (*OED*).

96:29–97:16 *and drawing . . . distance.* Extensively revised, as well as annotated, by Jervas for the 2d ed. (pp. 41, 43):

> That which is foremost and nearest to the Eye must be so distinctly express'd, as to be sharp or almost cutting to the Sight. Thus shall the Colours be disposed upon a Plane, which from a proper Place and Distance will seem so natural and round, as to make the Figures appear so many Statues.
>
> Solid Bodies subject to the Touch, are not to be painted transparent; and even when such Bodies are placed upon transparent Grounds, as upon Clouds, Waters, Air, and the like vacuities, they must be preserv'd *opaque, that their Solidity be not destroyed among those light, Aerial, transparent Species; and must therefore be express'd sharper and rougher than what is next to them, more distinct by a firm Light and Shadow, and with more solid and substantial Colours: That on the contrary the smoother and more transparent may be thrown off to a farther Distance.

*The French Translator here, as well as Mr. Dryden,
is unintelligible; which happen'd by their mistaking the
Meaning of the Word *Opaca,* which is not put for *dark;*
but *Opaque,* in Opposition to *transparent:* for a white
Garment may be *Opaque* &c.

98:27–35 *by their . . . Shadows.* For the 2d ed. Jervas substituted "there-
fore they painted each Figure with one Colour or with Colours of near
Affinity tho' the Habit were of different Kinds, distinguishing the upper
Garment from the under, or from the loose and flowing Mantle, by the
Tints, or Degrees, harmonizing and uniting the Colours, with whatever
was next to them" (pp. 47, 49).

100:14–16 *much painted . . . to them.* For the 2d ed. Jervas substituted
"carefully painted flat, in flowing Colours; then toucht up with spritely
Lights, and the true Lines of the Drawing restor'd, which were lost, or
confus'd in working the Colours together" (p. 53).

100:14 *unitedly.* Translating "uniment" (*L'Art de Peinture,* p. 39) and
evidently meaning "with colors that blend well together"; see the imme-
diately following reference to the ground of a painting "well united with
Colours which are of a friendly nature to each other."

100:22–23 *the bodies . . . ground.* For the 2d ed. Jervas substituted "those
Bodies that are back in the Ground be painted with Colours allied to those
of the Ground it self" (p. 53).

100:36–37 *and avoid . . . drily.* For the 2d ed. Jervas substituted "as if it
were painted from one Palette" (p. 55).

101:15–18 *As for . . . the other.* Translating de Piles' addition to the
Latin sense (*L'Art de Peinture,* p. 40).

101:27–31 *the degrees . . . places.* For the 2d ed. Jervas substituted (p. 57):
let those which are to be seen at a Distance, be varied
with fiercer Colours and stronger Tints.
Very large Figures must have Room enough, and strong,
or rather fierce colouring.

101:32–35 *paint . . . about.* For the 2d ed. Jervas substituted "take the
utmost Care, that broad Lights may be join'd to a like Breadth of Shadows"
(p. 57).

102:20–21 *Vertue . . . blameable.* For the 2d ed. Jervas substituted "Ex-
treams are always vicious" (p. 59), which is certainly closer to the Latin
(l. 415) than are Dryden's and de Piles' versions, but which seems an un-
necessary change.

108:6–12 *Correggio . . . Colours.* For the 2d ed. Jervas substituted "The
shining Eminence of Corregio consists in his laying on ample broad Lights
encompass'd with friendly Shadows, and in a grand Style of Painting, with
a Delicacy in the management of Colours" (p. 77).

OBSERVATIONS ON THE ART OF PAINTING

P. 111, ll. 20–21 *Hearing . . . sees.* Dryden substitutes a couplet for de
Piles' labored prose paraphrase (*L'Art de Peinture,* p. 61).

112:14 *Third Book.* "3. livre" in *L'Art de Peinture,* p. 61, and in the 2d
ed. of 1673, p. 97, but "5. livre" in the 3d ed. of 1684, p. 97. The first two edi-
tions are correct. The painters who checked the accuracy of Dryden's termi-

nology presumably made the change in Q (see headnote, p. 340 above).

112:19 *sidenote Mr. Le Brun*. Added by Dryden; de Piles merely refers to Louis XIV's "premier Peintre" (*L'Art de Peinture*, p. 62), which Charles Lebrun (1619–1690) became about 1661.

112:22 *sidenote Mr. Colbert*. Added by Dryden; de Piles merely refers to Louis XIV's "premier Ministre" (*L'Art de Peinture*, p. 62). In 1663 Jean Baptiste Colbert (1619–1683) reorganized the Académie des Beaux-Arts, founded in 1648.

120:12 *Raphael's Graver*. Added by Dryden (or the artists who checked his work). Marcantonio Raimondi (*c.* 1480–*c.* 1534) helped spread the fame of Raphael's paintings by his engravings of them.

120:16, 19 *Germany / Germany*. Substituted by Dryden (or the artists who checked his work) for "la Flandre" and "les Flamans" (*L'Art de Peinture*, p. 71; 1684 ed., pp. 112–113) in order to correct de Piles and his source (see Giorgio Vasari, *Le Vite de' Più Eccellenti Pittori Scultori ed Architettori*, ed. Gaetano Milanesi [1906; repr. 1973], V, 402).

121:24 *Theory . . . practice*. De Piles adds "& que la Pratique n'estoit rien sans la Theorie" (*L'Art de Peinture*, p. 73).

122:19 *6oth*. Thus corrected in the errata of Q; "51st." comes from *L'Art de Peinture*, p. 74.

124:18 *Pausiacâ . . . Tabellâ*. See *Satires*, II, vii, 95 (Loeb trans.: "madman, you stand dazed before a picture of Pausias").

124:21 *Opera da stupire*. A work that astonishes.

126:27 *O . . . pecus*. See 62:4–5 above and note.

128:17 *Virgil . . . Æneids*. Dryden's addition.

128:21 *and . . . Sandys*. Dryden's addition.

128:23–24 *translated . . . Volumes*. Dryden's addition, calling attention to the English translation of 1683–1686 to which Dryden contributed *The Life of Plutarch* and a dedication of the whole (*Works*, XVII, 227–288).

128:28–29 *This Author . . . make*. The lack of agreement is also in de Piles: "Cét Autheur avec Homere feroient" (*L'Art de Peinture*, p. 81).

128:30–31 *and . . . Antiquities*. Dryden's addition.

129:9 *by . . . Roscommon*. Dryden's addition.

129:13–16 *such as . . . Shere*. Dryden's addition.

130:4–6 *Quinctilian . . . eloquentiæ*. De Piles (*L'Art de Peinture*, p. 82) marginally attributes the dialogue to an unnamed author before quoting from a work now known as *Dialogus de Oratoribus* and usually attributed to Tacitus. In the seventeenth century the dialogue was sometimes attributed to Tacitus but was also identified with *De Causis Corruptae Eloquentiae*, a lost work by Quintilian, to which he several times referred in the *Institutio Oratoria*. For the variant attributions see *M. Fab. Quintiliani Declamationum Liber* (Oxford, 1675), pp. 207, 209. For Dryden's earlier reference to the dialogue as Quintilian's see *Works*, XI, 205:9–11 and note. In the preface to *Fables* (1700, sig. *B2v; Watson, II, 281), Dryden quotes from the dialogue and attributes it to Tacitus.

130:7–11 *That Painting . . . rightly*. Translating de Piles (*L'Art de Peinture*, p. 82), but the Latin compares oratory, not painting, with fire, and the two sentences (here separated by a colon) are not contiguous in the Latin (see *Dialogus de Oratoribus*, 36, 1; 37, 5).

134:2 *to be let*. For rent or hire.

135:11 *Monsieur Colbert.* Dryden's addition.

135:28 *dry.* "Characterized by stiff and formal outlines; lacking in softness or mellowness" (*OED*).

136:32 *principle.* Presumably the source of the muscle's contraction.

136:33–137:1 *insertion.* In the anatomical sense of the part of a muscle attaching it to the part to be moved.

137:24 *Tortebat.* Thus *L'Art de Peinture* (1668, p. 91; 1684, p. 144): de Piles' *Abrégé d'anatomie* was "mis en lumiere" (Dryden's "publish'd") by François Tortebat in 1667. Q's *Torrebat* may have been prompted by a worn and imperfectly inked "t" in the French editions of 1668 and 1684.

140:18 *That is.* For the 1673 edition of *L'Art de Peinture* de Piles added three introductory sentences to this remark which were included in the 1684 edition (p. 149); Dryden follows the 1668 edition (p. 94), from which the sentences are lacking.

140:31 *Cornish.* Cornice.

149:17–18 *See . . . Draperies.* I.e., 93:2–7 above.

153:31 *Lay-man.* In the now obsolete sense of "lay figure." The usual translation of the French "Manequin" (*L'Art de Peinture*, p. 110) would have been "puppet"; the technical term in the English, together with the explanatory sidenote, perhaps indicates the intervention at this point of the artists who corrected Dryden's work.

155:13 *sidenote Lib. 35.12.* Q's citation is here corrected from *L'Art de Peinture*, p. 111. The copying error could have been Dryden's or the compositor's; since the 1684 ed. lacks the citation on p. 179, the error could not have been introduced by Dryden's friends.

157:7 *Airs.* Q's reading is here corrected from *L'Art de Peinture*, p. 113: "Airs," in the sense of aspects or expressions.

160:3–4 *that is . . . Mockery.* Dryden's addition.

160:4 *the 3d. Satyre of.* Dryden's addition; the line is in fact *Satire* V, 91.

160:5–7 *Learn . . . dismounted.* Dryden's addition.

164:1 *Camus.* A now obsolete loanword (carried across from *L'Art de Peinture*, p. 120) meaning (of noses) flat.

167:23 *Relievo.* Relief: "distinctness of outline due to contrast of colour" (*OED*).

168:15 *turnings.* I.e., curved surfaces.

168:28 *Campaign.* I.e., champaign, or open country (*OED*).

169:24 *Furniture.* Trappings.

170:25 *Relievo.* See 167:23.

170:34 *reflects.* Reflections.

171:27 *Masticot.* Massicot: "yellow protoxide of lead, used as a pigment" (*OED*).

174:7–9 *of which . . . Conclusion.* The English is botched; cf. "dont vous pouvez faire essay, & vous éclaircir une fois pour toutes. (Voyez la fin . . . Couleur capitale) L'on peut neantmoins passer" (*L'Art de Peinture*, p. 132). Dryden neglected "pouvez," translated "faire" as an indicative, and took "vous éclaircir" as a simple infinitive instead of as the second infinitive governed by "pouvez." Some at least of the accidentals in Q may represent a printing-house attempt to impose grammar upon Dryden's English, but they move it even further from the French sense.

177:14–15 *He has . . . Reposes.* See 96:12–17, 165:10–14 above.

178:27 *Appion the Grammarian.* Presumably Apion, who flourished early in the first century A.D.; Dryden's spelling of the name is from the French (*L'Art de Peinture*, p. 137). He is called Apio in Pliny, XXXV, xxxvi, 88.

181:16–17 *as we . . . well.* Dryden's addition; for the proverb see Tilley, E156.

183:3 *which . . . Painting.* Dryden's addition.

183:16–24 *Let . . . work.* De Piles added this remark in the 1673 ed. and it was repeated in 1684 (p. 230). The catchphrase is taken from Dryden's translation of the *Art of Painting* (see 103:31–32 above); the remark itself seems not to have been translated by Dryden, who would not have encountered it in his 1668 edition of *L'Art de Peinture*, but presumably by one of the artists who checked his work while using the 1684 ed. Although Dryden for the most part translated de Piles closely and often awkwardly, this remark is more stiffly literal than the remainder of the translation. See headnote, p. 340 above.

184:2 *sidenote 35.2.* Q's "5.8." comes from the 1684 ed. of *L'Art de Peinture* (p. 231) and was presumably changed by the artists who corrected Dryden's work. In the 1668 ed. Dryden would have seen "35.2." (p. 143) and this citation also occurs in the 1673 ed. (p. 231). The passage quoted indeed occurs in Pliny's 35th book, although its placement within that book varies among editions; in the Loeb ed. it is in XXXV, xl, 133. This sidenote supplies the clearest evidence that the artists who corrected Dryden's work used a copy of *L'Art de Peinture* in the 1684 ed. rather than the 1668 or 1673 edition. See headnote, p. 340 above.

184:15 *sidenote Tuscul. lib. 5.* As in *L'Art de Peinture* (p. 143). Although Cicero glances at such a situation in *Tusculan Disputations*, V, iv, 10–11, he presents it more clearly at II, iii, 7–9.

184:21 *sidenote Georg. 3.* Thus in all editions of *L'Art de Peinture;* Q's additional "l.5." is an error: the line is in fact *Georgics*, III, 454. Dryden's artist-friends may have been responsible for the erroneous insertion. In the 1673 and 1684 editions of *L'Art de Peinture* (p. 232) the succeeding sidenote, citing a line from Horace, gives the obviously incorrect "L.5. ep. 16."; Horace wrote only two books of epistles, and the line is correctly identified in the 1668 ed. (p. 144) as from *Epistles*, I, xvi. Seeing this error, the artists may have thought that "L.5." belonged to the Virgilian citation and so transferred it from the Horatian citation, which appears only as "Ep. 16." in Q (see headnote, p. 340 above).

184:24 *sidenote L.I. Ep. 16.* See preceding note and Horace, *Epistles*, I, xvi, 24.

185:26–27 *That . . . them.* Q's sidenote is not taken from any edition of *L'Art de Peinture* but is presumably entered by mistake from the immediately succeeding sidenote. The Latin is in fact Martial, XII, xcviii, 8, and Dryden would certainly have known that Cicero's *De Officiis* was not in verse.

188:1 *Carraches.* The French form of Carraccis (cf. *L'Art de Peinture*, p. 148).

196:24 *218th.* Taken from *L'Art de Peinture* (1668, p. 158; 1673, 1684, p. 255). The remark is actually keyed to v. 217 in the French (1668, p. 108; 1673, 1684, p. 173) and in the English (152:16 above).

THE JUDGMENT OF DU FRESNOY

P. 199, l. 32–p. 200, l. 1 *Gaudens.* The French spelling, from *L'Art de Peinture*, p. 161. Gaudenzio Ferrari lived 1484?–1546.

200:12 *Tetrastyles.* "Structure[s] having four pillars or columns" (*OED*).

200:12 *Xistes.* The French form (from *L'Art de Peinture*, p. 161) of xysti or xysts. In Greece the xystus was "a long covered portico or court used for athletic exercises"; in Rome it was "an open colonnade, or walk planted with trees, used for recreation and conversation" (*OED*).

204:3 *Uncle.* As in *L'Art de Peinture*, p. 165: corrected to "Cousin" for the 1716 ed. of Dryden's translation, probably by Richard Graham, who was responsible in both editions for a supplementary "Account of the Most Eminent Painters."

204:8 *understood.* Translating "conduits" (*L'Art de Peinture*, p. 165) and presumably signifying "conceived and executed."

204:20 *35.* In *L'Art de Peinture*, p. 165, he "mourut à 23. ou 24. ans." Antonio Carracci's dates are now usually given as 1583–1618: he was 35 at his death, according to Giovanni Baglione, *Le Vite de' Pittori, Scultori, Architetti, ed Intagliatori* (ed. prin., 1642; Naples, 1733, pp. 142–143). We need not suppose that Dryden was responsible for the "35": one of the artists who corrected his work, or perhaps Richard Graham, may have made the change.

204:24, 25 *Lawrence.* Following *L'Art de Peinture*, p. 166. In the 2d ed. of 1716 the painter's name is corrected to "Denis Calvert" (p. 234): i.e., Denys Calvaert of Antwerp, with whom Guido Reni studied as a youth while Calvaert was in Bologna.

205:10 *Albani.* Q's "Albano" was corrected for the 2d ed. of 1716: Francesco Albani (1578–1660) studied under Calvaert.

205:12 *John Lanfranc.* I.e., Giovanni Lanfranco (1580–1647).

206:31 *Cabinet Pieces.* Following *L'Art de Peinture*, p. 167: "les Tableaux de Cabinets"; i.e., paintings to be displayed in small rooms rather than in galleries.

The Life of Lucian

In June 1693 Peter Motteux announced that "A New Translation of Lucian is preparing for the Press, and will probably appear in Michaelmas Term." In March 1694 he reported that the "Translation of Lucian is very forward," and optimistic promises of an imminent English Lucian appeared for the next sixteen years.[1] Finally, the translation materialized, the first, third, and fourth volumes bearing the date 1711 and the second, 1710. Prefatory to the first volume was Dryden's *Life of Lucian* which, the title page announced, included *A Discourse on his Writings, And A Character of some of the present Translators.*

Dryden probably wrote the *Life of Lucian* in 1696.[2] Samuel Briscoe, the

---

[1] See *Gentleman's Journal* (1693), p. 195, (1694), p. 63; and Benjamin Boyce, *Tom Brown of Facetious Memory* (1939), pp. 115–116.

[2] Boyce (*Tom Brown*, p. 116n) suggests "that Dryden's life was written before

publisher, asserted that it "and some of the Dialogues, were done before and in the Year 1696," and the preface to the second volume, dated 1710, claimed that the life "was Writ by Mr. Dryden near fifteen Years ago."[3] In the life itself Dryden praises the parliamentary service of Walter Moyle, who undertook heavy committee work that began in late November 1695 and continued far into 1696.[4] During 1696 Dryden was still occupied with Virgil, but his documented progress on that translation allowed time for the *Life of Lucian*. On 4 January he had almost finished the ninth Aeneid; the tenth was probably completed by June, the eleventh, by 3 September. Thereafter Dryden seems to have been continuously busy with Virgil, but, whereas during 1695 he had finished about eight Aeneids, in the months between 4 January and 3 September 1696 he translated not much more than two and perhaps drafted some of the notes to Virgil.[5] Although he may have been ill during those eight months, he certainly had time for the *Life of Lucian*, which need not have occupied more than a month. Dryden, of course, was still contracted with Tonson for the Virgil, and until Dryden completed the translation, the contract prohibited him from engaging in other work except for translating *De Arte Graphica*, contributing incidental material to his son's play, *The Husband His own Cuckold*, and writing "any New Originall Poem or book of Prose . . . which Shall not exceed the price of one Shilling Printed."[6] *The Works of Lucian* would certainly sell for more than a shilling, but Dryden's limited contribution could be construed as permitted by the terms of the contract.[7]

Dryden's association with the Lucian enterprise followed upon an earlier one of 1693, when he and Sir Henry Sheeres launched the Polybius translation for Samuel Briscoe. Both once more worked for Briscoe on the Lucian, but the second enterprise lagged, apparently for want of direction and immediately, it seems, because of reverses suffered by Briscoe. In 1696 he disappeared from the term catalogues, perhaps because between then and 1704 he was engaged in a legal battle with Wycherley. In 1699 Samuel Garth wrote that "Briscoe lately was undone by New" writers, and in 1701 he still lamented his lot. But he seems also to have "revived" by that time, having contracted "a friendship with Tom Brown," whose works he promoted and who contributed heavily to the Lucian.[8] Altogether, the project

---

August, 1693," when Charles Blount, mentioned in the life, committed suicide. But Dryden's reference can apply to a deceased Blount (see 223:23–26 above and note).

[3] *Works of Lucian*, I, sig. A3; II, sig. A6v.

[4] See 223:20–23 above and note.

[5] See *Works*, VI, 844.

[6] *Works*, VI, 1179.

[7] Cf. Swift, *On Poetry: A Rapsody*, ll. 251–254:
  Read all the Prefaces of Dryden,
  For these our Criticks much confide in,
  (Tho' meerly writ at first for filling
  To raise the Volume's Price, a Shilling.)

[8] For scattered references to Briscoe's hardships and revival see Henry R. Plomer, *A Dictionary of the Printers and Booksellers Who Were at Work in England, Scotland and Ireland from 1668 to 1725* (1922), p. 50; Howard P. Vincent, "William Wycherley's *Miscellany Poems*," *PQ*, XVI (1937), 145–148; Willard Connely, *Brawny Wycherley* (1930), p. 263; Garth, *The Dispensary*, IV, 6; Hardin

dragged on for some eighteen years, involving twenty-five named translators as well as anonymous contributors. Two of Walter Moyle's pieces and Charles Blount's date to 1693,[9] but others cannot be dated. A three-volume Lucian advertised in 1707 never appeared.[10] Although Briscoe remained the publisher, the booksellers and even their premises did not stay fixed.[11] And the second volume is dated 1710, whereas the others are dated 1711. That Dryden's *Life of Lucian* survived for fifteen years, ten of them after his death, presumably testifies to what Briscoe thought its economic value would be.

A recurring claim that Dryden acted as general editor in the project's early stages cannot be documented.[12] Peter Motteux, ever eager to advertise all he knew, Briscoe looking back in 1711, and Dryden himself, with no time to select and direct more than twenty-five translators, all said nothing about such a role. Tom Brown contributed more than anyone and in 1699 claimed that he planned "to prefix [a "Dissertation"] to the new Translation of Lucian's Works, done by several Gentlemen, which will be handed to the Press with all convenient Speed."[13] But Brown gave no hint that he was replacing Dryden and left behind no prefatory material supplanting Dryden's. It is certainly possible that Dryden recommended some of the contributors to Briscoe, but his phrasing in the *Life of Lucian* makes clear that he was unacquainted with others, and he names only three translators,[14] whose contributions account for just 137 of the 1,626 pages. Furthermore, Dryden compliments Briscoe on having "Interest" with good translators,[15] thus implying that Briscoe commissioned at least some of the work without reference to Dryden.

⎯⎯⎯⎯

For the *Life of Lucian* Dryden used eight sources. Three are gathered in Λουκιανοῦ Ἅπαντα: *Luciani Samosatensis Opera* (Basle, 1563). They are "Luciani Elogium" by Gilbertus Cognatus; "De Vita et Scriptis Luciani, Narratio," by Jacob Zvinger; and "Luciani Vita ex Suida." The other five are a brief life of Lucian by Joannes Bourdelotius (Jean Bourdelot) in

---

Craig, "Dryden's Lucian," *CP*, XVI (1921), 162; and John Dunton, *The Life and Errors of John Dunton* (1705), p. 365. Boyce, *Tom Brown*, p. 117, conjectures that Brown made his translation around 1699.

9 For Moyle's pieces see the *Works of Lucian*, I, 14, 25, 31 (2d pagination). Blount's contribution is dated by his death in 1693, the year the Lucian was first announced. Moyle published his Lucianic translations separately in 1710.

10 See Boyce, *Tom Brown*, p. 116n.

11 James Woodward moved from St. Christopher's Alley to Scalding Alley; J. Morphew dropped out.

12 For the claim see *DNB* under Walter Moyle; Charles Whibley, "Writers of Burlesque and Translators," *Cambridge History of English Literature* (1933), IX, 298; *Cambridge Bibliography of English Literature* (1941), II, 762; *New Cambridge Bibliography of English Literature* (1969–1977), II, 1492; and, where most elaborated, Arthur Sherbo, "The Dryden-Cambridge Translation of Plutarch's *Lives*," *Etudes Anglaises*, XXXII (1979), 177–184.

13 See Boyce, *Tom Brown*, p. 115. Brown contributed 43 of 347 pages in the first volume of the *Works of Lucian*, 302 of 488 in the third.

14 See 223:14–26 above.

15 See 226:3–7 above.

Luciani Samosatensis Philosophi Opera Omnia (Paris, 1615); Jasper Mayne, *Part of Lucian Made English* . . . *To which are adjoyned those other Dialogues of Lucian as they were formerly translated by Mr Francis Hicks,* published in 1663 and 1664; Nicolas Perrot, Sieur d'Ablancourt, *Lucien* (Paris, 1688); Ferrand Spence, *Lucian's Works* (1684); and the dialogues of Lucian himself.[16] Besides these eight sources, Dryden may have looked for one other, a life of Lucian by Thomas Hickes, but never found it.[17]

We may look first at Dryden's use of sources in his chronological account of Lucian's life, which he pieced together, as he noted at the outset, from fragmentary records. He drew most of his material from Zvinger, from Cognatus, and seemingly from the Suidas lexicon, adding some items from later sources, chiefly d'Ablancourt and Mayne, on points of special interest. Thus, identification of Lucian the satirist from among other Lucians, the family background of Lucian, his father's apprenticing him to a statuary because of a straitened family economy, his place and time of birth, his citizenship, the dream that persuaded him to replace statuary work with preparation for learning—all this material came from Zvinger.[18] Although Dryden twice cites Suidas, his citations came not from the Suidas lexicon or from the excerpt in the 1563 edition of Lucian, but from Zvinger's citations of Suidas. For Lucian's advance into rhetoric, which he in turn abandoned for writing, Dryden relied upon Cognatus, although Cognatus merely recorded the decision. Dryden's pejorative description of legal practice parallels those in d'Ablancourt and in two works Dryden despised: Spence's life of Lucian and Bruslé's *Lucien en belle Humeur.*[19] Dryden scanned all his sources when determining whether Lucian's death resulted from gout or from an attack by dogs.[20] Only the Suidas excerpt in the 1563 edition argued that dogs killed Lucian, but the story was retold, in order to be refuted, by both Mayne and d'Ablancourt.

The story mattered to Dryden because it had been used to support a

---

16 The first d'Ablancourt edition appeared in 1654, followed by at least eight more. We cite the edition of 1688. Since Dryden's reading texts of Lucian are unknown and unascertainable from the *Life of Lucian,* we cite the translation of 1710–1711 to which Dryden contributed the life. Although Dryden does not mention Bourdelot, he could have been directed to him by d'Ablancourt (I, sig. a4*v*). Eight sources served Dryden, but by 1550 more than 250 editions of works by Lucian had appeared, including at least 60 Greek texts (Harry L. Levy, *Lucian: Seventy Dialogues* [1976], p. xxiii). Hardin Craig ("Dryden's Lucian," pp. 141–150) refers to sixteenth-century editions of Lucian and lists seventeenth-century English translations as well as other Lucianic items published in Dryden's day.

17 Thomas Hickes, son of the translator of Lucian, contributed a life of Lucian to his father's version (Oxford, 1634; repr. 1666). The Hickes material was incorporated into Mayne's editions of 1663 and 1664 to form a second volume, and it was duly credited on the title pages. But many copies of Mayne's editions in fact lack the second volume (which was published at Oxford, whereas the first volume was published at London), and it seems likely that Dryden's was such a copy. Thomas Hickes's life contains material that Dryden would certainly have drawn upon had it been available to him.

18 See notes to 208:19–209:24, 209:25–33, 209:34–210:17, 210:18–24.

19 See note to 210:25–34.

20 See notes to 211:8–13, 212:1–15.

view of Lucian as an enemy of Christianity who was at last struck down ignominiously for his impiety. Such a view sorted ill with what Dryden calls charity and we may wish to call toleration. When Dryden moved from the chronological outline of Lucian's life to an assessment of Lucian's character and motives, he dwelt first on Lucian's relationship with Christianity and took the occasion to give his own view of proper Christian principles. In rehearsing this topic, Dryden sought to assess Lucian in the light of accumulated commentary upon his work, especially as that commentary was reflected in Dryden's sources. Here, though, Dryden modified his sources, as he had not when outlining the life, with judgments drawn from his own reading of Lucian.

Interest in Lucian as friend or foe of Christianity stemmed from his attack on the gods and his topical ridicule of figures, events, and institutions. Between the tenth and fifteenth centuries Lucian in Byzantium had provided forms and motifs for topical satire. From the beginning of the sixteenth century onward, Lucian's works were construed by Italian humanists as a blend of instruction and humor conveying an ethical system compatible with Christianity. Across the Alps, in the early sixteenth century, humanists from Cracow to London—Erasmus and More providing the main impetus— found in Lucian varying support for religious positions. In some of his works he was interpreted as elaborate allegorist of Catholic doctrine or of such virtues as literature and study, and the commentary in some early sixteenth-century editions presented him as an imaginative moralist. But Lucian the ridiculing skeptic also prompted condemnation. Partisan readings of his *Philopatris* as anti-Christian and his *Peregrinus* as containing allusions to Christians helped shape opinion against him. During the Reformation both Catholics and Protestants appropriated him as an example of skeptical disrespect for revealed religion, if not outright atheism. By 1559 the *Philopatris* and the *Peregrinus* were on the Index; by 1590, all his works.[21]

Seeking to disconnect Lucian from Christian polemics, Dryden began with d'Ablancourt's assertion that Lucian's works did not show him as a Christian.[22] To reinforce the supposition that Lucian bore no special animus toward Christianity, Dryden drew upon his second most respected source, the "learned and ingenious" Mayne, who had cited the current scholarship questioning Lucian's authorship of the dialogue of Triephon and Critias and of other dialogues satirizing Christians.[23] To counter those who accused Lucian of atheism, Dryden appropriated Mayne's questions about how odd it was that a Lucian who discredited the pagan gods and who pointed to Jupiter's sepulcher in Crete should be thought an atheist. Like Mayne, Dryden did not conclude that Lucian was a theist, insisting rather that nothing showed Lucian to be theist, atheist, or polytheist.[24] And just as he fended off the charge of atheism, so Dryden rescued Lucian from those who kidnaped him as friend or ally. Dryden agreed with Mayne

---

[21] Points in this paragraph are drawn from Christopher Robinson, *Lucian and His Influence in Europe* (1979), pp. 80–98.

[22] See 212:1–15 above and note.

[23] See 213:28–30 above and note.

[24] See note to 214:20–24.

that, although Lucian had served Christianity well by ridiculing the pagan gods, he had thereby furthered Christianity only unintentionally. Dryden rejected the step taken by those like Spence who appropriated Lucian as Christian comrade.[25]

Having, on cues from d'Ablancourt and Mayne, disentangled Lucian from Christian associations, Dryden next turned to the matter of Lucian's morals. On each issue, prompted by his sources, he went to the dialogues for evidence, emerging on the whole as Lucian's defender who, oftener than not, kept himself distinct from other defenders. Similarly, when discussing the philosophical basis of Lucian's satire and his rhetorical style, Dryden found points of departure in Mayne and d'Ablancourt but developed those points individually. We should remember that in the *Discourse of Satire* Dryden classified "many of *Lucian*'s Dialogues" as Varronian satire, perhaps because, in Dryden's taxonomy, such satire "temper'd Philology with Philosophy," where "Philology" evidently has its now obsolete sense of love of talk, speech, or argument.[26] Appropriately, then, Dryden turned in the *Life of Lucian* to discussion of the philosophical and rhetorical elements in Lucian's works.

Dryden concluded the *Life of Lucian* with some account of Lucian's translators and some observations on the practice of translation, perhaps to stretch out an unavoidably spare biography but no doubt also to offer a more immediate introduction to the translated text that was to follow. One of Fielding's characters stigmatized that text as "wretched," and it has been ignored in the twentieth century.[27] Dryden's contribution has suffered with it, eliciting little respect in the past two centuries, aside from occasional praise for Dryden's expression of tolerance.[28]

The *Life of Lucian* has an undeniable scrappiness, no doubt in part deriving from the paucity of facts at Dryden's disposal. His earlier *Life of Plutarch,* like his opening evocation of Plutarch himself, shows what he thought constituted sound biographical practice. Accuracy and impartiality are obvious desiderata, but so too is the ability to reveal character through the depiction of incident, especially domestic incident,[29] and there was virtually no record of such incident for Lucian. After all, "the Learned seldom abound with *Action.*" But if "it is *Action* only, that furnishes the Historian with Things agreeable and instructive," a learned man may nonetheless convey "his Reputation to Posterity by the remains of his Writings."[30] Much of Dryden's *Life of Lucian* accordingly offers to assess the character

25 See note to 214:30–34.

26 See *Works,* IV, 47–48.

27 See *Amelia* (1752), III, 143. No reference to the edition of 1710–1711 occurs in the Loeb text, ed. A. M. Harmon (1913).

28 For reaction to Dryden's *Life of Lucian* see Malone, III, 385n; George Saintsbury, *Dryden* (1881), p. 152; S-S, XVIII, 57; Craig, "Dryden's Lucian," pp. 150–151; Francis G. Allinson, *Lucian: Satirist and Artist* (1926), pp. 164–165; Watson, II, 209; William Myers, *Dryden* (1973), p. 134; Barry Baldwin, *Studies in Lucian* (1973), p. 8; Edward Pechter, *Dryden's Classical Theory of Literature* (1975), p. 157.

29 See *Works,* XVII, 275–277.

30 See 208:8–10, 209:10 above.

through a discourse on the writings. Here Dryden could display the biographer's or the critic's impartiality, especially when dealing with charges against Lucian for irreligion or pederasty.

Not all the scrappiness of the *Life of Lucian* can be attributed to inadequate records, for it conveys at times the air of having been written in discrete sections (prompted, it may be, by one or another of Dryden's sources), which were left side by side with little or no transition. The *Life of Lucian* nonetheless contains Dryden's fullest statement about prose translation, in which he applies to prose the principles he had already developed for verse.[31] It also contains in the discussion of Lucian and Christianity a sketch of the proper Christian life as founded on charity and a tolerance that never slides into mere permissiveness. Written in the closing years of Dryden's life, the *Life of Lucian* displays something of an old man's garrulousness or, it may be, that happy digressiveness which Dryden so admired in Plutarch and Montaigne.[32] But, perhaps for that reason, it also offers a personal statement. Three years later, Dryden wrote to Charles Montague that in *To My Honour'd Kinsman* "I have . . . given my Own opinion, of what an Englishman in Parliament oughto be; & deliver it as a Memorial of my own Principles to all Posterity."[33] What *To My Honour'd Kinsman* did for Dryden's political principles the *Life of Lucian* had earlier done for his religious and philosophical principles, for a man may convey "his Reputation to Posterity by the remains of his Writings."

P. 208, ll. 3–4 *we can . . . Perusal.* Cf. *Works*, XVII, 276:19–277:13.

208:10–12 *Diogenes . . . Philosophers.* Diogenes Laertius probably flourished in the first half of the third century A.D.; an English translation of his *Lives, Opinions, and Remarkable Sayings of the Most Famous Ancient Philosophers* was published in 1696. Thomas Stanley (1625–1678) produced his *History of Philosophy* between 1655 and 1662.

208:19–209:24 *There were . . . to him.* Based upon Jacob Zvinger, in *Lucian*, sigs. α6v–7, including the citations of the Suidas lexicon and of Gesner; the error that a Lucian murdered by Rufinus was a chief prefect, whereas Rufinus was the prefect; and the comment that merit incurs envy in courts.

208:21 *Suidas.* See *Works*, XVII, 446–447.

208:27 *Rufinus.* Malone (III, 359n) attributes O's *"Rafiany"* to a printer's copy that was "very carelessly written." By 395 A.D., when he was himself slain, Flavius Rufinus had become praetorian prefect, guardian of and minister to Arcadius, de facto head of the Eastern Roman Empire, and rival of Stilicho, general of the Western Empire. He had earlier killed a Lucian whom he had made count of the East.

209:9 *Gesnerus.* Konrad von Gesner (1516–1565) of Zürich, physician, naturalist, and classical scholar.

---

[31] It should be noted that, whereas Dryden's verse translations exemplify the theory he outlined in essays from the preface to *Ovid's Epistles* in 1680 to the dedication of the *Aeneis* in 1697, his prose translations rarely accord with the principles set out in the *Life of Lucian*, being for the most part metaphrastic rather than paraphrastic.

[32] See *Works*, XVII, 277.

[33] See Ward, *Letters*, p. 120.

209:25–33 *He was . . . Adrian.* Chiefly a close translation of Zvinger, in *Lucian,* sig. ᵃ7.

209:32–33 *the Reign of Adrian.* Hadrian was emperor from 117 to 138.

209:33 *it cannot be fix'd.* Barry Baldwin, *Studies in Lucian* (1973), p. 10, conjectures that Lucian was born about 117 A.D. or earlier.

209:34–210:17 *The Person . . . World.* Dryden follows Zvinger, in *Lucian,* sig. ᵃ7v, closely, but the ultimate source is Lucian's own *The Vision* (*Works of Lucian,* I, 1, 2d pag.).

210:2 *of his own Head.* Of his own accord (*OED*); cf. *The Annals of Tacitus, Book I,* 237:28 above.

210:8 *run.* This form of the past indicative survived into the nineteenth century, although "ran" was more common (*OED*).

210:18–24 *Tho' it . . . Statues.* Dryden condenses Zvinger, in *Lucian,* sigs. ᵃ7v–ᵃ8.

210:25–34 *In his . . . Egypt.* Some of these details occur either in Zvinger or in the excerpt from the Suidas lexicon in the 1563 edition of Lucian. But Dryden here relies upon the account by Gilbertus Cognatus in the same edition, sigs. ᵃ4v and ᵃ5r–v. Dryden's "the Noise of the Bar disgusting" him has no equivalent in Cognatus but finds parallels in d'Ablancourt, I, sig. a3v, Spence, I, sig. +4, and Jean-Chrysostôme Bruslé de Montpleinchamp (1641–1724), *Lucien en Belle Humeur ou Nouveau Entretien des Morts* (Amsterdam, 1694 [1st ed., 1691]), p. 7: "etant degouté des disputes du barreau."

210:34–211:5 *after . . . Rhetoric.* None of Dryden's sources claims that Lucian learned most about rhetoric in Gaul, but several of them suggest that it was then a very important center for rhetoric. Cf. Jean Bourdelot, sig. é5; Zvinger, in *Lucian,* sig. β1; and Spence, I, sig. +4.

211:5–7 *that Region . . . witness.* See Juvenal, Satire I, 44 (Dryden's ll. 65–66; *Works,* IV, 97), Satire VII, 148, and Satire XV, 111; Martial, IX, xcix, 3. See also Olwen Brogan, *Roman Gaul* (1953), p. 53.

211:9 *he died of the Gout.* So Cognatus, in *Lucian,* sig. ᵃ5v; Bourdelot, sig. é5v; and Spence, I, sig. †7v. Lucian's death by gout has not earned the ready endorsement of modern scholars (see Baldwin, *Studies in Lucian,* p. 9 and note), although it has also seemed less improbable than other causes (see Jennifer Hall, *Lucian's Satire* [1981], p. 44).

211:9–10 *Suidas . . . Dogs.* See the excerpt from the Suidas lexicon in *Lucian,* sig. β3v, where death by dogs is explained as punishment for Lucian's attacks on Christianity.

211:10 *returning from a Feast.* Mayne, sig. A5v, has the same phrase.

211:11–16 *which being . . . Apostacy.* Cf. d'Ablancourt, I, sig. a4r–v, and Mayne, sigs. a5v–A7; both, as Dryden goes on to say, rejected the story. Spence, I, sigs. +7v–+8v, uses the phrase "a Renegado from our Religion" when translating from d'Ablancourt.

211:25 *Fourscore, and Ten.* Accepting d'Ablancourt, I, sig. ã4 (also Spence, I, sig. 7v), rather than Cognatus, in *Lucian,* sig. ᵃ5v, who has Lucian die at eighty.

211:30–34 *Of his . . . to him.* Julian, born 331 A.D., could not have had as his favorite a son of Lucian, who was born some two centuries earlier. The mistake is also in Bourdelot, sig. é5v, and Spence, I, sig. 7v.

212:1–15 *I find . . . believing them.* See d'Ablancourt, I, sig. a4r–v.

212:15 *a muck.* The *OED* citations show that the word was sometimes separated, although it was always properly one.

212:20-24 *We have . . . Demonstration.* For an account of Dryden's skepticism, summarizing and modifying earlier views, see Phillip Harth, *Contexts of Dryden's Thought* (1968), pp. 1–31.

212:22 *Disquisition.* In its Latin sense of inquiry or investigation.

212:26-27 *the Doctrine . . . Church.* For an account of the doctrine from its beginnings through its validation in Augustine and Aquinas and others of the medieval church to its continuance after the Reformation in Calvin, see Ernest W. Nelson, "The Theory of Persecution," in *Persecution and Liberty: Essays in Honor of George Lincoln Burr* (1931; repr. 1968), pp. 3–20. Cf. *The Hind and the Panther,* I, 279–287 (*Works,* III, 131). In the preface to *The Hind and the Panther,* Dryden insisted (*Works,* III, 120: 16–21) that "Conscience is the Royalty and Prerogative of every Private man. He is absolute in his own Breast, and accountable to no Earthly Power, for that which passes only betwixt God and Him. Those who are driven into the Fold are, generally speaking, rather made Hypocrites then Converts."

212:29-30 *all . . . Church.* Cf. *Religio Laici,* ll. 432–444 (*Works,* II, 122).

212:30-32 *yet I cannot . . . the Indies.* Cf. Dryden's ironic reference in *The Hind and the Panther,* III, 1083 (*Works,* III, 193), to "this [Protestant] Inquisition in his [James II's] Yard."

212:32 *the Indies.* I.e., the West Indies. Concerning the Inquisition's efforts to extirpate the idolatry and superstitions of American Indians, see Richard E. Greenleaf, "The Inquisition and the Indians of New Spain: A Study in Jurisdictional Confusion," *The Americas: A Quarterly Review of Inter-American Cultural History,* XXII (October 1965), 138–166.

213:7-15 *I was . . . Apostacy.* D'Ablancourt, I, sig. a4r-v, also insisted that Lucian never showed himself a Christian in his writings, but he did not cite the *Peregrinus.*

213:13-14 *so severely . . . Proteus.* See *Peregrinus,* 1.

213:16-17 *I know . . . before me.* Cf. Thomas Hickes, in *Certain Select Dialogues of Lucian,* trans. Francis Hickes, in Mayne, sig. B3: "whosoever shall read [Lucian's] book *de morte Peregrini* . . . may soon perceive that he was never a Christian." Malone (III, 367n), followed by Scott (S-S, XVIII, 67n), claims that Cognatus had made the same point, but it is absent from Cognatus' contribution to the 1563 edition of Lucian.

213:17-19 *in this . . . Writings.* See, e.g., *Peregrinus,* 13, where Christians are dismissed as "poor wretches" so persuaded of their immortality that they despise death and imprisonment and Christ is referred to as "that crucified sophist" (Loeb trans.).

213:19-25 *the Dialogue . . . England-Men.* See James Drake's translation of *Philopatris,* XX–XXIII (in *Works of Lucian,* II, 37–39), where the description of early Christians includes "a Little Dwarfish, Old, Lean Scoundrel . . . who whistling at his Nose, . . . cough'd first something inwardly . . . and after this Exordium or Prelude he began in small whining low Voice to speak. . . . [A] certain Man who came out of the Mountains in bad Cloaths . . . [and] a Company of palefac'd Fellows, with their Faces bow'd down to the Ground . . . who ask'd me if I brought them any ill News? for they seem'd to wish for the worst, and were pleas'd with sorrowful and evil Events." For satiric descriptions of seventeenth-century sectarians such as those mentioned by Dryden, see, e.g., *The Character of a Quaker* (1671), sigs. A3, B1v–B3v, C1, and C3; and *The Character of a Fanatick* (1675), sig. A3v.

213:28–30 *The learned . . . Cognatus.* See Mayne, sig. A7v.

214:7–15 *There are . . . Communion.* See, e.g., the discussion in *Works*, XIX, 464, of Anglican attempts to reach an accommodation with dissenters and Catholics by publishing during Charles II's reign tracts that debated various points of doctrine. See also G. N. Clark, *The Later Stuarts, 1660–1714* (1955), p. 154, for unsuccessful attempts in the 1690s by some nonconformist sects to achieve reconciliation.

214:20–24 *One of . . . Atheist.* Dryden follows Mayne, sigs. A5v and A6, except that Mayne does not mention Tertullian, from whom Dryden may be recalling *Apologeticus*, XII, 5, XXV, 7, XXVIII, 2. For Lucian's use of Jupiter's Cretan birthplace to disprove his status as Olympian thunderer see *The Parliament of the Gods*, VI (*The Council of the Gods* in *Works of Lucian*, I, 195), and *Zeus Rants*, XLV (*Jupiter Tragœdus*, in *ibid.*, I, 235–236).

214:25 *Deist.* Here a believer in one God as opposed to a believer in none. Deist "was originally opposed to *atheist*, and was interchangeable with *theist*, even in the end of the 17th c." (*OED*). Dryden's usage here and at 216:12–13 may have led some modern scholars to associate seventeenth-century deism, as distinguished from theism, with interest in Lucian as a possible deist (see Hardin Craig, "Dryden's Lucian," *CP*, XVI [1921], 154, 157, 159, 160, and Christopher Robinson, *Lucian and His Influence in Europe* [1979], p. 67). But nothing supports the association.

214:27–30 *he might believe . . . at Court.* Flavius Claudius Julianus (331–363), Emperor of Rome, was the subject of a Restoration debate commenced by Samuel Johnson's *Julian the Apostate* (1682), which inspired retorts by George Hickes and William Hopkins as well as responses from Johnson, who used Julian to promote the exclusion of James. Dryden himself responded to Johnson with the character of Ben-Jochanan in *The Second Part of Absalom and Achitophel* (see ll. 352–372 and note in *Works*, II, 72–73, 331–332). The views of some modern scholars accord with Dryden's that Julian was not properly called an apostate (see, e.g., G. W. Bowersock, *Julian the Apostate* [1978], p. 18). Others (Giuseppe Ricciotti, trans. M. Joseph Costelloe, *Julian the Apostate* [1960], pp. 12–13; Robert Browning, *The Emperor Julian* [1975], p. 44) imply that Julian had been at one time a sincere Christian. Christianity had been established as the dominant religion in the empire by Julian's uncle, Constantine the Great, and was further promoted by Constantine's son and successor, Constantius II.

214:30–34 *Neither . . . intended us.* Mayne (sig. A6) similarly notes that Christians are indebted to Lucian for exploding paganism but does not attribute Christian intent to Lucian. On the other hand, Spence, I, sig. A8, while claiming to follow Mayne, sees loftier Christian purpose in Lucian and calls him "our Pretended Atheist."

215:2–8 *one of . . . framing them.* Derived from Mayne (sigs. A6, A7r–v).

215:17 *Elective.* Here in the sense of "eclectic."

215:28–31 *In one . . . the World.* See *Halcyon* (*The King Fisher* in *Works of Lucian*, II, 612–615).

215:31–216:1 *In another . . . Fate.* See *Zeus Catechized (Jupiter confuted and baffled* in *Works of Lucian,* IV, 206–218, esp. p. 208). Dryden seems to have recalled this dialogue in 1697 when putting his notes to Virgil into final form (see *Works,* VI, 1125).

216:13–15 *a Doubter . . . Sects.* See *Works of Lucian,* II, 532–611.

216:17 *Some . . . deserves.* E.g., the extract from the Suidas lexicon in *Lucian* calls Lucian a blasphemer, a curser, an atheist, and a wicked man (sig. *β3v*).

216:17–19 *his Defenders . . . Vertue.* E.g., Spence, I, sigs. A1*v*–A2, who, while not taxing Lucian's morals, feels Lucian should not be defended, "when he is prov'd a Delinquent."

216:20–21 *Nerva . . . Antonines.* The succession from Nerva to Marcus Aurelius, from 96 to 180, provided emperors of humanity, enlightenment, and discipline.

216:23–27 *He is more . . . condemns it.* See esp. *Amores (The Loves, or Difference of Sexes* in *Works of Lucian,* IV, 87–114). There are passing allusions in *Charidemus,* V (in *ibid.,* II, 4–5), *The Ship* II, XLIII (in *ibid.,* II, 471–472, 496), *The Carousel,* XV (*The Lapithæ,* in *ibid.,* III, 216), and in *The Dialogues of the Courtesans,* X (in *ibid.,* III, 307). Lucian's authorship of *Amores* and *Charidemus* is now questioned (see Loeb ed., VIII, 147, 467).

216:29–30 *He seems . . . Vice.* See *Amores,* XLVIII (*The Loves,* in *Works of Lucian,* IV, 111): Socrates "has advis'd us to the Love of Boys, as tending to the Improvement of the Republick."

217:9–10 *Lucian . . . Harlots.* See *The Dialogues of the Courtesans* (*Works of Lucian,* III, 280–323). The dialogue is reproved by Mayne (sigs. A7*v*–A8), who calls it "Obscoene Lucius, and Meretricious," and by d'Ablancourt (I, sig. â5); neither supplies the dialogue's title.

217:11–13 *But . . . Objection.* Cf. *To Mrs Anne Killigrew,* ll. 56–66 (*Works,* III, 111); *To My Friend, the Author* (Peter Motteux), ll. 15–16; preface to *Fables* (1700, D2*r*–*v*; Watson, II, 293–294); *Cymon and Iphigenia,* ll. 1–41; and the epilogue to *The Pilgrim,* ll. 1–47.

217:17–19 *exposing . . . Candle.* In *Philosophers for Sale (The Auction of the Philosophers,* in *Works of Lucian,* III, 323–344).

217:19 *sold . . . Candle.* By auction (*OED*). Spence (II, 25) uses the idiom when translating the passage in Lucian where the philosophers complain of being auctioned by Jupiter.

217:20–22 *their Opinion . . . honour'd.* In *The Dead Come to Life (The Fisherman,* in *Works of Lucian,* III, 345–376, esp. pp. 362–367). For another of Dryden's opinion see Mayne (sig. A7).

217:24–26 *he taught . . . the Snare.* In *The Dialogues of the Courtesans* (*Works of Lucian,* III, 280–323).

217:31 *Employment under Marcus Aurelius.* Earlier described by Dryden (210:34) as "Intendant of *Egypt.*" Cf. d'Ablancourt (I, sig. a4): "Intendant de l'Empereur en Egypte"; and Spence (I, sig. †7): "Procurator or Superintendent . . . in Ægypt." Modern scholars have demoted Lucian to *archistator praefecti,* the superintendent's chief usher or attendant (see, e.g., H.-G. Pflaum, "Lucien de Samosate, *Archistator Praefecti Aegypti,*" *Mélanges de l'École Française de Rome: Antiquité,* LXXI [1959], 281–286).

Lucian gives some glimpse of his duties in *Apologia*, XII (*An Apology for Those That Serve for a Pension*, in *Works of Lucian*, III, 107).

217:34–218:2 *to Herodian . . . Learned*. Herodian's history went from the death of Marcus Aurelius (A.D. 180) to the accession of Gordian III (A.D. 238). On Marcus Aurelius Dryden could also have recalled Eusebius and Dio Cassius (see A. E. Wallace Maurer, "Dryden's Knowledge of Historians, Ancient and Modern," *N&Q*, CCIV [1959], 264–266). In seventeenth-century England the *Meditations* of Marcus Aurelius were published in Greek, Latin, and English.

218:3–7 *As for . . . reform*. See Mayne (sigs. A6r–v): "they object That hee is too Satyricall, and puts too much Gall into his Inke. 'Tis much to be suspected That They who thus object, are guilty of the Follies, Hypocrisies, and Crimes, which he with so much pleasant wit labours to reforme."

218:7–8 *he rather . . . Juvenal*. Cf. *Discourse of Satire* (*Works*, IV, 63: 16–18).

218:17–18 *a Drunken . . . Lapithæ*. See *The Carousel* (*The Lapithæ*, in *Works of Lucian*, III, 207–240).

218:19–23 *he seems . . . a Body*. Cf. Mayne (sig. A7): "can they . . . say he was an Enemy to any thing but Vice? Was there ever a fairer Picture drawne of a truly Learned, Vertuous man then his Demonax? . . . Or was there ever such a Picture of Beauty mixt with Vertue, as he drew of the Lady, which gave the Title to his Images?" Adding the dialogue of *Nigrinus* (*Works of Lucian*, IV, 213–233, 2d pag.), Dryden accepts Mayne's examples of the *Demonax* (*ibid.*, IV, 128–141), and *Imagines* (*The Images* in *ibid.*, II, 381–398). In *Imagines* Lucian (Dryden's "Philosopher") depicts what ideal virtue would be when united with the ideal body.

218:23–24 *Alexander . . . Peregrinus*. The second is not in the *Works of Lucian;* for the first see I, 144–181.

218:27–31 *Some . . . Understanding*. Mayne (sig. A7) also disparages those who find fault with Lucian's wit.

218:32–219:16 *the wretched . . . him down*. Dryden refers to *Lucien en Belle Humeur* by Bruslé. Bruslé's Lucian dismisses his own dialogues as dull and wants to enliven his work with conversations between such as the Duke of Alva and the Prince of Orange or the King of Sweden and his daughter Christine (Amsterdam, 1694, p. 9). Bruslé's initial dialogue is between Lucian and d'Ablancourt.

219:1 *as insipid . . . Poet*. Bruslé was in fact Belgian, and the Dutch references here and subsequently were perhaps prompted by the Amsterdam imprint of his book. Cf. the prologue to *Amboyna*, ll. 33–34: "Wit; in Dutchmen . . . would be / As much improper as would Honesty."

219:8 *Slip*. A newspaper "printed in the form of a long slip of paper" (*OED*).

219:9–10 *Jaundice . . . him*. Cf. *Palamon and Arcite*, II, ll. 487–488.

219:13 *Frog-land*. I.e., Dutch (*OED*).

219:15 *of course*. According to the customary order or procedure (*OED*).

219:16–17 *Incipient . . . loqui*. Martial, V, lxix, 8 (Loeb trans.: "All men shall begin to speak for Cicero").

219:18–22 *'Tis to be . . . Arguing*. See d'Ablancourt (sigs. a4v–a5): "la façon dont il traite les matieres les plus importantes, fait assez voir qu'il n'êtoit pas fort profond dans la Philosophie, & qu'il n'en avoit apris que ce qui servoit à sa profession de Rhéteur, qui estoit de parler pour & contre, sur toutes sortes de sujets."

219:30–220:4 *For my . . . Lucian.* Condensed and rearranged from Mayne (sig. A6) but retaining most of his phrasing. Mayne does not there mention Lactantius but had earlier cited him as a likely borrower from Lucian (sig. A4*v*).

220:4–6 *the Treacherous . . . Author.* Cf. Mayne (sigs. A2*v*–A3): "of all Authours, I know none more hard to be render'd like Himselfe then Lucian: whose Greeke is . . . of such a new, and particular Stile . . . that his best Interpreters into Latine, Erasmus, Sʳ Thomas Moore, Melancthon . . . have but made him speake like a raw Traveller from one Country to another."

220:16–23 *It was . . . Isocrates.* Cf. Mayne (sigs. A2*v*–A3): Lucian's "Greeke is not of one uniforme Webbe, like Plato, Thucidides, Polibius, or Eunapius; but of . . . a new, and particular Stile. . . . [For] the Distribution, and close pursuit of the parts, the Roundnesse of his periods: the rare Art in the choyce of his words, and Transitions . . . musically tyed together, in a full floud, and torrent of perswasion . . . without Inæqualities, or swellings . . . [some of the dialogues may] stand in competition with the best Orations in Demosthenes, or Isocrates."

220:24–29 *His Wit . . . he liv'd.* D'Ablancourt (I, sig. a5) praises Lucian for "une humeur gaye & enjoüée, & cét air gallant que les anciens nommoient 'urbanité,'" as well as for "son élegance & . . . sa politesse," but adds: "Je le trouve seulement un peu grossier dans les choses de l'Amour, soit que cela se doive imputer au genie de son temps, ou au sien."

220:26 *Facetious.* "Polished and agreeable, urbane" (*OED*).

221:1–5 *If Wit . . . Subject.* See preface to *The State of Innocence* (1677, sig. C2*v*; Watson, I, 207): wit "*is a propriety of Thoughts and Words; or in other terms, Thought and Words, elegantly adapted to the Subject.*" Mayne (sigs. A4*v*–A5) perhaps prompted Dryden to recall his own definition, for Mayne, noting that wit is "a thing never yet perfectly defined," offers to remedy the deficiency.

221:3–4 *Aristotle . . . Terms.* Watson (II, 211) notes *Rhetoric,* III, ii, 1–7, and *Poetics,* XXII.

221:10–12 *not butchered . . . the stroke.* Cf. Dryden's *Discourse of Satire* (*Works,* IV, 71:8–11): "Yet there is still a vast difference betwixt the slovenly Butchering of a Man, and the fineness of a stroak that separates the Head from the Body, and leaves it standing in its place."

221:13 *Æneæ . . . cadis.* See *Aeneid,* X, 830, as Dryden translated it (l. 1180): "'Twas by the great *Æneas* hand I fell" (*Works,* VI, 714).

221:14–15 *I know . . . Aristophanes.* Dryden might be recalling Lucian's praise of Aristophanes in *A True Story,* I, 29 (*Of True History,* in *Works of Lucian,* III, 143), or he might have been prompted by Mayne's adjacent tributes to Aristophanes and Lucian (sigs. A4*v*, A5*r*–*v*).

221:17–18 *in Latin . . . Erasmus.* Erasmus translated 28 of Lucian's dialogues into Latin (Paris, 1506). See Craig R. Thompson, ed., *Collected Works of Erasmus* (1978), XXIV, 602–603.

221:18–19 *in French . . . Pleasure.* In *Nouveaux Dialogues des Morts* (Paris, 1683; 2d part, 1684), Bernard Le Bovier de Fontenelle (1657–1757) created dialogues between ancients (e.g., "Anacreon, Aristote"), between ancients and dead moderns (e.g., "Socrate, Montaigne"), and between dead moderns (e.g., "Elisabeth D'Angleterre, Le Duc D'Alencon"), and dedicated his work "A Lucien Aux Champs Elisiens": "Pour moy, je n'ay garde de pretendre à la gloire de vous avoir bien imité; je ne veux que celle d'avoir bien sçû qu'on ne peut imiter un plus excellent Modele que vous" (sig. A4*v*). Cf. Dryden's praise of Fontenelle when dedicating the *Pastorals* in *The Works of Virgil:* "the living Glory of the *French.* 'Tis enough for him to have excell'd his Master *Lucian*" (*Works*, V, 6).

221:20–21 *disnest.* A "rare" verb according to *OED,* which cites only this and one other example, both of them figurative and each with the verb governing a different preposition. The first example, from 1596, gives the sense of driving people from their abode and is thus plausibly analogous to dislodging someone or something, especially in the hunting term of dislodging a deer from hiding. Dryden's usage, if his it were, can only mean to disnest the abode of its occupants or, in *OED*'s gloss, "to void (as a nest) of its occupants." Such a usage seems semantically unlikely and Dryden may have written "divest"; but a change by copyist or compositor of "divest" into "disnest" is unlikely. "Disvest" (a now obsolete variant of "divest") could have been transmuted into "disnest," but *OED*'s only examples of "divest" evidently have only the literal sense of "disrobe." It should be noted that either the compositor or a copyist for O was prone to error and therefore untrustworthy.

221:25 *too Libertine.* See 216:17–217:10 and notes.

221:30–222:6 *Echard . . . Defence.* See John Eachard, *Mr Hobbs's State of Nature Considered; In a Dialogue Between Philautus and Timothy* (1672), and *Some Opinions Of Mr Hobbs Considered in a Second Dialogue Between Philautus and Timothy* (1673). See also Spence (I, sigs. C3*v*–C4), who alludes to Eachard without naming him and finds that he "has with the Greatest height of Wit, and depth of Reason, Writ Dialogue-wise against Mr. Hobbs, and done more then all the Grave and Magisterial Authors, Who have so formally taken that famous Man to Task."

222:1–2 *than those . . . Divinity.* See Samuel I. Mintz, *The Hunting of Leviathan* (1962), pp. 157–160.

222:7–11 *I will . . . accurately.* In *Of Dramatick Poesie* Dryden had earlier shown familiarity with the form of the classical dialogue from Plato to Cicero (*Works*, XVII, 348–359). Thereafter the dialogue became ubiquitous, with at least 2,000 appearing in England between 1660 and 1725 (see Eugene R. Purpus, "The 'Plain, Easy, and Familiar Way': The Dialogue in English Literature, 1660–1725," *ELH,* XVII [1950], 54 n. 30). Spence (I, sigs. C3*v*–C7) had in fact devoted some pages to distinguishing between kinds of dialogue, but his simple taxonomy fell far short of what could be performed in "an entire Volume."

222:13–14 *his discourse . . . Prometheus.* See *To One Who Said, "You're a Prometheus in Words"* (*Works of Lucian,* I, 9–13, 2d pag.).

222:19 *twelve.* Probably from d'Ablancourt (I, 7)—"une douzaine"—or possibly from Spence (I, 8). There are sixteen vultures in the 1563 edition of Lucian (Greek and Latin) and in Mayne (p. 2), as in modern texts. In the *Works of Lucian* (I, 11) there is "a whole Score."

223:5–6 *if you . . . Argument.* See d'Ablancourt, I, sig. a5.

223:6–8 *like Ovid . . . Stage.* Cf. *Of Dramatick Poesie* (*Works*, XVII, 67:

27–29); preface to *Ovid's Epistles* (*Works*, I, 112:17–20); and *Examen Poeticum* (*Works*, IV, 370:2–7).

223:17–20 *Sir Henry . . . Benefit.* See *Works*, XV, 421, and pp. 318–319 above.

223:20–23 *The Learning . . . Senate.* Upon election for Saltash, Walter Moyle served on committees from 25 November 1695 to 8 April 1696 (see *Journals of the House of Commons*, XI, 335–552; see also Caroline Robbins, ed., *Two English Republican Tracts* [1969], p. 24). For Dryden's other complimentary references to Moyle see *A Parallel betwixt Painting and Poetry*, 61:3–9, above; *Works*, V, 292:25–26.

223:23 *as his Father had done.* Sir Walter Moyle (1627–1701) represented Cornish constituencies in the parliaments of Oliver and Richard Cromwell; in the Convention Parliament which recalled Charles II and then became his first parliament until its dissolution early in 1661; and finally, after a long interval, in the Convention Parliament summoned by William of Orange, which became William & Mary's first parliament until its dissolution early in 1690 (see list of members in *Cobbett's Parliamentary History*, III [1808], 1428, 1479, 1531; IV [1808], 2; V [1809], 28). Moyle was not returned to subsequent parliaments. Earlier, he stood for election to Charles II's third parliament in 1679 but was not returned (his name appears on the list for that election drawn up by Shaftesbury but was crossed out when the returns became final; see J. R. Jones, "Shaftesbury's 'Worthy Men': A Whig View of the Parliament of 1679," *BIHR*, XXX [1957], 236). He was knighted on 4 February 1664 (William A. Shaw, *The Knights of England* [1906], II, 239).

223:23–26 *The Wit . . . a Herald.* Charles Blount (1654–1693) achieved considerable notoriety with his last work, *The Oracles of Reason* (1693) (see Phillip Harth, *Contexts of Dryden's Thought* [1968], p. 73; Craig, "Dryden's Lucian," p. 157). He had earlier praised Dryden and had also defended him against detractors (see *Dryden: The Critical Heritage*, ed. James and Helen Kinsley [1971], pp. 160, 80–88; see also *Works*, XI, 432, 527, 528). According to Luttrell, writing at the end of July 1693 (III, 149), Blount "shot himselfe for love of his former wifes sister," whom, according to the law of the time, he of course could not marry. Blount lingered for a month before dying (*ibid.*, III, 174). Winn, p. 605, argues that Blount's suicide may have been for Dryden among those "other Performances" that had "made too much noise in the World."

223:31–224:8 *For Criticism . . . common Sense.* For similar remarks throughout Dryden's writings see John M. Aden, *The Critical Opinions of John Dryden* (1963), pp. 43–45.

224:17–21 *what the . . . Work.* E.g., Jacques Amyot devoted nearly twenty years to making a translation of Plutarch first published in 1559 (René Sturel, *Jacques Amyot* [1908], pp. 90–92), a translation known to Dryden (*Works*, XVII, 257–258). Segrais' translation of Virgil, to which Dryden was referring in 1696 while making his own translation of Virgil, was published in two volumes, the first appearing in 1668, the second in 1681.

224:23 *the sincere . . . Eloquence.* Translating *Atticæ eloquentiæ exemplar syncerum* in an edition of Lucian (Amsterdam, 1687) introduced by Joannes Georgius Graevius, although the phrase occurs in a preface contributed to the edition by John Benedict (I, sig. **2*v*). For the seventeenth-century concept of "Attic" see *Style, Rhetoric, and Rhythm: Essays by Morris W. Croll,* ed. J. Max Patrick et al. (1966), pp. 45–101.

224:29–225:3 *D'Ablancourt . . . wrote.* With liberties, Spence more or less followed d'Ablancourt's French translation of Lucian, converting it into a clumsily colloquial English. Cf., e.g., d'Ablancourt, I, 196: "Cela est plaisant qu'il faille estre Violon, avant que d'estre Philosophe!" and Spence, II, 3: "Pleasant y gad, that a man must first be a Fidler, before he can be a Philosopher!"; also d'Ablancourt, I, 213: "Point de pardon, mon ami"; and Spence, II, 23: "Pardon with a murrain, no, no, no pardon, friend."

225:2 *a Jack-Pudding.* A buffoon or clown (*OED*).

225:6–8 *but it is . . . the whole.* In his "Table," Mayne (pp. 399–400) lists fifty dialogues. Among those "left . . . lockt up in their owne untranslated Greeke" are "an Obscœne Lucius, and Meretricious Dialogues, not fit for the Eyes or Eares of a Chaste, or Christian Reader" (sigs. A7*v*–A8).

225:8–9 *As for . . . never saw.* For the translations by Francis Hickes see headnote, p. 373.

225:14–15 *a Language . . . French.* For similar judgments see *Works,* V, 322:18–23; XVII, 246:21–23.

225:19–21 *In which . . . the French.* Translation of Latin and Greek classics flourished in sixteenth-century France (see Rudolf Pfeiffer, *History of Classical Scholarship from 1300–1850* [1976], pp. 99–123, 134).

225:22–226:2 *the Booksellers . . . Slavery.* An outburst perhaps prompted by Dryden's deteriorating relationship with Tonson while translating Virgil; see, e.g., "Upon triall I find all of your trade are Sharpers & you not more than others; therefore I have not wholly left you" (Ward, *Letters,* p. 80).

225:30 *bubbled Chapmen.* See Harry M. Geduld, *Prince of Publishers: A Study of the Work and Career of Jacob Tonson* (1969), p. 39: "Many of the lighter publications were distributed throughout London and the provinces by 'running booksellers'—an obscure body of hawkers and chapmen."

226:3–6 *when . . . Lucian.* See *Works,* XVII, 430.

226:12–15 *that Censure . . . Version.* Dorset may indeed have directed the witticism against Spence (as is assumed by Brice Harris, *Charles Sackville, Sixth Earl of Dorset,* in *Illinois Studies in Language and Literature,* XXVI, nos. 3–4 [1940], p. 99), but he certainly did not originate it; cf. d'Ablancourt's remark about painstakingly metaphrastic translation: "dont il faut lire l'Original pour entendre la Version" (I, sig. ã8*v*).

226:18–227:9 *The Qualification . . . Transfusion.* Cf. Dryden's remarks on verse translation in the preface to *Ovid's Epistles* (*Works,* I, 118:6–30) and the preface to *Sylvæ* (*Works,* III, 4:16–5:33).

226:24 *through.* I.e., thorough.

227:9 *Transfusion.* Cf. preface to *Fables* (1700, sig. *C2*v*; Watson, II, 288): "I grant, that something must be lost in all Transfusion, that is, in all Translations."

227:13 *More-Fields.* Outside the walls of London and then the site of brothels, taverns, and rowdy fighting between butchers and weavers (Arthur Bryant, *King Charles II* [1955], pp. 67, 73, 218).

227:13 *Bartholomew Fair.* Held annually on 24 August and, by the end of the seventeenth century, lasting a fortnight, resorted to by "idle Youth, and loose People . . . spend[ing] their Money in Vanity; and (that which was worse) in Debaucheries, Drunkenness, Whoredom" (Stow, *Survey*, ed. Strype, I, Book III, 240).

The Annals of Tacitus, Book I

At the end of June 1698 Matthew Gilliflower published in three volumes an evidently delayed translation of Tacitus' *Annals, Histories, Germania,* and *Agricola,* with Dryden's name and prestige attached to the initial piece, a translation of *Annals* I.[1] The translation may have been mooted as early as August 1692, when Peter Motteux noted with approval that Abraham Nicolas Amelot de la Houssaye had produced a French version of Tacitus superior to that of Nicolas Perrot, Sieur d'Ablancourt.[2] A year later Motteux reported that "three Persons of Quality" were to make Tacitus English and remarked that they could profit from Amelot's annotated translation into French.[3] Shortly thereafter, on 21 November 1693, the projected translation was entered in the *Stationers' Register* in language approximating that on the 1698 title page. Like the *Gentleman's Journal* two months earlier, the entry designates just three contributors, who are now identified as "Sr W. T. Sr H. S: Sr R. L.," possibly Sir William Temple and probably Sir Henry Sheeres and Sir Roger L'Estrange.[4] The entry further identifies Matthew Gilliflower and Samuel Briscoe as the publishers. Although absent from the original three, Dryden five years later headed a list of fifteen contributors in the published edition.

We have found no contemporary report showing how, when, or why Dryden became associated with the translation of Tacitus, but in 1693 Samuel Briscoe published Dryden's *Character of Polybius* as preface to Sir Henry Sheeres's translation of Polybius, where Sheeres is also identified

---

[1] For the date see *Correspondence of the Family of Hatton,* ed. Edward Maunde Thompson, Camden Society, n.s. XIII (1878), vol. 2, pp. 234–235. A second edition of the Tacitus appeared in 1716. Malone omitted Dryden's contribution, along with other translated works, from his collection of Dryden's prose. Scott also omitted it, although he included Dryden's complete translation of *The Life of St. Francis Xavier (Works,* XIX), together with excerpts from *The History of the League (Works,* XVIII).

[2] *Gentleman's Journal* (August 1692), p. 23. D'Ablancourt published a translation of the *Annals* (Paris, 1640), which was several times reprinted before he published a complete translation of *Les Oeuvres de Tacite* (Paris, 1658); the *Oeuvres* had received a number of editions, French and Dutch, by 1692. Amelot (properly Amelot de la Houssaye) published a translation of *Annals* I–VI at Paris in 1690, offering it as the first part of an evidently projected complete translation of Tacitus; a piracy of this first part appeared two years later at The Hague. Amelot added other books of the *Annals* early in the next century, but he died in 1706 with his project unfinished; it was completed by François Bruys.

[3] *Gentleman's Journal* (September 1693), p. 312. Macdonald, p. 177, gives the month as July; he was corrected by James M. Osborn, "Macdonald's Bibliography of Dryden," *MP,* XXXIX (1941), 98.

[4] The list of translators in 1698 includes L'Estrange and Sir H. S., but not Sir W. T., nor a name corresponding to those initials.

only as "Sir H. S." Dryden expressed admiration for Tacitus in *The Character of Polybius*,[5] and perhaps Briscoe, perhaps Sheeres, perhaps both together prevailed upon him to contribute to the Tacitus. Between entry of the Tacitus in the *Stationers' Register* in 1693 and its publication in 1698 the three men were evidently associated in another venture. A decade after Dryden's death, Briscoe published a translation of Lucian which numbered Sheeres among contributors and featured a prefatory life by Dryden, written, Briscoe claimed, in 1696.[6] But around 1696 Briscoe temporarily withdrew from publishing, discomfited by reverses,[7] and at this time, we may suppose, the Tacitus venture became the sole property of Matthew Gilliflower, who may, then, have inherited Dryden's commitment to translate part of Tacitus. For most of the years between 1693 and 1698, from June 1694 to July 1697, Dryden was under contract to translate Virgil for Jacob Tonson. The contract allowed Dryden time off from Virgil to discharge prior obligations, among them translation of *De Arte Graphica*.[8] There is, however, no mention of Tacitus (or of Lucian) in the contract, and Dryden, perhaps helping to delay publication, probably did not turn to Tacitus until the latter part of 1697 at the earliest, when he was free of Tonson's Virgil.[9]

---

[5] See 18:34–19:4, 34:24–35:23 above. Dryden frequently alluded to Tacitus: in *Of Dramatick Poesie* (*Works*, XVII, 6:20–21), *Tyrannick Love* (I, i, 162, and note; *Works*, X, 121, 411), *Notes and Observations on The Empress of Morocco* (*Works*, XVII, 85:30–31 and note), *The Hind and the Panther* (II, 706, and note; *Works*, III, 160, 407), the *Discourse of Satire* (*Works*, IV, 67:4–28), and the preface to *Fables* (1700, sig. B2v; Watson, II, 281). True, in *The Life of Plutarch* Dryden charged Tacitus with occasional "ill nature" and frequent "obscurity" (*Works*, XVII, 273:2, 276:30), but in the *Discourse of Satire* he declared that he strove to emulate Tacitus by divesting himself of "partiality, or prejudice" (*Works*, IV, 50: 33–34). See also Wallace Maurer, "Dryden's Knowledge of Historians, Ancient and Modern," *N&Q*, CCIV (1959), 264–266.

[6] *Works of Lucian*, I, sig. A3.

[7] See above, p. 371.

[8] For the text of the contract see *Works*, VI, 1179–1183.

[9] James Anderson Winn, *John Dryden and His World* (1987), pp. 454, 620, sets out an alternative hypothesis communicated to him by Steven N. Zwicker: Dryden's quotation of a sentence from Tacitus in the *Discourse of Satire* (*Works*, IV, 67:7–10), completion of which Dryden dated 18 August 1692 (*ibid.*, 90:6), "suggests that [by then] Dryden had already begun his part of the group translation of Tacitus." Dryden in fact quoted from near the end of *Annals* I, so that, if the quotation is indeed significant for the work of translating Tacitus, it ought, perhaps, to indicate that, by August 1692, Dryden had completed or almost completed the translation. To say as much places Dryden's work on Tacitus very early indeed, since, as we shall see, he made use when translating Tacitus of Amelot's *Tacite* in the second edition, which was not published until 1692 and perhaps not long before Motteux announced the availability of Amelot's version in the *Gentleman's Journal* for August 1692. In the *Discourse of Satire* Dryden followed the sentence from Tacitus with an English version, which differs from the version offered in 1698 (cf. *Works*, IV, 67:10–14, and 287:3–6 above). If we wish to connect the quotation in the *Discourse of Satire* with Dryden's other work at this time, we ought to remember that he was thinking of Tacitus when, shortly after completing his work for the *Satires* of Juvenal and Persius, he concluded his *Character of Polybius* with a comparison of Polybius and Tacitus. The quotation in the *Discourse of Satire* is taken from the Abbé Pichon's Delphin edition of Tacitus (*Works*, IV, 571), which Dryden also cited in *The Character of Polybius*

When we move from biography to textual analysis, from concern with how Dryden became involved in translating Tacitus to concern with what he translated, we must first ask just how much he contributed to Gilliflower's venture. The 1698 title page, like the entry in the *Stationers' Register,* announces that the translation (of *Annals* I–VI) is embellished with Amelot's political reflections and historical notes upon the text, and they duly appear at the foot of each page, Englished from Amelot's *Tacite.* The list of translators merely assigns the first book of the *Annals* to Dryden, thus implying that he translated the notes and reflections as well as the main text, and there is no known external evidence to deny (or confirm) the attribution. But the notes and reflections are translated in a manner uncharacteristic of Dryden, rendered for the most part word by word from the French, a procedure rare in Dryden's translations for more than a sentence or two at a time. Even the text above the notes, faithful enough to its original, treats that original, we shall see, more freely than do the notes. More striking is the frequent use in the notes of the -th ending for the third person singular of verbs: "saith," "hath," and "doth." To be sure, "says," "has," and "does" also occur, sometimes intermingled with -th endings, at other times, and for stretches of the notes, predominantly. We need not suppose from this inconsistency that two people translated the notes.

The -th ending was obsolescent by the end of the seventeenth century, although Halifax, for example, used it almost exclusively until his death in 1695. A year later, according to his own report, Swift wrote "the greatest part" of *A Tale of a Tub,* intermingling in it the -th and -s endings, sometimes in the same sentence and especially "hath" and "has."[10] Inconsistent usage by one author was, then, not without parallel. But Dryden, like Halifax, was not such an author, at least in his expository and argumentative prose. True, we find an occasional "hath" in the early essays,[11] and a scattering of -th endings in the dramatic verse and prose, although rarely more than once or twice in a play.[12] But the form is not found elsewhere

---

(14:23–24 above). It is certainly possible that Dryden was associated with the Tacitus project from its inception, perhaps at the request of Sheeres or Briscoe. He could even have made his translation early in the project's five- or six-year history and before Virgil descended upon him. But the evidence offered by Winn and Zwicker does nothing to confirm that possibility. Similarly, Dryden may have been associated with the Lucian project from its inception in 1693, although if he were, he evidently delayed the writing of his contribution. We should also remember that, although Motteux was able to announce Dryden's composition of *The Character of Polybius* before it was published, he mentioned Dryden in connection with neither the Lucian nor the Tacitus when he announced those projects in the *Gentlemen's Journal* for June and September 1693.

[10] See *A Tale of a Tub,* ed. Herbert Davis (1957), p. 1; for a sentence using both "hath" and "has" see the first sentence of Section I (p. 33).

[11] See *Of Dramatick Poesie* in *Works,* XVII, 54:13, 64:31; preface to *The Indian Emperour* in *Works,* IX, 7:5; and preface to *The Tempest* in *Works,* X, 4:36. There is also a "saith" in one of the notes to *Annus Mirabilis* (*Works,* I, 65).

[12] *The Tempest* has eleven -th endings, but their presence may reflect Davenant's stylistic influence, which Dryden acknowledged in the preface (*Works,* X, 4:13–36).

in his published prose,[13] including the translated text above the notes to Tacitus. So marked a stylistic divergence between text and notes supplies the strongest possible internal evidence for discounting Dryden's hand in the translated notes, and we have accordingly placed them in an appendix to show them as noncanonical material that was included with the canonical in our copy text. Dryden appears not to have consulted Amelot's political reflections, but he occasionally incorporated glosses from Amelot's historical notes into his translation of the main text, and in such a way that he once rendered a note virtually redundant.[14]

Dryden in fact looked at more than Amelot's notes, and early in the eighteenth century Thomas Gordon prefaced his rival translation of Tacitus by charging that, so far from turning Latin into English, Dryden translated "almost literally" and "servilely" from Amelot's French version of Tacitus, "never looked into the original [Latin], or understood not a word of it," and "was misled by the French which he appears to have as little understood."[15] This splenetic rival overstates the case, but, as we shall see, there is substance to his charge. Among other things of more weight, Dryden followed Amelot's paragraphing with only a few exceptions and adopted Amelot's idiosyncratic division of the text into chapters.

Early Renaissance editions of Tacitus show books of the *Annals* without subdivision, and the practice of breaking them into chapters seems not to have begun until the seventeenth century. Thus a posthumous reissue of the Lipsius edition (Antwerp, 1648) introduces chaptering absent from earlier issues, although it omits numbers 1–16 of *Annals* I and begins with 17, which corresponds with the seventeenth chapter in modern editions. Its subsequent chaptering also corresponds well enough with that in modern editions. An Amsterdam edition of 1649 inserts chapter numbers throughout and makes a point of doing so on its title page: *cum adjectis capitulorum numeris* (with chapter numbers added). Chaptering had in fact been used earlier for a French translation of Tacitus by Rodolphe Le Maistre (Paris, 1636), which agrees with the chaptering in later editions of the Latin, except that it omits numbering for the final chapter in *Annals* I, number 81. Chaptering was well established by the later seventeenth century, and although some editions still offered an undivided text, many broke it in the now accepted way. Such a chaptered edition was the Delphin (Paris,

---

[13] The form is also absent from Dryden's letters, except for the flirting, undergraduate letter to Honor Dryden, where he several times used a ceremonious "hath" (Ward, *Letters*, pp. 3–4).

[14] See our note to 244:28–29. The translator of the notes apparently worked both with the French and with Dryden's already made translation of the main text. At one point Dryden reversed the order of two clauses in the French, each keyed to a separate political reflection. The translator of the notes duly reversed the keys so that O's "*the first Occasion*,[3] *to seize it*[2]" (see 243:14 above) corresponds to Amelot's "de s'en saisir[2], s'il en trouvoit jamais l'occasion[3]" (I, 63–64), and the footnoted reflections correspond to the clauses upon which they are supposed to expatiate. On another occasion Dryden omitted a name given and glossed in the French, and the note is also omitted from the English version (see note to 273:4–5). It is of course true that such adjustments could also have been made by the publisher's supervisor or editor when preparing compositor's copy.

[15] Thomas Gordon, trans., *The Works of Tacitus* (1728–1731), I, 1–2.

1682–1687) by the Abbé Julien Pichon, which Dryden probably owned.[16] Pichon's chaptering of *Annals* I in fact corresponds with Le Maistre's of fifty years earlier: it omits, that is, numbering for what is the final, eighty-first chapter in other subdivided texts, seventeenth-century and modern.

Amelot imposed a different chaptering upon the *Annals*. In the first book he showed as an unnumbered and undivided prologue what were already and are now generally regarded as the first five chapters, so that his first chapter corresponds with the sixth in other chaptered editions. Later in the text, Amelot twice combines into one what are elsewhere two chapters and once separates into two what is elsewhere a single chapter, so that he contrives to end with six fewer chapters than can be found in other subdivided texts or five fewer than in the Delphin Tacitus. In other respects, Amelot supplies, with only minor variations, the same divisions as are found elsewhere. These are the divisions, Amelot's, which Dryden adopted for his translation of Tacitus, even though, as we shall see, he must have had a Latin text beside him also, most probably Pichon's, and perhaps others as well.[17] To help readers find their place in a Latin text with conventional chaptering we have bracketed the appropriate numerals in this edition. The unbracketed numerals are Dryden's, and Amelot's.

When Dryden made his translation of Tacitus, he had available a Latin text, probably in the Delphin first edition. He also had available Amelot's French translation, which had by then received two editions, at Paris in 1690 and at The Hague in 1692. Although the evidence is scanty, it suffices to show that Dryden used a copy of the Dutch piracy, not the Paris original.[18] Thus, he took from the Dutch edition the misprint "Martium" instead of the correct reading of 1690: "Mattium" (the Latin has *Mattio*).[19] But Dryden took more than misprints from the Dutch edition.

---

[16] Noyes (p. 1000) points out that in a paragraph of the *Discourse of Satire* (*Works,* IV, 67:6–68:21) Dryden drew upon Pichon's glosses to supplement a discussion of Tacitus. Dryden later acknowledged a debt to Pichon for material used in *The Character of Polybius* (see above, 14:23–24).

[17] Dryden used more than one edition when translating Virgil, although the Delphin predominantly (see *Works,* VI, 809:11–15). But he obviously made a much smaller commitment to the Tacitus than he did to the Virgil and may have relied upon a single text of the Latin.

[18] As he had done some years earlier when translating Maimbourg's *Histoire de la Ligue* (see *Works,* XVIII, 464–465). Cf. Dryden's translating Bouhours' *La Vie de S. François Xavier* from a Liège piracy rather than from editions produced in France (*Works,* XIX, 475–479). Lowland piracies may have been more available in England (and perhaps cheaper) than French originals (see *Works,* XIX, 453–454n).

[19] See above, 273:22. For the French readings see 1690, I, 84, and 1692, I, 174. For the Latin text see Pichon, I, 111 (ch. 56). The notes to *Annals* I were also translated from the 1692 rather than the 1690 edition. The political reflection on *Multitude* (272:5) concludes with "*Ch.* 13. *of his History*" (p. 471), following the 1692 reading (I, 167); 1690 (I, 81) has "Chap. 13 du livre 26. de son Hist." Again, the translated reflection on *Destiny* (272:26) concludes, as in 1692 (I, 171), with "*His History,* l. 6" (p. 473), whereas the reference in 1690 (I, 83) is to "Livre 16." Moreover, Gilliflower's edition follows 1692 in placing political reflections above historical notes at the foot of the page; 1690 places only historical notes at the foot and cuts the reflections into the text. Unless otherwise noted, all further citation of Amelot is from the 1692 edition.

To some extent at least, Dryden worked with both French and Latin versions, a procedure declared in his very first paragraph by the italicizing of scattered words and phrases that would not normally have been italicized in seventeenth-century practice. These words and phrases function as explanatory interpolations into the literal sense of the Latin and have a familiar precedent in the King James Bible, which also italicizes words, especially the copula, without equivalent in the original. Dryden, though, had a more immediate precedent than the King James Bible, for Amelot's opening paragraph also includes italicized words and phrases that function in the same way as Dryden's. As it happens, Dryden omitted all but one of Amelot's interpolations in that paragraph, while fashioning several of his own. Thus Amelot notes that Pompey and Crassus were Julius Caesar's *"colégues,"* whereas Lepidus and Antony were Augustus' *"rivaux."* While passing by those words, Dryden similarly notes that "the Dictatorship was granted, but *as necessity required,"* and that Julius had Augustus as *"his Successor"*: neither phrase has an equivalent in the Latin or the French. Again, Dryden refers to "the *Arbitrary* Dominion" of Cinna, in order, we may suppose, to catch the full sense of the Latin *dominatio* (which is muffled in the French "domination," although supplied in Amelot's note: "une puissance, qui n'a pas le droit & la raison pour fondement"). In these instances Dryden evidently translated from the Latin rather than from the French, or at least with an eye on both. But the final example in the first paragraph shows Dryden working principally from the French. When he offers "the *Modest* Title of Prince of the Senate" as, supposedly, a version of *nomine Principis* (with the title of prince), he is actually rendering Amelot's "le nom *modeste* de Prince *du Sénat."* Presumably by oversight, Dryden (or the printer) neglected to italicize "of the Senate" and signal an interpolation, along with *"Modest,"* into the literal sense of the Latin.[20]

Italicized words and phrases recur throughout the French and English versions, although with diminished frequency in the English. As in the opening paragraph, Dryden's interpolations usually differ from Amelot's. Frequently, moreover, Dryden will offer an unitalicized version of an italicized phrase in the French. Thus, Tacitus reports that, shortly before his death, Augustus made a voyage *electis consciis* (with chosen confidants).[21] For Amelot, Augustus had "choisi les plus confidens *de ses domestiques"* (I, 22), whereas Dryden's Augustus was "attended by some of his most trusty Servants" (ll. 160–161), a phrase corroborating, we might say, Thomas Gordon's charge that Dryden merely translated Amelot without an eye to the Latin. But the preceding sentence reverses the situation. There Dryden italicizes a word taken over, it seems, from the French, where it stands as an unitalicized substitute for a Latin word that Dryden also incorporates into his translation. Tacitus notes the rumor that Augustus' increasing ill health was owing to *scelus uxoris* (the wickedness of his wife). Amelot, specifying the wickedness or the crime, records that some suspected "sa femme de l'avoir empoisonné," and Dryden renders both the Latin gen-

---

20 For analysis of the opening paragraph stressing Dryden's dependence upon the Latin rather than the French see Steven N. Zwicker, *Politics and Language in Dryden's Poetry: The Arts of Disguise* (1984), pp. 236–238.

21 Pichon, I, 15 (ch. 5).

erality and the French particular, marking the latter as an interpolation: some suspected "the Impiety of his Wife by *Poison*."

On one occasion Dryden's italics apparently signal an interpolation into the literal sense of the French rather than of the Latin, the interpolated matter being taken from Amelot's note. Amelot describes popular discontent with "l'impôt du Centiéme" (I, 233), whereas Dryden records discontent with "the Impost laid on the Hundredth part of the *Gains by Commerce*" (ll. 2492–2493), his italicized phrase presumably corresponding to part of Amelot's note: "le centiéme de tout ce qui entroit en commerce." But Dryden's italicized phrase in fact corresponds well enough with a Latin phrase omitted from Amelot's text and instead translated in his note: *Centesimam rerum venalium* (a one percent [duty] on goods sold).[22] Here again, Thomas Gordon's charge would seem to stand.

However we explain Dryden's rendering of the *centesima* or the centiéme, the italicized words and phrases, other than proper names, almost always signal an interpolation into the literal sense of the Latin.[23] Since, moreover, we must suppose that they represent Dryden's decision rather than his compositor's whim, the otherwise irregular italics are preserved in this edition. After all, they usually provide clear evidence that Dryden consulted the Latin, even if intermittently. This evidence finds some confirmation from traces of the Latin diction and syntax in Dryden's sentences, especially in the earlier pages of the translation.

To say so is not to dismiss Gordon's charge, but only to modify it. Dryden unquestionably paid more attention to the French than to the Latin and increasingly so as the translation proceeded. The reasons are not far to seek. Dryden was almost certainly rushed, and however highly he valued Tacitus, he had once confessed that, when "troubled with the disease . . . of Translation," he always found "the cold Prose fits of it . . . the most tedious."[24] Tacitus, moreover, offers a text notoriously difficult to translate into English at once faithful and idiomatic; Dryden earlier remarked that Tacitus "often falls into obscurity."[25] Amelot, by contrast, provided a version that had already converted the elliptical Latin into a loose, expansive syntax, while his French idioms had, for the most part, established English equivalents. In his turn, Dryden generally adopts Amelot's syntax but treats the diction with more freedom, often, although not always, in the interests of idiomatic English.

The strong presence of an unimportant French intermediary unquestionably diminishes the stylistic interest of Dryden's translation, which would have been much greater had he confronted Tacitus directly and exclusively. There are nonetheless occasions when, by proceeding from Latin to French to English, we can gain some understanding of Dryden's stylistic preferences, simply because the Latin and French effectually supply alternatives between which Dryden chooses. Often enough, moreover, his choice of the French issues in something other than mere metaphrase, that

---

[22] *Ibid.*, p. 156 (ch. 78). The usual Renaissance reading; modern texts have *venatum*.

[23] See note to 260:9 for the only other example of an italicized phrase which cannot be construed as an interpolation into the sense of the Latin.

[24] Preface to *Sylvæ* in *Works*, III, 3:1–3.

[25] *The Life of Plutarch* in *Works*, XVII, 276:30.

"turning [of] an Authour word by word . . . from one Language into another" which he had dismissed in the preface to *Ovid's Epistles*.[26] Often enough, indeed, Dryden will enlarge upon the French in ways that respect its spirit while carrying us even further from the spirit of the Latin than the French had done. We should take our instance from the most compelling sequence in the first book of the *Annals*.

After some preliminaries devoted to the death of Augustus and the accession of Tiberius, the first book details events of A.D. 14–15, among them a continuing war in part undertaken to revenge the loss in A.D. 9 of three legions led by Quintilius Varus, which had been massacred in the forest of Teutoburg by Arminius and his Germans. By the summer of A.D. 15 Germanicus had brought an army close to the site of the massacre, had learned that the remains of Varus and his legions still lay unburied, and had determined to pay the last honors to his countrymen. Chapter 61 (Amelot's and Dryden's fifty-fifth) sets out the silent exploration of the place and concludes with reports from survivors of the disaster, who, we are to understand, now serve with Germanicus. The emphasis in all three versions—Latin, French, and English—falls upon shame and pain, the mingling of courage and weakness, the loss of three eagles, the suicide of Varus, and the contemptuous exultation of Arminius. But *quam mutatus!* Tacitus thus describes the discovery of bones:

> *Medio campi albentia ossa, ut fugerant, ut restiterant, disjecta vel aggerata: adjacebant fragmina telorum, equorumque artus, simul truncis arborum antefixa ora.*[27]

These evidences—almost an archeological report—invite interpretation, call for explanations that Tacitus himself declines to offer, though implying them in the remarkable sequence of *ut fugerant, ut restiterant, disjecta vel aggerata*. We know, what Tacitus leaves unsaid, that if these Romans were to die there, it would be better if countrymen in later years found their bones heaped together, not scattered around the edge of the battlefield. Undistracted by the historian's judgments, we are free to concentrate upon what these evidences must have meant to Germanicus and his legions, to Varus and his.

As soon as the Tacitean syntax, spare and elliptic, is translated into a more lightly inflected language the implied judgment easily becomes explicit, because the main words can no longer sit side by side, connected by inflection; instead they must be yoked by articles, pronouns of relationship, or adverbial phrases. Amelot does well enough by Tacitus according to his constraints. He elaborates a little and unnecessarily, but otherwise he remains as true to the Tacitean sense as an expansive syntax will permit (p. 186):

> Au milieu du champ paroissoient des carcasses & des os secs & blanchissans, dispersez, ou entassez, selon que les soldats avoient fui, ou resisté. Par tout des bouts de picques & de javelots, des membres & des mâchoires de cheval, des têtes d'hommes fichées à des troncs d'arbres.

---

26 *Works*, I, 114:25–26.

27 Pichon, I, 12 (in mid-plain were whitening bones, scattered or heaped, as they had fled, as they had stood firm; nearby were lying fragments of spears and horses' limbs; and [human] heads were fastened to tree trunks).

We see what Amelot adds to Tacitus: there are carcasses as well as bones, the bones dry as well as whitening; pikes as well as javelins; the jawbones of horses as well as their limbs. The heads are correctly specified as human, thus distinguishing them from the animal remains, and since the Latin *ora* is properly a synecdoche—mouths standing for heads—we can perhaps see why Amelot added the jawbones of horses. One other touch makes the French busier than the Latin, which notes only that broken weapons and horses' limbs lay nearby. For Amelot not only the weapons and limbs but also the human heads were everywhere: "par tout."

If Dryden glanced at the Latin while translating the discovery of bones— as we know he did elsewhere and as he almost certainly did a few sentences later—he set it aside and elaborated upon the French version, creating something unmistakably his own (277:31–38):

> The middle of the Field was strew'd with Carcasses, and white dry Bones, some scatter'd here and there, and others pil'd on heaps; by which might be observ'd, whether they receiv'd their Death in flight, or fell together in manly Resistance to the last. Every where were found their broken Pikes, and Javelins; the Limbs of Horses, and their Jaw-bones; and the Heads of Men, which were fix'd to the Trunks, or hung on the Branches of the Trees.

The opening phrase of the Latin implies the copula: in mid-plain (were) whitening bones. The French necessarily supplies a verb but makes it not much stronger than the copula: the bones were seen there. For Dryden, though, the field was "strew'd" with remains, thus preparing for the ubiquitous pieces of weapons, horses, and men. Dryden, of course, retains all of Amelot's additions, and embellishes them. Especially, he takes "re-sisté," itself faithful to *restiterant,* and stretches it into "fell together in manly Resistance to the last." "Manly" makes the implied judgment explicit and also, we must say, sentimentalizes the moment. So too, the replacement of *ut* or "selon que" with "by which might be observed" insists upon the process of passing judgment. Dryden prefers the French narrative, busier than the Latin, but he wants it even busier and wants it explained and judged in the moment of telling. We are certainly a long way from Tacitus, but we are also into an interesting, individual mind, as we are not with Amelot's French. Dryden's other major embellishment—the dangling of human heads from branches as well as fixing them to tree trunks—seems prompted more by the demands of cadence than of sense. Dryden, a master of the expansive syntax, ends fluently. Amelot, caught between syntaxes—his own and that of Tacitus—ends abruptly, the end of the sentence insufficiently felt for.[28]

Dryden continues to follow the French rather than the Latin version in the survivors' report, at one point accepting Amelot's explanatory amplification of *scrobes,* the trenches dug for executed Romans. Amelot stretches the single Latin word into "des fosses, *pour nous décoller à la Romaine*" (p. 187), which Dryden, omitting the italics that mark an interpolation,

---

[28] For further comparison of the Latin and English in this passage—without reference to the French—see Alan Roper, "Characteristics of Dryden's Prose," *ELH,* XLI (1974), 683–685.

duly renders as "Ditches, to behead and bury them according to the *Roman* Fashion" (ll. 1957–1958). Dryden, though, certainly knew that Amelot's italics marked an interpolation, because a phrase or two earlier he had evidently glanced at the Latin to learn from which raised spot Arminius made his harangue: *quo tribunali concionatus Arminius.* Amelot offers only "Voici, où Arminius haranguoit," and Dryden, accepting "voici," adds the tribunal from the Latin as well as specifying the recipients of the harangue: "Behold the Eminence from whence *Arminius* harangu'd his Soldiers." The exploration of the site ends with a report of how Arminius arrogantly scorned the standards and eagles: *signis & aquilis per superbiam inluserit.* Amelot adds a little—"ce superbe vainqueur se moquoit de nos Aigles & de nos Enseignes"—but Dryden specifies the form of insult and thus ends by dwelling upon the Roman humiliation: "the proud Conqueror forgot not to drag along the Ground, with Scorn, our Ensigns and our Eagles."

We can see, then, why Dryden for the most part preferred the French to the Latin. Amelot offered a syntax much closer to Dryden's own English syntax than did Tacitus. Amelot, moreover, was inclined to elaborate upon the literal sense of the Latin, incorporating explanations and not consigning everything to historical notes at the foot of the page. Some of those elaborations, at least in the forest of Teutoburg, involve not only gloss but a doubling and hence emphasizing of action or effect: carcasses as well as bones. We are familiar from elsewhere in Dryden's prose—as well as his verse—with his liking for reduplication: the synonymous clause or phrase, the saying things twice. Amelot had already moved Tacitean prose some way toward the kind of prose Dryden favored. It remained for Dryden to increase the doubling, to hang heads from branches as well as nailing them to tree trunks, and thus to make the scene even busier, filling it with actions and their results. He also, and as characteristically, added judgment or made judgment explicit, noting the manliness with which some resisted the Germans, or intensifying the scorn of an Arminius by making him "drag" the eagles "along the ground." We are indeed far from Tacitean restraint, the point touched but not dwelt upon, and Amelot certainly went before Dryden, in some sense showing the way. But Dryden goes so much farther, producing prose so characteristically his own, that it is hard to believe he would have translated Tacitus very differently had there been no French intermediary.

We can, though, hypothesize what might have been different if we describe in Dryden's own terms how the English relates to the Latin and how it relates to the French. Set beside the Latin, without reference to the French, the English appears to be "Paraphrase, or Translation with Latitude, where the Authour is kept in view by the Translator, so as never to be lost, but his words are not so strictly follow'd as his sense, and that too is admitted to be amplyfied, but not alter'd."[29] Set beside the French, without reference to the Latin, the English appears to be metaphrase, although not, it is true, the merely "servile, literal Translation"[30] which Gordon claimed it to be. Dryden, we have seen, modified Amelot, at times

[29] *Works,* I, 114:28–31.
[30] *Ibid.,* p. 116:21–22.

supplying his own embellishments, at others drawing upon Tacitus for details blurred or omitted by Amelot. Perhaps we should say that Dryden's English is close enough to the French to qualify, much of the time, as "literal," but not often so close as to be called "servile." The French, on the other hand, qualifies as paraphrase of the Latin in Dryden's terms; so we can say, if with caution, that Dryden metaphrased an existing paraphrase of the Latin. Had he made his own paraphrase, the result might have been different from what we have, as we can see from his practice at this time.

When Dryden took up Tacitus, he had recently completed (or just possibly was in the process of making) a paraphrase of Virgil. Soon after the Tacitus was published, Dryden turned to paraphrasing Homer, Ovid, Boccaccio, and Chaucer for the volume to be called *Fables Ancient and Modern*. His translations of Virgil and for *Fables* show us what paraphrase meant for Dryden in the 1690s, what he meant by saying he had "endeavour'd to make *Virgil* speak such *English*, as he wou'd himself have spoken, if he had been born in *England*, and in this present Age." [31] That amplification of the sense which Dryden admitted into paraphrase included (but was far from restricted to) turning the original toward acts and issues contemporary with the translator, toward, for example, the exile of James II, the bellicose policies of William III, or the nature of his title. The instances are many, and some have become familiar through frequent discussion. [32] They serve, we may suppose, to make the translated author current, to show his continuing relevance, and they do so, as it were, by inviting readers to apply the issues and actions of the past to their present equivalents. The translator's invitation becomes clear, its presence is confirmed, when we set his version beside the original and see how the literal sense differs. Such, in part, was paraphrase as Dryden practiced it in the 1690s.

Amelot's paraphrase, by contrast, issues no such invitations, and it was to this paraphrase that Dryden for the most part adhered, instead of making his own. To say so is by no means to deny that Dryden's Tacitus could be applied, if readers so chose, to English issues and actions. After all, Tacitus deals with power and rebellion, the calculations of politicians, the pathos and brutality of war, the burden of maintaining armies. These and other matters belong as much to Restoration England, or other ages, as to imperial Rome, and no doubt help account for the booksellers' interest in publishing an English Tacitus as well as Dryden's willingness to participate in the venture. The text, then, permitted applications, did not forbid the conversion of Roman particulars into English particulars. But we should not mistake permission for invitation, reader response for authorial intent, even though our ancestors certainly did.

An analogy from Dryden's earlier practice might help. Fourteen years before translating Tacitus, Dryden translated Louis Maimbourg's *Histoire de la Ligue*, thereby describing a period of French history which had already been paralleled with Restoration England in the years immediately preceding Dryden's translation. Dryden remained as faithful to Maim-

---

31 *Works*, V, 330:36–331:1.
32 See, e.g., Zwicker, *Politics and Language*, pp. 177–205; the commentary in *Works*, VI, 1038, on *Aeneis*, VI, 824–825; and, for Dryden's *Character of a Good Parson*, imitated from Chaucer, Alan Roper, *Dryden's Poetic Kingdoms* (1965), pp. 171–174.

bourg's text as he later did to Amelot's, adapting it in places, but only once turning it toward a Restoration particular, only once, that is, inviting an application.[33] To be sure, the translated text permitted readers to make applications if they so chose, and Dryden showed how to make them, both when dedicating the work to Charles II and in a lengthy postscript described by L'Estrange as "the Application" of the work.[34] Especially in the postscript, Dryden drew parallels between men, actions, and issues in late sixteenth-century France and late seventeenth-century England. By doing so he acted, in effect, as a reader of his own text, making applications permitted but not invited by that text.

The later translation of Tacitus, or of Amelot, has a status similar to that of *The History of the League*, except that it lacks a dedication and a postscript. It permits but does not invite applications, and Dryden supplies no instruction in how to make them, no examples of what they might be. We can of course guess at them, but any such applications are ours and are made without authorial assistance. If we choose to guess, we would perhaps do well to remember what Dryden once said of Tacitus, and when he said it. Tacitus, he pointed out, "describ'd the Times of Tyranny," and is "profitable, and instructive" to readers, especially "those who are born under a Monarchy."[35] Dryden said this, not while Charles reigned, or James, but in *The Character of Polybius*, when William reigned.

P. 230, ll. 1–13 *Rome . . . Senate.* See headnote, p. 391 above for discussion of this paragraph.

230:14 *But.* The disjunctive is from the Latin *Sed* (Pichon, I, 5); it is absent from the French (Amelot, I, 8).

230:17 *future Ages.* Dryden's addition.

230:20 *falsify'd through fear.* Translating *ob metum falsæ* (Pichon, I, 5; Loeb trans.: "falsified through cowardice") rather than Amelot's expansive "la crainte *de les ofenser*, fesoit écrire des mensonges" (I, 9).

230:21–22 *of their Historians.* Dryden's addition.

231:4–5 *the Title . . . Consul.* Dryden adds *"less invidious,"* perhaps prompted by Amelot's addition (I, 10), which Dryden passed by: "le nom odieux de Triumvir." Cf. Pichon, I, 6–7: *posito Triumviri nomine, Consulem se ferens* (after laying aside his title of triumvir and setting himself up as consul).

231:9 *Donatives . . . Provisions.* Cf. Amelot, I, 11: "l'abondance des vivres"; and Pichon, I, 7: *annona* (the price of corn).

232:12 *which . . . receiv'd.* Dryden's addition.

232:12 *not long.* Cf. Pichon, I, 12: *pridem* (long since); and Amelot, I, 16: "longtems."

232:18, 19 *no longer | as formerly.* The first phrase translates Amelot's "non plus" (I, 16); the second translates *ut antea* (Pichon, I, 12), which Amelot expands into *"lorsque son fils avoit des rivaux."*

233:16 *Masters.* With O's "Matters" cf. *dominos* (masters; Pichon, I, 13) and "Maîtres" (Amelot, I, 20).

---

[33] *Works*, XVIII, 244:4 and note.
[34] *Ibid.*, p. 423.
[35] 35:9–10, 35:20–22 above.

233:20–21 *mature . . . Warfare.* Translating *maturum annis, spectatum bello* (Pichon, I, 13; Loeb trans.: "mature in years and tried in war"), rather than "un homme fait, & qui a beaucoup de réputation militaire" (Amelot, I, 20–21).

233:24–25 *What . . . Man.* Translating Amelot's interpolated transition: "*Qu'atendre d'un homme*" (I, 21).

233:26 *amidst Arbitrary Power.* Dryden's addition.

234:5 *While . . . agitation.* A Latinism from *Hæc atque talia agitantibus* (Pichon, I, 14; Loeb trans.: "While these topics and the like were under discussion"); cf. Amelot, I, 22; "Pendant que l'on tenoit ces discours."

234:7 *the Impiety . . . Poison.* See headnote, pp. 391–392 above.

234:8–9 *attended . . . Servants.* See headnote, p. 391 above.

234:15 *It was farther reported.* Dryden's addition.

234:26 *Corps du Guard.* Accepting Amelot's version (I, 25) of *Acribus . . . custodiis* (Pichon, I, 15: with fierce guards).

235:14 *through fear of a Competitor.* Translating Amelot's "par la crainte d'avoir un Compétiteur" (I, 27), rather than the unelaborated *metu* (by fear) of the Latin (Pichon, I, 17).

235:19 *Sallustius Crispus.* The full name is from the Latin (Pichon, I, 17); Amelot (I, 30) has only "Saluste."

235:23–24 *either . . . Secret.* Dryden's addition.

235:27 *to execute his orders.* Accepting Amelot's addition: "*pour exécuter ses ordres*" (I, 30).

236:6 *in his name.* Accepting Amelot's explanatory "*en son nom*" (I, 32), rather than *apud . . . eos* (in their presence) in the Latin (Pichon, I, 19).

236:9–10 *affected . . . Consuls.* Accepting Amelot's "afectoit de commencer toutes les fonctions publiques par le ministére des Consuls" (I, 32–33), rather than *cuncta per Consules incipiebat* (he initiated everything through the consuls) in the Latin (Pichon, I, 19).

236:16 *funeral Honours.* Amelot's "honneurs *funébres*" (I, 33); cf. *honoribus* (Pichon, I, 19).

236:31 *from his Death.* Dryden's addition.

236:35 *the adoption . . . Man.* Tacitus has *senili adoptione* (Pichon, I, 20; by an elderly [perhaps senile] adoption). Cf. Amelot's "l'adoption d'un Vieillard *engeollé*" (I, 36); the interpolated "engeollé" (i.e., "enjôlé") presumably has the sense of "besotted" or "deceived" (see Randle Cotgrave, *A Dictionarie of the French and English Tongues* [1611]).

237:14–15 *to the People . . . five Thousand.* So Amelot, I, 38; Tacitus has *populo & plebi CCCCXXXV . . . millia* (435,000 to the nation and plebeians), which Pichon in his note (I, 22) apportions between the two groups in the same manner as Amelot and Dryden.

237:17 *small Sesterces, and three.* Modern texts of Tacitus include between the bequests to the praetorian guards and the legionaries a bequest of 500 sesterces to each of the urban troops; this bequest is omitted from Pichon and Amelot.

237:26 *interrupting . . . sudden.* Dryden's addition.

237:28 *of his own head.* Of his own accord (*OED*) and here translating Amelot's "de son chef" (I, 39: the Latin *sponte* [Pichon, I, 23] has a similar sense); cf. *The Life of Lucian*, 210:2.

237:35–238:1 *rather . . . Modesty.* Accepting Amelot's "plûtôt par vanité, *pour se faire honneur de ce refus,* que par un motif de modestie" (I, 39). Cf. *adroganti moderatione* (Pichon, I, 24; Loeb trans.: "with haughty moderation").

238:6 *for that Ceremony.* Accepting Amelot's substitution of *"pour céte cérémonie"* (I, 39) for *sede* (Pichon, I, 24; burial place).

238:12–13 *the superfluous . . . occasion.* Dryden's addition, anticipating 238:20–21.

238:16 *old.* Translating *senem* (Pichon, I, 24); Amelot omits the adjective.

238:16–17 *quietly . . . World.* Dryden's addition.

238:18 *of 44 years.* Also Amelot's addition (I, 40).

238:32 *or invented for him.* Accepting Amelot's interpretation of *aut nova* (Pichon, I, 25; or new): "ou inventez tout exprés en sa faveur" (I, 41).

239:2 *though . . . honest.* Also Amelot's addition: *"quoique la cause en fût juste"* (I, 42).

239:4 *because . . . assistance.* Also Amelot's addition: *"parce qu'il avoit besoin d'eux"* (I, 43).

239:11 *of the Senate.* Also Amelot's (italicized) addition (I, 44).

239:20 *Common-Wealth.* The historical note is miskeyed in O to 239:18 "Safety"; see Amelot, I, 45.

239:24 *Decimus Brutus.* Also Amelot's (italicized) addition (I, 45). Pichon (I, 27) glosses the unnamed consul as Mark Antony: the modern gloss.

240:13 *the forfeit.* Translating *pœnas* (Pichon, I, 28; penalty), which Amelot omits.

240:14 *was . . . ensue.* Probably influenced by Amelot's "Il est venu ensuite" (I, 47); cf. *sine dubio post hæc* (Pichon, I, 28; undoubtedly after that).

240:23 *Quintus Atedius.* The Latin text is corrupt at this point. Pichon, I, 30, gives *qui Atedii;* the full name is taken from Amelot, I, 48–49.

240:24 *his Minions.* Dryden is evidently translating Amelot's interpolated *"ses favoris"* (I, 50), but O's "minors" would not render "favoris." Dryden may have written "minions" or "minons," which the compositor misread as "minors."

241:31, 31–32 *Tributary / Conquer'd.* Also Amelot's additions: *"tributaires . . . sujétes"* (I, 58).

242:3–5 *which had . . . himself.* Also Amelot's (italicized) additions except for "or out of Jealousie" (I, 58).

242:27 *wherein . . . Affairs.* Also Amelot's (italicized) additions (I, 60).

242:30 *of Marcus Agrippa.* Cf. Amelot (I, 61): "d'Agrippa" and Pichon (I, 34): *M. Agrippæ.* The first name is spelled out in Pichon's paraphrase.

243:24 *for Emperour.* Explicating Amelot's addition: *"en sa faveur"* (I, 65–66).

244:8, 9 *Mother / Mother.* So Amelot: "Mere . . . Mere" (I, 67); cf. *parentem . . . matrem* (Pichon, I, 38).

244:8 *by . . . Distinction.* Elaborating upon Amelot's addition: *"par excellence"* (I, 67).

244:28–29 *the Assembly . . . Magistrates.* Translating Amelot's historical note (see p. 497 below) rather than his text—"les Comices" (I, 70) or the Latin *comitia* (Pichon, I, 40). As a result the translated note becomes virtually redundant.

245:1–2 *to . . . Election.* Accepting Amelot's addition: *"pour avoir sa faveur dans les élections"* (I, 71).

245:23 *This Disport began.* O's "Dispute" creates a non sequitur. Tacitus has only *Eo principio* (Pichon, I, 42; from this beginning); Amelot, seemingly followed by Dryden here, has "Ce relâchement commenca" (I, 74). Dryden may have written "disport," accurate in context and as translation of "relâchement," which the amanuensis or compositor misread as "dispute."

246:6 *a less.* From *paucioribus* (Pichon, I, 43; fewer), which Amelot (I, 75–76) omits.

246:9 *if need were.* Dryden's addition.

246:24 *Eight Pence.* Instead of ten asses in both Pichon (I, 44) and Amelot (I, 77). Amelot's note converts the Roman as into rather more than seven French deniers, and ten deniers would then have equaled an English penny (see Cotgrave, *Dictionarie*). Cf. the English conversion of Amelot's note, p. 498 below.

248:24 *Prefect . . . Camp.* First translating Tacitus (Pichon, I, 49–50): *præfectum castrorum,* and then reproducing Amelot's French equivalent (I, 84).

249:17 *as . . . Triumph.* Dryden's addition.

249:36 *Assistants.* In the now obsolete sense of "bystanders."

250:4 *by good Fortune.* Accepting Amelot's addition: *"par bonheur"* (I, 88).

250:11–12 *Cedo alteram.* Loeb trans.: "Fetch-Another."

250:13–14 *continue the Correction.* Dryden's addition.

251:20–21 *for . . . Augustus.* Accepting Amelot's (italicized) addition (I, 94).

253:9–11 *they imagin'd . . . Attempt.* Rendering the Latin (Pichon, I, 58): *sibi æternum laborem portendi, sua facinora aversari deos lamentantur* (Loeb trans.: "they began to bewail the eternal hardships thus foreshadowed and their crimes from which the face of heaven was averted"). Cf. Amelot, I, 99–100: "ils s'écrièrent avec douleur, que les Dieux . . . avoient leur désobéissance en horreur, & que leurs peines seroient éternelles."

253:21 *pretend.* In the now obsolete transitive sense of "put forward."

254:14–15 *which makes . . . timorous.* Dryden here follows Amelot but eliminates Amelot's elegant repetition, as Bouhours called the figure (see *Works,* XIX, 486–488): "qui se fait craindre quand elle ne craint pas, & qui peut être méprisée sûrement, lorsqu'elle craint" (I, 106).

254:23 *to keep . . . secret.* Accepting Amelot's (italicized) addition (I, 107–108).

254:25 *to their Companions.* Cf. Amelot (I, 108): "à leurs compagnons."

255:8–9 *attended.* In the now obsolete sense of "awaited" and here translating Amelot's "atendre" (I, 109).

255:18–19 *to prevent Subjection.* Accepting Amelot's addition: *"pour s'en soustraire"* (I, 109).

255:20 *reducing.* Bringing in; Amelot has "atirer" (I, 110).

256:8–9 *to dispose . . . pleas'd.* Dryden's addition to the sense in Amelot (I, 111), but in fact corresponding to *sitam* (Pichon, I, 66: "rested with," them, i.e.).

257:30 *Sequani and Belgæ.* The tribes are not named in Amelot's text

(I, 116), although they are specified in his note (see below, p. 500). They are also given in Pichon's text (I, 69): *Sequanos proximos, & Belgarum civitates* (the nearby Sequani and the Belgic cities). Modern texts reject *Sequanos proximos* in favor of *seque et proximos* (himself and those closest to him in rank).

258:22–23 *suffered in.* The reflection is keyed in Amelot (I, 118) to "fourage," the last item in Amelot's list but not in Dryden's; hence, presumably, the translator's decision to rekey to the beginning of the list instead of to the end.

259:10 *of bad Example.* A Gallicism from Amelot: "de pernicieux exemple" (I, 122).

260:8 *as ... Triumph.* Dryden's addition.

260:9 *extorted . . . General.* Not an addition, although italicized in O. Cf. Amelot (I, 127): "enlevé à leur Général"; and Pichon (I, 77): *fisci de imperatore rapti* (Loeb trans.: "the general's plundered coffers").

260:17 *Chauci.* The Latin form (Pichon, I, 77); Amelot (I, 127) has "Causses."

260:20 *Mennius.* Thus Amelot (I, 127) and Pichon (I, 79); modern editors believe the text corrupt at this point and that the name should be Manius Ennius (M' Ennius).

261:3–4 *for . . . committed.* Dryden's addition.

261:16 *they resolve.* Dryden omits the preceding clause, *ingerunt contumelias* (Pichon, I, 83; Loeb trans.: "They loaded them with insults"), and Amelot (I, 131): "ils leur font insulte."

263:24 *Rabble.* In fact, the word was *Quirites* (Pichon, I, 90; citizens), "bourgeois," as Amelot renders it (I, 140).

263:30 *Fifth.* An error for "First"; Pichon, I, 91: *primane;* Amelot, I, 142: "premiére."

264:24 *I behold . . . Ensigns.* Accepting Amelot's (italicized) addition (I, 143).

264:25 *these.* Properly "your" (i.e., Drusus'). Cf. Amelot (I, 143): "tes"; and Pichon (I, 92): *tui.*

266:7–8 *nothing mov'd . . . others.* O's text seems garbled at this point. Dryden is following Amelot (I, 146): "ni point touchées du repentir des autres," and the English should perhaps include a definite article before "Remorse."

266:23 *Dispose.* Disposal.

268:10–11 *On the ... opposite.* Translating the Latin, *discedunt in partes* (Pichon, I, 98: they separate into parties); Amelot (I, 154) offers no equivalent.

268:16 *Tribunes.* Carrying across *tribunus* (Pichon, I, 99) rather than Amelot's "Colonels" (I, 154).

269:18–20 *They thought . . . Rest.* Some of the diction derives from Amelot's alternative translations (I, 156), which offer between them "létargie" and "stupidité." But the sentence as a whole is closer to the Latin (Pichon, I, 101): *neque belli timor; ac ne pax quidem, nisi languida & soluta inter temulentos* (Loeb trans.: "there was no apprehension of war, and even their peace was the nerveless lethargy of drunkards").

269:32 *pass.* Followed by an additional phrase and clause in Amelot (I, 157): "mais Germanicus en étant averti, marcha toujours en bataille." See also Pichon, I, 103: *Quod gnarum duci: incessitque itineri & prælio* (Loeb trans.: "This came to the prince's ear, and he took the road prepared either to march or fight").

270:17–19 *it fill'd . . . Disturbance.* Dryden analyzes emotions that are merely juxtaposed in the Latin and French. Cf. Pichon (I, 103): *lætitiâ curaque adfecere* (Loeb trans.: "both relieved and disquieted" him); and Amelot (I, 158): "il en eut tout ensemble de la joie & de l'inquiétude."

270:33–34 *near the Coast of Sicily.* Cf. *Siculum fretum* (Pichon, I, 105; on the Strait of Sicily); and "en Sicile" (Amelot, I, 161).

271:6 *Gracchus, who.* Dryden omits *familia nobili* (Pichon, I, 106; from a noble family), which Amelot (I, 162) renders as "de famille illustre."

271:31–32 *of which Number were.* Cf. Amelot (I, 163): "ausquels furent adjoints"; and Pichon (I, 107): *adjiciuntur* (were added).

271:33–35 *began . . . Actor.* Translating both Tacitus and Amelot. Cf. Pichon (I, 108): *tunc primum cœpta* [modern editions have *coeptos*] *turbavit discordia, ex certamine histrionum* (Loeb trans.: "now first instituted, were marred by a disturbance due to the rivalry of the actors"); and Amelot (I, 164): "commencèrent alors d'être troublez par les diférentes inclinations des uns pour un Acteur, & des autres pour un autre."

271:37–272:1 *the Pantomime Bathyllus.* Cf. Amelot (I, 165): "le boufon Batillus"; in Tacitus the name is unmodified, but Pichon (I, 108) notes that Bathyllus was a pantomime.

272:17 *Germanicus.* An error for "Germany." Cf. Amelot (I, 168): "l'Alemagne"; and Pichon (I, 109): *Germaniæ.*

272:21 *Arminius.* Amelot (I, 169) here includes a brief note: "Fils de Sigimer, le plus grand seigneur du païs," which is omitted from O.

272:31 *Daughter Thusnelda.* She has no name in Amelot (I, 172) and Tacitus; Pichon (I, 110) supplies it in his note and in his paraphrase.

273:4–5 *having . . . Fortress.* Erected on Mount Taunus (Pichon, I, 110); cf. Amelot (I, 173): "sur le Mont Taurus" (1690, I, 83, has "Taunus"). Whoever translated the notes evidently knew that the name was omitted from the English version and accordingly passed by Amelot's note: "Dit aujourdui Der Heyrich."

273:22 *Martium.* From Amelot (I, 174); Amelot (1690; I, 84) has "Mattium," as does Tacitus (Pichon, I, 111).

274:27 *Divine Augustus.* The adjective is from Tacitus (*divo;* Pichon, I, 114); Amelot (I, 177) omits it.

275:22 *where . . . Danger.* Accepting Amelot's addition: "*afin qu'il y soit plus en sûreté*" (I, 181).

275:26 *when . . . Age.* Accepting Amelot's addition, "*quand il fut grand*" (I, 181), which in fact elaborates upon *mox* (Pichon, I, 116; afterwards).

276:29 *apprehended, lest.* I.e., feared that.

277:1 *pass'd.* "To make the passage of" (*OED*).

277:12 *Lippa.* The Latin and French have "Luppia" (Pichon, I, 120; Amelot, I, 185), which, as Amelot notes, is the Lippe ("La Lippe"); see also p. 505 below. Dryden's spelling, then, is an odd combination of modern stem and Latin ending. Cf. 291:7 and note.

277:14 *Teutburg.* Combining the spelling in Amelot, "Teutberg" (I, 185), and Tacitus, *Teutoburgiensi* (Pichon, I, 120).

277:27 *Voids.* Translating Amelot's gloss (see below, p. 505) rather than his text—"Principes" (I, 186)—or the Latin *principiis* (Pichon, I, 121).

277:31–278:13 *The middle . . . Eagles.* For discussion of this passage see headnote, pp. 393–395 above.

279:3–5 *being . . . for them.* Dryden elaborates upon both French and Latin in order to explicate the action. Cf. Amelot (I, 189): "embarassées de la foule des fuïars, qui tomboient sur elles"; and Pichon (I, 125): *fugientium agmine impulsæ* (Loeb trans.: "broken by the impact of the fugitive columns").

279:8 *from whence . . . themselves.* Translating Amelot's "d'où ils n'eussent jamais pû se tirer" (I, 189), which substitutes for *gnaram vincentibus, iniquam nesciis* (Pichon, I, 125; Loeb trans.: "familiar to the conquerors but fatal to strangers").

279:10 *Battalia.* Battle order.

280:21 *arrive.* In the now obsolete sense of "happen," carried across from Amelot's "ariver" (I, 193).

280:31–32 *rais'd . . . Romans.* Accepting Amelot's (italicized) addition (I, 193).

281:3 *his Assistance.* Accepting Amelot's (italicized) addition (I, 194).

282:21 *the Tribunes.* Cf. Amelot (I, 199): "les Tribuns & les Centurions"; and Pichon (I, 130): *tribuni & centuriones.*

282:23–24 *Place of Arms.* Accepting Amelot's version (I, 199) of *principia* (Pichon, I, 130), an open space in a camp where speeches were made and standards kept.

283:29 *crying out.* Dryden omits Amelot's addition, *"par bravade"* (I, 202).

284:5 *yet well contented.* Accepting Amelot's (italicized) addition (I, 203).

284:15 *who . . . Cold.* Dryden's addition.

285:10 *Campaign.* I.e., champaign, or open country (*OED*).

286:27 *Acts.* Dryden omits a phrase. Cf. Amelot (I, 213): "quoique le Sénat l'eût ordonné," translating *quamquam censente senatu* (Pichon, I, 137–138).

286:31–32 *the Law . . . Prince.* Explanatory elaboration. Cf. Amelot (I, 214): "la Loi de leze-majesté"; and Pichon (I, 138): *legem majestatis.*

287:3–6 *Augustus . . . Quality.* Dryden earlier quoted the Latin and offered a translation in the *Discourse of Satire* (see *Works*, IV, 67:7–14).

287:22 *Buffoon.* From Amelot's "boufon" (I, 217); cf. Pichon (I, 141): *mimum* (a mime).

287:36 *Jupiter.* Dryden omits Amelot's "Que c'est aux Dieux à vanger leurs injures" (I, 218), which translates *deorum injurias diis curæ* (Pichon, I, 142–143).

288:2 *Cæpio.* The spelling in Amelot, p. 219; Pichon, p. 143, and modern texts have *Cæpio.*

288:23 *without . . . aloud.* Dryden misconstrues. Cf. Amelot (I, 220–221): "rompant le silence, s'emporte jusqu'à crier tout haut"; and Pichon (I, 145): *exarsit adeo, ut rupta taciturnitate proclamaret* (Loeb trans.: "incensed the emperor to such a degree that, breaking through his taciturnity, he exclaimed"). Removing "without" from Dryden's translation would mend it.

288:25 *solemn . . . Jupiter.* Taking material from Amelot's note (see

p. 507 below) rather than translating Amelot's "avec serment" (I, 221) or *juratum* (Pichon, I, 145; under oath).

289:22 *to support his Quality.* Dryden's addition.

289:27–29 *all . . . unprofitably.* Dryden combines ingredients from the French and the Latin and adds a touch—"unprofitably"—of his own. Cf. Amelot (I, 226): "tous les autres préférérent la pauvreté à la honte de la déclarer au Sénat, & à l'espérance d'être soulagez"; and Pichon (I, 148): *cæteri silentium & paupertatem confessioni & beneficio præposuere* (Loeb trans.: "The rest . . . preferred silence and poverty to confession and charity").

291:7 *Terragona.* Latinizing the French form, "Terragone" (Amelot, I, 232); cf. Pichon (I, 155): *Tarraconensi.*

291:10 *Gains by Commerce.* See headnote, p. 392 above.

291:15 *virtually.* Dryden's addition.

291:18 *Capito.* From Amelot's "Capiton" (I, 234); Pichon has Ateius (*Atejo;* I, 157), as do modern editions.

291:24 *interess'd.* Accepting Amelot's (italicized) addition (I, 234).

TEXTUAL NOTES

Introduction

CHOICE OF THE COPY TEXT

The copy text is normally the first printing, on the theory that its accidentals are likely to be closest to the author's practice; but a manuscript or a subsequent printing may be chosen when there is reasonable evidence either that it represents more accurately the original manuscript as finally revised by the author or that the author revised the accidentals.

REPRODUCTION OF THE COPY TEXT

The copy text is normally reprinted *literatim*, but there are certain classes of exceptions. In the first place, apparently authoritative variants found in other texts are introduced as they occur, except that their purely accidental features are made to conform to the style of the copy text. These substitutions, but not their minor adjustments in accidentals, are recorded in footnotes as they occur. Second, the editors have introduced nonauthoritative emendations, whether found in earlier texts or not, where the sense seems to demand them. These emendations are also listed in the footnotes. Third, accidentals are introduced or altered where it seems helpful to the reader. All such changes also are recorded in footnotes as they occur. Fourth, turned b, q, d, p, n, and u are accepted as q, b, p, d, u, and n, respectively, and if they result in spelling errors are corrected in the text and listed in the footnotes. The textual footnotes show the agreements among the texts only with respect to the precise variation of the present edition from the copy text. For example, in *Character of Polybius* at 17:13, the footnote "one-ey'd man] O2; one-ey'd-man O1" refers only to the punctuation; O2 actually reads "one-ey'd Man" (as more fully noted on p. 411).

Certain purely mechanical details have been normalized without special mention. Long "s" has been changed to round "s," "VV" to "W"; swash italics have been represented by plain italics; captions, display initials, and any accompanying capitalization have been made uniform with the style of the present edition; stanza numbers have been corrected; wrong font and turned letters other than q, b, p, d, u, and n have been adjusted; italicized plurals in -'s have been distinguished (by italic final "s") from possessives (roman final "s"); quotations if marked with inverted commas have been marked at the beginning and end only and always; spacing between words and before and after punctuation has been normalized when no change in meaning results; the common contractions have been counted as single words, but otherwise words abbreviated by elision have been separated from those before and after if the apostrophe is present; if the elided syllable is written out as well as marked by an apostrophe, the words have been run together (*"speak'it"*).

TEXTUAL NOTES

The textual notes list the relevant manuscripts and printings, assign them sigla, and give references to the bibliographies where they are more fully described. The textual notes also outline the descent of the text, indicate which are the authorized texts, and explain in each instance how the copy text was selected. A list of copies collated follows. If differences among variant copies are sufficient to warrant a tabular view of them, it follows the list of copies collated.

The sigla indicate the format of printed books (F = folio, Q = quarto, O = octavo, etc.) and the order of printing, if it is determinable, within the format group (F may have been printed after Q1 and before Q2). If order of printing is in doubt, the numbers are arbitrary, and they are normally arbitrary for the manuscripts (represented by M).

Finally, the variants in the texts collated are given. The list is not exhaustive, but it records what seemed material, viz.:

All variants of the present edition from the copy text except in the mechanical details listed above.

All other substantive variants and variants in accidentals markedly affecting the sense. The insertion or removal of a period before a dash has sometimes been accepted as affecting the sense; other punctuational variants before dashes have been ignored. Failure of letters to print, in texts other than the copy text, has been noted only when the remaining letters form a different word or words, or when a word has disappeared entirely.

All errors of any kind repeated from one edition to another, except the use of -'s instead of -s for a plural.

Spelling variants where the new reading makes a new word (e.g., *then* and *than* being in Dryden's day alternate spellings of the conjunction, a change from *than* to *then* would be recorded, since the spelling *then* is now confined to the adverb, but a change from *then* to *than* would be ignored as a simple modernization).

In passages of verse, variants in elision of syllables normally pronounced (except that purely mechanical details, as *had'st, hadst*, are ignored). Thus *heaven, heav'n* is recorded, but not *denied, deny'd*.

When texts generally agree in a fairly lengthy variation, but one differs from the rest in a detail that it would be cumbrous to represent in the usual way, the subvariation is indicated in parentheses in the list of sigla. For example,

who, . . . Mediation,] ∼ᴧ . . . ∼ᴧ O1–2 (who, O2)

means that O2 agrees with O1 in lacking a comma after "Mediation" but has a comma after "who", where O1 lacks one.

When variants in punctuation alone are recorded, the wavy dash is used in place of the identifying word before (and sometimes after) the variant punctuation. A caret indicates absence of punctuation.

As in the previous volumes, no reference is made to modern editions if the editor is satisfied that reasonable care on his part would have resulted in the same emendations, even if he collated these editions before beginning to emend.

Preface to Walsh's Dialogue Concerning Women

Dryden's preface was printed only once in his lifetime, in 1691 (Macd 136; O). The copy text for the present edition is the Clark copy of O (*PR3757. W4D5), with which the following additional copies have been compared: Folger (W645), Harvard (*EC65.D8474.A691w), Texas (Aj.W168.691d), and Yale (Nqh80.691w).

The textual footnotes record the emendations introduced into the present edition.

A Character of Saint-Evremond

Dryden's continuation (sigs. A4–A7v) of a character of Saint-Evremond begun (sigs. A2–A4) by "A Person of Honour" was first published in 1692 in *Miscellaneous Essays: By Monsieur St. Euremont* (Macd 137[1]; O1). The relevant sheet (A) was reissued in 1695 (in the first volume of a two-volume edition of Saint-Evremond; Clark copy, *PR3419.M61.1695) with a new title page (*Miscellany Essays: By Monsieur St. Euremont*). A second edition, with additional lines entitled *"St Evremont's Character, Drawn by himself,"* appeared in 1700 (*The Works of Mr de St. Evremont,* Vol. I, sigs. A3–A7v; O2). Since Dryden seems not to have had a hand in the changes made in the second edition, the Yale copy of O1 (Hfc35.148), which contains a significant press variant ("*Mr. D. Cha.*"), has been chosen as the copy text.

In addition to the copy text, the following copies have also been examined: O1: Clark (*PR3419.M61), Folger (S305), Harvard (38542.19.6*), Texas (Aj.D848.692s); O2: Clark (*PQ1917.S5A2.1700,v.1).

7:3 *Evremont*] O2; *Euremont* O1.   7:6 Writers:] ~. O1–2.   7:9 Universal; they] ~. They O1–2.   7:10 *French*] French O1–2.   7:11 Empire] *Empire* O1–2.   7:14 *Evremont*] O2; *Euremont* O1.   7:22 Business; that] ~: That O1–2.   7:25 them; when] O1; ~. When O2.   8:6 of his] O1; of O2.   8:7 them.] O2; ~: O1.   8:10 said.] ~: O1; ~; O2.   8:11 it.] O2; ~: O1.   8:13 Hand.] O2; ~: O1.   8:19–21 Appetite. / ———— / *Mr. D. Cha.* / I] ~. *Mr. D. Cha.* / ———— / I O1 (*corrected form*); Appetite. / I O1 (*uncorrected form*); Appetite. / Character of *Monsieur de St. Evremont,* by *Mr. Dryden.* / I O2.   8:23 *Evremont*] O2; *Euremont* O1.   8:29 Speaking; an] ~. An O1–2.   9:3 Commonwealth] O1 (Com- / monwealth); Common-wealth O2.   9:5 If] *no paragraph break in O1–2.*   9:7 he has] O1; he O2.   9:13 Empire] *Empire* O1–2.   9:16 Mother-Goddess] S-S (mother-goddess); Mother Goddess O1–2.   9:17 *Virgil,*] ~∧ O1–2.   9:18 cou'd not] O2; cou'd O1.   9:26 undertakings:] ~. O1–2.   9:31 Preference, . . . Soldiers,] ~∧ . . . ~∧ O1–2.   9:32 *Antony*] *Anthony* O1–2.   10:8–9 Commonwealth] O1; Common-wealth O2.   10:13 Gods.] ~: O1–2.   10:23 *Evremont*] O2; *Euremont* O1.   10:24–25 Tempest (*Extemplo . . . &c.*), why] ~: ~ . . . *&c.*∧ Why O1–2 (&c. O2).   10:33 *Evremont*] O2; *Eure-*

mont O1.   11:5   *Grand*] Grand O1–2.   11:7   Theatre] *Theatre* O1–2.
11:19   *Evremont*] *Euremont* O1–2.   11:19   Writings:] O1; ~. O2.
11:19–23   and if . . . [*to*] . . . *Dryden.*] *omitted from O2.*

A Character of Polybius and His Writings

The first edition of *A Character of Polybius and His Writings* was pub-
lished in 1693 in *The History of Polybius the Megalopolitan*, I, sigs. A1–
D8 (O1; Macd 138a); the second, in 1698 in the second edition of *The His-
tory of Polybius, the Megalopolitan*, I, sigs. A1–C2 (O2; Macd 138b). The
copies of O1 collated for this edition disclosed press variants in outer B,
inner C, and outer D. Because Dryden seems not to have revised the acci-
dentals of O2, the Clark copy of O1 (*D58.P78) has been chosen as the
copy text.

The following additional copies of the two editions have also been ex-
amined: O1: Folger (P2786), Harvard (EC65.Sh372.693p), Yale (Gfp81.bg
693, v. 1); O2: Folger (P2787), Harvard (EC65.Sh372.693pb), Yale (Gfp81.bg
693b, v. 1).

Press Variants by Form

O1
Sheet B (outer form)

Uncorrected: Harvard
Corrected: Clark, Folger, Yale
Sig. B6*v*
    22:15   κακοπραγα'οσυνη] κακοπραγμόσυνη
Sheet C (inner form)
Uncorrected: Harvard
Corrected (first state): Folger
Sig. C2
    25:8   Yeteven] Yet even
       11   Cow-] cow-
       15   aSword] a Sword
Sig. C3*v*
    26:19   Terms.] ~∧
       19   in] in the
Sig. C4
    26:29   goes] ~,
Sig. C7*v*
    29:11   *Hanibal*] *Hannibal*
Sig. C8
    29:25   admirableforecast] admirable forecast
    Corrected (second state, the above corrections and the following): Clark,
       Yale
Sig. C1*v*
    24:27   Father;] ~.
    25:3   which] ~,

Sig. C2
  25:5 Him] ∼,
Sig. C5*v*
  27:26 scribes; for] ∼. For
Sig. C6
  28:11 to some] to

Sheet D (outer form)

Uncorrected (?): Clark
Corrected (?): Folger, Harvard, Yale
Sig. D1
  30:12 wherein] where
    23–24 indeed are his words.] are his words. Indeed
Sig. D3
  31:29 review] read
Sig. D6*v*
  34:23 to] and to

  13:4 *English*] English O1–2.   13:9 'Tis] *no paragraph break in O1–2.* 13:9 *English*] English O1–2.   13:14 clearest,] O2 (Clearest); ∼ₐ O1. 13:19 Manuscript,] O2; ∼ₐ O1.   13:27 own;] O2; ∼: O1.   13:28 kinds;] O2; ∼, O1.   14:1 History;] O2; ∼, O1.   14:5 it,] O2; ∼; O1. 14:6 Country; who,] O2; ∼. Whoₐ O1.   14:8 Navigation;] O2; ∼, O1. 14:8 and, . . . words,] O2 (Words); ∼ₐ . . . ∼ₐ O1.   14:9 Tacticks:] O2; ∼. O1.   14:14 *English*] English O1–2.   14:19 *Latin*] Latine O1–2. 14:23 Dauphin's] *Dauphin*'s O1–2.   14:24 work; which] O2 (Work); ∼. Which O1.   14:25 them,] O2; ∼; O1.   14:29 Fifth] O2; fifth O1. 15:3 possess; and] ∼. And O1–2.   15:4 *Polybius.* The] O2; ∼: the O1. 15:6 us] ∼, O1–2.   15:8 *Achaians*] O2; Achians O1.   15:16 *Polybius*] *no paragraph break in O1–2.* 15:18 Empire] ∼, O1–2.   15:18 World] ∼, O1–2.   15:19 known,] ∼; O1–2.   15:23 *Egypt;*] Ægypt, O1; *Egypt,* O2.   15:26 them;] ∼, O1–2.   16:6 The] *no paragraph break in O1–2.*   16:7 Fifth,] O2; ∼ₐ O1.   16:7 mention'd] O2; mention,d O1.   16:8 *Greek* Historians;] Greek ∼: O1–2.   16:10 him—] ∼; O1–2.   16:17 Politicks;] O2; ∼: O1.   16:22 *Aratus;*] ∼, O1–2. 16:22 *Africanus*] Affricanus O1–2.   16:24 Counsellour;] O2 (Consellor); ∼: O1.   16:24 good will] O1; Good-will O2.   16:25 *Egypt*] O2; Egyyt O1.   16:28 This] *no paragraph break in O1–2.*   17:3 (knowing] O2; ₐ∼ O1.   17:5 *Latin*] Latin O1–2.   17:7 him; which] ∼. Which O1–2.   17:12 *Greek*] Greek O1–2.   17:13 one-ey'd man] O2 (Man); one-ey'd-man O1.   17:19 *Greek*] Greek O1–2.   17:29 written,] ∼; O1–2 (Written O2).   17:30 Translator's] O2; Translators O1. 17:31 Our] *no paragraph break in O1–2.*   18:4 *Roman*] Roman O1–2. 18:5 *Latin*] Latin O1–2.   18:5 be excus'd] O2; beexcus'd O1.   18:19 which,] O2; ∼ₐ O1.   18:24 'Tis] *no paragraph break in O1–2.*   18:25 before] ∼, O1–2.   18:27 *English*] English O1–2.   18:30 know] O1; known O2.   19:4 but only] O1; but O2.   19:4 to] O1; with O2. 19:12 *Greece*] ∼; O1–2.   19:15 willfulness,] ∼: O1; ∼; O2 (Wilfulness).   19:15 vices] ∼, O1–2 (Vices O2).   19:15 to the] O2; the to O1.   19:16 *Greeks*] O2; Greeks O1.   19:17 *Romans*] O2; Romans

O1.　　19:21　Countrymen,] O2 (Country-men); ∼∧ O1 (Country- / men).
19:23　*Roman*] O2; Roman O1.　　19:32　People,] ∼; O1–2.　　19:34
remaining] ∼, O1–2.　　20:1　Fortune,] ∼; O1–2.　　20:3　foreseen.] ∼:
O1–2.　　20:20　misfortune] O1; Misfortunes O2.　　20:28　wisdom; in]
∼. In O1–2 (Wisdom O2).　　20:30　*Roman*] Roman O1–2.　　20:30–31
Government. And] ∼: and O1–2 (And O2).　　21:1　time] O2; tmie O1.
21:2　*Atlantick*] Atlantick O1–2.　　21:5　*Grecians*] Grecians O1–2.　　21:6
Statues] O2; Statutes O1.　　21:8　who, . . . Mediation,] ∼∧ . . . ∼∧ O1–2
(who, O2).　　21:9　Taxes] ∼, O1–2.　　21:11　Peace,] ∼; O1–2.　　21:
15　Yet] *no paragraph break in O1–2.*　　21:16　humane kind] O1;
Humane-kind O2.　　21:20　Philanthropy] *Philanthropy* O1–2.　　21:21
English] English O1–2.　　21:27　Standard] O2; Sandard O1.　　21:30
oblig'd,] ∼; O1–2 (Oblig'd O2).　　22:8　Servants; and] ∼. And O1–2.
22:11　and] O2; ∼, O1.　　22:12–13　Commonwealths,] ∼: O1–2 (Com-
mon- / wealths O1).　　22:15　κακοπραγμόσυνη] O1 *(corrected form),* O2;
κακοπραγα'οσυνη O1 *(uncorrected form).*　　22:17　common good] O1; Com-
mon-good O2.　　22:18　Light] ∼, O1–2.　　22:23　people;] ∼: O1–2
(People O2).　　22:24　Publick safety:] ∼ ∼, O1–2 (Publick-safety O2).
22:26　Government,] ∼; O1–2.　　22:29　frequently; in] ∼. In O1–2.
22:34　Youth] O1; ∼, O2.　　23:8　Knowledge,] O2; ∼: O1.　　23:8–9
Societies:] ∼. O1–2.　　23:11　I] *no paragraph break in O1–2.*　　23:11
perusal] perusual O1–2.　　23:12　History,] O2; ∼; O1.　　23:12　confess,]
O2; ∼∧ O1.　　23:12　Antients] O2 (Ancients); ∼, O1.　　23:19　us] O1;
me O2.　　23:23　We] *no paragraph break in O1–2.*　　23:25　Publick;]
O2; ∼: O1.　　23:26　Writer] O2; Writers O1.　　23:29　his,] ∼: O1; ∼;
O2.　　23:30　other,] O2; ∼; O1.　　23:31　men] O2 (Men); ∼, O1.　　23:
32　Affairs] ∼, O1–2.　　24:2　Tongue,] O2; ∼; O1.　　24:7　Mother-
tongue:] ∼-∼. O1–2 (Mother- / tongue O1).　　24:14　known] O2; ∼,
O1.　　24:17　*I believe*] O2; I believe O1.　　24:19　*mankind;*] O2 (*Man-
kind*); ∼: O1 (*man- / kind*).　　24:22　falshoods,] ∼; O1–2 (Falshoods O2).
24:23–24　*immediately,*] O2; ∼; O1.　　24:24　*time;*] O2; ∼, O1.　　24:27
Father.] O1 *(corrected form [second state]);* ∼; O1 *(uncorrected form and
corrected form [first state]),* O2.　　24:27　In . . . [to] . . . life] *in italics in
O1–2 (Life O2).*　　24:27–30　I . . . [to] . . . Truth] *in italics in O1–2.*
24:31　*Aratus*] *no paragraph break in O1–2.*　　25:1　and in] O1; and O2.
25:3　which,] O1 *(corrected form [second state]);* ∼∧ O1 *(uncorrected form
and corrected form [first state]),* O2.　　25:5　Him,] O1 *(corrected form
[second state]);* ∼∧ O1 *(uncorrected form and corrected form [first state]),* O2.
25:8　Yet even] O1 *(corrected form [first and second states]);* Yeteven O1
(uncorrected form); Yet, even O2.　　25:10　Enterprises,] O2; ∼; O1.
25:11　*Spanish*] Spanish O1–2.　　25:11　cowardly] O1 *(corrected form
[first and second states]),* O2; Cowardly O1 *(uncorrected form).*　　25:13
Plutarch,] O2; ∼: O1.　　25:15　a Sword] O1 *(corrected form [first and
second states]),* O2; aSword O1 *(uncorrected form).*　　25:17　accuses] O2;
cuses O1 *(but catchword on preceding page is "accuses".")*　　25:21　*Philip,*]
∼∧ O1–2.　　25:24　exquisitely] O1; exquisite O2.　　25:25　He] *para-
graph break in O1–2.*　　25:25　Judgment,] ∼: O1–2.　　25:28　*Grecians*;
and] ∼. And O1–2.　　25:33　*On this account*] *in romans in O1–2.*　　26:4
Agathocles,] ∼∧ O1–2.　　26:6　general] O2; genral O1.　　26:6–7　*Is . . .
[to] . . . thought*] O2; *in romans in O1.*　　26:12　pretermit] ∼, O1–2 (pre /

termit O2). 26:14 It] *no paragraph break in O1–2.* 26:17 *Egypt:*] O1; ~, O2. 26:19 Terms.] O1 *(uncorrected form)*, O2; ~ₐ O1 *(corrected form [first and second states])*. 26:19 in the] O1 *(corrected form [first and second states])*, O2; in O1 *(uncorrected form)*. 26:19 148th] O2; *148th.* O1. 26:20 *Olympiad*] Olympiad O1–2. 26:20 *Ptolemy*] O1; *Ptolomy* O2. 26:23 Lycortas,] ~ₐ O1–2. 26:29 goes,] O1 *(corrected form [first and second states])*, O2; ~ₐ O1 *(uncorrected form)*. 26: 29 afterward] O1; afterwards O2. 26:30 gives an] O1; gives O2. 27:5 *Ptolemy*'s] O1; *Ptolomy*'s O2. 27:6 (or] ₐ~ O1–2. 27:6 believe,] O2; ~ₐ O1. 27:6 contriv'd,)] ~,ₐ O1–2. 27:14 Law] O2; Law O1. 27:21 Another] *no paragraph break in O1–2.* 27:21 his] O1; this O2. 27:22 Reader (tho] ~: ~ O1; ~, ~ O2 (tho'). 27:23 judgment):] ~: O1; ~; O2 (Judgment). 27:26 describes; for] O1 *(uncorrected form and corrected form [first state]; catchword on preceding page is* "scribes;"), O2; ~. For O1 *(corrected form [second state])*. 27:31 proceeded] O1; preceeded O2. 28:3 spoken;] ~, O1–2 (Spoken O2). 28: 11 to] O1 *(corrected form [second state])*; to some O1 *(uncorrected form and corrected form [first state])*, O2. 28:13 *Hannibal*] O2; *Hanibal* O1. 28:14 *Alpes*] Alpes O1–2. 28:15 *New*] new O1; New O2. 28:17 approaches:] ~. O1–2 (Approaches O2). 28:33 Heroe,] O2; ~: O1. 28:34 fights,] O2 (Fights); ~: O1. 29:1 Actions:] ~. O1–2. 29:8 *Polybius*] O2; *Polybins* O1. 29:11 *Hannibal*] O1 *(corrected form [first and second states])*, O2; *Hanibal* O1 *(uncorrected form)*. 29:12 *Alpes*] Alpes O1–2. 29:14 General,] O2; ~ₐ O1. 29:16 Favour;] ~, O1–2. 29:20 *Scipio*,] O2; ~ₐ O1. 29:25 admirable forecast] O1 *(corrected form [first and second states])*, O2; admirableform O1 *(uncorrected form)*. 29:26 which,] O2; ~ₐ O1. 29:26–27 yet he had] O1; he yet had O2. 29:28 Expedition;] ~, O1–2. 29:30 and] O1; and with O2. 29:32 Whensoever] *no paragraph break in O1–2.* 29:34–30:1 undertaking,] O2 (Undertaking); ~; O1. 30:1 performance;] O2; ~: O1. 30:2 explains:] ~. O1–2 (Explains O2). 30:2 which,] ~ₐ O1–2. 30:4 17th] O2; *17th* O1. 30:11 overthrown] O2 (Overthrown); over thrown O1. 30:12 wherein] O1 *(uncorrected form [?])*, O2; where O1 *(corrected form [?])*. 30:14 of foreign] O1; of the foreign O2. 30:15 ill timing] O1; ill-timing O2. 30:23 Συμβαινόντων] O1 *(some copies)*, O2; Συμβαιν ντων O1 *(some copies)*. 30:23–24 indeed, are his words.] O1 (indeedₐ; *uncorrected form [?])*, O2; are his words. Indeed O1 *(corrected form [?])*. 30:25 her self] O1; herself O2. 30:26 whenever] O2; when ever O1. 30:28 understood.] O1; ~: O2. 30:29 But] *no paragraph break in O1–2.* 31:4 assertion,] ~ₐ O1–2 (Assertion O2). 31:19 farther,] O2; ~; O1. 31:20 stopp'd] O2; stop'd O1. 31:26 As] *no paragraph break in O1–2.* 31:27 Empire] *Empire* O1–2. 31:29 review] O1 *(uncorrected form [?])*, O2; read O1 *(corrected form [?])*. 31:32 And] O1; *paragraph break in O2.* 31:33 liv'd:] ~. O1–2. 32:1 People] ~, O1–2. 32:1–2 Government] ~, O1–2. 32:5 Senate] ~, O1–2. 32:14 By] *no paragraph break in O1–2.* 32:16 comprehend:] ~; O1. 32: 18 them,] ~; O1. 32:20 Endowments; being] ~. Being O1–2. 32: 22 *Egypt:*] ~. O1–2. 32:29 I] *no paragraph break in O1–2.* 32:33 Undertaking:] ~. O1–2. 33:5 Improvement;] ~: O1–2. 33:6 close:] ~; O1–2. 33:8 add,] O2; ~: O1. 33:9 already:] ~; O1–2. 33:

10 must] O1; might O2.   33:12 I] *no paragraph break in O1-2.*   33: 12 *Excerpta,* which] O2; ~ (~ O1.   33:14 finish'd;] O2; ~;) O1. 33:15 were] O1; are O2.   33:18 certain; the] ~. The O1-2.   33:30 Affairs;] ~, O1-2.   33:32 such] ~, O1-2.   34:1 this] ~, O1-2. 34:10 *Scipio's;*] *Scipio's,* O1-2.   34:15 *'Tis just*] ' 'Tis just O1-2.   34: 15 says he,] '~ ~ₐ O1-2 (he, O2).   34:15-19 *for . . . [to] . . . Commonwealth*] *in romans but set off by inverted commas in O1-2.*   34:23 *Rome;*] O2; ~: O1.   34:23 to] O1 *(uncorrected form* [?]*),* O2; and to O1 *(corrected form* [?]*).*   34:31 *Thucydides*] *Thucydydes* O1-2.   35:11 'Tis] O2; ,Tis O1.   35:12 accus'd] O2; accusd O1.   35:21 Reader;] O2; ~, O1.   35:22 Monarchy, *Polybius*] ~; ~, O1-2.   35:24 What] *no paragraph break in O1-2.*

De Arte Graphica

Only one printing (Macd 139a; Q) of *De Arte Graphica* appeared during Dryden's lifetime. In addition to Dryden's own preface ("PREFACE OF THE TRANSLATOR, With a Parallel Of *Poetry* and *Painting*," pp. i–lvi [sigs. (a)1–(g)4*v*]), the first edition (1695) contained Dryden's translation of the preface ("THE PREFACE OF THE French Author," pp. lvii–lxii [sigs. (h)1–(h)3*v*]) by the French translator of Du Fresnoy's Latin poem; Dryden's translation of the French table of the poem's precepts ("A *TABLE* of the *Precepts* Contain'd in this *TREATISE*," pp. [lxiii]–[lxiv] [sigs. (h)4–(h)4*v*]); the Latin text of Du Fresnoy's poem and Dryden's facing translation of the French translation of the Latin text ("DE ARTE GRAPHICA LIBER" and "THE Art of Painting," pp. 2–77 [sigs. B1*v*–L3]); Dryden's translation of the French observations on passages in Du Fresnoy's poem ("OBSERVATIONS ON THE Art of Painting OF *Charles Alphonse du Fresnoy*," pp. 79–212 [sigs. L4–Ee2*v*]); and Dryden's translation of Du Fresnoy's critique of recent painting ("THE JUDGMENT OF *Charles Alphonse du Fresnoy*, On the Works of the Principal and Best PAINTERS of the two last Ages," pp. 213–226 [sigs. Ee3–Gg1*v*]). Dryden seems to have had no connection with the last item published in *De Arte Graphica*, a history of painting from classical to modern times, pp. 227–355 (sigs. Gg2–Zz2). Zz2*v* contains a list of errata.

The copy text for the present edition of Dryden's preface and his translations of the preface by the French translator, the French table of precepts, the French translation of Du Fresnoy's Latin poem, the French observations on passages in Du Fresnoy's poem, and Du Fresnoy's critique is a Clark copy of Q (*PR3421.D86, cop. 1). The following copies of Q have also been examined: Clark (*PR3421.D86, cop. 2), Folger (D2458), Harvard (EC65.D8474.695da), Yale (Ij.D848–695, cop. 1). The Folger copy (originally owned by Dobell) contains marginal notes reflecting alterations and revisions prepared for the 1716 edition (see Macdonald, p. 175, n. 1, and p. 342 of this edition). The Folger copy also contains a sheet (B) for which the text was entirely reset but which yields only a few variant readings.

The Latin text of Du Fresnoy's poem has been reprinted in Appendix A.

In Q, annotations (such as "5." and "10." etc.) were placed in the margins of the pages containing Dryden's translation of Du Fresnoy's poem. These annotations roughly indicated similar locations in Du Fresnoy's Latin text. To avoid conflicts with the line numbering of the present edition, the editors have silently enclosed all such references within square brackets (for example, "[5.]") and have placed them at relevant locations in the text proper. Marginal markers (such as "¶1." and "¶2.") used on the pages of Dryden's translation of the observations to indicate relevant locations in Du Fresnoy's Latin text have for the same reason similarly been silently enclosed within square brackets (for example, "[¶1.]") and have been placed in the text proper, adjacent to the catchphrases to which they refer.

Press Variants by Form

Q
Sheet B (outer form)
Uncorrected: Clark (2 copies), Harvard, Yale
Corrected: Folger
Sig. B2*v*
  84:19 world] World
  85:6 only] onely
  85:9 only] onely
  85:11 wou'd] would
Sig. B3
  421:29 *negent*] *negant*
  421:31 *Artificum*] *Artificium*
Sig. B4*v*
  86:4 shou'd] should
  86:7 it is] is is
  86:12 errours] errors
  86:16 precipice] Precipice
Sheet B (inner form)
Uncorrected: Clark (2 copies), Harvard, Yale
Corrected: Folger
Sig. B2
  84:2–3 mu- / tually] mu/tually (?)
  84:7 wou'd] would
  84:17 flames] Flames
Sig. B4
  85:28–29 ignorant;] ~:

The Life of Lucian

The Life of Lucian was first published in 1711, as part (pp. 3–62; sigs. b2–e7*v*) of the first volume of *The Works of Lucian* (Macd 141; O). Dryden evidently had completed his part of the project in 1696 (see Macdonald, p. 179n). Although all the sheets that make up the *Life* were poorly printed, only sheet b (which was completely reset) appears to have been "corrected" in press. The copy text for this edition is the Clark copy (*PR3421.L93). The following additional copies have also been examined: Folger (PR3418. L9.1711.Cage), Harvard (G1.23.238), Huntington (25696), Yale (Gfl44.ag710, v. 1).

Press Variants by Form

O
Sheet b (outer form)

Corrected (?): Folger
Uncorrected (?): Clark, Harvard, Huntington, Yale
Sig. b2*v*
   208:11–12 written,] ~$_\Lambda$
   208:14   Entertainment] Entertainmeut
Sig. b5
   210:2 Head] head
   210:2 to make] make
Sig. b6*v*
   211:2 aud] and
Sig. b8*v*
   running title Lucian] ~.
   212:15 run] ran

Sheet b (inner form)

Corrected (?): Folger
Uncorrected (?): Clark, Harvard, Huntington, Yale
Sig. b2
   page number *om.*] 3
   208:1 Gir-] Cir-
Sig. b4
   209:18 *Lncian*] *Lucian*
   209:21 extradordinary] extraordinary
Sig. b6
   210:23 ter,] ter;
   210:24 Mind] Minds
   210:24 tures] tues
Sig. b7*v*
   211:28 *God's Govern-*] *God's Govern-*
Sig. b8
   212:5 *Suidas*] *Suidas*

The Annals of Cornelius Tacitus, Book I

Dryden's translation of Book I of *The Annals of Cornelius Tacitus* was first published in 1698 as part (pp. 1–159; sigs. B1–L8) of the first volume of *The Annals and History of Cornelius Tacitus* (Macd 140a; O). In addition to Dryden's translation of Book I of the *Annals,* the 1698 edition included "politick reflections" and "historical notes" (in a few cases inappropriately keyed), by Amelot De La Houssaye and Henry Savile, at the bottoms of relevant pages of Book I. Because those notes appear not to have been translated by Dryden (see above, pp. 388–389), they are in this edition printed in Appendix B. In the 1698 edition, lower-case superscript letters and superscript Arabic numbers were used in Dryden's translated text to mark words and phrases explained in these footnotes; in the present edition, superscript asterisks (*) signalling historical notes and superscript daggers (†) signalling political reflections have been silently (except for a few complex footnote sigla involving puncuation marks as well as reflection and note indicators) substituted for the original superscript letters and numbers which marked the existence of the explanatory passages. Accordingly, in Appendix B page and line numbers have been substituted for the Arabic numbers and lower-case letters that preceded the political and historical footnotes of the 1698 edition. Bracketed chapter numbers inserted into the text represent the conventional divisions of the book. For further explanation see the Commentary Headnote, p. 390. The copy text for this edition is the Clark copy (*PA6707.A1.1698. v. 1). The following additional copies of O were also examined: Harvard (*51–1702), Huntington (289488), Yale (Gnt1.ag698. Vol. 1).

APPENDIXES

Appendix A: Charles Alphonse Dufresnoy's De Arte Graphica

U T PICTURA POESIS ERIT; *similisque Poesi*
    Sit Pictura, refert par æmula quæq; sororem,
    Alternantque vices & nomina; muta Poesis
    Dicitur hæc, Pictura loquens solet illa vocari.
5 *Quod fuit auditu gratum cecinere Poetæ,*
  Quod pulchrum aspectu Pictores pingere curant:
  Quæque Poetarum numeris indigna fuêre,
  Non eadem Pictorum operam studiumque merentur:
  Ambæ quippe sacros ad Relligionis honores
10 *Sydereos superant ignes, Aulamque Tonantis*
  Ingressæ, Divûm aspectu, alloquioque fruuntur;
  Oraque magna Deûm & dicta observata reportant,
  Cœlestemque suorum operum mortalibus ignem.
  Inde per hunc orbem studiis coêuntibus errant,
15 *Carpentes quæ digna sui, revolutaque lustrant*
  Tempora. Quærendis consortibus Argumentis.
  Denique quæcumque in cœlo, terraque, marique
  Longius in tempus durare, ut pulchra, merentur,
  Nobilitate sua claroque insignia casu,
20 *Dives & ampla manet Pictores atque Poetas*
  Materies, inde alta sonant per sæcula mundo
  Nomina, magnanimis Heroibus inde superstes
  Gloria, perpetuoque operum miracula restant:
  Tantus inest divis honor Artibus atque potestas.
25 *Non mihi Pieridum chorus hic, nec Apollo vocandus,*
  Majus ut eloquium numeris aut gratia fandi
  Dogmaticis illustret opus rationibus horrens:
  Cum nitida tantum & facili digesta loquelâ,
  Ornari præcepta negent; contenta doceri.

30   *Nec mihi mens animusve fuit constringere nodos*
  Artificum manibus, quos tantum dirigit usus;
  Indolis ut vigor inde potens obstrictus hebescat,
  Normarum numero immani Geniumque moretur:
  Sed rerum ut pollens Ars cognitione gradatim
35 *Naturæ sese insinuet, verique capacem*
  Transeat in Genium, Geniusque usu induat Artem.
  Præcipua imprimis Artisque potissima pars est,   Primum Præ-
  Nôsse quid in rebus Natura creârit ad Artem   ceptum.
  Pulchrius, idque Modum juxta, Mentemque Vetustam,   De Pulchro.
40 *Qua sine barbaries cæca & temeraria Pulchrum*
  Negligit, insultans ignotæ audacior Arti,

Ut curare nequit, quæ non modo noverit esse,
Illud apud Veteres fuit, unde notabile dictum,
Nil Pictore malo securius atque Poeta.
45 *Cognita amas, & amata cupis, sequerisque cupita;*
Passibus assequeris tandem quæ fervidus urges:
Illa tamen quæ pulchra decent; non omnia casus
Qualiacumque dabunt, etiamve simillima veris:
Nam quamcumque modo servili haud sufficit ipsam
50 *Naturam exprimere ad vivum, sed ut Arbiter Artis*
Seliget ex illa tantùm pulcherrima Pictor.
Quodque minus pulchrum, aut mendosum corriget ipse
Marte suo, formæ Veneres captando fugaces.

Utque manus grandi nil nomine practica dignum
55 *Assequitur, purum arcanæ quam deficit Artis*
Lumen, & in præceps abitura ut cæca vagatur;
Sic nihil Ars operâ manuum privata supremum
Exequitur, sed languet iners uti vincta lacertos;
Dispositumque typum non linguâ pinxit Apelles.
60 *Ergo licet totâ normam haud possimus in Arte*
Ponere, (cùm nequeant quæ sunt palcherrima dici)
Nitimur hæc paucis, scrutati summa magistræ
Dogmata Naturæ, Artisque Exemplaria prima
Altiùs intuiti; sic mens habilisque facultas
65 *Indolis excolitur, Geniumque scientia complet,*
Luxuriansque in monstra furor compescitur Arte:
Est modus in rebus, sunt certi denique fines,
Quos ultra citraque nequit consistere rectum.

II. Præceptum.
De Speculatione
& Praxi.

His positis, erit optandum Thema nobile, pulchrum,
70 *Quodque venustatum circa Formam atque Colorem*
Sponte capax amplam emeritæ mox præbeat Arti
Materiam, retegens aliquid salis & documenti.

III. Præceptum.
De Argumento.

Tandem opus aggredior, primoque occurrit in Albo
Disponenda typi concepta potente Minervâ
75 *Machina, quæ nostris* Inventio *dicitur oris.*

INVENTIO
prima Picturæ
pars.

Illa quidem priùs ingenuis instructa Sororum
Artibus Aonidum, & Phœbi sublimior æstu.

Quærendasque inter Posituras, luminis, umbræ,
Atque futurorum jam præsentire colorum
80 *Par erit harmoniam, captando ab utrisque venustum.*

IV.
Dispositio, sive
operis totius
Oeconomia.

Sit Thematis genuina ac viva expressio juxta
Textum Antiquorum, propriis cum tempore formis.

V.
Fidelitas
Argumenti.

Nec quod inane, nihil facit ad rem, sive videtur
Improprium, miniméque urgens, potiora tenebit
85 *Ornamenta operis; Tragicæ sed lege sororis*
Summa ubi res agitur, vis summa requiritur Artis.

     VI.
    Inane rejici-
    endum.

   Ista labore gravi, studio, monitisque Magistri
Ardua pars nequit addisci rarissima: namque
Ni priùs æthereo rapuit quod ab axe Prometheus
90 *Sit jubar infusum menti cum flamine vitæ,*
Mortali haud cuivis divina hæc munera dantur,
Non uti Dædaleam licet omnibus ire Corinthum.

   Ægypto informis quondam Pictura reperta,
Græcorum studiis & mentis acumine crevit:
95 *Egregiis tandem illustrata & adulta Magistris*
Naturam visa est miro superare labore.

   Quos inter Graphidos gymnasia prima fuêre,
Portus Athenarum, Sicyon, Rhodos, atque Corinthus,
Disparia inter se, medicùm ratione Laboris;
100 *Ut patet ex Veterum statuis, formæ atque decoris*
Archetypis, queis posterior nil protulit ætas
Condignum, & non inferius longe Arte, Modoque:
Horum igitur vera ad normam Positura legetur,
Grandia, inæqualis, formosaque Partibus amplis
105 *Anteriora dabit membra, in contraria motu*
Diverso variata, suo liberataque centro:

     VII.
    GRAPHIS
    seu Positura,
    Secunda Picturæ
    pars.

   Membrorumque Sinus ignis flammantis ad instar
Serpenti undantes flexu, sed lævia plana
Magnaque signa, quasi sine tubere subdita tactu
110 *Ex longo deducta fluant, non secta minutim,*
Insertisque Toris sint nota ligamina juxta
Compagem Anathomes, & membrificatio Græco
Deformata Modo, paucisque expressa lacertis,
Qualis apud Veteres; totoque Eurithmia partes
115 *Componat, genitumque suo generante sequenti*
Sit minus, & puncto videantur cuncta sub uno;
Regula certa licet nequeant Prospectica dici,
Aut complementum Graphidos; sed in arte juvamen
Et Modus accelerans operandi: ut corpora falso
120 *Sub visu in multis referens mendosa labascit:*
Nam Geometralem nunquam sunt corpora juxta
Mensuram depicta oculis, sed qualia visa.

   Non eadem formæ species, non omnibus ætas
Æqualis, similisque color, crinesque Figuris:
125 *Nam variis velut orta plagis Gens disparevultu.*

     VIII.
    Varietas in
    Figuris.

Singula membra suo capiti conformia fiant	IX.
Unum idemque simul corpus cum vestibus ipsis:	Figura situna
	cum Membris
	& Vestibus.
Mutorumque silens Positura imitabitur actus.	X.
	Mutorum ac-
	tiones imitandæ.

130 *Prima Figurarum, seu Princeps Dramatis ultro*
Prosiliat media in Tabula sub lumine primo   XI.
Pulchrior ante alias, reliquis nec operta Figuris.   Figura Princeps.

Agglomerata simul sint membra, ipsæque Figuræ   XII.
Stipentur, circumque globos locus usque vacabit;   Figurarum
Ne, malè dispersis dum visus ubique Figuris   Globiseu
135 *Dividitur, cunctisque operis fervente tumultu*   Cumuli.
Partibus implicitis crepitans confusio surgat.

Inque figurarum cumulis non omnibus idem   XIII.
Corporis inflexus, motusque, vel artibus omnes   Positurarem
Conversis pariter non connitantur eodem,   diversitas in
140 *Sed quædam in diversatrabant contraria membra*   cumulis.
Transverséque aliis pugent, & cætera frangant.

Pluribus adversis aversam oppone figuram,
Pectoribusque humeros, & dextera membra sinistris,
Seu multis constabit Opus, paucisve figuris.

145 *Altera pars tabulæ vacuo ne frigida Campo*   XIV.
Aut deserta siet, dum pluribus altera formis   Tabulæ libra-
Fervida mole sua supremam exurgit ad oram: mentum.
Sed tibi sic positis respondeat utraque rebus,
Ut si aliquid sursum se parte attollat in unâ,
150 *Sic aliquid parte ex aliâ consurgat, & ambas*
Æquiparet, geminas cumulando æqualiter oras.

Pluribus implicitum Personis Drama supremo   XV.
In genere ut rarum est; multis ita densa Figuris   Numerus
Rarior est Tabula excellens; vel adhuc ferè nulla   Figurarum.
155 *Præstitit in multis quod vix bene præstat in unâ:*
Quippe solet rerum nimio dispersa tumultu
Majestate carere gravi requieque decorâ;
Nec speciosa nitet vacuo nisi libera Campo.
Sed si Opere in magno plures Thema grande requirat
160 *Esse figurarum Cumulos, spectabitur unà*
Machina tota rei, non singula quæque seorsim.

Præcipua extremis raro Internodia membris   XVI.
Abdita sint: sed summa Pedum vestigia nunquam.   Internodia & Pe-
  des exhibendi.

Gratia nulla manet, motusque, vigorque Figuras
165 *Retro aliis subter majori ex parte latentes,*
Ni capitis motum manibus comitentur agendo.

XVII.
Motus manuum
motui capitis
jungendus.

Difficiles fugito aspectus, contractaque visu
Membra sub ingrato, motusque, actusque coactos,
Quodque refert signis, rectos quodammodo tractus,
170 *Sive Parallelos plures simul, & vel acutas,*
Vel Geometrales (ut Quadra, Triangula,) formas:
Ingratamque pari Signorum ex ordine quandam
Symmetriam: sed præcipua in contraria semper
Signa volunt duci transversa, ut diximus anté.
175 *Summa igitur ratio Signorum habeatur in omni*
Composito; dat enim reliquis pretium, atque vigorem.

XVIII.
Quæ fugienda
in Distributione
& Compositione.

Non ita naturæ astanti sis cuique revinctus,
Hanc præter nihil ut Genio studioque relinquas;
Nec sine teste rei natura, Artisque Magistra
180 *Quidlibet ingenio memor ut tantummodo rerum*
Pingere posse putes; errorum est plurima sylva,
Multiplicesque viæ, bene agendi terminus unus,
Linea recta velut sola est, & mille recurvæ:
Sed juxta Antiquos naturam imitabere pulchram,
185 *Qualem forma rei propria, objectumque requirit.*

XIX.
Natura Genio
accommodanda.

Non te igitur lateant antiqua Numismata, Gemmæ,
Vasa, Typi, Statuæ, cælataque Marmora Signis;
Quodque refert specie Veterum post sæcula Mentem;
Splendidior quippe ex illis assurgit imago,
190 *Magnaque se rerum facies aperit meditanti;*
Tunc nostri tenuem sæcli miserebere sortem,
Cùm spes nulla siet redituræ æqualis in ævum.

XX.
Signa Antiqua
Naturæ modum
constituunt.

Exquisita siet formâ dum sola Figura
Pingitur, & multis variata Coloribus esto.

XXI.
Sola Figura
quomodotra-
ctanda.

195 *Lati amplique sinus Pannorum, & nobilis ordo*
Membra sequens, subter latitantia Lumine & Umbra
Exprimet, ille licet transversus sæpe feratur,
Et circumfusos Pannorum porrigat extra
Membra sinus, non contiguos, ipsisque Figuræ
200 *Partibus impressos, quasi Pannus adhæreat illis;*
Sed modicè expressos cum Lumine servet & Umbris:
Quæque intermissis passim sunt dissita vanis
Copulet, inductis subtérve, supérve lacernis.
Et membra ut magnis paucisque expressa lacertis,

XXII.
Quid in Pannis
observandum.

205 *Majestate aliis præstant forma atque decore;*
     Haud secus in Pannis quos supra optavimus amplos
     Perpaucos sinuum flexus, rugasque, striasque,
     Membra super versu faciles inducere præstat.
     Naturæque rei proprius sit Pannus, abundans
210 *Patriciis, succinctus erit crassusque Bubulcis*
     Mancipiisque; levis, teneris, gracilisque Puellis.
     Inque cavis maculisque umbrarum aliquando tumescet
     Lumen ut excipiens operis quà Massa requirit
     Latius extendat, sublatisque aggreget umbris.

215   *Nobilia Arma juvant virtutum, ornantque Figuras,*   XXIII.
         Qualia Musarum, Belli, Cultusque Deorum: Quid multum
         Nec sit opus nimiùm Gemmis Auroque refertum;   conferat ad
         Rara etenim magno in pretio, sed plurima vili.   Tabulæ or-
                                                                 namentum.
                                                                    XXIV.
                                                                 Ornamentum
                                                                 Auri &
                                                                 Gemmarum.

         Quæ deinde ex Vero nequeunt præsente videri,   XXV.
220 *Prototypum prius illorum formare juvabit.*   Prototypus.

         Conveniat locus atque habitus, ritusque decusque   XXVI.
     Servetur; sit Nobilitas, Charitumque Venustas,   Convenientia
     (Rarum homini munus, Cœlo, non Arte petendum.)   rerum cum
                                                                 Scena.
                                                                    XXVII.
                                                                 Charites &
                                                                 Nobilitas.

         Naturæ sit ubique tenor ratioque sequenda.   XXVIII.
225 *Non vicina pedum tabulata excelsa tonantis*   Res quæque
     Astra domus depicta gerent nubesque notosque;   locum suum
     Nec mare depressum Laquearia summa vel orcum;   teneat.
     Marmoreamque feret cannis vaga pergula molem:
     Congrua sed propriâ semper statione locentur.

230   *Hæc præter motus animorum & corde repostos*   XXIX.
     Exprimere Affectus, paucisque coloribus ipsam   Affectus.
     Pingere posse animam, atque oculis præbere videndam,
     Hoc opus, hic labor est: pauci quos æquus amavit
     Juppiter, aut ardens evexit ad æthera virtus:
235 *Dîs similes potuere manu miracula tanta.*
     Hos ego Rhetoribus tractandos desero tantum
     Egregii antiquum memorabo sophisma Magistri,
     Verius affectus animi vigor exprimit ardens,
     Solliciti nimiùm quam sedula cura laboris.

240   *Denique nil sapiat Gotthorum barbara trito*
    Ornamenta modo, sæclorum & monstra malorum;
    Queis ubi bella, famem & pestem, Discordia, Luxus,
    Et Romanorum res grandior intulit Orbi,
    Ingenuæ periere Artes, periere superbæ
245   *Artificum moles, sua tunc miracula vidit*
    Ignibus absumi Pictura, latere coacta
    Fornicibus, sortem & reliquam confidere Cryptis,
    Marmoribusque diu Sculptura jacere sepultis.
    Imperium interea scelerum gravitate fatiscens
250   *Horrida nox totum invasit, donoque superni*
    Luminis indignum, errorum caligine mersit,
    Impiaque ignaris damnavit sæcla tenebris:
    Unde Coloratum Graiis huc usque Magistris
    Nil superest tantorum Hominum quod Mente Modoque
255   *Nostrates juvet Artifices, doceatque Laborem;*
    Nec qui Chromatices nobis hoc tempore partes
    Restituat, quales Zeuxis tractaverat olim.
    Hujus quando magâ velut Arte æquavit Apellem
    Pictorum Archigraphum meruitque Coloribus altam
260   *Nominis æterni famam toto orbe sonantem.*
    Hæc quidem ut in Tabulis fallax sed grata Venustas,
    Et complementum Graphidos (mirabile visu)
    Pulchra vocabatur, sed subdola Lena Sororis:
    Non tamen hoc lenocinium; fucusque, dolusque
265   *Dedecori fuit unquam; illi sed semper honori,*
    Laudibus & meritis; hanc ergo nosse juvabit.

    Lux varium vivumque dabit, nullum Umbra Colorem.
    Quo magis adversum est corpus lucisque propinquum,
    Clarius est Lumen; nam debilitatur eundo.
270   *Quo magis est corpus directum oculisque propinquum,*
    Conspicitur meliùs; nam visus hebescit eundo.

    Ergo in corporibus quæ visa adversa rotundis
    Integra sint, extrema abscedant perdita signis
    Confusis, non præcipiti labentur in Umbram
275   *Clara gradu, nec adumbrata in clara alta repente*
    Prorumpant; sederit sensim hinc atque inde meatus
    Lucis & Umbrarum; capitisque unius ad instar
    Totum opus, ex multis quamquam sit partibus unus
    Luminis Umbrarumque globus tantummodo fiet,
280   *Sive duo vel tres ad summum, ubi grandius esset*
    Divisum Pegma in partes statione remotas.
    Sintque ita discreti inter se ratione colorum,
    Luminis umbrarumque anteorsum ut corpora clara
    Obscura umbrarum requies spectanda relinquat;
285   *Claroque exiliant umbrata atque aspera Campo.*

XXX.
Gotthorum
ornamenta
fugienda.

CHROMATICE
Tertia pars
Picturæ.

XXXI.
Tonorum,
Luminum &
Umbrarum
ratio.

Ac veluti in speculis convexis eminet ante
Asperior reipsa vigor & vis aucta colorum
Partibus adversis; magis & fuga rupta retrorsum
Illorum est (ut visa minùs vergentibus oris)
290 *Corporibus dabimus formas hoc more rotundas,*
Mente Modoque igitur Plastes & Pictor eodem
Dispositum tractabit opus; quæ Sculptor in orbem
Atterit, hæc rupto procul abscedente colore
Assequitur Pictor, fugientiaque illa retrorsum
295 *Jam signata minùs confusa coloribus aufert:*
Anteriora quidem directè adversa, colore
Integra, vivaci, summo cum Lumine & Umbra
Antrorsum distincta refert velut aspera visu.
Sicque super planum inducit Leucoma Colores.
300 *Hos velut ex ipsa natura immotus eodem*
Intuitu circum Statuas daret inde rotundas.

Densa Figurarum solidis quæ corpora formis
Subdita sunt tactu non translucent, sed opaca
In translucendi spatio ut super Aëra, Nubes
305 *Lympida stagna Undarum, & inania cætera debent*
Asperiora illis prope circumstantibus esse,
Ut distincta magis firmo cum Lumine & Umbra,
Et gravioribus ut sustenta coloribus, inter
Aëreas species subsistent semper opaca:
310 *Sed contra procul abscedant perlucida densis*
Corporibus leviora; uti Nubes, Aër & Undæ.

XXXII.
Corpora densa
& opaca cum
translucentibus.

Non poterunt diversa locis duo Lumina eâdem
In Tabulâ paria admitti, aut æqualia pingi:
Majus at in mediam Lumen cadet usqe Tabellam
315 *Latius infusum, primis qua summa Figuris*
Res agitur, circumque oras minuetur eundo:
Utque in progressu Jubar attenuatur ab ortu
Solis ad occasum paulatim, & cessat eundo;
Sic Tabulis Lumen, tota in compage Colorum,
320 *Primo à fonte, minus sensim declinat eundo.*
Majus ut in Statuis per compita stantibus Urbis
Lumen habent Partes superæ, minus inferiores,
Idem erit in tabulis, majorque nec umbra vel ater
Membra Figurarum intrabit Color atque secabit:
325 *Corpora sed circum Umbra cavis latitabit oberrans:*
Atque ita quæretur Lux opportuna Figuris,
Ut late infusum Lumen lata Umbra sequatur:
Unde nec immeritò fertur Titianus ubique
Lucis & Umbrarum Norman appellasse Racemum.

XXXIII.
Non duo ex
Cœlo Lumina
in Tabulam
æqualia.

330 *Purum Album esse potest propiusq; magisq; remotum:*
Cum Nigro antevenit propiùs, fugit absque remotum;
Purum autem Nigrum antrorsum venit usq; propinquum.

XXXIV.
Album &
Nigrum.

> *Lux fucata suo tingit miscetque Colore*
> *Corpora, sicque suo, per quem Lux funditur, aër.*

335 *Corpora juncta simul, circumfusosque Colores*
Excipiunt, propriumque aliis radiosa reflectunt.

XXXV.
Colorum
reflectio.

Pluribus in Solidis liquidâ sub Luce propinquis
Participes, mixtosque simul decet esse Colores.
Hanc Normam Veneti Pictores ritè sequuti,
340 *(Quæ fuit Antiquis Corruptio dicta Colorum)*
Cùm plures opere in magno posuêre Figuras,
Ne conjuncta simul variorum inimica Colorum
Congeries Formam implicitam & concisa minutis
Membra daret Pannis, totam unamquamque Figuram
345 *Affini aut uno tantùm vestire Colore*
Sunt soliti, variando Tonis tunicamque togamque
Carbaseosque Sinus, vel amicum in Lumine & Umbra
Contiguis circum rebus sociando Colorem.

XXXVI.
Unio Colorum.

Quà minus est spatii aërei, aut quà purior Aër,
350 *Cuncta magis distincta patent, speciesque reservant:*
Quàque magis densus nebulis, aut plurimus Aër
Amplum inter fuerit spatium porrectus, in auras
Confundet rerum species, & perdet inanes.

XXXVII.
Aër interpositus.

Anteriora magis semper finita remotis
355 *Incertis dominentur & abscedentibus, idque*
More relativo, ut majora minoribus extant.

XXXVIII.
Distantiarum
Relatio.

Cuncta minuta procul Massam densantur in unam,
Ut folia arboribus sylvarum, & in Æquore fluctus.

XXXIX.
Corpora procul
distantia.

Contigua inter se coëant, sed dissita distent,
360 *Distabuntque tamen grato & discrimine parvo.*

XL.
Contigua &
Dissita.

Extremia extremis contraria jungere noli;
Sed medio sint usque gradu sociata Coloris.

XLI.
Contraria ex-
trema fugienda.

Corporum erit Tonus atque Color variatus ubique
Quærat amicitiam retro, ferus emicet ante.

XLII.
Tonus &
Color varii.

365 *Supremum in Tabulis Lumen captare diei*
Insanus labor Artificum; cùm attingere tantùm
Non Pigmenta queant; auream sed vespere Lucem,
Seu modicam mane albentem, sive ætheris actam
Post Hyemem nimbis transfuso Sole caducam,
370 *Seu nebulis fultam accipient, tonitruque rubentem.*

XLIII.
Luminis
delectus.

Lævia quæ lucent, veluti Chrystalla, Metalla,
Ligna, Ossa & Lapides; Villosa, ut Vellera, Pelles,
Barbæ, aqueique Oculi, Crines, Holoserica, Plumæ;
Et Liquida, ut stagnans Aqua, reflexæque sub Undis
375 *Corporeæ species, & Aquis contermina cuncta,*
Subter ad extremum liquide sint picta, superque
Luminibus percussa suis, signisque repostis.

XLIV.
Quædam
circa Praxim.

Area vel Campus Tabulæ vagus esto, levisque
Abscedat latus, liquideque bene unctis amicis
380 *Tota ex mole Coloribus, una sive Patellâ:*
Quæque cadunt retro in Campum confinia Campo.
Vividus esto Color nimio non pallidus Albo,
Adversisque locis ingestus plurimus ardens;
Sed leviter parcéque datus vergentibus oris.

XLV.
Campus
Tabulæ.

XLVI.
Color vividus,
non tamen
pallidus.

385 *Cuncta Labore simul coëant, velut Umbrâ in eadem.*

XLVII.
Umbra.

Tota siet Tabula ex unâ depicta Patellâ.

XLVIII.
Ex una Patella
sit Tabula.

Multa ex Natura Speculum præclara docebit;
Quæque procul serò spatiis spectantur in amplis.

XLIX.
Speculum
Pictorum
Magister.

Dimidia Effigies, quæ sola, vel integra plures
390 *Ante alias posita ad Lucem, stet proxima visu,*
Et latis spectanda locis, oculisque remota,
Luminis Umbrarumque gradu sit picta supremo.

L.
Dimidia Figura
vel integra
ante alias.

Partibus in minimis imitatio justa juvabit
Effigiem, alternas referendo tempore eodem
395 *Consimiles Partes, cum Luminis atque Coloris*
Compositis justisque Tonis, tunc parta Labore
Si facili & vegeto micat ardens, viva videtur.

LI.
Effigies.

Visa loco angusto tenerè pingantur, amico
Juncta Colore graduque, procul quæ picta feroci
400 *Sint & inæquali variata Colore, Tonoque.*
Grandia signa volunt spatia ampla ferosque Colores.
Lumina lata unctas simul undique copulet Umbras
Extremus Labor. In Tabulas demissa fenestris
Si fuerit Lux parva, Color clarissimus esto:
405 *Vividus at contra obscurusque in Lumine aperto.*

LII.
Locus Tabulæ.

LIII.
Lumina lata.
LIV.
Quantitas
Luminis loci
in quo Tabula
est exponenda.

Quæ vacuis divisa cavis vitare memento:
Trita, minuta, simul quæ non stipata dehiscunt;
Barbara, Cruda oculis, rugis fucata Colorum,
Luminis Umbrarumque Tonis æqualia cuncta;
410 Fœda, cruenta, cruces, obscœna, ingrata, chimeras,
Sordidaque & misera, & vel acuta, vel aspera tactu,
Quæque dabunt formæ temerè congesta ruinam,
Implicitasque aliis confundent miscua Partes.

LV.
Errores & vitia
Picturæ.

Dumque fugis vitiosa, cave in contraria labi
415 Damna mali, Vitium extremis nam semper inhæret.

LVI.
Prudentia in
Pictore.

Pulchra gradu summo Graphidos stabilita Vetustæ
Nobilibus Signis sunt Grandia, Dissita, Pura,
Tersa, velut minime confusa, Labore Ligata,
Partibus ex magnis paucisque efficta, Colorum
420 Corporibus distincta feris, sed semper amicis.

LVII.
Elegantium
Idæa Tabula-
rum.

Qui bene cœpit, uti facti jam fertur habere
Dimidium; Picturam ita nil sub limine primo
Ingrediens Puer offendit damnosius Arti,
Quàm varia errorum genera ignorante Magistro
425 Ex pravis libare Typis, mentemque veneno
Inficere, in toto quod non abstergitur ævo.

LVIII.
Pictor Tyro.

Nec Graphidos rudis Artis adhuc cito qualiacumque
Corporaviva super studium meditabitur ante
Illorum quam Symmetriam, Internodia, Formam
430 Noverit inspectis docto evolvente Magistro
Archetypis, dulcesque Dolos præsenserit Artis.
Plusque Manu ante oculos quàm voce docebitur usus.

LIX.
Ars debet ser-
vire Pictori,
non Pictor
Arti.

Quære Artem quæcumque juvant, fuge quæque
repugnant.

LX.
Oculos recre-
ant diversitas
& Operis fa-
cilitas, quæ
speciatim Ars
dicitur.

Corpora diversæ naturæ juncta placebunt;
435 Sic ea quæ facili contempta labore videntur:
Æthereus quippe ignis inest & spiritus illis.
Mente diu versata, manu celeranda repenti.
Arsque Laborque Operis grata sic fraude latebit.
Maxima deinde erit ars, nihil artis inesse videri.

440 *Nec prius inducas Tabulæ Pigmenta Colorum,*
Expensi quàm signa Typi stabilita nitescant,
Et menti præsens Operis sit Pegma futuri.

LXI.
Archetypus
in mente,
Apographum
in tela.

Prævaleat sensus rationi quæ officit Arti
Conspicuæ, inque oculis tantummodo Circinus esto.

LXII.
Circinus in
oculis.

445 *Utere Doctorum Monitis, nec sperne superbus*
Discere quæ de te fuerit Sententia Vulgi.
Est cæcus nam quisque suis in rebus, & expers
Judicii, Prolemque suam miratur amatque.
Ast ubi Consilium deerit Sapientis Amici,
450 *Id tempus dabit, atque mora intermissa labori.*
Non facilis tamen ad nutus & inania Vulgi
Dicta levi mutabis Opus, Geniumque relinques:
Nam qui parte sua sperat bene posse mereri
Multivaga de Plebe, nocet sibi, nec placet ulli.

LXIII.
Superbia pic-
tori nocet
plurimúm.

455 *Cumque Opere in proprio soleat se pingere Pictor,*
(Prolem adeo sibi ferre parem Natura suevit)
Proderit imprimis Pictori γνῶθι σεαυτόν;
Ut data quæ genio colat, abstineatque negatis.
Fructibus utque suus nunquam est sapor atque venustas
460 *Floribus insueto in fundo præcoce sub anni*
Tempore, quos cultus violentus & ignis adegit;
Sic nunquam nimio quæ sunt extorta labore,
Et picta invito Genio, nunquam illa placebunt.

LXIV.
γνῶθι σεαυτόν.

Vera super meditando, Manus, Labor improbus adsit:
465 *Nec tamen obtundat Genium, mentisque vigorem.*

LXV.
Quod mente
conceperis manu
comproba.

Optima nostrorum pars matutina dierum,
Difficili hanc igitur potiorem impende Labori.

LXVI.
Matutinum
tempus La-
bori aptum.

Nulla dies abeat quin linea ducta supersit.

LXVII.
Singulis die-
bus aliquid
faciendum.

Perque vias vultus hominum, motusque notabis
470 *Libertate sua proprios, positasque Figuras*
Ex sese faciles, ut inobservatus habebis.

LXVIII.
Affectus in-
observati &
naturales.

Mox quodcumque Mari, Terris & in Aëre pulchrum
Contigerit, Chartis propera mandare paratis,
Dum præsens animo species tibi fervet hianti.

LXIX.
Non desint
Pugillares.

475 Non epulis nimis indulget Pictura, meroque
Parcit, Amicorum quantum ut sermone benigno
Exhaustum reparet mentem recreata, sed inde
Litibus & curis in Cœlibe libera vita
Secessus procul à turba strepituque remotos
480 Villarum rurisque beata silentia quærit:
Namque recollecto tota incumbente Minerva
Ingenio rerum species præsentior extat,
Commodiusque Operis compagem amplectitur omnem.

Infami tibi non potior sit avara peculi
485 Cura, aurique fames, modicâ quam sorte beato
Nominis æterni & laudis pruritus habendæ,
Condignæ pulchrorum Operum mercedis in ævum.

Judicium, docile Ingenium, Cor nobile, Sensus
Sublimes, firmum Corpus, florensque Juventa,
490 Commoda Res, Labor, Artis amor, doctusque Magister;
Et quamcumque voles occasio porrigat ansam,
Ni Genius quidam adfuerit Sydusque benignum,
Dotibus his tantis, nec adhuc Ars tanta paratur:
Distat ab Ingenio longè Manus. Optima Doctis
495 Censentur quæ prava minus; latet omnibus error,
Vitaque tam longæ brevior non sufficit Arti;
Desinimus nam posse senes cùm scire periti
Incipimus, doctamque Manum gravat ægra senectus,
Nec gelidis fervet juvenilis in Artubus ardor.

500 Quare agite, ô Juvenes, placido quos Sydere natos
Paciferæ studia allectant tranquilla Minervæ,
Quosque suo fovet igne, sibique optavit Alumnos!
Eja agite, atque animis ingentem ingentibus Artem
Exercete alacres, dum strenua corda Juventus
505 Viribus extimulat vegetis, patiensque laborum est;
Dum vacua errorum nulloque imbuta sapore
Pura nitet mens, & rerum sitibunda novarum
Præsentes haurit species, atque humida servat.

In Geometrali priùs Arte parumper adulti   LXX.
510 Signa Antiqua super Graïorum addiscite formam;   Ordo Studiorum.
Nec mora nec requies, noctuque diuque labori
Illorum Menti atque Modo, vos donec agendi
Praxis ab assiduo faciles assueverit usu.

Mox ubi Judicium emensis adoleverit annis
515 Singula quæ celebrant primæ Exemplaria classis
Romani, Veneti, Parmenses, atque Bononi
Partibus in cunctis pedetentim atque ordine recto,
Ut monitum suprà est vos expendisse juvabit.

434   *Appendix A*

Hos apud invenit Raphael *miracula summo*
520 *Ducta modo, Veneresque habuit quas nemo deinceps.*
Quidquid erat formæ scivit Bonarota *potenter.*
Julius *à puero Musarum eductus in Antris*
Aonias reseravit opes, Graphicaque Poësi
Quæ non visa priùs, sed tantùm audita Poëtis
525 *Ante oculos spectanda dedit Sacraria Phœbi:*
Quæque coronatis complevit bella triumphis
Heroüm fortuna potens, casusque decoros
Nobilius reipsa antiqua pinxisse videtur.
Clarior ante alios Corregius *extitit, ampla*
530 *Luce superfusa circum coëuntibus Umbris,*
Pingendique Modo grandi, & tractando Colore
Corpora. Amicitiamque, gradusque, dolosque Colorum,
Compagemque ita disposuit Titianus, *ut inde*
Divus appellatus, magnis sit honoribus auctus
535 *Fortunæque bonis: Quos sedulus* Annibal *omnes*
In propriam mentem atque Modum mira arte coëgit.

Plurimus inde labor Tabulas imitando juvabit
Egregias, Operumque Typos; sed plura docebit
Natura ante oculos præsens; nam firmat & auget
540 *Vim Genii, ex illaque Artem Experientia complet.*
Multa supersileo quæ commentaria dicent.

LXXI.
Natura &
Experientia
Artem perfi-
ciunt.

Hæc ego, dum memoror subitura volubilis ævi
Cuncta vices, variisque olim peritura ruinis,
Pauca Sophismata sum Graphica immortalibus ausus
545 *Credere Pieriis. Romæ meditatus: ad Alpes*
Dum super insanas moles inimicaque castra
Borbonidum decus & vindex Lodoicus Avorum
Fulminat ardenti dextrâ, Patriæque resurgens
Gallicus Alcides, premit Hispani ora Leonis.

Appendix B: Reflections and Notes on The Annals of Tacitus, Book I

I Politick Reflections

230:1 *Liberty*] When once the Regal Power begins to degenerate into Tyranny, the People aspire to Liberty; and when once a *Brutus* appears, that is, a Head who is capable to give it, they seldom fail to shake off the Yoke, not only of the King, who Tyrannizes, but also of the Regal Power, for fear there come another King, who might Tyrannize also *Occultior non Melior.*

230:5 *Years*] The surest way to preserve Liberty, saith *Livy,* is not to permit the Magistracy, wherein the Supreme Authority is lodg'd, to be of long duration. There is no place in the World, where this Maxim is so well observed as at *Venice;* and it may be this is the chief Cause which hath made it out-live so many Ages, and so many States, which were more powerful than theirs, and not surrounded with so many dangerous Neighbours. *Machiavel* saith that the short Duration of the Dictatorship, hinder'd the Dictator from transgressing the Bounds of his Duty. *Discourses,* lib. 1. ch. 34.

230:6 *space*] All Power that is Established by Sedition, as was that of these Tribunes, can never subsist long.

230:8 *continuance*] Nothing is so weak and so obnoxious to a reverse of Fortune, as a Power, which hath neither Right nor Reason for its Foundation. *Cinna* was slain in a Sedition by his own Soldiers, and *Sylla* constrain'd to renounce the Dictatorship. Upon which *Cæsar* said pleasantly, that *Sylla* could not Read, seeing he knew not how to Dictate.

230:12 *Government*] Ambition and the Quarrels of Great Men, are the Shelves on which the Liberty of Common-Wealths are always split; for the State is weaken'd in Proportion, as particular Persons fortifie themselves by Arms, under pretence of revenging their Injuries, or of securing themselves against the Resentments of their Enemies, or the Violence of these that are stronger. And as the People suffer themselves in the end to be the Prey of their Dissentions, they are constrain'd to receive an absolute Master, that they may have Peace; Thus *Tacitus* had good reason to say, that the Factions of Citizens are much more dangerous in Common-Wealths, and that Regal Power came not into the World but since Equality and Modesty went out of it, *Periculosiores sunt inimicitiæ juxta libertatem.* In Germania. *Postquam exui æqualitas, & pro modestia ac pudere ambitio & vis incedebat, provenere dominationes. Ann. 3.* To conclude, *Tacitus* seems to observe here, that *Rome* was never at rest, after the Expulsion of its Kings, until it return'd to the Government of a Single Person, as to its first principle; for in *Tully*'s Opinion it was not the Regal Power, but the Abuse of Regal Power which the Roman People hated, 3 *de Legib.*

230:13 *Prince*] A new Prince ought always to wave odious Titles, for besides that; Authority is not in Titles, those which he accepts give Men occasion to judge of the good or bad dispositions which he brings with him to the Government. It is natural to believe, that a Prince who voluntarily assumed a Title which shocks his Subjects, will take no great care to be belov'd, and will make it his principal Maxim, *Oderint, dum metuant.* Pope *Paul* II. gave People an ill opinion of his Pontificate from the Day of his Exaltation, by being desirous to take the name of *Formosus.* And indeed, his Vanity which sprang thence, made him to do many things unbecoming a Pope, for according to *Platina*'s Relation, he Painted and Dress'd like a Woman.

230:16 *Authors*] They who relate only these things which make for the Honour of their Country, and suppress the rest, are good Citizens, but very bad Historians,

> *Dum patriam laudat, dum damnat Poggius hostes,*
> *Nec malus est civis, nec bonus historicus.*

In *Tacitus*'s Opinion, History is always better written by the Subjects of a Republick, than by those of a Monarchy, because Flattery reigns less in Republicks.

230:18 *Flattery*] Flattery increases in proportion as Government is Establish'd. It began under the Reign of *Augustus,* but it was at its height under that of *Tiberius:* To see the Extravagant Progress which it made in a little time among Writers, we need only compare the History of *Paterculus,* with that of *Livy.* This was written under a Common-Wealth, the other under a Monarchy. If *Augustus* call'd *Livy* Pompeian, he would certainly have call'd *Paterculus* Tiberian.

230:22 *Historians*] The History of bad Princes is never Written faithfully, not during their life, because they are fear'd, nor after their Death, because they are calumniated. And besides, those who have made their Fortunes under them, believe that it is permitted to them to lye by way of gratitude. So that Posterity are equally deceived by both, *Ita neutris cura posteritatis inter infensos, vel obnoxios.* Hist. 1.

230:27 *Motive*] They who undertake to write History ought to indulge neither to the Love nor the Hatred which they have towards the Persons they are to speak of; Neither their Animosities, nor their Acknowledgments ought to pass from their Heart to their Writings; they should set themselves above Hope and Fear, that they may be at Liberty to speak Truth. Every one saith *d'Aubigne* protests at his setting out to make up his wants of Abilities, by an exact Fidelity, every one boasts of Liberty, and of laying his passions at his Feet, even such a one who in the very beginning shews, that his Pen and his Conscience are sold to Favour. *Preface of his Universal History.*

231:4 *Triumvir*] When a Prince ceases to be Cruel, and grows Merciful, all the Evil that he hath done, is attributed to Necessity, and the Unhappiness of the Times, and all the Good that he doth to his own Nature. *Augustus* effaced all the Footsteps of his Triumvirate, by quitting the Title of Triumvir; and it may be said, that his Clemency did the Roman Common-Wealth more mischief than his Triumvirate, seeing it made the People tame for Servitude, by making them love him for a Master, whom they before abhorr'd as a Triumvir.

231:7 *People*] They who have oppress'd the Liberties of Common-Wealths, have almost all of them begun by defending it; for the People accustom themselves insensibly to obey him who knows how to deceive them, under the specious Title of a Defender. It was by this fine Name *Pagano della Terra* made himself Lord of *Milan*, and the Duke of *Atenes*, of *Florence*.

231:8 *rewards*] An Army hath always a greater love for the Gifts which are bestow'd on them, and the Licentiousness which is allow'd them, than for the publick Liberty. *Donis corrumpebatur*, says *Livy*, *malebat licentiam suam, quam omnium libertatem.*

231:9 *Provisions*] The Common People love their Bellies better than their Liberty.

231:20 *Freedom*] It is as dangerous to attempt to restore Liberty to a People who desire to have a Master, as to endeavour to bring a People under Subjection, who desire to live free: In fine, it is to preserve the shadow and appearance of Liberty, to obey those willingly who have the power to force us to it, *Libertatis servaveris umbram*, says *Lucian*, *Si quicquid jubeare, velis.*

231:31 *Parentage*] The Prince who would be well served ought to honour Virtue wheresoever it is found, and to look upon him as the most Noble, who is the best able to assist him to govern well. A single Person, saith *Commines*, is sometimes the Cause of preventing great Inconveniencies to his Master, although he be not of Noble Birth, provided that he has only Sense and Virtue. *Ch. 5. Lib. 5. of his Mem. Cabrera* says, that *Philip* the II. in conferring Offices and Military Honours, preferred Spill'd Blood to Hereditary Blood, *Ch. ult. Lib. 2. of his History.*

232:5 *repugnance*] It is enough to guess, that a Prince does not Refuse a thing in good earnest, because he makes no resistance to accept it, when it is offered him again with greater importunity. The more Popes affect to shew in the beginning of their Pontificate, little inclination to call their Relations to the Administration of Affairs, the more the Cardinals, the Ambassadors and the Courtiers are importunate to persuade them to that which they knew they desire, *Vid. Reflection 6. of Ch. 7.*

232:9 *Livia*] The Death of Princes is frequently imputed to those, who have the greatest Advantage by it. As *Livia* desir'd to reign, even after *Augustus*'s death, she was suspected to have poyson'd *Lucius* and *Caius*, to make way for her Son. *Henry* Duke of *Orleance*, and *Catherine de Medicis*, his Wife, were supposed to be the true Authors of the Death of the Dauphine of *France*, because his Death secured the Crown to them.

232:21 *Age*] It is rarely seen, that a Prince growing old, maintains his Authority to the last. *Tacitus* saith, that the Power of an Old Man is precarious, *precarium seni imperium, & brevi transiturum. Hist. 1.* For under the colour of relieving his Old Age, his Wife, or his Son, or his Ministers assume the Government. Duke *Philip* being grown Old, *Commines* saith, that his Affairs were so manag'd by the Lords of *Crouy* and of *Chimay*, that he restor'd to the King the Cities upon the River of *Some*, at which the Count his Son was much troubled, for they were the Frontiers of their

Lordships. The Count call'd a great Council in the Bishop of *Cambray's* Palace, and there declar'd the whole House of *Crouy* mortal Enemies to his Father and himself: insomuch that they were all of them forc'd to fly. These proceedings were very displeasing to Duke *Philip,* but his great Age made him bear it with patience, *Ch.* 1. *&* 2. *Lib.* 1. *of his Memoirs.* That which also adds much to the Diminution of the Authority of an old and infirm Prince, is, that there being no more to be hop'd for from him, he is abandon'd by his Servants.

232:28 *Rhine*] It may be this was not so much to oppose the Incursions of the Germans, as to put a Check upon *Tiberius* if he should make an attempt upon the Authority of *Augustus.*

232:30 *Succession*] Adoption doth not only serve to multiply the Heirs of a Prince, who is too old for Procreation, but also to secure him from the reproach of Old Age, and incapacity to govern, when it is seen, that he makes a good Choice: And this was *Galba's* meaning in what he said when he adopted *Piso;* as soon as the Senate and the City shall hear of thy adoption, they'll no longer think me old. *Audita adoptione desinam videri senex. Tac. Hist.* 1.

233:1 *names*] *Arcanum novi status imago antiqui,* that is to say, the Art of a New Government is to resemble the Old. For the People ought not to be sensible of a Change, for fear of an Insurrection. After that *Philip* II. had taken possession of *Portugal,* he left Cardinal Arch-Duke *Albert,* Vice-Roy there; so that as to Habit, saith *Cabrera,* King Cardinal *Henry* seemed not to be dead, *History of Philip* II. *sub fin.* It was possibly for the same reason, that *Philip* gave the Government of the Low-Countrys to the Dutchess of *Parma* his Sister, considering that the Flemings having been accustomed to a Female Government for the space of 46 Years, that *Margaret* of *Austria,* Dutchess Dowager of *Savoy,* and *Mary* Queen of *Hungary,* his Aunt, had govern'd them; it was probable that a Governess would be more agreeable to them than a Governor. *Herrera* saith, that *Philip* having recall'd the Arch-Duke *Albert* from *Portugal* (in 1592.) the Government of this Kingdom remained in the hands of five Administrators, because that having promis'd the Portuguese to give them always one of the Royal Family for their Governor; and being either not able, or not willing to do it at that time, he thought to make no Innovation by placing in the room of *Albert* five Portuguese Lords, after the example of the King Cardinal *Henry,* who by his last Will had named five others, *Third Part of his Hist. Lib.* 10. *C.* 23. *Henry* IV. would make his Abjuration in the Church of St. *Denis,* to shew that he would follow the Religion and the Examples of the Kings, who were interr'd there. *Memoirs of the Chancellor* Chiverney.

233:16 *Masters*] When a Prince begins to break and grow infirm, all People turn their Eyes towards the Rising Sun, that is to say, towards his Successor, if there is an Heir apparent, as in Hereditary States there is: but if the Successors be uncertain, as in Elective Kingdoms, then every one reasons upon the good or bad Qualities of the several Pretenders, and destines to the Throne him that is most agreeable to himself. *Multi,* saith *Tacitus, occulta spe, prout quis amicus vel cliens, hunc vel illum ambitiosis rumoribus destinabans, Hist.* 1.

233:18 *suffer'd*] It has been often observed, that Princes who come from Exile to a Throne, have been cruel,

———*Regnabit sanguine multo, Quisquis ab exilio venit ad imperium. Apud Suet, in Vita Tib.*

and likewise those who have been despised or ill-treated under the Reign of their Predecessor. When once *Lewis* XI. was crowned and knew his Power, he thought of nothing but revenge. *Hist. Memoirs, Lib.* 1. *Ch.* 12.

233:27 *Youth*] It ought to be observed, saith the same Author, that all Men who have ever been great, or have done great things, began very Young. And this lies in Education.

233:30 *Luxury*] Princes of the Humour of *Tiberius* can never be in worse Company than with themselves. The fierce and cruel Temper of Don *Carlos,* Prince of *Spain,* according to *Cabrera,* was owing to the Inclination which he had for Solitude. C. 8. L. 1. *of his History.* For Solitude, saith he, makes young People Wild, Melancholly, Fantastical, Cholerick, and apt to form ill designs. That which none sees none reproves; and consequently temptation meets with no obstacle. *l.* 4. *c.* 2.

234:7 *Poison*] It is usual for People to impute the Death of Princes to Poyson; as if Princes could not dye of Diseases, or of Old Age; or that their Death must be render'd as mysterious as their Life.

234:15 *Grandfather*] *Augustus* being willing to repair the Error which he had committed in disinheriting his Grandson, made a greater by recalling him to the Succession of the Empire, after he had taken *Tiberius* for his Collegue. For besides that it was not in his power to undo what he had done, his Repentance which came too late, expos'd him to the Hatred and Revenge of *Livia* and *Tiberius,* who were no longer oblig'd to him for a Favour that he was sorry he had done them. When any one will do so great a thing, saith *Commines,* he ought to consult and debate it well, that he may take the safest side: For there is no Prince so wise, who doth not fail sometimes, and also very often, if he lives long; and this would be evident from his actions, if he always spoke the Truth of them. *His Memoirs, l.* 5. *c.* 13.

234:16 *Marcia*] *Cato* the Censor had good reason to say, that one of the three things whereof he repented, was, that he had told his Secret to a Woman; for, if you'l believe *Plautus,* none of that Sex have been Mutes. *Two or three contrary Examples,* saith a Modern Author, *are miracles, which do not make a Precedent. P. Bohours* keeping a Secret.

234:17 *Livia*] It is a general Custom, saith *Commines,* more to endeavour to please those whose future advancement we expect, than him who is already raised to such a Degree, that he can ascend no higher. *l.* 6. *c. uls.*

234:21 *Destiny*] Princes always destroy those who have discover'd their Secrets, not only for fear of treachery, but also because they are asham'd to be deceived in those they trusted. *Augustus,* who was a great discerner of Men, preferr'd *Fabius* before all the rest of his Friends, and yet this Confident through imprudence discover'd his Secrets. Therefore Princes ought not to confide in any Person, no more than *Metellus,* who said he would burn his Shirt, if it knew his secret design. By the way, 'tis fit to observe, that there is nothing more dangerous than to trust a married Woman with a Secret, because of her near relation to her Husband; for sooner or later the Bed discovers all, especially if 'tis the Woman's interest not to keep the Secret. Thus, we are not to wonder that *Livia,* knowing there was a design to set aside her Son *Tiberius,* and to bestow the Empire upon the Young *Agrippa* her Son-in-Law, sacrificed without respect and pity, *Fabius* and *Martia* to the anger of *Augustus,* to prevent him recalling his Grandson. In the last age Don *Antonio de Padilla* having discover'd to *Donna Anna* the Queen of *Spain,* that *Philip* II. had disappointed her of the Regency, by the Will which he had made at *Badajoz;* this Princess, who thought her self excluded for want of Love and Esteem, did not cease to make complaints, which soon after cost Don *Antonio* his Life, *Cabrera in his History Chap.* 3. *Lib.* 12. and *c.* 2. *l.* 13. He must never trust a Secret to a Person who is infinitely below him; for such is the case of Great Ones, that they reckon it a dishonour to stand in awe of their Inferiors; and a ridiculous Folly to be afraid of disobliging him, to whom they told a thing which may be for his advantage to reveal. *Antony Perez,* says, that the Tongue is that part of Man which the Ladies are most set against, because of the Secret which they wou'd have kept, and which they are afraid shou'd be discover'd. Men have more reason to be cautious, but especially they who live at Court, or who converse with the Court Ladies, ought to be more jealous of a Womans Tongue, and even of their own Wife's, than of their most dangerous Enemies.

234:35 *Posthumus*] A Prince who sheds the Royal Blood, gives an Example of most dangerous consequence. The Queen of *Naples, Joan* I. says *Ammirato,* when she caus'd *Andrew* her Husband to be strangled, taught *Charles* III. when he had it in his power to strangle her also. And after he had taken from the Queen his Mother her Crown and Life, he also lost his own Crown and Life, by the hands of the Hungarians who were taught by the example which he had given them. *Discourse* 7. *of the* 17 *Book of his Commentary upon Tacitus.* There are many Politicians, says *Cabrera,* who say on the contrary, that 'tis difficult to keep in Prison Princes of the Royal Blood, and that when they are dead they don't bite: which is the reason why *Charles* of *Anjou,* (that is *Charles* I. King of *Naples,)* put to death *Conradin,* the Nephew of *Manfrede* his Predecessor. But *Aragon* did not want Heirs, who happily recover'd the Kingdom, and who condemn'd to death the Son of *Charles.* And though this Sentence was not executed, *(for* Constance *the Eldest Daughter of* Manfrede, *and Wife of* Peter *III. King of* Aragon, *was more generous than* Charles *I.)* yet the innocent *Conradin* was reveng'd, by that mark of Infamy which his blood imprinted upon the House of *Anjou*——— *Philip* II. provided for the safety and preservation of Queen *Mary* of *England* his Wife, in opposing the execution of the Sentence of Death given against *Elizabeth,* his Sister-in-Law; for the Prince who puts those of his own blood into the hands of the Executioner, whets the Sword against himself. *Chap.* 10. *of Book* 1. *and* 5 *of Book* 2. *of his History of Philip* II. *Henry* IV. would never consent to the Death of *Charles* of *Valois,* Count of *Auvergne,* who conspir'd against him, saying, that he ought to have a respect for the blood of Kings; and Mr. *Villeroy,* one of his Ministers said well to the same purpose, that when the Question was put concerning the Life of Princes of the Blood, the Prince ought for Counsel to hear nature only. *Burnet* has declared, that the Death of the Queen of *Scotland* was the greatest Blot of Queen *Elizabeth*'s reign. And I wonder that Pope *Sixtus* V. who knew so well how to teach others to give respect to Royal Majesty, should envy this Queen the Happiness and Honour to have a Crown'd Head fall at her feet. And never was a Dream more full of instruction, than that Ladies, who usually lay in the Chamber of Queen *Elizabeth,* and who the Night before that Execution, awak'd in a Fright, crying out, that she saw the Head of *Mary Stuart* cut off, and that they would also have cut off the Head of Queen *Elizabeth* with the same Axe. *Leti Book 3. of part 2. of the Life of Sixtus* V.

235:17–18 *Commission*] 'Tis the Custom of Princes in hurtful cases to throw the Odium upon their Ministers. *Anthony Perez,* who found it so by sad experience in the Murder of *John* of *Escovedo,* which *Philip* II. gave leave to be enquir'd into; says, that Princes are advis'd to keep a Council of State to clear themselves of all unlucky accidents. Queen *Elizabeth* imprison'd the Secretary who dispatch'd an Order to hasten the Execution of *Mary Stuart,* Queen of Scots, saying, that she was surpris'd when she sign'd the Warrant. *Leti.*

235:24 *Guilty*] That Minister is unhappy, who is forc'd to accuse his Prince, to prove his own Innocence; or who must be Criminal, to make his Prince to be reputed Innocent. For if he keeps the Secret, the Judges condemn him; if he does not keep it, his Master sacrifices him as an unfaithful Servant. Besides, the Prince is always glad to rid himself of one who may be a Witness against him.

235:26 *Ministers*] Princes would often want Counsel, if it was dangerous to give them Counsel. *Defuturos qui suadeant, si suadere periculum sit. Curt. Lib.* 7. When a Prince keeps a Secret, says *Cabrera,* we freely tell him every thing that may do him hurt; which often preserves his State and Person. *Philip* II. was ignorant of nothing, because every one told him what he knew; and 'twas certain he would never discover what ought to be kept secret. *Chap. 3. of the 12 Book of his Life.*

235:29 *Senate*] 'Tis the Destruction of a Republick and introduces a Monarchy to commit the Sovereign Power to one alone, and 'tis the Overthrow of a Monarchy to give this Power to many. This was the mistake of *Philip* II. after the death of *Lewis* of *Requesen,* Governor of the Low-Countrys, in committing the Administration of the Affairs of *Flanders* to the Council of State of that Country. For the People, when they saw themselves delivered from the Yoke of a Spanish Governor, were not afraid of a Power, which being divided among many, seem'd unto 'em a kind of a Republick. Besides, the Interest and Advice of those who were of this Council never agreeing, the People had a fair pretence not to obey, standing neuter among so many Masters, who did not know how to command. 'Tis almost impossible, says *Commines,* that many great Lords of the same Quality and Estate, should be able to hold long together, unless there be one Superior to command 'em, and 'tis necessary that he should be Wife and well Approved whom they must all obey. And a little after, he gives this reason for it. Because, says he, they have so many things to dispatch and agree among themselves, that half of the time is lost before they can conclude any thing. *The last Chap. of Book 1. of his Memoirs. Cabrera* says, that a Prince has need of Counsel and of Ministers to assist him in the Government; for though he be an able Prince, yet he can't know every thing; but they must not be his companions in the Government, because being only his Instruments, 'tis fit he should use 'em as he pleases. *Chap. 7. of the first book of his History.*

236:10 *Consuls*] Because Liberty began with the Consulship, he affected to propose all things by the Consuls, to amuse the People, and even the Senate, by an image of the ancient Republick. *Arcanum enim novi status imago antiqui.*

236:15–16 *Augustus*] The Edicts of a Prince ought always to be short, for they are Laws and Commandments, of which it belongs not to Subjects to examine the reasons. 'Tis the business of a Doctor to alledge reasons, but not of a Legislator, who ought to make himself obey'd by Authority and not by Persuasion. If reasons were given to Subjects, they would examine them; and this Inquiry would carry 'em to Disobedience when they did not think those Reasons good. The force of a Law, does not formally consist in the Justice of it, but in the Authority of the Legislator; and therefore Kings, who are the Supreme Legislators, must be obeyed, because they have establish'd such and such Laws, and not because their Laws seem just to us.

236:27 *Senate*] He acted the part of a Republican in the Senate, because that was the only place where there yet remain'd any shadow of the ancient Liberty.

236:27–28 *dissimulation*] 'Tis the Interest of Courtiers to discover the Sentiments of the Prince, in the beginning of his Reign, to know how to behave themselves towards him; but 'tis the Interest of the Prince not to reveal or declare any thing in his affairs, that may exercise their Curiosity. For if they are before hand in discovering what is in his breast, he will never come to know what is in their hearts. *Lleva la ventaja,* says a Spanish Proverb, *el que vee el juego al companero.*

236:34 *Common-Wealth*] In an Elective Empire the Prince ought always to declare, that he holds the Kingdom from them who have a right to Elect, though he obtained it by other means; for otherwise he will be accounted an Usurper, and a declar'd Enemy to the publick Liberty, and by consequence his Life will be always in danger. Nothing can be said more judicious, nor more agreeable to a Republick, or to an Elective State, than that which *Galba* said of his Election to the Empire. Under the reigns of *Tiberius, Caligula,* and *Claudius,* said he, the Roman Common-Wealth has been as the Patrimony and Inheritance of one Family alone; but I who have been call'd to the Empire by the consent of the Gods and of Men, can say, that I have restored Liberty to the Common-Wealth, because Election has begun again in my Person; and that if the vast body of the Empire could be content to be govern'd by a single Person, I should be the Man, who would revive the ancient Common-Wealth.

236:35 *Woman*] In times past, the great Men thought it a dishonour, to be obliged to Women for their Fortune, as if they had been preferr'd by their Favour, rather than by their own Merit. But at this day, we are not so nice in that respect. The *Ruelle* advances far more than the Sword.

237:6 *Father*] The Prince who Honours and requires others to honour the Memory and Ashes of his Predecessors, gives an example to his Successors, which obliges them to pay him the same respect after his death. *Suetonius* relates, that 'twas said, *Cæsar* had secured his own Statues and Images from being broken, by restoring the Statues of *Sylla* and *Pompey,* which the People had thrown down during the Civil Wars. In *Poland* the King elect is not crown'd till the dead King be buried: (*Piasecki in his Chronicle.*) which is probably done out of respect to the dead, who surrenders not the

Crown till he has received burial. For the King Elect, does not act as King, nor Seals the Letters he writes to Foreign Princes with the Arms of the Kingdom, till after his Coronation. *Philip* II. King of *Spain,* built and founded the Monastery of *S. Laurence* of the *Escurial,* to be the burying place of the Emperor *Charles* V. his Father, and of the Empress *Issabella* his Mother, and all their Posterity, as he expresly declares in the act of the Foundation, reported by *Cabrera, Chap.* 11. *of book* 6. *of his History.* Before he left *Portugal* he staid three days at the Monastery of *Belem,* which is a little place of *Lisbon,* and caused to be interr'd the Bodies of the Kings *Sebastian* and *Henry,* and of twenty other Princes, the Children and Grand-Children of King *Emanuel,* which had been buried apart in divers Convents; being willing to make at least this acknowledgment to twenty two Heirs, who had given place to him to succeed in this Kingdom. *Spanish Relation of the Interment of* Philip *in* Portugal. *Chap.* 16. *and* Conestagio, *Book* 9. *of the Union of* Portugal *and* Castile.

237:12 *Ostentation*] In Princes, Clemency is often an effect of their Vanity, or of their good Nature.

238:15 *Justice*] The actions of great Men may be taken by two handles, some commend, others blame them. They receive divers names, according to the different inclinations of Persons who pass a Judgment of 'em. *Cataline* was blamed for what he would have done, and *Cæsar* was commended for what he did. When there are Parties, every one judges according to the Affection and Interest of that side he is of. The Doctors of the League durst compare *Clement* the Jacobin, who assassinated *Henry III.* with *Ebud* who delivered the Children of *Israel* out of bondage, by killing *Eglon* King of *Moab.* The Spaniards put into their Martyrology *Baltazar* of *Guerard,* who kill'd the Prince of *Orange* at *Delf,* whereas the Hollanders and Protestants have made him a Devil incarnate. In the 14 Book of the Second Part of the History of *Anthony* of *Herrera,* there are two Chapters (the 9. and the 10.) which make a Panegyrick upon this *Guerard,* whose death he calls a Martyrdom. I admire amongst others these words: *Considerando, como avia de executar sù intento, y estando firme con el exemplo de nuestro Salvador Jesu-Christo, y de sus Santos, &c. i. e.* Guerard, considering, how he ought to proceed to the Execution of his design, and continuing firm in his resolution, after the Example of our Saviour Jesus Christ, and his Saints, went the 10th of *July* to find the Rebel, *&c.* as if Jesus Christ and his Saints had given any example of murder! The Inquisition of *Spain* let this pass, as if they approved it. Moreover, this shews how much Men love their own Opinions, and how rash they are to believe things holy or wicked in the sight of God, as their passion moves them. Upon this occasion I shall observe, that the History of the Reformation of *England,* by Dr. *Burnet,* is full of this partiality, every where calling all those Rebels and Superstitious who would not acknowledge *H.* VIII. to be head of the Church of *England,* nor consent to the Laws which he made concerning Religion; nor to those which were made in the Reign of his Son *Edward* VI. and on the other side, giving the Glorious Title of Martyrs to the Protestants who suffered under the Reign of Q. *Mary,* the Sister of *Edward,* who restor'd the Catholick Religion in *England.*

239:1 *War*] We must not always ascribe to Princes the Cause of publick Evils; for sometimes the Times contribute more to them than the Men. A

Prince, who at his accession to the Throne, finds the Kingdom in disorder, and upon the brink of ruine, must of necessity use violent Remedies to give Life again to the Laws, to root out dissentions, and to set the Government upon a right foot.

239:4 *Lepidus*] Sometimes Princes shut their Eyes, that they may not see the Oppressions and Crimes they would be obliged to punish, if their Eyes were open. There are times when rigour wou'd be prejudicial to their Affairs, and particularly in the midst of a Civil War, when 'tis dangerous to encrease the Number of Male-Contents.

239:10 *King*] A Prince ought to forbear to assume new Titles and Honours; for instead of gaining by the new Power he pretends to, he runs the risque of losing that which no body denied him. *Augustus,* a wise Prince, was cautious of taking the Title, which a Thought of only cost his Predecessor his Life.

239:10–11 *Dictator*] The Dictatorship being an image of the ancient Regal Power, *Augustus* would never accept it, to shew that he avoided whatsoever had made his Uncle odious. *Ovid* makes the reign of *Augustus* and *Romulus* to oppose each other, as Liberty and Sovereign Power. *Tu domini nomen,* says he to *Romulus, principis ille gerit.*

239:13 *Rivers*] The greatest Contests which happen among Princes, arise upon the subject of limits, especially when their Lands lie one among the others, as those of the Dukes of *Savoy* and *Mantua* in *Montferrat;* of the King of *Spain,* and of the Dukedome of *Venice* in the *Milaneze;* of the same Republick and of the Grand Signior in *Dalmatia,* and in the Islands of the *Levant.* On the contrary, when Kingdoms are divided by the Sea, by Mountains, or by strong Forts, which hinder a Passage, Princes have less disputes with one another.

239:21 *pretext*] The actions of great Princes have always been liable to the Peoples censure, how wise soever they may have been, the Speculative have ever been able to give probable reasons for their conduct; nor do the Male-contents and the Envious, ever want matter to defame them. When *Philip* II. caused his Son Don *Carlos* to be arrested, all the Courtiers spoke of it as their inclinations led them, for the Father or the Son. Some call'd him Prudent, and others Severe, because his Sport and his Revenge met together. *Cabrera, Chap.* 22. *the* 7*th Book of his History. Commines* paints *John* II. King of *Portugal* as a Cruel and Barbarous Prince, because he kill'd his Cosin-German, the Duke of *Viseu,* and cut off the Head of the Duke of *Bragance,* Brother to the Queen his Wife. (*Chap.* 17. *of the last Book of his Memoirs.*) On the contrary, *Mariana* says, that he was a lover of Justice, and the Great Men of the Kingdom hated him, because he seiz'd the Criminals who withdrew for shelter into their Territories and Castles. And as for the Dukes of *Viseu* and *Bragance,* who had both conspired against the Person of the King and his Kingdom, I believe *Commines* would have agreed with *Mariana,* if he more narrowly examin'd this matter. *Chap.* 23. *of the* 14*th Book, and the* 11*th of the* 26 *Book of the History.* Where by the way we may observe, that the Resemblance between Vice and Virtue, often causes the Common People to confound and blend 'em together, giving to both the Name which belongs to its contrary.

240:22 *deliver'd*] Princes often make Religion yield to their Interests, whereas their Interests ought to give place to Religion. Dispensations for marriages within the Degrees forbidden are become so common, that 'tis not any longer a matter of scruple to marry two Sisters, or two Brothers. *Philip* II. who, according to Historians, had so nice a Conscience, was very near Marrying *Elizabeth* the Queen of *England*, and *Isabel* the Queen-Dowager of *France*, both his Sisters-in-Law, and the latter also the Daughter of the Empress *Mary* his Sister; and matching his Son, Don *Carlos*, with his other Sister, *Joan* the Princess-Dowager of *Portugal*, alledging for a President *Moses* and *Aaron*, who were the Sons of *Amram* by his Father's Sister. *Henry* the Cardinal King of *Portugal*, as devout a Priest and Arch-Bishop as he was, at the age of 67 years, was very earnest to obtain a Dispensation to marry the Duke of *Braganza's* Daughter, who was but 13 years old. Upon which *Cabrera* tells an odd Story; that Don *Duarte de Castelblanco* advised *Henry* to marry, and advised the Jesuits, who govern'd him absolutely, to make him take a Wife that was already with Child, there being no hopes, by reason of his Age and Infirmities, that he could otherwise have Children, *Lib.* 12. *Chap.* 14. *Paul Piasecki* saith, that the Poles abhor incestuous Marriages, and the Dispensations that permit them; and that the Famous *John Zamoyski*, Great Chancellor of *Poland*, who to his Death opposed the Marriage of *Sigismund* III. with *Constance* of *Austria*, Sister to his former Wife *Ann*, remonstrating to *Clement* VIII. that such a Marriage was repugnant to common honesty, and that the Polish Nation would never suffer this Decency to be Violated by his breeding Mares. Insomuch, that *Sigismund* was not able to procure the Dispensation he demanded, till after the Death both of the Pope and the Chancellor. *In his Latin Chronicle ad An.* 1604. I tremble, saith *Commines*, speaking of the Marriage of *Ferrand*, King of *Naples*, with the Sister of his own Father, King *Alphonso*, to speak of such a Marriage, of which Nature there have already been several in this Family within thirty years last past. *Memoirs, L.* 8. *Ch.* 14. Thus the Author of the Satyr *Menippe*, had reason to say, that the House of *Austria* do as the *Jews*, and lie with one another like *May*-Bugs.

240:23 *Pollio*] Princes are reproach'd, not only with their own Vices and Irregularities, but also with those of their Ministers and their Favourites. For people suppose they have the Vices which they tolerate in persons who are in their Service or their Favour.

240:25 *Livia*] Where is the Difference, saith *Aristotle*, in being govern'd by Women, or by Men who leave the Management of affairs to Women? *Polit. Lib.* 2. *Ch.* 7.

240:30 *him*] A Prince, who voluntarily chuses a bad Successor, instead of augmenting, effaces the Glory of his Reign; for his Memory becomes as odious as his Successor's person: To leave a good one, saith *Cabrera*, after the younger *Pliny*, is a kind of Roman Divinity, *Hist. Philip* II. *Lib.* 1. *Ch.* 8. If some of the better actions of the most moderate Princes are ill interpreted after their Deaths, as *Tacitus* sheweth, by the Example of *Augustus*, whom they railed at with so much Liberty, they have Hatred enough to bear, without loading themselves also with that, which the choice of an unworthy Successor draws upon them.

240:34 *Cruel*] In Princes, the Vices of the Man don't unqualifie him for good Government. Thus *Augustus* made no scruple to demand the Tribuneship for *Tiberius*, although he knew he had many Personal Vices, because he knew he had the Virtues of a Prince to ballance them. *Commines*, after having observed in several places of his Memoirs all the Vices of *Lewis* the Eleventh, his Inquietude, his Jealousie, his Levity in Discourse, his Aversion to great Men, his Natural Inclination to Men of mean Birth, his Insincerity, his Cruelty, concluded notwithstanding, that God had made him wiser, and more virtuous in all things, than the Princes, who were contemporary with him; because, without flattering him, he had more of the Qualities requisite to a King, than any Prince that he had ever seen: *Lib.* 6. *cap.* 10. And speaking of *John Galeas* Duke of *Millain,* he saith, That *he was a great Tyrant, but Honourable,* l. 7. c. 7. *Cabrera* speaking of Cardinal *Henry* King of *Portugal,* saith, That *he had the Virtues of a Priest, and the Faults of a Prince;* which was as much as to say, That he wanted the Qualities that are necessary to a King, *cap.* 24. *lib.* 12. of his *Philip* II. There have been, saith the same Author, Princes and Governours, who, notwithstanding great Vices, have been Venerable, for having had Qualities that deserve Reverence, as Eloquence, Liberality, Civility, the discernment of good and bad Counsels, the Art of governing Cities, and commanding Armies, and other Natural Virtues resembling Moral ones; whence arise great Advantages, which make the Persons who are the Authors of them, highly Esteemed and Respected. It is for this Reason, that some have said by way of Proverb, *A bad Man makes a good King.* A severe Prince, who doth not violate Natural and Divine Laws, is never called a Tyrant. The Imperious Majesty of King *Francis* I. although it was excessive, was more useful than the Sweetness and Humanity of his Son, who authorised Vice and Licentiousness, and who, by the Gifts and Favours which he conferred on Flatterers, converted the Publick Good into Private Interest, and left the People to the Mercy of Great Men, and never punished the Injustice of his Officers: *cap.* 8. *lib.* 2. of the same History.

241:4 *them*] This manner of Accusing, while we Excuse, is very much in fashion with Courtiers, who, according to the *Florentine* Proverb, have Honey in the Mouth, and a Razor under the Girdle.

241:11 *Affairs*] The Prince who immediately succeeds a Predecessor who hath performed great Things, doth himself an Honour in exalting him, for besides, that it is believed that the Esteem that he hath for him will spur him on to the imitation of him, he becomes himself more wonderful and more venerable to his Subjects, when he equals him, or excels him. *Tiberius* was not inferior to *Augustus* in Understanding and Experience. The Day that *Charles* the Fifth had abdicated the Kingdom of *Spain,* his Son *Philip* said in his Speech, That the Emperor laid an heavy Weight upon him; That he would not accept of a Crown which stood in need of the Prudence and Experience of his Imperial Majesty, were it not to contribute to the Preservation of so invaluable a Life. Concluding, that he would endeavour to imitate some of his Virtues; since to imitate them all, was a Thing impossible for the most perfect Man in the World. *Cabrera, lib.* 1. *cap.* 7. of his History.

241:12 *Emperour*] It would be a great Advantage to the Children of Sovereign Princes, if their Fathers would themselves take pains to instruct them, I mean those who are to succeed them; for, from whom shall they learn the Art of Government, if not from him who Governs? And, how can they be able to Govern when they ascend the Throne, if they have never been admitted to any Knowledge of the Affairs of their State? It must pass through the Hands of interested Ministers, who will make their Advantage of their Prince's Ignorance, to render themselves more necessary, and who, to maintain themselves in the Power they have gotten, will never let him see Affairs, but on that side which may give him a disgust of Business. On the contrary, a Prince who hath had some share in the Government in his Father's Life-time, enters trained up and accustomed to act the difficult part of a King. I don't pretend to say, that a King ought to trouble himself to teach him a thousand Things, which belong to the Office and Duty of a Præceptor *Majus aliquid & excelsius a Principe postulatur*. But setting Jealousie aside, he cannot fairly dispense with himself from teaching him certain Maxims, which are as the Principles and the Springs of Government, and which *Tacitus* calls *Arcana Dominationis*. And as the Children of Sovereign Princes, saith *Cabrera,* have been accustomed to believe themselves above the Laws, they have absolute need of the Instructions of their Fathers; for besides the Impressions which Blood and the Majesty of Sovereign Power make upon them, there are none but their Fathers, who have the Authority to command them, and the Means to make themselves obeyed: *cap.* 8. *lib.* 1. of his History.

241:18 *Labours*] It is very necessary for a Prince, saith *Commines,* to have several Persons of his Council; because the wisest sometimes err, and they help to set one another right: *l. 2. c. 2.* The chief Point is to know how to chuse them well, and to employ every one according to the Nature and Degree of their Abilities.

241:29 *Augustus*] Although Princes have Secretaries, whose Hand might save them the trouble of Writing, it is so far from being beneath them to write themselves Memoirs of this kind, which *Tacitus* calls *Dominationis Arcana;* that on the contrary, it would be Imprudence in them to commit them to the Ears and Hand of another. There is no Secretary, nor Confident, whosoever he be, that ought to be admitted to the Knowledge of these Secrets. A Prince, who is guilty of this Oversight, will become precarious to such a Subject. *Edward* the Sixth, King of *England,* wrote himself the Journal of his Life, whereof the three last Years are extant. So that if this Prince, who died at Sixteen, had lived longer, and continued his Labour, he would have proved a very great Man. In *Portugal* they have an Office which they call *Escrivaon da puridade,* as much as to say, The Writer or Register of the Confidence, or of the Secrets. And *Mariana* often makes use of this Word in this sense, when he saith, *Communicar sus consejos y puridades.* As this is the most important place of the Kingdom, and which hath never been held by any other, but by the chief Minister, it is probable, that it was erected on purpose to write the Secrets of the King's Cabinet, and thence to prepare Memoirs of State. *John* the Second King of *Portugal,* and *Ferdinand* the Fifth King of *Arragon* and *Castille,* wrote them themselves.

242:7 *Limits*] Whether this Counsel proceeded from Fear or Jealousie, it was certainly good. Power is not always augmented in proportion as it is extended. It is often with a vast State, as it is with prodigious Ships, whose Burden hinders their sailing. Besides, there are Conquests, which are burthensome because they can't be preserved. It was for this Reason, that *Edward* King of *England* would not hearken to the Proposals of *Lewis* the Eleventh, who would have engaged him in the Conquest of *Flanders,* after the Death of the last Duke of *Burgundy;* answering, "That the Cities of *Flanders* were strong and great, and the Country not easie to keep after it was conquered." *Memoires of* Commines, *l.* 6. *c.* 2. The King of *Spain* would gain more by giving up to *France* the remainder of the *Low-Countries,* than by keeping it; for besides, that this Country not only brings him in nothing, but costs him a great deal, it would be much more Honourable to give it up voluntarily, than to lose it by piece-meals after a shameful manner, as it were, by the Attachments of a Sergeant. *Pensees diverses, ch.* or *sect.* 40. This Counsel of *Augustus,* to shut up the Empire within its Limits, crossed, saith *Ammirato,* the inviolable Maxim of the *Romans,* who were ever endeavouring by all ways possible to enlarge their Empire; but *Augustus* knowing by his own Experience the Evils that might ensue thence, thought it his Duty to leave this Counsel to his Successors, to cut up the Root both of Foreign and Civil Wars. And if *Tacitus* gives the Name of Fear to this Advice, it is because it is the part of a wise Man to fear that which deserves to be feared, and to foresee how many Dangers he exposes himself to, who never ceases from invading others. *Commentary, lib.* 1. *disc.* 6. and *lib.* 12. *disc.* 1.

242:16 *silent*] Nothing gives greater Offence to a dissembling Prince, such as *Tiberius* was, than to endeavour to sound his Heart, or to let him see, that you perceive that he dissembles. We ought never to put Princes upon explaining themselves farther than they are willing; when they speak obscurely, it is a sign that there is some Mystery in it; and, consequently, it is dangerous to enquire into it. The Marquis of *Aitone,* saith M. *de Montresor,* went to visit Monsieur, who kept his Bed, pretending to have the Gout, and knew well enough that his Highness acted a Part, but he made no discovery thereof by any outward shew, or by any particular Act to prevent his Retreat out of the Territories of the King his Master. *In his Memoirs.*

242:19 *Burden*] This Answer of *Tiberius* plainly shews, that Princes do not love to be replied upon, and that it is want of Respect towards them to put them to the Trial. Princes desire to be thought sincere, because this conduces much to the obtaining their Ends; but they will not be so.

242:28 *Emperour*] The Praises which a Subject gives his Prince, after he has given him Offence by Words, are never a Plaister so broad as the Sore. The Affronts offered Princes are irreparable, because they impute the Reparations thereof to the Fear which the Offenders have of their Resentment, and not to their Repentance.

242:32 *Life*] A Prince never looks with a good Eye on him who hath married a Wife whom he hath divorced, whether he divorced her out of Aversion, or by Constraint; for if he did it out of Aversion, he looks on the Husband as a Person who hath taken her Part against him, or who knows the Secrets of the Family, whereof he may make an ill Use: If by Constraint, which was the case of *Tiberius,* he hates the Husband as a Rival, who hath enrich'd himself with his Spoils; or as an ambitious Person, who, by the advantage of his Marriage, hopes to advance his Fortunes. The Honour which *Asinius* had of being Father-in-Law to *Drusus,* one of the presumptive Heirs of the Empire, join'd with his ambitious Spirit, distinguished him too much, not to raise Jealousie in *Tiberius. Piasecki* relates, that *John* Duke of *Filandia,* who was afterwards King of *Poland,* was imprisoned by King *Eric,* his Brother, with his Wife *Catharine,* Sister to *Sigismund Augus-*

tus King of *Poland,* because he seemed to have compassed this high Alliance, to enable him to seize the Crown of *Suedeland,* as their Father *Gustavus* had done. *In the beginning of his Chronicle.*

243:6 *Merit*] Kings, saith *Salust,* are more afraid of Men of Virtue and Merit, than of ill Men. *Regibus boni, quàm mali, suspectiores sunt, semperque his aliena virtus formidolosa est.* In *Catilina. Tiberius* was well perswaded of what *Agrippa* had said to *Augustus,* That a Man of great Understanding, and great Courage, could not but be a Lover of Liberty, and in his Heart an Enemy to an absolute Master. *Dion, lib.* 52. *Commines* saith, that *Lewis* the Eleventh feared all Men, but especially those who were worthy to be in Authority. *Memoirs, l.* 6. *c.* 12.

243:14 *Occasion*] Ambition, Merit, Courage and Opportunity, are all that are necessary to make a Usurper. A Subject who hath been esteemed worthy to Govern, by a Prince who hath excelled in the Arts of Government, will always be suspected by the Successor of that Prince, and, which is worse, will fall a Sacrifice, if the Prince be of a sanguinary Temper. It was never doubted, but *Ferdinand d'Avalos,* Marquis *de Pesquera,* who commanded the Army of *Charles* the Fifth in *Italy,* was disposed to accept of the Kingdom of *Naples,* which *Francis Sforsa,* Duke of *Milain,* in the Name of the Pope and the *Venetians,* offered him with the Title of Captain-General of the *Italian* League; for he was a long time in Treaty with *Jerom Moron,* who was this Duke's chief Minister. And that he afterwards discovered all to the Emperour, was an effect of the difficulty of the Enterprize, rather than of his Fidelity, which *Charles* the Fifth ever after suspected.

243:14 *seize it*] A Prince can never give better instructions to his Successor, than to mark out what great Men he ought to distrust. This Knowledge is the most necessary thing to a Prince when he first ascends the Throne, and so much the more, because it is in the beginning that he is most easily deceived and the great Men most forward to make their Attempts upon an Authority that is not yet well established. In the last Counsels, which *David* on his Death-bed gave to his Son *Salomon,* he advised him not to let *Joab* go to the Grave in peace, who had slain two just Men, *Abner* and *Amasa;* to bring to the Grave with blood the hoar Head of *Shimei,* who had dared to curse him, and to cause the Sons of *Barzillai* to eat at his own Table, who had furnished him with Provisions and other Necessaries for his whole Army, when he fled before *Absalom:* 1 *Kings, chap.* 2. *Francis* the First, in the last Hours of his Life, advised his Son *Henry* not to admit the House of *Lorrain* to any share of the Government; foretelling, that the *Guises* would be the Ruine of the *Valois.* Counsel that would have saved *France* from many Wars and Calamities, had *Henry* the Second been wise enough to have made use of it. On the contrary, *Philip* the Second employed all those Ministers which *Charles* the Fifth recommended to him when he resigned the Crown of *Spain,* and especially the Duke *d'Alva,* the Bishop of *Arras,* who was afterwards *Granvelle, Diego de Bargas, Francis de Evaso,* and *Gonzalo Peres,* the Father of *Anthony,* who was so famous for his Misfortunes. And this he did with so much the more success, because *Charles* the Fifth, by a secret Memoir which he had sent him, had fully informed him of the true Character of their Minds, and of the difference of their Interests. This was a Paper of so excellent Instructions, saith the Commander of *Vera,* that if *Tiberius* had made the like, *Tacitus* would have given him Immortal Praises. *Epitome of the Life of* Charles *the Fifth, and* Cabrera, *cap.* 7. *lib.* 1. *of his History. Burnet* saith, that *Edward* the Sixth, King of *England,* wrote in a Book the Portraitures of the Lord-Lieutenants of his Counties, and of the principal Magistrates of his Kingdom, with all the Particulars that he was told of them: *Part.* 2. *l.* 1. *of his History.* Certainly, he had in this found the Secrets of knowing every thing, and consequently, of being well served.

243:22 *Head*] Subjects cannot reproach their Prince more, than to complain, that the State is without a Head, and consequently fallen into an Anarchy. From the moment that a Prince ascends the Throne, he ought to set upon Action, and not to give his Subjects space to doubt, whether they have a Master. *Anthony Perez* said, That the King and Kingdom make a Marriage; that the King is the Husband, and the Kingdom the Wife; and that a Kingdom is a Widow, that hath nor a laborious and vigilant King.

243:27 *offended*] Silence is the most certain sign of a deep Resentment; for whereas the Mouth gives the Heart vent, Silence nourishes in it Hatred, and the desire of Revenge. *Tacitus* saith, that *Agricola* was a little too sharp in his Reprimands, but that afterwards there remained no more in his Breast, so that none had any jealousie of his Silence.

243:32 *Requests*] Most Popes use this Policy; at first they seem not willing to hear any mention made of a Cardinal Nephew, or of the Acquisition of Principalities or Duchies for their Kindred, but after they have acted this Part some Weeks, they call their Nephews to the Administration of Affairs, to gratifie, as they say, the Ambassadors of Princes, for whom it would be inconvenient to treat always with the Pope himself in Person, whereas treating with their Nephews, they discharge their Office with less Ceremony, and consequently with greater Liberty and Confidence.

243:36 *forward*] When a great Man is fallen under the Hatred of his Prince, Accidents are imputed to him for Crimes, as well as voluntary Faults. Besides, there are always at Court, Persons who are ready to dispatch those, whose Death they know will be pleasing to the Prince.

244:12 *lavishly*] Kings are obliged, as all other Men, to honour their Mothers, and to have all the Complaisance for them, that domestick and civil Decency require; but as for Honours, which properly belong to Majesty, or which are of dangerous consequence, they ought not to permit them to be decreed to their Mothers. *Salomon* seeing his Mother coming to him, rose up to meet her, and caused her to sit on a separate Throne at his Right Hand; but as soon as she had asked *Abishag* in Marriage for *Adonijah, Salomon*'s elder Brother, he said to her, *Why do you not ask the Kingdom for him also?* And was so far from granting her Request, which was very imprudent, that he put *Adonijah* to death as a Traitor, who aspired to the Crown by marrying the Companion of his Father's Bed: 1 *Kings, ch.* 2. In *Poland,* they crown the Queen, but take no Oath of Allegiance to her; for the State allows her no Jurisdiction. *Martin Cromer, lib.* 2. *of Poland.*

244:14 *him*] Princes who will retrench superfluous Titles, and moderate the Vanity of their Subjects, ought to begin with themselves. And this is what *Philip* the Second did, to give Life and Vigour to the famous Ordinance of 1586, entituled, *Pragmatica,* where he commanded all those who should hereafter write to him, to give him no other Title in the beginning of their Letters, than *Senor;* nor any other Compliment in the end, than this Form, *Dios guarde la Catolica Persona de Vuestra Magestad;* and after that, the Subscription in the most simple manner, *viz.* only the Name of him that writes, without the flourish of, *Your most humble and most obedient Subject and Servant.* And for the Superscription, these Words, *Al Rey nuestro Senor. Cabrera* saith, that *Philip* made this Ordinance, that Ambition and Flattery might not come to usurp Divine Titles; and to set his Subjects an Example in all his Grants and Letters Patents, he stiled himself only *Don Filipe, &c.* without assuming the Sirnames of *Magnificent, Triumphant, Invincible,* which the Kings *Alphonso* the Sixth and Seventh, his Predecessors, had used: *cap.* 21. *lib.* 12. *of his History.* See *Note* 1. *Article* 38. *Lib.* 4. of these Annals.

244:22 *Augustus*] A Prince, who is disappointed of the Succession of a State, whereof he is the lawful Heir, hath much greater need to be comforted upon the account of the Injustice that is done him, than for the Death of him that hath done it.

244:25 *Augustus*] A wise Prince ought never to alter the Rules made by his Predecessor, if he is one whose Memory is had in Veneration by the People; or if he doth it, Prudence requires, that it be not in the beginning of his Reign, which is always the time wherein he is most exposed to Censure. *Lewis* the Twelfth, saith *Commines,* took possession of the Kingdom, without making any Alterations in the Pensions for that Year, which had yet six Months to come. He displaced few Officers, and said, That he would keep every Man in his Post, and in his Estate. And all this was very becoming him. *Cap. alt. of his Memoirs.*

244:26 *more*] The multiplication of the Officers of Justice, tends always to the Ruine of the People. Whereas it seems probable, that Affairs would be dispatched with more expedition by a great number of Officers, than by a small; on the contrary, they are spun out without end, because there are more People who have an interest to protract them, that they may subsist thereby, especially when Offices are venal. For, according to the common saying, He that buys Justice in Gross, will sell it by Retail.

244:33 *Tribes*] When a State is lately changed from a Democracy to a Monarchy, the Prince, as being new, ought to leave the People the Enjoyment of some of their ancient Rights, to accustom them insensibly to Obedience.

245:1 *Commons*] There is no Yoke which the great Men and the Nobility will not bear, rather than fall into the Hands of the People, and to make court to them to obtain Offices. It is for this Reason, that a Democracy is always of short duration in States where there is much Nobility.

245:3 *Naming*] A Prince newly established, who reserves to himself the naming but of a small number of Officers, so as his Nomination be liable to no Contest, establishes his Power much better, than if he attempted at first to name all. For, in process of Time, it will be easie for him to extend the Prerogatives of a Sovereignty, which the People have once acknowledged. When the Principality it self is in question, the Conditions ought never to be disputed whatsoever they are; it is sufficient to get possession of it, after which, all the rest follows as one would wish. *Ubi sis ingressus, adesse studia & Ministros.* Ann. 4.

245:6–7 *Augustus*] A remarkable Example of Flattery! Those, who by their Office and their Duty are obliged to preserve the publick Liberty, canonize the Person who destroyed it.

245:19 *War*] The beginnings of Reigns are ever subject to some Tempest; for it is then that all Male-contents are stirring, and are for selling their Obedience as dear as they can, by disturbing an Authority, that while it is in its growth hath need to keep fair with all, to gain Time to establish it self. Want of Power in a Prince, Ambition of great Men, who have always a good Opinion of their own Abilities and Discontents in the People, are the three ordinary Sources of Factions, as those are of Civil Wars. *France* saw sad Instances thereof during the Minority of *Lewis* the Great. GOD grant that these may be the last.

245:30 *Stage-Players*] Great Seditions are commonly raised by pitiful Fellows; and if a Rascal hath a Talent of speaking, the Rabble is always ready to lend an Ear to him. The common People need no other Oracles, especially if the Haranguer inveighs against some Minister that is much hated, as they all are. In the beginning of the Reign of *Charles* the Fifth, the famous Insurrection of the City of *Castille,* called *Las Communidades,* (because it was a Sedition of the common People against the Nobles, which afterwards degenerated into a direct Rebellion against the Prince;) This Revolt, I say, had for its Leaders, a Barber at *Medina del Campo;* a Fellmonger at *Salamanca;* a Carder at *Valenca;* a Tanner at *Segovia;* a Barber at *Avila;* and such other Deliverers at *Burgos,* at *Guadalaxara,* at *Siguenca,* at *Vailladolid,* at *Zamora, &c.* Epitome of the *Commandeur de Vera. Bussyle-Clerc* was one of the principal Supporters of the League; and *Peter de Brousell,* who was but an ordinary Counsellor, was the Oracle and the Idol of the *Fronde.*

246:6 *Tribunes*] An Army which comes to consider its own Multitude, and the small number of its Officers, is very apt to desire to free it self from Discipline, and makes a Jest of petitioning for those Things which they know well enough durst not be refused them, if they have recourse to Force.

246:8 *Emperour*] The Male-contents of a preceding Reign, find the beginning of the succeeding to be the most favourable time to have their Demands heard. This was the Policy the People of *Ghant* used towards *Charles* Duke of *Burgundy,* who was forced to grant them all they demanded, that he might not have two Wars on his Hands at once, Duke *Philip,* his Father, having left him one with *Liege. Memoirs of* Commines, *l. 2. c. 4.* Pope *Innocent* the Ninth said, That the beginning of a Reign was not a time for Negotiations, but for Congratulations and Rejoycings, to free himself by this handsom Excuse from the Importunities of those who came to beg Favours of him.

246:27 *Duties*] It is impossible, that an Army should be ever well disciplined, in which the Officers sell Exemptions from Watches, and other Military Duties; or that it should not abound with Male-contents, seeing that all the Soldiers who buy these Exemptions continuing useless, the rest must necessarily be oftner upon Duty, and withal, more exposed to Dangers. *Inter paucos pericula ac labor crebrius redibant.* Hist. 2.

247:19 *Severity*] Firmness is the best of Arms against Men in Sedition, especially in unforeseen Accidents; for in a surprise, a Man not having time to counterfeit, shews what he is, and consequently, all his Courage, or all his Weakness. Thus when a General immediately resists the Fury of a seditious Army, Admiration succeeds into the place of Insolence, and Fear seizes them, when once they see that they are not terrible enough to be feared; and that their General hath Courage and Resolution to despise them. In some occasions, saith Cardinal *de Richelieu,* to speak and act with Resolution, when one hath the Right of his side, is so far from making a Rupture, that, on the contrary, it is the way to prevent it, and stifle it in its Birth. *Second Part of his Politick Testament, ch.* 2.

247:28–29 *Well-speaking*] Eloquence in the Mouth of a General is a powerful means to suppress a Sedition, especially when he speaks *Ex tempore,* as *Blesus* did. But it must be a masculine, nervous, and vehement Eloquence, and without Art; for, according to *Tacitus,* Soldiers have not the subtilty nor delicacy of Gown-men. *In Agricola.*

247:30 *Sedition*] How just and necessary soever the Demands be, which Subjects make to their Princes, they ought to present them with Respect and Submission, otherwise the Circumstances totally change their Nature, *i. e.* of a good Cause, they make a bad one; and they are so far from deserving to be heard favourably, that they ought to be rigorously punished for their Insolence.

247:35 *Reign*] A Prince hath never more Business than in the beginning of his Reign; for besides, that his Authority is unsettled, he is employed in drawing up the Plan of his Government, which is an Affair of great difficulty. A Politick *Spaniard* said, That no Prudence nor Sagacity was sufficient for the beginning of a Reign; and that the case of Princes, at their Accession to the Throne, is much the same with that of Travellers, who meeting divers Paths, know not which to take for fear of losing their way. *Gratian in his Ferdinand.* To be short, what *Tacitus* makes *Blesus* say, *That it was illtiming their Business, to address so a Prince, whilst he was oppressed with the Weight of Affairs,* teaches Ambassadors, that there are Times which are not proper to negotiate successfully with the Princes, with whom they are resident, and that they ought to watch Opportunities, when the Prince is in a good Humour.

248:7 *Years*] There is nothing more dangerous for a Subject, than to take upon him the Commissions of Rebels, for it is in some sort to espouse their Interests against those of the Prince. And besides, the Prince hath always reason to take it ill, that his Subject will Capitulate with him. *Charles* the Fifth seeing Don *Pedro Laso* at the Head of the Deputies of the People of *Toledo,* who had made an uproar, told him, That he would punish him immediately, but that he considered whose Son he was: And he was very near cutting off the Head of *Anthony Vasques d'Avila,* for undertaking to deliver a Letter of the *Communeros, i. e.* of the Seditious of *Tordesillas. Dom Juan Antonio de Vera, in the Epitome of his Life.* The Prince of *Salerno,* of the House of *Sanseverino,* lost the Favour of this Emperour, and afterwards his Principality and his Reputation, for having undertaken an Embassy from the City of *Naples,* which had made an Insurrection against the Viceroy *Don Pedro de Toledo,* (in 1547.) The Duke *d'Alva* having Notice given him, that a Trumpeter had brought him a Letter from the Rebels of *Flanders,* commanded him to be hanged immediately. And this is the Answer, saith *Bernardin de Mendoza,* which Kings and other Sovereign Princes and their Ministers ought to give to Ambassadors, which are sent to them by Subjects in Rebellion, to teach them not to Treat with them as Equals, it belonging only to Princes to send Ambassadors and Trumpeters. Besides, there ought to be no Communication between the Officers of a Prince, and those of Rebels; for Malecontents seeing that Rebels have the liberty to Treat and to Negotiate with safety, are encouraged thereby to Revolt also, to endeavour to make their Condition better. *His Memoirs of the Wars of the Low-Countries, l. 4. c. 3.* The same Duke being General for *Charles* the Fifth in *Germany,* answer'd a Page and a Trumpeter, who came to declare War in the Name of the Princes of the League of *Smalkald,* That they deserved to be hanged, but that the Emperour was pleased to pardon them, and reserve the Punishment for their Masters. *Vera's Epitome of the Life of Charles V.*

248:24 *Camp*] Those Men, who from private Soldiers rise to the great Offices of an Army, are commonly the most severe, because they know better than others the Licentious Humour of Soldiers, and all the Tricks which they use to deceive the Vigilance of their Captains; as also, all the Debaucheries and Injuries which they commit in the Towns where they keep Garison. Such a one in the last Age was Colonel *Francis Veraugo,* who from a private Soldier, and a very poor Gentleman, rose by his Merit to be one of the General Officers of the *Spanish* Army, and Governour of *Frizeland.* He was wont to say, That he was *Francisco* for the good Soldiers, and *Verdugo* for the bad. A Name that in *Spanish* signifies a *Hangman. D. Carlos Coloma, lib. 8. of his Wars of Flanders.*

248:29 *Discipline*] Rigour is the Soul of Military Discipline, and we see every Day by Experience, that there are no worse Soldiers than those who serve under an indulgent Captain. But we must observe by the way, that as Military Seditions, which arise from the Severity of a General, are less frequent; so they are more dangerous, and of longer continuance than those, whereof Indulgence is the cause.

249:16 *Soldier*] *Nam & hi,* saith *Tacitus,* Hist. 1. *malis temporibus partem se Reipub. faciunt.* For, in troublesome Times, the meanest People make a Figure in a State, and private Soldiers have more Authority than Generals. *Civilibus bellis plus militibus, quam ducibus licere.* Hist. 2.

249:31 *Legions*] All Rebels and Traitors cover their wicked Designs with the Cloke of publick Good. The Count *de Charolois,* and other Princes of *France,* having taken Arms against *Lewis* the Eleventh; this War was afterwards called the *Publick Good,* because it was undertaken, as they said, for the Publick Good of the Kingdom. *Memoirs of Commines, l. 1. c. 2.* The Demands of the Lords, adds he in *cap.* 12. were great: The Duke of *Berry* demanded *Normandy* for his Share; the Count *de Charolois* the Cities seated on the River of *Somme,* as *Amiens, Abbeville, S. Quentin,* and *Perenne;* and several other Demands for each, with some Overtures for the Good of the Kingdom: But this was not the bottom of their Designs, for their Publick Good was turned into Private Interest; and, as *Salust* saith, speaking of *Cataline* and his Accomplices, *Bonum publicum simulantes pro sua quisque potentia certabant.*

249:36–250:1 *Revenge*] In Seditions, he is always the most mutinous, who is most hearkned to.

250:17 *Soldiers*] As Soldiers commonly exercise their Hands, more than their Minds; and consequently, understand how to Fight, better than how to Speak; they set a great Value upon a Man who is able to Speak well, and Negotiate, especially when they have Complaints to make at Court against their Generals, or Favours and Rewards to sollicit, which there is some difficulty to obtain.

250:26 *News*] Princes take great care to conceal ill Success from their Subjects, because they have the less Veneration for them when Fortune is against them. The Army of *Lewis* the Eleventh having taken several Towns in *Burgundy*, and defeated all the Forces that opposed them, the Duke, who was then in *Picardy*, caused a Report to be spread in his Camp, *That his Forces had had the better*, for fear left his Army should Revolt, if it should know the News of *Burgundy*. *Commines*, *l. 3. c. 3. of his Memoirs*. But of all Evils, a Sedition, or a Revolt, is that which Princes are most concerned to keep the Knowledge of from their Subjects, because it is an Example which never stops at the place where it begins. It is a Civil Contagion, which spreads from Province to Province, and whose Progress is so much the quicker, as it finds every where many Incendiaries, and very few Physicians.

250:29 *Affairs*] There are knotty Affairs, in which, Princes cannot take certain Measures. Seditions are of this Nature, Severity and Mildness being equally dangerous towards People, who must neither be altogether exasperated, nor wholly satisfied. When the Evil is pressing, the best Expedient is to send them a Person of eminent Quality, with Power to act according as the Occasion shall require, without expecting farther Orders, which would retard the conclusion of the Accommodation. But Commissions of this nature ought never to be given, but to Persons of approved Fidelity. And it was for this Reason, that *Tiberius* sent his Son and his Favourite to the mutinous Legions.

250:33 *Favourite*] When a Prince gives a Governor to his Son, he ought to chuse a Man of Authority, to the end, that the young Prince may have an Awe and Respect for him. "Education, (saith *Cabrera*) is the Source of all the good and bad Qualities of a Prince, and consequently, of the good or bad Fortune of his Subjects." For want of good Education, the Prince, in stead of being the Father and the Shepherd of his People, becomes the publick Scourge, and the universal Plague. The inward Counsel of a Prince comes both from Education and Nature which opens the first Windows to the Understanding, and displays there more or less Light, according to the disposition of the Constitution, which gives the first Lineaments to the Manners and Actions. . . . A Prince's Son is born with no more Understanding, than a common Man's; he is a Diamond that is hard to cut, but which casts a great Lustre after it is polished. *l. 4. c. 2. of his History*. *Mariana* saith, That *Peter* King of *Castile*, Sirnamed *The Cruel*, had a mixture of great Virtues, and of great Vices; that at his Accession to the Throne, which was at the Age of fifteen Years and a half, he shewed a Mind, a Courage, and Qualities, which gave great Hopes; that his Body was indefatigable, and his Courage invincible in all Difficulties; but that, with these Virtues, there began to appear Vices, which Age encreased, and Time multiplied, and which were owing to the ill Education which he had had under *Alphonso d'Albuquerque*, the Governour of his Childhood. Insomuch, that his Reign almost in every thing resembled *Nero*'s, for he put to Death two of his Natural Brothers, with their Mother; his Wife, *Blanche* of *Bour-*

bon, to gratifie his Concubine; the Queen of *Arragon,* his Aunt by the Mother's side; the Infant, *John* of *Arragon,* his Cousin-German; *Joan* of *Lara,* his Sister-in-Law; and many more Princes and Lords: *c.* 16, *&c.* l. 16, *& 17. of his History of Spain.*

251:12–13 *Threatenings*] In Seditions, whether Popular or Military, none dares speak singly, but all together; and all they say, is nothing but confused Complaints, and insolent Clamours and Demands.

251:14 *fear*] Nothing strikes so much Terror into Subjects that are in actual Fault, as the Prince's Presence; for *the Wrath of a King,* (saith *Salomon*) *is as the Messengers of Death:* Prov. 16.

251:20 *Wars*] It is a good way to appease a Mutiny, or a Revolt of Soldiers, to shew, that one remembers their former Services; for this Remembrance induces them to return to their Duty, in hopes of being rewarded for them. Besides, after Promises and fair Means have been tried, the Prince may justly treat them with Rigour, when once he hath reduced them by Force.

251:35 *Father*] *Drusus* had full Power, seeing his Father sent him with unlimited Instructions, *Nullis satis certis mandatis, ex re consulturum;* and yet he would not make use of them, although he ran no Hazard in doing it. An Example, which ought to be imitated by Ambassadors and Plenipotentiaries, who desire to keep the Favour of their Prince. For although the Prince is obliged to ratifie all that his Plenipotentiary hath done, that he may not break his Word; yet he hath a Right to chastise his Minister, who hath not made the best use of the Authority that he hath committed to him. *Lewis* the Thirteenth was willing, at the Desire of Pope *Urban* the Eighth, to sign the Treaty of *Moncon,* which *du Fargis,* his Ambassador, had made in *Spain, anno* 1626, but he might justly have sealed it with this Ambassador's Blood. It is very necessary to be exact in the choice of Ambassadors, and there can't be too great Severity used in the punishing those, which exceed their Powers, since thereby they put to hazard the Reputations of Princes, and the Safety of States. There are Men, who have such an itch to do something, that if they are not kept within the Bounds which are set them, by the fear of being ruined without Remedy, there will always some be found, who will chuse rather to make an ill Treaty, than none at all. *His Pol. Testament, part 2. ch.* 6.

252:10 *Soldiers*] It is usual for Princes to consult with none, when they will dispense Favours, that they may have the whole Honour thereof themselves: But when some unjust Action, or at least some odious Thing is to be done, they are willing to call in Counsellors, that the Hatred of the Malecontents may fall upon them. And this is what *Tiberius* did upon this Occasion, when finding it not convenient to grant the *Veterans* what they demanded of him, he referred them to the Senate, where he knew they would succeed worse, the Senate taking care not to grant that, which they perceived he would refuse.

252:22 *inflexible*] Counsels are always ascribed, to that Minister, who is believed to be of the greatest Power, or of the greatest Abilities. As such a Minister hath the greatest Share in the Glory of Successes, so he is also more exposed than others to the Hatred and Revenge of Disaffected Persons. The Duke of *Alva* was insupportable to the *Netherlanders,* because they knew, that he had been an Enemy to their Nation from the Time of *Charles* the Fifth, and the Author of all the Evil Counsels, which had been taken to bring the Country into absolute Subjection. *Sir W. Temple, c.* 1. *of his Remarks on Holland.* "But, saith *Pagliari,* I doubt much, whether they who attribute to the Ministers all odious Resolutions, are well informed whence they proceed; or rather, I believe, that they beat the Saddle, because they dare not beat the Horse." *In the* 71st *of his Observations on Tacitus.*

253:8–9 *Amazement*] There is nothing which makes the common People more Superstitious than Fear, nor which makes them more fearful than Superstition. For this Reason, Chance hath oftentimes greater Share in the good or ill Success of dangerous Enterprizes, than the Conduct of those who are the Authors of them. The Deputies of *Bohemia* having entred by Surprize into the Privy-Chamber of the Emperour *Frederick* the Second, and threatning him with their Arms in their Hands, That they would do themselves Right, if he did not grant them all their Demands, chang'd their Threats into Submission and Fear, upon the casual coming of *Walstein* with a new-rais'd Regiment, which he brought to shew the Emperour; and the Thunder ceased on a sudden.

253:11–12 *Wisdom*] To know how to make use of the Occasion, is an infallible Mark of the Ability of a Prince, and particularly of a General of an Army. Occasion is the Mother of great Events, *Opportunos magnis conatibus transitus rerum,* saith *Tacitus, Hist.* 1. The Definition, or rather Description, which *Cabrera* gives of it, deserves a place here, as an Instruction necessary for these who manage great Affairs. "They, (saith he) who boast of starting Occasions, discover sufficiently, that they know not what an Occasion is; for if Wit is the Contriver thereof, it is no longer an Occasion, but a Contrivance: And although it is sometimes founded with Industry, it is notwithstanding quite another Thing." It is necessary for a Prince to lay hold on it at the very nick of Time, equally avoiding the being too soon, or too late. Persons that are too quick, lose it by their Precipitation, because they scarce see the Shadow of it; but they run to catch it. They who are slow, miss it also; for as in its Nature it is perpetually in motion, they are not able to take notice of it at the moment it passes before them; nor to lay hold on it at the very instant that they do take notice of it. There is Understanding required to foresee it, and Patience to wait for it, till it comes. If Things depended only on Fortune, or only on our Wills, there would be no great difficulty in managing them, because Chance, or our Choice, would be our Guide; but when there is a necessity of joining Fortune, Art and Will together, there is need both of Patience and Judgment to make them act in Concert, which renders them twice stronger. We may easily make use of Art and Will when we please, but not of Fortune, with which we must absolutely comply, in observing the Seasons of her good Humour, without ever exacting of her what we see she obstinately refuses us, or drawing back when she gives us Encouragement to hope for what we desire. *His History, l.* 12. *c.* 9.

253:26 *Singly*] There are few People, who are Proof against the Charms of Interest. During the War of *Paris,* all the Generals of the Sling were meditating on their particular Accommodation, and each had his secret Correspondence with the Court, to make his Conditions the better. The Counsellor *Brousell* grew tractable, and *Mazaranized,* after he had a secret Promise of the Government of the *Bastille* for his eldest Son. *Memoirs of the*

Minority of Lewis *the Fourteenth.* The Sieur *de Villeroy,* saith the Chancellor *de Riverny,* was engaged as far as any in the League; notwithstanding he quitted it by a particular Treaty which he made for himself, and afterwards returned to serve the King in his former Office of Secretary of State. *In his Memoirs.*

253:27 *Resolution*] One Man of Parts is enough to reduce a whole Multitude to Obedience. Every Thing puts Fear into People who are in Sedition, when their first Heat is over, and a wise Man comes to deal with them, who excites in them the Desire of Impunity, which, according to *Tacitus,* battles all the Enterprizes which are formed against a Prince.

254:1 *Blood*] There is an Eloquence of the Looks, of the Gesture, of the Countenance, which oftentimes prevails more, than that of the greatest Orators. Subjects don't so much regard what their Prince says to them, as the manner after which he speaks it; every thing that he saith, is effectual, if he knows how to speak with Majesty. He ought to speak not as one who is about to Perswade, but as one who hath a Right to Command, and is able to make himself be Obeyed.

254:3 *Threatnings*] The Minister, whom a Prince sends to suppress a Sedition, or a Revolt of Soldiers, ought to take care of nothing more, than of doing any Thing; or suffering any Word to slip from him, that may be taken for a sign of Fear. For if once they come to perceive that he hath Fear, they shall impute it to the Knowledge which they will believe he hath of the Weakness of the Prince, rather than to his own want of Courage or Resolution. What *Commines* saith upon the occasion of the Town of *Nanci* surrendred to the Duke of *Lorraine* by a Lord of the House of *Crouy,* named *de Bievres,* who commanded in it for the Duke of *Burgundy,* shews of what Importance it is to be firm and resolved amongst Soldiers. "The *English,* (saith he) tired because the Duke of *Burgundy* delayed so long to relieve them, began to murmur, and to despair of Succours, and told the Lord *de Bievres,* that they would Capitulate without him, if he did not Capitulate." Although he was a good Officer, yet he had so little Resolution as to use Intreaties and Remonstrances, and if he had spoken more boldly, I believe, that it had been taken better from him; for the next Day, or two Days, after the Place was surrendred, the Duke of *Burgundy* came, well accompanied, as the Occasion required. *Memoirs, l.* 5. *c.* 5. In great Dangers, a General ought to put on a better Countenance; it is not always amiss to fear, but it is always unbecoming not to know how to conceal it. A Captain's Countenance ought to be armed with Dissimulation, as his Body with Steel, otherwise he will be betrayed sooner by his Eyes, than by his Soldiers.

254:14 *Multitude*] Shame is a Passion that is not to be found in the Multitude, but to compensate this, they are mightily subject to Fear. Thus Rigour hath the same Effect upon them, that the Point of Honour hath upon particular Persons.

254:19 *Mutiny*] Rebellions require an unrelenting Physician, that immediately cures by cutting and burning; for otherwise, the Cure will be long and difficult. Princes therefore never pardon the Ringleaders of a Revolt, or a Sedition, because they who sin without Example, are alone more culpable than all those who follow their Example, and consequently deserve less Compassion. Besides, there would be no Seditions or Rebellions, if there were no Incendiaries, forasmuch as the multitude sees only by Trust.

254:20 *Severity*] Of all Counsels which are given Princes, those appear to them to be the best, which are most agreeable to their Tempers. When a Prince is cruel or severe, and also affronted by Disrespect, it is in vain to advise him to Clemency. Cardinal *Spinosa,* and Prince *Rui Gomez,* found it not convenient to send the Duke of *Alva* Governour into the *Low-Countries,* because, in their Opinion, his Rigour would exasperate the Minds of that People, whereas they ought to have been softned; but as it was in this very Particular, that the Duke resembled and pleased *Philip* the Second, he was preferred before the Duke of *Feria,* [*Gomez Figueroa,*] whom the Cardinal and the Prince proposed, and who being equal to *Alva* in Quality, in Prudence, in greatness of Courage, and in Civil and Military Experience, surpassed him in Moderation and in Liberality, and was also more beloved by the King. *Cabrera's Hist. l. 7. c. 7.*

254:22 *Death*] It is the Fate of the Heads of Seditions and Rebellions, to be the Victims of their Party; sooner or later they are Delivered up to the Prince, or the Magistrate, to wash away with their Blood the Stain of the common Treason. There is nothing more dangerous, saith the *Florentine* Proverb, than to hang the Bell about the Cat's Neck. And this is what they do, who by a false Bravery, or rather by a fatal Rashness, put themselves at the Head of a Party, which upon the first Check, or the first Alarm, will sell them for an Amnesty.

254:23 *Tent*] If the Duke of *Alva* had put the Earls of *Egmont* and of *Horne* to Death in Prison, the *Flemmings* might perhaps have had less Compassion for them, and less Resentment against him and the Prince. This Execution, saith Sir *W. Temple,* put them beyond all Patience; so that one may say, that the end of the Lives of these Lords was the beginning of the Troubles, which spilt so much Blood in *Europe,* and which cost *Spain* a good part of these Provinces. *Remarks on the United Provinces, cap.* 1.

255:3 *Rebels*] Nothing hath a greater Force on the Multitude, saith *Quintus Curtius,* than Superstition; how inconstant and furious soever they be, they will always obey the Divines better than their Governours, if once their Minds be struck with false Images of Religion: *lib.* 4.

255:15 *rebell'd*] Nothing gives greater opportunity to an Army, that hath great pretentions, to Revolt, than the Absence of a General. The farther off Punishment is, the less they fear it. (*Germanicus* was then in the *Gaules.*)

255:19 *Legions*] It is very natural to believe, that a Prince, who hath his Sword in his Hand, and Soldiers entirely devoted to his Service, will not suffer himself to be deprived of a Kingdom that of Right belongs to him, especially if he, who hath taken Possession of it, be odious, both to the common People, and the Nobility, as *Tiberius* was. It is rather Cowardice, than Moderation, to suffer it. Want of Power may be excused, but never want of Courage, especially in a Person, who ought to inspire others with it.

255:28 *Cecina*] The Revolt of a Province, or of an Army, ought to be carefully concealed from other Armies and Provinces, for fear lest such an Example should draw them to Revolt likewise. It was for this Reason, that the *Burgundians* having been defeated, their Duke, who saw all his Affairs grow worse and worse, and his principal Servants desert him, and go over to *Lewis* the Eleventh, caused a Report to be spread in *Picardy,* and in *Flanders,* that his Army of *Burgundy* had had the better. *Commines's Memoirs, l. 3. c. 9.*

255:31 *Idleness*] There is nothing more contrary to Military Discipline than Idleness, saith *Paterculus. Res disciplinæ inimicissima otium: Hist.* 2. *c.* 78. It was for this Reason, that *Augustus* hardned his Soldiers by almost continual Expeditions in *Dalmatia* and *Illyria;* that *Cassius,* a Governor of *Syria,* exercised his Legions in times of Peace, with as much Care, as if he had been in open War. *Tacit. Ann.* 12. A *Lacedemonian* said, That nothing was to be done with an Army without Discipline, and that Soldiers ought to fear their General more than their Enemies.

256:26 *Caligula*] There is no Enemy, from whom Princes have more reason to fear Attempts against their Lives, than from an undaunted Man, who is animated with Resentment against them, and particularly, if he be a Man who hath a mighty Passion to make his Name memorable to Posterity. *Machiavel* describes, that *Jerom Olgiate,* who was one of the three Assassins of *Galeas* Duke of *Milain,* very much like this *Chærea,* when he saith, That this Cavalier, who was but 23 Years old, underwent his Punishment with no less Courage, than he had executed his Enterprize; and that seeing the Executioner with the Sword in his Hand, he spoke these Words; *Mors acerba, fama perpetua, stabit vetus memoria facti.* Lib. 7. of his History of *Florence.*

257:12 *unjust*] For, according to *Seneca,* The more Unjust our Hatred is, the more Obstinate it is: *Pertinaciores nos facit iniquitas iræ.* And, according to *Tacitus,* It is the Nature of Man always to hate those whom he hath injured: *Proprium humani ingenii est, odisse quem læseris.* In *Agric. Maugiron,* saith Queen *Margaret,* having quitted the Service of my Brother, [the Duke of *Alenson,*] bore so mortal a Hatred to him, (as 'tis usual for him that doth the Injury, never to forgive,) that he plotted his Ruine by all ways possible: *l.* 2. *of her Memoirs.*

257:14 *Empire*] The People always imagine fine Things of those, whom they desire should Reign. Possibly it might have fared with *Drusus* and *Germanicus,* had they come to the Empire, as it did with those two Kings of the *Suevi, Vangio* and *Sido,* who, *Tacitus* saith, were passionately loved before they Reigned, and as much hated when they Reigned: *Ann.* 12. At least, we may say of *Drusus* and his Son, what *Tacitus* saith of *Britannicus,* that *Periculis commendatus retinuit famam sine experimento;* that both of them dying in the Flower of their Age, (at the Age of 30 Years,) and both by Poison, their Misfortune hath preserved a grateful Fame of their Modesty, which possibly they would have lost, had they reigned. The Mildness, the Civility, and the Familiarity of Princes, who aspire, or who begin to Reign, are not so much the Effects of their Nature, as of their Policy. Add hereto, that the best Men are not always the best Princes. There is a *Spanish* Proverb, which saith, *De mal hombre buen Rey, i. e.* An ill Man makes a good King.

257:19 *Arrogance*] A proud and severe Prince can never love Ministers, who will be beloved by the People; for their popular Humour serves only to make him yet more odious, or at least more disagreeable to his Subjects. It often happens, that the People, and also the Courtiers, make Comparisons between the Prince and the Minister, which never fail of being reported sooner or later to the Prince, nor of ruining the Minister, when they are to his Advantage. And it was one of the Artifices, whereby the Grandees of *Spain* compassed the Disgrace of Cardinal *Espinosa,* whom they could not destroy by their Complaints. *Lewis Sforsa,* Duke of *Milain,* beheaded *Cecco Simoneta,* his Secretary of State, for saying to him, That he could not defend *Milain* against the *French,* but by the good-will of his People; because his Counsel gave him to understand, that his Minister was too popular. Now-a-days Princes have no jealousie in this Particular.

257:29 *Possession*] The next Heir of a Crown, or of a Principality, ought, according to all the Rules of good Policy, to shew himself the most zealous in the Service of the reigning Prince. As he hath more to lose, he hath more to fear; and, consequently, he ought to be more complaisant and submissive than all others. *Strada* attributes the cause of all the Misfortunes of *Francis,* Duke of *Alenson,* to the Envy which he had conceived against his Brother *Henry* the Third. For want of considering, that he was the Heir Apparent of the Crown, and, as it were, upon the point of being adored on the Throne, seeing his brother had no Children; he could not bear, that the casual order of Birth had made *Henry* his Sovereign. Thus looking on his Fortune only on the worse side, he lived in a continual Agitation, equally a Burden to his Brother, and to the State; so that being desirous to Command whatever it cost, not caring in what Country, he put himself at the Head of the Rebels in *Flanders,* who invited him rather to be the Pretext of the War, than to make him their Prince; and who hastned his Ruine, by the eager Desire which he discovered of imposing the Yoke on that People, who had not shaken off that of the King of *Spain,* but that they might live as a Free-State: *l.* 5. *of the Second Decad of his History.*

258:6 *could*] It is a Degree of Rebellion, for People to deliberate, whether they shall obey; they do not seem to have been willing to obey, who have a long time deliberated, whether they shall obey or no: *Qui deliberant, desciverunt.* Tacit. Hist. 2.

258:7 *Augustus*] As the Memory of *Augustus* was pleasing to them, he gained their Good-will by beginning with his Praises: And as they loved not *Tiberius,* whose Humour was wholly different from that of *Augustus,* he made them favourable to him, by putting them in mind, that they had a great Share in the Glory of his Exploits.

258:22–23 *suffered in*] Indeed, all this is worthy of Compassion, but Seditions and Revolts are evermore inexcusable, and consequently, Punishment is absolutely necessary, for fear lest Impunity open the Gate to Licentiousness. "Good and Evil are so contrary, that they ought not to be put in the Ballance against one another. They are two Enemies, betwixt whom there ought to be no Quarter, nor Exchange given: If one deserves Reward, the other doth Punishment; and both of them ought to be treated according to their Merit." *Chap.* 5. *of the Second Part of the Politick Testament.* Otherwise the Hopes, which every one will have of obtaining Pardon in consideration of past Services, will make them not care how they offend. *Manlius,* who had defended the Capitol against the *Gauls,* whence he was honoured with the Name of *Capitolinus,* and of *Protector of the People,* notwithstanding he recounted the long Services which he had done his Country, and shewed the Scars of Three and thirty Wounds which he had received in several Fights; the *Romans* condemn'd him to Death, as soon as his Adversaries had proved that he aspired to Regal Power. There is an indispensable Necessity of proceeding thus, according to the Opinion of *Machiavel,* in his 24*th chap. of l.* 1. *of his Discourses;* and of *Scipio Am-*

mirato, in the *7th Disc. of l. 2. of his Commentary on Tacitus.* And it is also the Opinion of *Tacitus* himself, who saith, That the City of *Treves* effaced by its Revolt all the Merit of the great Services which it had done to the *Romans.* Hist, 4.

258:31 *Age*] In a State which is governed by Military Maxims, and whose Subjects are Warlike, as were the *Romans,* the rewarding of Soldiers is the principal part of Government: For the expectation of Rewards, supports Emulation, Affection, Labour, and Discipline. And besides, there is nothing more Unjust, nor which doth greater Dishonour to the Prince, than to suffer People to die in Poverty, who have spent their whole Lives in the Dangers and Fatigues of War.

258:36 *Tribunal*] In such a Matter, to hear it, is to be Criminal. It is not enough to be innocent, especially under a jealous and mistrustful Prince, as *Tiberius* was; a Person must also act so, that the Prince may believe, that he hath neither Will nor Power to be culpable. With Princes, it is a Crime to be thought worthy to Reign; at least; it is a Rock, on which the Fortunes of the bravest Men have been split. *Vespasian,* by the Counsel of *Mucian,* his Chief Minister, put to Death *Calpurnius Galerianus,* who yet had never meddled with any dangerous Affair, because his illustrious Birth, his Youth, and his graceful Meen, made him talk'd of, as of a Man that was worthy to possess the Empire. Although *Verginius* had refused to accept it, he was yet always suspected by *Galba,* and kept near him to secure his Fidelity. *Tacit. Hist.* 4. & 1. Although Don *John* of *Austria* had not only rejected the Offers of the Sovereignty of the Low-Countries, but also punished with his own Hand the Person who had made him the Proposals of it. *Philip* the Second reported much, that he had given him the Government: For there are Suspicions, says *Strada,* which the greatest Innocence can never cure; and how good an Opinion soever Princes may have of the Fidelity of the great Men whom they employ, they have always a jealous Spirit, and are inclined to believe, that they grow weary of being Obedient and Faithful; and that it is Prudence to use such Precautions, that a Subject, who have once had the Moderation to refuse the Soveraignty, may never be capable to accept it: *L.* 10. *of his First Decad.* It was well the Marquis of *Pesquera* died a little time after he had revealed to *Charles* the Fifth, that the Pope, the Duke of *Milan,* and the *Venetians,* offered him the Kingdom of *Naples,* for certainly the Emperour would not have long left him the Command of his Armies in *Italy.*

259:16 *Revolt*] The first Remedy, which a Prince ought to employ against the Revolt of his Subjects, is to prevent the Rebels from gaining the Neighbouring Provinces and Cities which continue in Obedience.

259:25 *Contempt*] To use Rigour, is to exasperate their Minds, and to drive them to Despair; to dissemble, temporise or comply with the Will of the Mutineers, is to shew that they are feared, and, by consequence, is to increase their Insolence, and to expose to Contempt the Authority of the Prince and the General. What is to be done then in these Occasions, where Gentleness and Rigour are equally dangerous? He must not amuse himself about untying the Gordian-knot, for this will never be done; it must therefore be cut through. After the *Spanish* Soldiers were gone out of the *Low-Countries,* by Virtue of the *Perpetual Edict,* Don *John* of *Austria,* who was Governour there, soon perceived, that the intention of these Provinces was to govern themselves in the form of a Republick. Insomuch, that he was constrained to retire from *Brussels,* where he was at the Mercy of the Estates, to *Namur,* and immediately to recal the *Spanish* and *Italian* Troops, (which he had sent away) to appease the Rebels. (1577.)

259:31 *Years*] It is Prudence in a General, not to ingage the Prince; and yet to pretend to do that in Obedience, which he doth through Necessity. Thus *Germanicus,* by counterfeiting Letters from *Tiberius,* who ordered him to grant them their Demands, dextrously concealed his Inability to bring them to Reason, and *Tiberius* was not in the mean time obliged to make good any of the Promises contained in these forged Letters. And, probably, these Letters were only Blanks signed by the Prince; for otherwise, *Germanicus,* who knew too well how much he was suspected by *Tiberius,* durst not have made use of this Expedient.

259:36 *Design*] When seditious Persons, or Rebels, obtain of a Prince more than they have demanded of him, they have great Reason to believe, that he is much more concerned to deceive them, (as they deserve) than to satisfie them. This puts me in mind of what *Christian* the Fourth, King of *Denmark,* did on the like Occasion, who was so far from discovering any Resentment against Mutineers, who had made insolent Demands of him, that he handsomly pretended to yield to their Reasons, and to be willing to give them all the Satisfaction they desired. And, as a Testimony of this, he said, That he would drink with them; which appeared to them the more sincere, because he often did his Friends this Honour, and because in his Nature he was very familiar: But after he had made every one of them as drunk as Beasts, he caused them all to be hanged the same Evening. This Relation was given me by a *Danish* Envoy.

260:4 *Money*] Princes and Generals of Armies ought to avoid nothing more carefully, than the necessity of making Soldiers wait a long time for their Pay; for want of Pay is always followed with want of Respect and Obedience; and, in the mean time, the General dares not punish Men, whose Demands and Complaints are just. Besides, the opportunity of Acting and Fighting are lost, as long as the Mutiny continues; and there is no security in employing them, whilst they believe that they have a Right to do themselves Justice by Treachery. In fine, the longer their Pay is delayed, the more of their Insolence and cruelty must the People fear. Insomuch, that the Princes Authority remains in suspence betwixt the Impunity of one side, and the desperate Condition of the other. Some *Spanish* Troops (saith Sir *William Temple, c.* 1. of his Remarks) having mutinied for want of Pay, and seized the Town of *Alost* in the Neighbourhood of *Brussels,* the People of this City were in despair, the Tradesmen left their Shops, and the Husbandman his Work, and all ran to Arms: So that the Estates being assembled at *Ghent* in the Year 1576, it was there resolved to drive out of the *Low-Countries* all Foreigners, and to re-establish the ancient form of Government. Which gave the King of *Spain* to know by a fatal Experiment, that nothing is able to stop the Torrent of an inraged and obstinate People, who overturn all that stands in their way.

260:15 *it*] It's Wisdom for a Man to do that of his own accord, which he sees that he shall be obliged to do by force. This Anticipation makes that received as a Favour, which a little later would pass for Constraint.

260:22 *true*] There are Occasions, in which a greater Regard is to be had to the publick Service, than to the Laws; the Necessity being some time so pressing, that there is no means to expect their Assistance, which is often retarded by Formalities. Besides, it is not to cross the Laws to procure the publick Good, in prospect of which all the Laws were made. *Salus Populi suprema Lex esto,* says *Cicero.* 'Tis on these Occasions, said Cardinal *Richelieu* to the late King, in which your Authority ought to go beyond the Forms of Law to maintain Rule and Discipline; without which, a State is not able to subsist. *Part* 1. *of his Pol. Testament, sect.* 2. *ch.* 3.

260:26 *Emperour*] The Affronts offered to Magistrates, are reputed as done to the Prince; for it is his Authority which they resist, and not the Person of him who exercises it. It was for this, that *Charles* the Fifth would never recal from *Naples* the Viceroy Don *Pedro de Toledo,* against whom the City had made an Insurrection, and even with some appearance of Justice. *Ulloa, in his Life.* The Constable of St. *Pol* having given the Lie to the Lord *d'Himbercourt,* Ambassador from the Duke of *Burgundy,* he made him no other Answer, but, "That this Affront was not done to him, but to the King, under whose Protection he came thither as Ambassador; *(it was to the King in* Picardy;) and also to his Master, whose Person he represented, and to whom he would report it." *Memoirs of Commines, l.* 3. *ch.* 11. The greatest Kings, saith the same Cardinal *Richelieu,* cannot preserve their Authority inviolable, if they have not a great care to maintain it in the least of their Officers, whether near or distant from their Persons. For these are Outworks which are attack'd first, the taking of which emboldens them to make an Effort against those within, and afterward against the Person of the Prince himself. *Pol. Testament, part.* 1. *sect.* 7. *ch. ult.*

260:29 *Rank*] A Commander, who knows how to speak with Vigour, and to accompany his Words with some Action, wherein Resolution appears, will scarce ever fail of striking Terror into Seditious Persons, although they be numerous. The *German* Soldiers having made an Insurrection against *Alexander Farnese,* Governour and Captain-General of the *Low-Countries,* he went directly to these Mutineers, with his Sword in his Hand, and commanded the Colonel of the Regiment to send him immediately two Soldiers of each Company, which should be found most culpable, whom he caused to be hanged, to the number of Twenty, in the sight of his whole Army, without any Man daring to speak a Word. *Strada's Hist. Decad.* 2. *lib.* 5.

261:9 *Senate*] When once a Minister hath got the Reputation of a severe or violent Man, all rigorous Resolutions are imputed to him. The *Flemings* imputed all the Rigours of *Philip* the Second to the Counsels of the Duke of *Alva,* because they knew that he had said to *Charles* the Fifth, (who loved them and treated them with Respect, as having been born and educated among them,) that he ought not to give them so much liberty, nor so great a share in publick Affairs, to the great Discontent of other Nations of his Empire, who deserved to be preferred before them *Cabrera's Hist. l.* 5. *c.* 2.

261:12 *Prince*] It hath been a Maxim of several Princes, never to lie twice successively in the same Chamber. *Henry* the Third, King of *England,* and the Usurper *Cromwel,* changed almost every Day.

261:14 *Ensign*] Of two Evils, the least is to be chosen, and consequently, *Germanicus* did better in giving up the Colours to them, than to let them kill him.

261:17 *Character*] *Cicero,* in one of his Letters, saith, That the exterior

Marks of Dignities and great Offices, are but Obstacles to the safety of the Persons who wear them, that is to say, in Seditions; for at all other Times they are necessary to draw Respect from the People. One Day when *Otho* entertained the greatest Men of *Rome* at Supper, the *Prætorian* Soldiers having taken a false Alarm, came to force open the Doors of the Palace. *Otho,* who knew not whether their Design was against him, or the Guests, dismissed the Company; and every one, for his safety, stripp'd himself of the Marks of his Dignity. *Tac. Hist.* 1.

261:30 *Gods*] The General of an Army, which hath mutinied, doth prudently to attribute part of the Soldiers Faith to higher Causes, which have drawn them, as it were, by force; to the end, that this handsom manner of excusing them, may make them more readily return to their Duty, in hopes of obtaining a General Pardon.

261:34 *Ambassadors*] The Person of an Ambassador is so Sacred, that it is more inviolable than even that of the Prince himself, who sends him, would be, were he in the Places where he represents him. For a Prince, who is in the Territories of another, is but under the Security of the Laws of Hospitality, which make but a part of the Laws of Nations: But his Ambassador is under the Protection of the Laws of Nations themselves, taken in the utmost Extent of their Signification, and of their Privileges, provided that he be not in a strange Country, nor for his Pleasure, nor for his own private Affairs, but for the common Good of the two States. The Rights of Ambassadors are even so great, that they efface those which a Prince hath over his Natural Subjects. That is to say, a *French-man,* who should be Ambassador from the King of *Spain,* or a *Spaniard,* who should be Ambassador from the King of *France,* would efface and abolish, by his Character, the Jurisdiction, and all the Rights of Sovereignty which his Natural Prince had before over his Person. Local Customs, which ought to give Place to the Law of Nations, which is the Universal and Common Law of all People, who have a Form of Civil Government, in like manner as the Interest of private Men gives Place without contradiction to the publick Interest. And this is so true, that the Marquis *du Guast,* Governor of *Milan,* having caused to be assassinated on the *Po, Anthony Rinco,* a *Spaniard,* invested with the Quality of Ambassador from *Francis* the First, who sent him as such to *Constantinople; Charles* the Fifth loudly disowned this Action, and carefully avoided alledging amongst the Excuses, wherewith he coloured it, the Birth of *Rinco,* which he would not have failed to insist on, had he believed that it was his Right to have recalled him as his Subject, and to have punished him as a Deserter, who had been condemned for Contumacy in *Spain.* Don *Juan Antonio de Vera,* to justifie this Action of the Governour of *Milan,* which the force of Truth makes him vindicate by halves, when he saith, *Strangers say so, and I am willing to believe it, because it was much of his Character: Porque fue obra muy suya.* This Author, I say, complains of *John Bodin,* who making mention of the Death of *Rinco,* cunningly dissembles, that this Ambassador was a *Spaniard,* that he might give a false Colour to this Action; adding, that if *Bodin* had spoken the whole Truth, it was evident and undoubted, that *Charles* the Fifth might judicially condemn and punish *Rinco* with Death, seeing that he was his natural Sovereign, and that no subsequent acquired Privilege could skreen him from the Punishment of his antecedent Treason. But this

Reason doth not destroy those which I have alledged to the contrary. And the Example which Don *Juan Antonio* brings of *Joab,* whom *Salomon* caused to be slain at the Horns of the Altar, which he laid hold on, is not parallel in our Case, seeing that *Joab* was no Ambassador, as was *Rinco;* nor *Rinco a* wilful Murderer, as *Joab* was, (1 *King.* 2.) To conclude, the Example of *Joshua,* who would not kill the *Gibeonites,* although they circumvented him in obtaining the League which they came to make with him, *(Josh. ch.* 9.) may serve as a proper Answer to all the Reasons of this *Spanish* Lord. *See his Epitome of the Life of* Charles *the Fifth, and the first Dialogue of his* Enbaxador.

262:7 *Revolters*] When Mildness in a General is not seasoned with Severity, it cures Mutineers of nothing but of Fear; whereas they ought to have Terror struck into them, to reduce them to Obedience. The Instructions which *Philip* the Second gave in Writing to Don *Juan,* his Brother, when he sent him to the War; expresly recommended to him in all his publick Actions to observe a Decorum suitable to his Birth, and to his Office of General, in appearing grave with Sweetness, that he might be beloved; and modest with Authority, that he might be respected. *Cabrera's History, l. 7. c. 23.*

262:9 *Son*] The first Thing which a General of an Army ought to do in a Sedition or a Revolt of Soldiers, is to put his Wife and Children in some place of Safety, for fear lest the Mutineers, or the Rebels, seizing on their Persons, so precious a Pledge might serve them as a Buckler against him, and constrain him to grant them Demands prejudicial to his own Reputation, and to the Authority of the Prince who employs him. In a word, every Thing must be taken from Soldiers that may augment or foment their Violence.

262:15 *Danger*] There is nothing which makes a Woman more couragious, than the ardent Love which she hath for her Husband. *Dona Juana Cœlbo,* the Wife of *Anthony Perez,* and *Mary de Regelsberg,* the Wife of the famous *Hugo Grotius,* are two great modern Examples: And when History shall speak of the Disgrace of Monsieur the Surintendant *Fouequet,* it will not, it may be, forget to parallel his Wife with those two Foreign Ladies.

263:8 *Empire*] They who have the Management of publick Affairs, ought to prefer their Country to their Wives and Children. *Cari sunt parentes,* (saith *Cicero) cari liberi, propinqui, familiares, sed omnes omnium caritates Patria una complexa est.* Lib. 1. *de Off.* There is, in *Mariana's* History, a famous Example of what Governors and publick Ministers owe to their Country, in preference to their own Children. The Infant Don *Juan,* Brother of *Sancho* the Fourth, King of *Castille,* having besieged the Fortress of *Tarisa,* in which Don *Alonso Perez de Gusman* commanded, this General's only Son fell into the Hands of the Infant, the General of the *Moors* Army. The Besieged making a vigorous Defence, and the Infant beginning to lose all Hopes of taking the Place, he thought fit to expose to their Sight the young *Perez,* as a Victim to be slain, if they did not surrender. At this sad Spectacle, saith *Mariana,* the Father, without any Discomposure, protested, That if he had a thousand Sons, he would abandon them all, rather than stain his Honour, by surrendring the Place. And, to make good his Words, he threw over the Battlements of the Walls a Cuttle-Ax to the *Moors,* to make use of it against his Son, if their Design was such, and went away to Dinner. A little while after hearing the Outcries of the Soldiers, who saw their Master's Son executed before their Eyes, he ran at the Noise, and understanding what was the matter, he said with a Majestick Air, *I thought that the Enemies had entred the Town;* and returned to eat with his Wife, without discovering so much as any Alteration in his Countenance. So well did this Lord (worthy to be compared with the greatest Men of Antiquity) know how to master the impetuous Motions of Paternal Tenderness. From him are descended the Dukes of *Medina Sidonia. The History of Spain, l.* 14. *c.* 16.

263:9 *Empire*] These Words seem to contain a Sense, from which we may infer, that *Germanicus* did not refuse the Empire, but because it would have been dangerous to accept it, the other Armies and the other Provinces being faithful to *Tiberius.*

263:21–22 *Ambassadors*] To affront Persons who represent Kings, saith Cardinal *d'Ossat,* is to offend against the first Principles of the Policy, and Maintenance of Human Society. *Letter* 283.

263:23 *Rabble*] A seasonable Reproach given by a Prince, or a General of an Army, to People who have some Sense of Honour, or who begin to feel some Pricks of Repentance, is sufficient quickly to reduce them to their Duty, and to make them also more affectionate than ever to his Service. The Prisoners of the Army of the League of *Smalkald* imploring the Mercy of *Charles* the Fifth, by calling him their Father: *Such paultry Fellows as you,* said he, *are no Children of mine;* and added, (pointing to his Camp) *It is these, of whom I am the true Father.* Words which equally augmented the Shame of the Rebels, and the Love of the Soldiers of his Army, and were the cause, that most of the Cities, which took part with the League, returned to their Obedience; and that a certain Count, who thought his Repentance was not equivalent to his Fault, kill'd himself with his Sword, to give an undoubted Testimony of his Fidelity. *Epitome of the Life of Charles the Fifth, by Don Juan de Vera.*

263:27 *Loina*] The more illustrious Extraction a Person is of, the more the great Actions of his Ancestors give him confusion, if he doth not imitate them. As these Actions serve for Examples to others, they lay an indispensible Obligation upon him, who hath their Blood in his Veins, to tread in their Steps. He who boasts of their great Deeds without imitating them, is so far from doing himself Honour, that he makes the Difference that is between them and him taken notice of. Amongst the *Romans,* the Statues and Pictures of illustrious Persons were set up in the entrances of Houses, to put their Posterity in mind, that they had a great void Space to fill up, and that as many Images as they saw, would be so many Censors and Syndics, which would brand them with Infamy, if they should degenerate. *Boleslaus* the Chast, Prince of *Poland,* wore a Gold Medal about his Neck, with his Father's Effigies engraved upon it; and every time he held a Council, or went upon an Expedition, he kissed it with Respect, saying to his Father, as if he had been present, *God forbid, that I should do any thing unworthy of your great Name.*

266:30 *Peace*] Soldiers cannot love Peace, because it confounds them with the Citizens, and subjects them to the Laws, from which they set themselves at liberty with Impunity in time of War. *Militares artes per otium ignotæ, industriosque ac ignavos pax in æquo tenet.* Ann. 12. The Citizens, saith Sir

W. Temple, pretend to live in safety under the Protection of the Laws, which the Soldiers would subject to their Sword, and to their Will. *Chap. of his Remarks on the United Provinces.*

266:31 *Discourses*] An able Prince ought not to take his Measures from what the People say, who always speak by a Passion. *Non ex rumore statuendum.* Ann. 3. It is a good Commendation, which *Tacitus* gives *Tiberius,* that he was always a great Enemy to the Reports of the Town. *Tiberium spernendis Rumoribus validum.* An. 3. So that *Paterculus* ought not to be suspected of Flattery, in saying, That he was an excellent Judge of what he ought to do, and that he embraced not what the Multitude did approve, but what they ought to approve: For, saith he, he was more concerned for his Duty, than for his Reputation; and the Army never directed the Counsels, and the Designs of the General, but the General always gave Laws to his Army. *Ch.* 113, *&* 115. *Amirato* saith, That Princes who disquiet themselves with the Judgments of the People, fall into the same Error with those who scruple certain things which are not sinful; for as the Scrupulous sin by the Opinion which they have of sinning, altho they have not sinn'd; so Princes, who are concerned to hear the People blame what they have done, or are doing with good Counsel, and thorough Information, shew that they have not acted upon certain Principles, but by false Prejudices. *Disc.* 7. *of l.* 3. A Baron of *Chevreau,* who served in *Flanders* under the Duke of *Alva,* perceiving that the Duke would not hazard a Battel, which the Officers judged convenient to fight, threw his Pistol in Anger on the Ground, saying, "The Duke will never fight." To whom the Duke (who had heard him) answered, *That he was pleased to see the Desire which the Soldiers had to fight the Enemy, because their Profession required it; but that a General ought to consider nothing but conquering.* It is ordinary for Soldiers, (saith the Author who furnishes me with this Example) to desire to fight, to get Reputation by shewing their Courage; but the Reputation of Generals depends upon knowing how to conquer without losing a Soldier, if it be possible; and, consequently, not to fight, unless they are invited to it by the Necessity of relieving a Place, or by a most certain Advantage. Thus they ought never to comply with the Will of the Soldiers, if Reason doth not absolutely require it; for a Captain hath never suffer'd himself to be prevail'd on by the Discourses and Importunities of his Army, but he hath been afterwards beaten by his Enemies. *Bernard. de Mendozas's Memoirs, l.* 4. *ch.* 11.

266:32 *Empire*] The capital City of a Kingdom, according to *Tacitus,* is the Centre and Helm of Affairs, *Caput Rerum,* and consequently, the Prince's Presence is most necessary there, especially in the beginning of a Reign. If the Great *Pompey* had not left *Rome,* where he was the strongest, *Cæsar* would have had a great Difficulty to have entred it. *Philip* the Second consulting in his Council, Whether he should go into *Flanders,* Don *John Manriqua de Lara* said wisely, That the War being in a remote Country, the King ought not to leave the Heart of his Kingdom, whence issued out the Strength and the Preservation of all the other Parts. *Cabrera's Philip the Second, l.* 7. *c.* 7. In the Year 1591, the City of *Saragossa* having made an Insurrection against him about the Privileges of the Tribunal, which they call *El Justitia,* he would never go thither, although the People of *Madrid,* and several even of the Grandees aggravated the Danger; and when they had reported to him, what every one said of him on this Occasion, he answered, That it was not agreable to the Grandeur of the Monarchy, that the Prince, for a rebellious City, should quit that, whence he gave Motion to his whole Empire. *Herrera's Second Part of his History, l. 7. c. 20.* No Reason of State, nor of War, saith *Cabrera,* requires, that a King should hazard his Person, because neither Vigilance nor Fortune are sufficient Guarantees for the Safety of Princes, who ought not to ground their Deliberations on the Weakness of others, but upon their own Strength: *l. 12. c. 29.* Don *Juan Antonio de Vera* saith on the contrary, That *Charles* the Fifth had never found a more effectual Remedy against Seditions and Insurrections, than to go thither in Person; and that those who are of the other Opinion, upon the Maxim of *Tiberius,* don't consider the Difference that there is betwixt a Monarchy and a Commowealth; [*i. e.* What is safe for a Commonwealth, is pernicious to a Monarchy.] *Epitome of the Life of Charles the Fifth.*

267:17 *Business*] A Prince, who knows he is hated by his People, can never commit a greater Error, than in leaving his capital City; for if that once come to shake off the Yoke in his Absence, he immediately loses his whole State. The Complaints, which *Tacitus* saith, that the whole City of *Rome* made against *Tiberius,* sufficiently shew, how much his Presence there was a Burden to the Senate and to the People, and consequently, he did very wisely not to remove thence. If *Henry* Duke of *Guise,* who hath so highly extoll'd his Capacity in the Memoirs which he hath left us of his Government of *Naples,* had read *Tacitus,* perhaps he would not have been guilty of the Folly of going out of this City to give a Meeting to a Lady, who sold him to the *Spaniards.*

270:21 *it*] Such is the nature of Envy, that out of Actions which deserve Praise and Reward, it contrives the Ruine of the Authors; so that great Captains, and great Men, always run the risque of being blamed and despised for ill Successes, or of being envy'd and suspected of a dangerous Ambition on occasion of good Ones. Don *Carlos Coloma,* whose Reflection this is, saith, That the Duke of *Guise* having gained the Battel of *Auneau* in *Beausse* against the *Reitres* and the *Suisse,* who were sent as Succours to the *Huguenots, Henry* the Third pretended to be glad of this good Success, but by what followed, it was evident that it was not what he desired. *L. 1. of his History of the Wars of Flanders.* The Cardinal *Mazarin* rejoyced, that Monsieur the Prince had opened the Way for his return to *Paris,* upon which depended his Establishment in *France;* but his Joy was allay'd with jealousie of the great Actions of this Prince, to whom he offered the Command of the Army in *Flanders,* to remove so dangerous a Rival from Court. *Memoirs of M. de la Rochef.*

270:22 *Bounty*] The Largesses which are given to the Soldiers, by a General who is hated by the Prince, and who hath Pretensions to the Crown, pass for so many Corruptions, and, by consequence, for so many Crimes; and, particularly, when the General hath a great Military Reputation. The Enemies of the Duke of *Guise,* (saith *Coloma, ibid.*) said, That the manner after which he had made the War, and the Money which he dispersed into all Hands, (which was not the Custom of the *French*) sufficiently shew'd whence his Money came, and what were the Designs of him who sent it him; that he could never take a better Pretext, than that of Religion, to mount the Throne by the assistance of the King of *Spain;* that *Hugh Capet* ascended it, although his Right was less than that of the House of *Guise,* only because the Command of the Army was left to him; that *Henry* the Third nourished Vipers in his Bosom; that if he any longer deferred the Remedy of the Evils which threatned him, he would see his Fault, when it was too late. It is worth observing by the way, that *Coloma* himself believed, that the Duke of *Guise* had sold himself to the King of *Spain,* when he saith, That the Commander *John Moreo,* who managed the Money which *Philip* the Second distributed in *France,* so entirely gained this Duke, that he became wholly *Spanish. L. 3. of the same History.*

270:36 *Quality*] Unequal Marriages are almost always unfortunate, especially those of Gentlemen with Princesses of the Royal Blood. For commonly these Princesses will make up this Inequality at the Expence of the Honour, or the Estate, of their Husbands: And it is of them, that it is truly said, That Majesty and Love never dwell together. Add hereto, that the infinite Respect which they exact upon the account of their Rank, is insupportable to Husbands, who have reason to be highly displeased at Irregularities, which they dare not take notice of. We ought therefore to observe the Precept of the Wise Man of *Greece,* who advises not to marry a Wife of too great Riches, or too high a Birth, for fear of having a Master in stead of a Companion; or, as an old Poet said wittily, for fear of meeting with a Husband in stead of a Wife.

271:22 *Life*] Men are never throughly known till their Deaths. All the Stains of a Voluptuous and Irregular Life, are effaced by a Generous Death. The Count *de Chalais* did himself as great Honour by his Death, at which he called upon God to the Twentieth Stroke, of the Thirty six that he received from the Executioner's Hand, (an extraordinary Thing) as the Disorders of his Life, and his Conspiracy against the King, had dishonoured him. *Letters of the 19th of August,* 1626. *Tome I. of the Memoirs of Cardinal Richelieu.* Don *Rodrigo Calderon,* the Favourite of *Philip* the Third, King of *Spain,* by the Heroick Constancy of his Death, turned the Hatred under which he lay, into Esteem and Compassion. *Savadra,* Empr. 33. *Un bel morir* (saith *Petrarch*) *tutta la vita honora.*

271:25 *Murder*] How desirous soever Princes are to throw upon others the Hatred of the violent Resolutions, which are executed against Great Men, they are always believed to be the Authors thereof, when they let those Persons go unpunished, who have put them in execution. After that *Peter* the Cruel had secretly put to Death *John Nugnez de Prado,* Grand Master of *Calatrava,* this King (saith *Mariana*) expressed Grief for it, to avoid the Hatred and the Infamy which would be upon him by the unjust Death of a Lord, whose greatest Crime was his Friendship with a disgrac'd Favourite: But when he made no inquiry, and consequently inflicted no Punishment for so horrid a Fact, the whole Kingdom believed, that what all People before suspected of the King; was a Truth, which admitted of no Doubt. *History of Spain, lib.* 16. *cap.* 18.

271:32 *Germanicus*] The Orders of *Knighthood* are not esteemed, otherwise than they are confined to a small Number of Knights. This small Number ought also to consist of Persons illustrious for their Birth, or for their Merit; for otherwise the Great Men look on themselves to be disgraced in being associated with them, and, consequently, the Prince deprives himself of an easie way of rewarding them. *Tacitus* saith, That the Generals of the Army perceiving that the Senate of *Rome* granted the Triumphal Ornaments for the least Exploits in War, believed, that it would be more Honourable for them to preserve the Peace, than to renew the War, which would equal to themselves all those, to whom the Prince's Favour should procure a Triumph to be decreed. *Ann.* 13. In *Portugal,* it was pleasant to behold the Taylor and the Shoemaker of King *Alphonso* the Sixth to wear the Habit of Christ, although in truth they were as worthy of it, as most of those, to whom the Count of *Castelmelbor* sold it.

272:3 *Pleasures*] As there are certain Days in the Year, which the Fathers of Families spend in Rejoycings with their Children, it is very reasonable, that there should be also some, on which the Prince should live as in a Family with his People. *Tacitus* saith, That *Nero,* who was otherwise a very bad Prince, made Feasts in the publick Places, and shewed himself through the whole City, as if all the City had been his House. *Ann.* 15. Wise Princes, saith *Cabrera,* assist at the publick Plays, to gain the Affection of their Subjects, and these Plays, or Spectacles, are assigned to certain Days, to mitigate the ordinary Discontents of the People by Diversions, which deceive their Trouble. *Cap.* 1. *lib.* 9. *of his History. Commines* saith, That Princes, who divide their Time according to their Age, sometimes in serious Matters and in Council, at other times in Feasts and Pleasures, are to be commended, and the Subjects are happy who have such a Prince. *His Memoirs, l.* 6. *c.* 4.

272:5 *Multitude*] A Prince, upon his coming to the Throne, ought to make no alteration in Things, which he finds to have been of long Establishment, the People parting with old Customs with great difficulty. If the Memory of his Predecessor is dear to the People, he ought to conform himself to his manner of Government, at least until his Authority be well established. He must lead the People through long Turnings, and do it so, that they may go where he would have them, without perceiving whither they are going. *Lewis* the Eleventh had like to have lost all, by desiring to undo all that his Father had done. *When he came to the Crown,* (saith *Commines*) *he disappointed the best and most eminent Knights, who had faithfully served his Father in the recovery and settling of the Kingdom. But he oftentimes repented afterwards that he had treated them so, by acknowledging his Error, for thence sprang the War called* The Publick Good, *which was like to have taken from him his Crown. C.* 3. *of l.* 1. *and* c. 11. *of l.* 6. *of his Memoirs.* When he died, he therefore advised his Son not to do as he had done. *Elizabeth* Queen of *England,* at her coming to the Crown, acted directly contrary to *Lewis* the Eleventh, for she employed most of the Ministers of her Sister Queen *Mary,* by whom she had been ill Treated; and although in her Heart she was already entirely a Protestant, she was notwithstanding Crowned by a Bishop of the Church of *Rome,* and ordered *Karn,* who was *Mary*'s Ambassador at *Rome,* to make her Compliments to the Pope. *Burnet's History, Part* 2. *l.* 3, *Mariana* saith, That *Emanuel,* King of *Portugal,* made some difficulty to recall the Duke of *Braganza*'s Brother and Children, who were in Exile, that he might not in the beginning of his Reign shew, that he had a Design to change what *John* the Second, his Predecessor, had done; and that he might not make them his Enemies, to whom *John* had given their confiscated Estates. *Ch.* 13. *of his History.*

272:20 *Varus*] The good Opinion which most Great Men have of their Ability, or of their Strength, makes them often neglect to search the bottom of the Cabals and Conspiracies which are formed against them. I never (saith *Commines*) knew a Prince, who was able to know the difference betwixt Men, until he came into Necessity, and into Trouble. They who act in Fear, provide well against Contingencies, and oftner succeed, than those who proceed with Pride. For which Reason, 'tis no Shame to be Suspicious, but it is a great Shame to be deceived, and to be ruined by Negligence. *C. 12. of l. 1. the 4th of the 2d. and the 5th of the 3d.* About the middle of the last Age, there happened a Revolution at *Sienna*, which serves for a Lesson to Governours. A Spark of this general Conspiracy against the Emperour, saith *John Ant. de Vera*, flew from the Kingdom of *Naples* to *Sienna*, where Don *Diego de Mendosa* then commanded; but this Spark entred so subtilly, that although Don *Diego* had Notice given him of it, he yet found somewhat in the outward Carriage of the People wherewith to flatter his Incredulity, which in the end cost him very dear; for the People of *Sienna* coming to cry out *Liberty*, drove the *Spaniards* and the *Florentines* out of their City, and received a *French* Garison in their stead. *Epitome of the Life of Charles the Fifth.* And this was the cause that Don *Diego*, who had been so great a Man in his Youth, was not employed in his old Age, so that his riper Years paid for the Faults of his younger. Thus *Le Dom Baltazar de Suninga* speaks of him in the Extract of his Life, which he hath prefixed to his History of the Wars of *Grenada*, in which he hath very much imitated the Stile of *Tacitus*.

272:25 *Innocent*] This is what all Governours ought to do, upon Notice given them of Conspiracies which are a forming against the Prince and the State; immediately to secure (saith a Politician) the Persons suspected, and the Places which they command, that they may afterwards at leisure inform themselves what there is in it, and finding them guilty, punish them according to the Exigence of the Case. For, in such Occurrences, Incredulity is perilous; all Delays are dangerous; the least Jealousie is reputed a Crime; and the slightest suspicions make room for Justice to take place, which cannot be too rigorous; Rigour in such a case passing for Clemency, and Favour for Rigour. Thus Princes and Ministers of State, in Treasonable Practices, ought in the first place to take the Buckler of Resolution, and afterwards to unsheath the Sword of Justice, either against the Heads only of the Conspiracy, for Example, or against all that are engaged in it, for the Offence. *In the Memoirs of Montresor.* The Cardinal *de Richelieu* strongly maintains this Maxim: In the course of ordinary Affairs, (saith he) Justice requires an authentick Proof, but it is not the same, in those which concern the State. For in such a case, that which appears by pressing Conjectures, ought sometimes to be held to be sufficiently proved; because Conspiracies, which are formed against the publick Safety, are commonly managed with so much Cunning and Secrecy, that there is never any evident Proof thereof, but by their Event, which admits of no Remedy. In these cases, we must sometimes begin with the Execution, whereas in all others, legal Evidence by Witnesses, or undeniable Papers, is preferable to all other Ways. *Pol. Test. p. 2. c. 5.*

272:26 *Destiny*] The Power of the Destinies, saith *Paterculus*, is not to be surmounted, when they will destroy any one, they pervert his Counsels, and take away his Judgment. *Ch. 57. and* 118. *Commines* saith, *When God is so highly offended, that he will no longer endure a Person, but will shew his Power and his Divine Justice; then he first diminishes the Understanding* [of Princes], *so that they shun the Counsel of the Wise,* &c. *Cap. ult.* of *l.* 5. of his Memoirs. *Jerom Moron,* Chancellor of *Millain,* was esteemed the greatest Politician that was in *Italy,* and yet he fell into the Nets of the Marquis of *Pesquera,* whom all his Friends advised him to beware of, as of a Man, who would infallibly sacrifice him to *Charles* the Fifth. A Thing which appeared so much the stranger to me, saith *Guichardin,* because I remember, that *Moron* often told me in the time of *Leo* the Tenth, That there was not a worse, nor a more perfidious Man in *Italy,* than the Marquis of *Pesquera. His History, l.* 6.

272:26 *Arminius*] It is no small Question amongst Politicians and Soldiers, Whether it is better for a General of an Army to have great Courage with a moderate Understanding, or a great Understanding with moderate Courage. The Cardinal *de Richelieu* gives the Preference to great Courage, and afterwards adds: This Proposition will appear, it may be, surprising, it being contrary to what many have thought of this matter; but the Reason of it is evident. Men of great Courage are not put into a Consternation by danger: and consequently all the Understanding and Judgment, which God hath given them, is serviceable to them on such Occasions: On the contrary, Men of little Courage being easily put into a Consternation, find themselves so disordered at the least Danger, that how great an Understanding soever they have, it is utterly unserviceable to them, because their Fear deprives them of the Use of it. As a General of an Army should not have Courage that is void of Judgment; so neither ought he to have too much Flegm, or too much Speculation; because it is to be feared, that the foresight of many Inconveniencies which may happen, but which do not, may hinder him from attempting Things which would succeed in the Hands of others, who are less Speculative, and more Daring. *Political Test. par.* 2. *sect.* 4. *c.* 9.

272:34 *Enmity*] As Princes seldom marry but by Interest, not for Love, Alliance is so far from being a Band of Friendship betwixt them, that it opens a Gap to new Pretensions, which grow into Quarrels, and afterwards into Wars. The last Duke of *Burgundy* hated *Edward* King of *England,* and the whole House of *York,* against which he assisted the House of *Lancaster,* whence came his Grandmother by the Mother's side; and yet at last he married *Margaret,* Sister to *Edward,* only to strengthen himself against King *Lewis* the Eleventh. But as this Alliance was not made but by State-Interest, and that both of them might gain their Ends, the Duke notwithstanding hated *Edward,* on whom he made biting Jests; and *Edward* offer'd *Lewis* to joyn with him, and to bear part of the Charges, if he would continue the War against the Duke. *Commines, l.* 1. *c.* 5. *l.* 3. *c.* 4. *l.* 4. *c.* 8. & 11. *of his Memoirs.*

273:34 *War*] As there is nothing subject to greater Jealousie, nor more difficult to preserve amongst powerful Neighbours than Liberty, they who advise War, appear to have a greater Affection for their Country, than those who advise Peace, and consequently have more Credit amongst their Fellow-Citizens. It was by this Method that *Maurice,* Prince of *Orange,* who looked on the Treaty of 1609 as the Ruine of his Authority in *Holland,* where he aimed at the Sovereignty, found means to destroy *John Barnevelt,* who had been the principal Promoter of this Treaty, by perswading the People by Pamphlets, that this great Man was corrupted by the *Spanish* Gold, and held Intelligence with this King, for the reduction of the United Provinces to his Obedience.

274:2 *Employment*] When a Subject is conscious that he is guilty of Treason, he ought not to trust to the Prince's Clemency, if he hath not good Security of it. If my Mother was my Judge, said *Alcibiades,* I would not trust her, with much greater Reason, they who have the Prince for Judge and Party, ought to take good Security before they surrender themselves into his Hands. The Cardinal *Alphonso Petrucci* was no sooner come to *Rome,* but *Leo* the Tenth caused him to be arrested, and afterwards strangled in Prison, altho he came thither under the Security of the Pope's safe Conduct, whereof the *Spanish* Ambassador was Guarantee. The Landgrave of *Hesse* was cheated by the Confidence he reposed in *Charles* the Fifth, with whom he had two Electors, and several other Princes of the Empire, for Intercessors.

274:7 *received*] Sometimes Princes, who value themselves upon Gratitude, pardon the Children in consideration of Services done by the Fathers, or by the Ancestors. *Charles* the Fifth pardon'd Don *Pedro Laso,* (who brought him the Message from the Rebels of *Toledo,*) because he was the Son of a Gentleman, whose Memory was dear to him. *Philip* II. perceiving, whilst he was consulting about an Affair with *Mat. Vasquez,* his Secretary of State, that a certain Gentleman of his Chamber observed them both with some Curiosity: "Go tell that Man, *said he,* That if I do not take off his Head, he is beholden for it to his Uncle *Sebastian de Santoio,* who gave him to me." *Cabrera's History, l.* 12. *c.* 3.

274:14 *Temper*] It was much more glorious for *Thusnelda* to espouse the Interest of *Arminius,* who was the Deliverer of *Germany,* than that of *Segestes,* who was a Traitor to it. Traitors have this Misfortune, That they are oftentimes hated and contemned by their own Children.

274:28 *yours*] He obliquely reproached the Infidelity of *Arminius,* his Rival, who having been formerly in the Service of the *Romans,* had obtained, as well as himself, the Privileges of a Citizen, and the Quality of a *Roman* Knight. *Assiduus militiæ nostræ prioris comes, & civitatis Romanæ jus, equestremque consecutus gradum, segnitia ducis in occasionem sceleris usus est.* Patere. Hist. 2. c. 118.

274:31 *War*] Traitors never want Pretexts to colour over their Treason, nor specious Reasons to defend it. All their Remonstrances are full of those, which *Tacitus* puts in the Mouth of *Segestes.* There is scarce any Cause so bad, which a good Advocate can't colour over.

274:35 *you*] It is common with great Men to revenge their private Quarrel under the Name of the publick Quarrel. *Segestes* accused *Arminius* to *Varus,* as a Man who hated the *Romans,* and who rendred their Alliance suspected to the *Germans:* The Accusation was true, and the Defeat of *Varus's* Legions confirmed it; but the Motive of this Accusation, the Merit of which he so extols to *Germanicus,* was not so much an Effect of his Love and his Concern for the *Romans,* as an Effect of the Hatred which he bore to the Ravisher of his Daughter, and of the Jealousie which he had to see *Arminius* more Powerful and more Esteemed than himself in his Country. Thus we may apply to *Segestes* what *Paterculus* saith of the Consul *Opimius,*

That he sacrificed the Son of the Consul *Fulvius Flaccus* (who besides his tender Age was innocent) to the Hatred that he had born to his Father, rather than to the publick Vengeance. *Visa ultio privato odio magis, quam publicæ vindictæ data.* Hist. l. 2. c. 7.

274:36 *General*] Irresolution is the greatest Fault that can be in a General, or in any other Man who hath the Management of publick Affairs. What Advantage can be taken of Opportunities, where Execution is more necessary than Deliberation, by a Minister, who knows not what to resolve on, who fears every thing, and who is equally fruitful in Doubts, and barren in Expedients? Princes have but one good Remedy against Conspiracies, which is to prevent the Conspirators; and all Princes, who have not done it, have been overtaken by them. In a word, Whether in War, or in Peace, Irresolution is the Ruine of Affairs, and oftentimes even worse than a bad Resolution; because there is sometimes a Remedy for this, whereas the other renders the least Evils incurable, or lets slip all Occasions.

275:26 *Age*] It is fatal to great Men to be unfortunate Fathers, and to behold Fortune a Step-mother to their Children. If *Arminius* espoused the Interest of his Father and Mother, as it is to be presumed, he could not expect better Treatment from the *Romans* than what they gave him, it being the Maxim of all Princes, to revenge upon the Children the Injuries which they have received from the Parents. It may be also observed here, that great Men are often punished by the same Evils which they have inflicted on others. *Arminius* had taken away from *Segestes,* his Daughter, who was promised to another; and *Germanicus,* by a just return, took away from him his Wife, and his Son, whereby *Segestes* was doubly revenged. *Commines* makes many Reflections of this kind, whereof this is the most Instructive. Although, said he, the Duke of *Burgundy* had just cause to hate the Constable *S. Pol,* and to procure his Death, yet all the Reasons that can be alledged in this Matter, cannot justifie what he did, in selling him to the King out of Covetousness, in order to have him put to Death, after he had given him a good and authentick Safe-conduct. And as this was at the first Siege of *Nancy,* that he committed this Crime in dispatching the Order to deliver the Constable to the King's Men; God permitted, that at the second Siege of this City, he was betrayed by him in whom he put the greatest confidence, and justly paid for his Perfidiousness to the Constable. *His Memoirs, l. 5. c. 6.*

278:23 *Germanicus*] When a great Man begins to displease the Prince, a sinister Interpretation is put upon all his Actions. The Memoirs of Queen *Margaret* are full of Examples of this, and particularly the Second Book, in which are to be seen, all the Ombrages that *Henry* the Third took at the least Actions of the Duke of *Alenson,* his Brother.

278:24 *Soldiers*] Whereas *Germanicus* ought to have rouzed the Courage of his Soldiers, he ran the hazard of wholly sinking it, by letting them see that, which he should have carefully hid from them. The frightful Dream of *Cecina,* of which *Tacitus* speaks in one of the following Chapters, plainly shews the Effect, which this Spectacle was capable of producing in the Soldiers Imaginations. For,

> *Sommia fallaci ludunt temeraria nocte,*
> *Et pavidas menses falsa timere jubent.*
> Tibul. Epigr. l. 3.

So that although *Tiberius* was angry to see the Care which *Germanicus* took to gain the Affections of the Soldiers, he had yet most just cause to blame a General, who let his Army see, just as they were going to fight, the Remains of the Butchery of the *Roman* Legions.

280:19–20 *Fortune*] To be a great Man, it is necessary to have had the Trial of both Fortunes. He, that hath never had any but Good, knows but one side of Nature, and cannot be expert, because he hath had no occasion to exercise his Industry. He, that hath always lived in Adversity, and in Troubles, runs a great Hazard of being corrupted by Prosperity, which, according to *Tacitus,* hath sharper Goads than Misery. *Secundæ res acrioribus stimulis animum explorant, quia miseriæ tolerantur, felicitate corrumpimur.* Hist. 1. Which made one of the Ancients say, That he had rather Fortune should assault him with Adversity, than cherish him with her Delicacies. It is necessary therefore, that a Man employed in, or designed for the Administration of publick Affairs, should taste of good and bad Fortune, that he may be well acquainted with its Strength. *Anthony Perez,* who had had his Share of Adversity, said very judicially, That Nature hath two Carvers, which labour in polishing the Matter of Man, *viz.* Good, and bad Fortune that one of them is employed in polishing the coursest Part, whilst the others cuts and chisels that which is most excellent, to make a most accomplish'd Work thereof. In my Opinion, saith *Commines,* speaking of *Lewis XI.* the Hardships which he met with in his Youth, when he fled from his Father, were of great Advantage to him; for he was forced to please those whom he stood in need of; and this Good, which was not inconsiderable, he learned from Adversity. And in another place, I dare give him this Commendation, That I never knew a Man so wise in Adversity, nor who was more dextrous in winding himself out of Difficulties. *Memoirs, l.* 1. *c.* 10. *l.* 3. *c.* 12. Lastly, it hath been often observed, that of all Princes and Captains, those have proved the Bravest, and the most Able, who have had the least Share of good Fortune. And Don *Juan Antonio de Vera* saith very judiciously, That when *Cæsar* seeing himself taken with a furious Tempest, said to his Pilot: *Fear not, thou carriest Cæsar, and his Fortune;* He did not mean his good Fortune, but rather his invincible Courage; because, in such a Danger, it is certain, that he relied less on his Fortune, though that had never abandon'd him, than on his undaunted Spirit, and on his Experience, which he had acquired amidst the Labours, and the Hazards of War, which had never put him into any Consternation. *His. Enbax. Dial.* 2. The Cardinal *d'Ostat* speaking of *Henry* IV, I have observed, saith he, in the course of his Life, that of the many cross and troublesom Events, which he hath had in Peace and in War, God hath drawn out Good and Prosperity for him. *Letter* 339.

281:3 *him*] As we ought not to regard Dreams too much, so neither ought we wholly to slight them, especially when they nearly relate to the present State of Affairs, for the Contempt of them is the cause that we neglect to apply Remedies to those Evils, whereof they are the Fore-runners. There is a prudent Mean betwixt Superstition and Incredulity, which commonly proceeds from Self Love, which always flatters us, rather than from a true Solidity of Spirit. The Queen *Margaret* makes a Reflection which is of great weight. Some (saith she) hold, That God doth in an especial manner protect the Great, and that to Minds, in which there shines some uncommon Excellency, he gives by good Genius's some secret Warnings of Accidents that are like to happen to them, either of Good or Evil, as to the Queen, my Mother, who the Night before the unfortunate Race dream'd, That she saw the late King, my Father, wounded in the Eye, as it happen'd; and after she awaked, desired him several times not to run that Day. . . . Being dangerously sick at *Metz,* and having about her Bed the King *Charles* my Brother, my Sister, and my Brother of *Lorraine,* and many Ladies and Princesses, she cried out as if she had seen the Battel of *Jarnac; See how they ran away, my Son hath the Victory! behold in this Lane the Prince of* Conde *dead!* All that were there, believed that she raved: But the Night after, Monsieur *de Losses* bringing her the News of it, *I knew it well enough,* said she, *did I not see it yesterday?* Then they perceived, that it was not the raving of a Feaver, but a particular Notice, which God gives to illustrious and extraordinary Persons. And for my self, I own, that I was never near any signal Accident, either Unfortunate or Prosperous, of which I had not some Advertisement, either by Dream or otherwise; and may well say this Verse,

> *Of my Good, or my Evil,*
> *My Mind is my Oracle.*
> L. 1 of of her Memoirs.

281:32 *Retreat*] The greediness of Soldiers, who are commonly more intent upon Enriching themselves, than upon Fighting, is the cause that there is scarce ever a compleat Victory. This is an Evil that seems to be without Remedy, seeing, that after so many Ages, the Prudence and Severity of Princes and Generals have not been able to put a stop to it.

282:8 *Men*] Reflections of this kind do Soldiers no good, because they serve only to abate their Courage; witness the false Alarm, spoken of in the following Chapter.

282:13 *Germans*] When an Army hath been beaten, it is very subject to take false Alarms: And it is on these Occasions, saith *Xenophen,* that a General is much perplex'd, for the more he encourages his Soldiers, the greater they imagin is the Danger. *Quanto magis jubeat illos bono esse animo, tanto existimabunt in majore se esse discrimine.* Lib. 5. Cyropæd.

282:17 *Prayer*] When Foresight and Counsel have preceded the Danger, Fear is easily overcome; but when Fear hath prevented Foresight and Counsel, Advice and Exhortations will hardly find place.

282:19 *Issue*] If it happens, saith *Onosander,* that a vain Terrour, or even a reasonable Fear, hath seized the Spirits, it is then that a General ought to shew the Soldiers an assured Countenance, and unshaken Courage. *Stratag. cap.* 13. There is nothing that more perplexes the Prudence of a General, than these kind of false Alarms, in which the disorder'd Minds of an ignorant Multitude are not easily recovered of their Surprise. I observe in the Memoirs of *Commines,* that a Squib which fell on a Window, where *Charles* of *France,* the Duke of *Berry,* and *Charles* Count of *Charolois,* were talking together, was like to have confounded and disorder'd all the Princes and Lords who were in League against *Lewis* the Eleventh, if Mr. *John Bouteseu,* who threw it, had not come and declared that it was he, and had not thrown three or four more in their Presence, to take away the Suspicion which they had of one another. *L.* 1. *c.* 5.

283:13 *Councils*] It is rare, for two Generals to agree well together in one and the same Army, especially when they are both Men of great Parts and Experience, as *Arminius* and his Uncle were. The Protestants, who were in League against *Charles* the Fifth, lost the Battel of *Meissen,* because *John Frederick* Elector of *Saxony,* and *Philip* the Landgrave of *Hesse,* who commanded in conjunction the Army of this League, were both too great Captains, and besides, of too different a Humour, to yield to one another. This Battel was fought the 24th of *April, ann.* 1547. The *Turks* had not failed of taking *Malta, ann.* 1565, if *Piali,* the General at Sea, would have held good Correspondence with *Mustasa,* the General at Land.

283:21 *Barbarians*] Amongst barbarious People, the most violent and rashest Persons have always the greatest Credit, for Delays seem to them a sort of Slavery. *Barbaris, quanto quis audacia promptus, tanto magis fidus.* Ann. 1. *Barbaris cunctatio servilis; statim exequi, regium videtur.* Ann. 6.

283:36 *Resistance*] It seldoms happens, that an Army which is commanded by two Generals comes off Victorious. The *Roman* Armies were almost always defeated by *Hannibal,* when he had to do with two Consuls; whereas he was always beaten, or, at least, hindred from being Victorious, when a Dictator was at the Head of the *Roman* Army. As long as the Command of the Army was divided betwixt Monsieur *de Turenne,* and the Mareschal *de la Ferte-Senecterre,* their Jealousie rendred the fairest Enterprizes abortive; but from the time that the former was got rid of his Companion, who put every thing to hazard, Fortune always favoured him.

284:14 *Remedies*] It is not one of the least Praises of a General, to take care of the Health and Lives of his Soldiers. As there is nothing so Valuable as Life, so there is no Benefit, whereof Men have a more grateful Sense, than of it; especially Soldiers, who are exposed to more Dangers, than all the rest of Mankind. The *Spanish* Commentator on *Commines* saith, That the Soldiers set upon the Tomb of a certain Captain, who died at *Milain,* the Words of the Creed: *Qui propter nos, & propter nostram salutem, descendit ad inferos.* The *Spaniards,* adds he, gave not this Praise to the Prince of *Parma* in *Flanders;* for whilst his Army was in want of every thing, he must not want Mules to fetch Spaw-Waters for his Baths. *Ch.* 9. *l.* 6.

284:20–21 *innocent*] In the Opinion of *Livy,* Civility and Liberality are never free in a great Fortune. The Prince can't look upon a great Man, who studies to gain the People's Affections, but as a Rival, who would steal from him the Hearts of his Subjects, that he may afterwards deprive him of their Obedience. *Henry* the Third, saith a Politick *Spaniard,* one Day ask'd his Confidents this Question: What doth the Duke of *Guise* do, thus to charm the People's Hearts? Sir, (said a cunning Courtier,) he gives with both Hands, and when it is not in his Power to grant what they desire, he supplies it with Words: Let them invite him to a Wedding, he goes; to a Funeral, he assists at it; to be Godfather to a Child, he accepts it. He is affable, caressing, and liberal; he carries it fair to all People, and speaks ill of none; in short, he reigns in their Hearts, as your Majesty doth in your Territories. *Gracian's Heroes, ch.* 12. Of all that Don *Pedro Giron,* Duke of *Osson,* did to continue himself in the Viceroyship of *Naples,* and to hinder the Cardinal *Gaspar Borgia* from taking Possession of it, nothing rendred him more suspected, or rather more criminal, than what he did after the arrival of the Cardinal to *Prochira,* an Isle near *Naples.* Having assembled the common People, he threw among them abundance of Money, and when he had no more left, he pull'd off the Gold Buttons which he had on his Clothes, and a Girdle of Diamonds; and after that, by an extravagant Liberality, he also threw his Hat and his Cloke to them, imploring the Assistance of this Multitude against a Priest, who, he said, was not fit to govern a Kingdom, of which the Pope had a desire to possess himself. *Conjuratio Ossuniana* 1612, & 1620.

284:30 *Generals*] *Tiberius* transgressed through Distrust and Jealousie, but *Agrippina* through Imprudence; for the better remembred whence she descended, and whose Wife she was, than whose Subject. The same Commentator on *Comminus* saith, That Distrust is wont to take away the Judgment of Women, but that on the contrary it gives Judgment to Princes, and improves it; that it is a Passion that absolutely masters Ladies; whereas it is a Quality that is absolutely necessary to Kings. Witness *Edward* the Fourth, King of *England*, who, according to *Commines*, was driven out of his Kingdom by the Earl of *Warwick*, because he always lived without Suspicion. *Chap.* 1. *of the Commentary, let. E. and ch.* 5. *of l.* 1. *of the Memoirs.*

284:31 *Consideration*] Great Services draw Calamities on those who perform them, especially when they are Men, whose Birth, Courage, or Merit, gives Jealousie to the Prince. The younger *Pliny* saith, That it is seldom seen, that a Prince loves those, to whom he believes himself most obliged; and, according to the Testimony of *Commines, Lewis* the Eleventh was of the same Opinion. The Reason of this is, because Men do that more heartily which comes purely from Free-will, than that which they are obliged to do by a Motive of Gratitude. *Anthony Perez* saith, That it fares with the great Obligations which a Prince hath to his Subject, as with those Fruit-Trees, whose Boughs are broken by being overladen; and that to have performed extraordinary Services to his King, is a sort of Obligation, which ruines the Favourite.

284:33 *Tiberius*] There is nothing, which a Favourite, or a chief Minister, ought to take more Pains about, than throughly to know his Prince's Humour; for without this it is impossible, that his Favour should last long, or that he should not fall a Victim to his Enemies. *Cabrera* saith, That the Prince of *Eboli* was not so great a Statesman as the Duke of *Alva*, his Rival; but withal, that he far better understood his Master's Humour. And it is to this Knowledge, that he attributes the good Fortune of this Prince, to keep the Favour of *Philip* the Second, to the last moment of his Life. He preserved it, saith he, because he kept him company without being troublesom to him, and without importuning him when he was inclin'd to Solitude. He always bore him a great Respect, and this Respect always increas'd as his Favour, and the Obligations which he received. He discharged the Duties of his Place, without Artifice, and without Constraint. He digested and prepared with care what he had to Negotiate, and spoke his Opinion with a natural Modesty, and hearkned with Attention to his Master's Answer, without ever dilating in impertinent Discourses. He spoke advantagiously of those whom the King loved, and, by a handsom and prudent Dissimulation, he seemed to understand no more, than what the King was willing to tell him. He kept every thing secret which the King said to him, and if others spoke of it, he was the last that did it himself. When he went to Court, he moderated his Train, and never clothed his Domesticks in richer Liveries than the King's; and when he reprimanded any one in the King's Name, he avoided speaking with Heat, and keeping a wise Mean, he inveighed against the Fault, and not against the Person. *His History, l. 7. c. 7. & l. 10. c. 1.* *Anthony Perez* saith, That the Duke of *Alva* one Day speaking to him of this Favourite, expressed his Opinion of him in these words: The Lord *Ruy Gomez,* of whose Party you are so great a Favourer, is not one of the ablest Statesmen that we have had; but as for the Art of understanding the Nature of Kings, I acknowledge he hath been so great a Master, that how great soever all we that are here are, we meet with the Head where we think to have the Feet. *In a Letter to a great Favourite.* The Result of all which is, that a Favourite, or a Minister, who is only beloved by his Prince, is better establish'd, than he, who is highly esteem'd by him.

284:33 *Discontents*] A prudent Minister, and who loves the Reputation of his Prince, ought to avoid nothing more, than to nourish his Disquiets, and his Jealousies. This is so dangerous a Fault in Princes, and carries them to such troublesome Resolutions, and oftentimes so unjust, that there can't be too great a Care taken, to calm the Agitation of their Minds. Happy are the Kings, who have Ministers of such a Temper, as was Don *Antonio de Toledo,* Grand Prior of *Leon,* who having received an Order to bring a *Cassette,* in which were the Letters and secret Papers of Don *Carlos,* tore all those, which might prejudice this young Prince, and his Friends, before he put them into the Hands of *Philip* the Second. *Cabrera's History, l. 7. c. 22.*

284:34 *Ground*] When Princes dissemble their Resentment, it is a sign that they are meditating a cruel Revenge. The Constable of St. *Pol,* who had so much Wit, was so weak as to believe *Lewis* the Eleventh reconciled to him after the Interview at *Noion;* for if the Hatred was so great before, it was still greater on the King's side, who was ashamed that he had spoken with his Servant, with a Bar betwixt them. *Commines's Memoirs, l. 5. c. 11, & 12.*

285:9 *Equinox*] According to *Onosander,* Generals of Armies ought to understand Astronomy. *Inerrantium per noctem supra terras siderum Imperatori peritiam aliquam inesse oportet.* Strategici, c. 39. And *Polybius,* as great a Politician as an Historian, saith, That a General of an Army cannot take just Measures neither by Sea nor Land, if he doth not well understand the Summer Solstice, and the Equinoxes. *Debet perspicue cognoscere solstitium æstivale & æquinoctias, & intermedias dierum & noctium tam auctiones, quam diminutiones; sic enim duntaxat secundum rationera commensurare potest, quæ tam mari, quam terra perficienda sunt.* Lib. 9. *Christopher Columbus* saved his Army, which was perishing by Famine, by the Prediction which he made of an Eclipse to an *Indian* King, who refused to furnish him with Provisions. *Pagliari Observation* 74.

286:18 *Service*] Caresses and Praises are in stead of all Rewards to brave Men. Cardinal *de Richelieu* saith, That *Henry* the Fourth being under an extream Necessity, paid his Servants with good Words, and made them do Things with his Caresses, upon which his Weakness permitted him not to put them by other ways. *Pol. Test. part 1. c. 6.*

286:27 *Acts*] There is no Prince so wise, saith *Commines,* who doth not sometimes fail, and very often if he lives long; and thus would it be found in their Actions, if Truth had been always spoken of them. *Lib.* 5. *cap.* 13.

286:29 *Fall*] This Doctrine can never be too much inculcated on Princes, who, for the most part, presume much on their Power. Would to God, that each Prince, in the course of his Reign, might only meet with such a Minister, or a Confident, as he was, who said to *Philip* the Second, Sir, Be moderate, acknowledge God on Earth, as well as in Heaven, lest he grow weary of Monarchies, and provoked by the Abuse which Kings make of their Power, in usurping his, he give another form of Government to the World. *Anthony Perez, in one of his Spanish Letters.* It was very strange Discourse in the Mouth of a Pope, (*Paul* the Fourth,) who told the Cardinals, That he would make his Memory immortal by the Dominions which he would give his Family, according to the Grandeur of the Pontificate, by virtue of which, he had Emperours and Kings at his Feet. *Cabrera's Hist. l.* 2. *c.* 2.

286:34 *Extent*] Bad Princes turn all Offences into new Articles of Treason, to render them unpardonable, under a pretence of not going against Reason of State.

287:6 *Quality*] A wise Prince ought not to suffer those Satyrical Writers to go unpunished, who make a Trade to bespatter the Reputation of great Men, of Magistrates, and of private Persons. The Prince, who suffers them, draws upon himself the Hatred of those, who find themselves injured by these Verses, Portraitures, and secret Histories, wherewith they feed, or rather poison the Publick:

> ——————— *Jam sævus apertam*
> *In rabiem verti cæpit jocus, & per honestas*
> *Ire domos impune minax.*
> Hor. Ep. l. 2. ep. 1.

It was, perhaps, none of the least of the good Actions of Pope *Sixtus* the Fifth, in punishing that Poet, whom he sent to the Galleys; for a Sonnet which he made on an Advocate's Wife, wherein, whose Name he made to rhime with the word *Putana*, notwithstanding she was of an unblemished Life. A Punishment, to which this Pope condemned him for rhiming likewise with his Name, which was, *Matera. Leti's Life of this Pope, part 2. l. 3.* If the Prince is the Protector and the Preserver of the Lives and Estates of his Subjects, with much more Reason ought he to defend their Honour, which is the most valuable Thing they possess. *Charles* the Fifth did one day an Action, inwhich it is not easie to say, whether he discovered more his good Nature, or his Merit. Desiring to give one of those Divertisements, which they call in *Spain, Juego de canas, i. e.* silting with Canes or Reeds, he commanded the Grandees to divide themselves into Troops. Each Lord took care to make up his own Troop of the most considerable Gentlemen of his Acquaintance, but not one of them thought fit to take a certain Cavalier, a Man of Merit and Importance, because he had some sort of Blemish in his Birth. A Gentleman of the Emperour's Chamber speaking to the Emperour of the Mortification which this Cavalier was under upon this account, who was at that time also in the Antichamber; the Emperour, without seeming to know any thing of it, appearing at his Chamber Door, said to the Lords who attended at the Entrance; Sirs, Let none take Don *N*—— because he is to be of my Troop. *Epitome of his Life by the Com-*

mander of Vera. Cabrera saith, That *Philip* the Second turned his Back on those whom he heard speaking ill of others, and particularly if it was of his Ministers. *His History, l. 5. c. 17.* He answered a Canon's Letter in these Words: I am informed of what you say concerning your Bishop, and you ought to take care to be more reserved in speaking of such Persons. *L. 11. c. 11.*

287:11 *Mother*] Nothing offends a Prince more, than to attribute his Fortune, or his Exaltation, to those, whom it is not his Interest to acknowledge as the Authors of it. If the point of Honour is the most tender part of private Persons, how sensible must Princes be of it? *Ferdinand* the Catholick, who owed the whole Acquisition of the Kingdom of *Naples* to *Gonzalo Hernandez,* discover'd how uneasie he was under this Obligation, when he said; I do not see that I have reason to rejoyce for having acquired this Kingdom, seeing that there is no return of Profit to me from it; and that he, who hath conquered it in my Name, seems not to have had a Design to have acquired it for me, but only for himself and those, among whom he hath distributed the Lands and Revenues. *Paulus Jovius, l. 5. of the Life of the Grand Capitaine. Maurice,* Prince of *Orange,* could not endure to be told, That he owed his rise to *John* of *Barneveld,* who, by his Authority, made him leave the College, and put himself at the Head of the Armies of *Holland* in his Father's stead.

287:22 *Buffoon*] An Instance, how Scandalous the Profession of Players is accounted, as who have always been excluded from the Rites and Ceremonies of Religion, not only among Christians, but among Heathens likewise. In the Year 1687, the *Italian* Actors being desirous to offer up publick Prayers for the King's Recovery, had, under the Character of *Italian* Gentlemen, obtain'd Leave to perform their Devotions in the Church of the *Great Augustin*'s at *Paris;* but the Arch-Bishop discerning the Cheat, recalls his License, and would not permit it. *Impias preces, detestanda vota.*

287:29 *Citizens*] Religion ought never to be made use of, either as a colour, or instrument of Cruelty.

287:36 *Jupiter*] 'Tis for this Reason, that Crimes against Princes are punished with a greater Severity, than Blasphemy, and many other Offences against God, because the Prince hath no other way to make himself feared, than by present Punishment. In *Ireland,* where Oaths and Perjury are too usual, they who swear falsly by the Hand of the Governor, or Lord of the Place, are bound by the Payment of an heavy Mulct to repair the Injury done to his Name, whereas they who swear upon the Bible, upon the Altar, upon the Image of St. *Patrick,* their Apostle, or of any other Saint, are pass'd by without any other Censure, than that of being declared Forsworn.

288:6 *Practice*] For bad Examples, saith *Paterculus,* seldom or never stop at the first Author, who begins them; but when once a Gap is opened to them, how small soever, they soon spread themselves far and near.

288:7 *Fellow*] In matters of Report and Calumny, poor People, as living most in Obscurity, are more to be feared than others. Inasmuch as such Men are neither by Birth nor Merit qualified for any share in Business, nor yet honest enough to consider the publick Good, they stick not to set every place on fire, out of hopes to make their Fortunes in the confusion. They are sure to forget nothing, that lies in their power, to disturb, by flattering some, and libelling others, that order of Government, which hinders their

Advancement to Offices and Honours. *Ch. 8. of the Second Part of the Pol. Testament.*

288:22 *Tiberius*] When the Witness depos'd all the Ill that was either said or believed of himself, he shewed no Displeasure at it, lest he should be thought to confirm the Truth of those Reports, if he had appeared concerned at them; but as soon as any mention was made of an Injury done to *Augustus,* he immediately vents his Anger against *Marcellus,* thus, under pretence of what had been done to the Statue of his Father, revenging the Affront, which he took to be offered to himself. *Pro Augusto conquerens suum dolorem proferebat.* Further, a great many People use the Images and Pictures of Princes to the same purpose, to which Signs or Bushes are hung out at Taverns: and I remember, I my self have heard it said, That *Onofrio Camaiano,* President of the Apostolical Chamber, treated with great Respect the Portraiture of *Pius* the Fifth, his Friend and Benefactor, as long as that Pope lived; but as soon as he was dead, he orders the Head to be eraz'd, and that of his Successors to be put in its place. *Obs.* 162. I doubt not many have observed oftner than I, what happened a few years since upon the Death of a great Minister, whose Portraitures gave place to those of his Colleague in a great many Houses in *Paris,* but after this they were changed.

288:26 *Sentence*] A Prince, who desires to be well advised, must take care not to give his own Opinion first, because none will dare to contradict that. If he speaks first, it is a sign he expects Approbation, and not Counsel; and therefore it is dangerous for him to declare his own Judgment. Upon this account, *Philip* the Second seldom assisted at his Council of State, *Because* (saith he to *Antonio Perez) the Presence of the Prince intimidates the Spirits, restrains the Passions, and makes the Counsellors speak by Form, like Preachers from the Pulpit; whereas being by themselves, they Dispute, they Heat and Provoke one another, and shew without reserve their real Tempers and Interests. This serves much for the Information of the Prince, who, on the contrary, if he be present, is in hazard to disclose his Sentiments, and to argue with his Subjects as with Equals. A thing incompatible with Majesty, which is supported by outward Respects, in the same manner, as the Pontifical Ornaments procure to Prelates the Veneration of the People.* Perez, in his first *Spanish Letter.* A certain *Italian* Prince said, That when a Prince knows not what to resolve upon, he must hearken to the Advice of his Council, and speak his own Sense last; but that, on the contrary, if his Resolutions be fully fixed, he should give his own Opinion first, that so none may presume to oppose it.

289:1 *Treason*] It happens but too often, that Princes suffer for overtalking themselves. *Commines, chap.* 10. *of the First Book, and ch.* 10. *of the Fourth Book of his Memoirs.* When a Sovereign falls into Passion, (says a *Spanish* Cavalier,) he should call to mind that Emperour, whom his Confessor oblig'd to promise, never to have any Command put in Execution so hastily, as not first to allow himself time to say over all the Letters of the *Greek* Alphabet. *Don Carlos Coloma, in his Tenth Book of the Wars of Flanders.* Another speaking of *Charles* the Fifth, who, contrary to his Oath, granted a Pardon to the Duke of *Cleves,* says, That he never broke his Word, but when it had relation to something of Cruelty. *Don Juan Ant. de Vera, in the Abridgment of his Life.* Moreover, Prince *Ruy Gomez de Silva* had reason to say, That Words uttered in heat of Dispute, and unpremeditated, are more regarded by Princes, than all Remonstrances whatever. *Chinas y varillas arrojadas os descuydo ob ran mas que Lansas.* Ant. Perez, *in a Letter, entituled,* To a Grand Privado.

289:5 *Tribunal*] Those Princes very much deceive themselves, saith *Pliny* the younger, in his Panegyrick, who think they cease to be Princes, if at any time they condescend to do the Office of a Counsellor or Judge. There are some, says *Pagliari*, who blame Pope *Clement* the Eighth, for going in Person to visit the Courts of Judicature, the Parish-Churches, Convents, and even the very Cells of the Monks, as if so much Diligence and Concern were beneath the Dignity of the Supream Bishop. As for my self, I believ it was a matter of great trouble to this Pope, whose sole Study it was, to perform the full Duty of his Station, that he could not inspect all the Churches and Monasteries in *Christendom;* so throughly was he perswaded, that, for the discharge of his Conscience, he ought not to leave to the Care of others, the Administration of Things so material to the Salvation of Souls. *Observ.* 474. O! would all Bishops were effectually convinc'd of this momentous Truth, which that faithful Monitor within is always ready to exhort them to the Practice of.

289:21 *Poverty*] Wealth is a mighty Ornament to Greatness, and Men in Wealth, who receive such Advantage from outward Splendour, that of two Persons equal in Merit, it may without scruple be affirmed, that the richer is the better, for a poor Magistrate must have a Soul of a very resolute and virtuous Inclination, if he doth not suffer himself to act sometimes by Considerations of Interest. Besides, Experience assures us, that the Rich are under less Temptation to Extortion, than others. *Sect.* 1. *Ch.* 4. *of the First Part of the Polit. Testament of Card. Rich.* The Counsellor *Broussel,* whose Integrity the Parliament and People of *Paris* did so highly Extol, having been promis'd the Government of the *Bastile* for one of his Sons, became from that time, of a furious Bigot for the Faction of Slingers, a great Royalist, and wholly in the Service of *Mazarine. Memoirs of L. R.* However, the Chancellor of the Hospital, a Person the most considerable for Estate and Probity of any of his Age, affirm'd, He preferr'd the Poverty of the President *de la Vacquerie,* before the Riches of the Chancellor *Raulin;* (the one was first President of *Paris,* and the other Chancellor to the Duke of *Burgundy.* It is he who founded the Hospital of *Beaune.*)

289:25 *Senate*] Those who, to obtain their Suits, address themselves directly to the Prince, desire rather a present Denial, than to be referred to his Ministers who commonly are little respected for the Kindnesses they do, whether because in truth they are not the proper Donors, or because the number of Petitioners being almost infinite, the Discontented are a thousand times more than the others. Besides, the more Hands the Petition passes through, the less Share has the Prince in the acknowledgment of the Favour; whereas, indeed, 'tis all his Due. To give immediate Dispatch, and without reference to Officers, says a *Spanish* Gentleman, is to Reign more, and Disoblige less. *That is to say, when a Prince can, without Inconvenience, give a decisive Answer.* Don *Fadrique Moles,* in his *Audiencia de Principes. Hortalus* laid open the State and Reasons of his Poverty before a full Senate, and yet *Tiberius* made him a very rough and angry Reply. *See Articles the* 37th *and* 38th, *of the Second Book of Annals.*

289:26 *hard*] The Denials of a Prince, should be temper'd with Sweetness, and Courtesie of Behaviour. 'Tis not the refusal, but the manner, which occasions the Hatred and Ill-will; for nothing more affronts, than Rudeness. *Nihil est tam deforme, quam ad summum imperium etiam acerbitatem naturat adjungere.* Cicero, Ep. 1. ad Quint. fratr.

289:29 *unprofitably*] According to *Seneca,* Favours that must be extorted by the force of Cringes and Intreaties, are as Bread made of flinty Gravel. I had rather buy, than ask, says *Cicero,* speaking of those, who are forc'd to ask and beseech over and over again. *Pliny* the younger commends *Trajan,* for that he never put any to the trouble of attending, either for Audience or Courtesies in his Power to grant. *Audiuntur statim, dimittuntur statim.* Another says, silence is the best Cloke of Poverty.

289:34 *withstood*] A Prince newly advanced to the Throne, ought carefully to avoid the Introduction of Novelties among the People, especially in Matters pertaining to Religion. If *Tiberius* had given leave to make publick the Sibylline Books, the People, having no fondness for one of his Humour, would have been sure to expound reflectingly the ambiguous Oracles, as also the vain and fallacious Predictions, though, perhaps, they were never meant for a Prophecy of his Government. The Books of *Numa* having been found in his Grave, the Senate voted them to the Flames; being informed by the Prætor *Rutilius,* who by their Order had inspected them, that they contained Points contrary to the Religion then in Vogue with the People. The *Areopagus* condemned *Socrates,* because he endeavoured to make the People believe, there was but one God, when yet at the same time many of the Senators were verily perswaded, that it was true. Witness the Altar dedicated to the Unknown God, whom St. *Paul* affirmed to be the God whom they worshipped. *Acts* 17.

290:2 *present*] It is not fitting, a Prince should bestow all that a People may desire, because there will be no end of this; but when the Requests they sue for are reasonable, it then becomes him in Civility and Prudence to yield something, lest otherwise their Minds be exasperated. If a Country happen to be poor and barren, or hath been ruined by a long War, as it often befals Frontier Towns and Provinces, it is most equitable it should be Exempt, and Tax-free, not for ever, but for some very short time; I say, very short, for when the Time shall expire, if the Necessities of the Place still continue, the People will be obliged to crave a further Forbearance, and by this means an opportunity will be afforded for a second Favour, which will be esteemed greater than the first.

290:14 *Augustus*] A Prince, who knows he is hated, as *Tiberius* did, must industriously decline the giving any occasion of Comparison between himself and a Predecessor, that was popular; for the People, whose only Rule of Judging is wont to be their present Humour, will never do him Right, no not even in Things wherein he excels his Predecessor. *Inviso semel principe, seu bene, seu male facta premunt.* Tac. Hist. 1. I will add on this Occasion to the two Reasons, which Tacitus here assigns, Why *Tiberius* declin'd appearing at the publick Shews; another, which was, That he might not be constrained either to grant or refuse the People the Demands they were wont to make to the Prince in full Theatre.

290:16 *Complaisance*] A new Prince, as was *Augustus,* has no better way to keep quiet the People, whose Liberties he has invaded, than by Sights and publick Plays, especially if he seems to take Delight to be at them himself; for then the People, who mind only the outside and appearances of Things, receive it as a piece of Complaisance and Courtship to them; when it is in truth the main Instrument by which they are enslaved.

290:17 *People*] It was *Tiberius*'s Interest to have his Son *Drusus* better belov'd than *Germanicus*. Therefore, it is not probable, he ever intended to render his own Son odious, considering the terrible Jealousie he had of *Germanicus,* his adoptive Son.

290:30 *him*] It is sometimes an Advantage to the Prince, to say nothing during the Contest and Disputes his Ministers and Counsellors fall into one with another, for he may benefit himself at their Cost. In the heat of Opposition, something always happens to be said, which both Parties would been unwilling to have spoken in their sober Senses. *Tiberius,* who bore a mortal spight towards *Gallus Asinius,* for the Reasons alledged by *Tacitus* in the beginning of this Book, took, it may be, more Pleasure, to see him contending with so much earnestness and fury, than *Asinius* did in insulting his Colleagues.

290:35 *Edicts*] A Prince, who would establish his Government, must not venture to alter the Laws of his immediate Predecessor, but to be sure not, if this Predecessor is one much lamented; for such is the way of the People, that they constantly admit kinder Thoughts of a good Prince who is gone, than of him they have at present, though no less deserving. "What hath been setled by Princes, whose Management hath been esteemed judicious, must not reasonably be changed, unless an inconvenience be by Experience found to follow from it, or it evidently appear, that it may be altered for the better." *Sect.* 1. *ch.* 4. *of the First Part of the Pol. Testam.* As for the Regard *Tiberius* paid to all the Laws and Edicts of *Augustus,* it is not amiss to observe, That it proceeded as much at least from Policy and Precaution, as Gratitude, for he could not do otherwise, without weakening the Authority of all that *Augustus* had enacted in his Favour, for preferring him before *Germanicus.*

291:9 *part of*] Reason does not allow People to be excus'd from all Charges or Burdens, for if this Badge of their Subjection be wanting, they will be apt to forget their Condition, and by consequence, the Obedience they owe. Many Princes have lost their Kingdoms for want of maintaining Forces sufficient for their Defence, out of fear to burden their Subjects. And some People have become the Slaves of their Enemies, by aspiring to too much Liberty under their Natural Prince. But there is a stated Measure, which cannot be exceeded without Injustice, common Sense being able to inform every one, that a Proportion ought to be observed between the Burthen and the Strength of those who are to bear it. *Sect.* 5. *ch.* 4. *of the First Part of the Pol. Testament.*

291:16 *extorted*] Sooner or later Princes are sure to revoke the Priviledges and Acts of Grace, which were at first granted by Constraint. After *Charles* Duke of *Burgundy* had brought the City of *Liege* to Terms, he passed the Law to the Citizens of *Gaunt,* who, the very next day after his entry, mutini'd against him, forcing him to restore all Duke *Philip,* his Father, had taken from them, and to give them whatever Immunities they desired. But being returned to *Brussels,* he orders the 72 Banners of the Inhabitants of *Gaunt* to be fetched away, with all the Letters Patents signed in their Favour: The Banners he sent to *Boulogne,* nulled the Priviledge called that of the Law, which was, That of the Twenty six Sheriffs, the Duke should have power to create but Four; and condemned their City to an Amercement of 36000 Florins. *Commines, chap. 4. book 2. of his Memoirs.*

292:13 *died*] In *France,* where the Offices are for Life, the Maxim of *Tiberius* hath the Approbation of all the great Men, inasmuch as it favours their Interests; but it is it may be against that of the Prince, who, in some sort, ties up his own Hands, in giving what he cannot take away; and likewise against that of the Publick, where more Persons would be gratified and requited, if Places were Triennial, as in *Spain.* The Fable of the Fox, which being fallen into a Pit, where the Flies sorely stung and tormented him, refused the assistance of the Hedghog, who proffered to drive them away; Because (saith he) if you drive away these, others will come half starv'd, and exhaust all the Blood I have left. This Fable, I say; which *Tiberius* alledged as a Reason on which his Maxim was founded, concludes nothing in favour of Governments for Life; because the Fear of being no more employed and the hope of rising from one Post to another more considerable, will serve as a Curb and Restraint to Triennial Officers. Besides, such a frequent Removal, inclines People to bear the more patiently with the Governours they dislike, in hopes of better e're long. Cardinal *Richelieu* contends for the Custom of *France,* that is to say, for Governments during Life; but I may say, that in this matter he was influenced by the consideration, rather of the Ministry he was invested withal, than of the Publick; for seeing the Governments were disposed of absolutely at his Pleasure, 'twas his Interest they should be Perpetual, because his Relatives and Dependants, on whom he bestowed the most Valuable, might then render him more puisiant and favourable in the Provinces where they commanded, than they possibly could do, in case their Administration had been only Triennial. And this is so true, that if we compare the Arguments he offers for one and the other, (*in the Second Section of the Fifth Chapter in the First Part of his Politick Testament,*) it will be easie to discern, that the practice of *Spain,* in changing Governours so often, did not to himself appear altogether so pernicious for *France,* as he was willing to have it thought in this place. Insomuch, that had he remained Bishop of *Luson,* or Secretary of State, he had been able as well to defend the contrary Opinion, which he in part inclines to towards the close of the same Paragraph, where he thus speaks: *I am not afraid to say, it is better in this particular to keep to the Usage of* France, *than to imitate that of* Spain, *which nevertheless is grounded on such Policy and Reason, with respect to the largeness of its Territories, that although it cannot be conveniently reduced to Practice in this Realm, yet, in my Judgment, it would do well to be observed in such parts of* Lorrain *and* Italy, *as shall continue under the Dominion of* France. I conclude therefore agreeably with him, That since *Countries remote from the Residence of their Princes require change of Governours, because continuance for Life may make them have a mind to throw off the relation of Subjects or Subordinates, and set up for Supream, and Masters of themselves;* the Custom of *Spain* will become absolutely necessary to *France,* if she go on to extend her Frontiers.

292:17 *could*] A bad Policy this: For a Prince, who prefers few of his

Subjects, hath not only few Dependents, but always many Enemies, that is to
say, as many as deserve to be intrusted or considered, and are not. Thus
plurality of Places is as opposite to the true Interest of the Prince, as plu-
rality of Benefices is to that of the Church. I shall here remark by the way,
That the principal Support of the Regal Authority in *France* is the great
number of its Officers. And *Augustus* of old had never multiplied Offices,
but the better to secure his Authority by a multitude of Magistrates and
Expectants. *Commines* speaking of the last Duke of *Burgundy,* says, his
Favours were not well placed, because he was willing every one should share
in them. *Chap.* 9. *lib.* 5. *of his Memoirs.*

292:21 *Men*] A Person of ordinary Parts, and a moderate Capacity, is
more likely to make his Fortunes with Princes, than one of a sublime and
great Wit. For all Superiority being ungrateful to them, and they being
ambitious to be accounted Chief and Best at every Thing, will never love,
nor consequently prefer a Man, whose Understanding seems larger, and
more penetrating, than their own. The Letters of *Anthony Perez* contain
a great deal to this purpose. Among others, there is one directed to a *Grand
Privado,* wherein he thus speaks, when the Holy Spirit says, *Seem not wise
in the Presence of a King;* he meant not to say, *Be not wise,* but, *Seem not
to be so;* as if he had used these Words, *Conceal thy Parts, and thy Prudence,
shew not thy Intellectuals.* Prince *Rui Gomez de Silva,* the greatest Master
in this Art that has appeared for these many Ages, told me, he learned this
Rule from a mighty Favourite of the Kings of *Portugal;* and that in all the
Advices he gave, and in all the Consultations he at any time had with his
Prince, he took care to carry himself with all the Wariness and Circumspec-
tion he possibly could. . . . He further added, That he so contrived the
Matter, that the good Success of his Counsels might seem to be only the
effect of Chance, and not the return of any Care he had to please him, or of
an intent Application to his Business, but he seem'd to carry himself like
those Gamesters, who in Play depend more on the favour of Fortune, than
their Skill. On this Subject, continued he, the same Prince related to me,
what passed one day between *Emanuel* King of *Portugal,* and Count *Lewis
de Silveira.* The King having received a Dispatch from the Pope, composed
with great exactness, sends for the Count, and commands him to draw up an
Answer, whilst he himself was making another, for he had a strong inclina-
tion to be an Orator, and indeed was so. The Count obeys, but first declares
his Reluctancy to enter Competition with his Master, and the next day he
brings his Paper to the King, who, after he had heard it, was loth to read
his own; but when the Count had prevailed with him to read it, the King
acknowledging the Count's Answer to be the better, would have that sent
to the Pope, and not his own. The Count, at his return home, orders two
Horses to be saddled for his two Sons, and went immediately with them.
And when he was in the Fields, he saith to them: "My Children, seek ye
your Livelihood, and I mine, there is no farther means of living here; for
the King knows, that I am wiser than himself." Don *Juan Antonio de Vera,*
who relates the same thing in the First Discourse of his Ambassador, seems
to say and believe, that it is a Fable; but be it so or no, it is still very
Instructive.

293:4 *Words*] The Words of Princes seldom agree with their Actions; and
most frequently they act directly contrary to what they say.

II Historical Notes

230:1 *Kings*] viz. *Romulus* its Founder, who, according to *Tacitus*, rul'd with Absolute Power; *Romulus ut libitum imperitaverat. Ann.* 3. *Numa,* who Establish'd a Form of Divine Worship, with High-Priests, South-Sayers, and Priests, to perform the Ceremonies of the Sacrifices, *Numa religionibus & divine jure populum devinxit, Ibid. Tullus Hostilius,* who taught the Romans the Art of making War, and for this purpose Instituted Military Discipline. *Ancus Martius,* who adorn'd the City, and Peopled it with the Sabines, and the Latins, whom he had Conquer'd, and Built the City of *Ostia,* to be a Port for the Romans. *Tarquin* I. who built the *Cirque,* and distinguished the Senators and the Knights, by exterior marks of Honour, such as the *Ivory Chair,* call'd in Latin, *Cella Curulis;* the Gold Ring; the Purple Robe, call'd *Trabea;* the *Pretexta,* or the Robe edg'd with Scarlet. *Servius Tullius,* who, according to *Tacitus,* was the Chief Law-giver of the Romans, *Præcipuus Servius Tullius sanctor legum fruit, Ann.* 3. took into the City of *Quirinal,* the *Esquiline,* and the *Viminal* Hills, and caus'd his Laws to be engraven on Tables of Stone; and *Tarquin,* Sirnam'd, the Proud, who having ascended the Throne by Incest, and by the Murder of *Servius Tullius,* whose two Daughters he had Married, and endeavouring to maintain himself in it by Violence and Terror, was, with his whole Family, expell'd *Rome.*

230:1 *Liberty*] *Tacitus* always opposes Liberty to Regal Power, *Res dissociabiles, principatum & libertatem. In Agricola. Haud facile libertas & domini miscentur,* Hist. 4, a Master and Liberty are incompatible. *Tarquinius Priscus,* says he, *Lib.* 3. *of his Hist.* had laid the Foundation of the Capitol, and afterwards *Servius Tullius* and *Tarquin* the Proud, built it; one with the Gifts of the Allies, and the other with the Spoils of the Enemies, but the Glory of finishing this great Work, was reserved for Liberty: As for *Junius Brutus,* he was not only Author of the Consulship, but also the first who Exercis'd it, and with so great Zeal for his Country, that not being content with having banished *Collatine* his Collegue, only because he was of the Royal Family of the *Tarquins,* he caus'd his own Sons to be beheaded, who endeavoured to restore them to the Throne. The two Magistrates, on whom was transferr'd the Authority which the Kings had, were call'd *Consuls,* to signifie that they ought to assist the new Common-Wealth with their Counsels, and not to Govern it according to their humour, as the Kings had done.

230:3 *Dictatorship*] The Dictator was a Sovereign Magistrate, but whose Power lasted no longer than the Danger lasted, which threatned the Common-Wealth; so that he was no more than the Trustee of the Sovereign Authority. The first whom the Romans created was in the War against the Latins, who had given the *Tarquins* Protection, his Name was *Titus Lartius,* or *Largius.* He was call'd Dictator, *ab edicendo,* or *ab edictando, i.e.* because he had authority to make Edicts; or because he was not chosen by the Suffrages of the People, nor by the Scrutiny of the Senate, as other Magistrates were; but only *Dictus* named by the Consul, and afterwards proclaimed by the People. He was therefore named by the Consul, saith *Machiavel, Ch.* 34. *Lib.* 1. *of his Discourses,* because, as the Creation of a Dictator was a sort of a Dishonour to the Consul, who from being chief Governor of the City, became thereby subject, as the rest, to a Superior Power, the Romans would have him chosen by the Consuls themselves, to the end that as often as the City should stand in need of one, they might be the more willing to chuse him, and to have the less reluctance to obey him; the Wounds which we voluntarily give our selves, being far less sensible, than those which others give us. He had power to depose the Consuls, witness *Q. Cincinnatus,* who deposed the Consul *Minutius;* he suspended the Functions of all the Magistrates, except the Tribunes of the People, who sometimes had the better of him. At first, the Dictatorship was conferr'd only on the Nobles, but afterwards the Commons were admitted to it, as well as to the Consulship. The Dictatorship, saith *Machiavel,* deserves to be reckon'd amongst those things, which contributed most to the advancement of the Roman Empire. For in Republicks, which are always slow in their motions. (because no Magistrate can dispatch any business singly, and one having need of anothers agreement in their opinions, the time insensibly slips away.) The ordinary remedies are very dangerous, when they are to provide against some pressing Evil, which doth not give time to wait for the Consultation of many; whence I conclude, that Common-Wealths, which in pressing dangers have not recourse either to a Dictator, or some other Magistrate of the like Nature, will certainly run a-ground upon some sudden accident. Heretofore the Dutchy of *Brabant* created a *Ruvert,* or a Protector, on whom the Province conferr'd an Absolute Power for the time. The Prince of *Orange* got himself chosen *Ruvert, Anno.* 1577. *Cabrera, c.* 24. l. 11. *of his Philip* II. *and Strada lib.* 1. *dec.* 1.

230:4 *Decemvirate*] Ten Men who govern'd the Common-Wealth instead of Consuls. It was under them that the XII Tables were compos'd, *i. e.* a Compilation of the best Laws of *Greece,* but particularly of *Athens,* whose Polity was esteem'd the most Excellent. For all those which the Kings had made were abolish'd in hatred of Monarchy. The first year each made his Table according to the several matters, which fell to their lot, and the Year following, they made two more in common, to supply what was wanting in the ten former. But as they were endeavouring to perpetuate their Government, which began to degenerate into Tyranny, the Decemvirate was abolished for Ever, and the Consulship restored. The Decemvirs had greater Authority than the Dictator, for the Dictator could make no alteration in the ancient Laws of the City, nor do any thing which was prejudicial to the State, the Tribunes of the People, the Consuls and the Senate, who still subsisted, put a Bridle upon him, which kept him from breaking out of the right way, saith *Machiavel;* on the contrary the Consulship and the Tribuneship having been abolish'd by the Creation of the Decemvirs, to whom the People transferred all their Rights, these Ten, who had their hands at liberty, there remaining no appeal from them to the People, had an opportunity of becoming insolent.

230:5–6 *Military Tribunes*] The Patricii, or the Nobles being at discord with the People, who would have the Commons admitted to the Consulship, as well as the Nobles, found an Expedient to create Military Tribunes in the room of the Consuls: so that, as often as the People and the Nobility could not agree in the Election of the Consuls, they created Military Tribunes, who exercised all the Military Functions. A Testimony, saith *Machiavel, Discourse l. 1. c. 34.* that it was rather the Name of Consul that they hated, than the Authority of the Consulship. And this Custom lasted about 80 Years, not in a continu'd Succession, for there was sometimes of Consuls, and sometimes of Tribunes. *Tacitus* says nothing here of the Tribunes of the People, who held notwithstanding a considerable Rank in the ancient Common-Wealth, as having been instituted to moderate the Power of the Consuls, and to protect the meaner sort against the Insolence of the Great ones; besides, their Persons were Sacred and Inviolable. They were instituted fifty years before the Creation of Military Tribunes, when the People jealous of the Power of the Nobles, and weary of their Insults, retired to the *Crustumerin* Hill, call'd afterward the Sacred Hill, because of the happy accommodation of this quarrel. There was at first but two Tribunes of the People, but a little while after there was four other; and in process of time they were multiply'd to ten, and the Nobility excluded from this Office, which was not observed in following times. *C. Licinius Stolo,* and *Sextius Lateranus* put a stop to the Elections of Consuls, for the space of five years, and by these means the Senate was forced to admit *Plebeans* to the Consulship, which was conferr'd upon them the first time in the Persons of *Sextius* and *Licinius. Sylla,* the sworn Enemy of the Common People, had much humbled these Tribunes, but after his Death they resumed all their Authority.

230:13 *Senate*] He had yet no Superiority over the Senators, who was equal to him in every thing, except Precedency, and for this Reason *Dio* calls him πρόκριτον γερουσίας, *i. e.* the first of the Senate. This Title was in use under the ancient Common-Wealth. The first who was honour'd with it, was *Fabius Ambustus,* about the Year of *Rome,* 435. The Consuls were more than the Prince of the Senate, for they were Princes of the People.

BRUTUS and *CASSIUS.*

230:28 *Brutus*] *Paterculus* saith, that never any Persons had so favourable a Fortune in the beginning, as *Brutus* and *Cassius,* nor so short liv'd a one; *Brutus* was but 37 years old when he died; *Cassius* was a better Captain, *Brutus* a better Friend; the one had more Vigour, the other more Honesty. And as it was more advantageous to the Common-Wealth to have *Augustus* for its Master than *Anthony,* it would likewise have been more agreeable to obey'd *Brutus* than *Cassius.* They both kill'd themselves; the latter frighted by a Company of People who came to bring him News of the Victory, believing that they were Enemies; the Former a few days after in despair.

Young *POMPEY.*

230:29–231:1 *Pompey*] This young Man having possessed himself of *Sicily,* formed on Army of the broken remains of that of *Brutus,* and of multitudes of Slaves, Fugitives, and proscribed Persons, who flock'd to him. For although he was not much like his Father, and was not Valiant but in a Heat and in a Passion, any Leader was fit for People who had nothing to lose. When he infested the Seas by his Pyracies, *Augustus* and *Anthony* were oblig'd to make Peace with him to quiet the People of *Rome,* who were no longer able to bear the Scarcity of Provisions, which was caused by the Robbery of *Pompey's* Fleet. *Sicily* and *Greece* were yielded to him by this Treaty. But this turbulent Spirit being not content to keep within those bounds, *Augustus* declared War against him. In the beginning of which *Pompey* was successful, but *Augustus* in the latter end, for he forced him to fly into *Asia*, where he was slain by the Command of *Anthony*. *Paterc. Hist.* 2. *Chap.* 72, 73. and 79.

The Triumvir LEPIDUS.

231:1 *Lepidus*] After the defeat and flight of Young *Pompey*, *Lepidus*, who was come into *Sicily* with twelve Legions, incorporated with his Army *Pompey*'s Troops. Being therefore at the head of above twenty Legions, he had the boldness to send *Augustus* word, that *Sicily* belong'd to him by right of Conquest, although he had only been the Spectator of another's Victory, and which he had also a long time retarded, by giving advice upon every occasion, contrary to that, which all the rest approved. *Augustus*, notwithstanding he was unarm'd, entred *Lepidus* his Camp, and not regarding the Arrows which the other caused to be shot at him, he seised the Eagle of a Legion. *Lepidus* abandon'd by his Soldiers, and fortune which raised him to a degree of power which he no ways deserved, was forc'd to throw himself at *Augustus* his feet, who gave him his Life and his Estate.

MARK ANTHONY.

231:2 *Antony*] This Triumvir having resolved to make War on his Country, the Quarrel was decided by a Fight, which put an end to the Civil Wars. This Battle was fought near *Actium,* a Promontory of the Sea of *Albania.* After the two Fleets were engaged, Queen *Cleopatra* flying, *Anthony* chose rather to accompany a Woman who fled, than his Soldiers who fought. These brave Men however obstinately maintain'd the Fight, and they despaired of the Victory; they held it out a long time, being willing to die for a Deserter. But in the end *Augustus* having softned them by his Remonstrances, they threw down their Arms, and yielded the Victory to him who merited it as much by his Clemency, as by his Valour.

231:29 *Edile*] That is to say an Ædile, for there were Ædiles taken out of the Common People, who were not permitted to ride in the City with a Chariot, or to sit in an Ivory-Chair. But this distinction which was odious to the People, was afterwards abolished, and all the *Ædiles* were *Curules:* They had the oversight of the Government of the City of Publick *Games,* and of the Reparation of the Temples, and of all things relating to the Worship of the Gods.

232:6 *Robe*] A Robe edg'd with Scarlet, which Children of Quality wore from the time of the Reign of *Lucius Tarquinus,* Sirnamed *Priscus,* or the Old, they left it off at 17 years of Age.

232:15 *him*] According to *Paterculus, Tiberius* was adopted by *Augustus* in the Consulship of *Ælius Catus,* and of *Caus Sentius,* the 27th of *June Anno. Rome,* 754. *Hist,* 2. *Ch.* 103.

233:25 *Infancy*] *Tiberius* was not three years old when his Mother was married to *Augustus. Tiberius,* saith *Paterculus,* Educated under *Augustus,* season'd with his Divine Precepts, and endowed moreover with extraordinary Parts, discover'd very early somewhat which promis'd all that we behold in him at this day. *Hist.* 2. *Ch.* 94.

234:13 *tenderness*] The Elder *Pliny* saith, that *Augustus* lamented his Grandson *Agrippa,* after he had banish'd him, and that the Ambitious Designs of *Livia* and *Tiberius,* gave him anxious thoughts enough in the latter part of his life. *Abdicatio Posthumi Agrippæ post adoptionem, desiderium post relegationem.... Hinc uxoris & Tiberii cogitationes suprema ejus cura.* C. 45. L. 7. Lastly, concludes he, this Divine *Augustus* died, leaving his Enemy's Son his Heir and Successor. For *Tiberius* was the Son of *Claudius Nero* the High-Priest, who was the declared Protector of all the Malecontents after the Death of *Julius Cæsar,* and had raised the War in *Campania, Pater. Histor. c.* 75. *Sueton* adds, that the Father of *Tiberius,* was so passionate for Liberty, that he propos'd in the Senate, that rewards might be decreed for *Cæsar*'s Murderers. *In Tiberio.*

234:25 *when*] *Paterculus* says, that *Tiberius* came to *Nola* before the Death of *Augustus,* and that they had also some discourse together, *Chap.* 123.

234:30 *Augustus*] *Suetonius* says, that *Tiberius* wou'd not publish the Death of *Augustus* till he had caused the Young *Agrippa* to be assassinated. *In Tiberio.*

234:31 *Empire*] At the Age of Fifty five years.

235:14 *Competitor*] Paul Piasecki says, in his Chronicle, that *Constance* of *Austria,* the Second Wife of *Sigismond* III. King of *Poland,* used all her Interest to get her Eldest Son *John Casimir* to be chosen King, and her Son-in-Law and Nephew *Uladislaus* excluded, who being the Eldest Son of the King, according to the Law and Custom of the Country, was to be preferr'd before all others. Another Polonian says, *Nec unquam committunt, quin hic eligatur, cus ipso jure debetur successio.* Krzistanowic *in his description of the Government of Poland.*

235:32 *alone*] *Mary,* Queen of *Hungary,* Sister of *Charles* V. shew'd her self of the same opinion, when taking her leave of the Low-Countrys, which she had govern'd 23 years, she used this Expression: If I have fail'd in any thing, I may be excus'd, since I have done the best I could; but if any are dissatisfied with what I have done, I regard it not, since the Emperor my Brother is satisfied, and my care was only to please him. *Brantome disc.* 4. *of brave Women.*

236:2 *New*] *Don John Antonio de Vera* speaking of the Ceremony of the Abdication of *Charles* V. says, that they who assisted at it gave publick testimony of their sorrow, but however in such a manner as, without displeasing the Prince they received, shew'd what a Prince they lost. *Epitome of the Life of Charles* V.

236:15 *Power*] Under the ancient Republick, the Tribunes of the People had oftentimes assembled the Senate; so *Tiberius* acted popularly in convoking them. 'Tis true, the Tribunes had usurp'd this Power, for in the beginning they could only *vetare, aut intercedere, i. e.* hinder or oppose; whereas the Consuls had a right to command. *Consules jubent.*

236:18 *forsake*] Because *Augustus* dying at *Nola,* as *Tacitus* says, at the end of the Abridgment of his Life, he would in honour accompany his body to *Rome.*

236:20 *Edict*] *John Freinshemius* gives another sense to this passage: *neque abscedere a corpore, idque unum ex publicis muneribus usurpare;* making *Tiberius* say, that by this assembling the Senate, he did not pretend to a Superiority over it, or over any Senator, but only to acquit himself of his duty to his Father; and that for the future he would not take upon him to give any more commands. And in the Examen of the Translators of

Tacitus, which at the end of his Paraphrase, he says, most Interpreters understand these words, *abscedere a corpore,* of the Body of *Augustus;* but I understand 'em of the Body of the Senate. In which he has followed *Dati,* who renders them thus: *Ne voleva egli en cio partirsi dalla volonta de gli altera Senatori:* And *Rodolphus,* the Master, who interprets them in these terms, to be inseparably united to the body of the Senate.

237:9 *Augusta*] That is, with the Name of Empress, and with the Title of Majesty, which she had not while her Husband was living.

237:12–13 *Posterity*] We see here, says *Pagliari,* what slips sometimes the Wisest Men make. For if on the one side we consider, that *Augustus* made himself to be lamented, and esteem'd, by an unparallel'd demonstration of Humanity, yet without contributing any thing of his own; his last Will will appear to be made with great Wisdom and Policy, but if we examine more narrowly how he purchas'd the favour of the People, we shall find, that for a Prince of such Understanding he committed a great Fault, because by the bait of an apparent intail, he provoked the great Persons concerned in it, to plot against his Posterity, whom he had strengthen'd by many Adoptions. For if these Noble Persons were Politick Men, as 'tis probable, since *Augustus* mistrusted them; 'tis not likely that they would be contented with an hope, which according to the ordinary course of Nature, could not take effect in some hundreds of years, *Germanius* and *Drusus* with all their Children, being to succeed before she. *In the thirty third of his Observations upon* Tacitus.

238:15 *others*] Who call'd *Cæsar,* Tyrant, to authorise this Murther as Lawful. *Ita enim appellari Cæsarem facto ejus expiedebat;* says *Paterculus,* Book 1. Ch. 58. speaking of *Brutus.*

238:18 *years*] Counting from the Death of *Anthony* the Triumvir.

238:25 *Empire*] The 21. of *September,* compleat 20 years old, except one day, according to *Paterculus, Hist.* 2. *Chap.* 65.

238:26 *Octavius*] At the Death of Cardinal *de Richelieu,* the Parisians observ'd almost the same, that he was born and died in the same House: that he received Baptism and Extreme Unction in the same Parish. *History of Cardinal* de Richelieu, *Book* 6. *Chapter the Last. Conestagio* and *Cabrera* have likewise observ'd, that *Henry* Cardinal King of *Portugal,* died the same hour in which he was born 68 years before.

238:29 *Marius*] *Paterculus* says, that he was Consul eleven times, and refused to be Consul any more. *Book* 2. *Chap.* 89. Now *Marius* had been Consul seven times, and *Corvinus* six.

238:30–31 *Emperor*] That is, Victorious General, or Great Captain. *Tacitus* says, that 'tis an honour which Armies formerly gave to their Captains, when they were over-joy'd for having gain'd a Victory. So that, at the same time, there were many Emperors, who did not take place of one another. *At the end of the* 3 *Book of his Annals.*

239:4 *Lepidus*] 'Tis true, says *Paterculus,* they reviv'd again the Proscription which had been begun by *Sylla,* but this was not approved of by *Augustus,* though being single against two he could not oppose the Fury of *Anthony* and *Lepidus,* joyn'd together.

239:10 *Title*] *Paterculus* says, that *Cæsar* was become odious, from the day he assisted at the Feast of the *Lupercalia,* when *Mark Anthony,* his Coleague in the Consulship, put upon his Head a Royal Diadem; for *Cæsar* refused it in such a manner as shewed, that though the Action was rash, yet it had not much displeased him. *Hist. 2. Chap.* 56. Besides, he happen'd to say before, that they must take care how they spoke to him for the future, and that he meant what he said should be a Law. *Suetonius in his Life.*

239:13 *Ocean*] The Roman Empire was bounded on the West, by the Ocean; on the North by the *Danube* and the *Rhine;* on the East, by the *Euphrates* and the *Tygris;* on the South, by the Mountain *Atlas.*

239:20 *Common-Wealth*] *Paterculus* says, that *Augustus* was resolved to refuse the Dictatorship when the People offer'd it to him. *Chap.* 89.

239:28 *slain*] In the War of *Madena* against *Anthony*, *Hirtius* and *Pansa* were Consuls, and *Augustus* commanded there in quality of Proprætor. *Anthony* was forc'd to fly and leave *Italy.*

240:4 *Lands*] That is, That these Lands belonging to the Community, could not be given to private Persons, much less to the Soldiers, without wronging the Publick.

240:5 *Bruti*] *Marcus*, and *Decimus Brutus*, of whom the first kill'd himself, as I have already said, and the other was killed by the command of *Anthony*. A punishment he justly deserved for his ingratitude towards *Cæsar*, whom he was so hardy as to Murther, at the same time he received favours from him. He envy'd, says *Paterculus*, the Fortune of him who had made his, and after having taken away the Life of *Cæsar*, he thought it no injustice to keep the Estate he had received from him. *Hist. lib. 2. Chap.* 64. 'Tis fit to observe by the way, that of all the Murtherers of *Cæsar*, who were sixty in number, there was not one of them who did not die a Violent Death, nor did any of them out-live him more than three years.

240:6 *Father*]

> *Hoc opus, hæc pietas, hæc prima clementa fuerunt,*
> *Cæsaris, utcisci justa per arma patrem.* Ovid. l. 3. Fast.

Cato the Censor meeting a Young Man who came for a Decree to disgrace one of his Father's greatest Enemies. *See there,* says he, *how a well-bred Child ought to offer sacrifice to the Memory of his Father.*

240:15 *Egnatii*] *Rufus Egnatius*, who, according to *Paterculus*, was in every thing more like a Gladiator than a Senator, having form'd a Cabal of Men like himself; he resolved to kill *Augustus;* but his design succeeded no better than *Lucius Murena*'s, and *Fannius Cæpio's,* He was punished with the Accomplices of his Treason, by such a Death as his detestable Life deserved.

240:16 *Lollius*] *Marcus Lollius*, according to *Paterculus*, was more careful to enrich himself than to do his duty.

240:17 *Varus*] *Quintilius Varus*, a Peaceable Man, but heavy, and more fit to command an Army in time of Peace, than to make War. He was so imprudent, says *Florus, Book 4. Chap.* 12. as to assemble the Germans in the midst of his Camp to do them justice, as if he had been able to restrain the Violence of these barbarous People with a Serpent's Wand. He imagined, saith *Paterculus*, that they were plain honest People, who had little more than the Shape and voice of Men, and whom he could civilize by mild Laws, and tame by the Forms of Justice, those, who could not be subdued by the force of Arms. *Segestes* gave him notice of the intended revolt of *Arminius*, but he would not believe it, thinking the Germans had as much good will for him, as he had for them; In the mean time his Army is Surpris'd and Massacred by people whom they butcher'd before like Sheep. Poor *Varus,* more couragious to die than fight, stab'd himself.

240:34 *Proud*] *Dio* and *Sueton* don't differ much from *Tacitus. Suspicio,* saith the first, *quosdam tenuit, consulto Tiberium ab Augusto satis eum qualis esset cognoscente, successorem ordinatum, quo magis ipsius gloria floreret,* Lib. 56. *Nec illud ignoro,* saith the other, *aliquos tradidisse Augustum etiam ambitione tractum ut tali successore desiderabilior ipse quandoque fieret:* In *Tib. cap.* 23. So that *P. Bouhours* censures all at once these three *Roman* Historians, when he speaks thus: "Is it probable, that *Augustus* preferred *Tiberius* to *Agrippa* and *Germanicus,* for no other Reason, but to acquire Glory by the comparison which would be made of a cruel and arrogant Prince, such as *Tiberius* was, with himself, his Predecessor. For although *Tacitus* puts this in the Mouth of the *Romans,* 'tis visible enough, that the Reflection is his own, as well as that which he makes on the same *Augustus,* for having put in his Will, amongst his Heirs, the principal Persons of *Rome,* of whom the greatest part were odious to him; that he had put them in, I say, through Vanity, to make himself estemed by Posterity." *Dialogue* 3. *de sa manier de bien penser.* If this Reflection is *Tacitus*'s own, it ought to be attributed likewise to *Dio* and *Sueton,* who are esteemed nevertheless true and well-informed Historians. And consequently we may say of *Pere Bouhours;* what *Raphael dalla Torre* said of *Strada,* on occasion of the Censure of this Passage of History, and many others, that he knew better how to accuse *Tacitus,* than to justifie *Augustus:* For although *Sueton,* saith *Raphael,* declares in the place forementioned, that so sinister an Opinion is not agreeable to the Goodness of *Augustus,* yet in stead of confuting it by any Reason, he confirms it by the Knowledge which he owns *Augustus* had long before of the Evil Qualities of *Tiberius. Illa commota (Livia) veteres quosdam ad se Augusti codicillas de acerbitate & intolerantia morum ejus è sacrario protulit atque recitavit.* And by the Words which he saith *Augustus* spoke after the last Discourse which he had with *Tiberius,* crying out, *Unhappy is the People of* Rome, *who are to fall under such heavy Jaw-bones. Sueton* therefore may say as much as he will, that he cannot believe, that so prudent a Prince could be willing to choose a Successor of so Tyrannical a Temper to make himself the more regretted; but seeing he confesses, that *Augustus* knew the Ill-Nature of him that he chose, he ought at least to have given us some pertinent Reason to excuse so bad a Choice: *cap.* 4. of his *Astrolabe of State.*

241:2 *Tiberius*] He had exercised this Sovereign Power with *Augustus,* before his Retreat to *Rhodes. Paterculus Hist.* 2. *cap.* 99.

241:28 *Register*] *Sueton* calls this Registry, *Rationarium, i. e.* an Inventory, or a Journal.

242:30–31 *Tiberius*] *Dio* adds a Reason, which is of yet greater weight. That *Asinius* having married *Vipsania, Drusus* his Mother, he looked upon *Drusus* as his own Son. So that not being satisfied with having *Tiberius*'s first Wife, he also shared with him in his Prerogatives of a Father. It looked also as if he would have had a share also in *Drusus*'s Heart, *Cùm Drusum filii instar haberet:* These are *Dio*'s Words, *lib.* 57. Lastly, as *Tiberius* had always loved *Vipsania,* whom he had not divorced but to please *Augustus,* who gave him his own Daughter; he could not endure that *Asinius* should enjoy this Lady, who had as many good Qualities, as *Augustus*'s Daughter had bad ones.

243:27 *offended*] Because he discovered, that all *Tiberius*'s refusals of the Empire were not in earnest; whereas *Haterius* seemed to be perswaded, that his Refusal was sincere, when he conjured him not to suffer the Commonwealth to be longer without a Head; which was also an oblique way of flattering *Tiberius*, intimating thereby, that the Senate was not the Head of the Empire.

244:8 *Mother*] Which was as much as to say, the Empress-Mother.

244:16 *Lictour*] *i. e.* And Usher or Mace-bearer to walk before her.

244:28 *Assembly*] The Assembly, where they chose the Magistrates called *Comitia a cotundo vel comeundo*, which was held in the Fields of *Mars*.

244:33 *Suffrages*] *Romulus* divided the People into three Tribes, as the City was then divided into three Quarters; which Number gave occasion to the Name of *Tribe*. He afterwards divided these Tribes into thirty *Curiæ*, or Classes. The elder *Tarquin* doubled these Tribes, to equal their Number to the six Quarters of the City, which was much enlarged. *Servius Tullius*, the Successor of *Tarquin*, distributed it into nineteen Tribes, four of which were called *Tribus Urbanæ*, or the Citizens; and the other fifteen, which comprehended all the Inhabitants of the Country, were called *Tribus Rusticæ*. And in process of Time, the Number of Tribes encreased to Thirty five.

245:3 *Candidates*] So they call those who stood for Offices, because during the time of their Suit they wore a *White Garment*.

245:7 *Calendars*] In this Calendar, called *Fasti*, were set down the Festivals, the Ceremonies, and the Names of the Magistrates of the Cities.

245:10 *Robe*] It was a figured Robe, edged with Purple, with a Vest wrought with Branches of Palms.

245:16 *Pannonia*] These Legions, saith *Paterculus*, were for a new Head, a new Government, and, in a word, for a new Republick; they threatned to give Laws to the Senate, and even to the Prince himself; they would by main force augment their Pay, and shorten the time of their Service, to have their Reward before the set time. There was nothing wanting to them, but a Head, to have lead them on against the Government; and whosoever this Head had been, he would have found this Army ready to have followed him: *ch.* 125.

245:23 *Mourning*] *Ob Justitium*, saith *Tacitus*. The *Justitium* then was a Vacation or Suspension of all Civil Affairs, which was commanded by the Senate, or the Magistrates of the City, as may be gathered from these words of the Second Book of the Annals: *Ut ante Edictum Magistratuum, anti Senatus-consultum sumpto jùstitio desererentur fora, &c.*

246:6 *Tribunes*] In elder Times the Military Tribunes had none above them, but the General; but afterwards the Lieutenant-Generals took their Place. So that these Tribunes were much the same with our Colonels or Commanders of a thousand Men; for there were six of them in every Legion, which ordinarily consisted of six thousand Men. Their Office was to distribute the Generals Orders, to give the Word to the Sentinels, to take care of Fortifications, to try Deserters and Mutineers for their Lives, &c.

Sometimes *Tribunus Militum* is taken for the chief Commander of a Legion, and sometimes of a Cohort; and hence it came to pass, that the *Romans* had not so many Officers as we have.

246:19 *Name*] They were called *Veterans, i. e.* Soldiers, who had compleated their time of Service.

246:24-25 *Pence a Day*] The *Roman Denarius,* or Penny, was worth ten Asses, but under *Augustus* it was worth sixteen; about Sevenpence-Halfpenny of our Money.

246:29 *Summer*] Because they continued Day and Night.

246:32 *Denarius*] They demanded a Penny in Specie, in stead of ten Asses in Money, because the Penny was then worth sixteen Asses.

247:12 *one*] To make themselves more formidable by this Union, and to be always in a readiness to make a common Effort, if their General should think it to employ Force against them.

247:24 *Death*] Because of the Revenge which the Prince will take of it.

248:15 *Soldiers*] There was the great and the little *Manipulus,* or *Band.* The little one, called *Contubernium,* as much as to say, a Company that lies in one Chamber, and had but ten Men, but the great one consisted of a Hundred, or a Hundred and twenty. Each great Band had two Centurions, who commanded each sixty Men, as our Captains. Each Cohort had three Bands. These Companies were called *Manipuli,* 1. c. *Manualis herbarum fasciculus,* because they carried a Bottle of Hay, or a handful of Grass, for their Ensign, such as the Kings of *Sweden* and *Poland,* of the House of *Wasa,* bore in their Arms. The Emperours changed this Ensign into a Hand fixed on the point of a Pike. The little Band had a tenth Man, or *Decurio,* which was as a Corporal with us.

248:16 *Nauportum*] It was a City of *Pannonia,* called now *Laubac* in *Carniola,* a little Province of *Hungary.*

248:20 *Town*] That is, a City which enjoyed the Privileges and Franchises of the *Roman* People.

249:31 *Legions*] When the Duke of *Maine* heard at *Lyons* the News of the Duke and the Cardinal of *Guise* his Brothers, he caused it to be published through the whole City, that *Henry* the Third had taken away their Lives, for no other Reason, but because they protected and defended the Catholick Religion against the Huguenots. *Herrera, l. 5. of the Third Part of his History, c. 3.* Notwithstanding the Duke of *Guise* being at the Estates of *Blois,* had refused to sign a Declaration which the King caused to be offered to him by a Secretary of State, wherein he promised and swore to make War on the *Huguenots,* provided that his Subjects would assist him with their Forces, and would make no League with Foreigners without his Approbation; and that those who should act contrary to this Condition, should incur the Penalties of High-Treason: *c.* 11. *l.* 4. *of the same Part.* I cite this Historian here, because being a *Spaniard,* his Testimony is of greater force against the *Guises,* whom all the *Spanish* Writers make to be *Maccabees,* notwithstanding at the bottom they were acted only by Ambition, to make themselves Kings of *France* with the *Catolicon* of *Spain,* against all Laws both Divine and Humane.

250:12 *Baton*] The *Roman* Soldiers were chastized with a Wand of a Vine, and the Foreigners in their Service with Blows of Cudgels.

250:34 *Prætorium*] This Office was new, having been created by the Emperors. Some are of Opinion, that the *Præfectus Prætorio* was much the same with the *Magister Equitum,* or the General of the Horse under the ancient Commonwealth. For as this General held the first Place after the Dictator, to whom he was properly Lieutenant, the *Præfectus Prætorio* was the second Person of the Empire, especially after *Sejanus* thought fit to lodge in one Camp all the Prætorian Cohorts, or Companies of Guards, which were before dispersed in several Quarters of the City. (*Tacit. ann.* 4.) M. *de Chanvalon* speaks properly, in saying, That he was as the Constable of the Empire. His Authority grew so great, that there was no Appeal from his Judgments, whereas there lay an Appeal from those of the Consuls to the People, when *Rome* was a Commonwealth. In the Year 1631, *Urban* the Eighth having created his Nephew *Dom Tade Barberino* Præfect of *Rome,* this Lord by virtue of this new Dignity, which was but a Phantom of the Ancient, would have the Precedency of Ambassadors to *Salio.*

251:4 *Ensigns*] The *Roman* Army was wont to adorn their Ensigns with Garlands of Ribbands, and Bands of water'd Stuff: But on sad Occasions they carried them without Ornaments.

251:32 *Denarius*] That is to say, a Penny in Specie, which was then worth sixteen Asses.

253:8 *strucken*] Don *Juan Antonio de Vera* speaking of a Tempest by Sea and Land, which shook the Fleet of *Charles* the Fifth at his arrival to *Algiers,* saith, That it exercised its Fury not only on the material part thereof, that is to say, on the Galleys, and the rest of the Equipage, but also on the Courage of the Soldiers, who remained all under a Consternation, for there is nothing that makes them more Superstitious, than unexpected Accidents, which come from the Heavens, or the Elements. Witness the Legions of *Pannonia,* who having mutinied in the Reign of *Tiberius,* passed immediately from Fury to Repentance, upon an Eclipse of the Moon. *In the Epitome of the Life of* Charles *the Fifth.*

253:23 *seduc'd*] In the Year 1546, the Elector Palatine, who had declared for the League of *Smalkald* against *Charles* the Fifth, reduced some Cities to the Obedience of this Emperour by the same Remonstrance. "We are (said he) the last who have committed this Fault, let us be the first to repair it, that we may more easily obtain Pardon for it." *Epitome of the Life of Charles the Fifth, by John Antonio de Vera.*

253:26 *each*] The Memoirs of *Commines* furnish us with many notable Examples of this. "Of all Men that I ever knew, (saith he) *Lewis* the Eleventh was the wisest to get himself out of the Briars, and took the greatest Pains to gain a Man, who was able to serve him, or able to hurt him": *l.* 1. *c.* 10. The Accommodation which he made with the Duke of *Brittany* by the means of the Seigneur *de Lescun,* this Duke's Favourite, to whom he gave the Government of *Caen,* and of some other Places, was the cause that *Charles* of *France* his Brother lost the Duchy of *Normandy,* to the great Displeasure of the Duke of *Burgundy,* who had made him give him this great Apanage: *ch.* 15. *of the same Book.* The said *Lescun* obtained afterwards the Government of *Guienne,* of one of the Castles of *Bourdeaux;* the Government of *Blaie,* of *Bayonne,* of *Dax,* and of St. *Sever;* the Earldom of *Comminges,* the Order of the King, Eighty thousand Crowns in ready Money, and Six thousand Livres in Pension, to have Peace with the Duke of *Britany,* because so powerful a Duke managed by such a Man, was to be feared: *l. 3. c.* 11. Garter Herald of *England* being come into *France,* to declare War against *Lewis,* if he did not surrender the Kingdom to the King of *England,* immediately received a Reward from the King's hands, for the Promise he made to endeavour an Accommodation between the two Kings: *l. 4. c.* 15. The three Ambassadors from *England,* who concluded this Agreement, had great Presents in ready Money and Plate, and each of them Two thousand Crowns Pension: *c.* 8. *of the same Book.* A *Gascon* Gentleman, (*Lewis de Bretailles,*) who was much troubled at the Peace made between *France* and *England,* received a Thousand Crowns from King *Lewis* the Eleventh, after he had had the Honour to dine with him, to prevent him from telling the King of *England* his Master, that the *French* laugh'd in their Sleeves, for having driven the *English* out of *France,* by a Treaty of Peace, and by some Presents: *ch.* 10. *of the same Book.*

254:9 *Century*] *i. e.* Captain of the first Century or Company of the Band or Manipule, which, as I have already said, consisted of two Centuries or Companies, and consequently had two Captains or Centurions. And by *Centuriones primorum ordinum, Tacitus* means those whom we call Eldest Captains.

255:31 *Ubians*] The Country of *Collen.*

256:10 *Cæsars*] As *Tiberius,* who was Sirnamed *Germanicus,* in *Augustus's* Life-time; *Drusus,* and *Germanicus* his Son.

257:30 *Provinces*] By the *Sequani,* now the *French* Counties; and by the *Belgæ,* who are the *Flemings.*

258:34 *Empire*] In the Year 1577, a *Flemish* Lord having attempted the Fidelity of Don *John* of *Austria,* Governour of the *Low-Countries,* by offering him the Sovereignty thereof, if he would accept it; Don *John* transported with Rage, gave him a stab with a Ponyard. *Cabrera, l. 5. c.* 11 *of Philip II.* This Behaviour, in my Opinion, was more prudent, and also more sincere, than that of *Germanicus,* who would, or feign'd that he would, have kill'd himself. For, by immediately punishing so pernicious a Counsellor, he stopp'd their Mouths, and struck Terror into all those, who might be capable to draw him to this Design.

259:9 *sharper*] These two Circumstances of *Calusidius,* who presented *Germanicus* with his Sword as the sharper, and of the others who cried out, *Strike,* seemed to imply that the Soldiers believed, that *Germanicus's* Indignation was but acted, and that his Fidelity towards *Tiberius* had less of Reality in it, than of Art and Ostentation. For those who encouraged him to kill himself, would not have had occasion to cry *Strike,* had they not seen that it was only long of *Germanicus;* that it was not done; and *Calusidius* would never have thought fit to have presented him with his Sword, had he not been in a condition to make use of it. There is some Reason to believe, that the Faith of *Germanicus* was like that of young *Pompey,* who one Day, when he entertained *Octavius* and *Anthony* in his Gallery, being asked by the Corsair *Menas,* Whether he desired they should make him absolute Master, not only of *Sicily* and of *Sardinia,* but of the whole *Roman* Empire; answered, You should do it without giving me notice of it. *Plutarch, in the Life of Anthony.*

259:17 *Ubians*] Afterwards called *Collen.*

259:23 *Auxiliaries*] There was this difference betwixt Allies, and Auxiliaries; that the former took an Oath of Fidelity to the *Roman* Commonwealth, and received no Pay; whereas the others, who were Foreigners, and not under an Oath, took Pay. The Allies had Corn given them.

259:25 *Contempt*] *Cabrera* saith, That the Commander Dom *Luis de Requesens,* in stead of reducing the Rebels of *Flanders* to Obedience, by his Mildness, and by his Favours, increased their Obstinacy, it appearing to them that he treated them so, because he feared them. *Ch.* 15. *l.* 10. *of his History.*

259:33 *Duty*] These Soldiers, who were kept under the Colours, were Sirnamed *Vexilars; Quasi sub proprio Vexilla militantes:* For they were no longer under the Eagle, which was the Ensign of the Legions. And it is in this sense that *Tacitus* saith, *Vexillum Veteranorum.* Ann. 3.

260:8 *Silver*] This Money was Sacred.

260:17 *Chauci*] Now *Friseland.*

260:22 *Justice*] Because it belonged only to the General to punish with Death.

260:27 *Ensign*] The Ensigns were so highly reverenced by the *Romans,* that the Seditious themselves durst not refuse to follow them.

260:34 *Ubians*] Some are of Opinion, that this Altar stood where the City of *Bonn* is now, the ordinary place of Residence of the Arch-Bishop of *Collen.*

261:11 *Germanicus*] It was a Scarlet Ensign, which was set up on the General's Pavilion when they were going to give Battel, and it never was out of his Quarters, whence it could not be taken without Sacrilege.

261:20 *Ensigns*] Which were Sacred and Inviolable amongst the *Romans,* and which *Tacitus* calls, The particular Gods of the Legions, *Propria Legionum numina.* Ann. 2.

261:24 *Eagle-bearer*] The Person who carried the Eagle of the Legion.

262:38 *Boots*] These Boots were trimmed with Nails, and were worn only by the common Soldiers. Wherefore, in Latin Authors, *Miles Caligatus* is Synonymous to *Miles Gregarius,* or *Manipularis.*

263:24 *Service*] *Tradite nostra viris ignavi signa Quirites.* Whilst *Cæsar* was preparing for the War of *Africa,* whither *Curio* and *Cato,* Sirnamed *Uticensis,* were retired; the Soldiers, who saw he stood in need of them, thought fit to demand their Dismission, not with a design to obtain it, but to oblige him, for fear of being left without an Army, to grant them whatsoever they pretended to. But he, without any Concern, discharged them from their Oath, and disbanded them with these Words of Contempt: *Etenim, O Quirites, laboribus & vulneribus exhausti estis;* at which, they were so surprized, that they threw themselves at his Feet, to beg him to continue them in his Service. *Dio, l.* 42. He did an Action of like Resolution at the Battel of *Munda,* in the Kingdom of *Granada,* where seeing the Victory inclining to the Enemy's side, he alighted off his Horse, and cried out to his Soldiers, who gave Ground, *That, as for himself, he would not give Ground an Inch; that they should consider well what they were about to do; what a General they abandon'd, and in what Necessity.* Insomuch, that being spurr'd on by Shame, rather than by Honour, they rallied, and gain'd the Battel. *Patercul. Hist. c.* 55. It was in that Battel that he fought for his Life, whereas in others he fought but for the Victory.

263:25 *Actian-Legions*] After the Battel of *Actium, Augustus* having sent back most of the *Veterans* into *Italy,* without giving them any Rewards, these Soldiers being much discontented mutiny'd, whilst he was employ'd in *Asia* in observing the Steps of *Mark Anthony:* But after he was returned into *Italy,* his Presence brought such an Awe with it, that none durst stir. *Effectum est,* saith *Dio, ut nemo, rem novam tentare auderet.* Lib. 51.

265:12 *Legion*] He was as a Brigadier in our Armies; for our Brigades of Foot much resemble the *Roman* Legions, and the Battalions, which compose them, their Cohorts, of which the Legions were composed. The *Roman* Cohorts consisted of betwixt 5 or 600 Men, when the Legion was well supplied; our Battalions are 800 Men. In every Legion, there were 10 Cohorts; in every Brigade, there are always 5 or 6 Battalions.

265:14 *Tribune*] That is to say, a Colonel.

265:18–19 *Innocence*] Every one thought to merit his Pardon, by killing his Companion.

265:29 *Company*] *Ordo* in *Tacitus.*

266:3 *Vetera*] As much as to say, *Vetera Castra,* the old Camp.

266:31 *Discourses*] *Fabius Maximus,* whose Method was not to fight, slighted those envious Persons, who in a Jeer called him *The Temporiser,* and *Hannibal's Pædagogue,* saying, That it was greater Cowardice to fear the Judgments of the People, than to fear the Enemy. But all Captains (saith *Livy, l.* 4.) have not that strength of Mind which *Fabius* had, who would rather unjustly suffer the diminution of his Authority, than do otherwise than what was his Duty, to gain the Approbation of the People. *Seneca* saith, That there is nothing more ridiculous, than a Man who stands in fear of what others will say of him. *Nil stultius est homine verbs metuente.* Contradiction, in stead of Shocking, doth but fortifie and harden a resolved Mind.

267:1 *Italy*] Through the Cities of *Newport* and *Tergesta,* now *Triest,* with border on *Pannonia. Italiam* (saith *Paterculus*) *junctam sibi Nauporti ac Terrestis confinio.* Hist. 2. c. 120.

267:19 *suspence*] *Philip* the Second, King of *Spain,* used the same Artifice, sending word to *Margaret* of *Parma,* Governess of the Low-Countries, that every thing was ready for his Voyage, and that nothing retarded him but a Tertian Ague, and for which also, he would not stay till he was cured, although he was ready to die of it. *Strada, dec.* 1. *l.* 5. He communicated the same Advice to all Princes, and demanded a Passport of the King of *France,* and Counsel of the Duke of *Savoy* what Road was best to take. The whole Sixth Book of *Strada's* History is full of these Feints, and Pretences which *Philip* made use of to elude his own Promises, and the Entreaties of the Governess, and his other Ministers. But there was this difference betwixt him and *Tiberius,* that this Emperour sent his Sons to his revolted Armies, and that *Philip* feared nothing more, than to hear any Discourse of sending his Son Don *Carlos* into *Flanders,* and repented much that he had sent thither Don *John* of *Austria,* his Natural Brother.

267:29 *Commanders*] *Tacitus* saith, *Aquiliferis signiferisque, i. e.* the Ensign-Colonels, who carried the Eagles of their Legions; and the Ensigns of the Cohorts, who carried Wolves, Vultures, Lions, Dragons, Centaurs, Minotaurs, and other Figures in Relief, of Copper, Cast Brass, or Silver.

268:10 *Bed*] There happen'd in my Time a like Adventure at *Venice* betwixt the *Sbiri* and the Guards appointed for Entries, who having been condemned to Banishment for having shot with their Carbines at the

French Ambassador's Watermen, endeavoured to kill one another, that they might obtain their Pardon by bringing the Heads of their Companions.

268:35 *Cesia*] In the Territories of *Munster.*

269:23 *Revenge*] The *Romans* had conceived a most deep Resentment against the *Marsi,* because they had contributed, more than all the rest, to the Defeat of *Varus,* who with his Legions was also buried amongst them, in the Forest of *Teutberg.*

269:26 *Tanfane*] This was the most magnificent Temple of all *Germany,* dedicated to the *Origins of Things,* which could be no other than the Supreme Being.

269:29 *Bructeri*] People between the *Ems* and the *Rhine,* Neighbours of *Friseland.*

269:30 *Tubantes*] People of *Westphalia,* on the River *Ems.*

269:30 *Usipetes*] People, who inhabited along the *Lippe.* The *Tubantes,* and the *Marsi,* are now the Country of *Cleves* and *Gueldreland.*

270:26 *sincere*] It was his Desire, that they should believe that he exceeded in the Praises of *Germanicus,* thereby to lessen all the great Things which he had said of him. *Pessimum inimicorum genus laudantes.*

270:32 *Augustus*] *Julia* (saith *Paterculus*) utterly forgetting that she was *Augustus*'s Daughter, and *Tiberius*'s Wife, gave herself up to all manner of Debaucheries which a Woman was capable of, how shameful and infamous soever. She measured the Greatness of her Fortune by Licentiousness and Impunity. Her Adulterers were *Julius Antonius,* the Son of *Mark Anthony,* and Husband of *Marcella, Augustus*'s Niece; *Quintius Crispinus, Appius Claudius, Sempronius Gracchus,* and *Scipio,* besides some others of less Quality. *Hist. 2. c.* 100. She had four Children by *Agrippa* her second Husband, three Sons, and one Daughter, who inherited her Name and her Manners. *Sueton* saith, That when she was the Wife of *Marcellus,* she had a great Passion for *Tiberius;* as it is the way of Coquets, and lewd Women, always to love another better than their own Husband. *Seneca* saith, That *Augustus* perceiving too late the Error he had committed in publishing the Infamy of his Daughter by banishing her, said with Grief, That all this would not have befallen him, if *Agrippa* or *Mæcenas* had been alive.

270:33 *Pandataria*] Now *Pianosa,* in the Bay of *Pouzzoli.*

271:29 *Tatius*] These Priests or Knights were instituted, in *Romulus*'s Reign, after the Union of the *Sabines* with the *Romans,* who received the *Sabines* as Fellow-Citizens and Companions, whom the Day before they had Enemies; as *Tacitus* saith, *Eodem die hostes, dein cives habuerit.* Ann. 11. This *Tatius* was King of the *Sabines,* and was admitted a Partner in the Sovereignty of *Rome* by *Romulus,* who gave him the *Capitol* and the *Quirinal-Hill* for his Habitation. But his Death, which happen'd a little time after, reunited the Regal Power in the Person of *Romulus,* who thereby remained King of the *Romans* and of the *Sabines.*

271:35 *Actor*] *Cabrera* well observes, that the Spectacles and the publick Games were the Cause, that the People of *Rome,* who were before contented to obey the Magistrates and the Laws, thought fit to desire to have a Share in the Government. For taking upon themselves licentiously to Applaud what gave them the greatest Pleasure, as if they had been capable of Judging prudently, they began to perceive, that the Players set a great Value on their Approbation, and that their Favour gave them Reputation.

So that after they knew the Power which they had in the publick Feasts, they came to slight the Nobles and the Magistrates, and afterwards to create *Tribunes, Ædiles,* and *Quæstors.* At last they introduced the *Plebeians* into the Consulship and the Dictatorship, and made them thereby equal to the *Patritians. L.* 10. *c.* 22. *of his History.* So that we have no Reason to wonder, if *Tiberius,* who was so well skilled in the Arts of Government, had an Aversion to Spectacles, and all popular Concourses.

272:3 *People*] *Strada* saith, That *Octavius Farnese,* Duke of *Parma,* and Son-in-Law to *Charles* the Fifth, was a great Observer of this Maxim, and thereby was as much beloved by the People, as any Prince of his Time. *Laxamentis popularibus ipse se privato non absimilem immiscebat, essecitque, ut inter principes ea tempestace populorum studiis ac benevolentia claros meritò haberetur.* Lib. 9. dec. 1. *Burnet* saith, That *Elizabeth,* Queen of *England,* was a perfect Mistress of the Art of insinuating herself into the Hearts of the People; and although she was suspected of being too much a Comedian, she succeeded notwithstanding in her Designs, and made herself more beloved by her People, by little Complaisances and Affectations to shew herself, and to regard the People as she passed the Streets, than many Princes have done by scattering Favours with both Hands. *History of the Reformation, p. 2. l. 3.*

272:26 *Arminius*] This young Man, saith *Paterculus,* was of a robust Constitution, had a quick Apprehension, and a delicate and penetrating Wit, beyond what is to be imagined of a *Barbarian.* Considering, that nothing is more easie than to destroy those who fear nothing, and that overmuch Confidence is the most ordinary cause of great Misfortunes, he communicates his Design at first to very few People, but afterwards to many more: And this Resolution was so immediately followed with the Execution of it, that *Varus* having neglected the first Advice of *Segestes,* had not time to receive a second from him: *ch.* 118. *Charles,* Duke of *Burgundy,* committed the same Error that *Varus* did, and perished like him, by refusing to give Audience to a Country Gentleman named *Cifron,* who came to discover to him the Treason of the Count *de Campobasso;* and by not crediting the Intelligence which *Lewis* the Eleventh sent him by the Lord *de Contay,* his Ambassador in *France,* that this Count was selling his Life. *Whereby you see,* saith *Commines, that God infatuated him on this occasion. Memoirs, l.* 4. *c. ult. & l.* 3. *c.* 6, *& 2.*

273:16 *Adrana*] Now the *Eder.*

273:22 *Martium*] Now *Marpurg,* the Capital City of *Hesse.*

273:25–26 *Cherusci*] The People of *Brunswick,* and of *Thuring.*

274:4 *Fillets*] These were peculiar Ornaments of the Priests.

274:30 *espous'd*] *Philip* of *Macedon* being asked, whom he hated or loved most: *I love those very much,* saith he, *who will be Traitors to serve me, but I as much hate those who have been so.* The Count *de Campobache,* saith *Commines,* made an Offer to the King, (*Lewis* XI.) by a Physician, called Mr. *Simon* of *Pavia,* that if he would perform some Things which he demanded, *viz.* the Payment of 400 Lances, 20000 Crowns in ready Money, and a good County, he engaged to deliver the Duke of *Burgundy* into his Hands, or to kill him. The King had this Man's Wickedness in great Abhorrence, and acquainted the Duke of *Burgundy* with the whole Matter. *Memoirs, l.* 4. *c. ult. & l.* 5. *c.* 6. Upon the Count *de Campobach*'s Arrival to the Duke of *Lorrain*, to whom he had sacrificed his Master the Duke of *Burgundy*, the *Germans* gave him to understand, that he should retire, and that they would have no Traitors amongst them. *L. 5. c.* 8. I ought not to pass over in Silence the Praises which are due to *Elizabeth* of *England*, for the handsom Answer which she made to that *Graveston*, who gave her an Account of a Treacherous Act done to the *Spaniards* at *Berg-op-zoom*. After having gived him a Thousand Crowns for his Pains, and his Voyage; *Return home*, said she, *and if I should ever stand in need of a Man, who knows how to be a Traitor in perfection, I will make use of you.* Colomma, *l.* 1. *of his History of the Wars of* Flanders.

276:31 *Diversion*] *Alphonso*, King of *Naples*, said, That there was no succeeding in War but by Diligence and Diversion. *Guiccardin's Hist. l.* 1.

277:2 *Amisia*] This River is now called *Ems*, whence the City of *Embden* takes its Name.

277:9 *Varus*] *Piasecki* saith, That in the Defeat of *Varus*'s Legions, there were lost two Eagles, one White, and the other Black; that the White fell to the Auxiliary *Sarmatians*, and the other to the *Germans;* whence came the Arms of the Empire, which bears an Eagle *Sable*, in a Field *Or;* and of *Poland* which bears an Eagle *Argent*, in a Field *Gules. In his Chronicle.*

277:12 *Lippa*] The *Lippe.*

277:15 *unbury'd*] The Field, in which *Varus* was slain with his Legions, is called at this day *Winfeld, i. e.* in *High-Dutch*, the *Field of Victory. Bernardin de Mendoza* saith, That there remains also to this Day in the Bishoprick of *Munster*, a place called *Varendorp*, that is to say, the Borough of *Varus*, which was built by the People of the Country, to preserve the Memory of the Defeat of the *Romans. His Memoirs of the Low-Country Wars, l. 3. c. 3.*

277:23 *Bogs*] *Tacitus* saith, *Fallacibus Campis.* The same *Mendoza* saith, That *Fallaces Campi* are Lakes and Marshes of 30 Leagues extent, and make the Country almost a Desart. *Ibid.*

277:27 *Voids*] *Principia* was a void Place, where the Eagles and the Colours were set. As each Legion had its Eagle, it had also its *Principium;* so that by these three *Principia*, it was known that there had been three Legions.

278:2 *Orders*] That is to say, three Cohorts. For they rise from Cohort to Cohort, according to their Merit, or the time of their Service.

278:10 *Ditches*] These Ditches served for Burying-places for Malefactors, whom they covered with the Earth soked with their Blood.

278:20 *Sepulchre*] Don *Diego de Mendoza* hath finely imitated this whole Funeral Description, *in his History of the Wars of Grenada, L. 4. c. 9.* in his relating the Circumstances of the Defeat and the Death of Don *Alphonso d' Aquilar*, Brother to him whom in *Spain* they call the *Great Captain.* Which I have taken notice of here for the sake of those, who love to read Works written on the Model of *Tacitus*, whom Don *Diego* had much studied.

279:19 *Bridges*] It is a Causeway, made upon Piles with a great deal of Sand, above a League long. The *Hollanders* have made a Fort, by which they pass as they go into *Friseland.*

280:13 *indefatigable*] *Coriolanus* said, That Victory took away Weariness.

281:3 *Assistance*] Two or three Months before the Death of *Henry* the Fourth, the Queen, his Wife, being in Bed with him, saw in a Dream a

Man who stabb'd him to Death with a Knife. The News of his Death flew to *Lisle* in *Flanders,* to *Antwerp,* to *Bois-le-Duc,* and to *Mastrich,* ten Days before it happen'd. For it often comes to pass, that the News precedes the Accident. On the Eve of his Death, as he assisted at the Coronation of the Queen, a Maid, named *Jane Arnaud,* seeing him, said to her Sisters, *Behold a dead Man, who resembles the King, who are buried here!* The Day that he was slain, several Billets were thrown into his Chamber, which all gave him warning of his Fate. But he neglected all this as *Cæsar* did, and perished like him. *Homer* saith, That as the Dreams of common People are to be slighted, Because of the Weakness of their Brain; on the contrary, there ought to be a great Regard had to those of Persons who have the Management of State Affairs, because they arise from their Experience, and the continual Reflection, which they make upon the great Events of Civil Life. *L. 2. of the Iliads. Cabrera* saith, That *Joan* of *Austria,* Mother of *Sebastian* King of *Portugal,* being with Child of him, thought that one Night she saw enter into her Chamber a great many *Moors,* clad in Habits of divers Colours. The first Presage of what was to befal this Prince at the Battel of *Alcasar* in *Africk. His Philip II. l.* 11. *c.* 10.

282:14 *Decumane*] The Camp, which was always of a square Figure, had four Gates, the greatest of which was called the *Decumane,* and served for a Postern, through which the Soldiers passed, who were carried to Punishment. It was opposite to the *Prætorian,* so called from the *Prætorium,* or the General's Tent, which always stood towards the Enemy. The other two Gates, which were on the two Sides, were called *Principales.*

282:20 *General*] Don *Juan Antonio de Vera* relates an Action exactly like this done by *Fredrique Enriquez,* Admiral of *Castille,* at the Battel fought betwixt the *French* and the *Spaniards* near *Pampelune. In the Epitome of the Life of Charles the Fifth.*

282:24 *Arms*] *Tacitus* calls this place *Principia.*

283:25 *Palisade*] The Outworks of the Camp had three Things, *viz.* a Ditch, *(Fossa;)* a Rampart of Earth, *(Agger;)* and a Palisade all round made of great Stakes, *(Vallum.)*

284:13 *General*] In the Siege of *Tournay, ann.* 1581, *Mary* of *Lalain,* Princess of *Epinoy,* being not contented incessantly to exhort the Soldiers and the Burghers to a vigorous defence against the Duke of *Parma* and the *Spaniards,* she so valiantly exposed herself, that she had her Arm broken by the Shot of an Arquebuss, of which she died the Year following. Thus this Lady made good the Character which *Commines* gives of her Family. Messire *Philip de Lalain,* saith he, was of a Race, of which there have been few who have not been valiant, and have almost all died in serving their Princes in War. *Memoirs, l.* 1. *c.* 2. *Ann.* 1595, the Lady *De Balagny,* Wife of the Lord of *Cambray,* performed the Duty of a Captain, and of a private Soldier, in the defence of this Town against the *Spaniards.* Night and Day she went to visit the Sentinels, and to observe the Battery; she wrought on the Fortifications; she discharged the Cannon; with her Pike in her Hand, she exposed herself to all Dangers, and braved the *Spaniards,* and would not hear of a Capitulation. Which might have succeeded, if her Husband had not been so odious to the City, over which he tyrannized without Pity. *Herrera* calls this Lady, another *Bodicea,* another *Verulana. Hist. part* 3. *l.* 11. *c.* 16. *& Don Carlos Coloma, l.* 8. *of his Wars of Flanders.*

285:34 *Rhine*] The *Latin* hath the *Weser,* but it ought there to have the *Rhine,* where was the Winter Quarters of the Legions. For *Vitellius* carried the two Legions into the *Gaules,* whereas to have gained the *Weser,* which was beyond the *Ems,* had been to have carried them into *Germany.* There is more reason to conclude, that the word *Visurgim* is slipt in for *Vidrum,* called now the *Wecht,* which is one of the Mouths of the *Rhine,* than to attribute this Error to *Tacitus,* who always places the *Weser* where it is at this Day.

286:25 *Country*] *Sueton* saith, That he resolutely refused the Title of *Father of the Country,* and the Senates swearing to his Acts, for fear lest one Day they should think him unworthy of two so great Honours. *Ne mox majore dedecore impar tantis honoribus inveniretur.*

286:27 *Acts*] It was an Oath which the Magistrates took, to hold for well done whatsoever the Prince should do during his Reign. They renewed it every Year, on the First of *January.* It was by this Oath, that the *Romans* open'd the Gap to Slavery; for to ratifie and to hold for Authentick whatsoever the Prince should please to ordain, was to put an Arbitrary Power into his Hands, and to banish Liberty. *Lewis* the Eleventh seemed to exact a like Oath, when he said, That none ought ever to withstand the Prince's Will, no not when he was out of his Wits.

287:11 *Ingratitude*] He owed the Empire to her.

288:25 *Obstetation*] For, in Matters of great Importance, the Judges were wont to swear, That they judg'd according to their Conscience; using this Form, *Ex animi sententia;* or else this, *Si sciens fallam, ita me Diespiter bonis ejiciat, ut ego hunc lepidem;* The Oath was made on the Altar of *Jupiter Lapis.*

289:4 *Court*] With what Gravity, saith *Paterculus,* did *Tiberius* assist at the Tryals of Causes, not as a Prince, but as if he had been a meer Senator or Judge. *Ch. 129. of his Second Book.*

289:22 *Sesterces*] That is to say, 25000 Crowns.

289:33 *Sibils*] These Books were kept in a private Apartment of the Capitol, as an Instrument of Policy, to awe the *Populace* and Soldiery during the Calamities of the City and State. The People of *Rome* were always very inquisitive, to know what was contain'd in these and some other Books, which were in the custody of the Priests; witness the Reward one *Flavius* received, the Son of a Freeman, who was created Tribune, Senator, and Edile, for having given to the People a Register of the Ceremonies, which he had purloin'd from the Censor *Appius Claudius,* under whom he serv'd as a Clerk.

290:3 *Emperour*] For every Proconsul had three Lieutenants, which was an Oppression to the Provinces, whose Government was Proconsular; whereas those in the Emperour's Division were under the Government but of one Lieutenant, called a President, from whence they were called Presidial Provinces. The Proconsuls were Annual, but the Presidents continued in their Provinces, till the Emperour sent a Successor. The Proconsuls exercised more Authority than the Presidents, but sometimes the Emperour would advance these to a Power equal to that of others, by giving them a Commission for Consular Authority. The Presidents were sometimes only of the Order of Knights, whereas the Proconsuls were always of the Senatorial Body, and the Consular Rank. *Legatus Cæsaris,* and *Præses,* signifie the same in the *Latin* Historians. There are also Provinces called *Prætorian,* or *Publicæ Provinciæ,* according to *Tacitus, Ann.* 13. because the People disposed of the Governments; but when these Assemblies of the People were put down by *Tiberius,* these Provinces became annexed to the Jurisdiction of the Senate, and were held by Lot as the Proconsular. It may be useful to observe, by the way, That *Augustus,* who would assume no Title, but that popular one of *Prince of the Senate,* yet made no scruple to over-reach them in the distribution of these Provinces; for he took to his own Share all those, where the Legions were in Garison, under colour they were exposed more to danger, as lying nearer to the Enemy; but the true Reason was, That he might make himself Master of all the *Roman* Militia: *Ut in manu sua res omnis militaris esset,* says *Dion.* So that *Tacitus* had good Reason to say, *Patres & plebem invalida & inermia.* Ann. 1. And in another place, *Speciosa Senatus populique Romani nomina.* Hist. 1.

290:37 *Comedians*] *Tacitus* says, *De modo lucaris,* which, according to *Turnebius,* is *Merces Histrionum.*

290:36 *Favourers*] For every Comedian had his certain Followers, whose Employment it was to set the Spectators a clapping in his Favour, and to decry all others; whence came frequent Quarrellings and Tumults, in which every one took the Side he most fancied; and 'tis for this Reason, that *Tacitus* stiles them, *Operæ Theatrales, Histrionale Studium, Certamen Histrionura,* in several places of this very Book of Annals.

291:1 *Pantomimes*] Comedians, who play'd by Imitation and Posture, and counterfeited all sorts of Persons.

291:10 *War*] It was somewhat like the *Taillon* or the Extraordinary in *France,* in time of War. This Revenue had three Funds to maintain it; The Twentieth part of all Estates by Inheritance, and of Legacies; a Twentieth part in the Sale of Slaves; and an Hundredth part of all Goods imported in Trade. *Augustus* first laid this Duty.

291:26 *Interamnates*] Now the Inhabitants of *Terni.*

292:2 *Tiber*] Under the Popedom of *Sixtus* V. there was a Proposal to enlarge the Channel of the River *Tyber,* thereby to render it more commodious for Navigation; but the Pope changed his Mind, upon an Intimation that this would be a means to facilitate the passage of this River to the *Turks,* and other Enemies of the *Roman* Church.

292:14 *Civil*] *Cato* the Censor's saying was, That to continue the same Persons long in Offices, did demonstrate, either that the Commonwealth afforded few that were fit, or that they made small account of Magistrates.

292:23 *Insufficient*] These three Reasons, says *Scipio Amirato,* preceeded from his Vices: The first, from Laziness; the second, from Malice; and the third, from a mixture of Laziness and Folly. For, if he liked not to employ debauched Persons, he should have concerned himself to find out those that were good; and if he was afraid of virtuous and great Men, let him have but changed often, and he had been secure. *In the last Discourse of the First Book of his Commentaries. Commines* says, All crafty Princes are jealous, that all great Princes are so, and particularly, wise ones, and such as have made many Enemies, and injured many, as *Tiberius* had done. *Ch. 7. l. 6. of his Memoirs. Yet Jealousies are to be admitted with Slowness and Deliberation, for to be too much addicted to Jealousie, is not well.* L. 3. ch. 5.

293:2 *debarr'd*] *Tacitus* saith, *Posse profiteri. Profiteri* therefore was what we call, to stand for an Office, or to get his Name put into the List. *Quæsturam petentes,* (saith *Paterculus*) *quos indignos judicavis, profiteri vetuit. Hist.* 2. *cap.* 92. That is to say, the Consul forbid some of those, who pretended to the Questorship, to give in their Names, because he believed them unworthy of it.

INDEX TO THE COMMENTARY